A READER IN AMERICAN FOREIGN POLICY

EDITED BY

James M. McCormick
IOWA STATE UNIVERSITY

D1278019

F.E. PEACOCK PUBLISHERS, INC.
ITASCA, ILLINOIS 60143

Contents

Introduction

The intent of this collection of readings is to serve as a sourcebook to accompany a standard American foreign policy textbook. As the reader will quickly discover, the design fits well with the organization of *American Foreign Policy and American Values*,[1] but it surely could be used as a companion volume for any of the fine foreign policy texts currently available. The collection is also structured in a way that it could stand alone for any instructor who wants to provide an overview of American foreign policy but prefers not to use a standard text. Alternately, this selection of readings would be useful to the instructor who wants to provide an overview of past policy, so that students may be able to discuss current issues (e.g., Central America, the Middle East, or Soviet-American relations) in some broader American value context than current topical readings may allow. However this collection is ultimately used by the reader, my hope is that it will spark discussion over the values and beliefs that have (and should) inform American foreign policy. Moreover, it is my fervent personal belief that only out of confronting these value questions can sound foreign policy emerge.

The analysis of values and beliefs was consciously chosen as the organizing theme for this reader because such principles are ultimately the basis for both individual action and state behavior. Since values and beliefs are the motivating forces for an individual's actions—and since I make the assumption that foreign policy is ultimately the result of individual choice—their importance for foreign policy analysis becomes readily apparent. Put differently, by appreciating the underlying values and beliefs that shape a nation at any particular time, the analyst will be well prepared to understand and explain the foreign policy actions of the nation.

Social psychologists have provided the best analysis of the relationships between values, beliefs, and the behavior of individuals. Milton Rokeach, for example, stated the relationship between values and beliefs succinctly: "A value is a type of belief, centrally located within one's total belief system, about how one ought, or ought not, to behave, or about some end state of existence worth, or not worth, attaining." Furthermore, Rokeach reports that only a few values are at the core of an individual's belief system, but these are crucial toward understanding the attitudes and behaviors that an individual expresses.[2]

By extension, nation-states would operate in the same way, since ultimately individuals comprise nations. Inevitably, of course, there will be some slippage in any direct analogy between individual and nation-state behavior for at least two reasons. First, other factors such as the personality traits of individual leaders, the effects of bureaucratic politics, and the restraints of the governmental process will intrude into any complete identification of the national values and beliefs.[3] While recognizing these factors, and the wealth of research that has gone into their analysis, the role of underlying values and beliefs remains critically important and should not be overlooked. Even accepting this position, a second reason raises doubts about using this kind of values' perspective: the very definition of national values is likely to be problematic. Whose values are we to identify? Should they be those of the elites or the masses? Should they be the values of political leaders or the public at large? While the readings in this book will focus on the values held by the political elites, the values and beliefs of the public will also be examined.

In short, although recognizing the limitations of focusing upon national values and beliefs, the contention here is that this approach is a sufficiently useful first step to warrant more coverage than it has received. Further, the readings will not contend that the values and beliefs are immutable. Instead, the essays in this collection will emphasize the very opposite: the constancy of change. By doing that, these essays will show the dynamic nature of values and beliefs as a guide to foreign policy action.

Beyond the importance of the values themselves as an approach to understanding foreign policy, a values approach is especially germane to analyzing American foreign policy for at least three reasons. First, the nation was explicitly founded on particular sets of values—for example, freedom and equality—and these values made the United States view itself as "different" from the nations of the Old World from which it originated. In this view, politics was not to be conducted upon the principles of power politics, but it was to be conducted on the basis of democratic principles. To many, then, America could act in the world only on the basis of moral principles or in defense of such principles. Domestic values, at all times, were to be the guide to political behavior. Whether the United States lived up to these standards of course is debatable, but the inevitable desire to justify actions within a value context emphasizes the role of such principles as guides to U.S. foreign policy.

A second important reason for employing a values perspective in analyzing American foreign policy is due to the fact that American values toward the world are changing—especially recently. For instance, we have witnessed a sharp break with America's past as it moved from isolationism to an active globalism in the immediate post-World War II. From the late 1940s to the time of America's involvement in Vietnam, a particular set of values that came to be labeled the cold war consensus dominated the motivations for the actions that the United States took toward the rest of the world. In the post-Vietnam period, too, American value orientation to the world has changed. In fact, American foreign policy orientation has tended to vacillate from the power politics of the Kissinger-Nixon-Ford years to the moralism of the Carter administration and back to a revival of the cold war values by the Reagan administration. With such identifiable value orientation throughout various periods of U.S. foreign policy, understanding these particular value orientations serves as a useful approach to understanding American behavior abroad in those periods.

Finally, an important third reason exists for employing a value approach to analyzing American foreign policy: the lack of a foreign policy consensus at the present time. According to both elite and mass survey data, none of the value perspectives of the post-Vietnam period has been fully embraced by the American public or their leaders. Furthermore, both the public at large and the American leadership are deeply divided as to the appropriate set of values to guide American policy for the future. Three distinct value orientations have formed among the public and the elites. One portion of the public and the elites hold to traditional cold war values and to a continued involvement of the United States in world affairs (the Cold War Internationalists); another segment shares the commitment to internationalism but desires to take a more differentiated view of global politics, beyond the principles of the cold war (the Post-Cold War Internationalists); and a third segment wants the United States to reduce its global involvement and take a more self-interested view toward its own problems (the Semi-Isolationists).[4] Until these divisions are overcome or until a new approach emerges, the role of values and beliefs in understanding policy will remain a potent force.

The collection of readings is divided into three parts to help the student appreciate the different aspects of the role of values and beliefs in American foreign policy. Part I focuses on the evolution of foreign policy values and beliefs from the beginning of the nation through the 1980s. Part II is a collection of readings which illustrates the competition among different sets of domestic values and beliefs in the shaping of American foreign policy. The roles of the president, the Congress, the bureaucracy, various interest groups, and the public at large are examined in this part of the volume. Part III discusses some problems of building a new foreign policy consensus and offers sets of values and beliefs that may shape American foreign policymaking in the future.

NOTES

1. James M. McCormick, *American Foreign Policy and American Values* (Itasca, Ill.: F. E. Peacock Publishers, Inc., 1985).
2. See Milton Rokeach's discussion under "Attitudes" in the *International Encyclopedia of the Social Sciences* (New York: The Macmillan Company and the Free Press, 1968), pp. 449–457. The quotation is from p. 454. Also see, Milton Rokeach, *Beliefs, Attitudes and Values* (San Francisco: Jossey-Bass, Inc., 1968).

3. A recent book which surveys the research done within the context of these various factors to explain foreign policy is Lloyd Jensen, *Explaining Foreign Policy* (Englewood Cliffs, N.J.: Prentice-Hall, 1982).
4. These divisions within American society have been developed and thoroughly examined in Ole R. Holsti and James N. Rosenau, *American Leadership in World Affairs* (Boston: Allen & Unwin, 1984).

The Evolution of American Foreign Policy Beliefs

The essays in Part I provide the reader with an overview and a critique of American foreign policy values and beliefs from the beginning of the nation to the present. Three different kinds of essays were selected to accomplish this end: Some describe the basic values and beliefs during a particular period or administration; others portray foreign policy actions taken during these time periods which seem to reflect the underlying values; and still other readings critique the values and beliefs of a particular time period or a particular administration. In the main, the selections concentrate on the post-World War II period because this was the period of greatest U.S. involvement in international politics. Further, in the interest of portraying the dominant foreign policy values of the elites, the primary emphasis is on the value approaches advanced by the principal political leaders and their advisers; nevertheless, the view of the public will be readily apparent in some of these selections.

To make this review of the evolution of U.S. foreign policy values more manageable, Part I is divided into four different sections. The first covers the historical values that have shaped American policy, while the other three sections cover the period from the end of World War II to the present. The second section, for example, focuses on the values and beliefs during the cold war and the challenges that emerged to this approach. The third section covers the period beginning with America's efforts to extricate itself from Vietnam through the Carter administration. The aim at that juncture is to illustrate the changes in values and beliefs that guided foreign policy during the years in which Henry Kissinger largely shaped U.S. policy to the years of the Carter administration in which a more moralistic approach to foreign policy was the dominant theme. During these years, the United States sought to develop a new foreign policy consensus to replace the one shattered by the Vietnam experience and adopted orientations that were markedly different from one another in the space of a few years. The last section of Part I focuses

1

on the values and beliefs of the Reagan administration and offers some critique of its basic foreign policy approach. While the Reagan approach continued the search for a new post-Vietnam consensus, the selections on the Reagan period are treated separately to allow some evaluation of present policy.

Section I–A. THE HISTORICAL LEGACY

Because the United States was explicitly founded on political values and beliefs that were believed to be different from the prevailing European political ones of the time, two important values shaped the foreign policy historically and continue to affect how the United States approaches the world. These two values were an emphasis on isolationism and moralism as the guiding principles to American foreign policy. Isolationism essentially referred to America's reluctance to become involved in global politics, and especially the politics as practiced in Europe, while moralism referred to the view that America's foreign policy actions needed to be justified on firm ethical principles.

Isolationism held particular appeal for the United States for both philosophical and practical reasons. On a philosophical level, isolationism was attractive because it meant that the United States would stay out of the quarrels of Europe and thus would preserve its distinctive values and beliefs. On a practical level, it meant that the United States would concentrate on the development of the American political system and the American continent, unencumbered by foreign politics.

Moralism was appealing because it further signaled the uniqueness of the United States in the world. Unlike other nations that seemed to be motivated primarily by the requirements of power politics, the United States would only take actions out of moral convictions. Moreover, since the United States developed in such an isolationist tradition, a certain self-righteousness about its moral principles was only reinforced.

The first two essays in this section examine both of these major tenets of America's past. In the first essay, Cecil Crabb outlines the origins and the implications of the isolationist sentiment for American foreign policy. Beginning with a congressional resolution during the period of the Articles of Confederation and gaining more formal status with the pronouncements of Washington's Farewell Address, Jefferson's admonition against "entangling alliances," and the declaration of the Monroe Doctrine, isolationism, according to Crabb, had been an important component of American foreign policy for the first 150 years of the Republic. Further, the effects of isolationism are far from ended: This political value, in fact, remains attractive for many people to this day.

The concept of isolationism changed over time and came to have a variety of meanings and many different implications for U.S. action in the world. On the one hand, for instance, isolationism meant both a geographic separation and a political and ideological separation from other nations, although especially Europe. On the other hand, it also emphasized the effort of the United States to steer its own course in global affairs and to maintain its national independence. By doing that, the United States was able to enjoy its noninvolvement in the politics and the wars of the Old World. Crabb discusses all of these meanings and their implications in some detail, but the basic message in this essay is that isolationism was pervasive throughout the history of the nation, even if it assumed many different meanings for the public and its leaders.

In the second essay, Dexter Perkins examines in some detail the strong emphasis on moralism in America's historical approach to foreign policy. He first discusses several ways in which moralism was manifested in American diplomacy—a strong commitment to democratic values, a rejection of conquest as a legitimate tactic of policy, an abiding commitment to openness in diplomatic bargaining, and an attempt to impose a direct relationship between individual morality and state morality. By his analysis, these unique American characteristics produced a "highly moralistic flavor to our diplomacy." By reviewing numerous episodes of American diplomatic history, Perkins wants to "make clear how strong this moralistic emphasis has been and how often it has played a part in foreign policy."

His survey covers from the moralism that shaped Washington's and Jefferson's response to the British and the French in the early 1790s to the idealism manifested in the actions of President Woodrow Wilson in the early part of the 20th century. Perkins also uses illustrations from the 1930s and into the years of the cold war to show the continued influence of this tradition in the present era. His message is thus similar to Crabb's: Moralism, like isolationism, was pervasive when America did take action in the international system and remains so to the present. Furthermore, Perkins's conclusion is an apt one: " . . . *ideas,* and ideas connected with certain moral preoccupations, are a factor, and a substantially important factor, in the conduct of [American] diplomacy."

In the last essay, Hans J. Morgenthau offers an alternate interpretation and a forceful critique of the manner in which U.S. foreign policy has been conducted, especially in the early part of the 20th century. Although he acknowledges that the United States has "tended to conceive of our actions in non-political, moralistic terms" and to pursue an isolationist—albeit not a detached—policy toward the world, America's political leaders—at least until the rise of Wilsonianism—acted in ways generally compatible with the national interest. In this sense, America, like any nation, acted in a way consistent with the requirements of power politics in the current nation-state system. He illustrates this approach by dividing U.S. diplomatic history into three periods. In the first period, the realistic phase, dating from President Washington to President Jefferson, the United States pursued a policy of isolationism tempered by a desire to maintain equilibrium in Europe. In this period, there was the least discrepancy between the words and actions of America's leaders, especially when compared to the second period. During this second period, the ideological phase, covering the presidencies from Jefferson to McKinley, the rationale for policy took on high moral tones, but the actions, in Morgenthau's assessment, still focused on achieving the national interest.

In the last period of his analysis, the utopian phase, depicted mainly by the philosophy of President Woodrow Wilson, showed similarity between words and actions in seeking to eliminate the balance of power system from international politics. Yet such an approach, Morgenthau contends, is impossible for states to pursue. For political leaders to deny the role of power politics in the affairs of states is "like a scientist not believing in the law of gravity," Morgenthau argues. Even Wilson himself, despite his efforts, Morgenthau explains, could not escape the requirement of the balance of power system. Thus Wilson "pursued the right policy" in entering World War I, "but he pursued it for the wrong reasons." Power considerations, not moral justification, should have been the motivating factor.

The last part of Morgenthau's essay is an elaboration of his critique of the inadequacy of either Wilsonianism, isolationism, or internationalism as a guide to foreign policy. In addition, it is the classic statement in defense of the national interest, rather than universal moral principles, as the basis for foreign policy. Note how he argues that pursuing the national interest is not an amoral or immoral strategy for states, but, in effect, a more moral posture than those who would seek a universal set of standards to guide state action. In fact, the use of "moral abstractions" to shape policy is truly the immoral policy for a state to pursue because it could well lead to "national suicide." This issue of nation-state morality versus a universal morality to guide the foreign policy of nations remains a great debate and will occur once again in this book, in the survey of the value approaches in the post-World War II period.

1. THE ISOLATIONIST HERITAGE

Cecil V. Crabb, Jr.

On June 12, 1783, the Congress of the United States resolved that "the true interests of these states [i.e., the United States] require that they should be as little as possible entangled in the politics and controversies of European nations."[1]

Thirteen years later, in one of the most celebrated state papers in the nation's history, President George Washington's Farewell Address, Americans were solemnly warned against "permanent antipathies against particular nations and passionate attachments for others"; instead, the new Republic should cultivate "just and amicable feelings toward all" nations. Then, in what came to be referred to widely in later years as "Washington's rule," the President declared:

The great rule of conduct for us in regard to foreign nations is, in extending our commercial relations to have with them [the nations of Europe] as little political connection as possible. . . . Europe has a set of primary interests which to us have none or a very remote relation. Hence she must be engaged in frequent controversies, the causes of which are essentially foreign to our corners. Hence, therefore, it must be unwise in us to implicate ourselves by artificial ties in the ordinary vicissitudes of her politics or the ordinary combinations and collisions of her friendships or enmities. . . . It is our true policy to steer clear of permanent alliances with any portion of the foreign world. . . . Taking care always to keep ourselves by suitable establishments on a respectable posture, we may safely trust to temporary alliances for extraordinary emergencies.

Source: Cecil V. Crabb, Jr., *Policy-Makers and Critics: Conflicting Theories of American Foreign Policy* (New York: Praeger Publishers, 1976), pp. 1–15. Copyright 1976 by Cecil V. Crabb.

Referring to the existence of warfare in Europe, President Washington reaffirmed America's "neutral position" toward the conflict. A neutral stance would "gain time to our country to settle and mature its yet recent institutions, and to progress without interruption to that degree of strength and consistency which is necessary to give it . . . the command of its own fortunes."

Later Presidents and statesmen amplified the meaning of "Washington's rule," applying it to concrete issues that arose in American foreign relations and adapting it to new conditions confronting the United States abroad. Despite a popular tendency to attribute the phrase to Washington, for example, it was President Thomas Jefferson who in 1801 admonished Americans to shun "entangling alliances" with other nations.[2] In a message to Congress on December 2, 1823, President James Monroe reaffirmed and amplified these principles, applying them specifically to the twofold threat of intervention by the Holy Alliance in the Western Hemisphere and Czarist Russia's territorial ambitions in the Pacific Northwest. In what came to be known in the years thereafter as the "Monroe Doctrine," Monroe stated that "the American continents, by the free and independent condition which they have assumed and maintain, are henceforth not to be considered as subjects for future colonization by any European powers." At the same time Monroe pledged, "In the wars of the European powers in matters relating to themselves we have never taken any part, nor does it comport with our policy to do so." He observed that "the political system of the allied [i.e., European] powers is essentially different ... from that of America." Accordingly, the United States would "consider any attempt on their part to extend their system to any portion of this hemisphere as dangerous to our peace and safety." Yet with Europe's "existing colonies" in the New World, Monroe added, "we have not interfered and shall not interfere."

For more than a century and a half—from the time it declared its independence in 1776 until the outbreak of World War II—the United States was devoted to an "isolationist" position in world affairs.[3] As we shall see, isolationism is not an easy or simple concept to define. Throughout the course of American history, the doctrine acquired numerous implications and tenets, some of which were not always mutually consistent or compatible. From the time of Washington's Farewell Address onward, isolationism was in reality a *cluster of attitudes and assumptions* about America's proper relationship with the outside world. Isolationism had several components from the beginning, and every age tended to modify its content as the concept was applied to specific conditions prevailing at home and abroad.

We shall examine the main components or facets of isolationism at a later stage. Meanwhile, two points about the doctrine require emphasis at the outset. The first is that, for a hundred and fifty years or so after the United States became an independent nation, a foreign policy of isolationism was viewed by most citizens as an *indispensable condition* for their national security, the continued success of their democratic experiment, their political stability, their economic prosperity—in brief, for all the benefits conferred by successful pursuit of the "American way of life." However much they often disagreed upon domestic issues, most Americans subscribed to the view that the "timeless principles" enunciated by Presidents Washington, Jefferson, and Monroe must be adhered to diligently in foreign relations. Continued devotion to them would enable the society to realize the promises implicit in the American society's unique way of life. Conversely, departure from them risked a host of evils: foreign intervention in the political and economic affairs of the nation; the growth of "militarism" and escalating armaments expenditures; the loss of freedoms guaranteed by the Bill of Rights and other liberties; the emergence of presidential "dictatorship" and the consequent "decline" of Congress; a steadily mounting national debt; internal divisiveness and acute political factionalism; economic retrogression, precipitated by the loss of foreign markets—to mention but a few of the dangers that proponents of an isolationist position sought to avoid. As time passed, prominent American historians discerned a *direct causal relationship* between stability and progress at home, and steadfast adherence to a policy of isolationism abroad. Thus one of the nation's most eminent historians in the pre-World War II period, Charles A. Beard, was convinced that an isolationist policy had " ... enabled the American people to go ahead under the principles of 1776, conquering a continent and building a civilization which, with all its faults, has precious merits for us and is, at all events, our own." Under the shelter provided by this doctrine, Beard was convinced, " ... humans beings were set free to see what they could do on this continent, when emancipated from the privilege-encrusted institutions of Europe and from entanglement in the endless revolutions and wars of the continent."[4]

Some fifty years earlier, the perceptive British observer Lord Bryce had said much the same thing about the United States: "America lives in a world of her own. . . . Safe from attack, safe even from menace, she hears from afar the warring cries of European races and faiths. . . . But for the present at least—it may not always be so—she sails upon a summer sea."[5]

Such viewpoints are not cited to prove that a foreign policy of isolationism was in fact directly responsible for the promise and progress that Americans identified with their way of life. But what people believe to be true is sometimes even more crucial in accounting for their behavior than what is objectively true. Correctly or not, down to World War II millions of Americans were prone to view an isolationist position in foreign affairs abroad as part of the unchallenged "wisdom" of the Founding Fathers; the soundness of their advice appeared to have been reinforced by a century and a half of secure existence as a free nation.

A second point requires emphasis at the outset of our study of the isolationist approach to American foreign relations. Pervasive and deeply rooted as it was down to World War II, today isolationism *per se* no longer commands the allegiance of the American society. Following the most destructive global conflict in the history of the world, the American people and their leaders overwhelmingly rejected an isolationist stance for the United States in the postwar period.[6] One of the most vocal and influential spokesmen for pre-World War II isolationism, Senator Robert A. Taft (Republican of Ohio), said in 1950: "I don't know what they mean by isolationism, nobody is an isolationist today."[7] Even before the end of World War II, another prominent spokesman for the isolationist viewpoint, Senator

Arthur H. Vandenberg (Republican of Michigan) delivered a widely circulated "confession" on the floor of the Senate, in which he formally renounced his isolationist principles and called for a "hard-and-fast treaty" between the United States and the principal wartime Allies to assure peace and security in the postwar period.[8] After Senator Vandenberg's dramatic conversion to an internationalist point of view, he emerged as a leading architect of a bipartisan approach to foreign relations, based on collaboration between the Democratic and Republican parties in behalf of common foreign policy principles and programs.[9] In Vandenberg's new role as advocate of a bipartisan approach to external problems, one of his outstanding contributions to a unified foreign policy was "to keep in line the obstructionists and diehard isolationists in his own party."[10]

The transformation witnessed in the viewpoints of figures like Senators Taft and Vandenberg about foreign affairs may be taken as representative of the fundamental shift in American opinion toward the outside world as a result of World War II. A substantial majority of Americans now accepted the fact that after World War II isolationism no longer served as a viable foreign policy posture for the most influential nation on the world scene. Indeed, by the end of World War II the concept of isolationism not only had few overt adherents; the very term had rapidly fallen into disrepute and had become something of an epithet, signifying myopia toward the course of world events and an unwillingness to accept the most elementary realities about America's involvement in them. Thus one of the most tireless champions of the doctrine prior to World War II, Senator Gerald P. Nye (Republican of North Dakota), said in 1944 that isolationism had become identified with "everything that was bad, terrible, un-American, and indecent."[11] In the postwar period, very few Americans have been willing to identify themselves openly as "isolationists," out of fear perhaps that whatever they said about America's proper course in foreign relations would be discredited by virtue of that admission.

Admittedly, therefore, it is difficult for the contemporary student of American foreign policy to evaluate the traditional isolationist point of view sympathetically and with due regard for its more positive and beneficial features. Isolationism often seems as relevant for the successful conduct of foreign policy in the modern period as mercantilism for the operation of the economic system or an understanding of pre-Copernican astronomy for insight into the problems of the space age. Yet it is an assumption of this chapter that—while very few Americans subscribe to an avowedly isolationist position—the nation's more or less consistent adherence to an isolationist stance for over a century and a half *profoundly affected the American approach to foreign relations after World War II, as well as before it*. The doctrine of isolationism may no longer be in vogue—and likely will never be again. But many of the assumptions, preconceptions, popular images, attitudes, sentiments, and the like associated with the isolationist mentality for more than one hundred and fifty years remain deeply embedded in the American ethos and continue to affect the thinking of the American people and their leaders about events outside of their own borders. As we shall see, since 1945 there has often been a remarkable continuity between the reaction displayed by Americans toward developments overseas and the assessment of Americans in the mid-nineteenth century or during the 1930s.

Despite America's formal renunciation of isolationism, many citizens in the postwar period continue to exhibit behavior tendencies and attitudes toward foreign affairs remarkably akin to those identified with the traditional isolationist mentality. At this stage, let us take note merely of two recent examples. By the 1970s, a substantial number of citizens had become convinced that perhaps America's most useful contribution to global peace and security would be to "set its own house in order," thereby providing a worthy example (contemporary political scientists tended to call it an attractive "model") that other societies would be motivated to follow. As we shall see, this conviction—the idea that the solution of major *domestic* problems had first claim upon the energies and resources of the American society—was also a fundamental tenet of classical isolationist outlook.[12]

Toward a different problem in the contemporary period—American military intervention in Southeast Asia or other regions—a significant number of Americans have become persuaded that the intervention of the United States in political or ideological controversies far from its own shores was indefensible for a number of reasons. One of them was the conviction that America's involvement in such crises will in the end "make no difference" in their outcome. Critics of the nation's prolonged involvement in the Vietnam conflict, for example, frequently contended that it did not lie within the power of the United States to determine the result of political contests in settings like Southeast Asia. Other critics applied the same reasoning to crises in the Middle East, Black Africa, and Latin America. This same conviction underlay the thinking of early isolationists with regard to American involvement in Europe's political rivalries. It was particularly prominent during the 1930s in the opposition of isolationists to American policies designed to limit Axis expansionism in Europe or to curb Japanese aggression in the Far East. These two instances are cited to illustrate a more general phenomenon: While "isolationism" is no longer a doctrine commanding the overtly enthusiastic support of the American people, an understanding of the traditional isolationist mentality yields many insights applicable to the American approach to foreign relations in the modern period.

THE MANY FACETS OF "ISOLATIONISM"

A remarkable quality of the concept of isolationism—and a characteristic that was crucial in enabling it to serve as the basis for the nation's foreign policy over a century and a half—was the richness and adaptability of the doctrine. During no era of American history did isolationism comprise a coherent, internally consistent body of foreign policy principles. Instead, the exact content of isolationism tended to vary from era to era; even within any given historical period, no two proponents of the doctrine were likely to define it identically. The isolationism of the late eighteenth century Jeffersonian was likely to differ in several important respects from the isolationism espoused by the "agrarian radicals" a century later, and the foreign policy viewpoints of this latter group in turn could be contrasted at several points with the isolationism of the America First Committee and other groups that attacked the Roosevelt Administration's foreign policies during the 1930s. From the time of Washington's Farewell Address onward, there has always been a tendency for isolationism to be defined by reference to concrete policy issues confronting the United States in its foreign and domestic affairs.

Moreover, as Rieselbach has emphasized, isolationist thought could and did exist *on several levels.* The concept might emphasize America's *geographic separation* from other continents, particularly Europe. It might stress mainly America's *spiritual and philosophical separation* from Europe, underscoring the contrast between the progressive "American way of life" versus Europe's stagnant social and economic systems. It might call attention primarily to *fundamental political and ideological distinctions* between the democracy of the New World and the authoritarian or despotic political systems and ideologies of the Old World. By the twentieth century, isolationism might also have reference to America's relative *economic self-sufficiency* and its ability to prosper, if need be, without access to the markets of the world. After 1900 isolationism might denote the nation's *relative military security and invincibility in the Western Hemisphere.* Many of the isolationists of the 1930s, for example, were convinced that an Axis victory in Europe, or even worldwide, posed no serious military consequences for the security of the United States. Isolationism could also convey the American people's inherent *apathy and antipathy toward foreign affairs generally vis-à-vis domestic affairs.* The former was a realm abounding in problems, frustrations, unwanted burdens, and dangers for the American Republic, whereas the latter was a sphere in which the promises and benefits implicit in the "American way of life" could be, and were being, rapidly realized. The "isolationism" expressed by a particular individual or school of thought might embody an almost infinite combination of these and other elements; or it might give almost exclusive attention to one of the above dimensions of the idea, while largely ignoring other dimensions.

Within these general limitations, let us take note of several specific facets or connotations of the term "isolationism," recognizing at all times that the concept never comprised a universally accepted or internally consistent set of foreign policy guidelines. Throughout the course of American history, perhaps the most widely accepted definition for isolationism—the idea viewed by many authorities as its "core" or most intrinsic meaning—was the idea of *diplomatic and military nonentanglement,* as illustrated by President Jefferson's admonition in 1801 against "entangling alliances."[13] The variant phrase—"no entangling alliances"—in time became the watchword of isolationism and a keynote of the American national credo. After 1800 nearly every American president was compelled to reassure the nation that his policies were designed to avoid "entangling alliances" with other countries, in conformity with principles enunciated by the Founding Fathers.

It must be emphasized that Jefferson was merely giving authoritative and forceful expression to a principle that had already found wide acceptance among the American people and their leaders.[14] Adherence to the principle of "no entangling alliances" was designed to safeguard the new Republic against a specific danger: involvement in the upheavals that gripped Europe during the period of the French Revolution and the Napoleonic era. French assistance during the American Revolution had been of inestimable importance—some historians have regarded it in fact as absolutely essential—for an American victory and the achievement of independence from England. On February 6, 1778, the United States and France signed a treaty of alliance; according to its terms, the United States was obligated to assist France "forever" in retaining possession of its New World colonies, like the French West Indies.[15] Even before the pact was signed, and even more so while it was in force, French officials had repeatedly intervened in the internal affairs of the United States (vigorous French efforts designed to prevent ratification of the Jay Treaty, signed with England on November 19, 1794, was a case in point). As new conflicts erupted among the European powers at the end of the eighteenth century, there was the real danger that the United States might find itself involved in another war with England to fulfill its obligations under the alliance with France. As had occurred many times in the past, the risk existed that Americans would find themselves "entangled" once more in a European struggle, in which their interests were secondary to those of the more powerful belligerents and in which their capacity to affect the outcome was minimal. This was the specific danger against which Jefferson's admonition against "entangling alliances" was directed.

As was not unusual with later principles of American foreign policy (such as those associated with the Monroe Doctrine in 1823), the injunction against "entangling alliances" in time came to be universalized and sanctified into a kind of law. The tendency was to interpret and apply it far more rigidly and indiscriminately that its early advocates had intended. The principle was enunciated, we need to be reminded, *in response to a particular set of circumstances,* which appeared to threaten the security and well-being of the young and vulnerable American democracy. The threat arose from the machinations of *European powers.* As with nearly all other tenets of isolationism, it was at prevention of American involvement in *European conflicts* that the maxim was aimed. Note should also be taken of the fact that the specific danger identified was "entangling" *alliances.* Neither Washington nor Jefferson, nor any other early statesman had urged the United States to avoid involvement in foreign (and certainly not in foreign economic and commercial) affairs; the injunction of Washington and Jefferson contained no suggestion that America could be indifferent to events outside its own borders, take its precarious security for granted, or pretend tha. its destiny was otherwise unaffected by the behavior of other countries.

A closely related connotation of "isolationism" from the infancy of the Republic to the period of World War II was preservation of *national sovereignty and independence in decision-making.* Why should the United States avoid "entangling alliances" with more powerful European states? It should do so primarily because, as a weak and vulnerable country, its independence might be jeopardized by close diplomatic and military association with more powerful nations. For example, Secretary of State Timothy Pickering believed that the government of France had aided the colonial cause during the American Revolution chiefly to promote its own interests—a leading French objective being *to keep the United States dependent upon France for an indefinite period thereafter.*[16]

President Monroe's famous message to Congress (December 2, 1823) laying the foundation for what came to be called the Monroe Doctrine, was directed against two (real or imaginary) dangers: a threatened intervention by the Holy Alliance in Latin America and expansionism by Czarist Russia in the Pacific Northwest. Although the principles enunciated by President Monroe became well known in

the years to follow, it was sometimes overlooked that his paramount concern was *the security and independence of the United States.*[17] Invited to join with Great Britain in asserting the concepts contained in his doctrine, President Monroe refused. A joint declaration with the vastly more powerful England, Secretary of State John Quincy Adams wrote, would have reduced the United States to "a cock-boat in the wake of the British man-of-war."[18]

Another facet of the doctrine of isolationism was *unilateralism;* during the twenty years that followed World War I, this was perhaps the doctrine's dominant connotation. According to Paul Seabury, the term signified America's "preference for autonomous action in world politics and a disinclination to be bound by alliances or by any supranational agreements committing the nation in advance to policies which might involve the use of force or war."[19] In 1924, Secretary of State Charles Evans Hughes declared that, although the United States was willing to participate in certain forms of international collaboration (like arms reduction), it "would not tolerate the submission of such questions which pertain to our own policy to the determination of any group of Powers. . . . We should not be willing to enter any organization through which a group of Powers would be in a position to intervene to attempt to determine our policies for us."[20] Called the "perfect isolationist," Senator William E. Borah once declared: "What I have opposed from the beginning is any commitment of this nation to a given line of procedure in a future exigency, the facts as to which could not be known before the event."[21]

As war clouds gathered in Europe (and more specifically after Italy invaded Ethiopia in 1935), the Roosevelt Administration tried to take limited steps to prevent further aggression. In this process, one commentator has written, Secretary of State Cordell Hull "was careful to avoid any appearance of being led by the League [of Nations]."[22] Irrespective of what America's particular response to Axis expansionism might be—and there was a considerable range of opinion, even among isolationists, on this issue—the United States was required to act unilaterally. It was precluded by the isolationist heritage from using its military, economic, and frequently even its moral influence abroad in concert with other nations.

Still another component or facet of the isolationist credo was its insistence upon *America's nonparticipation in foreign wars.* In the Monroe Doctrine, President Monroe had declared:

In the wars of the European powers in matters relating to themselves we have never taken any part, nor does it comport with our policy to do so. It is only when our rights are invaded or seriously menaced that we resent injuries or make preparation for our defense.

As with other aspects of the isolationist mentality, America's desire to escape involvement in foreign wars was no abstract principle formulated by the fathers of the Republic. To the contrary, it was a determination which had evolved out of the American society's experience during the colonial period and the early years under the Constitution. The diplomatic historian, Thomas A. Bailey, has noted that between 1689 and 1815 England and France fought each other seven times, engaging in conflict for 60 out of 126 years. Americans had been involved in every one of these major and minor wars, irrespective of their own wishes in the matter.[23] The benefits accruing to Americans from avoidance in Europe's wars had been one of the main advantages of "separa-

tion" from England, as advocated by Thomas Paine in *Common Sense* and by other pre-Revolutionary leaders.[24]

Something of the dominant American attitude on this point is conveyed by President Woodrow Wilson's mental anguish during World War I, after he had prepared his "war message" (presented to Congress on February 26, 1917). According to one historian, Wilson feared that America's entry into the First World War would "overturn the world we had known."

Down to World War II, the connection between staunch adherence to a policy of isolationism and nonparticipation in war was twofold. First, *if* the American society could successfully avoid becoming embroiled in foreign conflicts, it could escape such evils as infringement upon its independent decision-making by more powerful states, a tendency toward militarism at home, the possible loss of such liberties as those incorporated in the Bill of Rights, higher taxes, and distraction from more important and promising domestic pursuits. Second, the evident success of their isolationist stance, in enabling the United States to avoid involvement in major foreign conflicts for more than a century after the War of 1812, tended to confirm Americans in the wisdom of their behavior toward other countries. (As Sheldon Appleton has pointed out, Americans tended to overlook the fact that for some one hundred years after the defeat of Napoleon in 1815, in fact there was no general European war!)[25]

Yet, fundamental as it was to the concept of isolationism, we should not imagine that the principle of avoiding war was unqualified or free of ambiguities and limitations. The Monroe Doctrine's provisions, for example, were more heavily qualified than most Americans realized. President Monroe had pledged the United

States to abstain from participation in Europe's wars; as with certain other dimensions of the isolationist viewpoint, the restrictions envisioned upon American diplomatic behavior were directed primarily at "èntanglement" *in Europe's rivalries and conflicts.* But President Monroe had gone even further: He affirmed that the United States would not participate in "the wars of the European powers *in matters relating to themselves* [italics added]." Moreover, he had emphatically warned the European Powers that "when our rights are invaded or seriously menaced" America would "make preparation for our defense." Despite the mythology that came to surround it, the Monroe Doctrine, in other words, *contained no blanket prohibition against American participation in foreign wars.* The United States proposed to be a nonbelligerent—or adopt a position of "neutrality"—(1) toward wars involving the major powers of Continental Europe, (2) with regard to disputes that were of concern to these states, (3) so long as America's own security was not jeopardized. This is quite literally what President Monroe announced to the world. As time passed, the American people (not excluding sometimes their leaders) lost sight of the qualifications surrounding the nonbelligerency principle. Thus, President Franklin D. Roosevelt informed the Australian Prime Minister, Joseph A. Lyons, in 1935 that the United States would never again be drawn into a European war *for any reason.*[26]

Although the nonbelligerency concept became associated with the isolationist credo, we must not imagine that isolationism was synonymous with pacificism or total indifference toward the problem of national defense and security. As with other specific connotations of the isolationist doctrine, the meaning and rela-

tive importance of the nonbelligerency idea tended to vary, depending upon circumstances at home and abroad. Those Americans who opposed interventionism in Europe's conflicts during the 1930s, for example, were convinced that isolationism *was* a viable diplomatic strategy, which would enable the United States to defend its interests and security successfully. For many isolationists, a salient feature of their approach to foreign policy, for example, was the premise that *within the Western Hemisphere, the power of the United States was supreme, and it must continue to be supreme.* As long as this was the case, American security was not endangered by the Axis Powers.[27] Robert E. Sherwood has emphasized that most pre-World War II isolationists were in no sense pacifists. Their attitude toward Japan ànd Soviet Russia, for example, was sometime very belligerent! More generally, they favored reliance upon armed force to achieve national policy goals under two conditions: All battles must be waged on America's so-called home ground in the Western Hemisphere, and the United States must fight its military engagements *alone,* without allies, thereby presumably avoiding the "mistakes" of World War I.[28]

Isolationists of an earlier era had sometimes taken a different view of the proper use of military force for the achievement of American foreign policy objectives. Thus, in the period from the end of the nineteenth century to World War I, one school of thought, typified by Senator Henry Cabot Lodge (Republican of Massachusetts), advocated a "large" American policy, involving expansionism and territorial annexations. Lodge entered political life at a time when the advantages accruing from America's geographic isolation were being undermined by modern means of communication and transportation. In this period America was "coming of age," emerging as one of the most powerful nations on the globe. A disciple of Admiral Alfred Mahan, America's foremost advocate of seapower and of control over sea lanes and bases upon which its effective exercise depended,[29] Lodge called for an energetic and expansionist foreign policy for the United States, entailing a rapid buildup in naval strength, particularly in the Pacific region. Thus, Lodge favored America's annexation of Hawaii on strategic-military grounds: Possession of these islands gave the United States mastery of the Pacific sea lanes, and the United States had to deny ownership of them to any foreign power.[30] Similarly, on the eve of World War I, Senator William E. Borah urged the Republican party to "make our position strong for America first, for the protection of American rights here and abroad." Responding to President Wilson's assertion (May 10, 1915) that "there is such a thing as a man [or nation] being too proud to fight," Borah stated: "A nation which declares itself too proud to fight will soon be regarded by the nations of the earth as too cowardly to live." In Borah's view, "weakness is a source of war." Borah was the author of the phrase (from which the "America First" movement, one of the most influential organizations during the 1930s, took its name): "America first, let it cost what it may."[31]

In connection with a controversy with Great Britain, on January 21, 1821, Secretary of State John Quincy Adams had informed London: "Keep what is yours, but leave the rest of the [American] Continent to us."[32] This highlights another component of isolationist thought: the idea of *continentalism*. After independence, one of the goals served by an isolationist stance was "filling out" America's boundaries westward and extending the

hegemony of the United States up to its "natural frontiers" on the Pacific Ocean, the Canadian border, and the Gulf of Mexico. (Some Americans of course believed that eventually Canada, and perhaps Cuba, were destined to form part of the American Union.) This aspiration was unquestionably implicit in the "noncolonization" principle of the Monroe Doctrine and reiterated many times after 1823. As expressed in President James K. Polk's celebrated "corollary" to the Monroe Doctrine (December 2, 1845), the United States was dedicated to the "settled policy that no future European colony or dominion shall with our consent be planted or established on any part of the North American continent." Polk continued that the United States was committed to

... the principle that the people of this continent alone have the right to decide their own destiny. Should any portion of them, constituting an independent state, propose to unite themselves with our Confederacy, this will be a question for them and us to determine without any foreign interposition.[33]

A generation earlier, Congress had forcefully asserted another concept—the "no-transfer" principle—in connection with Spanish possessions in Florida. On January 15, 1811, a congressional resolution announced that the United States could not, "without serious inquietude, see any part of the said territory [East and West Florida] pass into the hands of any foreign Power." Proponents of the no-transfer injunction were unquestionably aware that ultimately the United States might wish to annex Florida and other European colonial possessions in North America.[34] When the Monroe Doctrine and the no-transfer principle were invoked against outside powers, therefore, this was done in some degree on the premise that it was the destiny of the

United States to incorporate foreign territorial possessions on the North American continent.

To the American mind, such expansionist impulses had little in common with the hegemonial tendencies of nations in the Old World. Pursuit of "continentalism" not only would benefit the United States but ultimately would uplift human society at large, not excluding the conduct of international affairs. This mentality perhaps reached its culmination in the approach of Wilsonian idealists to foreign policy questions. Compelled by events to abandon America's preferred position of neutrality toward the belligerents in World War I, President Wilson was determined that, as a result of America's entry into the war, the basic pattern of international relations would thereafter be fundamentally changed. For Wilsonians, this conflict became "the war to end wars" and to "make the world safe for democracy." As Walter Lippmann expressed the idea, "The Wilsonian doctrine was the adaptation of the American tradition to an unexpected necessity—that of returning to Europe, of fighting on the soil of Europe, and of reuniting politically with the European nations." In order to achieve these Wilsonian ends, "the principles of democracy would have to be made universal throughout the world. The Wilsonian ideology is American fundamentalism made into universal doctrine."[35]

NOTES

1. Quoted in Richard W. Leopold, *The Growth of American Foreign Policy: A History* (New York: Alfred A. Knopf, 1962), p. 18.

2. See Jefferson's First Inaugural Address (March 4, 1801), in House of Representatives, *Miscellaneous Documents.* 53d Congress, 2d Session, 1893-94 (Washington, D.C.: U.S. Government Printing Office, 1895), pp. 321–24.

3. When the United States "abandoned" isolationism is a debatable question, which elicits diverse answers from commentators. Some believe that President Franklin D. Roosevelt's "Quarantine Speech" of October 5, 1937, in which he likened Axis aggression to a disease and called on the nations of the world to quarantine it, marked the end of America's isolationist posture. See William L. Langer and S. Everett Gleason, *The Challenge to Isolation: 1937-1940* (New York: Harper & Row, 1952), p. 11.

4. Quoted from Charles A. Beard, *Giddy Minds and Foreign Quarrels* (New York: Macmillan, 1939), reprinted in Robert A. Goldwin, Ed., *Readings in American Foreign Policy,* 2d ed. (New York: Oxford University Press, 1971), pp. 131–33.

5. Quoted in Norman A. Graebner, "Isolationism," *International Encyclopedia of the Social Sciences* (New York: Crowell Collier and Macmillan, 1968), vol. 8, p. 218.

6. After analyzing the results of public opinion polls in the early postwar period, one commentator concluded that no more than 10 percent of the American people could accurately be described as "isolationists." See Alfred O. Hero, *Americans in World Affairs* (Boston: World Peace Foundation, 1959), pp. 10–11.

7. Quoted in Graebner, "Isolationism," p. 219.

8. See Arthur H. Vandenberg, Jr., Ed., *The Private Papers of Senator Vandenberg* (Boston: Houghton Mifflin, 1952), pp. 131, 139.

9. For a detailed discussion of Senator Vandenberg's role, see Cecil V. Crabb, Jr., *Bipartisan Foreign Policy: Myth or Reality?* (New York: Harper & Row, 1957), esp. pp. 44–116.

10. Vandenberg, *The Private Papers of Senator Vandenberg,* p. 139.

11. Quoted in Wayne S. Cole, *Senator Gerald*

P. Nye and American Foreign Relations (Minneapolis: University of Minnesota Press, 1962), p. 216.

12. The idea that America's most beneficial contribution to global peace and security was to solve its own internal problems and conduct itself in an exemplary manner is one of the most consistent themes associated with traditional isolationist thought. President Millard Fillmore in 1851 said that America's "true mission" was "to teach by example and show by our success ... the advantages of free institutions." Quoted in Leopold, *The Growth of American Foreign Policy,* p. 26, and in Arthur A. Ekirch, Jr., *Ideas, Ideals and American Diplomacy* (New York: Appleton-Century-Crofts, 1966), pp. 36–37. Many years later, Secretary of State Cordell Hull declared in a speech in 1937 that America's most effective contribution to world peace was "to have this country respected throughout the world for integrity, justice, good will, strength, and unswerving loyalty to principles." Quoted in Julius W. Pratt, "Cordell Hull," in Samuel F. Bemis, Ed., *The American Secretaries of State and Their Diplomacy* (New York: Cooper Square Publishers, 1964), p. 288.

13. Although Jefferson did not use the term "isolationism," in time the phrase "no entangling alliances" became synonymous with it. See Samuel F. Bemis, *A Diplomatic History of the United States,* 2d ed. (New York: Holt, Rinehart & Winston, 1942), pp. 202–3, and Leopold, *The Growth of American Foreign Policy,* pp. 22–23.

14. As we have already observed, the warning had been foreshadowed in Washington's Farewell Address (1796).

15. Despite the fact that supposedly its terms were to last *in perpetuo,* on July 7, 1798, Congress declared the French alliance void on the grounds that the French government had violated its terms. Thomas A. Bailey, *A Diplomatic History of the American People,* 8th Ed. (New York: Appleton-Century-Crofts, 1969), p. 95.

16. Henry J. Ford, "Timothy Pickering," in Bemis, Ed., *The American Secretaries of State,* pp. 205–6. Pickering served as Secretary of State during the period 1795–1800.

17. Frank Donovan, *Mr. Monroe's Message: The Story of the Monroe Doctrine* (New York: Dodd, Mead, 1963), p. 9.

18. Quoted in Bailey, *A Diplomatic History of the American People,* p. 182, citing C. F. Adams, *Memoirs* (November 7, 1823), p. 179.

19. Paul Seabury, *Power, Freedom, and Diplomacy: The Foreign Policy of the United States of America* (New York: Random House, 1963), p. 38.

20. Quoted in Charles C. Hyde, "Charles Evans Hughes," in Bemis, Ed., *The American Secretaries of State,* p. 356.

21. John C. Vinson, *William E. Borah and the Outlawry of War* (Athens: University of Georgia Press, 1957), p. 1.

22. Quoted in Pratt, "Cordell Hull," p. 199.

23. See the views of Thomas A. Bailey, as cited in Sheldon Appleton, *United States Foreign Policy: An Introduction with Cases* (Boston: Little, Brown, 1968), p. 39.

24. Bemis, *A Diplomatic History of the United States,* p. 12.

25. Appleton, *United States Foreign Policy,* p. 56.

26. For Roosevelt's views, see Robert H. Ferrell, *American Diplomacy: A History* (New York: W. W. Norton, 1959), p. 367.

27. See Burton K. Wheeler, *Yankee from the West* (Garden City, N.Y.: Doubleday Publishing, 1962), p. 22, and Pratt, "Cordell Hull," p. 251.

28. See Robert E. Sherwood, *Roosevelt and Hopkins* (New York: Bantam Books, 1950), pp. 1–161.

29. Admiral Alfred Mahan (1840-1914) exercised a profound influence upon American military strategy for perhaps a half-century or more after 1900. He was a prolific author and well-known lecturer; his most famous book was *The Influence of Seapower upon History* (1918). For a succinct discussion of Mahan's views, see Margaret T. Sprout, "Mahan: Evangelist

of Sea Power," in Edward M. Earle, Ed., *Makers of Modern Strategy* (New York: Atheneum, 1966), pp. 415–46.

30. John A. Garraty, *Henry Cabot Lodge: A Biography* (New York: Alfred A. Knopf, 1953), pp. 150–55.

31. Marian C. McKenna, *Borah* (Ann Arbor: University of Michigan Press, 1961), pp. 138–43.

32. See Adams's views as quoted in Leopold, *The Growth of American Foreign Policy,* p. 42.

33. Julius W. Pratt, *A History of United States Foreign Policy* (Englewood Cliffs, N.J.: Prentice-Hall, 1955), pp. 243–44.

34. See ibid., pp. 129, 165.

35. See Walter Lippmann, *Isolation and Alliances: An American Speaks to the British* (Boston: Little, Brown, 1952), pp. 21–22.

2. THE MORALISTIC INTERPRETATION OF AMERICAN FOREIGN POLICY

Dexter Perkins

The realistic student of foreign affairs will perforce admit the very large role that is played by sheer physical power in the intercourse of nations. But those who assume that physical power operates apart from all other considerations, and especially apart from what may well be described as moral considerations, display a shallow kind of cynicism that is far removed from the facts. The most absolute and the most unscrupulous dictators are themselves the refutation of this point of view. In international affairs, as in life in general, hypocrisy is the tribute that vice pays to virtue. Adolf Hitler had no public morals whatsoever, so far as his diplomacy was concerned. Yet he constantly branded other people as warmongers in an effort to make war palatable to his own people; again and again he fabricated stories of atrocities suffered by Germans outside the Reich in order to give some kind of moral validity to his projects of aggrandizement; and he created an ideology around which loyalties could center in an opposition to Communism. In the same way the present leaders of the Soviet Union, while quite oblivious of any precepts of international morality, constantly talk in terms of such precepts, constantly invoke the Hitlerian device of describing other people as bellicose and sinister in their ambitions, pretend to be

Source: Reprinted by permission of the publishers from *The American Approach to Foreign Policy,* Rev. Ed., pp. 72–97, Dexter Perkins, Cambridge, Mass.: Harvard University Press. Copyright © 1962 by the President and Fellows of Harvard College.

interested in disarmament while maintaining the largest armed forces in the world in proportion to their population, and make appeal to an ideology which becomes a kind of faith, with all the moral implications that faith implies and with the declared end the betterment of the fortunes of the human race. No government in the modern world could treat its people as if moral ideas did not exist, and none would try.

The degree, however, to which moral ideas influence diplomacy will vary, and the expression of these ideas will vary with the political constitution and mores of the individual state. In Hitlerian Germany or Soviet Russia, ethical concepts may be a mere device for the advancement of the national interests, a mere support to a largely cynical diplomacy. But we must not imagine that it is only in the dictatorships that this is true. It has been true of states which were not autocratic in form. In Europe in the nineteenth century, foreign policy was conducted very largely in secret and by professional diplomats, who acted independently, to a very large degree though not absolutely, without regard to public opinion. In such conditions it is not strange that there were many "deals," which were not supposed to see the light of day, and that agreements were often entered into which concerned third parties and perhaps sacrificed their interests, agreements which might have met with considerable condemnation if they had been made public. In general, putting the matter in another way, a very free hand was left to the professionals by the people themselves, and the professionals naturally made such use as they chose of this freedom, promoting the national interest as they understood it, no doubt, but referring to public opinion only when they felt compelled to do so, or when they found in it a useful support for their own objectives. Nor have we seen the last of professional diplomacy in our own age. There is still in many countries a long tradition of relative freedom of action for government in the conduct of foreign affairs, and while this tradition is no doubt declining in force, it is still a factor in the actual conduct of foreign relations.

In the United States, on the other hand, to a degree remarkable at least by comparison, a different way of thinking and acting with regard to these matters has developed. American democracy is not by any means precisely like the democracy of European states. There has not been a governing class in America since the Federalists aspired to that title at the end of the eighteenth century. The professional diplomat hardly existed in much of the nineteenth century, and he has never occupied the secure position that he once occupied, and to some degree still occupies, in the Old World. To an extent that is true in no other country, the motivating force in government has come up from the people, rather than down from a political or diplomatic elite. The average man in America, be he well informed or ill informed, is likely to think that he has a right to express an opinion in politics and to have that opinion considered. When complex issues are submitted to examination in such a mechanism as the *Fortune* poll, the amazing thing is often the small number of persons who will say that they do not know the answer. The spirit of American politics suggests that

the citizen *does* know the answers, and, in any case, the citizen is likely to think that he knows. In addition to all this, there has been from the beginning of American politics (and here we anticipate what we are to examine in more detail later) a dislike of secrecy with regard to foreign affairs and a habit of public debate on foreign issues. The great questions of foreign policy have often been submitted to public debate, often discussed with great frankness from more than one point of view, and often decided by the test of public opinion. No one can understand American diplomacy who does not grasp the importance of the democratic motif in its historic evolution.

Now the mass of men are, of course, not equipped to understand in their infinite ramifications and details the problems that confront a nation in the field of foreign affairs. If they exercise an influence on policy (and it has just been stated they *do* exercise such an influence in America), they are almost bound, in the nature of the case, to attach themselves to relatively simple concepts, to principles easy to understand and relevant to their general democratic experience, or to emotional attitudes that spring from the circumstances of the moment. Among these considerations, for example, may be the idea that democratic government is the best government on earth (irrespective of the particular situation of a given nation), or the idea that conquest is inherently immoral (without too sharp a scrutiny of the American past in this regard), or the idea that it is wrong to negotiate in secret (though it is hard to see how diplomacy could be carried on if there were not at least some secrecy), or the idea that the state is bound by the same moral code as is the individual (though this is a knotty question even for philosophers). And if views such as these are widely diffused throughout the community, and if they are also strongly held, they are bound, of course, to affect the tone of our diplomatic action and to influence very strongly the actual conduct of our public men. In other words, principles, strongly fused with emotions, will play a very great part in the foreign policy of such a country as the United States. Because this is so (and again the point must be elaborated later), high-sounding declarations and general appeals to international morality will often characterize the utterances of our statesmen and even their private diplomatic notes. When we say this, we by no means imply that Americans are unique in this regard. But it is, I think, fair to say that there is a highly moralistic flavor to our diplomacy as compared with the other nations. To foreigners this lofty moral tone no doubt sometimes seems like cant or a mere device of the diplomats themselves. But these people do Americans injustice; and the best test of this is to be found in the fact that, on occasion, the government of the United States has put ethical considerations ahead of national interest as it would be defined in the narrow sense of the term.

Before we examine, however, the moralistic overtones in American diplomacy, we must pause to remark that these overtones do not necessarily and inevitably mean that American foreign policy is therefore "better" than the diplomacy of other nations, even if we maintained, which we do not, that the difference was one in kind and not in degree. For one thing, the oversimplification of the issues which results from an appeal to moral principle may or may not be desirable in practice. The conviction, for example, that democratic government is the best of all governments may lead us to try to impose it on others, without success and with the result that international irritation ensues. A moral repugnance to imperialism and conquest may blind Americans to the practical difficulties in the way of giving complete independence to nations not yet very well prepared for it. A dislike of secrecy may lead to a degree of publicity in international affairs which makes compromise difficult and which arouses rather than allays the passions that often play a part in international affairs. The notion that the state must be bound by the same code as the individual may lead to quixotic action and naive judgment in the real world of international affairs. Principles are both useful and dangerous, both inspiring and exacerbating.

Indeed, one of the major difficulties with the moralistic view of foreign policy is that it makes for rigidity. The business of diplomacy is often the business of adjusting rival interests and rival points of view, of giving a little here and there and of getting a little in return. But if every question is to be invested with the aura of principle, how is adjustment to take place? There is no more difficult problem in the world of individuals than that of bringing together contestants who, each from his own point of view, are clad in the armor of unsullied righteousness. The same thing applies to nations.

Furthermore, moral judgments, since they rest on a foundation of deep feeling, rather than on precise analysis, may and sometimes do verge on sentimentality. A moral judgment may be very naive in the manner in which it assesses the elements of a complex problem. It has been difficult for some good people to accept the fact that the ushering in of an era of good will is not a prime objective of foreign policy for the Soviet Union; they cannot persuade themselves that some such ethical objective does not underlie the action of the Kremlin, as it would, no doubt, underlie their own action if they were where they could act effectively. Or, to take another example, it was easy for most Americans to believe, more deeply than on the basis of the facts they ought to have believed, in the efficacy of the Kellogg Pact, by which nations who signed pledged themselves not to resort to war as an instrument of policy. The promise to be virtuous is not virtue, as the generation which followed discovered before long. In the field of international organization, too, Americans are sometimes deceived by their feelings. World government, for example, is an appealing ideal so long as one feels about it rather than thinks about it. But it is by no means certain that the institutional approach to peace is the best approach, and it is certainly not the only one.

It is not, however, the object of this essay to make a moral judgment on the moralistic approach of the Americans to diplomacy; it is rather my purpose, by reviewing the national story, to make clear how strong this moralistic emphasis has been and how often it has played a part in foreign policy. Let us look first of all at the strong influence exerted by the democratic ideal upon American action. And here we may begin with the events of the second Washington administration and with the difficulties of the first President in shaping a course which was to the interest of the nation. There seems to me little doubt about what was wise policy for the United States in this initial period. An intellectual or realistic view of the matter would surely have led to an understanding with Great Britain, our principal source of imports, our best customer, our neighbor in North America, and the holder of our border posts at a time when we were little equipped to afford the luxury of British hostility. So, of course, Washington viewed the matter; on this basis he acted in the despatch of the Jay mission. Yet such men as Jefferson and Madison, representing a powerful section of opinion, advocated measures of commercial reprisal against Great Britain, which would probably have been fruitless, and opposed bitterly the treaty of 1794. The basis of their action lay, without question, in their sympathy for the French Revolution—in other words, in ideological and moral considerations.

The revolutions in Latin America had a substantial repercussion in the United States. There were certainly many distinctions between the course of the events in that part of the world and the course of events at home. But the judgment of such an American as Henry Clay took none of these factors into account. In his speeches in Congress in 1818, he put great stress on the similarity of the institutions of North and South America, and laid the basis for the structure that was later to become known as Pan-Americanism. The more cautious and intellectual Adams saw a very different picture; he was influenced by motives at once more realistic and more selfish; and the recognition of the colonies, for which Clay clamored, was postponed till 1822, when the United States had safely acquired the Floridas from Spain. But the ideological note is strong, indeed, in the policy of the Monroe administration itself when we come to the famous declaration of December 2, 1823. In a sense, the message is an ideological tract, praising the democratic principle and exalting democratic forms in contrast to the monarchies of Europe. And if Monroe had had his way, its ideological character would have been still more complete, for he proposed to add to the message a sympathetic reference to the Greeks and a commentary on the suppression of constitutional government in Spain. Of course it is not to be contended that none but idealistic and moral considerations entered into Monroe's pronouncement. In one sense, it was based upon the principle of national security, on the assumption that the restoration of monarchical rule in Latin America was "dangerous to our peace and safety." But this hypothesis would have been difficult to prove if submitted to the acid test of analysis, especially at the time that the President issued his famous challenge. The prime significance of the message was ideological, and its prime origin lay in Americans' feeling of moral association with their "southern brethren." Europeans clearly recognized this fact; Metternich was by no means alone among European conservatives in bewailing what he foresaw as the separation of the New World from the Old. Indeed, any careful study of the period will make it clear that the young republic of the West was regarded by Continental Europeans as having deliberately and arrogantly laid down a principle which flew in the face of European doctrine and which was primarily based on very different assumptions from the assumption of legitimacy. The immense enthusiasm which the message aroused in the United States, the press comment of the time, dwelt for the most part very little upon the sense of immediate peril and very much upon the distinction between the institutions of Europe and the institutions of America.

The moral factor in diplomacy, the sympathy with the democratic ideal, was again expressed in the European revolutions of 1848. The American government acted promptly, almost precipitately, in recognizing the Second French Republic in 1848. The Hungarian revolt was followed with intense enthusiasm by many Americans, and the Taylor administration sent an American representative to Hungary, with instructions to hold out assurances of recognition if the circumstances warranted. When the Austrian government protested this action, Secretary of State Daniel Webster responded in a despatch whose flowing periods and flamboyant tone make it one of the most remarkable in American diplomatic intercourse. And though with Russian aid the independence movement was put down, the patriot Kossuth, when he came to this country, was received with transports of acclaim and honored by a banquet at which Webster himself was one of the speakers. True, it was not possible for Americans to do anything effective; armed intervention was out of the question, for reasons of geography, if nothing else; but the tension created by this episode was great enough to lead to a temporary interruption of relations between the Austrian minister and the Secretary of State.

The clash of political ideals was again illustrated in the course of events in Mexico in the fifties and the sixties. In the struggle between the liberal and reactionary elements in that country, the United States was naturally impelled to take the side of the liberals. It supported the Juarez regime from an early period, and the Buchanan administration even went so far as to negotiate what was virtually a treaty of protectorate with that regime. French intrigues in behalf of monarchy, from the first regarded with suspicion, became the object of pointed reprobation on the part of Seward even in the course of the Civil War, and they aroused such widespread indignation during that struggle that in April 1864 the House of Representatives passed unanimously a resolution condemning the policy of Napoleon III. And, at the end of the war, there was still more emphatic expression of public sentiment, which might conceivably have led to war had it not been for the adroit diplomacy of Seward and the reaction in France itself against the adventure in Mexico.

The theme of democratic idealism runs through the whole history of Pan-Americanism, which began to find expression in positive form with James G. Blaine. The economic determinist will doubtless discover ulterior motives behind the calling of the Latin American conference of 1889; and such motives there undoubtedly were. But would it have been possible to weld together the nations of the New World in so close an association on the basis of a trade infinitely less significant than that with Europe? Is it not certain that the belief, whether justified or not, that there existed a similarity of institutions among the states of North and South America had something to do with the success of this important movement? And have not Pan-American conferences again and again asserted the validity of democratic principles and paid tribute to the democratic ideal?

Nor is this the only way that the United States has attempted to promote democracy on this side of the Atlantic. Sometimes it has gone further and attempted to use its influence more directly. The Central American treaties of 1907 and 1923, with their doctrine that governments arising from revolution ought not to be recognized, was, in a sense, an attempt to impose the American way of orderly election and popular choice upon some of our weaker neighbors. Largely ineffective in practice it has certainly been; today not many students of American diplomacy would advocate such policy. But this does not alter the fact that democratic principle affected action. Nor must we forget the still more striking case in which the same idea was applied: Woodrow

Wilson's attitude towards Mexico. The refusal of the President to recognize the blood-stained regime of Victoriano Huerta was based squarely upon principle, and ironically enough this insistence on principle came very near to leading to intervention. No doubt Wilson's policy came in for very sharp criticism from some of those who described themselves as realists, but it was, nonetheless, resolutely adhered to, and it led, of course, to the fall of the Mexican dictator.

We have already discussed the interventions in the Caribbean. Here the motives, as we have seen, were largely strategic. But in every case, be it noted, the final act was an election conducted according to democratic principle, and the notion that somehow or other the unruly little peoples of this area could be instructed—and coerced—into accepting American conceptions of popular government was at all times present.

In the evolution of American public opinion with regard to the world war, a sense of democratic morality was certainly one of the factors that shaped the course of policy. Americans, from the beginning, contrasted the political institutions of France and Britain with the institutions of Germany. They were by no means always fair in this regard; to describe Germany as an autocracy in 1914 was stretching things pretty far. They overlooked, also, the fact that the Russian regime was far closer to political absolutism than the governments of the Central Empires. But although the generalization that the war was a struggle of autocracy against democracy had only a partial validity, this did not in any way diminish the force of the popular sentiment in this regard. The policy of partiality toward the Allies, and of discrimination against Germany, was in no small degree due to moral considerations. It explains why the Wilson administration dealt gently with British violations of international law and held rigidly to principle in dealing with the government in Berlin. It explains why the President himself, highly trained though he was, could echo the popular generalization in some of the very greatest of his speeches, and why he could proclaim the struggle to be in very truth a struggle involving political forms.

Wilson's war message, indeed, is largely based on this theory. Democratic governments, he seems to be saying, are peaceful governments; they act on principles of international morality different from those of autocratic governments. They do not (here Wilson was either misinformed or disingenuous) fill their neighbor states with spies; they do not embark upon ambitious enterprises of conquest. The peace of the world depends upon the breaking of the force of autocracy and upon the setting up of democratic regimes. "The world must be made safe for democracy." The President goes further. In a passage more remarkable for its rhetoric than for its prescience, he welcomes "the great naive Russian people" to the ranks of the democrats and actually, in his optimism and exaltation, goes so far as to say that the autocracy which "crowned the summit of Russian political life" was "not in fact Russian in origin, character, or purpose." Idealism could hardly go further than this.

This same faith in the democratic ideal animated Wilsonian diplomacy in dealing with Germany. The avowed theory of his speeches was that not the German people, but the rulers of Germany, were to blame for the war, that if the democratic forces in Germany could be liberated a new nation, to all intents and purposes, would arise. And insistence on this point of view was certainly a factor, and a very important factor, in bringing

about the flight of the Kaiser and the establishment of a republic in the Reich. It may be that, in this respect, Wilson's policy was not entirely wise; it is possible to argue that a constitutional monarchy would have offered a more successful resistance to the madness of National Socialism than the republican regime could have done; but, however this may be, the moral conviction that lay behind Wilson's policy cannot be denied. To him popular government was something of a religion. And that he echoed a deep-seated popular sentiment can hardly be doubted.

In another sense, too, the notion of democracy deeply affected the policy of the war years and the making of the peace. For the democratic ideal is obviously closely connected with the principle of self-determination, and to this principle Woodrow Wilson gave pronounced allegiance. That the peace should rest upon the will of the peoples concerned was clear to him, clear to him even before the United States entered the war, set forth in some detail in the famous address of January 22, 1917. This idea was enunciated again and again after America entered the conflict; it is one of the dominating conceptions in the famous speech of the Fourteen Points. And, of course, it plays an important part in the negotiation of the treaty of peace. It was respect for this principle that made Wilson fight tenaciously French ambitions for the annexation of the Saar and that led to the setting up of an international regime in that important region, with provision for a plebiscite at the end of a fifteen-year period; it was on the basis of this principle that the President contested French designs to detach the Rhineland from Germany; it was still from the same point of view that he either actively encouraged or easily acquiesced in the various plebiscites which determined the frontiers of the Reich on the north in regard to Denmark and on the east with regard to Poland; the internationalization of Danzig was based on the same conceptions; and preoccupation with self-determination influenced the arrangements for the Italian boundary in Istria. Finally, respect for the democratic ideal led to a wholly new treatment of the problem of the backward peoples, as we have already seen. It is of course not contended that Wilson was consistent to the last degree in his attachment to principle. Few men are. The veto in the treaty on the possible union of Austria and Germany was hardly defensible; and though the question of the German population in the Sudetenland was hardly raised while the President was at Paris, he seems never to have been much troubled by the attitude of the Czechs towards this problem. He wavered, in other words, in the pressing of his own standards of rectitude, as others have done before him and will do after him. But that democratic idealism played an important part in the negotiation of the Treaty of Versailles, and an especially important part in American diplomacy at Paris, it would be difficult to deny.

The same idealism, whether misguided or not, directed Wilsonian policy towards Soviet Russia. It was characteristic of the President that his remedy for the Russian civil war in 1919 was a conference of all factions, presumably to decide upon a peace based on democratic principle; and it is understandable that as the autocratic character of the Russian regime made itself more and more apparent the reaction of the administration was that of nonrecognition. It may perhaps be questioned whether a sound sense of political realism dictates abstention from diplomatic intercourse with governments of whose origins or principles we

disapprove. It may be that it is wiser to keep the channels of communication open and hope that some breath of freedom will penetrate from the outside world. But moral reprobation is in some ways a very human form of satisfaction, and no country has carried it further in the evolution of its policy than the United States. The policy determined upon by Wilson, and enunciated by his Secretary of State Bainbridge Colby, was followed by the Harding and Coolidge administrations, and long after the other great nations of the world had established relations with the Kremlin, our own government stood aloof. It was not indeed until 1933 that the diplomatic boycott was ended.

The dislike of the Communist regime did not end with the advent of the Roosevelt administration. Anti-Communist sentiment, it is true, influenced policy to a considerably less degree in the thirties and was naturally suppressed, from motives of convenience, in the years of the war. But it was not slow to revive as soon as the struggle was over. From the pure point of view of national interest, there was really very little reason for the United States to concern itself with the character of the governments that were set up in Bulgaria and Rumania. Yet the United States made itself from the outset the defender of democracy in this part of the world and sought to prevent the transformation of these two states into satellites of the Kremlin. The case of Poland was, in many respects, similar, though here the anti-Russian feeling of American Poles rested on a broader basis than pure ideology. But a diplomacy less affected by considerations of principle might well have tried to bargain and to agree to let the Soviet government pursue its own course in Eastern Europe in exchange for a policy more considerate of American interests in Western Europe. I do not say, let it be clear, that such a policy would have succeeded. It probably would not have done so. But the fact that it was not even attempted is surely significant.

Ideological considerations have played a substantial part, also, in the American attitude towards Communist China. The question of the recognition of the Peiping government, it is true, is a complicated one, and the fact that this regime waged war against the United States and that it has consistently violated the armistice ending that war no doubt goes far to explain such an attitude. But another factor, beyond a doubt, is a deep repugnance to the brutality and violence which are so evident in the regime of Mao Tse-tung.

It is not only dictatorships of the left that have fallen under American condemnation on moral grounds. It is impossible to weigh accurately the elements which entered into the equation in fixing American hostility to Adolf Hitler. But surely among them was the brutal persecution of the Jews and the outrageous bad faith of the Third Reich in the international sphere. In the same way there existed in the forties a deep repugnance to the regime of General Franco. From the purely objective point of view, Americans might have judged the Spanish government less harshly than they did. In retrospect, whatever the sympathies of the Caudillo, it seems fairly clear that cautious neutrality was the watchword of Spanish policy, and that the chances of Spanish intervention on the side of Germany were extremely small. Yet dislike of the government at Madrid led the government of the United States to recall its ambassador in 1946 and to support the resolution in the Assembly of the United Nations which recommended such action to the members of the international body. To take another case, during the war the United States refused to deal with the Farrell regime in

Argentina, and in the elections of 1946 the weight of the United States was exerted quite openly against the authoritarian elements which rallied behind Colonel Peron. It is by no means clear that such a policy was wise; it had its roots in feeling rather than in self-interest.

Another striking case of repugnance to a dictatorship of the right is to be found in the severance of relations with the Dominican Republic in 1960. The regime of Rafael Leonidas Trujillo fostered the development of American capital and sought in many ways to woo the United States. But the repulsive character of the dictator, his unbridled acquisitiveness, his intrigues against other Latin American states whose rulers he disliked, the iron character of his rule, led to a resolution of the Organization of American States looking to a rupture of diplomatic intercourse. The United States representative supported this resolution. And the antagonism to Trujillo in the State Department over a substantial period of time is a matter of record. The repugnance was moral.

We need spend less time on the American reaction towards imperialism, since the subject has already been discussed. Yet some examples of the uneasy conscience that often goes with acquisitiveness, in the case of the United States, may be cited. Take, for example, the ill-timed attempt of President Grant to bring about the annexation of the Dominican Republic in 1870. The attempt was no doubt absurd, a kind of shoddy deal, with overtones of land speculation, with a government that could only maintain itself by a treaty with a stronger neighbor; but what is interesting is the strong moral reprobation which the enterprise aroused in the breast of Charles Sumner and the refusal of the Republican majority, in days of intense partisanship, to go along with the President. Or take again the attitude of Grover Cleveland with regard to the Hawaiian revolution of 1893. This revolution was encouraged, if not actually assisted, by the American minister at Honolulu, and it was followed by a treaty of annexation with the United States. But Cleveland sent a special commissioner to the islands, established to his own satisfaction the fact that the course of the United States had not been free from blame, and withdrew the treaty. Indeed, he went further and, with a fine gesture of moral indignation, demanded of the authorities of the islands that they restore the deposed Queen Lilioukalani to the throne. The gesture, it is true, was futile; it was met with prompt defiance. But it illustrates well enough the moralistic emphasis which sometimes intrudes itself into American diplomacy.

Another and a rather amusing illustration of American bad conscience where acquisition is concerned is to be found in the payments the United States has been ready to make for territory acquired by the sword. For example, the treaty of Guadalupe Hidalgo, in 1848, stipulated that the Mexican government should receive the sum of $20 million for the cession of California. Perhaps, in this case, cynics would suggest that the motive for such generosity was not one of undiluted altruism but that a desire to "grease the way" for the acceptance of the treaty by Mexico was also present. But no such consideration could possibly have had a part in the 1898 treaty of Paris, when we paid $20 million for the cession of the Philippines by Spain. Another instance of this kind of action is to be found in the famous treaty of 1914 with Colombia. The Colombian government had been understandably incensed at the role of the United States in the revolution in Panama in 1903 and at the hasty recognition of the Panamanian government by Wash-

ington. The Wilson administration, coming into power in 1913, sought to allay this resentment and negotiated a treaty which contained a virtual apology for the incident of a decade before, and which stipulated a payment of $25 million to the government at Bogota. True, this treaty was delayed for some time, and the discovery of oil in Colombia may have altered the moral aspects of the problem for some senators, such as Henry Cabot Lodge of Massachusetts. Yet no such considerations prompted the original negotiation or the widespread support which the treaty obtained from the outset on the Democratic side of the Senate.

In a little different category, but illustrating again the impulse of conscience in our dealings with weaker powers, is the attitude of the United States with regard to the Boxer indemnity of 1900. The Americans had joined with the European powers in that year to relieve the legations at Peking, besieged by Chinese revolutionists, and had, in common with the rest, demanded an indemnity from the Chinese government. But this did not sit well on the national conscience, and it was not long before the indemnity was remitted to the Chinese government, with the understanding that it should be used for the education of Chinese students in the United States.

There are many larger issues with regard to the American attitude towards imperialism that have been already treated. Domination of other peoples, as we have seen, has always created an uneasy feeling in Americans; they naturally look towards establishing the institutions of freedom wherever they go; and their natural instincts lead them to look with favor on movements of independence from foreign control wherever these movements arise.

We spoke of a third manner in which

the American moral impulse expressed itself in American diplomacy, that is, in a dislike of secrecy, especially of secret deals. The general question of secret diplomacy is to be treated later. But the matter of making bargains with one power at the expense of another, a practice of which the history of Europe is full, may well be considered here. On the whole, the American record is a very good one. There are some exceptions. A case in point is the not very scrupulous attempt of Thomas Jefferson to bribe the French government into putting pressure on the satellite regime in Spain to cede the Floridas to the United States. Yet this attempt met with violent condemnation from John Randolph, until then one of Jefferson's followers, and it came to nothing. We have to come down to relatively recent times to find another episode of doubtful morality of the same general kind. The Taft-Katsura memorandum of 1905, by which the United States bound itself to the recognition of the Japanese position in Korea in exchange for a pledge to respect the independence of the Philippines, has an extremely "practical" significance. We may cite also the action of Franklin D. Roosevelt at Yalta, in pledging himself in writing to support the claims of the Soviet Union to their former privileges in Manchuria, at the expense of China and really behind the back of the government at Peking. It is true that the President was told by his military advisers that it was essential to bring the Russians into the war against Japan. It is also true that the Chinese Nationalists later accepted the arrangement. But it is significant that this "deal" was not even recorded in the archives of the State Department and that, when discovered, it met with severe reprobation from large sections of American public opinion. Speaking generally, it is fair to say that

such oblique transactions have by no means been characteristic of American diplomacy.

But there is a still larger sense in which moral judgment enters into the formation of American foreign policy. We have spoken of the democratic ideal as influencing American conduct with regard to the First World War. There was more to the matter than that. The simple judgment of many Americans condemned the Central Empires in 1914 because it was believed that these empires had started the war. A more refined judgment might point to a long train of causes and to errors and provocations on both sides. But what was seen in that fateful August was that the Austro-Hungarian government had launched an attack on Serbia, and Germany an attack on Russia. And when these initial acts of aggression (as they were widely regarded) were followed by the violation of Belgian neutrality, in contemptuous disregard of solemn treaty obligations, the partiality of many citizens for the cause of the Allies was heightened. It would be foolish to deny the influence of these events on the course of American diplomacy. If Woodrow Wilson did not hold the balance even between the two sets of contestants in the mighty struggle that was unleashed, the reason was that he, like hosts of others, had made a moral judgment with regard to the war from which he could not free himself.

Equally striking is the American attitude towards both Japanese and German imperialism in the thirties. The American government, in 1931, could not sit still in the face of the Japanese conquest of Manchuria. The foreign offices of Europe were by no means so disposed to a moral judgment, and the British, in particular, hesitated to take any stand against Japan. But the United States insisted that the question be thoroughly ventilated, and though it was not ready to challenge Tokyo to armed conflict, it put forward the famous Stimson Doctrine and even secured its acceptance by the assembly of the League of Nations. By this doctrine, as is well known, the powers of the world refused to recognize any situation, treaty, or agreement brought about by means contrary to the obligations of the Kellogg Pact, that is, by acts of force. Whether such moral pillorying of another government is wise or foolish, a futile gesture or a useful clarification of the record, is beside the point. It represents very clearly the influence of an ethical ideal in the practice of diplomacy.

The same thing can be seen in later relations with Japan. When it came to the Sino-Japanese war, there was certainly a case for a policy of appeasement from the American point of view. Our trade with Japan and our investments in Japan were far greater than our trade with or our investments in China. True, the conquest of the Middle Kingdom by Nippon tended to restrict our commerce, but true, too, we would jeopardize a far more valuable commerce by war. And, in addition, prudential considerations might well have suggested the gentle handling of Tokyo at a time when the situation was increasingly serious in Europe. The British government (of course in a far more critical situation) seemed to be acting on just such calculations when it closed the Burma Road in the spring of 1940. But none of these elements determined American policy. It was impossible for the Roosevelt administration to frame its policy in the Far East without regard to the moral revulsion felt by the American people at the Japanese invasion of China. In the conversations of 1941, the Japanese negotiators at least hinted that a way might be found to evade Japan's obligations to

Germany under the treaty of alliance of September 1940, if only the United States would grant it a free hand in its ambitious designs on its great neighbor. But it would have been practically and morally impossible for the United States to take any such position, as the polls of public opinion amply attest. Indeed, the attempted modus vivendi of November 1941 broke down just because it was out of the question to tolerate the continued domination of the Tokyo government on the Asian continent. And so the country found itself involved in a two-front war from the outset, a war that might conceivably (wisely or unwisely, as you will) have been postponed.

The same sense of moral reprobation with regard to aggression showed itself in the American attitude towards Hitler. Not only dislike of totalitarian political forms but indignation at the aggressions of the National Socialist regime, not only fear of consequences but moral indignation at the methods of aggrandizement, played a part in the steadily mounting tide of feeling against the Third Reich. By the end of the thirties, too, the American people were coming to a conviction that is more and more influencing policy, the conviction that the use of force for the purposes of domination is inherently immoral and intolerable. Opinion expressed itself decisively with regard to the rape of Austria and the violent methods that preceded Munich, and rarely have more sincere moral homilies been written by a Secretary of State than those which flowed from the indignant pen of Cordell Hull in this period. It was the same when the Russians attacked Finland. There was, perhaps, something of a case for the Soviet Union, from the point of view of the protection of its own territory. But the war against the Finns was almost universally denounced in the

United States. And, in the period since 1945, the steady imposition of Communist power on the satellite states, though not necessarily dangerous to American security, though hardly more, from one angle, than the consolidation of a position already attained by the victories of Russian armies in the war itself, has met with a steady stream of condemnation in this country.

But the most striking of all examples of American moralism in international affairs is to be found in the doctrine of collective security. The very root of this doctrine lies in the idea that the use of force in the settlement of international disputes is morally wrong and that the social interest requires that all states shall combine against an aggressor. Not national interest, narrowly defined, but the public peace becomes the foundation of policy. It is true that the United States declined to accept the responsibilities implicit in this point of view in the twenties and thirties, and repudiated at the polls the great leader who propounded it. But the doctrine survived, and we have heard much of it since the end of the Second World War. Consider, for example, the American action in Korea in 1950. The cold-blooded could have given many reasons why the issue raised by the invasion of South Korea might have been allowed to pass unchallenged. The government of Syngman Rhee, to judge from the elections of May 1950, had few roots in Korean opinion. The military problem presented by the giving of aid to that government was a difficult one, both because the weather conditions were peculiarly unfavorable to counteroperations against the forces of the North and because the problems of supply were peculiarly difficult. Moreover, the Americans had to fight with their backs to the sea, in a position where defeat would mean nothing less than evacuation. Finally, there was always the risk that Russia or China would intervene (as actually happened in the case of China). Yet none of these things affected the issue. The decision taken by President Truman at this time received the almost unanimous support of the nation; it was a decision based in no small degree on fundamental principles of international morality. There was, of course, an argument of another kind, and a good one, the argument that appeasement would only lead to new challenges, until an explosion was inevitable. But this does not invalidate the conclusion that a strong moral impulse influenced American action.

A still more striking case is the position taken by the American government in 1956 when the Israelis, the British, and the French invaded Egypt. The French and British were our allies; the Israelis were our friends and had many sympathizers among the Jews of the United States. On the other hand, we had no particular reason to admire the Egyptian leader, Colonel Nasser. Yet the United States sharply denounced the invasion, aligned itself in the General Assembly of the United Nations with the Soviet Union in the voting, and had a hand in bringing a halt to the whole enterprise. A less moralistic view of the matter might have led the administration either to hold its hand or, perhaps more wisely, to have offered its services as a go-between. The hurt inflicted on our relations with France and Great Britain was deep. But an austere view of American duty was what prevailed.

Still another example of American moralism in the world of today may be given. It has been impossible for the United States to accept the *fait accompli* with regard to Soviet expansion in Eastern Europe, especially Soviet aggression in Hungary. There are those who would argue that it is wise to accept accomplished facts. But this is not the attitude assumed by most Americans, nor has it been the attitude of the Truman, the Eisenhower, or (so far) the Kennedy administration.

To assert these things, be it said in conclusion, is not to fall into that kind of oversimplification which attributes to a single factor a total influence over events. It is not to say that American foreign policy is always altruistic, that it is not directed by conceptions of national interest, that it is always either in its methods or its objectives to be unqualifiedly commended. It is only to say that *ideas,* and ideas connected with certain moral preoccupations, are a factor, and a substantially important factor, in the conduct of diplomacy. And there are Americans who would add that some of the strength of the nation flows from just these facts. When men go to war, they are actuated by many motives, by mere conformity, by patriotism, by the fear of danger, by understood self-interest, but also, and not infrequently, by the belief that they are defending right and justice. And whether this belief is justified or not in the eyes of the skeptical analyst, it is one of the mainsprings of that courageous devotion which brings victory.

3. THE MAINSPRINGS OF AMERICAN FOREIGN POLICY

Hans J. Morgenthau

It is often said that the foreign policy of the United States needs to mature and that the American people and their government must grow up if they want to emerge victorious from the trials of our age. It would be truer to say that this generation of Americans must shed the illusions of its fathers and grandfathers and relearn the great principles of statecraft which guided the republic in the first decade and—in moralistic disguise—in the first century of its existence. The United States offers the singular spectacle of a commonwealth whose political wisdom has not grown slowly through the accumulation and articulation of experiences. On the contrary, the full flowering of its political wisdom was coeval with its birth as an independent nation; indeed, it owed its existence and survival as an independent nation to those extraordinary qualities of political insight, historical perspective, and common sense which the first generation of Americans applied to the affairs of state.

This classic age of American statecraft came to an end with the disappearance of that generation of American statesmen. Cut off from its vital sources, the rich and varied landscape in which they had planted all that is worth while in the tradition of Western political thought was allowed to go to waste. That age and its wisdom became a faint and baffling remembrance, a symbol to be worshipped rather than a source of inspiration and a guide for action. Until very recently the American people have appeared content to live in a political desert whose intellectual barrenness and aridity was relieved only by some sparse and neglected oases of insight and wisdom. What passed for foreign policy was either improvisation or—especially in our century—the invocation of some abstract moral principle in whose image the world was to be made over. Improvisation was largely successful, for in the past the margin of American and allied power has generally exceeded the degree to which American improvidence has failed the demands of the hour. The invocation of abstract moral principles was in part hardly more than an innocuous pastime; embracing everything, it came to grips with nothing. In part, however, it was a magnificent instrument for marshaling public opinion in support of war and warlike policies— and for losing the peace. The intoxication with moral abstractions, which as a mass phenomenon started with the Spanish-American War and which in our time has become the prevailing substitute for political thought, is indeed one of the great sources of weakness and failure in American foreign policy. Much will have to be said about this later.

Still it is worthy of note that underneath this political dilettantism, which is nourished by improvidence and a sense of moral mission, there lives an almost instinctive awareness of the perennial in-

Source: Hans J. Morgenthau, *In Defense of the National Interest* (New York: Alfred A. Knopf, 1952), pp. 3–39. Reprinted by permission of Matthew Morgenthau and Susanna Morgenthau.

terests of the United States. This has been especially true with regard to Europe and the Western Hemisphere, for in these regions the national interest of the United States has always been obvious and clearly defined.

THE NATIONAL INTEREST OF THE UNITED STATES

In the Western Hemisphere we have always endeavored to preserve the unique position of the United States as a predominant power without rival. We have not been slow in recognizing that our predominance was not likely to be effectively threatened by any one American nation or combination of nations acting without support from outside the hemisphere. This peculiar situation has made it imperative for the United States to isolate the Western Hemisphere from the political and military policies of non-American nations. The interference of non-American nations in the affairs of the Western Hemisphere, especially through the acquisition of territory, was the only way in which the predominance of the United States could have been challenged from within the hemisphere itself. The Monroe Doctrine and the policies implementing it express that permanent national interest of the United States in the Western Hemisphere.

Since a threat to our national interest in the Western Hemisphere can only come from outside it—historically, from Europe—we have always striven to prevent the development of conditions in Europe which would be conducive to a European nation's interfering in the affairs of the Western Hemisphere or contemplating a direct attack upon the United States. These conditions would be most likely to arise if a European nation, its predominance unchallenged within Europe, could

look across the sea for conquest without fear of being menaced at the center of its power; that is, in Europe itself.

It is for this reason that the United States has consistently—the War of 1812 is the sole major exception—pursued policies aiming at the maintenance of the balance of power in Europe. It has opposed whatever European nation—be it Great Britain, France, Germany, or Russia—was likely to gain that ascendancy over its European competitors which would have jeopardized the hemispheric predominance and eventually the very independence of the United States. Conversely, it has supported whatever European nation appeared capable of restoring the balance of power by offering successful resistance to the would-be conqueror. While it is hard to imagine a greater contrast in ways of thinking about matters political than that between Alexander Hamilton and Woodrow Wilson, in this concern for the maintenance of the balance of power in Europe—for whatever different reasons—they are one. It is with this concern that the United States has intervened in both World Wars on the side of the initially weaker coalition, and has pursued European policies so largely paralleling those of Great Britain; for from Henry VIII to this day Great Britain has had a single objective in Europe: the maintenance of the balance of power.

Asia has vitally concerned the United States only since the turn of the century, and the relation of Asia to our national interests has never been obvious or clearly defined. In consequence, our policies in Asia have never as unequivocally expressed our permanent national interest as have the hemispheric and European policies; nor have they commanded the bipartisan support the latter have largely enjoyed. In addition, they have been subjected more fully to moralistic influence than the European and hemispheric policies. Yet underlying the confusions, reversals of policy, and moralistic generalities of our Asiatic policy since McKinley, one can detect a consistency that reflects, however vaguely, the permanent interest of the United States in Asia. And this interest is again the maintenance of the balance of power. The principle of the "open door" in China expresses this interest. Originally its meaning was purely commercial, but when other nations, especially Japan, threatened to close the door to China not only commercially but also militarily and politically, the "open door" was interpreted to cover the territorial integrity and political independence of China for not commercial but political reasons. However unsure the United States has been in its Asiatic policy, it has always assumed that the domination of China by another nation would lead to so great an accumulation of power as to threaten the security of the United States.

THE AMERICAN EXPERIENCE IN FOREIGN AFFAIRS

Wherever American foreign policy has operated, political thought has been divorced from political action. Even where our long-range policies reflect faithfully, as they do in the Americas and in Europe, the true interests of the United States, we think about them in terms that have at best but a tenuous connection with the actual character of the policies pursued. We have acted on the international scene, as all nations must, in power-political terms; but we have tended to conceive of our actions in non-political, moralistic terms. This aversion to seeing problems of international politics as they are, and the inclination to view them in non-political and moralistic terms, can be attributed both to certain misunderstood peculiarities of the American experience in foreign affairs and to the general climate of opinion in the Western world during the better part of the nineteenth and the first decades of the twentieth centuries. Three of these peculiarities of the American experience stand out: the uniqueness of the American experiment; the actual isolation, during the nineteenth century, of the United States from the centers of world conflict; and the humanitarian pacifism and anti-imperialism of American ideology.

The uniqueness of the American experiment in foreign policy resides in two elements: the negative one of distinctness from the traditional power-political quarrels of Europe, and the positive one of a continental expansion that created the freest and richest nation on earth, apparently without conquest or subjugation of others.

When the founders of the republic broke our constitutional ties with Britain, they were convinced that this meant the beginning of an American foreign policy distinct from that of Europe. As Washington's Farewell Address put it: "Europe has a set of primary interests, which to us have none, or a very remote relation. Hence she must be engaged in frequent controversies, the causes of which are essentially foreign to our concerns. Hence, therefore, it must be unwise in us to implicate ourselves, by artificial ties, in the ordinary vicissitudes of her politics, or the ordinary combinations and collisions of her friendships or enmities." In 1796, European politics and power politics were identical; there were no other power politics but those engaged in by the princes of Europe. "The toils of European ambition, rivalship, interest, humor or caprice" were all that the American eye could discern of the international struggle for power. The retreat from European politics, as proclaimed by Washington, could therefore be taken to mean retreat from power politics as such.

The expansion of the United States up to the Spanish-American War seemed to provide conclusive proof of both the distinctness and the moral superiority of American foreign policy. The settlement of the better part of a continent by the thirteen original states—an act of civilizing rather than of conquering—appeared essentially different from, and morally superior to, the imperialistic ventures, wars of conquest, and colonial acquisitions with which the history of other nations was replete. Yet what permitted this uniqueness in American expansion was not so much political virtue as the contiguity of the sparsely settled object of conquest with the original territory of departure. As was the case with Russia's simultaneous eastward expansion toward the Pacific, the United States, in order to expand, did not need to cross the oceans and fight wars of conquest in strange lands, in the manner of the other great colonizing nations. Furthermore, the utter political, military, and numerical inferiority of the Indian opponent tended to obscure the element of power, which was no less real though less obtrusive in our continental expansion than in the expansionist movements of other nations. Thus what actually was the fortuitous conjunction of two potent historic accidents could take on in the popular imagination the aspects of an inevitable natural development, a "manifest destiny," confirming the uniqueness of American foreign policy in its freedom from those power-political blemishes that degrade the foreign policies of other nations.

Yet American isolation from the European tradition of power politics was more than a political program or a moralistic illusion. In the matter of involvement in the political conflicts centering in Europe, and the commitments and risks implied in such involvement, American isolation was an established political fact until the end of the nineteenth century. This actuality was a result of deliberate choice as well as of the objective conditions of geography. Popular writers might see in the uniqueness of America's geographic position the hand of God unalterably prescribing the course of American expansion as well as isolation, but more responsible observers, from Washington on, were careful to emphasize the conjunction of geographic conditions and of a foreign policy choosing its ends in the light of geography and using geographic conditions to attain those ends. Washington referred to "our detached and distant situation" and asked: "Why forego the advantages of so peculiar a situation?" When this period of American foreign policy drew to a close, John Bright wrote to Alfred Love: "On your continent we may hope your growing millions may henceforth know nothing of war. None can assail you; and you are anxious to abstain from mingling with the quarrels of other nations."

From the shores of the North American continent, the citizens of the new world watched the strange spectacle of the struggle for power unfolding in distant Europe, Africa, and Asia. Since for the better part of the nineteenth century their foreign policy enabled them to keep the roles of spectators, what was actually the result of a passing historic configuration appeared to Americans as a permanent condition, self-chosen as well as naturally ordained. At worst they would continue to watch the game of power politics played by others. At best the time was near when, with democracy established everywhere, the final curtain would fall and the game of power politics would no longer be played.

Aiding in the achievement of this goal was conceived to be part of America's mission. Throughout our history, the national destiny of the United States has been understood in anti-militaristic, libertarian terms. Whenever that national mission finds a non-aggressive, abstentionist formulation, as in the political philosophy of John C. Calhoun, it is conceived as the promotion of domestic liberty. Thus we may "do more to extend liberty by our example over this continent and the world generally, than would be done by a thousand victories." When the United States, in the wake of the Spanish-American War, seemed to desert this anti-imperialist and democratic ideal, William Graham Sumner restated its essence: "Expansion and imperialism are a grand onslaught on democracy . . . expansion and imperialism are at war with the best traditions, principles, and interests of the American people." Comparing the tendencies of European power politics with the ideals of the American tradition, Sumner thought with Washington that they were incompatible. Yet, as a prophet, he saw that with the conclusion of the Spanish-American War America was irrevocably committed to the course that was engulfing Europe in revolution and war.

To understand the American mission in such selfless, humanitarian terms was all the easier because the United States, in contrast to the other great powers, was generally not interested—at least outside the Western Hemisphere—in particular advantages definable in terms of power or of territorial gain. Its national interest was exhausted by the preservation of its predominance in the Western Hemisphere and the balance of power in Europe and Asia. And even this interest in general stability rather than special advantage was, as we know, not always clearly recognized.

Yet while the foreign policy of the United States was forced, by circumstance if not by choice, to employ the methods, shoulder the commitments, seek the objectives, and run the risks, from which it had thought itself permanently exempt, American political thought continued to uphold that exemption at least as an ideal. And that ideal was supposed to be only temporarily beyond the reach of the American people, because of the wickedness and stupidity of either American or, preferably, foreign statesmen. In one sense, this ideal of a free, peaceful, and prosperous world, from which popular government had forever banished power politics, was a natural outgrowth of the American experience. In another sense, this ideal expressed in a particularly eloquent and consistent fashion the general philosophy that dominated the Western world during the better part of the nineteenth century. This philosophy rests on two basic propositions: that the struggle for power on the international scene is a mere accident of history, naturally associated with non-democratic government and therefore destined to disappear with the triumph of democracy throughout the world; and that, in consequence, conflicts between democratic and non-democratic nations must be primarily conceived not as struggles for mutual advantage in terms of power but as fights between good and evil, which can only end with the complete triumph of good, and with evil wiped off the face of the earth.

The nineteenth century developed this philosophy of international relations from its experience of domestic politics. The distinctive characteristic of this experience was the domination of the middle classes by the aristocracy. The political philosophy of the nineteenth century identified this aristocratic domination with political domination of any kind, and concluded that by ending aristocratic domination one could abolish all political domination. After the defeat of aristocratic government, the middle classes developed a system of indirect domination. They replaced the traditional division into the governing and governed classes and the military method of open violence, characteristic of aristocratic rule, with the invisible chains of economic dependence. This economic system operated through a network of seemingly equalitarian legal rules which concealed the very existence of power relations. The nineteenth century was unable to see the political nature of these legalized relations, considering them to be essentially different from what had gone, so far, under the name of politics. Therefore, politics in its aristocratic—that is, open and violent—form was identified with politics as such. The struggle, then, for political power, in domestic as well as in international affairs, appeared to be only a historic accident, coincident with autocratic government and bound to disappear with the disappearance of such government.

It is easy to see how this general climate of opinion in the Western world nourished similar tendencies that the specific experiences of American history had planted in the American mind. Thus it is not an accident that nowhere in the Western world was there greater conviction and tenacity in support of the belief that involvement in power politics is not inevitable but only accidental, and that nations have a choice between power politics and another kind of foreign policy conforming to moral principles and not tainted by the desire for power. Nor is it by accident that this philosophy of foreign policy found its most dedicated and eloquent spokesman in an American President, Woodrow Wilson.

THE THREE PERIODS OF AMERICAN FOREIGN POLICY

The Realistic Period

The illusion that a nation can escape, if it wants to, from power politics into a realm where action is guided by moral principles rather than by considerations of power is deeply rooted in the American mind. Yet it took more than a century for that illusion to crowd out the older notion that international politics is an unending struggle for power in which the interests of individual nations must necessarily be defined in terms of power. Out of the struggle between these two opposing conceptions, three types of American foreign policy have emerged: the realistic—thinking and acting in terms of power—represented by Alexander Hamilton; the ideological—thinking in terms of moral principles but acting in terms of power—represented by Thomas Jefferson and John Quincy Adams; and the moralistic—thinking and acting in terms of moral principles—represented by Woodrow Wilson. To these three types, three periods of American foreign policy roughly correspond, the first covering the first decade of the history of the United States as an independent nation, the second covering the nineteenth century to the Spanish-American War, and the third covering the half century after that war. This division of the history of American foreign policy—as will become obvious in our discussion—refers only to prevailing tendencies, without precluding the operation side by side of different tendencies in the same period.

It illustrates both the depth of the moralistic illusion and the original strength of the opposition to it that the issue between these two opposing conceptions of foreign policy was joined at the very beginning of the history of the United States, was decided in favor of the realistic position, and was formulated with unsurpassed simplicity and penetration by Alexander Hamilton. The memorable occasion was Washington's proclamation of neutrality in the War of the First Coalition against revolutionary France.

In 1792, the War of the First Coalition had ranged Austria, Prussia, Sardinia, Great Britain, and the United Netherlands against revolutionary France, which was tied to the United States by a treaty of alliance. On April 22, 1793, Washington issued a proclamation of neutrality, and it was in defense of that proclamation that Hamilton wrote the "Pacificus" and "Americanus" articles. Among the arguments directed against the proclamation were three derived from moral principles. Faithfulness to treaty obligations, gratitude toward a country that had lent its assistance to the colonies in their struggle for independence, and the affinity of republican institutions, were cited to prove that the United States must side with France. Against these moral principles, Hamilton invoked the national interest of the United States:

There would be no proportion between the mischiefs and perils to which the United States would expose themselves, by embarking in the war, and the benefit which the nature of their stipulation aims at securing to France, or that which it would be in their power actually to render her by becoming a party.

This disproportion would be a valid reason for not executing the guaranty. All contracts are to receive a reasonable construction. Self-preservation is the first duty of a nation; and though in the performance of stipulations relating to war, good faith requires that its ordinary hazards should be fairly met, because they are directly contemplated by such stipulations, yet it does not require that extraordinary and extreme hazards should be run. . . .

The basis of gratitude is a benefit received or intended which there was no right to claim, originating in a regard to the interest or advantage of the party on whom the benefit is, or is meant to be, conferred. If a service is rendered from views relative to the immediate interest of the party who performs it, and is productive of reciprocal advantages, there seems scarcely, in such a case, to be an adequate basis for a sentiment like that of gratitude. . . . It may be affirmed as a general principle, that the predominant motive of good offices from one nation to another, is the interest or advantage of the nation which performs them.

Indeed, the rule of morality in this respect is not precisely the same between nations as between individuals. The duty of making its own welfare the guide of its actions, is much stronger upon the former than upon the latter; in proportion to the greater magnitude and importance of national compared with individual happiness, and to the greater permanency of the effects of national than of individual conduct. Existing millions, and for the most part future generations, are concerned in the present measures of a government; while the consequences of the private actions of an individual ordinarily terminate with himself, or are circumscribed within a narrow compass.

Whence it follows that an individual may, on numerous occasions, meritoriously indulge the emotions of generosity and benevolence, not only without an eye to, but even at the expense of, his own interest. But a government can rarely, if at all, be justifiable in pursuing a similar course; and, if it does so, ought to confine itself within much stricter bounds. . . . Good offices which are indifferent to the interest of a nation performing them, or which are compensated by the existence or expectation of some reasonable equivalent, or which produce an essential good to the nation to which they are rendered, without real detriment to the affairs of the benefactors, prescribe perhaps the limits of national generosity or benevolence. . . .

But we are sometimes told, by way of answer, that the cause of France is the cause of liberty; and that we are bound to assist the nation on the score of their being engaged in the defence of that cause. . . .

The obligation to assist the cause of liberty must be deduced from the merits of that cause and from the interest we have in its support.

* * * * *

An examination into the question how far *regard to the cause of Liberty* ought to induce the United States to take part with France in the present war, is rendered necessary by the efforts which are making to establish an opinion, that it ought to have that effect. In order to a right judgment on the point, it is requisite to consider the question under two aspects.

I. Whether the cause of France be truly the cause of Liberty, pursued with justice and humanity, and in a manner likely to crown it with honorable success.

II. Whether the degree of service we could render, by participating in the conflict, was likely to compensate, by its utility to the cause, the evils which would probably flow from it to ourselves.

If either of these questions can be answered in the negative, it will result, that the consideration which has been stated ought not to embark us in the war. . . .

The certain evils of our joining France in the war, are sufficient dissuasives from so intemperate a measure. The possible ones are of a nature to call for all our caution, all our prudence.

To defend its own rights, to vindicate its own honor, there are occasions when a nation ought to hazard even its existence. Should such an occasion occur, I trust those who are most averse to commit the peace of the country, will not be the last to face the danger, nor the first to turn their backs upon it.

But let us at least have the consolation of not having rashly courted misfortune. Let us have to act under the animating reflection of being engaged in repelling wrongs, which we neither sought nor merited; in vindicating our rights, invaded without provocation; in defending our honor, violated without cause. Let us not have to reproach ourselves with having voluntarily bartered blessings for calamities.

But we are told that our own liberty is at stake upon the event of the war against France—that if she falls, we shall be the next victim. The combined powers, it is said, will never forgive in us the origination of those principles which were the germs of the French revolution. They will endeavor to eradicate them from the world.

If this suggestion were ever so well founded, it would perhaps be a sufficient answer to it to say, that our interference is not likely to alter the case; that it would only serve prematurely to exhaust our strength.

But other answers more conclusive present themselves. . . .

It is therefore matter of real regret, that there should be an effort on our part to level the distinctions which discriminate our case from that of France, to confound the two cases in the view of foreign powers, and to pervert or hazard our own principles by persuading ourselves of a similitude which does not exist. . . .

But let us not corrupt ourselves by false comparisons or glosses, nor shut our eyes to the true nature of transactions which ought to grieve and warn us, nor rashly mingle our destiny in the consequences of the errors and extravagancies of another nation.

Must a nation subordinate its security, its happiness, nay, its very existence to the respect for treaty obligations, to the sentiment of gratitude, to sympathy with a kindred political system? This was the question Hamilton proposed to answer, and his answer was an unequivocal "no." To the issues raised by the opposition to Washington's proclamation of neutrality Hamilton unswervingly applied one standard: the national interest of the United States. He put the legalistic and moralistic arguments of the opposition, represented by Madison under the pseudonym "Helvidius," into the context of the concrete power-situation in which the United States found itself on the international scene, and asked: If the United States were to join France against virtually all of Europe, what risks would the United States run, what advantages could it expect, what good could it do to its ally?

The Ideological Period

Considerations such as these, recognized for what they were, guided American foreign policy for but a short period; that is, as long as the Federalists were in power. *The Federalist* and Washington's Farewell Address are their classic expression. Yet we have seen that these considerations, not recognized for what they were or even rejected, have determined the great objectives of American foreign policy to this day. During the century following their brief flowering, their influence has persisted, under the cover of those moral principles with which from Jefferson onward American statesmen have liked to justify their moves on the international scene. Thus this second period witnessed a discrepancy between political thought and political action, yet a coincidence in the intended results of both. What was said of Gladstone could also have been said of Jefferson, John Quincy Adams, Grover Cleveland, Theodore Roosevelt, the war policies of Wilson and of Franklin D. Roosevelt: what the moral law demanded was by a felicitous coincidence always identical with what the national interest seemed to require. Political thought and political action moved on different planes, which, however, inclined to merge in the end.

John Quincy Adams is the classic example of the political moralist in thought and word, who cannot help being a political realist in action. Yet even in Jefferson, whose dedication to abstract morality was much stronger and whose realist touch in foreign affairs was much less sure, the moral pretense yielded often, especially in private utterance, to the impact of the national interest upon native good sense.

Thus during the concluding decade of the Napoleonic Wars Jefferson's thought on international affairs was a reflection of the ever changing distribution of power in the world rather than of immutable moral principles. In 1806, he favored "an English ascendancy on the ocean" as being "safer for us than that of France." In 1807, he was by the logic of events forced to admit:

I never expected to be under the necessity of wishing success to Buonaparte. But the English being equally tyrannical at sea as he is on land, & that tyranny bearing on us in every point of either honor or interest, I say "down with England" and as for what Buonaparte is then to do to us, let us trust to the chapter of accidents, I cannot, with the Anglomen, prefer a certain present evil to a future hypothetical one.

However, in 1812, when Napoleon was at the pinnacle of his power, Jefferson hoped for the restoration of the balance. Speaking of England, he said:

it is for the general interest that she should be a sensible and independent weight in the scale of nations, and be able to contribute, when a favorable moment presents itself, to reduce under the same order, her great rival in flagitiousness. We especially ought to pray that the powers of Europe may be so poised and counterpoised among themselves, that their own security may require the presence of all their forces at home, leaving the other quarters of the globe in undisturbed tranquility.

In 1814, again compelled by the logic of events, he came clearly out against Napoleon and in favor of a balance of power which would leave the power of Napoleon and of England limited, but intact.

Surely none of us wish to see Bonaparte conquer Russia, and lay thus at his feet the whole continent of Europe. This done, England would be but a breakfast; and, although I am free from the visionary fears which the votaries of England have effected to entertain, because I believe he cannot effect the conquest of Europe; yet put all Europe into his hands, and he might spare such a force to be sent in British ships, as I would as leave not have to encounter, when I see how much trouble a handful of British soldiers in Canada has given us. No. It cannot be to our interest that all Europe should be reduced to a single monarchy. The true line of interest for us, is, that Bonaparte should be able to effect the complete exclusion of England from the whole continent of Europe, in order, as the same letter said, "by this peaceable engine of constraint, to make her renounce her views of dominion over the ocean, of permitting no other nation to navigate it but with her license, and on tribute to her, and her aggressions on the persons of our citizens who may choose to exercise their right of passing over that element." And this would be effected by Bonaparte's succeeding so far as to close the Baltic against her. This success I wished him the last year, this I wish him this year; but were he again advanced to Moscow, I should again wish him such disasters as would prevent his reaching Petersburg. And were the consequences even to be the longer continuance of our war, I would rather meet them than see the whole force of Europe wielded by a single hand.

Similarly, in 1815, Jefferson wrote:

For my part, I wish that all nations may recover and retain their independence; that those which are overgrown may not advance beyond safe measures of power, that a salutary balance may be ever maintained among nations, and that our peace, commerce, and friendship, may be sought and cultivated by all.

It was only when, after 1815, the danger to the balance of power seemed to have passed that Jefferson allowed himself again to indulge in the cultivation of moral principles divorced from political exigencies.

From this tendency, to which Jefferson only too readily yielded, John Quincy Adams was well-nigh immune. We are here in the presence of a statesman who had been reared in the realist tradition of the first period of American foreign policy, who had done the better part of his work of statecraft in an atmosphere saturated with Jeffersonian principles, and who had achieved the merger of these two elements of his experience into a harmonious whole. Between John Quincy Adams's moral principles and the traditional interest of the United States there was hardly ever a conflict. The moral principles were nothing but the political interests formulated in moral terms, and vice versa. They fit the interests as a glove fits the hand. Adams's great contributions to the tradition of American foreign policy—freedom of the seas, the Monroe Doctrine, and Manifest Destiny—are witness to this achievement.

In the hands of Adams, the legal and moral principle of the freedom of the seas was a weapon, as it had been two centuries earlier when Grotius wielded it on behalf of the Low Countries, through which an inferior naval power endeavored to safeguard its independence against Great Britain, the mistress of the seas. The Monroe Doctrine's moral postulates of anti-imperialism and mutual non-intervention were the negative conditions for the safety and enduring greatness of the United States. Their fulfillment secured the isolation of the United States from the power struggles of Europe and, through it, the continuing predominance of the United States in the Western Hemisphere. Manifest Destiny was the moral justification as well as the moral incentive for the westward expansion of the United States, the peculiar American way—foreordained by the objective conditions of American existence—of founding an empire, the "American Empire," as one of the contemporary opponents of Adams's policies put it.

The Utopian Period

Jefferson and John Quincy Adams stand at the beginning of the second period of

American thought on foreign policy, both its most eminent representatives and the heirs of a realist tradition that continued to mold political action, while it had largely ceased to influence political thought. At the beginning of the third period, McKinley leads the United States as a great world power beyond the confines of the Western Hemisphere, ignorant of the bearing of this step upon the national interest, and guided by moral principles completely divorced from the national interest. When at the end of the Spanish-American War the status of the Philippines had to be determined, McKinley expected and found no guidance in the traditional national interests of the United States. According to his own testimony, he knelt beside his bed in prayer, and in the wee hours of the morning he heard the voice of God telling him—as was to be expected—to annex the Philippines.

This period initiated by McKinley, in which moral principles no longer justify the enduring national interest as in the second, but replace it as a guide for action, finds its fulfillment in the political thought of Woodrow Wilson. Wilson's thought not only disregards the national interest, but is explicitly opposed to it on moral grounds. "It is a very perilous thing," he said in his address at Mobile on October 27, 1913.

to determine the foreign policy of a nation in the terms of material interest. It not only is unfair to those with whom you are dealing, but it is degrading as regards your own actions. . . . We dare not turn from the principle that morality and not expediency is the thing that must guide us, and that we will never condone iniquity because it is most convenient to do so.

Wilson's wartime speeches are but an elaboration of this philosophy. An excerpt from his address of September 27, 1918, opening the campaign for the Fourth Liberty Loan, will suffice to show the continuance of that philosophy.

It is of capital importance that we should also be explicitly agreed that no peace shall be obtained by any kind of compromise or abatement of the principles we have avowed as the principles for which we are fighting. . . .

First, the impartial justice meted out must involve no discrimination between those to whom we wish to be just and those to whom we do not wish to be just. It must be a justice that plays no favorites and knows no standard but the equal rights of the several peoples concerned;

Second, no special or separate interest of any single nation or any group of nations can be made the basis of any part of the settlement which is not consistent with the common interest of all;

Third, there can be no leagues or alliances or special covenants and understandings within the general and common family of the League of Nations.

Fourth, and more specifically, there can be no special, selfish economic combinations within the League and no employment of any form of economic boycott or exclusion except as the power of economic penalty by exclusion from the markets of the world may be vested in the League of Nations itself as a means of discipline and control.

Fifth, all international agreements and treaties of every kind must be made known in their entirety to the rest of the world.

Special alliances and economic rivalries and hostilities have been the prolific source in the modern world of the plans and passions that produce war. It would be an insincere as well as insecure peace that did not exclude them in definite and binding terms. . . .

National purposes have fallen more and more into the background and the common purpose of enlightened mankind has taken their place. The counsels of plain men have become on all hands more simple and straightforward and more unified than the counsels of sophisticated men of affairs, who still retain the impression that they are playing a game of power and playing for high stakes. That is why I have said that this is a peoples' war, not a statesmen's. Statesmen must follow the clarified common thought or be broken.

Yet in his political actions, especially under the pressure of the First World War, Wilson could not discount completely the national interest of the United States, any more than could Jefferson before him. Wilson's case, however, was different from Jefferson's in two respects. For one thing, Wilson was never able, even when the national interest of the United States was directly menaced, to conceive of the danger in other than moral terms. It was only the objective force of the national interest, which no rational man could escape, that imposed the source of America's mortal danger upon him as the object of his moral indignation. Thus Wilson in 1917 led the United States into war against Germany for the same reasons, only half-known to himself, for which Jefferson had wished and worked alternately for the victory of England and France. Germany threatened the balance of power in Europe, and it was in order to remove that threat—and not to make the world safe for democracy—that the United States put its weight into the Allies' scale. Wilson pursued the right policy, but he pursued it for the wrong reasons.

Not only, however, did Wilson's crusading fervor obliterate awareness of the traditional interest of the United States in maintaining the European balance of power, to be accomplished through the defeat of Germany; it also had politically disastrous effects, for which there is no precedent in the history of the United States. Wilson's moral objective required the destruction of the Kaiser's autocracy, and this happened also to be required by the political interests of the United States. The political interests of the United States required, beyond this immediate objective of total victory, the restoration of the European balance of power, traditional guarantor of American security. Yet it was in indignation at

the moral deficiencies of that very balance of power, "forever discredited," as he thought, that Wilson had asked the American people to take up arms against the Central Powers! Once military victory had put an end to the immediate threat to American security, the very logic of his moral position—let us remember that consistency is the moralist's supreme virtue—drove him toward substituting for the concrete national interest of the United States the general postulate of a brave new world where the national interest of the United States, as that of all other nations, would disappear in a community of interests comprising mankind.

Consequently, Wilson considered it to be the purpose of victory not to restore a new, viable balance of power, but to put an end to the balance of power once and forever. "You know," he told the English people at Manchester on December 30, 1918,

that the United States has always felt from the very beginning of her history that she must keep herself separate from any kind of connection with European politics, and I want to say very frankly to you that she is not now interested in European politics. But she is interested in the partnership of right between America and Europe. If the future had nothing for us but a new attempt to keep the world at a right poise by a balance of power, the United States would take no interest, because she will join no combination of power which is not the combination of all of us. She is not interested merely in the peace of Europe, but in the peace of the world.

Faced with the national interests of the great Allied powers, Wilson had nothing to oppose or support them with but his moral principles, with the result that the neglect of the American national interest was not compensated for by the triumph of political morality. In the end Wilson had to consent to a series of uneasy compromises, which were a betrayal of his moral principles—for principles can, by their very nature, not be made the object of compromise—and which satisfied nobody's national aspirations. These compromises had no relation at all to the traditional American national interest in a viable European balance of power. Thus Wilson returned from Versailles a compromised idealist, an empty-handed statesman, a discredited ally. In that triple failure lies the tragedy not only of Wilson, a great yet misguided man, but of Wilsonianism as a political doctrine.

Yet Wilson returned unaware of his failure. He offered the American people what he had offered the Allied nations at Paris: moral principles divorced from political reality. "The day we have left behind us," he proclaimed at Los Angeles on September 20, 1919,

was a day of balances of power. It was a day of "every nation take care of itself or make a partnership with some other nation or group of nations to hold the peace of the world steady or to dominate the weaker portions of the world." Those were the days of alliances. This project of the League of Nations is a great process of disentanglement.

WILSONIANISM, ISOLATIONISM, INTERNATIONALISM—THREE FORMS OF UTOPIANISM

Whereas before Paris and Versailles these moral principles rang true with the promise of a new and better world, afterwards they must have sounded rather hollow and platitudinous to many. Yet what is significant for the course American foreign policy was to take in the interwar years is not so much that the American people rejected Wilsonianism, but that they rejected it by ratifying the denial of the American tradition of foreign policy which was implicit in the political thought of Wilson. We are here indeed dealing with a tragedy not of one man, but of a political doctrine and, as far as the United States is concerned, of a political tradition. The isolationism of the interwar period could delude itself into believing that it was but the restorer of the early realistic tradition of American foreign policy. Did it not, like that tradition, proclaim the self-sufficiency of the United States within the Western Hemisphere? Did it not, like that tradition, refuse to become involved in the rivalries of European nations? The isolationists of the twenties and thirties did not see—and this was the very essence of the policies of the Founding Fathers—that both the isolated and the preponderant position of the United States in the Western Hemisphere was not a fact of nature, and that the freedom from entanglements in European conflicts was not the result of mere abstention on the part of the United States. Both benefits were the result of political conditions outside the Western Hemisphere and of policies carefully contrived and purposefully executed in their support. For the realists of the first period, isolation was an objective of policy, and had to be striven for to be attained. For the isolationists of the interwar period, isolation was a natural state, and only needed to be left undisturbed in order to continue forever. Conceived in such terms, it was the very negation of foreign policy.

Isolationism, then, is in its way as oblivious to political reality as is Wilsonianism—the internationalist challenge, to which it thought to have found the American answer. In consequence, they are both strangers not only to the first, realistic phase of American foreign policy, but to its whole tradition. Both refused to face political reality either in realistic or ideological terms. They refused to face it at all. Thus isolationism and Wilsonianism have more in common than their historic enmity would lead one to suspect. In a profound sense they are brothers under the skin. Both are one in maintaining that the United States has no interest in any particular political and military configuration outside the Western Hemisphere. While isolationism stops here, Wilsonianism asserts that the American national interest is not somewhere in particular, but everywhere, being identical with the interests of mankind itself. Both refuse to concern themselves with the concrete issues upon which the national interest must be asserted. Isolationism stops short of them, Wilsonianism soars beyond them. Both have but a negative relation to the national interest of the United States outside the Western Hemisphere. They are unaware of its very existence. This being so, both substitute abstract moral principles for the guidance of the national interest, derived from the actual conditions of American existence. Wilsonianism applies the illusory expectations of liberal reform to the whole world, isolationism empties of all concrete political content the realistic political principle of isolation and transforms it into the unattainable parochial ideal of automatic separation.

In view of this inner affinity between isolationism and Wilsonianism, it is not surprising that the great debate of the twenties and thirties between internationalism and isolationism was carried on primarily in moral terms. Was there a moral obligation for the United States to make its contribution to world peace by joining the League of Nations and the World Court? Was it morally incumbent upon the United States, as a democracy, to oppose Fascism in Europe and to uphold international law in Asia? Such were the questions raised in that debate, and the answers depended upon the moral position taken. The question central to the national interest of the United States, that of the balance of power in Europe and Asia, was hardly ever faced squarely, and when it was faced it was dismissed on moral grounds. Mr. Cordell Hull, Secretary of State of the United States from 1933 to 1944, and one of the most respected spokesmen of internationalism, summarizes in his *Memoirs* his attitude toward this central problem of American foreign policy:

I was not, and am not, a believer in the idea of balance of power or spheres of influence as a means of keeping the peace. During the First World War I had made an intensive study of the system of spheres of influence and balance of power, and I was grounded to the taproots in their iniquitous consequences. The conclusions I then formed in total opposition to this system stayed with me.

When internationalism triumphed in the late thirties, it did so in the moral terms of Wilsonianism. That in this instance the moral postulates inspiring the administration of Franklin D. Roosevelt happened to coincide with the exigencies of the American national interest was again, as in the case of Jefferson and of the Wilson of 1917, due to the impact of a national emergency upon innate common sense, and to the strength of a national tradition that holds in its spell the actions of even those who deny its validity in words. However, as soon as the minds of the American leaders, freed from these inescapable pressures of a primarily military nature, turned toward the political problems of the Second World War and its aftermath, they thought and acted again as Wilson had acted under similar circumstances. That is to say, they thought and acted in moral terms, divorced from the political conditions of America's existence.

The practical results of this philosophy of international affairs, as applied to the political problems of the war and post-war period, were therefore bound to be quite similar to those which had made the Allied victory in the First World War politically meaningless. Conceived as it was as a "crusade"—to borrow from the title of General Eisenhower's book—against the evil incarnate in the Axis powers, the purpose of the Second World War could only be the destruction of that evil, brought about through the instrumentality of "unconditional surrender." Since the threat to the Western world emanating from the Axis was conceived primarily in moral terms, it was easy to imagine that all conceivable danger was concentrated in that historic constellation of hostile powers and that with its destruction political evil itself would disappear from the world. Beyond "unconditional surrender" there was to be, then, a brave new world after the model of Wilson's, which would liquidate the heritage of the defeated nations—evil and not "peace-loving"—and establish an order of things where war, aggressiveness, and the struggle for power itself would be no more. Thus Mr. Cordell Hull could declare on his return in 1943 from the Moscow conference that the new international organization would mean the end of power politics and usher in a new era of international collaboration. Three years later, Mr. Philip Noel-Baker, then British Minister of State, echoed Mr. Hull by stating in the House of Commons that the British government was "determined to use the institutions of the United Nations to kill power politics, in order that by the methods of democracy, the will of the people shall prevail."

With this philosophy dominant in the West—Mr. Churchill provides almost the sole, however ineffective, exception—the strategy of the war and of the peace to follow could not help being oblivious to those considerations of the national interest which the great statesmen of the West, from Hamilton through Castlereagh, Canning, and John Quincy Adams, to Disraeli and Salisbury, had brought to bear upon the international problems of their day. War was no longer regarded as a means to a political end. The only end the war was to serve was total victory, which is another way of saying that the war became an end in itself. Hence, it became irrelevant how the war was won politically, as long as it was won speedily, cheaply, and totally. The thought that the war might be waged in view of a new balance of power to be established after the war, occurred in the West only to Winston Churchill—and, of course, it occurred to Joseph Stalin. The national interest of the Western nations was, then, satisfied in so far as it required the destruction of the threat to the balance of power emanating from Germany and Japan; for to that extent the moral purposes of the war happened to coincide with the national interest. However, the national interest of the Western nations was jeopardized in so far as their security required the creation of a new viable balance of power after the war.

How could statesmen who boasted that they were not "believers in the idea of balance of power"—like a scientist not believing in the law of gravity—and who were out "to kill power politics," understand the very idea of the national interest which demanded, above all, protection from the power of others? Thus it was with deep and sincere moral indignation that the Western world, expecting a utopia without power politics, found itself confronted with a new and more formidable threat to its security as soon as the old one had been subdued. There was good reason for moral indignation, however misdirected it was. That a new balance of power will rise out of the ruins of an old balance and that nations with political sense will avail themselves of the opportunity to improve their position within it, is a law of politics for whose validity nobody is to blame. Yet they are indeed blameworthy who in their moralistic disdain for the laws of politics endanger the interests of the nations in their care.

THE MORAL DIGNITY OF THE NATIONAL INTEREST

The fundamental error that has thwarted American foreign policy in thought and action is the antithesis of national interest and moral principles. The equation of political moralizing with morality and of political realism with immorality is itself untenable. The chcice is not between moral principles and the national interest, devoid of moral dignity, but between one set of moral principles divorced from political reality, and another set of moral principles derived from political reality.

The moralistic detractors of the national interest are guilty of both intellectual error and moral perversion. The nature of the intellectual error must be obvious from what has been said thus far, as it is from the record of history: a foreign policy guided by moral abstractions, without consideration of the national interest, is bound to fail; for it accepts a standard of action alien to the nature of the action itself. All the successful statesmen of modern times from Richelieu to Churchill have made the national interest the ultimate standard of their policies, and none of the great moralists in international affairs has attained his goals.

The perversion of the moralizing approach to foreign policy is threefold. That approach operates with a false concept of morality, developed by national societies but unsuited to the conditions of international society. In the process of its realization, it is bound to destroy the very moral values it sets out to promote. Finally, it is derived from a false antithesis between morality and power politics, thus arrogating to itself all moral values and placing the stigma of immorality upon the theory and practice of power politics.

There is a profound and neglected truth hidden in Hobbes's extreme dictum that the state creates morality as well as law and that there is neither morality nor law outside the state. Universal moral principles, such as justice or equality, are capable of guiding political action only to the extent that they have been given concrete content and have been related to political situations by society. What justice means in the United States can within wide limits be objectively ascertained; for interests and convictions, experiences of life and institutionalized traditions have in large measure created a consensus concerning what justice means under the conditions of American society. No such consensus exists in the relations between nations. For above the national societies there exists no international society so integrated as to be able to define for them the concrete meaning of justice or equality, as national societies do for their individual members. In consequence, the appeal to moral principles by the representative of a nation vis-à-vis another nation signifies something fundamentally different from a verbally identical appeal made by an individual in his relations to another individual member of the same national society. The appeal to moral principles in the international sphere has no concrete universal meaning. It is either so vague as to have no concrete meaning that could provide rational guidance for political action, or it will be nothing but the reflection of the moral preconceptions of a particular nation and will by that same token be unable to gain the universal recognition it pretends to deserve.

Whenever the appeal to moral principles provides guidance for political action in international affairs, it destroys the very moral principles it intends to realize. It can do so in three different ways. Universal moral principles can serve as a mere pretext for the pursuit of national policies. In other words, they fulfill the functions of those ideological rationalizations and justifications to which we have referred before. They are mere means to the ends of national policies, bestowing upon the national interest the false dignity of universal moral principles. The performance of such a function is hypocrisy and abuse and carries a negative moral connotation.

The appeal to moral principles may also guide political action to that political failure which we have mentioned above. The extreme instance of political failure on the international plane is national suicide. It may well be said that a foreign policy guided by universal moral principles, by definition relegating the national interest to the background, is under contemporary conditions of foreign policy and warfare a policy of national suicide, actual or potential. Within a national society the individual can at times afford, and may even be required, to subordinate his interests and even to sacrifice his very existence to a supraindividual moral principle—for in national societies such principles exist, capable of providing concrete standards for individual action. What is more important still, national societies take it upon themselves within certain limits to protect and promote the interests of the individual and, in particular, to guard his existence against violent attack. National societies of this kind can exist and fulfill their functions only if their individual members are willing to subordinate their individual interests in a certain measure to the common good of society. Altruism and self-sacrifice are in that measure morally required.

The mutual relations of national societies are fundamentally different. These relations are not controlled by universal moral principles concrete enough to guide the political actions of individual nations. What again is more important, no agency is able to promote and protect the interests of individual nations and to guard their existence—and that is emphatically true of the great powers—but the individual nations themselves. To ask, then, a nation to embark upon altruistic policies oblivious of the national interest is really to ask something immoral. For such disregard of the individual interest, on the part of nations as of individuals, can be morally justified only by the existence of social institutions, the embodiment of concrete moral principles, which are able to do what otherwise the individual would have to do. In the absence of such institutions it would be both foolish and morally wrong to ask a nation to forego its national interests not for the good of a society with a superior moral claim but for a chimera. Morally speaking, national egotism is not the same as individual egotism because the functions of the international society are not identical with those of a national society.

The immorality of a politically effective appeal to moral abstractions in foreign policy is consummated in the contemporary phenomenon of the moral crusade. The crusading moralist, unable in the absence of an integrated national society to transcend the limits of national moral values and political interests, identifies the national interest with the manifestation of moral principles, which is, as we have seen, the typical function of ideology. Yet the crusader goes one step farther. He projects the national moral standards onto the international scene not only with the legitimate claim of reflecting the national interest, but with the politically and morally unfounded claim of providing moral standards for all mankind to conform to in concrete political action. Through the intermediary of the universal moral appeal the national and the universal interest become one and the same thing. What is good for the crusading country is by definition good for all mankind, and if the rest of mankind refuses to accept such claims to universal recognition, it must be converted with fire and sword.

There is already an inkling of this ultimate degeneration of international moralism in Wilson's crusade to make the world safe for democracy. We see it in full bloom in the universal aspirations of Bolshevism. Yet to the extent that the West, too, is persuaded that it has a holy mission, in the name of whatever moral principle, first to save the world and then to remake it, it has itself fallen victim to the moral disease of the crusading spirit in politics. If that disease should become general, as well it might, the age of political moralizing would issue in one or a series of religious world wars. The fanaticism of political religions would, then, justify all those abominations unknown to less moralistic but more politically-minded ages and for which in times past the fanaticism of other-worldly religions provided a convenient cloak.

In order to understand fully what these intellectual and moral aberrations of a moralizing in foreign policy imply, and how the moral and political problems to which that philosophy has given rise can be solved, we must recall that from the day of Machiavelli onward the controversy has been fought on the assumption that there was morality on one side and immorality on the other. Yet the antithesis that equates political moralizing with morality and political realism with immorality is erroneous.

We have already pointed out that it is a political necessity for the individual members of the international society to take care of their own national interests, and that there can be no moral duty to neglect them. Self-preservation both for the individual and for societies is, however, not only a biological and psychological necessity but, in the absence of an overriding moral obligation, a moral duty as well. In the absence of an integrated international society, the attainment of a modicum of order and the realization of a minimum of moral values are predicated upon the existence of national communities capable of preserving order and realizing moral values within the limits of their power.

It is obvious that such a state of affairs falls far short of that order and realized morality to which we are accustomed in national societies. The only relevant question is, however, what the practical alternative is to these imperfections of an international society that is based upon the national interests of its component parts. The attainable alternative is not a higher morality realized through the application of universal moral principles, but moral deterioration through either political failure or the fanaticism of political crusades. The juxtaposition of the morality of political moralism and the immorality of the national interest is mistaken. It presents a false concept of morality, developed by national societies but unsuited to the conditions of international society. It is bound to destroy the very moral values it aims to foster. Hence, the antithesis between moral principles and the national interest is not only intellectually mistaken but also morally pernicious. A foreign policy derived from the national interest is in fact morally superior to a foreign policy inspired by universal moral principles. Albert Sorel, the Anglophobe historian of the French Revolution, summarized well the real antithesis when he said in grudging admiration of Castlereagh:

He piqued himself on principles to which he held with an unshakable constancy, which in actual affairs could not be distinguished from obstinacy; but these principles were in no degree abstract or speculative, but were all embraced in one alone, the supremacy of English interests; they all proceeded from this high reason of state.

In our time the United States is groping toward a reason of state of its own—one that expresses our national interest.

The history of American foreign policy since the end of the Second World War is the story of the encounter of the American mind with a new political world. That mind was weakened in its understanding of foreign policy by half a century of ever more complete intoxication with moral abstractions. Even a mind less weakened would have found it hard to face with adequate understanding and successful action the unprecedented novelty and magnitude of the new political world. American foreign policy in that period presents itself as a slow, painful, and incomplete process of emancipation from deeply ingrained error, and of rediscovery of long-forgotten truths.

What are the characteristics of the new political world which affect the United States in its foreign relations, and how have they affected it?

Section I–B. GLOBALISM AND THE COLD WAR: THE RISE AND DECLINE OF A FOREIGN POLICY CONSENSUS

With the advent of America's involvement in World War II, the isolationism of the past was permanently shattered, and the nation was thrust into global politics from which it has not departed. Although some desired to revert to isolationism after World War II, the actions of its leaders, the global political circumstances, and the perceived threat from the Soviet Union would not allow such a policy. Instead, the United States set into motion a globalist foreign policy course, highly motivated by its domestic values.

President Franklin D. Roosevelt was determined to maintain U.S. global involvement after the war and had already devised a plan to do just that, albeit based primarily upon the principles of the balance of power.[1] This plan was to establish global order through the concerted global cooperation of the "Four Policemen": China, the Soviet Union, the United States, and Great Britain. Although he initiated such a plan with his wartime Allied conferences, he was not able to carry his plan very far before his death in April 1945. Harry S Truman, upon succeeding President Roosevelt, tried to follow this plan of great power cooperation for a time.

This cooperative strategy was challenged by both the weakened conditions of Europe and Asia and by the perception that the United States would be unable to cooperate with the Soviet Union because of its revolutionary designs. Europe had been devastated by the war; none of the traditional powers—France, Germany, or Great Britain—was in a position to continue a global role immediately. Asia, too, remained in turmoil with the civil war erupting in China between the forces of Chiang Kai-Shek and Mao Tse-tung. In effect, then, the United States and the Soviet Union—despite their heavy losses in World War II—were in a position to assume global responsibility.

Even with this global predominance of the Soviet Union and the United States, mutual suspicion of the intentions of the other shattered any real hope for postwar cooperation. Although President Roosevelt optimistically saw the Soviet Union as motivated by power considerations like any nation (and thus restrained by the power capabilities of others), this assumption was not the one followed by Truman and his advisers.[2] They rather quickly adopted the more pessimistic view that the Soviet Union was primarily motivated by Marxist-Leninist thought and was bent on global revolution. The threatening statements against Western capitalism by Soviet leader Joseph Stalin only served to emphasize this view. This perception, moreover, came to summarize the values and beliefs that were the motivating force of American policy throughout the post-World War II years.

The first two readings set forth this value perspective in more detail, and each outlines the policy that the United States should pursue, especially against the Soviet Union. The first reading is President Harry Truman's speech to a joint session of Congress on March 12, 1947. The immediate occasion of the speech was to seek $400 million worth of aid for Greece and Turkey, two nations that were beset by internal unrest. The ultimate impact of the speech was to prepare Congress and the public for a particular kind of global involvement, based upon opposition to the Soviet Union. Furthermore, the speech set into motion the emergence of the "cold war" between these two nations. Although this cold war was not fought on battlefields between these two states, it was to be an ideological battle fought for decades over alternate ways of organizing society.

The Truman speech is particularly important in how it defined the world for the United States and noted the important foreign policy values that were at stake. The speech first of all provided a stark bipolar view of international politics: "Nearly every nation must choose between alternative ways of life. . . . One . . . is based upon the will of the majority, and is distinguished by free institutions. . . . The second way . . . is based upon the will of a minority forcibly imposed upon the majority. It relies upon terror and oppression, a controlled press and radio, fixed elections, and the suppression of personal freedoms." President Truman also boldly states what U.S. policy must be in such an international circumstance: " . . . to support free peoples who are resisting attempted subjugation by armed minorities or by outside pressures." While President Truman does not mention the Soviet Union by name, the target of his remarks is clear.

The second reading, "The Sources of Soviet Conduct," appeared shortly after the Truman speech in *Foreign Affairs* magazine in July 1947 under the pseudonym of "Mr. X." The author was quickly revealed to be George Kennan, the director of policy planning at the Department of State. His essay directly confronts the challenge to the United States from the Soviet Union and then outlines the basic strategy that the United States ought to pursue. His essay begins by identifying the values and beliefs that motivate the Soviet Union, how these clash directly with American beliefs, and how they challenge free institutions everywhere. Consequently, a great global struggle was likely to result between these two powers. Beyond that important discussion, however, the article is closely associated with the policy that it recommends against this Soviet threat: "a long-term, patient but firm and vigilant containment of Russian expansive tendencies." Kennan's discussion was quickly seized by others and became the rationale for the containment strategy that the United States was to begin to implement in the late 1940s and early 1950s. Moreover, it was to be the rationale for the formulation of such military alliances as NATO, SEATO, the Rio Pact, and CENTO, the development of military and economic assistance programs throughout the world, and the rapid buildup of America's conventional and nuclear forces.

The third reading, "How the Cold War Was Played," from *Foreign Affairs,* by Zbigniew Brzezinski, noted scholar and national security adviser to President Jimmy Carter, provides a detailed discussion on how the United States and the Soviet Union conducted international politics during some 25 years of the cold war from 1947 to 1972. The essay divides the cold war into six different phases and compares the Soviets and the Americans on political, military, and economic factors during each phase. Brzezinski makes clear that the cold war ebbed and flowed from greater to lesser periods of hostilities and to the periodic advantage of one power over the other. Each party gained from this process, but each was "essentially prudent and restrained." Neither gained all the values that had motivated this conflict at the outset, but neither was able to dominate the other completely in this encounter. Morever, as these nations changed in their own capabilities, as the international system changed, the possibility of a détente relationship between the United States and the Soviet Union became possible at least for a time in the early 1970s.

The next essay, "The Changing Terrain of International Politics," was excerpted from *Beyond the Cold War* originally published in 1966 by Marshall Shulman and reprinted in 1985 by Westview Publishers (Boulder, Colorado). This reading discusses the series of changes that he saw taking place in the international system which required the United States to move beyond the values and beliefs of the cold war. His discussion moves beyond the changes in Soviet-American relations that Brzezinski had discussed and illustrates how global technological and political changes had begun to alter the dynamics of the cold war. With the benefit of hindsight, we can attest to the accuracy of his assessment and the substantial effects of the factors that he identifies.

Shulman first notes, for instance, the impact of modern technology on the military capabilities of states and on the conduct of diplomacy. With these technological changes, the effects of time and space in insulating nations or regions from the impact of international affairs has been reduced. Similarly, rapid economic growth in Western Europe and Japan has changed those nations' roles in international politics. Further, the rapid decolonization of Asia and Africa, and the concomitant rise of nationalism, and the changed nature of China has altered the dynamics of the cold war approach. The result for Shulman is "how much the Cold War has lost its centrality. . . . [T]he confrontation between the Soviet Union and the United States . . . no longer holds the center of the stage."

Along with the global changes that Shulman discusses and the bilateral changes in Soviet-American relations which Brzezinski had analyzed, one major foreign involvement precipitated important alterations in U.S. foreign policy orientation, beginning in the late 1960s. That major influence was the American involvement in the Vietnam War. In the last essay in this section, "Misadventure Revisited," Richard Betts describes and analyzes the impact of that war on U.S. foreign policy. More than any other action, the Vietnam War was responsible for the shattering of the cold war consensus and producing a reassessment of America's approach to international affairs.

At the outset of the involvement, as Betts argues, there was little domestic opposition to the United States seeking to contain Communist expansion in South Vietnam; the cold war consensus was alive and well. (" [T]he remarkable American consensus behind the initial intervention, from 1961 to the 1968 Tet offensive, has been obscured in retrospect by the force of later disillusionment.") Instead the internal debate was over means, not ends. The means chosen were consistently of a limited nature, following a policy that avoided defeat, but one that also precluded victory. (Presidents Kennedy, Johnson, and Nixon "increased U.S. deployments of men and/or firepower simply to stave off defeat, with no real expectation of victory.") The American hope was that over time the will of the North Vietnamese could be broken and that the United States could "reshape the fragile, war-battered South Vietnamese political system."

When neither of these occurred, and as the length of the American involvement increased, disillusionment at home increased as well in both the Congress and the public at large. The upshot was a shattering of the cold war consensus and the call for a reexamination of America's approach to the world. Despite attempts by succeeding presidents to replace this value consensus, Betts concludes that this "bipartisan consensus . . . behind containment" has not reemerged.

NOTES

1. See John Lewis Gaddis, *The United States and the Origins of the Cold War 1941–1947* (New York: Columbia University Press), pp. 1 and 2.
2. See Daniel Yergin, *Shattered Peace: The Origins of the Cold War and the National Security State* (Boston: Houghton Mifflin, 1977), p. 55.

4. ADDRESS OF THE PRESIDENT OF THE UNITED STATES—GREECE, TURKEY, AND THE MIDDLE EAST (H. DOC. NO. 171)

Harry S Truman

The PRESIDENT: Mr. President, Mr. Speaker, Members of the Congress of the United States, the gravity of the situation which confronts the world today necessitates my appearance before a joint session of the Congress.

The foreign policy and the national security of this country are involved.

One aspect of the present situation, which I wish to present to you at this time for your consideration and decision, concerns Greece and Turkey.

The United States has received from the Greek Government an urgent appeal for financial and economic assistance. Preliminary reports from the American economic mission now in Greece and reports from the American Ambassador in Greece corroborate the statement of the Greek Government that assistance is imperative if Greece is to survive as a free nation.

I do not believe that the American people and the Congress wish to turn a deaf ear to the appeal of the Greek Government.

Greece is not a rich country. Lack of sufficient natural resources has always forced the Greek people to work hard to make both ends meet. Since 1940, this industrious and peace-loving country has suffered invasion, 4 years of cruel enemy occupation, and bitter internal strife.

When forces of liberation entered

Greece they found that the retreating Germans had destroyed virtually all the railways, roads, port facilities, communications, and merchant marine. More than a thousand villages had been burned. Eighty-five percent of the children were tubercular. Livestock, poultry, and draft animals had almost disappeared. Inflation had wiped out practically all savings.

As a result of these tragic conditions, a militant minority, exploiting human want and misery, was able to create political chaos which, until now, has made economic recovery impossible.

Greece is today without funds to finance the importation of those goods which are essential to bare subsistence. Under these circumstances the people of Greece cannot make progress in solving their problems of reconstruction. Greece is in desperate need of financial and economic assistance to enable it to resume purchases of food, clothing, fuel, and seeds. These are indispensable for the subsistence of its people and are obtainable only from abroad. Greece must have help to import the goods necessary to restore internal order and security so essential for economic and political recovery.

The Greek Government has also asked for the assistance of experienced American administrators, economists, and technicians to insure that the financial and other aid given to Greece shall be used effectively in creating a stable and self-sustaining economy and in improving its public administration.

Source: *Congressional Record,* vol. 93–Part 2, March 12, 1947, pp. 1980–1981.

The very existence of the Greek state is today threatened by the terrorist activities of several thousand armed men, led by Communists, who defy the Government's authority at a number of points, particularly along the northern boundaries. A commission appointed by the United Nations Security Council is at present investigating disturbed conditions in northern Greece and alleged border violations along the frontier between Greece on the one hand and Albania, Bulgaria, and Yugoslavia on the other.

Meanwhile, the Greek Government is unable to cope with the situation. The Greek Army is small and poorly equipped. It needs supplies and equipment if it is to restore the authority of the Government throughout Greek territory.

Greece must have assistance if it is to become a self-supporting and self-respecting democracy.

The United States must supply this assistance. We have already extended to Greece certain types of relief and economic aid but these are inadequate.

There is no other country to which democratic Greece can turn.

No other nation is willing and able to provide the necessary support for a democratic Greek Government.

The British Government, which has been helping Greece, can give no further financial or economic aid after March 31. Great Britain finds itself under the necessity of reducing or liquidating its commitments in several parts of the world, including Greece.

We have considered how the United Nations might assist in this crisis. But the situation is an urgent one requiring immediate action, and the United Nations and its related organizations are not in a position to extend help of the kind that is required.

It is important to note that the Greek Government has asked for our aid in utilizing effectively the financial and other assistance we may give to Greece, and in improving its public administration. It is of the utmost importance that we supervise the use of any funds made available to Greece [applause], in such a manner that each dollar spent will count toward making Greece self-supporting, and will help to build an economy in which a healthy democracy can flourish.

No government is perfect. One of the chief virtues of a democracy, however, is that its defects are always visible and under democratic processes can be pointed out and corrected. The Government of Greece is not perfect. Nevertheless it represents 85 percent of the members of the Greek Parliament who were chosen in an election last year. Foreign observers, including 692 Americans, considered this election to be a fair expression of the views of the Greek people.

The Greek Government has been operating in an atmosphere of chaos and extremism. It has made mistakes. The extension of aid by this country does not mean that the United States condones everything that the Greek Government has done or will do. We have condemned in the past, and we condemn now, extremist measures of the right or the left. We have in the past advised tolerance, and we advise tolerance now.

Greece's neighbor, Turkey, also deserves our attention.

The future of Turkey as an independent and economically sound state is clearly no less important to the freedom-loving peoples of the world than the future of Greece. The circumstances in which Turkey finds itself today are considerably different from those of Greece. Turkey has been spared the disasters that have beset Greece. And during the war, the United States and Great Britain furnished Turkey with material aid.

Nevertheless, Turkey now needs our support.

Since the war, Turkey has sought financial assistance from Great Britain and the United States for the purpose of effecting that modernization necessary for the maintenance of its national integrity.

That integrity is essential to the preservation of order in the Middle East.

The British Government has informed us that, owing to its own difficulties, it can no longer extend financial or economic aid to Turkey.

As in the case of Greece, if Turkey is to have the assistance it needs, the United States must supply it. We are the only country able to provide that help.

I am fully aware of the broad implications involved if the United States extends assistance to Greece and Turkey, and I shall discuss these implications with you at this time.

One of the primary objectives of the foreign policy of the United States is the creation of conditions in which we and other nations will be able to work out a way of life free from coercion. This was a fundamental issue in the war with Germany and Japan. Our victory was won over countries which sought to impose their will, and their way of life, upon other nations.

To insure the peaceful development of nations, free from coercion, the United States has taken a leading part in establishing the United Nations. The United Nations is designed to make possible lasting freedom and independence for all its members. We shall not realize our objectives, however, unless we are willing to help free peoples to maintain their free institutions and their national integrity against aggressive movements that seek to impose upon them totalitarian regimes. [Applause.] This is no more than a frank recognition that totalitarian regimes imposed on free peoples, by direct or indirect aggression, undermine the foundations of international peace and hence the security of the United States.

The peoples of a number of countries of the world have recently had totalitarian regimes forced upon them against their will. The Government of the United States has made frequent protests against coercion and intimidation, in violation of the Yalta agreement, in Poland, Rumania, and Bulgaria. I must also state that in a number of other countries there have been similar developments.

At the present moment in world history nearly every nation must choose between alternative ways of life. The choice is too often not a free one.

One way of life is based upon the will of the majority, and is distinguished by free institutions, representative government, free elections, guaranties of individual liberty, freedom of speech and religion, and freedom from political oppression.

The second way of life is based upon the will of a minority forcibly imposed upon the majority. It relies upon terror and oppression, a controlled press and radio, fixed elections, and the suppression of personal freedoms.

I believe that it must be the policy of the United States to support free peoples who are resisting attempted subjugation by armed minorities or by outside pressures.

I believe that we must assist free peoples to work out their own destinies in their own way.

I believe that our help should be primarily through economic and financial aid, which is essential to economic stability and orderly political processes.

The world is not static and the status quo is not sacred. But we cannot allow changes in the status quo in violation of the Charter of the United Nations by such methods as coercion, or by such subterfuges as political infiltration. In helping free and independent nations to maintain their freedom, the United States will be giving effect to the principles of the Charter of the United Nations.

It is necessary only to glance at a map to realize that the survival and integrity of the Greek nation are of grave importance in a much wider situation. If Greece should fall under the control of an armed minority, the effect upon its neighbor, Turkey, would be immediate and serious. Confusion and disorder might well spread throughout the entire Middle East.

Moreover, the disappearance of Greece as an independent state would have a profound effect upon those countries in Europe whose peoples are struggling against great difficulties to maintain their freedoms and their independence while they repair the damages of war.

It would be an unspeakable tragedy if these countries, which have struggled so long against overwhelming odds, should lose that victory for which they sacrificed so much. Collapse of free institutions and loss of independence would be disastrous not only for them but for the world. Discouragement and possibly failure would quickly be the lot of neighboring peoples striving to maintain their freedom and independence.

Should we fail to aid Greece and Turkey in this fateful hour, the effect will be far reaching to the West as well as to the East.

We must take immediate and resolute action.

I therefore ask the Congress to provide authority for assistance to Greece and Turkey in the amount of $400,000,000 for the period ending June 30, 1948. In requesting these funds, I have taken into consideration the maximum amount of relief assistance which would be furnished to Greece out of the $350,000,000 which I recently requested that the Congress authorize for the prevention of starvation and suffering in countries devastated by the war.

In addition to funds, I ask the Congress to authorize the detail of American civilian and military personnel to Greece and Turkey, at the request of those countries, to assist in the tasks of reconstruction, and for the purpose of supervising the use of such financial and material assistance as may be furnished. I recommend that authority also be provided for the instruction and training of selected Greek and Turkish personnel.

Finally, I ask that the Congress provide authority which will permit the speediest and most effective use, in terms of needed commodities, supplies, and equipment, of such funds as may be authorized.

If further funds, or further authority, should be needed for purposes indicated in this message, I shall not hesitate to bring the situation before the Congress. On this subject the executive and legislative branches of the Government must work together.

This is a serious course upon which we embark.

I would not recommend it except that the alternative is much more serious. [Applause.]

The United States contributed $341,000,000,000 toward winning World War II. This is an investment in world freedom and world peace.

The assistance that I am recommending for Greece and Turkey amounts to little more than one-tenth of 1 percent of this investment. It is only common sense that we should safeguard this investment and make sure that it was not in vain.

The seeds of totalitarian regimes are

nurtured by misery and want. They spread and grow in the evil soil of poverty and strife. They reach their full growth when the hope of a people for a better life has died.

We must keep that hope alive.

The free peoples of the world look to us for support in maintaining their freedoms.

If we falter in our leadership, we may endanger the peace of the world—and we shall surely endanger the welfare of our own Nation.

Great responsibilities have been placed upon us by the swift movement of events.

I am confident that the Congress will face these responsibilities squarely. [Applause, the Members rising.]

5. THE SOURCES OF SOVIET CONDUCT

Mr. X [George Kennan]

The political personality of Soviet power as we know it today is the product of ideology and circumstances: ideology inherited by the present Soviet leaders from the movement in which they had their political origin, and circumstances of the power which they now have exercised for nearly three decades in Russia. There can be few tasks of psychological analysis more difficult than to try to trace the interaction of these two forces and the relative rôle of each in the determination of official Soviet conduct. Yet the attempt must be made if that conduct is to be understood and effectively countered.

It is difficult to summarize the set of ideological concepts with which the Soviet leaders came into power. Marxian ideology, in its Russian-Communist projection, has always been in process of subtle evolution. The materials on which it bases itself are extensive and complex. But the outstanding features of Communist thought as it existed in 1916 may perhaps be summarized as follows: (*a*) that the central factor in the life of man, the factor which determines the character of public life and the "physiognomy of society," is the system by which material goods are produced and exchanged; (*b*) that the capitalist system of production is a nefarious one which inevitably leads to the exploitation of the working class by the capital-owning class and is

incapable of developing adequately the economic resources of society or of distributing fairly the material goods produced by human labor; (*c*) that capitalism contains the seeds of its own destruction and must, in view of the inability of the capital-owning class to adjust itself to economic change, result eventually and inescapably in a revolutionary transfer of power to the working class; and (*d*) that imperialism, the final phase of capitalism, leads directly to war and revolution.

The rest may be outlined in Lenin's own words: "Unevenness of economic and political development is the inflexible law of capitalism. It follows from this that the victory of Socialism may come originally in a few capitalist countries or even in a single capitalist country. The victorious proletariat of that country, having expropriated the capitalists and having organized Socialist production at home, would rise against the remaining capitalist world, drawing to itself in the process the oppressed classes of other countries."[1] It must be noted that there was no assumption that capitalism would perish without proletarian revolution. A final push was needed from a revolutionary proletariat movement in order to tip over the tottering structure. But it was regarded as inevitable that sooner or later that push be given.

For 50 years prior to the outbreak of the Revolution, this pattern of thought had exercised great fascination for the members of the Russian revolutionary movement. Frustrated, discontented, hopeless of finding self-expression—or too

Source: Reprinted by permission of *Foreign Affairs* July 1947, pp. 566–82. Copyright 1947 by the Council on Foreign Relations, Inc.

impatient to seek it—in the confining limits of the Tsarist political system, yet lacking wide popular support for their choice of bloody revolution as a means of social betterment, these revolutionists found in Marxist theory a highly convenient rationalization for their own instinctive desires. It afforded pseudo-scientific justification for their impatience, for their categoric denial of all value in the Tsarist system, for their yearning for power and revenge and for their inclination to cut corners in the pursuit of it. It is therefore no wonder that they had come to believe implicitly in the truth and soundness of the Marxian-Leninist teachings, so congenial to their own impulses and emotions. Their sincerity need not be impugned. This is a phenomenon as old as human nature itself. It has never been more aptly described than by Edward Gibbon, who wrote in *The Decline and Fall of the Roman Empire:* "From enthusiasm to imposture the step is perilous and slippery; the demon of Socrates affords a memorable instance how a wise man may deceive himself, how a good man may deceive others, how the conscience may slumber in a mixed and middle state between self-illusion and voluntary fraud." And it was with this set of conceptions that the members of the Bolshevik Party entered into power.

Now it must be noted that through all the years of preparation for revolution, the attention of these men, as indeed of Marx himself, had been centered less on the future form which Socialism[2] would take than on the necessary overthrow of rival power which, in their view, had to precede the introduction of Socialism. Their views, therefore, on the positive program to be put into effect, once power was attained, were for the most part nebulous, visionary and impractical. Beyond the nationalization of industry and the expropriation of large private capital holdings there was no agreed program. The treatment of the peasantry, which according to the Marxist formulation was not of the proletariat, had always been a vague spot in the pattern of Communist thought; and it remained an object of controversy and vacillation for the first ten years of Communist power.

The circumstances of the immediate post-revolution period—the existence in Russia of civil war and foreign intervention, together with the obvious fact that the Communists represented only a tiny minority of the Russian people —made the establishment of dictatorial power a necessity. The experiment with "war Communism" and the abrupt attempt to eliminate private production and trade had unfortunate economic consequences and caused further bitterness against the new revolutionary régime. While the temporary relaxation of the effort to communize Russia, represented by the New Economic Policy, alleviated some of this economic distress and thereby served its purpose, it also made it evident that the "capitalistic sector of society" was still prepared to profit at once from any relaxation of governmental pressure, and would, if permitted to continue to exist, always constitute a powerful opposing element to the Soviet régime and a serious rival for influence in the country. Somewhat the same situation prevailed with respect to the individual peasant who, in his own small way, was also a private producer.

Lenin, had he lived, might have proved a great enough man to reconcile these conflicting forces to the ultimate benefit of Russian society, though this is questionable. But be that as it may, Stalin, and those whom he led in the struggle for succession to Lenin's position of leadership, were not the men to tolerate rival political forces in the sphere of power which they coveted. Their sense of insecurity was too great. Their particular brand of fanaticism, unmodified by any of the Anglo-Saxon traditions of compromise, was too fierce and too jealous to envisage any permanent sharing of power. From the Russian-Asiatic world out of which they had emerged they carried with them a skepticism as to the possibilities of permanent and peaceful coexistence of rival forces. Easily persuaded of their own doctrinaire "rightness," they insisted on the submission or destruction of all competing power. Outside of the Communist Party, Russian society was to have no rigidity. There were to be no forms of collective human activity or association which would not be dominated by the Party. No other force in Russian society was to be permitted to achieve vitality or integrity. Only the Party was to have structure. All else was to be an amorphous mass.

And within the Party the same principle was to apply. The mass of Party members might go through the motions of election, deliberation, decision and action; but in these motions they were to be animated not by their own individual wills but by the awesome breath of the Party leadership and the overbrooding presence of "the word."

Let it be stressed again that subjectively these men probably did not seek absolutism for its own sake. They doubtless believed—and found it easy to believe—that they alone knew what was good for society and that they would accomplish that good once their power was secure and unchallengeable. But in seeking that security of their own rule they were prepared to recognize no restrictions, either of God or man, on the character of their methods. And until such time as that security might be achieved,

they placed far down on their scale of operational priorities the comforts and happiness of the peoples entrusted to their care.

Now the outstanding circumstance concerning the Soviet régime is that down to the present day this process of political consolidation has never been completed and the men in the Kremlin have continued to be predominantly absorbed with the struggle to secure and make absolute the power which they seized in November 1917. They have endeavored to secure it primarily against forces at home, within Soviet society itself. But they have also endeavored to secure it against the outside world. For ideology, as we have seen, taught them that the outside world was hostile and that it was their duty eventually to overthrow the political forces beyond their borders. The powerful hands of Russian history and tradition reached up to sustain them in this feeling. Finally, their own aggressive intransigeance with respect to the outside world began to find its own reaction; and they were soon forced, to use another Gibbonesque phrase, "to chastise the contumacy" which they themselves had provoked. It is an undeniable privilege of every man to prove himself right in the thesis that the world is his enemy; for if he reiterates it frequently enough and makes it the background of his conduct he is bound eventually to be right.

Now it lies in the nature of the mental world of the Soviet leaders, as well as in the character of their ideology, that no opposition to them can be officially recognized as having any merit or justification whatsoever. Such opposition can flow, in theory, only from the hostile and incorrigible forces of dying capitalism. As long as remnants of capitalism were officially recognized as existing in Russia, it was possible to place on them, as an internal element, part of the blame for the maintenance of a dictatorial form of society. But as these remnants were liquidated, little by little, this justification fell away; and when it was indicated officially that they had been finally destroyed, it disappeared altogether. And this fact created one of the most basic of the compulsions which came to act upon the Soviet régime: since capitalism no longer existed in Russia and since it could not be admitted that there could be serious or widespread opposition to the Kremlin springing spontaneously from the liberated masses under its authority, it became necessary to justify the retention of the dictatorship by stressing the menace of capitalism abroad.

This began at an early date. In 1924 Stalin specifically defended the retention of the "organs of suppression," meaning, among others, the army and the secret police, on the ground that "as long as there is a capitalist encirclement there will be danger of intervention with all the consequences that flow from that danger." In accordance with that theory, and from that time on, all internal opposition forces in Russia have consistently been portrayed as the agents of foreign forces of reaction antagonistic to Soviet power.

By the same token, tremendous emphasis has been placed on the original Communist thesis of a basic antagonism between the capitalist and Socialist worlds. It is clear, from many indications, that this emphasis is not founded in reality. The real facts concerning it have been confused by the existence abroad of genuine resentment provoked by Soviet philosophy and tactics and occasionally by the existence of great centers of military power, notably the Nazi régime in Germany and the Japanese Government of the late 1930s, which did indeed have aggressive designs against the Soviet

Union. But there is ample evidence that the stress laid in Moscow on the menace confronting Soviet society from the world outside its borders is founded not in the realities of foreign antagonism but in the necessity of explaining away the maintenance of dictatorial authority at home.

Now the maintenance of this pattern of Soviet power, namely, the pursuit of unlimited authority domestically, accompanied by the cultivation of the semi-myth of implacable foreign hostility, has gone far to shape the actual machinery of Soviet power as we know it today. Internal organs of administration which did not serve this purpose withered on the vine. Organs which did serve this purpose became vastly swollen. The security of Soviet power came to rest on the iron discipline of the Party, on the severity and ubiquity of the secret police, and on the uncompromising economic monopolism of the state. The "organs of suppression," in which the Soviet leaders had sought security from rival forces, became in large measure the masters of those whom they were designed to serve. Today the major part of the structure of Soviet power is committed to the perfection of the dictatorship and to the maintenance of the concept of Russia as in a state of siege, with the enemy lowering beyond the walls. And the millions of human beings who form that part of the structure of power must defend at all costs this concept of Russia's position, for without it they are themselves superfluous.

As things stand today, the rulers can no longer dream of parting with these organs of suppression. The quest for absolute power, pursued now for nearly three decades with a ruthlessness unparalleled (in scope at least) in modern times, has again produced internally, as it did externally, its own reaction. The excesses of the police apparatus have fanned the potential opposition to the régime into something far greater and more dangerous than it could have been before those excesses began.

But least of all can the rulers dispense with the fiction by which the maintenance of dictatorial power has been defended. For this fiction has been canonized in Soviet philosophy by the excesses already committed in its name; and it is now anchored in the Soviet structure of thought by bonds far greater than those of mere ideology.

So much for the historical background. What does it spell in terms of the political personality of Soviet power as we know it today?

Of the original ideology, nothing has been officially junked. Belief is maintained in the basic badness of capitalism, in the inevitability of its destruction, in the obligation of the proletariat to assist in that destruction and to take power into its own hands. But stress has come to be laid primarily on those concepts which relate most specifically to the Soviet régime itself: to its position as the sole truly Socialist régime in a dark and misguided world, and to the relationships of power within it.

The first of these concepts is that of the innate antagonism between capitalism and Socialism. We have seen how deeply that concept has become imbedded in foundations of Soviet power. It has profound implications for Russia's conduct as a member of international society. It means that there can never be on Moscow's side any sincere assumption of a community of aims between the Soviet Union and powers which are regarded as capitalist. It must invariably be assumed in Moscow that the aims of the capitalist world are antagonistic to the Soviet régime, and therefore to the interests of the peoples it controls. If the Soviet Government occa-

sionally sets its signature to documents which would indicate the contrary, this is to be regarded as a tactical manoeuvre permissible in dealing with the enemy (who is without honor) and should be taken in the spirit of *caveat emptor*. Basically, the antagonism remains. It is postulated. And from it flow many of the phenomena which we find disturbing in the Kremlin's conduct of foreign policy: the secretiveness, the lack of frankness, the duplicity, the wary suspiciousness, and the basic unfriendliness of purpose. These phenomena are there to stay, for the foreseeable future. There can be variations of degree and of emphasis. When there is something the Russians want from us, one or the other of these features of their policy may be thrust temporarily into the background; and when that happens there will always be Americans who will leap forward with gleeful announcements that "the Russians have changed," and some who will even try to take credit for having brought about such "changes." But we should not be misled by tactical manoeuvres. These characteristics of Soviet policy, like the postulate from which they flow, are basic to the internal nature of Soviet power, and will be with us, whether in the foreground or the background, until the internal nature of Soviet power is changed.

This means that we are going to continue for a long time to find the Russians difficult to deal with. It does not mean that they should be considered as embarked upon a do-or-die program to overthrow our society by a given date. The theory of the inevitability of the eventual fall of capitalism has the fortunate connotation that there is no hurry about it. The forces of progress can take their time in preparing the final *coup de grâce*. Meanwhile, what is vital is that the "Socialist fatherland"—that oasis of power which has been already won for Socialism in the person of the Soviet Union—should be cherished and defended by all good Communists at home and abroad, its fortunes promoted, its enemies badgered and confounded. The promotion of premature, "adventuristic" revolutionary projects abroad which might embarrass Soviet power in any way would be an inexcusable, even a counter-revolutionary act. The cause of Socialism is the support and promotion of Soviet power, as defined in Moscow.

This brings us to the second of the concepts important to contemporary Soviet outlook. That is the infallibility of the Kremlin. The Soviet concept of power, which permits no focal points of organization outside the Party itself, requires that the Party leadership remain in theory the sole repository of truth. For if truth were to be found elsewhere, there would be justification for its expression in organized activity. But it is precisely that which the Kremlin cannot and will not permit.

The leadership of the Communist Party is therefore always right, and has been always right ever since in 1929 Stalin formalized his personal power by announcing that decisions of the Politburo were being taken unanimously.

On the principle of infallibility there rests the iron discipline of the Communist Party. In fact, the two concepts are mutually self-supporting. Perfect discipline requires recognition of infallibility. Infallibility requires the observance of discipline. And the two together go far to determine the behaviorism of the entire Soviet apparatus of power. But their effect cannot be understood unless a third factor be taken into account: namely, the fact that the leadership is at liberty to put forward for tactical purposes any particular thesis which it finds useful to the

cause at any particular moment and to require the faithful and unquestioning acceptance of that thesis by the members of the movement as a whole. This means that truth is not a constant but is actually created, for all intents and purposes, by the Soviet leaders themselves. It may vary from week to week, from month to month. It is nothing absolute and immutable— nothing which flows from objective reality. It is only the most recent manifestation of the wisdom of those in whom the ultimate wisdom is supposed to reside, because they represent the logic of history. The accumulative effect of these factors is to give to the whole subordinate apparatus of Soviet power an unshakeable stubbornness and steadfastness in its orientation. This orientation can be changed at will by the Kremlin but by no other power. Once a given party line has been laid down on a given issue of current policy, the whole Soviet governmental machine, including the mechanism of diplomacy, moves inexorably along the prescribed path, like a persistent toy automobile wound up and headed in a given direction, stopping only when it meets with some unanswerable force. The individuals who are the components of this machine are unamenable to argument or reason which comes to them from outside sources. Their whole training has taught them to mistrust and discount the glib persuasiveness of the outside world. Like the white dog before the phonograph, they hear only the "master's voice." And if they are to be called off from the purposes last dictated to them, it is the master who must call them off. Thus the foreign representative cannot hope that his words will make any impression on them. The most that he can hope is that they will be transmitted to those at the top, who are capable of changing the party line. But even those are not likely to be swayed by any normal logic in the words of the bourgeois representative. Since there can be no appeal to common purposes, there can be no appeal to common mental approaches. For this reason, facts speak louder than words to the ears of the Kremlin; and words carry the greatest weight when they have the ring of reflecting, or being backed up by, facts of unchallengeable validity.

But we have seen that the Kremlin is under no ideological compulsion to accomplish its purposes in a hurry. Like the Church, it is dealing in ideological concepts which are of long-term validity, and it can afford to be patient. It has no right to risk the existing achievements of the revolution for the sake of vain baubles of the future. The very teachings of Lenin himself require great caution and flexibility in the pursuit of Communist purposes. Again, these precepts are fortified by the lessons of Russian history: of centuries of obscure battles between nomadic forces over the stretches of a vast unfortified plain. Here caution, circumspection, flexibility and deception are the valuable qualities; and their value finds natural appreciation in the Russian or the oriental mind. Thus the Kremlin has no compunction about retreating in the face of superior force. And being under the compulsion of no timetable, it does not get panicky under the necessity for such retreat. Its political action is a fluid stream which moves constantly, wherever it is permitted to move, toward a given goal. Its main concern is to make sure that it has filled every nook and cranny available to it in the basin of world power. But if it finds unassailable barriers in its path, it accepts these philosophically and accommodates itself to them. The main thing is that there should always be pressure, unceasing constant pressure, toward the desired goal. There is no trace of any feeling in Soviet psychology that that goal must be reached at any given time.

These considerations make Soviet diplomacy at once easier and more difficult to deal with than the diplomacy of individual aggressive leaders like Napoleon and Hitler. On the one hand it is more sensitive to contrary force, more ready to yield on individual sectors of the diplomatic front when that force is felt to be too strong, and thus more rational in the logic and rhetoric of power. On the other hand it cannot be easily defeated or discouraged by a single victory on the part of its opponents. And the patient persistence by which it is animated means that it can be effectively countered not by sporadic acts which represent the momentary whims of democratic opinion but only by intelligent long-range policies on the part of Russia's adversaries—policies no less steady in their purpose, and no less variegated and resourceful in their application, than those of the Soviet Union itself.

In these circumstances it is clear that the main element of any United States policy toward the Soviet Union must be that of a long-term, patient but firm and vigilant containment of Russian expansive tendencies. It is important to note, however, that such a policy has nothing to do with outward histrionics: with threats or blustering or superfluous gestures of outward "toughness." While the Kremlin is basically flexible in its reaction to political realities, it is by no means unamenable to considerations of prestige. Like almost any other government, it can be placed by tactless and threatening gestures in a position where it cannot afford to yield even though this might be dictated by its sense of realism. The Russian leaders are keen judges of human psychology, and as such they are highly conscious that loss of temper and of self-control is never a source of strength in political affairs. They are quick to exploit such evidences of weakness. For these reasons, it is a *sine qua non* of successful dealing with Russia that the foreign government in question should remain at all times cool and collected and that its demands on Russian policy should be put forward in such a manner as to leave the way open for a compliance not too detrimental to Russian prestige.

In the light of the above, it will be clearly seen that the Soviet pressure against the free institutions of the western world is something that can be contained by the adroit and vigilant application of counter-force at a series of constantly shifting geographical and political points, corresponding to the shifts and manoeuvres of Soviet policy, but which cannot be charmed or talked out of existence. The Russians look forward to a duel of infinite duration, and they see that already they have scored great successes. It must be borne in mind that there was a time when the Communist Party represented far more of a minority in the sphere of Russian national life than Soviet power today represents in the world community.

But if ideology convinces the rulers of Russia that truth is on their side and that they can therefore afford to wait, those of us on whom that ideology has no claim are free to examine objectively the validity of that premise. The Soviet thesis not only implies complete lack of control by the west over its own economic destiny, it likewise assumes Russian unity, discipline and patience over an infinite period. Let us bring this apocalyptic vision down to earth, and suppose that the western world finds the strength and resourcefulness to contain Soviet power over a period of ten to fifteen years. What does that spell for Russia itself?

The Soviet leaders, taking advantage of the contributions of modern technique to the arts of despotism, have solved the question of obedience within the confines of their power. Few challenge their authority; and even those who do are unable to make that challenge valid as against the organs of suppression of the state.

The Kremlin has also proved able to accomplish its purpose of building up in Russia, regardless of the interests of the inhabitants, an industrial foundation of heavy metallurgy, which is, to be sure, not yet complete but which is nevertheless continuing to grow and is approaching those of the other major industrial countries. All of this, however, both the maintenance of internal political security and the building of heavy industry, has been carried out at a terrible cost in human life and in human hopes and energies. It has necessitated the use of forced labor on a scale unprecedented in modern times under conditions of peace. It has involved the neglect or abuse of other phases of Soviet economic life, particularly agriculture, consumers' goods production, housing and transportation.

To all that, the war has added its tremendous toll of destruction, death and human exhaustion. In consequence of this, we have in Russia today a population which is physically and spiritually tired. The mass of the people are disillusioned, skeptical and no longer as accessible as they once were to the magical attraction which Soviet power still radiates to its followers abroad. The avidity with which people seized upon the slight respite accorded to the Church for tactical reasons during the war was eloquent testimony to the fact that their capacity for faith and devotion found little expression in the purposes of the régime.

In these circumstances, there are limits to the physical and nervous strength of people themselves. These limits are absolute ones, and are binding even for the cruelest dictatorship, because beyond them people cannot be driven. The forced labor camps and the other agencies of constraint provide temporary means of compelling people to work longer hours than their own volition or mere economic pressure would dictate; but if people survive them at all they become old before their time and must be considered as human casualties to the demands of dictatorship. In either case their best powers are no longer available to society and can no longer be enlisted in the service of the state.

Here only the younger generation can help. The younger generation, despite all vicissitudes and sufferings, is numerous and vigorous; and the Russians are a talented people. But it still remains to be seen what will be the effects on mature performance of the abnormal emotional strains of childhood which Soviet dictatorship created and which were enormously increased by the war. Such things as normal security and placidity of home environment have practically ceased to exist in the Soviet Union outside of the most remote farms and villages. And observers are not yet sure whether that is not going to leave its mark on the overall capacity of the generation now coming into maturity.

In addition to this, we have the fact that Soviet economic development, while it can list certain formidable achievements, has been precariously spotty and uneven. Russian Communists who speak of the "uneven development of capitalism" should blush at the contemplation of their own national economy. Here certain branches of economic life, such as the metallurgical and machine industries, have been pushed out of all proportion to other sectors of economy. Here is a nation striving to become in a short period one of the great industrial nations of the world while it still has no highway network worthy of the name and only a relatively primitive network of railways. Much has been done to increase efficiency of labor and to teach primitive peasants something about the operation of machines. But maintenance is still a crying deficiency of all Soviet economy. Construction is hasty and poor in quality. Depreciation must be enormous. And in vast sectors of economic life it has not yet been possible to instill into labor anything like that general culture of production and technical self-respect which characterizes the skilled worker of the west.

It is difficult to see how these deficiencies can be corrected at an early date by a tired and dispirited population working largely under the shadow of fear and compulsion. And as long as they are not overcome, Russia will remain economically a vulnerable, and in a certain sense an impotent, nation, capable of exporting its enthusiasms and of radiating the strange charm of its primitive political vitality but unable to back up those articles of export by the real evidences of material power and prosperity.

Meanwhile, a great uncertainty hangs over the political life of the Soviet Union. That is the uncertainty involved in the transfer of power from one individual or group of individuals to others.

This is, of course, outstandingly the problem of the personal position of Stalin. We must remember that his succession to Lenin's pinnacle of preëminence in the Communist movement was the only such transfer of individual authority which the Soviet Union has experienced. That transfer took 12 years to consolidate. It cost the lives of millions of people and shook the state to its foundations. The attendant tremors were felt all through the international revolutionary movement, to the disadvantage of the Kremlin itself.

It is always possible that another transfer of preëminent power may take place quietly and inconspicuously, with no repercussions anywhere. But again, it is possible that the questions involved may unleash, to use some of Lenin's words, one of those "incredibly swift transitions" from "delicate deceit" to "wild violence" which characterize Russian history, and may shake Soviet power to its foundations.

But this is not only a question of Stalin himself. There has been, since 1938, a dangerous congealment of political life in the higher circles of Soviet power. The All-Union Congress of Soviets, in theory the supreme body of the Party, is supposed to meet not less often than once in three years. It will soon be eight full years since its last meeting. During this period membership in the Party has numerically doubled. Party mortality during the war was enormous; and today well over half of the Party members are persons who have entered since the last Party congress was held. Meanwhile, the same small group of men has carried on at the top through an amazing series of national vicissitudes. Surely there is some reason why the experiences of the war brought basic political changes to every one of the great governments of the west. Surely the causes of that phenomenon are basic enough to be present somewhere in the obscurity of Soviet political life, as well. And yet no recognition has been given to these causes in Russia.

It must be surmised from this that even within so highly disciplined an organization as the Communist Party there must be a growing divergence in age, outlook and interest between the great mass of Party members, only so recently recruited into the movement, and the little self-perpetuating clique of men at the top, whom most of these Party members have never met, with whom they have never conversed, and with whom they can have no political intimacy.

Who can say whether, in these circumstances, the eventual rejuvenation of the higher spheres of authority (which can only be a matter of time) can take place smoothly and peacefully, or whether rivals in the quest for higher power will not eventually reach down into these politically immature and inexperienced masses in order to find support for their respective claims? If this were ever to happen, strange consequences could flow for the Communist Party: for the membership at large has been exercised only in the practices of iron discipline and obedience and not in the arts of compromise and accommodation. And if disunity were ever to seize and paralyze the Party, the chaos and weakness of Russian society would be revealed in forms beyond description. For we have seen that Soviet power is only a crust concealing an amorphous mass of human beings among whom no independent organizational structure is tolerated. In Russia there is not even such a thing as local government. The present generation of Russians have never known spontaneity of collective action. If, consequently, anything were ever to occur to disrupt the unity and efficacy of the Party as a political instrument, Soviet Russia might be changed overnight from one of the strongest to one of the weakest and most pitiable of national societies.

Thus the future of Soviet power may not be by any means as secure as Russian capacity for self-delusion would make it appear to the men in the Kremlin. That they can keep power themselves, they have demonstrated. That they can quietly and easily turn it over to others remains to be proved. Meanwhile, the hardships of their rule and the vicissitudes of international life have taken a heavy toll of the strength and hopes of the great people on whom their power rests. It is curious to note that the ideological power of Soviet authority is strongest today in areas beyond the frontiers of Russia, beyond the reach of its police power. This phenomenon brings to mind a comparison used by Thomas Mann in his great novel *Buddenbrooks.* Observing that human institutions often show the greatest outward brilliance at a moment when inner decay is in reality farthest advanced, he compared the Buddenbrook family, in the days of its greatest glamour, to one of those stars whose light shines most brightly on this world when in reality it has long since ceased to exist. And who can say with assurance that the strong light still cast by the Kremlin on the dissatisfied peoples of the western world is not the powerful afterglow of a constellation which is in actuality on the wane? This cannot be proved. And it cannot be disproved. But the possibility remains (and in the opinion of this writer it is a strong one) that Soviet power, like the capitalist world of its conception, bears within it the seeds of its own decay, and that the sprouting of these seeds is well advanced.

It is clear that the United States cannot expect in the foreseeable future to enjoy political intimacy with the Soviet régime. It must continue to regard the Soviet Union as a rival, not a partner, in the political arena. It must continue to expect that Soviet policies will reflect no abstract love of peace and stability, no real faith in the possibility of a permanent happy coexistence of the Socialist and capitalist worlds, but rather a cautious, persistent pressure toward the disruption and weakening of all rival influence and rival power.

Balanced against this are the facts that Russia, as opposed to the western world in general, is still by far the weaker party, that Soviet policy is highly flexible, and that Soviet society may well contain deficiencies which will eventually weaken its own total potential. This would of itself warrant the United States entering with reasonable confidence upon a policy of firm containment, designed to confront the Russians with unalterable counter-force at every point where they show signs of encroaching upon the interests of a peaceful and stable world.

But in actuality the possibilities for American policy are by no means limited to holding the line and hoping for the best. It is entirely possible for the United States to influence by its actions the internal developments, both within Russia and throughout the international Communist movement, by which Russian policy is largely determined. This is not only a question of the modest measure of informational activity which this government can conduct in the Soviet Union and elsewhere, although that, too, is important. It is rather a question of the degree to which the United States can create among the peoples of the world generally the impression of a country which knows what it wants, which is coping successfully with the problems of its internal life and with the responsibilities of a World Power, and which has a spiritual vitality capable of holding its own among the major ideological currents of the time. To the extent that such an impression can be created and maintained, the aims of Russian Communism must appear sterile and quixotic, the hopes and enthusiasm of Moscow's supporters must wane, and added strain must be imposed on the

Kremlin's foreign policies. For the palsied decrepitude of the capitalist world is the keystone of Communist philosophy. Even the failure of the United States to experience the early economic depression which the ravens of the Red Square have been predicting with such complacent confidence since hostilities ceased would have deep and important repercussions throughout the Communist world.

By the same token, exhibitions of indecision, disunity and internal disintegration within this country have an exhilarating effect on the whole Communist movement. At each evidence of these tendencies, a thrill of hope and excitement goes through the Communist world; a new jauntiness can be noted in the Moscow tread; new groups of foreign supporters climb on to what they can only view as the band wagon of international politics; and Russian pressure increases all along the line in international affairs.

It would be an exaggeration to say that American behavior unassisted and alone could exercise a power of life and death over the Communist movement and bring about the early fall of Soviet power in Russia. But the United States has it in its power to increase enormously the strains under which Soviet policy must operate, to force upon the Kremlin a far greater degree of moderation and circumspection than it has had to observe in recent years, and in this way to promote tendencies which must eventually find their outlet in either the break-up or the gradual mellowing of Soviet power. For no

mystical, Messianic movement—and particularly not that of the Kremlin—can face frustration indefinitely without eventually adjusting itself in one way or another to the logic of that state of affairs.

Thus the decision will really fall in large measure in this country itself. The issue of Soviet-American relations is in essence a test of the over-all worth of the United States as a nation among nations. To avoid destruction the United States need only measure up to its own best traditions and prove itself worthy of preservation as a great nation.

Surely, there was never a fairer test of national quality than this. In the light of these circumstances, the thoughtful observer of Russian-American relations will find no cause for complaint in the Kremlin's challenge to American society. He will rather experience a certain gratitude to a Providence which, by providing the American people with this implacable challenge, has made their entire security as a nation dependent on their pulling themselves together and accepting the responsibilities of moral and political leadership that history plainly intended them to bear.

NOTES

1. "Concerning the Slogans of the United States of Europe," August 1915. Official Soviet edition of Lenin's works.
2. Here and elsewhere in this paper "Socialism" refers to Marxist or Leninist Communism, not to liberal Socialism of the Second International variety.

6. HOW THE COLD WAR WAS PLAYED

Zbigniew Brzezinski

The dates May 22, 1947, and May 22, 1972, span exactly 25 years. On May 22, 1947, President Truman signed a congressional bill committing the United States to support Greece and Turkey against Soviet designs, and the United States thereby assumed overtly the direct leadership of the West in the containment of Soviet influence. Twenty-five years later to the day, another American President landed in Moscow, declaring to the Soviet leaders that "we meet at a moment when we can make peaceful coöperation a reality."

Viewing the past 25 years of the cold war as a political process, this study seeks to evaluate the conduct of the two competitors and to draw some implications from the experience of a quarter-century's rivalry for the future of U.S.-Soviet relations. Its purpose is thus neither to seek the causes of the cold war nor to assign moral or historical responsibility for it.

To accomplish the above, two preliminary steps must be taken. The first is to identify the principal phases of the cold war, viewing it as a process of conflict and competition. The purpose of the periodization is to delineate phases of time in which the competitive process was dominated by a discernible pattern of relations; in its simplest form, this involves identifying phases in which one or the other side seemed to hold the political initiative, either on the basis of a rela-

Source: Reprinted by permission of *Foreign Affairs* October 1972, pp. 181–204. Copyright 1972 by the Council on Foreign Relations, Inc.

tively crystallized strategy and/or through more assertive behavior.

Second, it is necessary to focus on several dynamic components at work in the competitive process, the interaction of which shaped the relative performance of the two powers. Reference will be made within the several phases of the competition to the relative international standing of the two rivals, to their relative economic power, to their relative military power, and to the relative clarity and purposefulness of national policy, including the degree of domestic support for that policy.

Finally, it must be acknowledged that this writer sees the cold war as more the product of lengthy and probably ineluctable historical forces and less as the result of human error and evil. Two great powers, differentiated by divergent centuries-long experience and separated by sharply differing ideological perspectives, yet thrust into political proximity as a consequence of the shattering of the earlier international system, could hardly avoid being plunged into a competitive relationship. In brief, this was less a matter of Stalin or of Dulles and more of de Tocqueville.

PHASE I—SHAPING OF THE CONFRONTATION, 1945–1947

This phase was essentially a preliminary one. Neither the United States nor the Soviet Union was yet directly pitted against the other. Within both societies active debates concerning the likely nature of postwar developments were yielding conflicting estimates and advice: in the United States the issue came out in the open with the Truman-Wallace split; in the Soviet Union there were overtones of it in Zhdanov's more militant posture, while the Varga debate about the postwar prospects of capitalism—though more muted than the corresponding discussions in the United States—indicated analytical disagreements concerning the future of the capitalist system.

Neither side thus was yet operating on the basis of clear-cut policies, backed by firm domestic support. Internal U.S. divisions continued into the presidential campaign of 1948, and it was only in 1947–1948 that a more crystallized American view emerged, backed by bipartisan support. George Kennan's famous article in *Foreign Affairs* of July 1947 represented in that respect a historic watershed. On the Soviet side, while the assumption of Western hostility was deeply ingrained in the official ideology, widespread popular disaffection, economic dislocations and the gradual reimposition of Stalinist controls after relative wartime relaxation—all reflected a very basic domestic weakness of the system as a whole, sharpening for Stalin the dilemmas of moderation or militancy (with the latter apparently advocated not only by Zhdanov but in very early postwar phases also by Tito and his associates in Jugoslavia and Bulgaria).

The international context in which the emerging hostility was crystallizing was clearly to America's advantage. While the Soviet Union emerged from the war with vastly enhanced prestige, with much accumulated good will even within the United States, and with highly subservient and influential Communist parties playing key roles in such countries as France and Italy, the Soviet position in

the world was still very inferior to that of the United States. The Western Hemisphere was firmly in the American grip; Africa and the Middle East were politically controlled by America's allies (with American economic assets expanding particularly rapidly in the Middle East); the southern Asian arc was still part of the British Empire, while Iran already in 1946 was seeking U.S. political assistance against the Soviet Union; Nationalist China was striving to consolidate its authority; and Japan was subject to an exclusive U.S. occupation.

Economically and militarily, the relationship favored the United States, though the military aspect was clouded by some uncertainties. The United States emerged from the war with its GNP actually increased, while the Soviet Union, on the other hand, had suffered grievously during the war and by 1947 its GNP was probably less than one-third that of the United States (roughly equal to that of contemporary India or China).

The military picture was not as clearcut. Neither side could afford to maintain the enormous forces that were at its disposal at the conclusion of the war. American armed forces, which at their peak numbered some 12.3 million men, were rapidly demobilized because of domestic political pressures and economic need. By 1947, American ground forces had shrunk to only about 670,000 men. At their peak, Soviet armed forces numbered about 11.3 million men. Contrary to postwar myths, the Soviet Union did not refrain from large-scale demobilization, which was an economic necessity, given wartime devastation, and enormous manpower losses; by 1947 the Soviet Union had only approximately 2.8 million men under arms.

For political reasons, the Soviet government chose to keep its demobilization a secret. As a result, contemporary Western estimates of Soviet military strength were considerably higher than reality. The element of uncertainty in the military relationship was also introduced by the U.S. monopoly in atomic bombs. Presumably because of this fact, it suited the Soviet Union not to disabuse the West of the otherwise politically costly notion that it was only the United States (and Great Britain) that disarmed following the war. This provided an important counter to the American atomic monopoly, perhaps inhibiting the American side from exploiting it politically. Moreover, in the immediate postwar era there was considerable uncertainty both as to the actual destructiveness of the new atomic weapons and the American capacity to deliver these weapons on Soviet targets. Because of lags in production and the termination of some atomic facilities, the U.S. atomic stockpile by 1947 was well under 100 bombs, with a cumulative damage-inflicting capacity roughly equal to that imposed on Nazi Germany during World War II, and thus not on a scale sufficient to guarantee the effective destruction of the Soviet Union.

Both sides were thus in an ambiguous position. Unsettled political and social conditions in the West as well as the Soviet advantage on the ground favored the Soviet Union in the event of hostilities in Europe. The U.S. nuclear monopoly as well as the vastly superior American economy—not to speak of the general exhaustion of the Soviet society—boded ill for the Soviet Union in the event of any protracted conflict. The standoff that followed, in a variety of limited confrontations, was the logical outcome, especially given the absence of directly conflicting political goals. The West, vastly overestimating Soviet strength, did not contest Soviet primacy in Central Europe, fear-ing instead a Soviet push westward. The Soviet Union, preoccupied with consolidating its wartime gains and concerned lest the West exploit its weaknesses, only half-heartedly probed the newly established perimeters.

PHASE II—SOVIET PROBES, 1948–1952

The confrontation between the United States and the Soviet Union crystallized during the next phase. Within both societies there emerged a form of political consensus: in America the crushing defeat of Henry Wallace and the appearance of bipartisan support for an actively anti-Soviet policy signaled the end of postwar uncertainty; in the Soviet Union (as well as in Eastern Europe) the imposition of Stalinist terror created an atmosphere of a beleaguered camp ("imperialist encirclement") dominated by implacable ideological hostility toward its rivals.

The cold war now became primarily an American-Soviet affair. By 1947 the United States had assumed responsibility for British undertakings in Greece and Turkey and, more generally, taken the lead in fashioning the strategy of the West. American goals were succinctly expressed in the concept of "containment." Essentially, the strategy rested on two premises: Soviet expansion must be halted, by both military and political means; and this in turn would create the preconditions for an eventual mellowing or even breaking up of the Soviet system. Soviet actions indicated an accelerated effort to subordinate Eastern Europe to full Soviet control, while Soviet probes in Berlin and Korea appeared to have been aimed both at the consolidation of existing Communist power and, had an American response been lacking, also the expansion of the Soviet sphere.

During this phase, the United States continued to enjoy the decisive advantage in economic power and international influence, though its relative military position in some respects actually worsened. The U.S. economy grew during this phase to over $400 billion (in 1966 dollars), and the United States was able to undertake a massive program in injecting its capital into Western Europe, thus reinforcing a vital political link. Soviet postwar recovery was pressed energetically and the Soviet economy passed its prewar levels with the GNP crossing the $150 billion mark (in 1966 dollars) by the time of Stalin's death.

The international climate was similarly skewed to U.S. advantage. The coup in Czechoslovakia, the Berlin blockade, the defection of Jugoslavia (with its overtones of Soviet bullying), the purge trials in Eastern Europe and eventually the invasion of South Korea all created a distinctly anti-Soviet mood. In some respects, however, this was misleading. Probably a more accurate measure of international attitudes was provided by the February 1951 vote condemning the Chinese intervention in the Korean War. The pro-U.S. vote was 47 to seven with ten abstentions. India and Burma joined the Soviet Union in opposition to the resolutions, while Egypt, Indonesia, Pakistan, Saudi Arabia, Sweden, Syria, Yemen, Jugoslavia, Algeria and Afghanistan abstained. The southern arc of the Eurasian continent was thus beginning to divorce itself from a clear-cut identification with the United States.

Heightened international tensions, especially after the outbreak of Korean hostilities, prompted both powers to step up their military preparedness. Paradoxically, the tendency in the West at the time—in contrast to the earlier phase—was somewhat to underestimate Soviet strength. Soviet ground forces were being built up rapidly in order to offset any Western atomic threat. Soviet defense spending—despite a decline to under $30 billion in 1948 from its wartime high of about $50 billion—was still more than twice that of the United States, and Soviet armed forces grew in manpower to almost five million men by the time of Stalin's death, a figure approximately one million above prevailing Western estimates and considerably in excess of the U.S. 1.6 million men under arms. American defense spending did not rise until the Korean War (having dropped precipitously from over $70 billion in 1945 to under $12 billion by 1950), but then it did so rapidly, exceeding by 1952 in total dollar value Soviet military allocations.

More important in the shifting military relationship was the development by the Soviet Union of the atomic bomb. That development came earlier than American planners had expected and by 1951 the Soviet Union already possessed a modest stockpile of atomic bombs (numbering about 60 weapons, or roughly one-tenth of the U.S. stockpile). Increasingly binding U.S. political and military commitments to Europe were hence designed to cancel any advantage the Soviet Union could derive from this new situation and thus to preserve the inherent asymmetry in the American-Soviet relationship.

On balance, this phase of the cold war can be said to have involved clashes reflecting a more assertive Soviet pattern of behavior, with the United States essentially responding to perceived threats. The consequences of the clashes were three major developments, all to U.S. advantage: the launching of Western economic recovery and the shaping of a new political coalition; the initiation of a rapid U.S. military build-up designed to erase the

Soviet advantage on the ground; the rebuff of the Soviet Union in two, and possibly three, crisis areas: Berlin, Korea and Jugoslavia. Soviet military power was effective only in shielding the Soviet political predominance in Eastern Europe, an area not even actively contested by the West.

The historical significance of the Korean War, in addition to its crucial impact on U.S. rearmament, poses an especially tantalizing question: to what extent was it merely a Soviet miscalculation, based on the assumption of U.S. disengagement from the mainland of Asia and perhaps also stimulated by Stalin's desire (reflecting long-standing Russian interests) to transform a united Korea into a Soviet dependency (instead of a Chinese or eventually a Japanese one), and to what extent was it a calculated move deliberately designed to stimulate American-Chinese hostility? Stalin's suspicions of China are well documented, while the predominant U.S. inclination prior to the Korean War was to seek some sort of an accommodation with the new government on the Chinese mainland. In any case, the opportunity to stimulate a head-on clash between America and China must have been welcomed by Stalin, and deservedly so. The ensuing 20 years of American-Chinese hostility were certainly a net gain for the Soviet Union.

PHASE III—ASSERTIVE RHETORIC VS. POLICY OF STATUS QUO, 1953–1957

The coincidence of apparent external successes with domestic political change in the United States (not only in leadership but, even more notably, in ideological climate) led to the next phase in the rivalry, a phase seemingly dominated by greater U.S. assertiveness.

The new American policy, articulated by the winning Republican side during the presidential election of 1952, seemed to signal a basic departure from the U.S. strategy of containment: the adoption, instead, of an offensive "policy of liberation" designed to roll back the Soviet Union from its newly acquired East European satellites.

Soviet leaders had cause to view this change in American tone with some anxiety. Their insecurity was doubtless heightened by a series of internal crises, the cumulative effect of which was to sharpen the contrast between the self-confident and, on the whole, self-satisfied America of the early Eisenhower years and the troubled Russia torn by post-Stalin dissensions. A grave and enduring political crisis ensued in the wake of Stalin's death, with internecine conflicts consuming the energies of the top Soviet leaders. Its eruption precipitated a marked decline in the effectiveness of Soviet control over Eastern Europe—the area at which the new U.S. policy ostensibly pointed—and it sparked a series of violent uprisings. Finally, Soviet uncertainty about the future of Sino-Soviet relations caused Soviet leaders to redress the more overtly irritating aspects of the relationship established between Stalin and Mao in 1949, but without quieting entirely Soviet anxieties about the future.

More urgent from the Soviet point of view was the fact that during this phase the United States was beginning to acquire a strategic capability for inflicting significant damage on the Soviet Union which, coupled with the generally more crusading mood of Washington, seemed to lend credibility to the offensive character of U.S. policy. U.S. military spending, though it declined somewhat from the Korean War peak of $61 billion, stabilized around the mid-$30 billion mark during the first Eisenhower administration, while manpower under arms ranged from 3.5 million to 2.8 million men. In effective manpower, the Soviet Union still retained a considerable edge (almost 2 to 1), since by 1955 its armed forces numbered some 5.7 million men, with Soviet defense spending for this period estimated as roughly equivalent to $30 billion per annum. The big margin, strategically and politically, was in respective nuclear vulnerability. The United States proclaimed itself committed to the doctrine of massive retaliation, and the modernization and expansion of the Strategic Air Command (SAC) did create during this phase, probably for the first time, a situation of high Soviet vulnerability to a large-scale U.S. atomic attack. By 1955, the U.S. nuclear-weapons bomber fleet capable of undertaking two-way attack missions on the Soviet Union had grown to about 400 aircraft, and the total number of U.S. bombers capable of executing an atomic attack on the Soviet Union was in the vicinity of 1,350; the corresponding Soviet figures were only about 40 and 350, respectively.

The Soviet atomic insecurity was heightened still further by the continuing economic gap and by persisting international isolation. On the international plane, despite stepped-up Soviet activity, the isolation of the Soviet Union remained as complete as it had been since the days of the early fifties. The economic asymmetry also remained roughly what it had been at the time of Stalin's death: if anything, the gap widened slightly in absolute figures, with the U.S. GNP reaching in 1955 the figure of $508 billion (in 1966 dollars), and the Soviet Union increasing its to about $185 billion. Relatively, the Soviet Union moved up somewhat, with a GNP about 36 percent of that of the United States. None the less, the death of Stalin and the subse-

quent temptation on the part of competing Soviet leaders to cater more to domestic aspirations prompted a debate whether to enhance the Soviet standard of living, necessarily at the expense of defense budgeting.

However, the U.S. side during this phase also began to be increasingly apprehensive about its security. Even the very limited Soviet striking power created, for the first time, some domestic U.S. vulnerability to a Soviet nuclear attack. This heightened sense of insecurity was reinforced by the unexpectedly rapid Soviet acquisition of an H-bomb, with the Soviet Union testing an operational weapon before the United States. A special RAND study concluded that even with an inferior striking power the Soviet Union might be able to launch a devastatingly effective first strike against the American Strategic Air Command bases.

The combination of domestic and international strains led the Soviet side to initiate a series of steps pointing toward a détente in East-West relations. Even before Stalin's death, the Soviet side hinted that it might be willing to explore the possibility of a reunited but neutralized Germany, and some of the post-Stalin successors appeared to have been inclined to pursue this path. More significant was the Soviet readiness to conclude a peace treaty with Austria, resulting in the withdrawal of Soviet forces from that country. Khrushchev's accommodation with Jugoslavia terminated that particular crisis, while "the spirit of Geneva"—following the 1955 summit meeting—prompted on both U.S. and Soviet sides publicly announced troop cuts.

On the Soviet side, the critical turning point, prompting the termination of this particular phase in the cold war and initiating a new one, probably came with the October-November crisis of 1956. The almost total U.S. passivity in the face of enormous Soviet indecision regarding what seemed for a while like the imminent collapse of Soviet rule throughout Eastern Europe apparently convinced the Soviet leaders that American assertiveness was in fact only a domestically expedient myth. The skillful Soviet exploitation of the unprecedented allied differences over the Suez affair also fed Soviet optimism, and a novel tone of assertiveness increasingly began to be heard from the Kremlin.

This phase of the cold war was thus essentially one of missed U.S. opportunities. It was the American side which failed to capitalize on the political and military momentum generated by the repulsion of Stalin's probes—either by exploiting to its own advantage the surfacing Soviet weaknesses or by taking advantage of the Soviet interest in a détente. The doctrine of massive retaliation, accompanied by cuts in U.S. ground forces, left too narrow a margin between the extremes of war or peace for the U.S. policy-makers to exploit the U.S. strategic preponderance. The post-1953 Soviet anxiety about U.S. capabilities and intentions now gave way to a radically different Soviet reading of the rivalry. If during 1953 to 1956 the Soviet Union can be said to have exaggerated its own strength in order to deter the United States from acting assertively, from 1957 on the Soviet leaders were inclined to exaggerate their own strength in order to exploit it on behalf of a more assertive Soviet behavior.

PHASE IV—PREMATURE SOVIET GLOBALISM, 1958–1963

"The East Wind Prevails Over the West Wind": These words uttered in the Kremlin by Mao Tse-tung in late 1957 set the tone for the next phase of the cold war. The Soviet concept of détente changed accordingly. If in the early fifties it was primarily designed to shore up a threatened status quo, in the late fifties it was meant to help effect a change in it. Soviet leaders thus sought to combine summit diplomacy from a position of apparent strength with a recourse to open threats in order to compel the removal of the United States from Berlin, still the most sensitive spot in the East-West relationship.

Soviet international activity acquired for the first time a distinctly global range. Soviet involvement in the Middle East was widened and politically deepened; Soviet ties with North Africa expanded; the Soviet Union became deeply involved in the Congo crisis, and it developed close political and even some ideological links with the new African governments of Mali and Guinea; the Soviet Union provided extensive support to President Sukarno of Indonesia, and—most symbolic of its new policy—the Soviet Union began to aid, though at first rather cautiously, the new Castro government in Cuba.

If Mao Tse-tung's remarks can be said to have set the tone for the next phase, perhaps the key signal—in any case, so interpreted by the other side—was provided by Khrushchev's so-called "national liberation struggle" speech of early 1961. Delivered almost literally on the eve of the inauguration of the new U.S. President—and read avidly by him—his speech represented for the United States what almost a decade earlier Dulles' concept of the "policy of liberation" probably meant to the Soviet leaders: an ominous warning of an activist policy based on force, even if not exercised through the application of direct force.

What Khrushchev appeared to be saying was that the balance of power had tipped; that ideologically decisive change could now be effected by "national liberation struggles" carried on under the protective umbrella of Soviet power; that Communist gains could be securely protected; and that the West would have to yield even in Berlin, where Soviet tactical advantages could be asserted under the protection of the newly acquired Soviet strategic capabilities. In effect, Khrushchev's policy seemed emulative of Dulles'; "massive retaliation" would deter U.S. counteractions, enabling the desired changes to be effected at a lower threshold of risk.

This more assertive policy was pursued in an international atmosphere which, for the first time since World War II, was turning distinctly less favorable to the United States. By 1960, the United States was finding itself in a minority on the China question (i.e., those abstaining as well as opposed to the U.S. position were now more numerous), and on the defensive on such issues as Cuba or the Congo. The question of Cuba became for the United States (especially after the débâcle of the Bay of Pigs) what Hungary had been earlier for the Soviet Union: a source of embarrassment and strain.

All of this contributed to an atmosphere which seemed to pit an energetic and assertive Soviet Union against a fumbling and defensive America. Though John F. Kennedy assumed the presidency after waging a campaign in which American weakness (particularly the so-called missile gap) was one of his principal charges, events shortly after the inauguration seemed to bear out the self-confident mood of Soviet leaders. U.S. ineptitude during the abortive invasion of Cuba was followed shortly thereafter by American passivity when the Soviet Union took unilateral action to partition Berlin effectively.

Yet the underlying reality of the relationship was more complex than its appearance, and that underlying reality was to surface before long. Politically, the change in the U.S. leadership did bring to the top a new and younger élite, which gained increasing self-confidence and which proceeded rapidly to build up U.S. military power. Within the Soviet Union, on the other hand, Khrushchev's personal position remained far from consolidated, with internal political struggles surfacing again, with unprecedented public displays of continued disagreement within the leadership manifesting themselves at the Twenty-second Party Congress. Moreover, the increasingly bitter struggle with China further complicated Soviet decision-making, both forcing the Soviet Union to compete with China's militancy and somewhat reducing the Soviet Union's own room for maneuver.

The Soviet rate of growth also began to wobble in the early 1960s. Moreover, the American economy, after the slowdown of the second half of the fifties, began to accelerate, so much so that not only the absolute but even the relative gap between the two economies widened between 1961 and 1965.

Most significant of all, however, were developments in the military field. This phase marked the beginning of a new strategic competition, with power measured increasingly by the number of missiles capable of inflicting strategic damage on the respective homelands of the two rivals. On the Soviet side, the number of men under arms actually decreased during these years. By 1960, the level had dropped to some 3.6 million men, and Khrushchev even proposed to cut it down further to 2.4 million. At the same time, Soviet military expenditures continued to rise, to approximately $40 billion per annum, with the priorities put on modernization of equipment, and particularly on expansion of Soviet missile strength.

The atmosphere created by Soviet boasting was very conducive to highly exaggerated U.S. estimates of Soviet power. In 1960, Soviet intercontinental ballistic missile (ICBM) strength was semi-officially estimated as already around 100 missiles, and publicly was projected to reach the impressive figure of 500 missiles by 1961. In fact, during the Cuban missile crisis of October 1962 the Soviet Union had only about 70 liquid-fueled ICBMs (of somewhat dubious reliability) capable of being targeted on the United States, and it did not reach the 500 mark until 1966–67. The new Kennedy administration, responding to what appeared to be both aggressive Soviet intentions as well as capabilities, sharply increased U.S. defense spending, passing the $50 billion mark in 1962. Both U.S. strategic and conventional forces were reinforced. The former were designed to deny the Soviet Union the advantage of strategic threat; the latter were designed to meet head-on the new threat of insurgency and to enable the United States to wage the so-called 2½ wars, i.e., both in Asia and Europe simultaneously. The United States was in fact widening its strategic edge. At the time of the Cuban missile crisis, the United States was in a position to deliver several times as devastating an attack on the Soviet Union as the Soviet Union could on the United States, even though by then American civilian losses might have been on the prohibitive scale of some 30 or so million fatalities.

From the Soviet point of view, however, the politically decisive factor was the realization by the Soviet decision-makers of the fact that their society was several times more vulnerable than the American. This imposed a constraint on the Soviet use of strategic pressure even on behalf of moves in areas where the Soviet Union enjoyed a tactical advantage, as for example in Berlin. Furthermore, the rapid increase by the United States in NATO's nuclear strength (by some 60 percent in 1961 to 1963, as a consequence of deployment, according to Secretary McNamara, of "thousands of U.S. warheads") meant that a European confrontation would quickly become a strategic one.

It was this asymmetry in power that led the Soviet Union to introduce medium-range ballistic missiles (MRBMs) covertly into Cuba. Mikoyan confirmed this to a closed meeting of Communist ambassadors, held in Washington after the Cuban missile crisis (as recounted later by the Hungarian chargé present). By early 1962, the top Soviet leaders knew that in fact they did not have the strategic advantage they had claimed (and that American leaders *knew* this as well). What is even more important, the Soviet leaders probably knew what American leaders at the time could not yet know: that during the next several years the strategic gap would further widen in U.S. favor.

The Cuban confrontation was thus in all likelihood a last desperate gamble to achieve a payoff for an assertive Soviet strategy undertaken back in 1958. But that strategy rested on an insufficient base of power; it did not enjoy a sufficiently dynamic economic foundation or the backing of an adequately developed military technology; and it overestimated the revolutionary potential for global radical change. As events during the next phase were to demonstrate, conditions were not yet ripe for a Soviet policy that was meant to be both global and revolutionary. The casualty of this policy was the East-West détente, which seemed within grasp in 1958 or 1960; the consequences were the massive U.S. strategic build-up of the early 1960s and a new phase in the cold war, a phase dominated by increased U.S. assertiveness.

PHASE V—THE CRESTING OF AMERICAN GLOBALISM, 1963–1968

The ideology for American globalism was provided by John Kennedy's inaugural address; American preponderance was dramatized by the Soviet backdown during the Cuban confrontation in 1962; the globalist policy came into its own during Lyndon Johnson's presidency, which coincided with the high watermark of the progressive post-World War II expansion of a worldwide U.S. presence.

The Soviet backdown in Cuba was widely regarded as signaling a protracted setback to Soviet global ambitions. American predominance was taken for granted, and American strategic superiority was blissfully portrayed as unchallengeable. Secretary McNamara went so far as to assert in 1965 that the "Soviets have decided that they have lost the quantitative race, and they are not seeking to engage us in that contest. It means there is no indication that the Soviets are seeking to develop a strategic nuclear force as large as ours."[1]

However, the new phase did not involve a return to the mutual hostility of the fifties. Indeed, American global assertiveness was initially accompanied by a stepped-up search for accommodation with the Soviet Union. The test-ban agreement of 1963 and the establishment of the Washington-Moscow "hot line" represented major breakthroughs, signaling the growing recognition on the part of both powers of their stake in somehow stabilizing the arms race. On the political plane, the new phase saw also a more active U.S. interest in developing closer ties with Eastern Europe. President Kennedy stressed during his electoral campaign the desirability of peaceful economic and cultural engagement with Eastern Europe, and President Johnson carried this approach even further, altering in October 1966 the postwar U.S. priorities in Europe. Heretofore German reunification had been held to be the precondition for a European settlement; henceforth, East-West reconciliation was seen as laying the basis for a European settlement, eventually pointing to some resolution of the German question. Moreover, East-West reconciliation, it was expected, would help to increase East European independence from Soviet control.

If confident self-assertiveness was characteristic of the American mood during the initial years of this phase, anxiety and ambiguity appear to have dominated the Soviet outlook. At first, the change from Khrushchev to Brezhnev-Kosygin coincided with a distinct sense of letdown. The heroic competition with America— economic, political and even spatial —had clearly ended in a defeat, symbolized toward the end of the decade by the American landing on the moon. The Soviet leaders were evidently jolted by the directness of the 1962 American threat of a strategic attack on the Soviet Union, and the Cuban débâcle doubtless contributed to Khrushchev's fall from power in 1964. In addition, there is circumstantial evidence indicating that the post-Khrushchev Soviet leaders concluded that world affairs more generally were in a "reactionary" or "counterrevolutionary" phase, with the United States instigating the various international setbacks for "progressive" forces, deprived of Soviet nuclear protection. That appears to have been the meaning attached by Soviet leaders to the fall of Goulart in March of 1964 in Brazil, of Ben Bella in June of 1965 in Algeria, of Papandreou in July of 1965 in Greece, of Nkrumah in February of 1966 in Ghana, and of Sukarno in March of 1966 in Indonesia—all statesmen whom Khrushchev had actively cultivated. In the words of the official organ of the Italian Communist Party (August 4, 1967):

For the policy of the *status quo* and the attempts to divide the world into zones of influence between the two super-powers, U.S. imperialism is gradually substituting a revised and corrected re-edition of the old policy of *roll back,* giving birth, within the framework of nuclear coexistence with the USSR (caused by reasons of *force majeure*), to a series of local interventions (economical, political, military) designed to modify the world equilibrium by means of setting up reactionary regimes, or by support given to them, and liquidation of the progressive forces and movements in individual countries.

Soviet confidence was even further damaged by the widening rift with China, by the surfacing of liberal sentiments in Czechoslovakia, and by the shattering defeat by Israel of Nasser's army, equipped and trained by the Soviet Union (including the embarrassing capture by the Israelis of some Soviet military advisers). The international gains of the preceding years appeared everywhere to be in jeopardy, with the prematurely assertive Soviet globalism prompting not only the massive U.S. military build-up but the global political American counteroffensive.

The Soviet response was, accordingly, cautious. In effect, for a while the new Soviet team did not have a foreign policy beyond that of retrenchment and very ad hoc responses to new situations. The drift contributed to a rather widespread sense of malaise, and perhaps even emboldened the Chinese to step up both their anti-Soviet polemics and border tensions.

However, as in the Soviet case during the preceding phase, American global assertiveness obscured a reality which was becoming steadily less favorable to the American side. The mounting U.S. engagement in the war in Vietnam, transforming what initially appeared to be a relatively limited shoring-up operation into a more massive and costly intervention, significantly reduced American freedom of action, prompted severe strains in the U.S. economy and society, absorbed much of the U.S. defense budget, and weakened the U.S. international position. As a result, America neither translated into deeds the vision held up in President Johnson's 1966 speech on East-West reconciliation in Europe nor made the slightest move to complicate the Soviet decision to occupy forcibly in August 1968 the increasingly liberalized Czechoslovakia. Similarly, diplomatic passivity marked the U.S. posture in the Middle East, with the result that before long the Soviet Union was able to reëstablish and even widen its badly shaken position in the Mediterranean area.

In the meantime, Soviet diplomacy with regard to the Vietnam War became increasingly skillful. Its essence can be described with the words: "exploitation of opportunities" and "reduction of risks." The war had the effect of increasing disproportionately the U.S. stake in Soviet good will, and at the same time it significantly decreased American international standing.

On the economic plane, the situation was more mixed. The American economy continued to grow steadily, but the Soviet economy regained much of its forward momentum and resumed its upward climb relative to the United States. By 1967, the U.S. GNP stood at $762 billion; the Soviet at $372 billion, or 49 percent of the U.S. total, although the Soviet economy continued to be plagued by operational inefficiency and lack of adequate technological innovation. However, inflationary trends were beginning to beset the United States, with the war in Vietnam making it increasingly difficult for the United States to pursue its domestic programs of social renewal.

The biggest change, however, was to come in the military relationship. On the surface, U.S. supremacy seemed secure. In 1965, Defense Secretary McNamara estimated that in terms of delivery systems "we have a superiority of approximately 3 or 4 to 1. . . . In qualitative terms, it's impossible to come up with a precise evaluation but it far exceeds 3 or 4 to 1. . . . The programs we have under way are more than adequate to assure our superiority in the years ahead." By 1968, the steady build-up in U.S. ground forces also gave the United States for the first time in the history of the rivalry a lead in the number of men under arms (3.5 million *vs.* 3.47 million). However, this particular increase was due primarily to the Vietnam War, as was also the case with the continuing increase in U.S. military expenditures from $52 billion in 1965 to over $80 billion in 1968.

In reality, despite Secretary McNamara's extraordinary optimism, the military balance was quietly shifting away from U.S. supremacy. It gradually became clear that some time earlier in the decade—presumably some time before the Cuban crisis, though the outcome of the crisis obviously reinforced the decision—the Soviet leadership decided to respond to the American missile build-up with one of its own, thereby eventually making good on Khrushchev's premature claims. Soviet defense spending moved steadily upward, crossing the $50 billion mark in 1967 and reaching $55 billion in 1968, thereby effectively matching and even surpassing U.S. defense spending, outside of the Vietnam War effort. By 1968, Russia (with some 900 operational

ICBMs and America leveling off at 1,054) was well on the way to erasing the margins of superiority authoritatively claimed by Secretary McNamara three years earlier.

Though by 1968 the United States still enjoyed a marked strategic edge (especially in strategic bombers—over 600 to less than 200 for the Soviets—and submarine-launched missiles targetable on respective homelands—656 to 45), in reality both sides had the capacity to destroy each other as viable societies, with neither possessing a decisive first-strike capability. Although this changed relationship imposed on both sides a far greater obligation than heretofore to take closely into account the likely consequences of any unilateral application of force on the international scene, it meant a greater change for America, till then relatively invulnerable.

Most important of all, however, was the conjunction between this change and the collapse within the United States of the postwar consensus concerning foreign affairs. Like the Soviet Union after the death of Stalin, by the latter part of the sixties the United States found itself in the midst of a deep political crisis, involving major convulsions within the ruling élite and a general crisis of social values. With the Vietnam War precipitating a divisive national debate about foreign policy aims, the U.S. global engagement became increasingly devoid of positive domestic support. As a result, the initiative thus gradually passed to the Soviet side.

PHASE VI—THE SHAPING OF A MIXED RELATIONSHIP, 1969–

Just as Khrushchev's fall from power ushered in a period dominated by American assertiveness, Johnson's fall from power in 1968 opened a new phase, dominated by rising Soviet self-confidence and expanding global involvement. Soviet analysts began to evaluate the world again in terms of the general crisis of capitalism, and Soviet leaders—though much more cautious in their pronouncements than Khrushchev—were apparently concluding that the world was again shifting from a quiescent state into a dynamic condition, more favorable to "revolutionary" than to "reactionary" trends.

This new phase also saw the consequence of a policy that was no longer primarily regional or handicapped—as had been particularly the case under Khrushchev—by a vast disproportion between ends and means. Exploiting both the domestic American malaise and the Vietnam conflict, the Soviet leaders proceeded to fashion their own equivalent of the earlier Kennedy-Johnson combination of American globalism and bridge-building. The wider scope of the new Soviet strategy involved a rather different kind of policy from that pursued earlier by Khrushchev: his was not only globally premature but globally undifferentiated, spreading thinly still thin Soviet resources, relying heavily on economic aid and ideology. His successors, putting more reliance on diplomacy and military presence, exploiting nationalism even while significantly reducing Soviet economic aid (and concentrating it on a few key targets), not only have been pursuing a more selective strategy, but have appeared to focus it on the vast Eurasian continent: isolating China in the East, and flirting with Japan; consolidating the Soviet position in South Asia, while the United States was tied down to the war in Vietnam; expanding their presence in the Mediterranean and in the Middle East; and seeking to draw Western Europe into closer economic and political ties—hopeful-

ly pointing to the "Finlandization" of Western Europe. Continentalism rather than, as in the past, either regionalism (focused on Europe almost entirely) or premature globalism (undifferentiated in form), was the central character of the new Soviet policy.

This strategy coincided with the American reëxamination of its foreign policy. The redefinition of American policy by 1972 was clearly leading the United States into increased reliance on a triangular pattern of politics, exploiting the Sino-Soviet cleavage to gain increased leverage in bilateral American-Soviet relations. In response, the Soviet Union, obviously concerned about the new Washington-Peking relationship, sought to balance the negative consequences of any American-Chinese accommodation through its own initiatives vis-à-vis Washington, designed to convince the American side of the greater desirability of an American-Soviet accommodation. Beyond that, the Soviet Union appeared to be still counting on the possibility of a more pro-Soviet leadership emerging in China after Mao; in the meantime Soviet military pressure on China did result in the cooling down of Chinese border pressures. None the less, China came to represent a growing source of Soviet security concerns, necessitating a major redeployment of forces and reallocation of resources.

The military dimensions of the American-Soviet relationship during this phase have been dominated by a new element of uncertainty. The pace of the Soviet strategic and tactical build-up, as well as intensive development of home civil defense, appeared to indicate a desire to acquire a war-fighting capability in the context of parity—which, if attained, could give the Soviet Union a significant edge in any protracted crisis-bargaining. Soviet defense spending continued to rise (crossing the $55 billion mark by the late sixties), while American defense expenditures outside of the Vietnam War remained unchanged. With the American strategic forces on a plateau since 1967, the Soviet Union was able by 1970 roughly to match the United States in the strategic sector, while some of its programs could even be interpreted as seeking to obtain by the mid-1970s a decisive first-strike capability. Moreover, the Soviet Union made major strides toward the acquisition of effective naval power and long-range air- and sea-lift capabilities, and began to develop the argument (in the words of one Soviet commentator) that these forces would be able in the future to induce a U.S. recognition of "the inevitability and irreversibility of the social changes dictated by the will of the peoples."

The result was that both powers were now checking each other, and—more dangerous—their power frequently overlapped (as in the Mediterranean). This prompted heightened pressures on them to develop more stable rules of behavior (e.g., the 1972 agreement on avoidance of naval incidents), but it also increased the probabilities of friction.

The improved Soviet military posture was purchased at a very high economic price, especially given the continuing disparity between the two economies. With a GNP in the early 1970s of about $500 billion (or under one-half that of the United States), the Soviet Union was attempting to match—perhaps even exceed—the U.S. military effort, with the costs and complexity of that effort growing at an almost exponential rate. Increased Soviet interest in somewhat moderating the military competition was doubtless thus stimulated in part by economic pressures, even if some sectors of the Soviet leadership (especially the military) may have continued to press in favor of a military posture that at a minimum assured the Soviet Union a reliable warfighting capability and at the maximum eventually a decisive first-strike capability.

None the less, this most recent phase in the American-Soviet relationship also saw increased Soviet optimism concerning longer-range economic prospects. In 1971 Premier Kosygin even revived— though in a moderated form—the earlier Soviet prognosis of an eventual victory over the United States in economic competition. U.S. economic difficulties and tensions between America and her European and Japanese allies reinforced the Soviet expectations, even though the Soviet economy continued to suffer from inadequate scientific-technological innovation for which it sought remedies in periodic domestic economic reorganizations and in increased technological importation from the more advanced West.

What made for even greater uncertainty about the eventual outcome of this particular phase was the increasing importance of domestic political changes within both systems. The new bipolar checking relationship, even though it heightened the risks of a crisis, also meant that both sides were being pushed by the very nature of the checking relationship into a new competition, one in which the domestic performance of the two systems was becoming an increasingly vital aspect of the competition. Their respective abilities to cope with the rising demands for the implementation of the concepts of liberty and equality (the former more in the Soviet Union; the latter more in the United States) was becoming an important ingredient in a competition that was now less a purely traditional one and more and more part of a global political process, increasingly inimical to sharp demarcating lines between the foreign and the domestic.

In this regard, both sides were plagued by major intangibles. Turbulent change in America made for uncertainty about the character of America's involvement in world affairs and that, in turn, nurtured some of the Soviet optimism about the historical significance of this particular phase in the rivalry. Soviet—particularly Great Russian—nationalism was obviously attracted by the prospect of the Soviet Union emerging as the number-one world power, and this feeling, even more than ideology, provided the social propellant for sustained competition with the United States. Yet change in the Soviet Union, less visible and more repressed, is also taking place, and its eventual surfacing could have enormous implications. Increased social demands for a higher standard of living, intellectual dissent, generational unease, rising tensions between Great Russian nationalism and the more aroused nationalisms of the non-Russian nations, coupled with the conservative reaction of the ruling party élite—all cumulatively increased the importance of domestic considerations in Soviet foreign policy decision-making.

The combined effect of increasing external complexity (symbolized by Vietnam for the United States and by China for the Soviet Union) and of rising domestic demands was to pressure both powers into limited but expanding accommodations. The number of bilateral U.S.-Soviet agreements continued to expand, and the process culminated in May 1972 with the Moscow summit. That meeting was held within days of an act of U.S. military compulsion directed largely against the Soviet Union: the mining of North Vietnamese ports. The Soviet failure to respond indicated the high Soviet political stake in the accords, even though these agreements involved calculated gambles on both sides.

In essence, the Moscow accords represented a clear short-term political gain for the Soviet side, and a short-term strategic gain for the American side; in the longer run, they could turn out to be politically more beneficial to the American side, provided the longer run does not see the strategic relationship skewed to a considerable Soviet advantage. On the political plane, the agreements involved an American acknowledgment of U.S.-Soviet parity as well as the legitimization of postwar Soviet gains in Eastern Europe (symbolized also by the related visit by Nixon to Warsaw, the first presidential visit to a capital of an East European state not defying Moscow). In the longer run, the process of accommodation could dilute Soviet ideological militancy, provided that the relationship of strategic parity is not upset. In that strategic relationship the agreements had the effect of halting the quantitative momentum of the Soviet deployment while leaving open the competition in its qualitative aspects, where the United States remains clearly superior; in the longer run, however, the existing Soviet quantitative advantage could become quite significant if the qualitative U.S. lead is erased.

This is why there is a sensitive interdependence between the political and the strategic aspects of the Moscow agreements, and the character of the next phase in the competitive relationship will be very much affected by the degree to which the U.S. Congress recognizes the interdependence. There is little reason to doubt that the Soviet leadership is sensitive to it.

CONCLUSIONS

Several broader observations emerge from our analysis of the different phases of the cold war. They are as follows:

Cyclical pattern. The American-Soviet relationship appears to have been punctuated by alternating offensive and defensive phases, with neither side demonstrating the will or the capacity for sustained political momentum. After the initial skirmishing had gradually given way to a sharper rivalry, the Soviet Union adopted a more offensive policy during the years 1948 to 1952; the United States then gained the initiative and appeared to be on the political offensive during the years 1953 to 1957; the Soviet Union in turn became more assertive and maintained an offensive posture between 1958 and 1963; that policy collapsed in 1963, and between 1963 and 1968 the United States pursued an activist global policy; however, by the late sixties the Soviet Union regained its momentum, while the United States was experiencing "an agonizing reappraisal" of its foreign policy. This has initiated the present phase in the relationship.

As the Soviet side gained in strength and self-confidence, its policies—both strategic and political—tended to emulate the American. In many respects, Soviet policy during the premature fourth phase was imitative of the American during the third phase; American reliance on "massive retaliation" and "the policy of liberation" were later matched by Soviet nuclear threats and promises of support for "national liberation struggles." Similarly, the present phase of the relationship has seen strong reverse overtones of the political and strategic postures adopted by the United States during the fifth phase.

Relative performance. In a narrow sense, the Soviet performance may be said to have been superior to the American, at least in so far as the relative Soviet position improved considerably. From a general position of inferiority (in the context of reciprocal hostility) the Soviet Union has moved to a level approaching a global condominium with the United States (in the context of a more mixed coöperative-competitive relationship); there are probably still some Soviet leaders arguing on behalf of preponderance as the Soviet goal for the next stage, and this is what makes the present phase so very critical. However, such a judgment must be qualified by the consideration that both sides succeeded in their basic defensive aims, even though in the last several years the Soviet Union has pierced southward (into the Middle East and Asia), through the weakest parts of the perimeters drawn by the U.S. policy of containment. (The rebuff Moscow has recently suffered from Egypt modifies but does not substantially change the picture.) Moreover, the Soviet leaders did botch up their alliance relationship with China, whereas the American side showed greater skill in maintaining complex alliance relationships.

Given the nature of the Soviet system, Soviet leaders have been in a better position than the American policy-makers to exploit politically whatever assets they had at their disposal. In that sense, Soviet policy has tended to be somewhat freer from objective restraints than the American. The Soviet Union thus adopted offensive postures when opportunity seemed to beckon, even if at a relative disadvantage in two or even three of the four comparable elements noted during each phase: relative international influence, respective military and economic power, domestic cohesion on behalf of national policy. In contrast, the United States has tended to become more asser-

Phase I	1945–1947 Preliminary Skirmishing	
	1 International standing	U.S. advantage
	2 Military power	Probably a Soviet advantage
	3 Economic power	Overwhelming U.S. advantage
	4 Domestic policy base	Uncertainty in both
Phase II	1948–1952 Soviet Union Assertive	
	1 International standing	U.S. advantage
	2 Military power	Marginal Soviet advantage?
	3 Economic power	Decisive U.S. advantage
	4 Domestic policy base	U.S. advantage
Phase III	1953–1957 United States Assertive	
	1 International standing	U.S. advantage
	2 Military power	U.S. advantage
	3 Economic power	U.S. advantage
	4 Domestic policy base	U.S. advantage
Phase IV	1958–1963 Soviet Union Assertive	
	1 International standing	Declining U.S. advantage
	2 Military power	Uncertain U.S. advantage
	3 Economic power	U.S. advantage
	4 Domestic policy base	Probable U.S. advantage
Phase V	1963–1968 United States Assertive	
	1 International standing	Marginal U.S. advantage
	2 Military power	Clear U.S. advantage
	3 Economic power	U.S. advantage
	4 Domestic policy base	Declining U.S. advantage
Phase VI	1969– Soviet Union Assertive	
	1 International standing	Roughly equal
	2 Military power	Marginal U.S. advantage?
	3 Economic power	U.S. advantage
	4 Domestic policy base	Soviet advantage

tive only when all or most of these factors were favorable, as the [above] table indicates.

On the whole, throughout the relationship, both sides have been essentially prudent and restrained. Each has avoided pushing the other beyond the point of no return. In this regard, note must be taken of the extraordinarily salutary effect of nuclear weapons; in a more traditional setting, without the restraining effect of nuclear weapons, it is likely, given mutual hostility and occasionally very sharp provocations, that a major American-Soviet war would have occurred.

NOTE

1. Congressional Record, Vol. III, Part 6, 89th Congress, 1st session, April 7, 1965, p. 7271.

7. THE CHANGING TERRAIN OF INTERNATIONAL POLITICS

Marshall Shulman

Let us turn now to another thread in the argument. It is sometimes misleading, I believe, to deal with the Cold War as an encapsulated problem, to focus attention too narrowly upon the esoteric developments of the Communist world as detached from the underlying forces of international politics. The whole terrain of international politics has been radically transformed since the end of the war, and it is illuminating to begin with this fact and to trace from the source some of the forces that have been inducing change not only in the Soviet system and policies but in our own as well.

It is not the revolution of Marx and Lenin that is transforming the world, but the radical effects of modern military technology; the new forms and uses of energy in nonmilitary technology, such as transportation and communications; the continued upsurge of industrial techniques in the already industrial areas, with profound consequences for their societies; and the explosive force of nationalism in the former colonial areas and, to some extent, in the industrial parts of the world as well. These are all more or less familiar phenomena, and it has become a commonplace to speak of them as "the revolutions of our time," but we are in truth a long way from having absorbed the implications of these transformations into

our analysis of international politics and even less so into our policies. As a step in this direction, let us reflect for a few moments on some of the ways in which these factors have been affecting the conditions within which the Cold War has been evolving.

To begin with, it seems evident that the radical increase in the destructiveness and cost of modern weapons has had a curious paradoxical effect upon the configuration of power in the world, and has even called into question our familiar conceptions about the very nature of national power. In the current debate about whether we have moved from a bipolar world toward some multipolar configuration of power, the paradox is especially evident in the confusion of the different senses in which the notion of national power is applied. If we are thinking of the power to wage a large-scale nuclear war, the world is still in a fundamentally bipolar situation, and seems likely to remain so for some time to come. Even if a number of other countries develop the capacity to discharge some nuclear weapons, sufficient to carry out local nuclear military operations or to trigger a larger war, only two nations have the resources sufficient to conduct a strategic nuclear war. On the other hand, if we consider the inhibitions against the use of strategic nuclear weapons, so disproportionate to most political purposes, it is apparent that many nations (not only the medium powers, but small as well) have indeed become multiple poles in the

Source: Marshall D. Shulman, *Beyond the Cold War* (New Haven, Conn.: Yale University Press, 1965), pp. 18–32, 107–111. It has now been reprinted by Westview Press, Boulder, Colorado, in 1985. Copyright 1965 by Marshall D. Shulman.

distribution of other forms of power—power to influence the course of events through small wars, through economic and political strength, ideas, diplomatic energy, and even, on occasion, through statesmanship.

In this sense—that is, apart from the conditions of general war or extreme tension—the significant design in international politics is not bilateral but polygonal. In the shade of the nuclear umbrella, varieties of alignment and demialignment have flourished. It is no longer possible to think in unitary terms of broad categories of nations or of continental groups of nations, in simplifying the design of international politics. Significant subgroupings within the Soviet bloc, the Western alliance, and the "third world" require such a variety of cross-hatchings on a political map as would tax the ingenuity of a mapmaker. What is implied in this variegated cross-hatching is a growing international acceptance of degrees of allegiance and a certain flexibility in political action outside the alliance systems.

The effect upon the Cold War has been to create a certain schizotic confusion about the various levels of conflict that dominate the forefront of our consciousness at various times. Much of the time we are preoccupied with lower levels of political, economic, or guerrilla conflict within a loose polygonal structure, but on occasion we find ourselves reminded that the gross bipolar structure in the background is still ultimately significant because of the potential consequences of a general nuclear war.

In the ambiguous twilight zone of potential nuclear war, we become aware how much the developments in military technology have been changing the relationship between war and politics, and how greatly this has affected the evolution of the Cold War. For a nation committed to a process of change, the realization that modern large-scale war cannot be a continuation of politics is a difficult one to absorb even if it has no deliberate intention of launching an attack, since the stabilization of the military environment tends to create a certain détente in the political realm as well, and a constraint on political action. This condition has been one of the forces working toward the attenuation of the revolutionary impulse in Soviet policy. Another consequence of this realization has been an increasing Soviet attention to other instrumentalities, especially economic power, as levers for achieving the ultimate transformations to which the Soviet ideology is committed. Along with this goes an increasing concern for the *political effects* of weapons systems, as distinguished from their putative usefulness in the actual event of war—that is, a choice of weapons systems in part at least based upon the effect they are thought to have upon political behavior. The Soviet Union has been more consistently conscious than the United States of the role of force as a backdrop to international politics, and this concern for the peacetime political utility of weapons has been one factor that has made the introduction of arms control measures more difficult.

On a few vivid occasions, the Soviet Union and the United States have found themselves drawn into playing a kind of poker game test of will around a crisis point, in the twilight zone where the implied willingness to use nuclear weapons is a marginal form of diplomatic pressure. Sober afterthoughts about the risks that pure chance and possible miscalculation may introduce into such encounters have created transient periods of receptivity for safeguards against inadvertent war, but the political imagination has not been retentive enough, and the minatory image has faded before substantial safeguards could gain acceptance.

This leads us directly to consider a related effect of the transformation in military technology—the way in which changing conceptions of security have had a bearing upon the evolution of the Cold War. The primary paradox here has grown out of the fact that the tenuous security of mutual deterrence has emerged out of the universal increase in vulnerability to total destruction. . . . [W]e have already touched upon some of the consequences for the Cold War of this strategic balance, and we will be returning to the subject once again later when we come to a discussion of arms control, but it is worth reminding ourselves at this point that there are many reasons for regarding the present strategic stabilization as a temporary lull rather than as a long-term basis for security. One of the reasons for this is the uncertain effect of future technological change upon the weapons equilibrium. Many scientists believe that there do not appear to be on the near horizon many great scientific leaps like those that made their appearance during the war and in the early postwar years, but that wider application of presently available science to military technology could make the situation ten years from now as different from the present as the present is from the situation ten years ago—that is, before the age of missiles. The rate at which science is applied to military technology, however, depends somewhat on the level of tension, since these measures are extremely costly, and the incentives appear to be chiefly negative—that is, the desire not to be without something the other side may be developing.

This prospect of qualitative leaps in the arms competition as the result of such potential technological developments as an antiballistic missile system, together with the risks of miscalculation around crisis points, the apparent probability of the spread of nuclear weapons, and the possibility of the enlargement of local wars—all raise the urgent question whether the present plateau of strategic stabilization can long remain a sufficient security against nuclear war, without being underpinned by safeguards against these specific hazards. This question is more fully examined . . . [later], but the point that is relevant here is that the strategic stabilization, however temporary it may turn out to be, has already had a qualitative effect upon the Cold War. The arms race has taken on a dual character. One of its aspects is marked by deadly competition for advantages that may be decisive in case of war, or may be vital in the political conflict. The other aspect reflects the interests that the adversaries have in common against the factors that tend to increase the danger of inadvertent war. Perhaps it is more accurate to speak of overlapping interests than mutual interests, but each side has slowly begun to accept the realization that more military power does not always produce more security, that there is an interacting process at work between the adversaries, and that in an ultimate sense the security of each side is interlocked with that of the other. The result has been a gradual acceptance of certain restraints in practice, and a certain amount of guarded communication between adversaries. Although they appear to be contradictory in their effect, both aspects are part of the present reality, and the coexistence of these conflicting conceptions is perhaps the major change in the situation as contrasted with, say, fifteen years ago. The question posed by these dual aspects of the military confrontation is whether it will be possible to find ways of introducing safeguards into the arms race without sacrificing the political interests of those who are still fundamentally adversaries. I believe it *is* possible, as I shall try to show later on.

Outside the military field, other technological applications have also been exerting a transforming effect upon international politics and the Cold War. This is a subject that will bear much further study, but it is obvious when we stop to think of it that advances over the past twenty years, particularly in transportation and communications, have been changing both the mechanics and the substance of diplomacy perhaps more than most of us have realized. Some of these changes affect the general environment of international politics, and a few are directly relevant to the evolution of the Cold War.

One of the most striking effects of advances in transportation and communications upon the conduct of diplomacy is the extent to which the command and control of foreign policy have become increasingly centralized. The consul on the spot has become a lesser adjunct of the console of communications before the head of state and his foreign office. That it is now possible for a chief executive to take direct responsibility for day-to-day developments in remote places, or to send personal envoys overnight anywhere in the world, or to engage in frequent "summitry" by jet or by television with friends or adversaries—all these technical possibilities have tended to transfer to the machinery and the top leadership at home many of the details of foreign policy management. Moreover, the line between domestic and foreign policies has become less distinct as world developments are impressed vividly and even insistently upon both leaders and the public, and it has become increasingly difficult for the leadership of any major nation to keep foreign issues in the background, even when it wishes to do so.

The pace and immediacy of diplomatic activity have also been affected. Time and distance once cushioned remote encounters; today the major capitals are directly involved with each other within a matter of hours over developments anywhere in the world. Diplomatic reaction times to events in areas formerly remote are now virtually instantaneous—faster sometimes than the speed of thought. Policies change more quickly, and interact much faster, so that the alternations in the climate of the Cold War, which once could be charted in periods of several years at a time, must now be measured from month to month.

Also, the area of encounter has become worldwide. Contiguity has become a diminishing factor in defining areas of contact and conflict. Hardly a problem anywhere remains local in character or escapes involvement in global politics. Such traditional political-geographic concepts as "buffer zones" and "lines of communication" have been losing some of their significance. As a consequence, traditional diplomatic techniques for reducing tension by easing points of peripheral contact or for encouraging stability by a physical separation of "zones of influence" have become less meaningful than they once were, particularly in the advanced industrial areas.

Another consequence of geographical mobility is that the reach of organized political activity has been extended. Demonstrations have been synchronized in a dozen places around the world to respond to events the day before. For better or for worse, apparently limitless possibilities have unfolded for the propagation of slogans, propaganda, ideas, and information into every rice paddy and jungle clearing. But the substance as well as the techniques of international politics have been affected as travel and various forms of communication across cultures and continents have multiplied. Inevitably, as more people have had some form of direct contact with other countries, the effect has been to reduce the "foreign" quality of other cultures and systems. The diffusion of cultural patterns, social values, political institutions, and even popular fads has been markedly accelerated. For totalitarian societies, it has become increasingly difficult to close off a population from foreign influences or to rely upon secrecy as a source of security. To a significant degree, Soviet institutions have had to be adapted to the irresistible flow of information to and from the rest of the world. The historical Russian isolation from foreign influences was in part at least a result of difficulty in travel; today, police techniques may impede but they cannot indefinitely hold off the reduction of this isolation by modern technology, particularly if the political leadership regards the flow of information as a necessary concomitant to the industrial development of the country.

We have touched upon only a few of the ways in which technology has been affecting international politics, and once the mind turns in this direction innumerable illustrations begin to present themselves. But if we ask ourselves what, in gross terms, the dominant effect of changing nonmilitary technology has been upon the Cold War, perhaps the answer would be that it has stimulated the shift of focus from Europe to the underdeveloped areas. On the one hand, technology has contributed to the stabilization of the European theater of the Cold War by providing the technical underpinning of integration, and by narrowing the logistic distance between Europe and the United States. On the other hand, technology has

made the underdeveloped areas more readily accessible as a theater of competition in the Cold War, not only to the Soviet Union and the Western countries, but also to China. There are other reasons for this shift of focus, some of which we will come to in a moment, but technology is certainly an important contributory factor.

A related factor of change in international politics has been the phenomenal and unanticipated further growth of the advanced industrial areas—particularly in Western Europe and Japan—partly as a result of government policies favoring investment and growth, and in part the effect of an extraordinary continuing increase in productivity through the application of modern technology, some of it borrowed from the United States. One major consequence of this development has been the return of Europe to a greater prominence in international politics.

Much has been written about the effect of the high growth rate in Western Europe in stimulating what has sometimes been called "a search for identity" and sometimes "a new nationalism," and I shall with difficulty limit myself here to a brief enumeration of a few consequences of this development that may be immediately relevant to our purposes.

It is apparent that the weakening of the Western alliance as a result of the growth of European self-confidence and self-reliance has raised the possibility of a new major economic and political power center in the world, whose degree of association with, or opposition to, American power is a principal determining question for the immediate future. . . . [T]his development has been an important factor in the evolution of Soviet policy. The rise of Europe has also raised the thorny question of nuclear proliferation, which lies at the heart of the thrust for European self-reliance, for the ambiguity of the nature of national power in the present period ... leaves it unclear whether the power to exert a major influence in world affairs can only be based upon an independent strategic nuclear capability. This issue too has exerted a shaping influence on Soviet foreign policy.

Also, the rate of growth in Western Europe and in the other advanced industrial countries has further widened the gap between themselves and the underdeveloped areas, with possibilities for exacerbating future conflicts between these two parts of the world.

Further, the European (and Japanese) growth rates have been a fundamental contradiction of the Marxist-Leninist expectations concerning the decline of capitalism. Moreover, the social and political consequences of this economic growth have been inhospitable to proletarian revolutionary dynamism. High growth rates have weakened the class struggle and encouraged the spread of a middle-class outlook in European societies. What some writers have referred to as "the decline of ideology" at least in the revolutionary sense of ideology, has been reflected in the movement of European socialism in the direction of non-Marxist reformism, and even of the Communist parties of Italy and France toward conservative operation within the existing political and social system.

What the long-term effects of this advancing industrialization are likely to be upon the social and political organization of modern societies—the Soviet as well as Western—has been the subject of an interesting literature; such questions have been explored as whether industrialization is inevitably accompanied by pluralist trends, or trends toward technocracy and bureaucratism, and whether such trends will moderate Soviet totali-

tarianism and conversely will increase centralization in Western political systems. . . .

Finally, among the factors in international politics that have been changing the external environment have been of course the rapid decolonization in Asia and Africa and the explosion of nationalism throughout the underdeveloped world. The swiftness and lack of preparation with which the four-century-old European colonial system was liquidated has left a legacy of turbulent upheaval that now appears destined to dominate international politics for some time to come.

The many new nations which have been formed, once described as a "third world" in international politics, have been prevented from functioning as a unitary bloc by intense ethnic, religious, tribal, and nationalist conflicts, as well as by their involvement in the broader currents of international politics. In some areas, the disintegrative phase of nationalism appears to be yielding to regional economic and political groupings, perhaps foreshadowing the next phase in this development. The political life of the United Nations, still congested by the sudden enlargement of its membership, is just beginning to reflect the sorting-out of the new regional groupings.

The major complicating factor in the upheavals throughout the underdeveloped world has been the rise of China as an independent power, with its radical revolutionary involvement throughout Asia, Africa, and Latin America. The responsiveness of some revolutionary cadres in these areas to the dynamism of the Chinese appeal seems to have become the major inhibiting factor operating against trends toward moderation in Soviet policy. Economic development in these areas has for the most part been slower and more difficult than was optimistically forecast a few years ago (recall the optimism with which the "Point Four" program was launched), often not keeping up with population growth, and the widening gap between the "haves" and "have-nots," stirred by venomous and irrational resentments against the West, darkened by ominous racial overtones, has in it the potentiality of making the coming decade in international politics one of continuing violence.

These are in brief some of the forces that have been at work transforming the terrain of international politics in recent years. The value of beginning with these conditions in considering the evolution of the Cold War is that it increases our sensitivity to the *process of adaptation* to the external environment which is often overlooked in the study of Soviet policy. This process—partly conscious and partly unintended—by which the Soviet leadership seeks to make its efforts effective under changing conditions, has had a transforming effect upon Soviet policies and the Soviet system, and has been an important factor in opening up the dispute with the Chinese.

Before we go on to analyze how this has operated, there is one general observation I should like to make about the developments we have been discussing. The main impression that emerges from this perspective is how much the Cold War has lost its centrality. Whereas in its first postwar phase the confrontation between the Soviet Union and the United States was the dominating fact of international politics, and of internal politics in both countries, today this confrontation no longer holds the center of the stage. The conflict of purposes between these two systems has become caught up in the turbulent currents of international politics.

It is no longer sufficient—if indeed it ever was—for the leaders of either country to define their policies simply by reference to the other. These countries are like two tired wrestlers whose ring is swirling with many former spectators, and whose bout has become something of a free-for-all. The attention of the leaders of both countries is less narrowly focused upon the other. The first decade of the Cold War, as we have seen, was chiefly characterized by the redefinition of power lines in Europe and by the development of stability in Western Europe as well as some measure of stability in the strategic military relations between the United States and the Soviet Union. We have now passed into a stage whose main characteristic appears to be a differentiation between the limited field of maneuver in the still decisive but largely stabilized European theater, and the trackless movement of revolutionary conflict in the underdeveloped areas, complicated by the Chinese effort to establish its influence by militant policies.

If this is true, it is evident that old habits of thought, rooted in the simplified drama of the early years of the Cold War, will not lead to adequate responses to the kinds of problems that now confront us.

* * * * *

This brings us to the point at which we must consider the major conclusion . . . . our relations with the Soviet Union cannot be discussed without reference to the broader context of international politics today. Indeed, the central problem for the United States or the West is not the Soviet Union, which is another way of saying that the Cold War is not the all-embracing issue in international politics. The Soviet Union is a serious complicating factor in a time in which the main characteristics are the strengthening of tendencies toward nationalism, violence, and international anarchy. The central problem is how to survive this period without general war, and how to influence the direction of events toward the strengthening of international processes which can accommodate change without violence.

The problem of dealing with local manifestations of Communism in the underdeveloped areas is inseparable from the problem of the widening gap between the industrialized and the underdeveloped parts of the world. The only effective kind of anti-Communism in these areas is that which, like an antibiotic, inhibits the growth of a microorganism by destroying the nutrients on which is feeds.

In association with our allies—for this is their problem as much as it is ours, whether they are ready to recognize this responsibility or not—we should address ourselves to the necessity of providing a democratic alternative to the totalitarian model of development in Asia, Africa, and Latin America, and of encouraging the forces of nationalism in these areas to find their expression, not in identification with Communism and not in demagogic violence, but in the tradition of a constructive and integrative nationalism. This is the most potent source of political energy in the world today, and it should be channeled into the drive to discover what modernization should mean for each people on its own terms.

It is relevant to remind ourselves here that the West has a persistent and fundamental interest, in the background at all times, in encouraging the growth and acceptance of an international system among the nation-states—"system" here not necessarily meaning a particular institutional form, but more broadly referring to the deepening of habits of cooperation and restraint, the strengthening of accepted procedures for managing change and limiting conflict. This is why we must have an interest in the process as well as the substance of the resolution of international problems. That this is a central part of our purpose gives added importance to the "how" of doing things, in order that the manner of our conduct shall have the effect of strengthening the patterns of international behavior we would wish to see prevail. No advice can be more pernicious than that we should "fight fire with fire"—to contribute to the degradation of international conduct because of the jungle ethics of an adversary.

The United Nations now has the possibility of becoming an universal institution, but it is in a phase of growth in which it is absorbing a greatly enlarged constituency. As with any living political organism, it must rediscover in experience how it must function under changed circumstances, and this will take time, and faith. Its purposes meanwhile must be supported by a host of instrumentalities.

Among these, a central responsibility devolves upon the Atlantic group of nations. Perhaps the most important rationale for the closer association of this group today is to be found in the fact that among their shared values is a common interest in strengthening international habits of cooperation. In the present period, their sense of community can best be expressed, not through large institutional innovations, but through myriad forms of consultation, planning, cooperative action, and division of labor on problems everywhere in the world which are, or ought to be, as much a matter of concern to our allies as they are to us. What is required, however, is that we should define our national interests in terms of sufficient breadth and vision that they will have relevance for people in all countries who are our natural allies.

The shift of emphasis in policy that is required must begin with the recognition that the Cold War—as a term, and as a conception—does not provide an adequate framework for thinking about the kinds of problems that need our attention. Not that the Cold War is over, but it has been transformed and merged into a larger and more complex setting.

What lies beyond the Cold War, then? No surcease of conflict, surely, nor some alternative slogan, but an urgent and tangled array of challenges to international order which defy any simplified catchphrase. It may be that there is a public need for a few schematic notions to make the complexities of foreign affairs fit into a comprehensible pattern, but the guiding popular conceptions must be made more adequate to the situation that exists. Even the wisest of policies cannot be effective if public support has to be won for them by the manipulation of outworn and oversimplified themes. The public should share in the difficult revision of thought which experience has been forcing on the decision-makers.

It is not utopian, I believe, to expect public acceptance for the notion that our relations with the Soviet Union are and should be multidimensional in order that we may oppose where necessary and collaborate where possible, having always in mind a longer-term sense of direction toward the moderation of conflict.

Even in the containment of Chinese power, which now begins to preoccupy us, the lesson of past experience with the Soviet Union would be lost if we did not understand and respond to the sources of conflict which go far beyond Communism. Our perspectives must be broad enough to encompass the period of violent transitions into which we are moving, in which the varied forms of Communism are understood as complicating factors entwined among the many sources of conflict to which our attention must also be directed.

And in responding to these immediate needs, we must give greater emphasis than we have to process as well as purpose, in order that our actions will strengthen the habits and institutions of international cooperation and deepen the restraints on the use of force which are essential to the kind of environment in which free societies can survive and flourish. It is this sense of the direction toward which we would like to see things move that should be reflected in everything we do, as well as in what we say.

8. MISADVENTURE REVISITED

Richard K. Betts

Each November 22nd, representatives of the U.S. Army Special Forces—the Green Berets—join members of the Kennedy family at a memorial ceremony at President John F. Kennedy's grave. This joint tribute symbolizes the ambiguous legacy of the U.S. venture in Vietnam. Kennedy had personally championed the Green Berets as an elite vanguard combating Communism revolution and subversion in the Third World. But just four years after the President's assassination, his brothers Robert and Edward had moved into the vanguard of congressional opposition to this commitment.

Last autumn, there was an added irony; the Reagan administration had recently moved, as Kennedy did two decades ago, to re-emphasize the role of the Special Forces. The United States was once again speaking as if it would "pay any price, bear any burden" to oppose challenges to the free world.

To the extent that Ronald Reagan's assertive policy in El Salvador recalls that early period of U.S. involvement in Vietnam, it is useful to re-examine the White House assumptions, deliberations, and expectations of the 1960s. One finds lessons and nonlessons.

The U.S. commitment to South Vietnam was impelled by the overarching post-1945 goal of "containing" Communist expansion, first in Europe, then, with the Korean War, in Asia.

In the case of Vietnam, a few critics in Washington and in academe quarreled with applying "containment" to a theater low in priority to the West. Indeed, scholar-diplomat George F. Kennan, the Soviet affairs specialist who had coined the term, was an early critic of the Johnson administration's involvement in Indochina. But not until late 1965, after Lyndon Baines Johnson started bombing North Vietnam and sent 184,000 troops to the South, did many in Congress, the press, the universities, or the politically sensitive public begin to doubt that South Vietnam was a vital testing ground in the global East-West struggle to keep the world safe for democracy.

By the time Richard Nixon and Henry Kissinger gained the White House in 1969, the war had become a political fiasco; the whole notion of containment was under heavy attack. Disillusionment over Vietnam, Sino-American rapprochement, and high hopes for détente and arms control soon eroded the bipartisan constituency for maintaining a strong U.S. military presence overseas, even outside the Third World.[1] But the reaction proved more transient than the consensus that led to Vietnam. As the Soviets or their allies advanced in Angola, Ethiopia, and Yemen, as revolutionary Iran humiliated the United States, and as Soviet troops went into Afghanistan, assertiveness slowly became popular again.

The U.S. experience in Vietnam will not inevitably repeat itself elsewhere, despite all the recent hue and cry over Central America. But it is worth examining

Source: From *The Wilson Quarterly*, Summer 1983, pp. 95-110. Copyright 1983 by The Woodrow Wilson International Center for Scholars.

what circumstances, beliefs, and judgments make Presidents and their advisers in Washington decide that in certain cases they have only one choice, and that they are better off enduring high costs rather than backing off from further engagement.

The United States became gradually involved in Indochina after 1950. Even before the outbreak of the Korean War, President Harry S Truman began to take on the financial burden of the vain struggle of America's NATO ally, France, to defeat Ho Chi Minh's Viet Minh, which was assisted by Communist China, America's foe in Korea. Dwight D. Eisenhower continued and increased that support, and committed the United States to the new regime in South Vietnam after French withdrawal. South Vietnam did not become a high U.S. priority until Kennedy's Presidency, and it did not become the highest overseas priority until the Johnson era.

The 1960s were, of course, a turning point, but not because Washington's goals changed. Ever since the Korean War, U.S. policy in Indochina had vacillated between contrary objectives—preventing a Communist takeover while avoiding American participation in a major war in Asia. Yet the contradiction between these two aims did not become acute until 1965. The efforts of Kennedy and Johnson differed in scale—the 1961 decision to increase the number of U.S. advisers (from 948 in November 1961 to 2,646 in January 1962) pales beside the 1965 decisions to bomb the North and to dispatch combat troops to the South. But in both cases, U.S. involvement grew dramatically in order to prevent imminent South Vietnamese collapse under Communist pressure and to shift momentum to the anti-Communist side. What was required to do this in 1961 was far less than what was required four years later.

All in all, Kennedy was less willing to disengage than later apologists suggested, and Johnson less deceptive about his goals and less anxious to escalate than later detractors believed. The notion that Kennedy intended to extricate the United States from South Vietnam after the 1964 U.S. election is belied by his actions right up to his death: a continuing build-up of aid and advisers, presidential reaffirmations[2] that would have been gratuitous if he were looking forward to withdrawal, and prior endorsement of the 1963 Saigon coup against President Ngo Dinh Diem. Johnson's campaign rhetoric against Barry Goldwater in 1964 exploited public fears of war, but he never suggested that defeat would be an acceptable alternative.[3] And, although Johnson ordered contingency planning for direct U.S. military action before November 1964, he continued to search for alternatives *after* the election.

LOSING AND WINNING

Indeed, LBJ was a most reluctant warrior. Like his predecessor, he refused to accept any radical options proposed by subordinates that promised *victory*. Early in 1965, he authorized the bombing of North Vietnam, but only in limited, gradually increasing doses—not the quick and overwhelming effort sought by the Air Force. In July 1965, he ordered a build-up to 125,000 men in South Vietnam, despite the lack of promises of a long-term solution from Army leaders. In late 1965, Defense Secretary Robert S. McNamara privately estimated that 600,000 U.S. troops (10 percent more than the highest level ever reached during the war) might be needed by 1967 and admitted that even that number "will not guarantee success."

Once the air strikes against the North

began, Johnson abstemiously expanded them (rejecting military protests that such gradualism vitiated their effect) in consonance with his civilian advisers' hopes that mounting pressure might induce Hanoi to negotiate on U.S. terms.

As U.S. troop strength grew, General William C. Westmoreland's ground operations in the South expanded too, and soon, after Hanoi's spectacular but costly 1968 Tet Offensive, their cumulative effect—even if blunt and wasteful—forced the Communists, both regulars and guerrillas, onto the defensive and rolled back many of their earlier gains. But, in most circumstances, guerrillas win as long as they do not lose, and government forces lose as long as they do not win. And Hanoi, with its sanctuaries at home and its bases and routes of reinforcement in Laos and Cambodia, could keep from "losing" indefinitely. Colonel Harry G. Summers ruefully described his encounter in 1973, during negotiations on American MIAs (Missing-in-Action) in Hanoi, with a North Vietnamese officer who, confronted with the assertion that the Communists had never beaten U.S. troops in a major battle, replied, "That is correct. It is also irrelevant."

In March 1967, Westmoreland told LBJ and McNamara that unless his forces were allowed to cut off Hanoi's infiltration of men and supplies, the war could continue indefinitely. Later in the year, despite their public optimism, Westmoreland and General Earle Wheeler, Chairman of the Joint Chiefs of Staff, told the President that with current U.S. troop levels, the war would continue as an indecisive "meat-grinder"; with a reinforcement of 95,000, it could drag on for three years; and with one of 195,000 (to a total of 665,000), it could last two years. Yet Johnson authorized an increase of only 55,000.

A QUEST FOR COMPROMISE

Like JFK, LBJ chose a *limited* strategy. He chose to nibble the bullet rather than bite it. He feared provoking Chinese intervention and undertaking a full-scale war (or withdrawal) that could wreck his primary ambition: to build the Great Society.

Most important was his unwillingness to provoke a domestic political assault from either the Right (for "selling out" Vietnam) *or* the Left (for going too far militarily). In effect, he preferred to compromise on the battlefield and to suffer limited attacks at home from both ends of the political spectrum rather than face the full fury of either—although until the Tet Offensive, he feared the hawks more than the doves. A consensus-seeking, centrist political strategy drove the White House military policy. In this, too, Johnson's approach reflected that of his predecessors.

Nixon also sought to follow a middle path between his own instincts (more hawkish than Johnson's) and the growing opposition in Congress and the broader public. He successfully appealed to the "Silent Majority"—who, polls indicated, wanted to withdraw but not to lose—by combining "re-escalations" (secretly bombing Communist bases in Cambodia in 1969, briefly invading Cambodia in 1970, supporting a short-lived Army of the Republic of Vietnam [ARVN] invasion into Laos in 1971, renewing the bombing of North Vietnam and mining Haiphong harbor in 1972) with peace talks, the phased withdrawal of U.S. troops, and "Vietnamization."

Actually, Nixon's approach was no less contradictory than that of his predecessors. Like Kissinger, Nixon overestimated his ability to solve the problem through the negotiations at Paris that

A BRIEF CHRONOLOGY
1954–1975

1954 Geneva Accords end Indochina War between French and Viet Minh, dividing Vietnam into North and South. Eisenhower offers aid to South Vietnamese government.

1955 U.S. advisers take over training of South Vietnamese army (ARVN) from French. Diem becomes leader of South Vietnam.

1958 Growth of Communist guerrilla war against Diem regime.

1959 Hanoi decides to unify Vietnam by force, organizes Ho Chi Minh Trail infiltration routes to South Vietnam.

1960 Hanoi forms southern National Liberation Front (Viet Cong). Kennedy elected President.

1961 As Viet Cong pressure grows, JFK increases aid to Saigon, raises number of U.S. military advisers from 685 to 16,000— by late 1963.

1962 Soviet-American agreement in Geneva provides for "neutral" Laos, but does not end Hanoi's use of Ho Chi Minh Trail or CIA counterinsurgency effort.

1963 After suppressing Buddhist dissidents, Diem is ousted and killed by army; Kennedy assassinated; Johnson becomes President. McNamara notes Viet Cong gains after anti-Diem coup.

1964 Hanoi starts sending regular army (PAVN) units to South. United States pledges assistance to South Vietnam as required to defeat "Communist aggression"; issues warnings to Hanoi. After clash between North Vietnamese PT boats and U.S. destroyers, Congress passes Tonkin Gulf Resolution supporting U.S. efforts to "prevent further aggression."

Johnson elected president, as his Great Society gets under way. 23,000 U.S. advisers are in Vietnam.

1965 Communists batter ARVN; U.S. planes start bombing North Vietnam; Marines land at Da Nang to protect air base; Nguyen Cao Ky becomes Premier of South Vietnam; LBJ announces build-up to 125,000 men but refuses to call up reserves; Hanoi rejects U.S. offers to negotiate.

1966 U.S. Senate hearings on war policy; many antiwar demonstrations; Cultural Revolution in China; the *New York Times* reports from Hanoi on civilian damage caused by U.S. air strikes. Cambodia's Norodom Sihanouk secretly allows Hanoi to use Sihanoukville (Kompong Som) as supply port. War of attrition grinds on in South Vietnam. Filipinos, Australians, New Zealanders, South Koreans send troops.

1967 Guam "summit": Westmoreland tells LBJ more decisive strategy is required to end the war, but LBJ does not respond. Johnson raises U.S. troop ceiling in South Vietnam to 525,000, calls for 10 percent surtax. Elections of Thieu and Ky. McNamara privately urges end of U.S. bombing and limit on U.S. manpower in Vietnam, resigns to become president of World Bank in 1968.

1968 LBJ curbs most direct U.S. investment abroad and restricts overseas travel of U.S. citizens to cut growing balance-of-payments deficit. North Korea seizes *Pueblo*, U.S. Navy "spy ship." In Vietnam, Giap's forces besiege Khe Sanh, launch countrywide Tet Offensive and, later, "mini-Tet" attacks against Saigon.

Eugene McCarthy, peace candidate, wins 42.4 percent of Democratic vote in New Hampshire presidential primary; Johnson receives 49.5 percent. LBJ orders partial bombing halt and announces he will not run for re-election; Hanoi agrees to peace talks in Paris. Clifford fixes 549,500-man U.S. troop ceiling and gradual transfer of war burden to South Vietnamese. LBJ ends all bombing of North. Nixon elected President with 43.4 percent of popular vote.

1969 In "Vietnamization" effort, Nixon withdraws 68,000 troops during year; Ho Chi Minh dies; mass antiwar march in Washington. Peace talks continue.

1970 Joint U.S.-South Vietnamese invasion of Cambodia after Lon Nol coup ousts Sihanouk. Four protesters at Ohio's Kent State University are slain by National Guardsmen; students close 100 colleges.

1971 South Vietnamese troops, with U.S. air support, invade southern Laos, in raid on Ho Chi Minh Trail. The *New York Times* begins publication of "Pentagon Papers." Re-election of Thieu. U.S. troop strength in Vietnam drops below 200,000. Congress votes to end draft in 1973.

1972 U.S. election year. Equipped by Soviets, North Vietnamese launch massive tank-led Easter Offensive; Nixon orders mining of North Vietnam's ports and renews bombing. He attends summits in Beijing, Moscow. Watergate break-in. Hanoi's offensive stalls. Kissinger says "peace is at hand," but year ends with peace agreement unsigned. Nixon re-elected President, orders all-out "Christmas bombing" of Hanoi area to force North Vietnam back to Paris conference table.

1973 Nixon halts all air operations against North Vietnam. After he privately assures Thieu that the United States will react with force to Communist violations, the United States, North and South Vietnam, and Viet Cong sign peace pact in Paris. In August, obeying Congress's mandate, United States ends bombing of Khmer Rouge insurgents in Cambodia, and thus all direct U.S. military intervention in Indochina. As Watergate disclosures engulf White House, Congress passes War Powers Act.

1974 Both sides violate cease-fire in South Vietnam. U.S. Senate and House cut back military aid to Saigon requested by Nixon. In August, climaxing Watergate scandal, Nixon resigns as President, and is succeeded by Gerald Ford.

1975 Communists triumph in Laos, Cambodia, and South Vietnam. North Vietnamese take Phuoc Long province against feeble resistance, then open Great Spring Offensive that routs South Vietnamese forces and ends with capture of Saigon. Americans help 150,000 escape. Pol Pot's Khmer Rouge capture Phnom Penh, begin massacres across Cambodia. Pro-Hanoi Pathet Lao forces occupy Vientiane, Laos's capital. Peace.

Johnson had initiated in 1968. Nixon milked his "madman" theory—that the Communists would quail before the threat of his irrational behavior—but his hopes (like those of LBJ) of enlisting Moscow's aid to sway Hanoi did not materialize, and Nixon, not the enemy, made the crucial negotiating concession in May 1971 by implicitly accepting the presence of North Vietnamese troops in the South after any cease-fire.[4]

Under Kennedy, Johnson, and Nixon, senior policy-makers in Washington were seldom deluded that the odds of routing the Communists in Vietnam were high. Indeed, in most cases, they increased U.S. deployments of men and/or firepower simply to stave off defeat, with no real expectation of victory. What made the men in Washington believe that they were making efforts that with luck might pan out, rather than marching *inevitably* toward defeat?

THE IRON COMBINATION

The answer lies between hubris and hope. During the early 1960s, both civilian and military theorists of "counterinsurgency" promoted the fateful illusion that American tutelage could reshape the fragile, war-battered South Vietnamese political system, creating a new nationalism among the South Vietnamese that could confront Marxist revolutionary élan with some sort of vigorous Asian Jeffersonianism—through land reform, free elections, better government.

Some U.S. "pacification" techniques proved successful—in the short term. For all their much-publicized deficiencies, the sheer weight of allied manpower and economic resources produced major gains in rural prosperity, population control, and road security during the years between Tet and the 1972 Easter Offensive. In-creasingly unable to enlist new recruits, the southern Communist guerrillas (Viet Cong) were ground down by attrition; North Vietnamese forces took over the chief burden of combat. Large-scale *conventional* North Vietnamese attacks, with bases in Laos and Cambodia, rather than Viet Cong guerrilla insurgency, brought on the 1975 collapse of the Saigon regime.

Even more important was limited war theory,[5] an outgrowth of opposition to the Eisenhower administration's post-Korea "massive retaliation" policy. The focus was on using measured doses of force to induce an adversary to negotiate and to compromise. The 1965–67 air war against North Vietnam exposed the holes in some versions of the theory. The Pentagon civilians who had designed the air war originally expected to "calibrate" the U.S. response to each enemy provocation and to use incremental pressure to convince Hanoi to desist. This aim was inevitably subverted by practical difficulties—targeting, timing, communications—that derailed Washington's "orchestration" of words and deeds.

Most of all, the theory foundered because its proponents vastly underestimated Hanoi's determination and overestimated the basis for a negotiated compromise. The Vietnam War was primarily a civil war, and, overall, a struggle involving *incompatible* ideologies and visions of society, not just a proxy conflict between great powers over influence in a third area. Both American leaders and their critics in Congress and the press found this reality hard to understand. As Kissinger reflected with hindsight,

Because the United States had become great by assimilating men and women of different beliefs, we had developed an ethic of tolerance; having had little experience with unbridgeable schisms, our mode of settling conflicts was to seek a solution somewhere between the contending positions. But to the Vietnamese this meant that we were not serious about what we put forward and that we treated them as frivolous. They had not fought for forty years to achieve a compromise. [Kissinger, *White House Years,* p. 259.]

Professional military men never agreed with the civilians' game-theory logic. Yet, with few exceptions, until 1968 both military and civilian leaders in Washington assumed that South Vietnam *had* to be saved. The United States could not just walk out on its ally. The disputes, seldom publicized, were over means, not ends.

Only if President Johnson, McNamara, and Secretary of State Dean Rush had known for *sure* in early 1965 that "graduated pressure" would fail and that the most pessimistic military estimates of what would be required to bend Hanoi's will were correct would there have been a chance for a White House decision to disengage. Like Kennedy, Johnson distrusted the Joint Chiefs of Staff (JCS). Some of his civilian lieutenants viewed bleak JCS estimates or pleas for "decisive" strategies as "worst-case" ploys designed to maximize their options and to protect their reputations in case of failure.

This tragic misjudgment aside, the fact remains that LBJ & Co. knew that gradually building up U.S. strength in Vietnam offered no assurance of victory. Yet at each juncture until Tet 1968, they saw no alternative to pressing on, *hoping* that the Politburo in Hanoi would grow weary and negotiate.

The air war strategy was flawed, but the details of its rationale fade in significance beside the overarching White House decision in 1965 to keep the war effort, as a whole, limited. Except for the military, who did not protest in public, there were virtually no officials in the executive branch—and few newspaper editors or legislators—who in 1965 questioned the premise of limitation.

The tragedy stemmed from the iron combination of this consensus with the premise that the war still had to be fought.

The one high-ranking official who opposed escalation was Under Secretary of State George W. Ball. Beginning in 1963, he argued that Vietnam was of secondary importance, and that our commitment there drained resources away from NATO. LBJ's negative reaction was ironic, since the initial U.S. involvement in Indochina was spurred by the priority of NATO—to support France in the early 1950s even though Washington had no love for colonialism. But not until 1965, after the first Marines went ashore at Da Nang in March, did Ball recommend outright withdrawal.

In 1964–65, Congress was quite complaisant; only Senate mavericks like Wayne L. Morse (D.–Ore.) and Ernest H. Gruening (D.–Alaska) opposed crucial decisions of the mid-1960s. When J. W. Fulbright, chairman of the Senate Foreign Relations Committee, turned against the war in 1966, he was still countered by colleagues of equal rank such as John C. Stennis, chairman of the Armed Services Committee.

There was little early active support for Johnson administration policy on Capitol Hill, but, contrary to myth, even well after Tet, nearly all congressional war foes, from Edward M. Kennedy (D.–Mass.) to George S. McGovern (D.–S.D.) issued calls for faster troop withdrawals and greater concessions in peace talks, *not* for unconditional U.S. withdrawal. Though opposition on Capitol Hill mounted with time, it was not until *after* U.S. troops had been withdrawn and the POWs returned in 1973 that the raft of legislation was passed constraining both presiden-

THE ANTIWAR MOVEMENT, THE NEW LEFT, AND PUBLIC OPINION

On March 31, 1968, President Lyndon Baines Johnson announced on TV that he would not seek re-election. "With America's sons in the fields far away, with America's future under challenge right here at home," he could not both serve as the nation's wartime Commander-in-Chief and fight the partisan battles of a political campaign.

The growing antiwar movement claimed credit for Johnson's decision. But did its efforts hasten the war's end? Probably not.

Mild dissent first surfaced in 1964–65. A few prominent intellectuals, notably Hans J. Morgenthau, argued that the Free World's interests in South Vietnam did not justify a massive expenditure of U.S. blood and treasure. Said columnist Walter Lippmann in July 1965, "We can search the globe and look in vain for true and active supporters of our policy." Liberal doves—Arthur Schlesinger, Jr., Richard H. Rovere, the *New York Times's* John Oakes—variously called for bombing halts, cease-fires, and talks leading to a coalition regime in Saigon that would include the southern National Liberation Front (Viet Cong), which, some of these writers suggested, enjoyed autonomy from Hanoi.

New Left intellectuals demanded much more. Besides condemning LBJ, the U.S. military, and South Vietnamese leaders, they cheered on Ho Chi Minh. Visiting Hanoi in 1968, the *New York Review of Books's* Susan Sontag discovered "an ethical society" whose government "loves the people." Her hosts' only defect was that they "aren't good enough haters"; Hanoi's jailers "genuinely care about the welfare of the hundreds of captured American pilots. . . ." No less impressed was novelist Mary McCarthy, who concluded that Prime Minister Pham Van Dong presided over "a moral, ascetic government, concerned above all with the *quality* of Vietnamese life." And MIT's Noam Chomsky described his own country as "the most aggressive power in the world"; he urged "a kind of denazification" of U.S. leaders.

More widespread was a larger movement centered at first in the elite universities. As higher draft calls came in 1966–67, such groups as Students for a Democratic Society (SDS) conducted "teach-ins" on college campuses and then mounted protest rallies in cities across the nation. Against such opposition, Lyndon Johnson's failure to offer "a convincing moral justification" for the U.S. war effort, *Commentary's* Norman Podhoretz argued in 1982, doomed his quest for stronger support at home.

Yet through most of the 1960s, nearly two-thirds of the public, judging by polls, favored a continuation or intensification of the struggle. The Vietnam War, political scientist John E. Mueller has shown, only became more unpopular (in September 1969) than the Korean War after U.S. casualties in

Vietnam had substantially surpassed those of the earlier, shorter conflict. . . . Moreover, Mueller argues, the protesters' disruptive style was in some ways self-defeating. In a 1968 poll by the University of Michigan Institute for Social Research in which the public was asked to rate various groups on a 100-point scale, one-third gave antiwar protestors a zero, while only 16 percent put them anywhere in the upper half of the scale.

The dramatic efforts of antiwar Democrats to elect presidential peace candidates gained only Pyrrhic victories. The surprising 42.2 percent vote that Senator Eugene J. McCarthy won in the party's 1968 New Hampshire primary largely reflected "anti-Johnson" rather than "antiwar" sentiment. Among McCarthy voters, hawks outnumbered doves by nearly three to two. Moreover, the Democratic Left, Mueller contends, "helped to elect Richard Nixon twice": in 1968, by convincing a sufficient number of disaffected liberals to sit out the election and give Nixon a narrow victory over Hubert H. Humphrey, and in 1972, by securing the Democratic nomination for a landslide loser, Senator George S. McGovern.

The antiwar movement crested in 1969-70, as moderate Democrats, notably Humphrey and Edward S. Muskie, came out against what was now Richard Nixon's war. But when the last great Washington protest march occurred in April 1971, the heterogeneous antiwar coalition was already fragmenting into a number of single-issue groups, notably feminists, environmentalists, homosexuals. And as draft calls dwindled with Nixon's gradual withdrawal of U.S. troops from Vietnam, campus unrest noticeably subsided.

The Vietnam conflict did not cause the "cultural revolution" of the late 1960s in America (and Western Europe). "If there had been no Vietnam War, we would have invented one," Yippie leader Jerry Rubin wrote in 1970. Rather, the war came to represent all that dissident groups believed was wrong with the United States: It offered, in Sontag's words, "the key to a systematic criticism of America."

In the end, as Mueller suggests, antiwar protest (and congressional outcries) inhibited administration policy-makers, but it was not decisive. It may have prompted Nixon to speed up U.S. troop withdrawals, to pull back from his 1970 incursion into Cambodia earlier than planned, and to join Democrats in ending the draft. It did not prevent him from bombing the North in 1972. Congress adopted the most consequential antiwar measure, the restrictive War Powers Act of 1973, well after street protest had faded.

Still, most scholars agree, the disarray of the Vietnam era brought one long-term consequence: It helped to shatter the U.S. foreign policy consensus forged during the early Cold War, greatly complicating the task of later Presidents in defending U.S. interests abroad.

tial war powers and aid to the South Vietnamese ally.

RUNNING OUT OF TIME

In short, the remarkable American consensus behind the initial intervention, from 1961 to the 1968 Tet Offensive, has been obscured in retrospect by the force of later disillusionment. Only *after* it became clear that the cost of prolonged U.S. intervention in Vietnam was prohibitive did it begin to seem to large segments of Congress, the media, and academe that the alternative, a Communist victory in South Vietnam, was not so grave a disaster (for America). But by that time, compromises that had seemed radical during the Johnson administration seemed insufficient. As Kissinger recounts:

By August of 1969 we had offered or undertaken unilaterally all of the terms of the 1968 *dove* plank of the Democrats (which had been defeated in Chicago). We had exceeded the promises of the Republican platform, expecting by our demonstration of flexibility to foster moderation in Hanoi and unity at home. We were naively wrong in both expectations. [Kissinger, *White House Years,* p. 256.]

The American effort in 1965–72 was not subverted by moral objections (such objections remained those of a minority even to the end), but by a gradually building public perception that all the blood and treasure was simply being *wasted* to no visible end. The United States may be able to fight a major limited war again, say, in the Persian Gulf, but only if it is not long and inconclusive. As Harvard's Samuel P. Huntington observed: "The most crucial limitation ... is not the limitation on weapons or geographical scope or goals, but rather the limitation on *time.*"

Wide recognition of such U.S. political realities reinforces the military's argument against limitations on the use of conventional forces. But this recognition provides no guarantee against future mistakes. The necessary scale and duration of successful military operations can never be known for sure in advance. What the Vietnam record shows is that Washington's top decision-makers knew in 1964–65 that, given the limits they imposed on U.S. strategy, victory would not come quickly, if it came at all. A similar prognosis by the White House in a future case, with the Vietnam experience in mind, could produce a presidential choice between a decisive hard-hitting use of force or no military intervention at all.

HINDSIGHT IS EASIER

Should future U.S. ventures overseas be undertaken only if a cut-off point is decided in advance? Political scientist Richard Neustadt has criticized the White House National Security Council staff in 1964–65 for not seriously addressing "the option of getting out of Vietnam. . . . It was always taken to be unacceptable on the face of it." Doing this, however, is politically dangerous; any leak to the press about such a study would surely subvert the commitment's support and credibility.

White House decisions on what is vital to U.S. interests abroad are affected by limited information and by official perceptions that may not be known to be— or may not *be*—incorrect until later. For example, as Rusk was wont to explain, part of the rationale for sending U.S. troops to South Vietnam was to prevent Chinese advances further into Southeast Asia. The problem was not simply an obtuse U.S. failure to recognize the Sino-Soviet split. Despite their dispute,

Moscow and Beijing were seen in Washington as having parallel interests in promoting violent Communist revolution. Because a Sino-American rapprochement occurred during the 1970s does not mean that it could have happened during the 1960s—before the 1969 Soviet-Chinese border clashes and before Soviet hints of a future preventive attack on China's new nuclear facilities pushed Beijing toward accommodation with Washington.

A YEARNING IN WASHINGTON

Moreover, the President does not act in a vacuum. Had North Korea, armed by the Soviets, not attacked South Korea in 1950 (shaking Washington into revision of judgments about whether Communist leaders would resort to armed conquest), Truman might have felt no urge to become more involved in support of the French in Indochina. Had Eisenhower not just concluded the Korean War and scored anti-Communist successes in Iran and Guatemala, he might not have felt secure enough in 1954 to accept the partition of Vietnam (though his acceptance resulted in a U.S. commitment to the new regime in the South). Had Kennedy not experienced the unsettling Vienna summit with Nikita Khrushchev, the Bay of Pigs, a new Berlin crisis, and setbacks in Laos—all in 1961—he might have felt he had more leeway in avoiding a major increase in the U.S. advisory effort in South Vietnam later that year.

The crucial phase of any overseas commitment is the formative period, when presidential rhetoric becomes mortgaged and initial costs are sunk. Yet during this early phase, the long-range consequences are least certain and the commitment is a secondary matter, rather than the centerpiece it may become later as U.S. involvement and costs accumulate. When costs are still limited, the alternative seems bleaker than when the commitment burgeons into full-blown national sacrifice.

John F. Kennedy, Lyndon B. Johnson, and lesser policymakers during the 1960s faced these pressures and ambiguities and decided that a gamble in South Vietnam was preferable to the alternative; uncertain prospects of victory were better than certain prospects of defeat. The results make clear the folly of this judgment.

By 1975, the dominant "lesson" was that Washington should take no risks, that it should not begin messy involvements in the Third World if there is *any* danger that they cannot be concluded without considerable sacrifice. Despite President Jimmy Carter's creation of a much-publicized Rapid Deployment Force in 1978–80, the lesson still has a powerful hold. In 1983, Congress has shown little enthusiasm for the Reagan administration's modest efforts to counter Marxist guerrillas in Central America, and none at all for direct combat involvement of U.S. military men, even as advisers. Yet "containment," in theory at least, has been reinvigorated. Reagan's rhetoric recalls the staunchness of the New Frontier. The Pentagon speaks of a global "maritime strategy."

What has not rebounded to the same degree is the bipartisan consensus among politicians and in the press behind containment. If anything, there seems to be a yearning in Reagan's Washington for the containment of the Eisenhower years, to bestride the globe and confront Soviet power without spilling blood, to be strong but at peace, to support anti-Communist allies or clients with money and arms but not men, all without raising the spectre of war.

Dwight Eisenhower could accomplish all that because the predicament that his successors faced—imminent collapse of the whole row of Indochina dominoes— did not develop while he was in office. We know more now, but we still do not know how a disastrous war could have been avoided except at the price foreseen in 1961 as in 1965—apparently disastrous defeat. John Kennedy and Lyndon Johnson were wrong in moving into Vietnam on so grand a scale, but neither was wrong in thinking that his failure to do so could produce unpleasant reactions at home and abroad. Now, as then, neither containment nor disengagement is risk-free.

NOTES

1. In May 1971, Senate Majority Leader Mike Mansfield (D.-Mont.) offered an amendment to a military draft bill that would have required the United States to withdraw one-half of its 300,000 troops in Europe as of December 31, 1971. After intense White House lobbying, the Senate defeated that amendment by a margin of 61–36.

2. E.g., on September 12, 1963: "In some ways I think the Vietnamese people and ourselves agree: we want the war to be won, the Communists to be contained, and the Americans to go home.... But we are not there to see a war lost, and we will follow the policy which I have indicated today of advancing those causes and issues which help win the war."

3. In Akron, Ohio, on October 21, 1964, Johnson stated: "[We] are not about to send American boys 9 or 10,000 miles away from home to do what Asian boys ought to be doing for themselves." But Johnson added that "we are going to assist them [the South Vietnamese] against attack as we have" in the past and "[we] will not permit the independent nations of the East to be swallowed up by Communist conquest."

4. Henry A. Kissinger, *White House Years* (Boston: Little, Brown, 1979), p. 1,018.

5. Its chief academic proponents were Robert Osgood and Thomas Schelling; their views found many echoes in the Army, notably in writings by Generals Maxwell Taylor (*The Uncertain Trumpet,* 1959) and James Gavin (*War and Peace in the Space Age,* 1959).

Section I–C. THE SEARCH FOR A NEW CONSENSUS: FROM THE NIXON TO THE CARTER ADMINISTRATIONS

With the breakdown of the cold war consensus finalized by America's agonizing defeat in the Vietnam War, succeeding administrations attempted to bring forth new foreign policy perspectives to replace this shattered world view. In this section on the evolution of American foreign policy beliefs, the focus is on readings that illustrate the values and beliefs that the Nixon and Carter administrations brought to U.S. foreign policy.[1] Each relied upon considerably different value perspectives to inform foreign policymaking. The Nixon administration, primarily through its chief spokesman, Henry Kissinger, sought to bring a "power politics" approach to U.S. policy, while the Carter administration tried to employ a "global politics" approach. Neither approach, however, succeeded in producing a new consensus; instead, each met with substantial criticism. To illustrate the opposition that each approach encountered, readings are provided which critique each approach. In this way, the discerning reader will be in a good position to evaluate and criticize the Nixon and Carter approaches.

To a large degree, the Nixon administration tried to break with many assumptions of the cold war consensus and even with America's historical traditions in its approach to foreign affairs. These changes are reflected in the first two essays of this section. The first one, drawn from a report, "U.S. Foreign Policy for the 1970's," by President Richard Nixon to the U.S. Congress, outlines a new strategy of foreign policy for the United States based upon three principles: partnership, strength, and negotiation. Such principles are directly tied to the balance of power system. In that system, building a stable international order requires establishing working alliances with other states, using strength—essentially the reliance on military strength—when necessary, and employing diplomacy judiciously. While the United States had surely relied upon these instruments in the past, the explicit formulation—and acceptance of them—as the cornerstone of policy was new. Furthermore, President Nixon also officially accepted the fact that the international system has changed with the shattering of monolithic Communism and the rise of nationalism in the Third World. As a result, and unlike the period of the cold war when a bipolar approach—East versus West—was dominant, a new design was now necessary.

The philosophical underpinnings to this new balance of power approach were provided by Henry A. Kissinger. A good portion of his perception of the international system, and the U.S. role in that system, is captured in the second reading, "The Central Issues of American Foreign Policy." (Even though the essay was written prior to Kissinger joining the Nixon administration, it foreshadows the resulting Nixon approach outlined in the first essay.) For Kissinger, the principal issue for the United States in the late 1960s was "to develop some concept of order in a world which is bipolar militarily but multipolar politically." Translated into concrete problems, such an imperative meant the United States needed to develop a way to produce greater "political legitimacy" in the new nations of the world, so that these states could contribute to international order; it needed to develop a more consistent policy toward the Soviet Union, so that order could be created in that relationship; and it needed to examine its own national interest, so that it could play a more positive role in the world. Kissinger, in particular, spends a considerable portion of the essay on this last issue. What is clear from his treatment of this question, moreover, is that the American moralism and idealism of the past, its reluctance to use power and seek its own national interest, and the failure to conceive a legitimate international order are now inappropriate for the new [Nixon] administration.

Richard Falk's "What's Wrong with Henry Kissinger's Foreign Policy," continues this discussion of Kissinger's approach by showing the evolution and consistency in his thinking about international politics. More important-ly, though, the Falk essay offers a telling critique of Kissinger's approach to foreign policy. While granting that Kissinger had some success in stabilizing the international system, Falk is seriously troubled by the lack of moral content in the Kissinger approach (e.g., his seeming indifference to human rights questions in dealing with some states and his tragic view of human nature) and by the long-term implications of following this design (a foreign policy "that embodies indifference to the poor and weak" and that "tempts changed-minded groups to adopt some variant of 'desperate politics.' "). In sum, then, Kissinger's effort to stabilize the existing state system does not address what Falk sees as the essential problem of the international system— "the need to evolve a new system of world order based on principles of peace and justice."

The Carter administration also proposed a new approach to foreign poli-cy—one based upon American domestic values and one more attuned to global political change. The next series of readings focus upon that approach. The first reading on the Carter approach utilizes the commencement address at the University of Notre Dame by President Carter himself in May 1977. Since the address was early in the Carter presidency and since it was virtually his first major foreign policy speech, his remarks were important both in the tone that it set and the policy priorities it identified.[2] At the outset of his remarks, President Carter emphasizes the role that domestic values will play in policymaking: "I believe we can have a foreign policy that is democratic, that is based on fundamental values, and that uses power and influence . . . for humane purposes." In addition, he asserts that America's policy will not only emphasize the traditional political and military issues of foreign policy, but will endeavor to address the emerging global agenda: "We can no longer separate the traditional issues of war and peace from the new global ques-tions of justice, equity, and human rights." Furthermore, because President Carter sets forth a list of foreign policy issues and discusses them in a particular order, the reader can begin to appreciate the relative importance of some issues for this administration.

The second reading, "Meeting the Challenges of a Changing World," by former Secretary of State Cyrus Vance expands upon the values and beliefs and basic policy orientation of the Carter administration. While Secretary Vance recognizes the economic, political, and military capabilities of the United States, he particularly emphasizes that American policy must adjust to, and attempt to shape, the substantial changes that are going on in global affairs. In effect, then, the United States must adopt a more global perspective in its foreign policy.

Vance divides his discussion into an assessment of five types of change and their global implications: (1) the movement from a period of strategic supremacy by the United States to one of strategic equivalence with the Soviet Union; (2) the recognition of the dangers posed by regional conflicts; (3) the effects of changes within the nations of the world; (4) the development of a pluralistic international system; and (5) the changes in the international economy. The overriding message of Vance's analysis is that the United States must recognize its limitations and work with others in addressing these changes; the United States can no longer try to provide "American solutions to every problem." Yet, the United States is far from impotent in global affairs; it can still play an important global role "by welcoming change and working with it, not by resisting it."

The final selection in this section, "Requiem," by Stanley Hoffmann, provides an incisive analysis and critique of the values and beliefs that the Carter administration brought to American foreign policy. Despite what some of his critics may contend, the foreign policy approach of President Jimmy Carter did yield some successes. His approach, for instance, restored the American idealism of the past—largely through his human rights campaign; it attempted "to come to terms with the world" as it was—by recognizing the limits of American power; it sought "to cope with major long-term problems," such as nuclear proliferation, arms sales, and international trade issues; and it addressed some crucial security and political issues, such as NATO modernization and the normalization of relations with the People's Republic of China.

While acknowledging these successes, the Carter approach suffered from serious difficulties less related to the basic values and beliefs that it espoused than to how those imperatives were translated into American foreign policy. According to Hoffmann, the Carter administration suffered from a failure of style (the use of "erratic tactics" in dealing with friend and foe), a failure of strategy (a "strategic incoherence" in dealing with the Soviet Union), a failure of economics (the absence of understanding the linkage between a healthy domestic economy and foreign policy), and the failure in "the politics of foreign policy" (the failure to explain satisfactorily complex policies to the American public).

While Hoffmann draws out several important lessons for American foreign policy from his analysis, he also suggests why Ronald Reagan was successful in gaining the presidency in 1980. Because President Carter—and even President Nixon and Henry Kissinger before him—had offered more complex approaches to foreign policy than Americans were accustomed to during the cold war, these leaders were subject to attacks from those who provided simpler solutions to U.S. foreign policy. Since Ronald Reagan's approach to foreign policy was reminiscent of this earlier period, it struck a receptive chord within the American belief system.

NOTES

1. The approach of the Ford administration (1974–76) to foreign policy is not treated separately here because National Security Adviser and Secretary of State Henry Kissinger continued to dominate policy during those years.
2. The only other major foreign policy address prior to the Notre Dame speech by President Jimmy Carter was to the United Nations in March 1977.

9. UNITED STATES FOREIGN POLICY FOR THE 1970'S: A NEW STRATEGY FOR PEACE

Richard M. Nixon

A nation needs many qualities, but it needs faith and confidence above all. Skeptics do not build societies; the idealists are the builders. Only societies that believe in themselves can rise to their challenges. Let us not, then, pose a false choice between meeting our responsibilities abroad and meeting the needs of our people at home. We shall meet both or we shall meet neither.

The President's Remarks
at the Air Force Academy
Commencement, June 4, 1969

When I took office, the most immedi ate problem facing our nation was the war in Vietnam. No question has more occupied our thoughts and energies dur ing this past year.

Yet the fundamental task confronting us was more profound. We could see that the whole pattern of international politics was changing. Our challenge was to understand that change, to define America's goals for the next period, and to set in motion policies to achieve them. For all Americans must understand that because of its strength, its history and its concern for human dignity, this nation occupies a special place in the world. Peace and progress are impossible without a major American role.

This first annual report on U.S. foreign policy is more than a record of one year. It is this Administration's statement of a new approach to foreign policy, to match a new era of international relations.

Source: *U.S. Foreign Policy for the 1970's: A New Strategy for Peace,* A Report to the Congress by Richard Nixon, President of the United States, February 18, 1970, pp. 1–13.

A NEW ERA

The postwar period in international relations has ended.

Then, we were the only great power whose society and economy had escaped World War II's massive destruction. Today, the ravages of that war have been overcome. Western Europe and Japan have recovered their economic strength, their political vitality, and their national self-confidence. Once the recipients of American aid, they have now begun to share their growing resources with the developing world. Once almost totally dependent on American military power, our European allies now play a greater role in our common policies, commensurate with their growing strength.

Then, new nations are being born, often in turmoil and uncertainty. Today, these nations have a new spirit and a growing strength of independence. Once, many feared that they would become simply a battleground of cold-war rivalry and fertile ground for Communist penetration. But this fear misjudged their pride in their national identities and their determination to preserve their newly won sovereignty.

Then, we were confronted by a monolithic Communist world. Today, the nature of that world has changed—the power of individual Communist nations has grown, but international Communist unity has been shattered. Once a unified bloc, its solidarity has been broken by the powerful forces of nationalism. The Soviet Union and Communist China, once bound by an alliance of friendship, had become bitter adversaries by the mid-1960's. The only times the Soviet Union has used the Red Army since World War II have been against its own allies—in East Germany in 1953, in Hungary in 1956, and in Czechoslovakia in 1968. The Marxist dream of international Communist unity has disintegrated.

Then, the United States had a monopoly or overwhelming superiority of nuclear weapons. Today, a revolution in the technology of war has altered the nature of the military balance of power. New types of weapons present new dangers. Communist China has acquired thermonuclear weapons. Both the Soviet Union and the United States have acquired the ability to inflict unacceptable damage on the other, no matter which strikes first. There can be no gain and certainly no victory for the power that provokes a thermonuclear exchange. Thus, both sides have recognized a vital mutual interest in halting the dangerous momentum of the nuclear arms race.

Then, the slogans formed in the past century were the ideological accessories of the intellectual debate. Today, the "isms" have lost their vitality—indeed the restlessness of youth on both sides of the dividing line testifies to the need for a new idealism and deeper purposes.

This is the challenge and the opportunity before America as it enters the 1970's.

THE FRAMEWORK FOR A DURABLE PEACE

In the first postwar decades, American energies were absorbed in coping with a cycle of recurrent crises, whose fundamental origins lay in the destruction of World War II and the tensions attending the emergence of scores of new nations. Our opportunity today—and challenge— is to get at the causes of crises, to take a longer view, and to help build the international relationships that will provide the framework of a durable peace.

I have often reflected on the meaning of "peace," and have reached one certain conclusion: Peace must be far more than the absence of war. Peace must provide a durable structure of international relationships which inhibits or removes the causes of war. Building a lasting peace requires a foreign policy guided by three basic principles:

1. Peace requires *partnership*. Its obligations, like its benefits, must be shared. This concept of partnership guides our relations with all friendly nations.
2. Peace requires *strength*. So long as there are those who would threaten our vital interests and those of our allies with military force, we must be strong. American weakness could tempt would-be aggressors to make dangerous miscalculations. At the same time, our own strength is important only in relation to the strength of others. We— like others—must place high priority on enhancing our security through cooperative arms control.
3. Peace requires a *willingness to negotiate*. All nations—and we are no exception—have important national interests to protect. But the most fundamental interest of all nations lies in building the structure of peace. In

partnership with our allies, secure in our own strength, we will seek those areas in which we can agree among ourselves and with others to accommodate conflicts and overcome rivalries. We are working toward the day when *all* nations will have a stake in peace, and will therefore be partners in its maintenance.

Within such a structure, international disputes can be settled and clashes contained. The insecurity of nations, out of which so much conflict arises, will be eased, and the habits of moderation and compromise will be nurtured. Most important, a durable peace will give full opportunity to the powerful forces driving toward economic change and social justice.

This vision of a peace built on partnership, strength and willingness to negotiate is the unifying theme of this report. In the sections that follow, the first steps we have taken during this past year—the policies we have devised and the programs we have initiated to realize this vision— are placed in the context of these three principles.

Peace Through Partnership—The Nixon Doctrine

As I said in my address of November 3, "We Americans are a do-it-yourself people—an impatient people. Instead of teaching someone else to do a job, we like to do it ourselves. This trait has been carried over into our foreign policy."

The postwar era of American foreign policy began in this vein in 1947 with the proclamation of the Truman Doctrine and the Marshall plan, offering American economic and military assistance to countries threatened by aggression. Our policy held that democracy and prosperity, but-

tressed by American military strength and organized in a worldwide network of American-led alliances, would insure stability and peace. In the formative years of the postwar period, this great effort of international political and economic reconstruction was a triumph of American leadership and imagination, especially in Europe.

For two decades after the end of the Second World War, our foreign policy was guided by such a vision and inspired by its success. The vision was based on the fact that the United States was the richest and most stable country, without whose initiative and resources little security or progress was possible.

This impulse carried us through into the 1960's. The United States conceived programs and ran them. We devised strategies, and proposed them to our allies. We discerned dangers, and acted directly to combat them.

The world has dramatically changed since the days of the Marshall Plan. We deal now with a world of stronger allies, a community of independent developing nations, and a Communist world still hostile but now divided.

Others now have the ability and responsibility to deal with local disputes which once might have required our interventions. Our contribution and success will depend not on the frequency of our involvement in the affairs of others, but on the stamina of our policies. This is the approach which will best encourage other nations to do their part, and will most genuinely enlist the support of the American people.

This is the message of the doctrine I announced at Guam—the "Nixon Doctrine." Its central thesis is that the United States will participate in the defense and development of allies and friends, but that America cannot—and will not—

conceive *all* the plans, design *all* the programs, execute *all* the decisions and undertake *all* the defense of the free nations of the world. We will help where it makes a real difference and is considered in our interest.

America cannot live in isolation if it expects to live in peace. We have no intention of withdrawing from the world. The only issue before us is how we can be most effective in meeting our responsibilities, protecting our interests, and thereby building peace.

A more responsible participation by our foreign friends in their own defense and progress means a more effective common effort toward the goals we all seek. Peace in the world will continue to require us to maintain our commitments—and we will. As I said at the United Nations, "It is not my belief that the way to peace is by giving up our friends or letting down our allies." But a more balanced and realistic American role in the world is essential if American commitments are to be sustained over the long pull. In my State of the Union Address, I affirmed that "to insist that other nations play a role is not a retreat from responsibility; it is a sharing of responsibility." This is not a way for America to withdraw from its indispensable role in the world. It is a way—the only way—we can carry out our responsibilities.

It is misleading, moreover, to pose the fundamental question so largely in terms of commitments. Our objective, in the first instance, is to support our *interests* over the long run with a sound foreign policy. The more that policy is based on a realistic assessment of our and others' interests, the more effective our role in the world can be. We are not involved in the world because we have commitments; we have commitments because we are involved. Our interests must shape our commitments, rather than the other way around.

We will view new commitments in the light of a careful assessment of our own national interests and those of other countries, of the specific threats to those interests, and of our capacity to counter those threats at an acceptable risk and cost.

We have been guided by these concepts during the past year in our dealings with free nations throughout the world.

1. In Europe, our policies embody precisely the three principles of a durable peace: partnership, continued strength to defend our common interests when challenged, and willingness to negotiate differences with adversaries.

2. Here in the Western Hemisphere we seek to strengthen our special relationship with our sister republics through a new program of action for progress in which all voices are heard and none predominates.

3. In Asia, where the Nixon Doctrine was enunciated, partnership will have special meaning for our policies—as evidenced by our strengthened ties with Japan. Our cooperation with Asian nations will be enhanced as they cooperate with one another and develop regional institutions.

4. In Vietnam, we seek a just settlement which all parties to the conflict, and all Americans, can support. We are working closely with the South Vietnamese to strengthen their ability to defend themselves. As South Vietnam grows stronger, the other side will, we hope, soon realize that it becomes ever more in their interest to negotiate a just peace.

5. In the Middle East, we shall continue

to work with others to establish a possible framework within which the parties to the Arab-Israeli conflict can negotiate the complicated and difficult questions at issue. Others must join us in recognizing that a settlement will require sacrifices and restraints by all concerned.

6. Africa, with its historic ties to so many of our own citizens, must always retain a significant place in our partnership with the new nations. Africans will play the major role in fulfilling their just aspirations—an end to racialism, the building of new nations, freedom from outside interference, and cooperative economic development. But we will add our efforts to theirs to help realize Africa's great potential.

7. In an ever more interdependent world economy, American foreign policy will emphasize the freer flow of capital and goods between nations. We are proud to have participated in the successful cooperative effort which created Special Drawing Rights, a form of international money which will help insure the stability of the monetary structure on which the continued expansion of trade depends.

8. The great effort of economic development must engage the cooperation of all nations. We are carefully studying the specific goals of our economic assistance programs and how most effectively to reach them.

9. Unprecedented scientific and technological advances as well as explosions in population, communications, and knowledge require new forms of international cooperation. The United Nations, the symbol of international partnership, will receive our continued strong support as it marks its 25th Anniversary.

America's Strength

The second element of a durable peace must be America's strength. Peace, we have learned, cannot be gained by good will alone.

In determining the strength of our defenses, we must make precise and crucial judgments. We should spend no more than is necessary. But there is an irreducible minimum of essential military security: for if we are less strong than necessary, and if the worst happens, there will be no domestic society to look after. The magnitude of such a catastrophe, and the reality of the opposing military power that could threaten it, present a risk which requires of any President the most searching and careful attention to the state of our defenses.

The changes in the world since 1945 have altered the context and requirements of our defense policy. In this area, perhaps more than in any other, the need to reexamine our approaches is urgent and constant.

The last 25 years have seen a revolution in the nature of military power. In fact, there has been a series of transformations—from the atomic to the thermonuclear weapon, from the strategic bomber to the intercontinental ballistic missile, from the surface missile to the hardened silo and the missile-carrying submarine, from the single to the multiple warhead, and from air defense to missile defense. We are now entering an era in which the sophistication and destructiveness of weapons present more formidable and complex issues affecting our strategic posture.

The last 25 years have also seen an important change in the relative balance of strategic power. From 1945 to 1949, we were the only nation in the world possessing an arsenal of atomic weapons.

From 1950 to 1966, we possessed an overwhelming superiority in strategic weapons. From 1967 to 1969, we retained a significant superiority. Today, the Soviet Union possesses a powerful and sophisticated strategic force approaching our own. We must consider, too, that Communist China will deploy its own intercontinental missiles during the coming decade, introducing new and complicating factors for our strategic planning and diplomacy.

In the light of these fateful changes, the Administration undertook a comprehensive and far-reaching reconsideration of the premises and procedures for designing our forces. We sought—and I believe we have achieved—a rational and coherent formulation of our defense strategy and requirements for the 1970's.

The importance of comprehensive planning of policy and objective scrutiny of programs is clear:

1. Because of the lead-time in building new strategic systems, the decisions we make today substantially determine our military posture—and thus our security—five years from now. This places a premium on foresight and planning.
2. Because the allocation of national resources between defense programs and other national programs is itself an issue of policy, it must be considered on a systematic basis at the early stages of the national security planning process.
3. Because we are a leader of the Atlantic Alliance, our doctrine and forces are crucial to the policy and planning of NATO. The mutual confidence that holds the allies together depends on understanding, agreement, and coordination among the 15 sovereign nations of the Treaty.

4. Because our security depends not only on our own strategic strength, but also on cooperative efforts to provide greater security for everyone through arms control, planning weapons systems and planning for arms control negotiations must be closely integrated.

For these reasons, this Administration has established procedures for the intensive scrutiny of defense issues in the light of overall national priorities. We have reexamined our strategic forces; we have reassessed our general purpose forces; and we have engaged in the most painstaking preparation ever undertaken by the United States Government for arms control negotiations.

Willingness to Negotiate—An Era of Negotiation

Partnership and strength are two of the pillars of the structure of a durable peace. Negotiation is the third. For our commitment to peace is most convincingly demonstrated in our willingness to negotiate our points of difference in a fair and businesslike manner with the Communist countries.

We are under no illusions. We know that there are enduring ideological differences. We are aware of the difficulty in moderating tensions that arise from the clash of national interests. These differences will not be dissipated by changes of atmosphere or dissolved in cordial personal relations between statesmen. They involve strong convictions and contrary philosophies, necessities of national security, and the deep-seated differences of perspectives formed by geography and history.

The United States, like any other nation, has interests of its own, and will defend those interests. But any nation today must define its interests with special concern for the interests of others. If some nations define their security in a manner that means insecurity for other nations, then peace is threatened and the security of all is diminished. This obligation is particularly great for the nuclear superpowers on whose decisions the survival of mankind may well depend.

The United States is confident that tensions can be eased and the danger of war reduced by patient and precise efforts to reconcile conflicting interests on concrete issues. Coexistence demands more than a spirit of good will. It requires the definition of positive goals which can be sought and achieved cooperatively. It requires real progress toward resolution of specific differences. This is our objective.

As the Secretary of State said on December 6:

We will continue to probe every available opening that offers a prospect for better East-West relations, for the resolution of problems large or small, for greater security for all.
In this the United States will continue to play an active role in concert with our allies.

This is the spirit in which the United States ratified the Non-Proliferation Treaty and entered into negotiation with the Soviet Union on control of the military use of the seabeds, on the framework of a settlement in the Middle East, and on limitation of strategic arms. This is the basis on which we and our Atlantic allies have offered to negotiate on concrete issues affecting the security and future of Europe, and on which the United States took steps last year to improve our relations with nations of Eastern Europe. This is also the spirit in which we have resumed formal talks in Warsaw with Communist China. No nation need be our permanent enemy.

AMERICA'S PURPOSE

These policies were conceived as a result of change, and we know they will be tested by the change that lies ahead. The world of 1970 was not predicted a decade ago, and we can be certain that the world of 1980 will render many current views obsolete.

The source of America's historic greatness has been our ability to see what had to be done, and then to do it. I believe America now has the chance to move the world closer to a durable peace. And I know that Americans working with each other and with other nations can make our vision real.

10. CENTRAL ISSUES OF AMERICAN FOREIGN POLICY

Henry A. Kissinger

. . . . .

BIPOLARITY AND MULTIPOLARITY: THE CONCEPTUAL PROBLEM

In the years ahead, the most profound challenge to American policy will be philosophical: to develop some concept of order in a world which is bipolar militarily but multipolar politically. But a philosophical deepening will not come easily to those brought up in the American tradition of foreign policy.

Our political society was one of the few which was *consciously* created at a point in time. At least until the emergence of the race problem, we were blessed by the absence of conflicts between classes and over ultimate ends. These factors produced the characteristic aspects of American foreign policy: a certain manipulativeness and pragmatism, a conviction that the normal pattern of international relations was harmonious, a reluctance to think in structural terms, a belief in final answers—all qualities which reflect a sense of self-sufficiency not far removed from a sense of omnipotence. Yet the contemporary dilemma is that there are no total solutions; we live in a world gripped by revolutions in technology, values, and institutions. We are immersed

Source: "Bipolarity and Multipolarity: The Conceptual Problem" is excerpted from *American Foreign Policy,* Third Edition, pp. 79–97, by Henry A. Kissinger, by permission of W. W. Norton & Company, Inc. Copyright © 1977, 1974, 1969 by Henry A. Kissinger.

in an unending process, not in a quest for a final destination. The deepest problems of equilibrium are not physical but psychological or moral. The shape of the future will depend ultimately on convictions which far transcend the physical balance of power.

The New Nations and Political Legitimacy

This challenge is especially crucial with respect to the new nations. Future historians are likely to class the confusion and torment in the emerging countries with the great movements of religious awakening. Continents which had been dormant for centuries suddenly develop political consciousness. Regions which for scores of years had considered foreign rule as natural struggle for independence. Yet it is a curious nationalism which defines itself not as in Europe by common language or culture but often primarily by the common experience of foreign rule. Boundaries—especially in Africa—have tended to follow the administrative convenience of the colonial powers rather than linguistic or tribal lines. The new nations have faced problems both of identity and of political authority. They often lack social cohesiveness entirely, or they are split into competing groups, each with a highly developed sense of identity.

It is no accident that between the Berlin crisis and the invasion of Czechoslovakia, the principal threats to peace came from the emerging areas. Domestic weakness encourages foreign intervention. The temptation to deflect domestic dissatisfactions into foreign adventures is ever present. Leaders feel little sense of responsibility to an over-all international equilibrium; they are much more conscious of their local grievances. The rivalry of the superpowers offers many opportunities for blackmail.

Yet their relations with other countries are not the most significant aspect of the turmoil of the new countries. It is in the new countries that questions of the purpose of political life and the meaning of political legitimacy—key issues also in the modern state—pose themselves in their most acute form. The new nations weigh little in the physical balance of power. But the forces unleashed in the emergence of so many new states may well affect the moral balance of the world— the convictions which form the structure for the world of tomorrow. This adds a new dimension to the problem of multipolarity.

Almost all of the new countries suffer from a revolutionary malaise: revolutions succeed through the coming together of all resentments. But the elimination of existing structures compounds the difficulty of establishing political consensus. A successful revolution leaves as its legacy a profound dislocation. In the new countries, contrary to all revolutionary expectations, the task of construction emerges as less glamorous and more complex than the struggle for freedom; the exaltation of the quest for independence cannot be perpetuated. Sooner or later, positive goals must replace resentment of the former colonial power as a motive force. In the absence of autonomous social forces, this unifying role tends to be performed by the state.

But the assumption of this role by the state does not produce stability. When social cohesiveness is slight, the struggle for control of authority is correspondingly more bitter. When government is the principal, sometimes the sole, expression of national identity, opposition comes to be considered treason. The profound social or religious schisms of many of the new nations turn the control of political authority quite literally into a matter of life and death. Where political obligation follows racial, religious, or tribal lines, self-restraint breaks down. Domestic conflicts assume the character of civil war. Such traditional authority as exists is personal or feudal. The problem is to make it "legitimate"—to develop a notion of political obligation which depends on legal norms rather than on coercive power or personal loyalty.

This process took centuries in Europe. It must be accomplished in decades in the new nations, where preconditions of success are less favorable than at comparable periods in Europe. The new countries are subject to outside pressures; there is a premium on foreign adventures to bring about domestic cohesiveness. Their lack of domestic structure compounds the already great international instabilities.

The American role in the new nations' efforts to build legitimate authority is in need of serious reexamination. The dominant American view about political structure has been that it will follow more or less automatically upon economic progress and that it will take the form of constitutional democracy.

Both assumptions are subject to serious questions. In every advanced country, political stability preceded rather than emerged from the process of industrialization. Where the rudiments of popular institutions did not exist at the beginning of the Industrial Revolution, they did not receive their impetus from it. To be sure, representative institutions were broadened and elaborated as the countries prospered, but their significant features antedated economic development and are not attributable to it. In fact, the system of government which brought about industrialization—whether popular or authoritarian—has tended to be confirmed rather than radically changed by this achievement.

Nor is democracy a natural evolution of nationalism. In the last century, democracy was accepted by a ruling class whose estimate of itself was founded outside the political process. It was buttressed by a middle class, holding a political philosophy in which the state was considered to be a referee of the ultimately important social forces rather than the principal focus of national consciousness. Professional revolutionaries were rarely involved; their bias is seldom democratic.

The pluralism of the West had many causes which cannot be duplicated elsewhere. These included a church organization outside the control of the state and therefore symbolizing the limitation of government power; the Greco-Roman philosophical tradition of justice based on human dignity, reinforced later by the Christian ethic; an emerging bourgeoisie; a stalemate in religious wars imposing tolerance as a practical necessity and a multiplicity of states. Industrialization was by no means the most significant of these factors. Had any of the others been missing, the Western political evolution could have been quite different.

This is why Communism has never succeeded in the industrialized Western countries for which its theory was devised; its greatest successes have been in developing societies. This is no accident. Industrialization—in its early phases—multiplies dislocations. It smashes the traditional framework. It requires a system of values which makes the sacrifices involved in capital formation tolerable and which furnishes some integrating principles to contain psychological frustrations.

Communism is able to supply legitimacy for the sacrifices inseparably connected with capital formation in an age when the maxims of laissez faire are no longer acceptable. And Leninism has the attraction of providing a rationale for holding on to power. Many of the leaders of the new countries are revolutionaries who sustained themselves through the struggle for independence by visions of the transformations to be brought about after victory. They are not predisposed even to admit the possibility of giving up power in their hour of triumph. Since they usually began their struggle for independence while in a small minority and sustained it against heavy odds, they are not likely to be repelled by the notion that it is possible to "force men to be free."

The ironic feature of the current situation is that Marxism, professing a materialistic philosophy, is accepted only where it does not exist: in some new countries and among protest movements of the advanced democratic countries. Its appeal is its idealistic component and not its economic theory. It offers a doctrine of substantive change and an explanation of final purposes. Its philosophy has totally failed to inspire the younger generation in Communist countries, where its bureaucratic reality is obvious.

On the other hand, the United States, professing an idealistic philosophy, often fails to gain acceptance for democratic values because of its heavy reliance on economic factors. It has answers to technical dislocations but has not been able to contribute much to building a political and moral consensus. It offers a procedure for change but little content for it.

The problem of political legitimacy is the key to political stability in regions containing two-thirds of the world's population. A stable domestic system in the new countries will not automatically produce international order, but international order is impossible without it. An American agenda must include some conception of what we understand by political legitimacy. In an age of instantaneous communication, we cannot pretend that what happens to over two-thirds of humanity is of no concern or interest to the United States. This does not mean that our goal should be to transfer American institutions to the new nations—even less that we should impose them. Nor should we define the problem as how to prevent the spread of Communism. Our goal should be to build a moral consensus which can make a pluralistic world creative rather than destructive.

Irrelevance to one of the great revolutions of our time will mean that we will ultimately be engulfed by it—if not physically, then psychologically. Already some of the protest movements have made heroes of leaders in repressive new countries. The absurdity of founding a claim for freedom on protagonists of the totalitarian state—such as Guevara or Ho or Mao—underlines the impact of the travail of the new countries on older societies which share none of their technical but some of their spiritual problems, especially the problem of the nature of authority in the modern world. To a young generation in rebellion against bureaucracy and bored with material comfort, these societies offer at least the challenge of unlimited opportunity (and occasionally unlimited manipulativeness) in the quest for justice.

A world which is bipolar militarily and multipolar politically thus confronts an additional problem. Side by side with the physical balance of power, there exists a psychological balance based on intangibles of value and belief. The presuppositions of the physical equilibrium have changed drastically; those of the psychological balance remain to be discovered.

The Problem of Soviet Intentions

Nothing has been more difficult for Americans to assimilate in the nuclear age than the fact that even enmity is complex. In the Soviet Union, we confront an opponent whose public pronouncements are insistently hostile. Yet the nuclear age imposes a degree of cooperation and an absolute limit to conflicts.

The military relationship with the Soviet Union is difficult enough; the political one confronts us with a profound conceptual problem. A society which regards peace as the normal condition tends to ascribe tension not to structural causes but to wicked or shortsighted individuals. Peace is thought to result either from the automatic operations of economic forces or from the emergence of a more benign leadership abroad.

The debate about Soviet trends between "hard-liners" and "soft-liners" illustrates this problem. Both sides tend to agree that the purpose of American policy is to encourage a more benign evolution of Soviet society—the original purpose of containment was, after all, to bring about the *domestic* transformation of the U.S.S.R. They are at one that a settlement presupposes a change in the Soviet system. Both groups imply that the nature of a possible settlement is perfectly obvious. But the apostles of containment have never specified the American negotiating program to be undertaken from the position of strength their policy was designed to achieve. The advocates of relaxation of tensions have been no more precise; they have been more concerned with atmosphere than with the substance of talks.

In fact, the difference between the "hawks" and "doves" has usually concerned timing: the hawks have maintained that a Soviet change of heart, while inevitable, was still in the future, whereas the doves have argued that it has already taken place. Many of the hawks tend to consider all negotiations as fruitless. Many of the doves argue—or did before Czechoslovakia—that the biggest step toward peace has already been accomplished by a Soviet change of heart about the cold war; negotiations need only remove some essentially technical obstacles.

The difference affects—and sometimes poisons—the entire American debate about foreign policy. Left-wing critics of American foreign policy seem incapable of attacking U.S. actions without elevating our opponent (whether it happens to be Mao or Castro or Ho) to a pedestal. If they discern some stupidity or self-interest on our side, they assume that the other side must be virtuous. They then criticize the United States for opposing the other side. The right follows the same logic in reverse: they presuppose *our* good intentions and conclude that the other side must be perverse in opposing us. Both the left and the right judge largely in terms of intentions. In the process, whatever the issue—whether Berlin or Vietnam—more attention is paid to whether to get to the conference room than what to do once we arrive there. The dispute over Communist intentions has diverted attention from elaborating our own purposes. In some quarters, the test of dedication to peace has been whether one interprets Soviet intentions in the most favorable manner.

It should be obvious, however, that the Soviet domestic situation is complex and its relationship to foreign policy far from obvious. It is true that the risks of general nuclear war should be as unacceptable to Moscow as to Washington; but this truism does not automatically produce détente. It also seems to lessen the risks involved in local intervention. No doubt the current generation of Communist leaders lacks the ideological dynamism of their predecessors who made the revolution; at the same time, they have at their disposal a military machine of unprecedented strength, and they must deal with a bureaucracy of formidable vested interests. Unquestionably, Soviet consumers press their leaders to satisfy their demands; but it is equally true that an expanding modern economy is able to supply *both* guns and butter. Some Soviet leaders may have become more pragmatic; but in an elaborated Communist state, the results of pragmatism are complex. Once power is seized and industrialization is largely accomplished, the Communist Party faces a difficult situation. It is not needed to conduct the government, and it has no real function in running the economy (though it tries to do both). In order to justify its continued existence and command, it may develop a vested interest in vigilance against outside danger and thus in perpetuating a fairly high level of tension.

It is beyond the scope of this essay to go into detail on the issue of internal Communist evolution. But it may be appropriate to inquire why, in the past, every period of détente has proved stillborn. There have been at least five periods of peaceful coexistence since the Bolshevik seizure of power, one in each decade of the Soviet state. Each was hailed in the West as ushering in a new era of reconciliation and as signifying the long-awaited final change in Soviet purposes. Each ended abruptly with a new period of intransigence, which was generally ascribed to a victory of Soviet hard-liners rather than to the dynamics of the system. There were undoubtedly many reasons for this. But the tendency of many in the West to be content with changes of Soviet tone and to confuse atmosphere with substance surely did not help matters. It has enabled the Communist leaders to postpone the choice which they must make sooner or later: whether to use détente as a device to lull the West or whether to move toward a resolution of the outstanding differences. As long as this choice is postponed, the possibility exists that latent crises may run away with the principal protagonists, as happened in the Middle East and perhaps even in Czechoslovakia.

The eagerness of many in the West to emphasize the liberalizing implications of Soviet economic trends and to make favorable interpretation of Soviet intentions a test of good faith may have the paradoxical consequence of strengthening the Soviet hard-liners. Soviet troops had hardly arrived in Prague when some Western leaders began to insist that the invasion would not affect the quest for détente while others continued to indicate a nostalgia for high-level meetings. Such an attitude hardly serves the cause of peace. The risk is great that if there is no penalty for intransigence there is no incentive for conciliation. The Kremlin may use negotiations—including arms control—as a safety valve to dissipate Western suspicions rather than as a serious endeavor to resolve concrete disputes or to remove the scourge of nuclear war.

If we focus our policy discussions on Soviet purposes, we confuse the debate in two ways: Soviet trends are too ambiguous to offer a reliable guide—it is possible that not even Soviet leaders fully understand the dynamics of their system; it deflects us from articulating the purposes we should pursue, whatever Soviet intentions. Peace will not, in any event, result from one grand settlement but from a long diplomatic process, and this process requires some clarity as to our destination. Confusing foreign policy with psychotherapy deprives us of criteria by which to judge the political foundations of international order.

The obsession with Soviet intentions causes the West to be smug during periods of détente and panicky during crises. A benign Soviet tone is equated with the achievement of peace; Soviet hostility is considered to be the signal for a new period of tension and usually evokes purely military countermeasures. The West is thus never ready for a Soviet change of course; it has been equally unprepared for détente and intransigence.

These lines are being written while outrage at the Soviet invasion of Czechoslovakia is still strong. There is a tendency to focus on military implications or to speak of strengthening unity in the abstract. But if history is a guide, there will be a new Soviet peace offensive sooner or later. Thus, reflecting about the nature of détente seems most important while its achievement appears most problematical. If we are not to be doomed to repeat the past, it may be well to learn some of its lessons: we should not again confuse a change of tone with a change of heart. We should not pose false inconsistencies between allied unity and détente; indeed, a true relaxation of tensions presupposes Western unity. We should concentrate negotiations on the concrete issues that threaten peace, such as intervention in the third world. Moderating the arms race must also be high on the agenda. None of this is possible without a concrete idea of what we understand by peace and a creative world order.

AN INQUIRY INTO THE AMERICAN NATIONAL INTEREST

Wherever we turn, then, the central task of American foreign policy is to analyze anew the current international environment and to develop some concepts which will enable us to contribute to the emergence of a stable order.

First, we must recognize the existence of profound structural problems that are to a considerable extent independent of the intentions of the principal protagonists and that cannot be solved merely by good will. The vacuum in Central Europe and the decline of the Western European countries would have disturbed the world equilibrium regardless of the domestic structure of the Soviet Union. A strong China has historically tended to establish suzerainty over its neighbors; in fact, one special problem of dealing with China—Communism apart—is that it has had no experience in conducting foreign policy with equals. China has been either dominant or subjected.

To understand the structural issue, it is necessary to undertake an inquiry, from which we have historically shied away, into the essence of our national interest and into the premises of our foreign policy. It is part of American folklore that, while other nations have interests, we have responsibilities; while other nations are concerned with equilibrium, we are concerned with the legal requirements of peace. We have a tendency to offer our altruism as a guarantee of our reliability: "We have no quarrel with the Communists," Secretary of State Rusk said on one occasion; "all our quarrels are on behalf of other people."

Such an attitude makes it difficult to develop a conception of our role in the world. It inhibits other nations from gearing their policy to ours in a confident way—a "disinterested" policy is likely to be considered "unreliable." A mature conception of our interest in the world would obviously have to take into account the widespread interest in stability and peaceful change. It would deal with two fundamental questions: What is it in our interest to prevent? What should we seek to accomplish?

The answer to the first question is complicated by an often-repeated proposition that we must resist aggression anywhere it occurs since peace is indivisible. A corollary is the argument that we do not oppose the fact of particular changes but the method by which they are brought about. We find it hard to articulate a truly vital interest which we would defend however "legal" the challenge. This leads to an undifferentiated globalism and confusion about our purposes. The abstract concept of aggression causes us to multiply our commitments. But the denial that our interests are involved diminishes our staying power when we try to carry out these commitments.

Part of the reason for our difficulties is our reluctance to think in terms of power and equilibrium. In 1949, for example, a State Department memorandum justified NATO as follows:

[The treaty] obligates the parties to defend the purposes and principles of the United Nations, the freedom, common heritage and civilization of the parties and their free institutions based upon the principles of democracy, individual liberty and the role of law. It obligates them to act in defense of peace and security. It is directed against no one; it is directed solely against aggression. It seeks not to influence any shifting balance of power but to strengthen a balance of principle.

But principle, however lofty, must at some point be related to practice; historically, stability has always coincided with an equilibrium that made physical domination difficult. Interest is not necessarily amoral; moral consequences can spring from interested acts. Britain did not contribute any the less to international order for having a clear-cut concept of its interest which required it to prevent the domination of the Continent by a single power (no matter in what way it was threatened) and the control of the seas by anybody (even if the immediate intentions were not hostile). A new American administration confronts the challenge of relating our commitments to our interests and our obligations to our purposes.

The task of defining positive goals is more difficult but even more important. The first two decades after the end of the Second World War posed problems well suited to the American approach to international relations. Wherever we turned, massive dislocations required attention. Our pragmatic, *ad hoc* tendency was an advantage in a world clamoring for technical remedies. Our legal bent contributed to the development of many instruments of stability.

In the late sixties, the situation is more complex. The United States is no longer in a position to operate programs globally; it has to encourage them. It can no longer impose its preferred solution; it must seek to evoke it. In the forties and fifties, we offered remedies; in the late sixties and the seventies our role will have to be to contribute to a structure that will foster the initiative of others. We are a superpower physically, but our designs can be meaningful only if they generate willing cooperation. We can continue to contribute to defense and positive programs, but we must seek to encourage and not stifle a sense of local responsibility. Our contribution should not be the sole or principal effort, but it should make the difference between success and failure.

This task requires a different kind of creativity and another form of patience than we have displayed in the past. Enthusiasm, belief in progress, and the invincible conviction that American remedies can work everywhere must give way to an understanding of historical trends, an ordering of our preferences, and above all an understanding of the difference our preferences can in fact make.

The dilemma is that there can be no stability without equilibrium but, equally, equilibrium is not a purpose with which we can respond to the travail of our world. A sense of mission is clearly a legacy of American history; to most Americans, America has always stood for something other than its own grandeur. But a clearer understanding of America's interests and of the requirements of equilibrium can give perspective to our idealism and lead to humane and moderate objectives, especially in relation to political and social change. Thus our conception of world order must have deeper purposes than stability but greater restraints on our behavior than would result if it were approached only in a fit of enthusiasm.

Whether such a leap of the imagination is possible in the modern bureaucratic state remains to be seen. New administrations come to power convinced of the need for goals and for comprehensive concepts. Sooner, rather than later, they find themselves subjected to the pressures of the immediate and the particular. Part of the reason is the pragmatic, issue-oriented bias of our decision-makers. But the fundamental reason may be the pervasiveness of modern bureaucracy. What started out as an aid to decision-making has developed a momentum of its own. Increasingly, the policy-maker is more conscious of the pressures and the morale of his staff than of the purpose this staff is supposed to serve. The policy-maker becomes a referee among quasi-autonomous bureaucratic bodies. Success consists of moving the administrative machinery to the point of decision, leaving relatively little energy for analyzing the decision's merit. The modern bureaucratic state widens the range of technical choices while limiting the capacity to make them.

An even more serious problem is posed by the change of ethic of precisely the most idealistic element of American youth. The idealism of the fifties during the Kennedy era expressed itself in self-confident, often zealous, institution building. Today, however, many in the younger generation consider the management of power irrelevant, perhaps even immoral. While the idea of service retains a potent influence, it does so largely with respect to problems which are clearly *not* connected with the strategic aspects of American foreign policy; the Peace Corps is a good example. The new ethic of freedom is not "civic"; it is indifferent or even hostile to systems and notions of order. Management is equated with manipulation. Structural designs are perceived as systems of "domination"—not of order. The generation which has come of age after the fifties has had Vietnam as its introduction to world politics. It has no memory of occasions when American-supported structural innovations were successful or of the motivations which prompted these enterprises.

Partly as a result of the generation gap, the American mood oscillates dangerously between being ashamed of power and expecting too much of it. The former attitude deprecates the use or possession of force; the latter is overly receptive to the possibilities of absolute action and overly indifferent to the likely consequences. The danger of a rejection of power is that it may result in a nihilistic perfectionism which disdains the gradual and seeks to destroy what does not conform to its notion of utopia. The danger of an overconcern with force is that policy-makers may respond to clamor by a series of spasmodic gestures and stylistic maneuvers and then recoil before their implications.

These essentially psychological problems cannot be overemphasized. It is the essence of a satisfied, advanced society that it puts a premium on operating within familiar procedures and concepts. It draws its motivation from the present, and it defines excellence by the ability to manipulate an established framework. But for the major part of humanity, the present becomes endurable only through a vision of the future. To most Americans—including most American leaders—the significant reality is what they see around them. But for most of the world—including many of the leaders of the new nations—the significant reality is what they wish to bring about. If we remain nothing but the managers of our physical patrimony, we will grow increasingly irrelevant. And since there can be no stability without us, the prospects of world order will decline.

We require a new burst of creativity, however, not so much for the sake of other countries as for our own people, especially the youth. The contemporary unrest is no doubt exploited by some whose purposes are all too clear. But that it is there to exploit is proof of a profound dissatisfaction with the merely managerial and consumer-oriented qualities of the modern state and with a world which seems to generate crises by inertia. The modern bureaucratic state, for all its panoply of strength, often finds itself shaken to its foundations by seemingly trivial causes. Its brittleness and the world-wide revolution of youth—especially in advanced countries and among the relatively affluent—suggest a spiritual void, an almost metaphysical boredom with a political environment that increasingly emphasizes bureaucratic challenges and is dedicated to no deeper purpose than material comfort.

Our unrest has no easy remedy. Nor is the solution to be found primarily in the realm of foreign policy. Yet a deeper non-technical challenge would surely help us regain a sense of direction. The best and most prideful expressions of American purposes in the world have been those in which we acted in concert with others. Our influence in these situations has depended on achieving a reputation as a member of such a concert. To act consistently abroad we must be able to generate coalitions of shared purposes. Regional groupings supported by the United States will have to take over major responsibility for their immediate areas, with the United States being concerned more with the over-all framework of order than with the management of every regional enterprise.

In the best of circumstances, the next administration will be beset by crises. In almost every area of the world, we have been living off capital—warding off the immediate, rarely dealing with underlying problems. These difficulties are likely to multiply when it becomes apparent that one of the legacies of the war in Vietnam will be a strong American reluctance to risk overseas involvements.

A new administration has the right to ask for compassion and understanding from the American people. But it must found its claim not on pat technical answers to difficult issues; it must above all ask the right questions. It must recognize that, in the field of foreign policy, we will never be able to contribute to building a stable and creative world order unless we first form some conception of it.

11. WHAT'S WRONG WITH HENRY KISSINGER'S FOREIGN POLICY

Richard A. Falk

A Hero of Our Time, gentlemen, is indeed a portrait, but not of a single individual; it is a portrait composed of all the vices of our generation in the fullness of their development.

Mihail Lermontov, "The Author's Introduction," *A Hero of Our Time* (1958)

PRELIMINARIES

My purpose in this paper is to criticize the workings of the state system in the latter part of the twentieth century. One means of doing so is to examine the role of its most exemplary practitioner, Henry Kissinger. There is much to admire in Kissinger's role. He has helped moderate tensions among the superpowers and used his formidable intelligence and energies to work toward the settlement of the most dangerous international conflicts. Indeed, Kissinger has dramatically revealed how much peace-making can still be done by way of traditional diplomacy.

Given these achievements, it may seem almost perverse to single Kissinger's foreign policy out for critical attack. Indeed, Kissinger has realized the dream of every political figure—to become so valuable a public servant that it seems irresponsible to criticize him; in almost every part of the world, including those most anti-American, Kissinger appears to stand above criticism.[1] Of course, this widely shared appreciation of Kissinger may not last; it is precarious, and could vanish as soon as U.S. diplomacy turned hard in

Source: *Alternatives: A Journal of World Policy,* 1 (March 1975), pp. 79–100.

an unpopular direction. For there is no doubt that Kissinger's activities are predicated on what is good for the U.S., and not necessarily on what is good for the world. Nevertheless, for the moment, Kissinger seems like the only diplomat whose skill and stature are so great as to make his services indispensable to the cause of moderation and peace among sovereign states.

I am not out to shatter this Kissinger myth, only to discuss its geopolitical significance for the central problems confronting an increasingly tormented mankind. My main point is decidedly not that Kissinger is a worse spokesman for U.S. foreign policy than his principal predecessors such as William Rogers, Dean Rusk, or John Foster Dulles. Nor am I implying that a politically feasible successor to Kissinger, regardless of which party prevails in the 1976 elections, is going to be an improvement. Quite the contrary. I believe that Kissinger is about the best that the U.S. political system can produce under present circumstances, given prevailing political beliefs and consciousness. Nor do I wish to imply that governments in most other large states are presently capable of pursuing a consistently more progressive foreign policy.[2] I find no evidence at all to suggest that the Soviet Union or Japan or most European countries would not gladly exchange their current foreign minister for a national equivalent of Kissinger.

I also do not in any sense want to make the more limited point that Kissinger has been contaminated by Watergate involvement or by his close association with now a discredited President (although there is room for argument that Kissinger should have quit, or at least that he compromised himself by exhibiting the Watergate mentality to the extent of wiretapping his own staff). But I am prepared to go along with the view that Kissinger was obliged to this degree of participation in the Nixon ethos in order to sustain his own effectiveness, and that this effectiveness was and remains far more important to the country and the world than any conceivable expression of indignation through acts of opposition or resignation.

On a more problematical basis, I would not even condemn Kissinger for his willingness to implement and justify cruel and illegal U.S. policies in Indochina. Kissinger's public endorsement of the 1972 Christmas bombings of Hanoi, after peace agreements had already been negotiated, manifested Kissinger's Vietnam role in its most objectionable form. This role persists. Kissinger received a Nobel Peace Prize for negotiating the Paris Peace Agreement of 1973, which he allowed (perhaps even encouraged?) Saigon to repudiate in numerous ways before the ink was even dry. In addition, Kissinger has led the political fight to sustain high levels of U.S. military and economic aid for the Thieu regime and shares some responsibility for the various covert means being used by the U.S. to avoid the obligations solemnly assumed in Paris.

I do not want to emphasize Kissinger's personal frailties either. His personal biography is only relevant to the extent that it helps us understand his access to power and his broad political support despite an identification with the dramatic efforts to end, or at least moderate, the Cold War. Kissinger has achieved diplomatic success mainly because of structural features of the contemporary world and also because he has put his intelligence, energy, and charm to work on behalf of an essentially correct reading of diplomatic possibilities presented by this structure during this time period.

My principal aim is to show that Kissinger's foreign policy, successful as it seems, does not sufficiently address the central task of our time—namely, the need to evolve a new system of world order based on principles of peace and justice. Kissinger's effort to settle international conflicts which threaten large-scale warfare is certainly admirable from almost any point of view, but it may be dangerously deceptive if it is not associated with a wider program of global reform. Indeed, Kissinger's historical importance may be to have provided a specious stability to a disintegrating state system, on behalf of the few states that are both powerful and rich. This policy reflects a global ideology of domination that embodies indifference to the poor and weak. It is a foreign policy based on the presumption that the governments of sovereign states can achieve security and prosperity for their populations, despite the growing interdependence of life on the planet. In essence, I am arguing that Kissinger's foreign policy is oblivious to the deeper self-destructive tendencies and inequities of the state system, and hence to the need and desirability of adapting geopolitics to an emergent global situation of *de facto* integration.[3]

Another preliminary issue of a related

nature is the extent to which Kissinger's influence on foreign policy should be regarded as a reflection of Richard Nixon's outlook. I believe that Nixon and Kissinger shared an interpretation of the dynamics of the state system and of the main targets of diplomatic opportunity that existed in 1969. I do not mean that Kissinger was always in agreement with the tactical judgments of Nixon, only that for our purposes we can ignore the fact that Kissinger was acting on behalf of Nixon. While Nixon's view of the state system seems indistinguishable from that of Kissinger, Kissinger's diplomatic flair has probably added a measure, perhaps a decisive measure, of effectiveness to what Nixon might have achieved with ordinary as distinct from exemplary execution of his policies.

ELEMENTS OF KISSINGER'S APPROACH

As a matter of backgrond, it is helpful to examine Kissinger's approach to foreign policy developed over the years when he was a university professor.[4] His scholarly work exhibits an unusual singlemindedness of purpose. From the time Kissinger was a graduate student at Harvard he seemed preoccupied with the achievement of stability in international society. It is, perhaps, not surprising that someone who had spent the formative years of his life in Nazi Germany would be concerned with stability and its concomitant affirmations of the *status quo* and moderation. It is even less surprising, I think, that Kissinger should identify revolutionary actors, whether from the left or the right, as the main threat to stability. Despite this apparent rejection of *all* revolutionary actors, Kissinger's work actually deals mainly with the threat from the left. There are several apparent explanations.

Kissinger obviously believes that the Soviet challenge is historically paramount. As his career progresses Kissinger comes to write more and more with the outlook of a U.S. geopolitician rather than that of a social scientist; and increasingly seems to regard his most significant audience as U.S. opinion leaders and policy-makers.

In his earliest work Kissinger's approach was oriented around the discovery of "crucial" truth in a relatively detached manner. In that spirit Kissinger found it most useful to understand the present and future by penetrating an analogous historical setting in the past.

As he put it in his Harvard doctoral dissertation (Graubard, 1973, p. 10):

> The success of physical science depends on the selection of the "crucial" experiment; that of political science in the field of international affairs, on the selection of the "crucial" period. I have chosen for my topic the period between 1812 and 1822, partly, I am frank to say, because its problems seem to me analogous to those of our day.

Kissinger has sometimes been accused of modeling himself on the nineteenth-century Austrian diplomat Metternich. I think Graubard (1973, p. 14) is correct when he writes that "Kissinger's interest was not in a historical personage, Metternich, but in the problems that Metternich was compelled to deal with. He chose the Napoleonic period because he believed it resembled his own." The modern resemblance arises from Metternich's successful confrontation of revolutionary France under Napoleon and the creation of a moderate war-free period of international diplomacy. Kissinger himself, in his famous interview with Oriana Fallaci (1972), has made it plain that he does not regard Metternich as a *model* for his own statesmanship:

Most people associate me with Metternich. And that is childish ... there can be nothing in common between me and Metternich. He was chancellor and foreign minister at a time when it took three weeks to travel from Central Europe to the ends of the Continent. He was chancellor and foreign minister at a time when wars were conducted by professional soldiers and diplomacy was in the hands of the aristocracy. How can one compare such conditions with the ones prevailing in today's world, a world where there is no homogeneous group of leaders, no homogeneous internal situation and no homogeneous cultural background?[5]

What Kissinger admired was Metternich's understanding of the revolutionary character of the Napoleonic challenge and his leadership in bringing about a new era of international stability after Napoleon's military defeat [see Kissinger (1954)]. But Kissinger never intended such admiration to be understood as proposing a Metternichian recipe for the solution of comparable contemporary problems.

In his *A World Restored,* Kissinger (1954) examines the efforts of Metternich and Castlereagh to rebuild the international order of Europe after the revolutionary challenge posed by Napoleonic France had been turned back. Kissinger's backward glance at history was intended as an acerbic commentary on post-World War II U.S. diplomacy which, in Kissinger's view, had not clearly enough come to terms with the revolutionary nature of the Soviet challenge.

What was implicit in *A World Restored* became the central argument of *Nuclear Weapons and Foreign Policy* (Kissinger 1958), the book that made Kissinger an academic celebrity. Kissinger states his case in strong terms that link revolutionary challenges by Napoleon and Hitler with the contemporary challenge posed by the Soviet bloc (1958, p. 43):

Time and again states boldly proclaim that their purpose is to destroy the existing structure and to recast it completely. And time and again, the powers that are the declared victims stand by indifferent or inactive while the balance of power is overturned. Indeed, they tend to explain away the efforts of the revolutionary power to upset the equilibrium as the expression of limited arms or specific grievances, until they discover—sometimes too late and always at excessive cost—that the revolutionary power was perfectly sincere all along, that its call for a new order expressed its real aspirations. So it was when the French Revolution burst on an unbelieving Europe and when Hitler challenged the system of Versailles. So it has been with the relations of the rest of the world toward the Soviet bloc.[6]

Kissinger argues that Soviet (and, under Mao, Chinese) words and deeds exhibit an unswerving commitment to revolutionary objectives which are antithetical to the realization of his own utopia —namely, international stability in the face of revolutionary challenges.[7] In this regard he is openly scornful of those who think that a more forthcoming attitude by the liberal democracies would be rewarded by a more pliant and moderate Soviet foreign policy. In a sense, Kissinger's whole approach is an attempt to learn and teach the lesson of Munich in the altered setting of the nuclear age. He believes that the liberal democracies are inherently complacent about safeguarding stability against major challenges. He is critical of the failure of the U.S. in the 1950s to evolve the only sort of military strategy that he believed capable of averting either World War III or some sort of political catastrophe for the non-communist world: For Kissinger, the inadequate response to Hitler confirms his anxiety (1969, p. 14): "In 1936, no one could know whether Hitler was a misunderstood nationalist or a maniac. By the time certainty was achieved it had to be paid for with millions of lives."

Kissinger even turns on its head the argument that Soviet leaders seek nothing more than defensive security. He acknowledges that Soviet leaders were "probably sincere" about feeling threatened, but he notes: "the point to bear in mind is that nothing can reassure them" (1958, p. 77). Extending this line of reasoning, Kissinger (1958, pp. 45, 77) arrives at the startling conclusion that

Because their doctrine *requires* them to fear us, they strive for absolute security: the neutralization of the United States and the elimination of our influence from Europe and Asia. And because absolute security for the USSR means absolute insecurity for us, the only safe United States policy is one which is built on the assumption of a continued revolutionary struggle, even though the methods may vary with the requirements of the changing situation.

This assessment of the Soviet system was frequently reiterated by Kissinger, even in an article published shortly before he joined the Nixon administration in early 1969 (Kissinger, 1968).

Given this perception of the international setting, the only way to turn back the revolutionary challenge is to mobilize military capabilities on behalf of *status quo* interests (Kissinger, 1958, p. 76).

In *The Necessity for Choice,* published in 1961, Kissinger in even more pointed terms emphasizes the danger to American interests that arises from the Soviet challenge. Indeed, he begins his book (1961, p. 1) on an alarmist note:

... the United States cannot afford another decline like that which has characterized the past decade and a half. Fifteen years more of a deterioration of our position such as we have experienced since World War II would find us reduced to Fortress America in a world in which we had become largely irrelevant.

Kissinger's main policy argument involves a strategy for coping with the Soviet-led challenge. Because he feels that, above all, it is necessary to understand the challenge as revolutionary in character, he does not see the Soviet challenge as likely to be dissipated by the domestic evolution of the Soviet system or by a change in the fundamental outlook of its leadership. Indeed, Kissinger's reading of history stresses military responses: a revolutionary movement subsides "when such a movement came to be opposed with equal fervor or when it reached the limits of its military strength" (1958, p. 76). On this basis, Kissinger urges upon the U.S. a determination to fight throughout the world where and when it is necessary, rather than resting its security upon a capacity to deter a nuclear attack upon itself.

At the same time, Kissinger acknowledged that the prospects for world peace could be improved because of the apparent rationality of the communist side, at least with respect to avoiding all-out mutually destructive nuclear war. For this reason Kissinger believed, for instance, that if "the free world gains in purpose, cohesion, and safety," then it may be possible to negotiate seriously with communist leaders on "how to reduce the tensions inherent in an unchecked arms race," (1961, p. 7). When confronted with strong political and military opposition even a revolutionary actor may be willing to strike certain bargains with his *status quo* adversaries, and the quality of international stability will thereby be enhanced. Kissinger seemed to believe that the possibility of such bargaining, even during a revolutionary phase, constituted one of the distinct effects of nuclear weaponry on the international system. However, Kissinger qualified his receptivity to bargaining with a revolutionary

Soviet actor by insisting that negotiations deal with concrete issues on the basis of mutual interest, and that negotiating initiatives derive from strength rather than from false hopes for a new era of friendly relations. Kissinger was worried that Soviet leaders would lull their American counterparts to sleep with the false rhetoric of harmony, while working apace to advance their revolutionary program of geopolitical expansion.

In *The Necessity for Choice,* Kissinger's analysis already showed a shift in emphasis from the revolutionary actor to the revolutionary situation. By broadening his analysis, Kissinger meant to emphasize several rapid changes in the international setting—the spread of communism, the rise of new post-colonial nations, and the proliferation of nuclear weapons—that made it appropriate to regard "our period as an age of revolution" (1961, p. 2). The struggle with communism remains at the top of the agenda, but these additional factors complicate the maintenance of stability which is, we should remember, the *sine qua non* for Kissinger of an acceptable world order structure.

In 1968 this shift in focus becomes even more central to Kissinger's interpretation of the international scene, and apparently reflects his mood at the time he entered policy-forming arenas. As Kissinger depicts this revolutionary background of international relations (1969, p. 53):

The revolutionary character of our age can be summed up in three general statements: (a) the number of participants in the international order has increased and their nature has altered; (b) their technical ability to affect each other has altered; (c) the scope of their purposes has expanded.

As a result of the Sino-Soviet split, the rise of Afro-Asian states, and the weakening of the Western alliance, multipolarity has generally superseded bipolarity. The nature of the revolutionary challenge, even the identity of the challenger, may differ from context to context. Such issue areas as resource flows, monetary relations, and military security suggest the variances that occur in a multipolar setting. As a consequence, a statesman needs to be more flexible and sophisticated than in the simpler circumstances of earlier centuries. In Kissinger's words (1969, p. 57):

Many of the elements of stability which characterized the international system in the nineteenth century cannot be re-created in the modern age. The stable technology, the multiplicity of major powers, the limited domestic claims, and the frontiers which permitted adjustments are gone forever. A new concept of international order is essential; without it stability will prove elusive.

What is revealing about this statement, especially when compared with his earlier analyses of international situations, is that it anticipates a diplomatic stance that is post-Cold War in character. Having become antagonists of one another, the Soviet Union and China become potential (if limited) partners for the U.S. This partnership option available to an adept U.S. diplomat provides geopolitical leverage in meeting a revolutionary challenge from a given national source. Still Kissinger remains wary of the Soviet Union (1969, pp. 85–90). He is impressed by its political absolutism and hostile propaganda toward the West, and skeptical of any short-term prospect of fundamental change, although he urges (1969, p. 89) that "a serious endeavor to resolve concrete disputes" be undertaken. The Nixon-Kissinger diplomacy of the past few years has made this serious endeavor but, given

Kissinger's earlier arguments, at the cost of generating undue and premature optimism about the future of Soviet-U.S. relations.

Détente diplomacy has proceeded cautiously, seeking to test the extent to which Soviet-U.S. tensions can be moderated. Although conservatives are uneasy about the new approach to the Soviet Union, Kissinger has made it clear by both words and deeds that the U.S. government has no illusions about Soviet liberalization or about the permanence of the détente atmosphere.

The fracturing of the world communist movement and the U.S. failure in Indochina created an international atmosphere where both sides were eager to compromise their differences and enter into specific negotiations across a wide spectrum. True, Nixon and Kissinger, as well as their Soviet counterparts, have sustained a posture of wariness and a willingness to resume antagonistic postures, as in the Middle East, when their interests clashed.[8] Nevertheless, the Nixon-Kissinger "structure of peace" is based on the conviction that no substantial revolutionary threat is at work in world affairs and that, therefore, present international disputes can be settled by negotiations among the great powers—especially if they defer to each other's zones of imperial or hegemonial control over the third world and other areas.

To Kissinger it makes almost no difference whether a revolutionary is red or white.[9] Both are equally dangerous to international stability, which is the overriding, virtually the exclusive, objective of a statesman. Thus, any kind of ideological or moralistic posturing by a government or its leaders is abhorrent to Kissinger. For this reason, he dislikes the liberal wing of the American establishment, because it tends to confuse the quest for stability with reforming the character of international order. Presumably for this reason also, although he nowhere says so, Kissinger is not concerned as a statesman with the occurrence of domestic repression in a foreign country.[10] It is not that he necessarily likes the Greek or Chilean juntas, but he believes that they do not pose the sort of threat to international stability that is created by governments such as those of Castro's Cuba or Allende's Chile which tend to be anti-American and espouse solidarity with oppressed peoples everywhere. The attractiveness of Kissinger's approach derives, in part, from its simplicity and clarity. As soon as issues of dignity and equity are taken into account, matters of choice and policy enter a more complex, ambiguous frame of reference.[11] It is difficult for either conservatives or liberals to oppose the moderation of conflict in international relations; Kissinger's tendency to remove the moral question from the sphere of international diplomacy is a tremendous asset in the search for domestic political support within the U.S.

There is a further element in Kissinger's approach. It is his tragic view of human nature. He repeatedly asserts that it is the man of good will and idealistic fervor who brings bloodshed and grief into the world: "Rousseau killed a lot of people with optimism which resulted in the French Revolution. ... When you know history, how many tragedies have been touched off by good will, you have to admit the tragic elements of existence."[12] Similarly, Kissinger rails against those anti-war Americans who demonstrated their disapproval of the U.S. invasion of Cambodia in 1970 (Hunebelle, 1972, p. 174): ". . . those short-sighted professors, partisans and ideologists, incapable of maturity or objectivity in reaching judgment."[13] In contrast, Kissinger believes that the man alive to the evil aspiration of others and prepared to do whatever is necessary to thwart them is likely to exert a beneficial force in world history.[14] The war-maker becomes the only reliable peace-maker. Hence, for Kissinger it is probably a glorious confirmation of this basic belief that he could serve as the model for Dr. Strangelove in Stanley Kubrick's film and yet be the recipient of a Nobel Peace Prize a decade or so later.

Kissinger believes that Americans exhibit a peculiar susceptibility to the flow of optimism that it is his special vocation to be on guard against. As he puts it (1961, p. 1), "Nothing is more difficult for Americans to understand than the possibility of tragedy. And yet nothing should concern us more." Before entering the government Kissinger was concerned about the tragedy of general nuclear war. He believed that this tragedy was more likely to take place if Americans did not anticipate it as a plausible prospect. By preparing for nuclear holocaust, it was necessary to be strong and to manifest a readiness to fight with nuclear weapons in quite destructive limited wars.[15] In essence, it was necessary above all else to avoid any impression of appeasement whenever revolutionary conditions existed in international life; if such conditions should disappear, then an international atmosphere of "reasonableness"—the bargaining of differences—could become possible.[16]

A final element in Kissinger's approach is to plan for the future (Hunebelle, 1972, p. 26): ". . . I admire people who don't try to monkey around with the present, but see further than that and do all they can to set up the future." Such a futurist perspective should be understood in relation to Kissinger's preoccupation with international stability. Kissinger thinks that threats to stability can be dealt with

less destructively if they are identified and countered as early as possible. To achieve a *stable* world order for Kissinger requires that great powers feel content with their status, that leaders avoid ideological fervor or grand designs, and that dominant states and alliances stay strong and militant enough to avoid any revolutionary temptation on the part of those who are dissatisfied.[17] He is therefore sensitive to "the lesson of Versailles" as well as to "the lesson of Munich," namely, that the purpose of force is to remove the revolutionary element in world society, but not to humiliate or dismember a major constituent state. To impose excessive burdens on a defeated country, as was done to Germany at Versailles after World War I, is to plant a revolutionary seed in the soil of the defeated enemy. The defeated society harbors resentment against the international *status quo,* and becomes more receptive to an extremist leader like Hitler who promises to regain the nation's rightful place in the world system. Again, Kissinger should be seen as rather single-minded. The role of war as an instrument of non-revolutionary diplomacy (i.e., by *status quo* or dominant states) is *exclusively* counter-revolutionary. It has few ulterior ends, whether moral or geopolitical.

There is an important confusion embedded in Kissinger's academic writing. This confusion derived mainly from Kissinger's intermingling of neutral analysis of the conditions of international stability with policy analysis of the conditions of U.S. geopolitical primacy. As a consequence of this intermingling, we get no clear analysis of why Kissinger is mainly preoccupied with exposing the destabilizing effects of radical politics whereas his theoretical and historical expositions, for instance in relation to Bismarck, make no distinction, as we noted, between the revolutionaries of the left and of the right. At the same time, Kissinger is no mere geopolitical maximalist as he is sensitive to the dangers of overreaching by the U.S. and he believes that geopolitical rationality generally conforms with the requirements for international stability. My point is that Kissinger has never clearly resolved the relationship between a national interest (or foreign policy) perspective and a world order perspective.

There is one other point of qualification. Kissinger's career as a public servant seems more responsive to considerations of diplomatic climate than his academic writing would lead one to suspect. In part, this may reflect a concession to the Nixon presidency with its overall obsession with public relations. But I suspect it more directly reflects Kissinger's appreciation of the extent to which bargaining possibilities in diplomacy are increased by an atmosphere of "good feelings." Of course, this side of Kissinger's public image is quite at odds with the apparent message of his earlier writing to the effect that raising public hopes about friendly relations with geopolitical rivals tends to undermine the morale, and hence, the security of a liberal democracy like the U.S. And it is precisely on this kind of point that Senator Henry Jackson has led a domestic counter-attack against the détente diplomacy of Nixon-Kissinger.

THE MIRACLE OF HENRY KISSINGER

Why is Kissinger so effective and celebrated as a statesman? What has made him the most dramatic diplomat on the contemporary scene? Why, especially, has he been so successful and admired at a time when the world prestige of the U.S. is at a low ebb?

The American columnist, James Res-

ton, has written of "the miracle of Henry Kissinger" implying that his success defies any rational explanation. In a later section we shall challenge the view that Kissinger's overall impact has been benign, much less miraculous, but here my interest is in giving an account of his undeniable potency as a statesman.

The first point to note is that there is nothing distinctive about his version of world affairs. He understands and accepts the logic of the state and in this sense, despite his protestations, belongs to the Machiavellian tradition of statesmen.

He accepts balance of power mechanisms and political pluralism, and is willing to use force if necessary, and diplomacy if possible, to settle international conflicts. This orientation hardly differs from that held by many other diplomats on the world scene, including such prominent Americans as John Foster Dulles, Dean Acheson, Jr. and Dean Rusk who were active during the period when the U.S. had more leverage to exert in international relations than it has had during the Kissinger years. It seems clear, then, that Kissinger's influence cannot be understood by reference to some new set of ideas about either the means or goals of foreign policy.

Coherence

Although Kissinger reflects conventional wisdom on the conduct of foreign relations, he has a deeper penetration of its nuances and characteristics than other major diplomats. In that sense his orientation is reassuring to others, and yet its greater coherence lends to its exposition a quality of authoritativeness. Kissinger's background of study and reflection adds a dimension of personal assurance, as well as historical depth and precision, to his perception of diplomatic possibilities. In this regard, his stature as a former Harvard professor has been consciously underlined by references to him as "Dr. Kissinger." This kind of professional claim has not been asserted by other academics in the American government, e.g., Schlesinger, Galbraith and Rostow, all of whom tried to play down the egghead connotations of their intellectual background as much as possible.

Whereas an academic background has been usually a liability in the upper echelons of American government and has been particularly scorned during the Nixon presidency, Kissinger turned it into an asset. First of all, his academic qualifications seemed to contribute directly to the discharge of his governmental responsibilities; the claims of expert status made on his behalf had an unusual degree of plausibility. Secondly, Kissinger's approach was not at all threatening to the main power brokers in the Pentagon or elsewhere in Washington. His advocacy of a strong defense posture had been a consistent ingredient of his policy advocacy through the years. Thirdly, he brought to his job none of those threatening forms of morality or idealism that Washington professionals associate with liberal academicians. On the contrary, he tended to indicate in an effective way their own amoral approach to geopolitics. Furthermore, his dislike of ambiguity or uncertainty, as well as the focus on revolutionary danger, made him temperamentally akin to the military and business mentality that has been so prominent in U.S. government circles during the Nixon years.[18]

The main point is that Kissinger has a coherent view of the state system which allows politicians and policy-makers to pursue their interests without fear of moral encumbrance or judgment. It would not occur to anyone to accuse Kissinger of false sentimentality. He has demonstrated a stomach for power, whether it entails the mindless bombing of Indochinese peasants or wiretapping his own personnel.

Kissinger's flexible view of the state system presents a more positive side of his diplomatic role. Although his approach to international relations resembles that of his predecessors, it is less ideological in two respects. First, he has been more willing to regard the Cold War as a *phase* rather than a *condition* in international affairs. Kissinger's historical studies seem relevant to this posture. Metternich understood that the objective of diplomacy was to neutralize a revolutionary challenge with as little dislocation as possible, and not to mount an ideological counter-offensive aimed at disabling the revolutionary state. By this reasoning, it would be far more preferable to induce the Soviet Union to exchange revolutionary policies for beneficial participation in the world economic and political *status quo,* than to endure a persisting confrontation among nuclear superpowers. Secondly, Kissinger's indifference to domestic conditions in foreign societies makes him able to forego judgments about the inequities or indecencies of other national systems, as long as repressive governments renounce their revolutionary stance. In this sense, Kissinger is able to bargain without ambivalence with governmental leaders from any part of the world. Since many powerful governments do have skeletons in their closets, they welcome this non-judgmental appreciation of the limits of diplomacy in the state system. Part of Kissinger's international success, therefore, arises from this very unconcern with human rights, and from the extent to which this unconcern is a shared premise of mainstream statecraft.

Timing

Given his views, Kissinger arrived on the diplomatic scene at a very opportune moment. The Sino-Soviet split, U.S. weariness with Vietnam, common dangers from an unchecked arms race, and the growing difficulties of the world economy created unusual opportunities for diplomatic maneuver. Kissinger prudently took advantage of this situation to generate a new political climate of great power relations. The Cold War mentality no longer seemed plausible to many Americans, and its ideological overtones were not accepted by Kissinger. Leaders in China and the Soviet Union, preoccupied with domestic problems and with one another, were much more concerned with moderating their relations with the U.S. than with pursuing revolutionary goals by continuing the tactics and rhetoric of confrontation. A few years earlier, neither American nor Western public opinion would have been ready, nor would leaders in Peking or Moscow have likely been so responsive. In the earlier world setting Kissinger probably could not have succeeded, and might not even have tried, to moderate great power conflict. Therefore the *timing* of his access to power was perfectly adapted to the search for new modes of international stability in a phase of great power relations of diminished ideological and revolutionary intensity.

Credibility

Kissinger has been a credible diplomat. He is backed up by a President who shares his essential interpretation of the world scene and who seemed able, until Watergate, to generate bipartisan public enthusiasm for his international policies. Nixon had such impeccable Cold War credentials that his Chinese and Soviet overtures could be undertaken without fear of provoking substantial accusations of being soft on communism.

Kissinger was similarly reassuring. He is one of the few prominent American intellectuals with a long period of identification with the Republican Party. For several years he had worked closely with Nelson Rockefeller, known even in his former period of relative domestic liberalism, for his hawkish views on national security and the Cold War. Kissinger's earlier intellectual mentors were also ultra-conservative.[19] More significantly, Kissinger credibly presented himself as a man virtually free from human compassion—the quality that so often antagonizes conservatives in the U.S. either because they regard such sentiments as hypocritical or because they fear that they are not. Kissinger's role is compatible with the dominant neo-Darwinian ethos that is the inversion of the ethics of empathy characteristic of the world's great religious and humanistic traditions. As for the liberals, they found Kissinger's geopolitical initiatives so constructive that they were even almost willing to go along with Nixon on "peace with honor" in Vietnam. As a consequence, the main thrust of the Kissinger diplomacy gained domestic credibility across a wide political spectrum; this base of bipartisan domestic support greatly strengthened Kissinger's international bargaining power. The Kissinger-Nixon initiatives were unlikely to be rebuffed by Congress or a hostile public opinion, or even to be repudiated by subsequent elections.

Edgar Snow noted long before Nixon that Chinese leaders indicated a preference for dealing with a conservative American administration, feeling that any understandings reached would be more durable than if made with a liberal American government that was negotiating ahead of its domestic public opinion. The solidity of Kissinger's domestic position undoubtedly strengthened his credibility as he approached leaders in foreign capitals. I believe, also, that Kissinger's Machiavellian posture has been a welcome relief to many foreign statesmen who had developed a distaste for and suspicion of the self-righteous pretensions of U.S. diplomacy since the time of Woodrow Wilson. Kissinger, at least, was playing "the game of nations" as it is and should be played—that is, to maximize the player's advantage. Such a style encouraged focus on specific negotiating bargains that could be achieved in various international settings; less rhetoric, more results. As the time was ripe for bargaining toward détente the results appeared spectacular. In other settings where the contours of bargains are not yet apparent, as in Euro-U.S. or Japan-U.S. relations, the results have been less promising. The impact of Kissinger's diplomacy on the Middle East is not yet clear, although Kissinger's energy and skill have been well deployed as a designer of reasonable bargains, that is, of conceiving and proposing settlement terms which neither party can reasonably turn down. To the extent that governments want a settlement, then, such an intermediary role is invaluable, as it liberates the antagonists from ideological entrapment.

Kissinger is effective wherever the game of nations can be pursued without ideological or moral imperatives. It is ineffectual elsewhere, as for instance in relation to overcoming any of the more extreme patterns of injustice in the Third World areas, or even in parts of the international system where the heavy hand of U.S. influence is strong. It is not only that Kissinger is silent about the abuses, but that he evidently supports the covert and indirect moves of U.S. diplomacy used to maintain or create such injustices. This observation may appear to slip over into an appraisal, but it is not yet so intended. My point here is that Kissinger's effectiveness arises from his capacity to deal with foreign governments without making any unpleasant representations about their domestic indecencies. One can almost visualize Kissinger justifying embarrassed representations to the Soviets on Jewish emigration policy not by the human rights at stake, but because Congress would interfere with the Administration's efforts to achieve trade liberalization. Statesmen can accept this language of gains and losses without feeling threatened.

Conclusion

It would be a mistake to assume that Kissinger has been an opportunist. Indeed, I accept his own protestation (Hunebelle, 1972, p. 27): "I'm intelligent, true; but that's no source of pride to me. But I am proud of having character." Kissinger has never wavered. He was uncomfortable with liberal administrations in Washington, and held back from identifying himself with their efforts. He believes there is no place for morality in foreign policy, beyond the overarching morality of securing as much stability as the system will really permit at a given time. His genius, if this is the term, lies in his deep understanding of what is possible and in his ability to ground that understanding on a strong domestic political base. Furthermore, foreign statesmen who grasp Kissinger's view of things can enter the game fairly confident of what it is they are bargaining toward. There are no illusions, hence few disappointments.

Perhaps the North Vietnamese were somewhat deceived by Kissinger's negotiating posture, but it is more likely that they expected the U.S. not to implement the Paris Agreement of 1973.[20] In that setting, Kissinger probably had the narrow task of negotiating the return of American POW's in exchange for an end to a direct U.S. military role. Although the Agreement promised much more by way of converting a military struggle into political competition between the Provisional Revolutionary Government of South Vietnam and the Saigon Administration, this promise was clearly dependent on either Saigon's good faith (for which there was no hope) or Washington's willingness to pressure Saigon into compliance (for which there was virtually no hope). Therefore, in his most celebrated negotiations for which he was awarded the Nobel Peace Prize, Kissinger probably did not purport to do much more than was achieved—that is, achieve, a provisional narrowing of the military struggle.[21] To call such an outcome "peace" is of course grotesque, given the high casualty rates since the settlement came into effect at the end of January 1973. That the Nobel Committee should celebrate such an illusion provides a revealing insight into the low state of contemporary statecraft.

But was the Paris Agreement an illusion when it comes even to the issue of peace? Yes, if you count Indochinese corpses, or if you count American corpses; no, if you consider "peace" to involve only relations among great powers. Kissinger succeeded in removing the obstacles to détente posed by the continuing U.S. combat involvement in the Indochina War. The so-called "structure of peace" involves moderating great power relations so as to reduce the danger of general warfare by cutting tensions and slowing down the arms race. It does not promise to eliminate violence from international relations, and especially not

from those marginal sectors (i.e., the entire Third World) in which exploitation and mass misery are the norms of existence.

WHAT'S WRONG WITH HENRY KISSINGER?

As indicated at the outset, Kissinger embodies, in exemplary form, the strengths and weaknesses of the existing international system. Those who approve of the system, or think that it defines the realistic outer limits of what can be achieved, tend to applaud Kissinger's role and accomplishments. Those who believe the system is deeply tainted by injustice and imperialism or by an avoidable escalation to self-destruction powered by the war machine and its technological and ecological accompaniments tend to view Kissinger either as a dangerous throwback to nineteenth-century diplomacy or as an evil genius who is inflicting such brain damage on the collective wisdom of the human race that people increasingly believe war is peace and injustice is justice. In the middle are those of liberal persuasion who believe that a moderate balance of power is the best we can hope for in international relations, but believe it is possible, desirable, perhaps even necessary, to display a bit more concern than Kissinger shows for small power politics and for the impoverished billions in the third world. Such a position tends to praise Kissinger for seeking to end the Cold War and resolve the dangerous inter-governmental conflict in the Middle East, but criticizes his do-nothing posture on Third World issues.

The remark attributed by Márquez (1974, p. 46) to Kissinger, "I am not interested in, nor do I know anything about, the southern portion of the world from the Pyrenees on down," may not have been actually said, but it undoubtedly expresses the Kissinger outlook. As far as I know, Kissinger has given virtually no thought to the world food crisis that, according to the latest UNICEF figures, threatens as many as 500,000,000 children of Africa and Asia with famine, disease, and deformation. Kissinger is not alone among world leaders in passing over such a massive human tragedy, but he is part of a conspiracy of silence that is directed by the rich and powerful with regard to the deprivations of the poor. It is inconceivable that afflictions of this magnitude in the northern hemisphere would not be perceived as a catastrophe of historic significance. Kissinger cannot be held accountable for this discrepancy, which is more properly attributable to the hegemonic dimension of the state system, but his behavior does provide important evidence for our appraisal of the system's adequacy to meet human needs. Kissinger's outlook presupposes that it is possible to manage international relations mainly by moderating conflictual relations among governments in the northern hemisphere.[22] This conviction is the underlying conceptual flaw in Kissinger's approach to global reform. Kissinger's strategies for accommodating revolutionary challengers and stabilizing great power relations in moderate phases presuppose the continuity of the state system that has dominated international society since the Peace of Westphalia in 1648. However, in my view, international society can learn a far more relevant lesson from the *pre-Westphalia* context, because it was a period in which the system itself was undergoing a fundamental transition from *non-territorial central guidance* of Medieval Europe to the *territorial central guidance* of post-Westphalia Europe.[23] This regional system became the nucleus of the world system because cultural, eco-

nomic and political forms of imperialism eventually gave it a global outreach. At the present stage of world history, as a result of increasing *interdependence* and a rediscovery of resource scarcity and limits to growth, we are beginning to experience the early stages of a new transition process that is moving the world political system toward some form of non-territorial central guidance.[24] What matters now is which actors will control this process of transition for what ends, with what effects. Will it be the multinational corporation operating a global market? Will it be a coalition of powerful governments? Will it be an alliance of governmental and corporate actors? Will poor countries succeed in creating significant centers of power capable of sharing in the central guidance process? Will it become possible to organize a transnational populist movement seeking to orient central guidance processes around humanistic world order values?

Kissinger is participating in this transition process by apparently seeking to establish a cooperative directorate among great powers. Such a vision of the future is short-sighted in the sense that it won't work at all, or at least not for long. It is also stultifying so far as human potentialities are concerned. It accepts as inevitable the persistence of large-scale misery and repression. It enables the disfavored many to be kept under control by the favored few. The global structure of control that Kissinger envisages and endorses tempts change-minded groups to adopt some variant of "desperate politics" to achieve their goals of liberation from social, political and economic oppression.

Any conception of international relations that is confined to actions among principal governments is profoundly deficient. It is insensitive to the historical forces that are enlivening human awareness of inequities and that are shifting the locus of authority toward a non-territorial center. It is the choice of options surrounding the shape and orientation of that center that is the major global issue of the day. Kissinger's approach solidifies the position of neo-Darwinian ethics—the rich and strong are entitled to prevail because they are the most fit—and is likely to be embodied in a scheme by which the great power governments forge a working alliance with the major multinational corporations. For those of us who fear or oppose such a new world order, the imprint of Kissingerian diplomacy is an apt occasion for alarm. At the same time we can acknowledge the importance in the nuclear age of his major premise if it could be relegated to the position of minor premise in an adequate movement for global reform, i.e., it is desirable to moderate conflict among great powers while a process of transition (the major premise) is shaping the world order system to foster peace, equity, dignity and ecological balance for the world *as a whole*. Without an ethics of global concern, the attempt to merely smooth out relations among great powers is a recipe for disaster.

POSTSCRIPT

Since this article was written a number of developments have strengthened its central contention that Secretary Kissinger's status as miracle worker was ill-deserved and precarious. First of all, Kissinger has been held widely responsible for the Cyprus debacle, both by underreacting to the anti-Makarios coup and, then, by appearing to acquiesce in the Turkish invasion and seizure of Cypriot territory. Second, and most notably, testimony by William Colby, Director of the CIA, revealed that the U.S. had for several years spent large sums of money to interfere with Allende's governance of Chile. The expenditures had been authorized by the 40 Committee presided over by Kissinger, a role that flatly contradicted such sworn reassurances to Congress and the public as the following assertion before the Senate Foreign Relations Committe just weeks earlier: "The CIA had nothing to do with the coup, to the best of my knowledge and belief, and I only put in that qualification in case some madman appears down there who without instruction talked to somebody. I have absolutely no reason to suppose it."

It is hardly integrity becoming a public servant to defend the quoted statement by claiming that efforts to destabilize Allende's political control were completely separate from the tragic sequel of bloody coup and brutal repression. And, finally, *Kissinger,* the widely respected study of Kissinger's role by the Kalb brothers, has demonstrated in great detail that it was Nixon rather than Kissinger who deserves most of the credit for seeking détente with the USSR and normalization of Sino-American relations.

NOTES

1. At the same time, there is a widespread uneasiness generated by Kissinger's role. As Kristol (1974) notes, Kissinger "is a much admired and much distrusted Secretary of State. . . . The anxiety as to the meaning of Kissinger pervades the entire political spectrum—right, left, and center." Kristol believes that "this widespread apprehension" arises because there is a "dim but nagging recognition that he has a new conception of American foreign policy." Nevertheless, I think that for the present the admiration clearly overshadows the uneasiness.

2. This criticism is directed mainly at the rich and powerful states of the most industrialized sector of world society. Such other large and important states as China and India have pursued a more progressive course in foreign policy on global issues, partly because they have a natural basis for solidarity with the poor and weak, and seek a more equitable distribution of wealth and income in the world.
3. In effect, it is not enough to restore "balance" to the relations among principal states; this traditional search by prudent statesmen assumed the sufficiency of decentralized control over the main life and wealth processes of planetary existence. My argument is that objective conditions are producing circumstances of global integration and interdependence that require some mode of central guidance [see Falk (1971, 1975)].
4. The best comprehensive treatment of Kissinger's *pre-government* thinking is by a friend and academic colleague; see Graubard (1973).
5. For a more intellectual formulation in which Kissinger displays his awareness that the problems for the statesman of today are dramatically different from those confronting Metternich, see Kissinger (1969, p. 57).
6. On "dynamism of the Soviet system" in relation to its revolutionary objectives, see Kissinger (1958, pp. 47-48).
7. "From Lenin, to Stalin, to Mao, and to the current Soviet leadership, the insistence on superior historical understanding, on endless and inevitable conflict with non-Soviet states, on ultimate victory, has been unvarying." (Kissinger, 1958, pp. 50-51; see generally pp. 44-80.)
8. In the 1968 essay Kissinger writes (1969, p. 89): "The obsession with Soviet intentions causes the West to be smug during periods of détente and panicky during crises. ... The West is thus never ready for a Soviet change of course; it has been equally unprepared for détente and intransigence." Since his career as policymaker Kissinger has sought to be steadfast in both pursuing lines of convergent interest (i.e., readiness for détente) and sustaining a firm defense posture (e.g., the willingness during the October 1973 crisis in the Middle East to put U.S. nuclear forces on a global alert so as to dissuade the Soviet Union from sending troops to Egypt to implement the UN cease-fire).
9. See Kissinger (1970), especially p. 317 where he quotes approvingly the German liberal Bamberger who wrote with Bismarck in mind, "People are born revolutionaries. ... The accident of life decides whether one becomes a Red or a White revolutionary."
10. Recalling Kissinger's quest for stability, he seems only to regard domestic political orientation as a factor if it embodies a missionary ideology. Of course, it is not quite so simple, because Kissinger perceives the requirements of stability primarily from the U.S. outlook. Thus an anti-U.S.-Latin American dictatorship of the left is perceived as an "adverse" development whereas an anti-communist dictatorship is not.
11. This kind of analysis is perceptively presented in Ajami (1975).
12. Attributed to Kissinger in a rather illuminating account by a French T.V. journalist of her infatuations and impressions (Hunebelle, 1972, p. 24).
13. In contrast, when asked about the military, Kissinger responded "Oh me, I'm an agnostic where the military is concerned. ... I'm neither for nor against on that score ..." (Hunebelle, 1972, p. 16).
14. Over and over again Kissinger refers to the paradoxical relationship between the quest and the attainment of a peaceful world order. One characteristic formulation is in the Introduction to *A World Restored* (Kissinger, 1954): "But the attainment of peace is not as easy as the desire for it. Not for nothing is history associated with the figure of Nemesis, which defeats man by fulfilling his wishes in a different form or by answering his prayers too completely. Those ages which in retrospect seem most peaceful were least

in search of peace." Kissinger starts *Nuclear Weapons and Foreign Policy* on the same note (1958, p. 1): "In Greek mythology the gods sometimes punished man by fulfilling his wishes too completely. It has remained for the nuclear age to experience the full irony of this penalty." See also the same idea in Kissinger's Bismarck essay (1970, p. 319).

15. Such a posture attracts establishment support as it reconciles the rhetoric of decency and peace-mindedness with the necessity for high rates of defense spending and an aggressive foreign policy.

16. But by characterizing the age as "revolutionary," the importance of military strength and wariness are stressed as constant ingredients of a rational foreign policy.

17. Two assertions by Kissinger further illuminate his view on the conduct of foreign relations. In his Bismarck essay (Kissinger, 1970, p. 348) he writes: "The bane of stable societies or of stable international systems is the inability to conceive of a mortal challenge." In other words, stability collapses when its architects grow too self-assured. In his general appraisal of the world scene in 1968, Kissinger (1969, p. 97) writes: " . . . we will never be able to contribute to building a stable and creative world order unless we first form some conception of it." Kissinger opposes the *ad hoc,* anti-doctrinal, anti-conceptual cast of mind that has so often dominated U.S. policy-making in world affairs. He favors general interpretations that are realistic and establish a basis for coherent behavior across a series of contexts and through a period of time.

18. According to Hunebelle, Kissinger actually regarded Nixon as a personal confidant during his early years at the White House. Kissinger is quoted (Hunebelle, 1972, p. 43) as saying that it is "too dangerous" to keep a personal diary: "Suppose I died or got robbed. . . . Even so, when you're permanently under pressure and in control of yourself, you really feel like opening up sometimes. So, at night, I often go up and chat with the President." Little did Kissinger realize that while he was "opening up" Nixon was evidently taping their conversations!

19. Kissinger attended Harvard at the suggestion of Fritz Kraemer, a Pentagon official, whom Kissinger describes as more conservative than himself. (See Hunebelle, 1972, p. 46.) At Harvard he worked mainly with William Y. Elliott, the most conservative member of the Government Department, to whom Kissinger dedicated his first book, *A World Restored.*

20. For a revealing account of the Paris negotiations that details Kissinger's role in misleading North Vietnam (and others), see the article by Szulc (1974).

21. As Anthony Lewis puts it, on the basis of the evidence contained in the Szulc (1974) article " . . . the record is clear that the United States backed off an agreement, then bombed the other party to mollify a recalcitrant ally. Whatever other diplomatic accomplishments history credits to Henry Kissinger and Richard Nixon, that episode will forever blacken their names, and their country's."

22. Such indifference to Third World needs and aspirations is accentuated, not alleviated, by Kissinger's new effort at idealistic rhetoric of compassion and concern. His statements, part of the role of an U.S. Secretary of State, create confusion because the right phrases are used but no behavioral consequences seem to follow. Nothing illustrates this pattern better than Kissinger's effort to foster good relations with Latin America based on what he calls "a new process of collaboration and inspired by a new attitude—the spirit of Tlatelolco." (Address before General Assembly, Organization of American States, 20 April, 1974.)

23. I have developed this analysis in some detail in a series of lectures delivered at Yale Law School in March 1974, a mimeographed copy of which is available upon request. The reference to "territorial" and "non-territorial" models of world order

has to do with the connections between *authority, control and physical space.* The Catholic Church, the Holy Roman Emperor, the World Communist Party, the multinational corporation, the organs of the UN are all examples of non-territorial actors whose orbit of authority is not based upon jurisdiction over events in space, whereas the sovereign state or its political subdivisions enjoy degrees of authority and control that are operative within boundaries fixed in space.

24. See Camps (1974). For a more normative and political response to the challenge of interdependence, see the principal manuscripts published under the auspices of the World Order Models Project and the volume of essays from the Project (Mendlovitz and Baldwin, 1975).

REFERENCES

Ajami, F. (1975). The global populists: third-world nations and world-order. *Alternatives,* 1; Princeton University, Center of International Studies, Research Monograph, No. 41, May (1974).

Camps, M. (1974). *The Management of Interdependence: A Preliminary View.* Council on Foreign Relations: New York.

Falk, R. A. (1971). *This Endangered Planet: Prospects and Proposals for Human Survival.* Random House: New York.

Falk, R. A. (1975). *A Study of Future Worlds.* Free Press: New York.

Fallaci, O. (1972). Kissinger. *New Republic,* 16 Dec., 21.

Graubard, S. (1973). *Kissinger: Portrait of a Mind.* Norton: New York.

Hunebelle, D. (1972). *Dear Henry.* Berkeley: New York.

Kissinger, H. (1954). *A World Restored: Europe after Napoleon.* Grosset and Dunlap: New York.

Kissinger, H. (1958). *Nuclear Weapons and Foreign Policy.* Doubleday Anchor: Garden City, N.Y.

Kissinger, H. (1961). *The Necessity for Choice: Prospects of American Foreign Policy.* Harper: New York.

Kissinger, H. (1968). Central issues of American foreign policy. In: Gordon, K. (Ed.) *Agenda for the Nation.* Washington, D.C.

Kissinger, H. (1969). *American Foreign Policy.* Norton: New York.

Kissinger, H. (1970). The white revolutionary: reflections on Bismarck. In: Rustow, D. A. (Ed.) *Philosophers and Kings: Studies in Leadership.* Braziller: New York, 317-353.

Kristol, I. (1974). The meaning of Kissinger. *Wall Street Journal,* 11 Apr. 12.

Lermontov, M. (1958). *A Hero of Our Time.* Doubleday Anchor: Garden City, N.Y. (Nabokov translation). 1.

Márquez, G. G. (1974). The death of Salvador Allende. *Harper's Magazine,* May, 46-53.

Mendlovitz, S. H. and Baldwin, J. (Jr.) (Eds.) (1975). *On Creating a Just and Peaceful World Order.* Free Press: New York.

Szulc, T. (1974). Behind the Vietnam cease-fire agreement. *Foreign Policy,* 15, 21-69.

12. COMMENCEMENT ADDRESS AT THE UNIVERSITY OF NOTRE DAME

Jimmy Carter

Thank you very much. To Father Hesburgh and the great faculty of Notre Dame, to those who have been honored this afternoon with the degree from your great university, to the graduate and undergraduate group who I understand is the largest in the history of this great institution, friends and parents:

Thank you for that welcome. I'm very glad to be with you. You may have started a new graduation trend which I don't deplore; that is, throwing peanuts on graduation day. [*Laughter*] The more that are used or consumed, the higher the price goes. [*Laughter*]

I really did appreciate the great honor bestowed upon me this afternoon. My other degree is blue and gold from the Navy, and I want to let you know that I do feel a kinship with those who are assembled here this afternoon. I was a little taken aback by the comment that I had brought a new accent to the White House. In the minds of many people in our country, for the first time in almost 150 years, there is no accent. [*Laughter*]

I tried to think of a story that would illustrate two points simultaneously and also be brief, which is kind of a difficult assignment. I was sitting on the Truman Balcony the other night with my good friend, Charles Kirbo, who told me about a man who was arrested and taken in to court for being drunk and for setting a bed on fire. When the judge asked him

how he pleaded, he said, "not guilty." He said, "I was drunk but the bed was on fire when I got in it." [*Laughter*]

I think most of the graduates can draw the parallel between that statement and what you are approaching after this graduation exercise. But there are two points to that, and I'll come to the other one in just a few minutes.

In his 25 years as president of Notre Dame, Father Hesburgh has spoken more consistently and more effectively in the support of the rights of human beings than any other person I know. His interest in the Notre Dame Center for Civil Rights has never wavered. And he played an important role in broadening the scope of the center's work—and I visited there last fall—to see this work include, now, all people in the world, as shown by last month's conference here on human rights and American foreign policy.

And that concern has been demonstrated again today in a vivid fashion by the selection of Bishop Donal Lamont, Paul Cardinal Arns, and Stephen Cardinal Kim, to receive honorary degrees. In their fight for human freedoms in Rhodesia, Brazil, and South Korea, these three religious leaders typify all that is best in their countries and in our church. I'm honored to join you in recognizing their dedication, their personal sacrifice, and their supreme courage.

Quite often, brave men like these are castigated and sometimes punished, sometimes even put to death, because they enter the realm where human rights is a

Source: *Weekly Compilation of Presidential Documents* 13, no. 22 (May 30, 1977), pp. 773–79.

struggle. And sometimes, they are blamed for the very circumstance which they helped to dramatize, but it's been there for a long time. And the flames which they seek to extinguish concern us all and are increasingly visible around the world.

Last week, I spoke in California about the domestic agenda for our Nation: to provide more efficiently for the needs of our people, to demonstrate—against the dark faith of our times—that our Government can be both competent and more humane.

But I want to speak to you today about the strands that connect our actions overseas with our essential character as a nation. I believe we can have a foreign policy that is democratic, that is based on fundamental values, and that uses power and influence, which we have, for humane purposes. We can also have a foreign policy that the American people both support and, for a change, know about and understand.

I have a quiet confidence in our own political system. Because we know that democracy works, we can reject the arguments of those rulers who deny human rights to their people.

We are confident that democracy's example will be compelling, and so we seek to bring that example closer to those from whom in the past few years we have been separated and who are not yet convinced about the advantages of our kind of life.

We are confident that democratic methods are the most effective, and so we are not tempted to employ improper tactics here at home or abroad.

We are confident of our own strength, so we can seek substantial mutual reductions in the nuclear arms race.

And we are confident of the good sense of American people, and so we let them share in the process of making foreign policy decisions. We can thus speak with the voices of 215 million, and not just of an isolated handful.

Democracy's great recent successes—in India, Portugal, Spain, Greece—show that our confidence in this system is not misplaced. Being confident of our own future, we are now free of that inordinate fear of communism which once led us to embrace any dictator who joined us in that fear. I'm glad that that's being changed.

For too many years, we've been willing to adopt the flawed and erroneous principles and tactics of our adversaries, sometimes abandoning our own values for theirs. We've fought fire with fire, never thinking that fire is better quenched with water. This approach failed, with Vietnam the best example of its intellectual and moral poverty. But through failure, we have now found our way back to our own principles and values, and we have regained our lost confidence.

By the measure of history, our Nation's 200 years are very brief, and our rise to world eminence is briefer still. It dates from 1945 when Europe and the old international order lay in ruins. Before then America was largely on the periphery of world affairs, but since then we have inescapably been at the center of world affairs.

Our policy during this period was guided by two principles: a belief that Soviet expansion was almost inevitable but that it must be contained, and the corresponding belief in the importance of an almost exclusive alliance among non-Communist nations on both sides of the Atlantic. That system could not last forever unchanged. Historical trends have weakened its foundation. The unifying threat of conflict with the Soviet Union has become less intensive even though the competition has become more extensive

The Vietnamese war produced a profound moral crisis sapping worldwide faith in our own policy and our system of life, a crisis of confidence made even more grave by the covert pessimism of some of our leaders.

In less than a generation, we've seen the world change dramatically. The daily lives and aspirations of most human beings have been transformed. Colonialism is nearly gone. A new sense of national identity now exists in almost 100 new countries that have been formed in the last generation. Knowledge has become more widespread; aspirations are higher. As more people have been freed from traditional constraints, more have been determined to achieve for the first time in their lives social justice.

The world is still divided by ideological disputes, dominated by regional conflicts, and threatened by danger that we will not resolve the differences of race and wealth without violence or without drawing into combat the major military powers. We can no longer separate the traditional issues of war and peace from the new global questions of justice, equity, and human rights.

It is a new world—but America should not fear it. It is a new world—and we should help to shape it. It is a new world that calls for a new American foreign policy—a policy based on constant decency in its values and on optimism in our historical vision.

We can no longer have a policy solely for the industrial nations as the foundation of global stability, but we must respond to the new reality of a politically awakening world.

We can no longer expect that the other 150 nations will follow the dictates of the powerful, but we must continue—confidently—our efforts to inspire, to persuade, and to lead.

Our policy must reflect our belief that the world can hope for more than simple survival and our belief that dignity and freedom are fundamental spiritual requirements. Our policy must shape an international system that will last longer than secret deals.

We cannot make this kind of policy by manipulation. Our policy must be open; it must be candid; it must be one of constructive global involvement, resting on five cardinal principles.

I've tried to make these premises clear to the American people since last January. Let me review what we have been doing and discuss what we intend to do.

First, we have reaffirmed America's commitment to human rights as a fundamental tenet of our foreign policy. In ancestry, religion, color, place of origin, and cultural background, we Americans are as diverse a nation as the world has ever seen. No common mystique of blood or soil unites us. What draws us together, perhaps more than anything else, is a belief in human freedom.

We want the world to know that our Nation stands for more than financial prosperity. This does not mean that we can conduct our foreign policy by rigid moral maxims. We live in a world that is imperfect and which will always be imperfect—a world that is complex and confused and which will always be complex and confused.

I understand fully the limits of moral suasion. We have no illusion that changes will come easily or soon. But I also believe that it is a mistake to undervalue the power of words and of the ideas that words embody. In our own history, that power has ranged from Thomas Paine's *Common Sense* to Martin Luther King, Jr.'s "I Have a Dream."

In the life of the human spirit, words are action, much more so than many of us may realize who live in countries where freedom of expression is taken for granted. The leaders of totalitarian nations understand this very well. The proof is that words are precisely the action for which dissidents in those countries are being persecuted.

Nonetheless, we can already see dramatic, worldwide advances in the protection of the individual from the arbitrary power of the state. For us to ignore this trend would be to lose influence and moral authority in the world. To lead it will be to regain the moral stature that we once had.

The great democracies are not free because we are strong and prosperous. I believe we are strong and influential and prosperous because we are free.

Throughout the world today, in free nations and in totalitarian countries as well, there is a preoccupation with the subject of human freedom, human rights. And I believe it is incumbent on us in this country to keep that discussion, that debate, that contention alive. No other country is as well-qualified as we to set an example. We have our own shortcomings and faults, and we should strive constantly and with courage to make sure that we are legitimately proud of what we have.

Second, we've moved deliberately to reinforce the bonds among our democracies. In our recent meetings in London, we agreed to widen our economic cooperation, to promote free trade, to strengthen the world's monetary system, to seek ways of avoiding nuclear proliferation. We prepared constructive proposals for the forthcoming meetings on North-South problems of poverty, development, and global well-being, and we agreed on joint efforts to reinforce and to modernize our common defense.

You may be interested in knowing that at this NATO meeting, for the first time in more than 25 years, all members are democracies. Even more important, all of us reaffirmed our basic optimism in the future of the democratic system. Our spirit of confidence is spreading. Together, our democracies can help to shape the wider architecture of global cooperation.

Third, we've moved to engage the Soviet Union in a joint effort to halt the strategic arms race. This race is not only dangerous, it's morally deplorable. We must put an end to it.

I know it will not be easy to reach agreements. Our goal is to be fair to both sides, to produce reciprocal stability, parity, and security. We desire a freeze on further modernization and production of weapons and a continuing, substantial reduction of strategic nuclear weapons as well. We want a comprehensive ban on all nuclear testing, a prohibition against all chemical warfare, no attack capability against space satellites, and arms limitations in the Indian Ocean.

We hope that we can take joint steps with all nations toward a final agreement eliminating nuclear weapons completely from our arsenals of death. We will persist in this effort.

Now, I believe in détente with the Soviet Union. To me, it means progress toward peace. But the effects of détente should not be limited to our own two countries alone. We hope to persuade the Soviet Union that one country cannot impose its system of society upon another, either through direct military intervention or through the use of a client state's military force, as was the case with Cuban intervention in Angola.

Cooperation also implies obligation. We hope that the Soviet Union will join with us and other nations in playing a larger role in aiding the developing world, for common aid efforts will help us build a bridge of mutual confidence in one another.

Fourth, we are taking deliberate steps to improve the chances of lasting peace in the Middle East. Through wide-ranging consultation with leaders of the countries involved—Israel, Syria, Jordan, and Egypt—we have found some areas of agreement and some movement toward consensus. The negotiations must continue.

Through my own public comments, I've also tried to suggest a more flexible framework for the discussion of the three key issues which have so far been so intractable: the nature of a comprehensive peace—What is peace? What does it mean to the Israelis? What does it mean to their Arab neighbors? Secondly, the relationship between security and borders—How can the dispute over border delineations be established and settled with a feeling of security on both sides? And the issue of the Palestinian homeland.

The historic friendship that the United States has with Israel is not dependent on domestic politics in either nation; it's derived from our common respect for human freedom and from a common search for permanent peace.

We will continue to promote a settlement which all of us need. Our own policy will not be affected by changes in leadership in any of the countries in the Middle East. Therefore, we expect Israel and her neighbors to continue to be bound by United Nations Resolutions 242 and 338, which they have previously accepted.

This may be the most propitious time for a genuine settlement since the beginning of the Arab-Israeli conflict almost 30 years ago. To let this opportunity pass could mean disaster not only for the Middle East but, perhaps, for the international political and economic order as well.

And fifth, we are attempting, even at the risk of some friction with our friends, to reduce the danger of nuclear proliferation and the world-wide spread of conventional weapons.

At the recent summit, we set in motion an international effort to determine the best ways of harnessing nuclear energy for peaceful use while reducing the risks that its products will be diverted to the making of explosives.

We've already completed a comprehensive review of our own policy on arms transfers. Competition in arms sales is inimical to peace and destructive of the economic development of the poorer countries.

We will, as a matter of national policy now in our country, seek to reduce the annual dollar volume of arms sales, to restrict the transfer of advanced weapons, and to reduce the extent of our co-production arrangements about weapons with foreign states. And, just as important, we are trying to get other nations, both free and otherwise, to join us in this effort.

But all of this that I've described is just the beginning. It's a beginning aimed towards a clear goal: to create a wider framework of international cooperation suited to the new and rapidly changing historical circumstances.

We will cooperate more closely with the newly influential countries in Latin America, Africa, and Asia. We need their friendship and cooperation in a common effort as the structure of world power changes.

More than 100 years ago, Abraham Lincoln said that our Nation could not exist half slave and half free. We know a peaceful world cannot long exist one-third rich and two-thirds hungry.

Most nations share our faith that in the long run, expanded and equitable trade will best help the developing countries to help themselves. But the immediate problems of hunger, disease, illiteracy, and repression are here now.

The Western democracies, the OPEC nations, and the developed Communist countries can cooperate through existing international institutions in providing more effective aid. This is an excellent alternative to war.

We have a special need for cooperation and consultation with other nations in this hemisphere—to the north and to the south. We do not need another slogan. Although these are our close friends and neighbors, our links with them are the same links of equality that we forge for the rest of the world. We will be dealing with them as part of a new, worldwide mosaic of global, regional, and bilateral relations.

It's important that we make progress toward normalizing relations with the People's Republic of China. We see the American and Chinese relationship as a central element of our global policy, and China as a key force for global peace. We wish to cooperate closely with the creative Chinese people on the problems that confront all mankind, and we hope to find a formula which can bridge some of the difficulties that still separate us.

Finally, let me say that we are committed to a peaceful resolution of the crisis in southern Africa. The time has come for the principle of majority rule to be the basis for political order, recognizing that in a democratic system the rights of the minority must also be protected.

To be peaceful, change must come promptly. The United States is determined to work together with our European allies and with the concerned African States to shape a congenial international framework for the rapid and progressive transformation of southern African society and to help protect it from unwarranted outside interference.

Let me conclude by summarizing: Our policy is based on an historical vision of America's role. Our policy is derived from a larger view of global change. Our policy is rooted in our moral values, which never change. Our policy is reinforced by our material wealth and by our military power. Our policy is designed to serve mankind. And it is a policy that I hope will make you proud to be Americans.

Thank you.

13. MEETING THE CHALLENGES OF A CHANGING WORLD

Cyrus Vance

From the first days of our nation, Americans have held a staunch optimism about the future. We have been a self-confident people, certain about our ability to shape our destiny. And we are a people who have not only adapted well to change, we have thrived on it.

We are now living in a period of history marked by deep and rapid change. Tonight, I want to talk about change and how America can use its extraordinary strength to meet the challenges of a changing world.

America's optimism has been jarred in recent years—by a bitter war, by domestic divisions that tested our democratic institutions and left many of our people skeptical about government, by the sudden awareness that our economic life at home can be shaped by actions abroad, and by the realization that there are events which affect us but which we can only partly influence.

There is much that we can and have learned from these experiences. But fear of the future is not one of them.

Let me share with you frankly my concern that the distorted proposition being advanced by some that America is in a period of decline in the world is not only wrong as a matter of fact but dangerous as a basis for policy.

For we would imperil our future if we lost confidence in ourselves and in our strength and retreated from energetic lead-

Source: *Department of State Bulletin,* June 1979, pp. 16–19.

ership in the world. And we would imperil our future, as well, if we reacted in frustration and used our power to resist change in the world or employed our military power when it would do more harm than good.

The realization that we are not omnipotent should not make us fear we have lost our power or the will to use it. If we appreciate the extraordinary strengths we have, if we understand the nature of the changes taking place in the world, and if we act effectively to use our different kinds of power to shape different kinds of change, we have every reason to be confident about our future.

AMERICA'S STRENGTHS

We must begin with a clear understanding of our own strengths as a nation.

America's military strength today is formidable. I know of no responsible military official who would exchange our strategic position for that of any other nation.

1. We have friendly neighbors on our borders.
2. We have strong and reliable security relationships. Together, these allies more than double our overall military strength.
3. We have easy access to the sea, which enables us to have diversified strategic forces and the ready capacity to project our power.

Our economy, and those of our allies, are more than three times as productive as those of the Soviets and their allies.

The industrial democracies continue to lead the way in technological innovation and in harnessing that technology to serve mankind.

And the way of life of our people and what we stand for as a nation continue to have magnetic appeal around the world.

Because we and our allies are the engines of creative change in almost every field, because of the vitality of our political institutions and the strength of our military forces, we have a capacity for leadership—and an ability to thrive in a world of change—that is unsurpassed.

The issue is not whether we are strong. We are. The challenge is to use these unquestioned strengths appropriately and effectively to advance our interests in a world undergoing different kinds of change.

What are these changes, and how can we use our strength effectively?

STABLE STRATEGIC EQUIVALENCE

The first element of change is the evolution from an earlier period of American strategic supremacy to an era of stable strategic equivalence.

We should harbor no illusion that we could return to the earlier era. Neither side will permit the other to hold an exploitable strategic advantage. Each side has the financial and technical resources to keep pace with the other. With the stakes so high, we know that both of us will do whatever is necessary to keep from falling behind. That is why essential equivalence has become the only realistic strategy in today's nuclear world.

This rough balance can also serve the cause of stability—even if some find it

unsettling compared with our earlier supremacy. It is this essential equivalence in strategic arms which allows us to move ahead on arms limitation. For if one side were far ahead, it would feel no special urgency about arms control, and the side that was behind would refuse to negotiate from a position of weakness. Only when both sides perceive a balance, as is now the case, can we hope for real arms control progress.

Our response to this broad change in the security environment has several elements.

We will assure that essential equivalence in nuclear arms is maintained. We will not be overtaken by the momentum of Soviet military programs.

We have undertaken a far-reaching modernization of our strategic forces. We are improving each leg of our strategic triad—with cruise missiles for our B-52 bombers, with a new Trident I missile for existing submarines and the development of a new Trident submarine and Trident II missile, and with development funding for the M-X missile. And we are examining, in a timely fashion, the options for offsetting the probable future threat to the land-based portion of our missile force.

At the same time, we are equally determined to enhance our security by applying mutual limits to nuclear arms. We are at the threshold of a SALT II treaty. It is a critical step in the process of bringing strategic weapons under sensible control. As its terms become known and debated, I am confident that the Senate will agree that it will enhance our national security and that of our allies. Its rejection would lead to an intensification of the nuclear arms race. The risk of nuclear war would increase. The costs to our taxpayers would rise sharply. It would heighten tensions with the Soviets, trouble our allies, and deal a crippling blow to future arms control prospects.

The American people, and our allies, understand the importance of decreasing tensions with the Soviet Union and seeking common ground where our interests may converge.

While we address strategic issues, we must also be especially sensitive to the importance of maintaining a balance of conventional forces. At the NATO summit last summer, we and our allies committed ourselves to real increases of 3% in defense expenditures and to modernize and upgrade NATO forces. Last year's repeal of the arms embargo against Turkey was an important step to help bolster NATO's southern flank.

In Europe and elsewhere, we are committed to maintain strong conventional forces. And no one should doubt that we will use those forces if our vital interests or those of our allies are threatened.

In these ways, we will maintain, and strengthen, our security in an age of essential equivalence by meeting the new problems it presents and by seizing the new arms control opportunities it affords.

GROWING RISKS OF REGIONAL CONFLICTS

A second change is the reality that the risks posed by regional conflicts have grown. Many of these conflicts are long standing. They have roots deep in history, in geography, in religious and ethnic differences.

But as more nations acquire more sophisticated arms, regional conflicts become more dangerous. They pose a constant threat of wider confrontation. As a result, the United States must be more active in working to help settle these disputes peacefully.

The fact is that no nation is more intensively engaged in the continuing effort to dampen the flames of conflict around the world than the United States.

No other nation could have played the role that the United States has played in helping Israel and Egypt achieve an historic peace treaty. And we will continue to remain actively involved in the effort to achieve a comprehensive peace—a peace in which Israel, the neighboring Arab states, and the Palestinian people can live with security and with dignity.

In southern Africa, in the eastern Mediterranean, in Southeast Asia, and elsewhere in the world, we are using the influence we have for peace. Progress does not come easily or quickly. There will be setbacks, for the path to peace is often more difficult than the road to war. But with persistence and steadiness, we *can* help provide the parties to conflict with an alternative to violence—if they choose to take it.

In some cases, these efforts will involve working with other interested nations as a catalyst for bringing the parties together. In other situations, we will support international and regional institutions that provide a framework for easing tensions. When we believe it will contribute to regional stability, we will assist nations threatened by external force to strengthen their ability to defend themselves.

In all cases, we will oppose attempts by others to transform local disputes into international tests of will. Every nation has a responsibility to recognize that there is greater safety in healing, rather than fueling, local conflicts.

CHANGES WITHIN NATIONS

A third kind of change we must address is change *within* nations.

As a result of mass communications,

better education, urbanization, and growing expectations for a better life, there is a new tide in many Third World nations, as more and more people demand a fuller share in their government and their economy. These demands can place extraordinary pressures on economic, social, and political institutions.

This ferment can at times cause the kind of turmoil that adversely affects our interests, at least in the short run. But rather than reacting in opposition to such change, or assuming that it necessarily works against us, let us look at two central questions: Is this kind of change generally in the interest of our nation? And what are the best instruments through which we can help others meet popular aspirations in an orderly and peaceful fashion?

The answer to the first question, in my judgment, is that the growing demand of individuals around the world for the fulfillment of their political, social, and economic rights *is* generally in our interest. These aspirations are producing new or strengthened democratic institutions in many nations throughout the world. And America can flourish best in a world where freedom flourishes.

Should we not gain confidence from this expansion of democracy, which is taking place not because we force it but because of its inherent appeal?

And what is that inherent appeal? Surely it lies in the enhanced opportunity that democracy provides for the realization of fundamental human rights—the rights to political and religious expression, to political participation, and to economic justice.

These values are remarkably attuned to the demands of change. The change which confronts many nations—particularly the less developed nations—challenges cultures, ways of living and communicating, notions of individual and national autonomy. The great strength of democratic processes is their flexibility and resilience. They allow accommodation and compromise. By giving all groups a voice in the decisions which affect their lives, democratic societies are far better able to shape a peaceful and stable balance between tradition and progress.

Internal change in other countries will sometimes be turbulent and difficult. At times, it may run in repressive directions. But we must not let our concerns about the crosscurrents blind us to the tide running in favor of freedom.

In seeking to help others meet the legitimate demands of their peoples, what are the best instruments at hand?

Let me state first that the use of military force is not, and should not be, a desirable American policy response to the internal politics of other nations. We believe we have the right to shape our destiny; we must respect that right in others. We must clearly understand the distinction between our readiness to act forcefully when the vital interests of our nation, our allies, and our friends are threatened and our recognition that our military forces cannot provide a satisfactory answer to the purely *internal* problems of other nations.

In helping other nations cope with such internal change, our challenge is to help them develop their own institutions, strengthen their own economies, and foster the ties between government and people.

To do so, we must continue to provide them with increasing levels of development assistance. We must maintain human rights policies which work in practical ways to advance freedom. And we must accept the fact that other societies will manage change and build new institutions in patterns that may be different from our own.

Third World nations will fiercely defend their independence. They will reject efforts by outsiders to impose their institutions. We should welcome this spirit. For our national interest is not in their becoming like us; it is that they be free of domination by others.

This strategy of affirmative involvement and support for the independence and the diversity of developing nations serves us well. It capitalizes on the West's inherent strengths. And it improves our ties to developing countries in a context which does not force them to make an explicit choice between East and West.

The test of our will in dealing with domestic change abroad will come not in how we use our military might but in whether we are willing to put our resources behind our words—and to make them work effectively.

AN INCREASINGLY PLURALISTIC WORLD

A fourth kind of change that we are seeing is in the international system itself. Building on our experience as a pluralistic nation, we must learn to deal effectively with an increasingly pluralistic world.

Since the early 1960's, we have seen the emergence of dozens of new nations, each with its distinctive identity, each fiercely intent on fulfilling its national aspirations.

We have seen the development of new powers in the world, nations which play an increasingly important role in international economic and political life.

And we have come to recognize that many of the challenges we face are genuinely global in scope. Halting the spread of nuclear weapons, managing the world's resources sensibly and fairly, preserving an environment that can sustain us—

these problems do not derive from any single nation nor can any single nation, working alone, resolve them.

A world where many must participate in designing the future rather than a few, where progress often requires cooperative effort, demands more—not less—American leadership. It requires us to exercise that leadership creatively, to inspire others to work with us toward goals we share but cannot achieve separately. It calls for a new kind of diplomacy.

We must practice, wherever possible, an inclusive form of diplomacy, working together with others to achieve common goals. Such multilateral efforts are time consuming and complex. But they can often be more productive than working alone.

The core around which these broader efforts must be built is a strong and solid relationship with our traditional allies. We have worked hard in this Administration to strengthen that partnership, and we have done so.

Working together with our allies we are able, on an increasing number of issues, to engage others in collective efforts to resolve some of the more intractable problems we face. Let me cite just one example—our effort to find a more proliferation-resistant nuclear fuel cycle.

At our initiative, 44 nations have come together to search for ways—both technical and institutional—to enable nations to pursue peaceful nuclear energy without adding to the danger of nuclear weapons proliferation. There is no "American" answer to the threat of nuclear weapons proliferation; there is only an international answer, and we are working with others to find it.

We are strengthening our ties with those developing nations which exert increasing economic and political influence. We have worked to bring these and other developing nations more fully and fairly into the decisionmaking of international institutions which affect their life and ours. For enduring solutions to problems we face in common can be found only if all who have a stake also have a role and recognize their responsibilities as well as their rights in the world community.

To work effectively in a changing international system we must be prepared to work with nations whose ideologies are different from our own. By establishing full diplomatic relations with the People's Republic of China, for example, we are now in a better position to deal directly and forthrightly with a government that represents one-fourth of the world's people.

We have embarked on a deliberate effort to enhance the role of the United Nations and regional institutions such as the Organization of American States, the Association of South East Asian Nations, and the Organization of African Unity. These institutions often can provide the most effective setting for resolving international disputes and for broadening the realm of international cooperation.

To secure the cooperation of other nations, we must deal with them on a basis of mutual respect and independence. Our achievement of a new Panama Canal treaty, which secures our use of the canal for coming generations, has demonstrated that fair dealing with other nations, whatever their size, can serve our interests as well as theirs. Our relations throughout this hemisphere have benefited as a result.

A CHANGING WORLD ECONOMY

Let me turn finally to the change we are seeing in the international economy— the growing stake every nation has in economic decisions made beyond its borders.

America's strength rests on the vitality of America's economy. Our economy continues to provide expanding opportunity for our people and continues to fuel growth around the world. We must also recognize the other side of this coin—the health of other economies around the world increasingly affects the health of our economy.

Our exports provide Americans with jobs—in fact, one out of every eight jobs in the manufacturing sector—and income for our firms and farmers. Every third acre of our farmland produces for export. Imports from abroad provide us with essential raw materials, they afford our consumers greater choice, and they dampen our inflation.

This growing economic interdependence requires that our government work with others to help create international conditions in which all nations can thrive. We cannot seek to build our own economic future at the expense of others, nor will we allow others to compete unfairly. For a new era of economic nationalism could have tragic consequences, just as it did during the protectionist warfare of the 1930's.

We are deeply involved in working with other nations to meet the challenges of a changing world economic order.

We have been successful in strengthening economic cooperation among the industrial nations. We have instituted regular economic summits to coordinate our economic policies so that they reinforce rather than undermine one another. And there has been far closer collaboration among our monetary authorities in restoring order to foreign exchange markets.

We have initaled an important new multilateral trade agreement that will establish fair trading rules for the next decade. It will have a direct and positive impact on our economy.

We have agreed with the other industrialized members of the International Energy Agency to cut back our collective
demand for oil by 2 million barrels a day.
To fulfill this commitment—and to reduce our own costly and dangerous dependence on oil imports—the President
has initiated a sensible program for
achieving greater domestic conservation
and production. For we must begin to
deal urgently with a markedly changed
global energy environment.

We recognize that a well-managed foreign assistance program contributes to the
economic performance of the developing
countries. Their growth has become an
increasingly important factor in the health
of our own economy. Aiding that development is not only an investment in the
future of others, it is an investment in
our own future as well.

THE PATH WE WILL FOLLOW

In the foreign policy choices we are
now making, we are determining the path
we will follow in a new era. In unsettled
times, each of us has a responsibility to
be clear about how we would deal with
the world as we find it.

Most Americans now recognize that we
alone cannot dictate events. This recognition is not a sign of America's decline;
it is a sign of growing American maturity
in a complex world.

We are stronger today because we recognize the realities of our times. This recognition, together with an equally clear
understanding that we remain the most
powerful of nations, should make every
American as staunchly optimistic about
our nation's future as we have always
been.

There can be no going back to a time
when we thought there could be American solutions to every problem. We must
go forward into a new era of mature American leadership—based on strength, not
belligerence; on steadiness, not impulse;
on confidence, not fear.

We have every reason to be confident.
For 200 years, we have prospered by welcoming change and working with it, not
by resisting it. We have understood, at
home and abroad, that stability is not the
status quo. It comes through human
progress. We will continue in this American tradition.

14. REQUIEM

Stanley Hoffmann

Rarely has an administration had as few defenders as Jimmy Carter's. The election of Ronald Reagan has been generally interpreted as a repudiation both of Carter's economic policies and of his foreign policy. Thus, it may be useful to ask three questions: What was done well, what went wrong, and what should be learned from the Carter presidency?

At a time when realpolitik is regaining prestige, it may not be very popular to state that the almost aggressive reassertion of American idealism by the Carter administration in its first year was one of its greatest achievements. There have been too many disappointments and difficulties since then for most Americans to appreciate today how welcome the tone set by Carter and his team was at that time. At home, he appealed to the national reservoir of moral enthusiasm and the urge to behave in world affairs not merely as a great power but also as the champion of certain values. He was determined to redefine the national interest to make it coincide with the moral impulse. These efforts did much to help Americans overcome the bitter divisions, and the sense of shame and guilt, engendered by the war in Vietnam and by the Watergate scandal.

Abroad, many governments were as suspicious of American flings of idealism—easily translated into, or perceived as, alarming mixes of naiveté and benevolent arrogance—as they usually are of

brutal or cynical power plays by big states. But it soon became apparent that Carter's human rights emphasis was not merely rhetorical, that steps were actually taken to turn it into a policy, and that even mere sermons or lofty pronouncements by an American president cannot fail to have some effect when they clearly reflect his wishes and his will. As this policy began to liberate political prisoners, put repressive governments on the defensive, and encourage dissidents everywhere, the prestige of the United States—tarnished by American behavior in Vietnam, Chile, Cyprus, and Bangladesh—soared again in many parts of the world.

Good Machiavellians will discount the sympathy for America felt by opponents of Filipino President Ferdinand Marcos or by Indonesians released from camps or by many black Africans or by citizens of Panama. But just as it is not enough to be loved in the global contest for influence, it is certainly not sufficient to be feared. The Soviet quandary in Poland testifies both to the subversive potential of human rights and to the unenviable choices facing a power that relies almost entirely on fear.

The second merit of the Carter administration was its attempt to come to terms with the world as it is. The administration may have harbored far too many illusions about the ease with which this world, or even the United States, could be managed. But in important respects, the original analysis was right. The Carter administration understood that, in an

Source: *Foreign Policy* 42 (Spring 1981), pp. 3–26.

era marked by the diffusion of power to new actors insistent on asserting themselves and on rejecting the dependencies fashioned by colonialism or by long economic subordination to more advanced nations, the conditions for U.S. influence had changed. In a world characterized both by the contagion of independence and by the complex bonds, restraints, and manipulations of interdependence, Marina v. N. Whitman's formula of "leadership without hegemony"[1] was the only possible one.

That this was later denounced as a quasiretreat from leadership, as an abdication from power, says more about the critics than about the administration. Those who tend to equate power with displays of military might, or with periodic military outbursts, have failed to understand that power is neither a mystical gift nor a stock of goods, but a relationship. If the purpose of the exercise of power is to influence the behavior of others, the first requirement is to understand the concerns, interests, and fears of those one tries to affect and the costs and limits of control.

There was often too much glibness in the proclaimed intention to be on the side of change: Not all changes are desirable, and there was always a tension between the drive for human rights and the accommodation of the developing nations' desires. But those very Americans who were disturbed by U.S. defeats in the United Nations in the early 1970s and unresigned to the spectacle of the United States as a mere, albeit vocal, opposition in the General Assembly, should have been the first to note that under Carter the United States ceased being on the defensive and achieved some remarkable successes in the U.N. General Assembly and Security Council. The negotiation of the Panama Canal treaties symbolized the new U.S. willingness to accept, even in its own domain, the reality of a postcolonial era.

LOSSES AND VICTORIES

The Carter administration's original analysis was correct again in stressing that this ever more complex world could be neither managed by the superpowers nor reduced to the relationship between them. Until his last years as secretary of state, Henry Kissinger had maintained an intensely bipolar view of the world. In 1973 it became clear that superpower control of regional conflicts and internal developments in Third World countries was limited and imperfect. Opportunities for superpower influence arose from local politics and could not be easily eliminated or offset unless the local circumstances were propitious.

The best way of coping with Soviet advances and maneuvers in the Third World is through preventive diplomacy. Not every Soviet success can be avoided at a reasonable cost or constitutes a threat to a major U.S. interest. Not every loss is a defeat. And the division of the world into two camps—moderates versus radicals—is an artificial and ultimately self-defeating procrustean formula. It gives up as lost and treats as foes countries or forces whose extremism, or whose ties to the Soviets, may well be temporary and counts as allies regimes or groups whose internal weaknesses or external ambitions may turn them into liabilities for the United States and opportunities for the Soviet Union. Carter's steadfast refusal to apply this mischievous Manichaean division to Rhodesia was entirely justified.

A third merit of the Carter administration was its determination to cope with major, long-term problems, rather than to concentrate only on the most urgent ones. The emphasis on global issues, many of which had been dealt with only timidly before, was far sighted, whatever one may say about the way in which policies were carried out. Human rights, non-proliferation, arms sales, arms control beyond the confines of SALT or of Europe, the law of the seas, international trade, and the Arab-Israeli conflict were all subjects of enormous long-range importance.

In some instances, little more was achieved than consciousness raising. In others, partial victories were won: The rate of nuclear proliferation has slowed, and the range of consensus among suppliers of nuclear fuels and technology has increased; the Tokyo round of the General Agreement on Tariffs and Trade has been a success; an agreement on the law of the seas is in sight.

Fourth, those who now speak of the Carter legacy as one of disaster and peril will soon realize that the great improvements of which they will undoubtedly boast in a few months were all carefully prepared by the Carter administration. Thus, Carter and Harold Brown, the secretary of defense, initiated a variety of programs designed to neutralize the Soviet strategic nuclear build-up by increasing America's counterforce capabilities; obtained West European consent to a modernization of North Atlantic Treaty Organization (NATO) forces and to the establishment of long-range theater nuclear weapons in Western Europe; pressured Japan, with some success, for an increase in its defense effort; and created the Rapid Deployment Force and negotiated access to various bases and facilities for it. Also, the Carter administration normalized relations with the Soviet Union's most uncompromising enemy—China— and began to fashion a strategic relationship with the new Chinese leadership.

Critics of the Carter administration ritualistically deplore what they view as its major defeats—Moscow's grip on Ethiopia, Vietnamese control of Kampuchea, the Soviet invasion of Afghanistan, the collapse of America's position in Iran, and turmoil in Central America. But there were also major victories—the solidity of America's main alliances, the progress in relations with China, the breakthrough at Camp David, the decline of Soviet influence in the Arab world, the trend of elections in the Caribbean, the end of the Rhodesian civil war, and the support of Angola and Mozambique for major Western objectives in Southern Africa. This is not a picture of decline and retreat. Yet it has been so perceived by many, at home and abroad.

The general impression of failure is not caused by the fact that Carter pursued policies at the end of his term that were far different—indeed almost the opposite—from those he had announced when he first took office. A team that had wanted to conduct a diplomacy freed from the "inordinate fear" of communism and to play down the relationship between the superpowers ended up so preoccupied with the bipolar conflict that it had little time and energy left for anything else, except the Iran hostage crisis. But other administrations had shown the same contradiction between their original course and their later trajectory: The Harry Truman of the Cold War was far different from the Truman of 1945–1946; Kissinger's global diplomacy of 1975–1976 was vastly different from his détente policy of 1971–1973.

Nor is the impression of failure caused largely by the hostage crisis. Most Americans agreed that the return of the hostages was the primary national objective. A declaration of war followed by military operations would have been fatal to the hostages, dangerous for America's relations with its allies, and rich in opportunities for Soviet gain. A blockade with or without a declaration of war would have embroiled the United States in confrontations with third powers and jeopardized the world's oil supply without necessarily helping the hostages. Waiting until the dust settled in Iran and until other events—such as the Iran-Iraq war—changed Iranian priorities proved to be frustrating; but few outside the United States believe that America practiced appeasement or was humiliated because of its show of restraint.

Indeed, the contrast between American patience toward Iran and Soviet brutality in Afghanistan has not been unnoticed. Those who believe that the United States should have put national honor or pride ahead of the lives of the hostages ought to ask themselves what the spectacle of a great power bombing or otherwise assulting a weaker country with which it had been previously involved—to put it mildly—in an unhappy and unfortunate relationship would have done for America's prestige.

DIVERSITY OR CACOPHONY?

The main failures of the Carter administration can be found in four different but interrelated areas: style, strategy, economics, and politics. Style is almost as important as substance. A policy based on a faulty design can impress friends and skeptics abroad and generate enthusiasm at home, if it is carried out with a sense of mastery and a dash of drama. Style can convey the illusion of coherence and continuity at a time when a policy is floundering, the original design is in pieces, and diplomacy is reduced to improvisation.

Any student of the late French President Charles de Gaulle or of Kissinger's diplomacy knows that skill in manipulating the perceptions of the public and of leaders can go a long way toward offsetting miscalculations or even a deficiency of power. But the Carter administration from the very beginning developed a style of clumsiness that amplified misgivings and specific grievances abroad into a general conviction of incompetence.

The administration suffered from an almost total addiction to erratic tactics. The complaint of friends and foes alike—that Carter was unpredictable—was based in large part on the bumpiness of the administration's style. There were policy zigzags on the status of U.S. troops in South Korea, the neutron bomb, high technology transfers to the Soviet Union, relations with Somalia, the Soviet role in a Middle East settlement, the March 1980 U.N. resolution on Israeli settlements, and other issues.

There was plain incoherence, such as when the president authorized the hostage rescue mission in Iran immediately after he had obtained allied support for economic sanctions by promising military restraint. Moments of complacency—the absence of reaction to the April 1978 communist coup in Afghanistan and Carter's failure at and immediately after Camp David to press Israeli Prime Minister Menachem Begin on the issue of Israeli West Bank settlements—alternated with brusque, screeching fortissimos—the initial confrontation with Bonn over the West German-Brazilian nuclear deal, the "discovery" of a Soviet brigade in Cuba, and the post-Afghanistan avalanche of sanctions against the Soviet Union. There was, above all, what might be called tactical fission: some officials sounding the alarm about African or Caribbean developments while others were shrugging it off, the U.S. embassy in Tehran pursuing one course at the time of the fall of Shah Mohammad Reza Pahlavi while Washington seemed to be pursuing at least two others—one non-interventionist, one pro-shah.

This tactical infelicity had three causes. One was institutional. A president may want to receive diverse kinds of advice. He may even want to institutionalize diversity. But then he must be able to impose his own views, achieve his own synthesis, and be the master of the administration's tactics. Otherwise, diversity enshrined in different administrative sanctuaries becomes cacophony. At no point, except at Camp David, did the president give the impression of being in command of the daily course.

There was not only the well-publicized conflict of views and of styles between the national security adviser and the secretary of state, and between either of these and Andrew Young, the U.S. ambassador to the United Nations. There were also tensions between the domestic advisers, with their eyes on the polls—and on the Jewish vote—and the foreign policy experts; between the regional bureaus and the champions of global or functional issues; between the arms controllers and the military or its supporters. Such divergencies are inevitable. But when each group or clan is allowed, or feels free, to launch its own initiatives, and the others then try to cancel these moves or to neutralize them with moves of their own, the style that emerges is deplorable.

The second cause was personal. Each of the main players had his own flaws. Carter has often been blamed for his addiction to detail; but detail and tactics turned out not to be synonymous. The attempt to master detail—always a dubious goal for a president—becomes particularly futile when specific knowledge is not translated into a steady course of action. In domestic as well as in foreign affairs, Carter often behaved as if his minute understanding of a problem and his definition of goals were all a policy needed for success.

Former Secretary of State Cyrus Vance was a believer in case-by-case negotiation. Tactically, this was a fine bent, but one that failed to address two problems: the need or itch for occasional spectaculars—a need neglected at great peril not only in democracies but also in multilateral diplomacy, which tends toward paralysis if there are not some crescendos from time to time—and the opportunity a lack of style gives to flashier, if clumsier, players, who then provide the crescendos on their own, at the wrong moment or far too loud. National Security Adviser Zbigniew Brzezinski's fascination with tactics was not wedded to talent for negotiation or regard for steadiness. In his case, institutional and personal characteristics merged to handicap the administration: No national security adviser should be a principal negotiator, an enforcer of policy, and a public spokesman; but this is especially true when the adviser likes quick moves, grand gestures, and tough tactics.

DISCOMBOBULATED GROPING

The third cause of the clumsy style was the most important and resulted in part from the other two: the Carter administration's strategic incoherence. This factor is of such importance that it must be treated as an independent one. Never did the administration succeed in integrating its excellent intuitions and assumptions into a strategy. Contradictions remained unmanaged until the end.

From the beginning, the core of the failure was in the area of Soviet-U.S. relations. It was impossible both to improve these relations and to pursue—in the Middle East, the Far East, and with respect to human rights—a policy the Soviets would view as one of exclusion or confrontation. It was impossible simultaneously to demote the Soviet-U.S. relationship from its perch as the top American concern and to expect the Soviets—keen on competition and unhappy with the U.S. interpretation of the "Basic Principles of U.S.-Soviet Relations" agreed to in 1972—to let themselves be relegated to the periphery of American concerns. It was wrong to believe that world affairs could somehow be packaged into two separate categories: the Soviet-U.S. contest, to be dealt with by the alliances and by a mix of military and arms control measures; and all the rest.

Indeed, the more one wanted to be able to concentrate on that remainder, to cope with global issues, to make progress on regional ones, to examine them on their own merits, the more important it was to manage the Soviet-American contest intelligently. Otherwise, the duel between the superpowers would again spill over into all areas and dominate U.S. attention, either totally obscuring or distorting the other issues. Third World conflicts and global problems do have roots autonomous of the superpowers. But when superpower competition moves toward confrontation, world-wide strategic considerations—the fear of the cumulative effect of discrete, and perhaps separately insignificant, Soviet advances; the worry about U.S. credibility and reliability—begin to overwhelm the concern for local realities. U.S. ability to deal with these, and with global issues, is at the mercy of the superpower contest: The latter is not the only or even the determining force in world affairs, but it remains the central one.

The biggest charge that can be made against the Carter administration is that it failed to define what it wanted out of Soviet-U.S. relations. It failed to decide and to communicate, through deeds as well as words, which Soviet activities were intolerable, and which were compatible with Washington's concept of the bipolar contest. The Carter administration thus compromised its own innovative insights and intentions.

Those who believe that the superpower contest is the one overriding issue and that foreign policy and security policy are synonymous have of course been critical of Carter's initial belief that the competition could lose its saliency and of his persistent, discombobulated groping for a mix of cooperation and confrontation. But those who think that the administration was right in trying to remove the blinders of bipolarity from American eyes have a very different reason for being critical of Carter. At the time of his victory, the American people had already gone through one rich experience. The détente policy of Richard Nixon and Kissinger aimed at moderating Soviet behavior through incentives, punishments, and barricades had already run into formidable obstacles: Many Americans were suspicious of providing the Soviets with economic rewards, the Soviets were unwilling to forgo political gains in the Third World, Washington was unwilling to interpret the 1972 statement of principles in the way Moscow read it—as a promise of condominium and an assertion that the arms race would continue, especially on the Soviet side.

Three lessons seemed clear. First was the difficulty of waging a long-range, mixed policy toward Moscow, which could lead to Soviet restraint in the long run even if there were, on the way, occasional setbacks and confrontations. For every such setback tends to be seen as a reason to remove rewards, and every resort to a sanction is treated not as a normal application of the theory of incentives, but as evidence of failure of the whole policy. The second lesson was the difficulty of waging such a policy when the climate is poisoned by a quickening arms race. The third was the formidable reservoir of antagonism in the United States to any policy other than one of hostility and traditional containment toward the Soviet Union—a state rightly felt to be a threat both to U.S. power and to America's most fundamental values, and, much more questionably, held to have few genuinely common interests with America.

The Carter administration did not draw the consequences from these lessons. Kissinger's failed attempt at an integrated strategy was replaced not with a different integrated policy, but with a declaratory policy of juxtapositions. The United States would, in Brzezinski's words, both "recognize the continuing relevance of power" and be "responsive to the new political realities of the world."[2] It would have both competition and cooperation in Soviet-American relations. Amen! Yet how would the search for either half not drown out the other?

The administration never made up its mind on linkage. Kissinger's attempt had apparently not worked after 1972. But rather than determining why it had failed—because it had not really been tried, thanks to the Jackson-Vanik amendment; or because it had attempted to achieve the impossible by demanding Soviet acceptance of the U.S. concept of stability; or even because it could never work once the Soviets had reached the original objectives of their switch to détente—the members of the Carter administration oscillated from moments when the very notion of linkage seemed abandoned, to others when linkage-as-punishment was discussed, to the final orgy of linkage after the invasion of Afghanistan.

POLICY SCHIZOPHRENIA

But linkage is above all a means to an end; and the end—defining acceptable Soviet behavior—was never clarified. If a modicum of cooperation with the Soviet Union was deemed essential, both as a way to curtail the growth of the Soviet war machine and as a way to make the new Carter global strategy possible, then a very clear priority ought to have been given to arms control. The longer it took to negotiate SALT II, the more the United States exposed itself to dangerous schizophrenia in the realm of security—to a situation in which there would appear to be a contradiction between U.S. arms control policy and a renewed U.S. military effort, required by the failure to curb the Soviet build-up by mutual agreements and intended to prevent a further deterioration of the balance.

The adminstration appeared divided between a security policy increasingly driven by mounting fears of Soviet capabilities and intentions and an arms control policy based on moderate assumptions about the two sides' strategic plans. And such schizophrenia could not fail to lead to the defeat of the arms control component, if global political and military events appeared to vindicate what might be called the Committee on the Present Danger's analysis of Soviet behavior. The imperatives were therefore either a quick arms control agreement as a major component of the cooperative dimension or, if no such rapid success seemed possible, a major attempt at joint U.S.-Soviet crisis management in the meantime to accompany America's military efforts. Neither was achieved, and the latter was not even undertaken.

In the absence of either, decisions about redressing the military balance seemed to be a vindication of the committee's warnings and a frantic effort to buy votes for SALT II, rather than a part of a balanced strategy. With a deteriorating diplomatic climate at the end of the SALT II negotiations, attention increasingly was concentrated not on the future of Washington's political relationship with Moscow but on the nightmare scenarios of Minuteman missile vulnerability. The shrinking of the cooperative dimension with Moscow tended to make of a most improbable worst-case hypothesis—a disarming Soviet first strike—not only the tail that wagged the dog of strategic decisions and doctrines, but also, absurdly enough, an additional reason for rejecting SALT II, since the treaty did nothing to remove that particular threat.

Indeed, U.S. military policy is increasingly driven by an apparent belief that the United States needs capabilities that mirror theoretical Soviet ones, either those required to win a nuclear war or those in the Persian Gulf area. The questions that ought to be asked are: What are American objectives, and what is entailed by them? Instead, Americans seem to ask: What are, or rather what might be, Soviet goals, and what does the United States need to match Soviet capabilities?

Another unfortunate effect of this U.S. failure was the gap between Washington's Soviet policy and that of its European allies. The West Europeans have clearly chosen a mixed strategy, one that does not entail linkages and aims above all at stability in Europe. Given their economic and diplomatic links with Moscow, they see little contradiction between those links and an arms effort. France began to increase its defense budget sev-

eral years before NATO and West German Chancellor Helmut Schmidt raised the issue of the Euro-strategic balance. As long as the United States has no network of relations with Moscow of comparable density, Washington will be quick to resort to sanctions—suspending grain sales or shelving SALT II when Moscow misbehaves. As long as Western Europe, in its bundle of bonds with Moscow, does not have any arms agreement of its own, it will insist on arms control—at both the central and the theater level. Moreover, arms control is a necessary companion of any rearmament effort, if for no other reason than domestic opinion. This trans-Atlantic contrast is a perfect recipe for mutual recrimination.

A third consequence was the administration's inability to choose between a policy of balance toward Moscow and Beijing, and a quasi-alliance with China. Each has had its champions. A fourth consequence has been felt in those very areas that the administration wanted to rescue, so to speak, from bipolarity. The prerequisite for such a rescue was a better and more stable, but not necessarily uncompetitive, Soviet-U.S. relationship. In the absence of that kind of relationship, the Carter administration did not feel free to pursue its own instincts and postulates in sensitive areas; but by continuing to act as if the Soviet-American contest had to be the determining factor, the administration often made mistakes, or worse. In other words, the weakness of its political strategy both compromised what was right and new, and reinforced what was old and wrong.

Carter inherited the policy of regional influentials in the Middle East. He continued to see in the shah of Iran a bulwark for stability, and so, American policy in Iran continued to depend on the shah. Once the revolution began, there was—

short of military intervention nobody advocated—no way of avoiding that the shah's fall would also be a U.S. debacle. The fear of Soviet influence in the Middle East and the habit of looking at Israel as a bastion of security there partly explain Carter's failure to try to extract bigger concessions on the Palestinian issue from Begin. The fear of Cuban influence, or of the charge of being blind to Cuban expansionism, largely explains the administration's protracted unwillingness to acknowledge a revolutionary situation, first in Nicaragua, later in El Salvador. The same zero-sum-game view has thwarted efforts to recognize Angola or Vietnam in order to diminish the strength of their ties to Moscow.

Asserting that nothing was thought through does not mean that devising a strategy radically different from the two varieties of containment—the Cold War and the détente versions—would have been easy. Establishing a mixed relationship with Moscow will remain a most difficult undertaking. It must be acceptable to the U.S. public and deemed satisfactory in Moscow. It must provide for enough cooperation with the Soviets to restrain the means and intensity of the contest in gray areas, without amounting to the superpower condominium Moscow seeks but nobody else wants. It must not lead to a division of the world into exclusive spheres of domination that would risk self-destruction whenever turbulence attributable to one side's efforts hits a zone of influence of the other.

Nor is it easy, when the Soviets behave in an unacceptable way, to choose between a response "in the area and in kind"[3] only (for this may be deemed too weak, both within the United States and in Moscow) and linkage across the board (for every incident then threatens to unravel the whole policy). Nor is it easy to inte-

grate arms control and security concerns: What is best for the former may not always be the best solution for the latter. But the tragedy of the Carter failure is that, far from furthering an intelligent discussion of the issues, it has thrown us back to the simplicities of cold war containment and bipolarity. The absence of a strategy has paved the way for those who seem to have one, however inadequate or antiquated it may be.

Strategic incoherence explains many of the daily fluctuations, such as the tendency to look at the Ayatollah Ruhollah Khomeini's Iran sometimes as a baffling enemy, sometimes as a potential friend against the Soviets or even the Iraqis. It also explains why the Carter administration itself, as its relations with Moscow grew more sour, began to abandon some of its earlier dispositions about the local causes of Third World conflicts, in North and East Africa and in Central America, while trying to preserve, at least rhetorically, its original inspiration. Had Carter been re-elected, the task of devising a strategy would have had to be started from scratch.

INTERNATIONAL ECONOMIC TURMOIL

A third major failure was the inability to understand quickly enough that the soundness of the U.S. economy was as important a precondition for an effective foreign policy as a strong military establishment. In the realm of energy, the reponsibility for failure lies largely with Congress. However, it remains true that U.S. policy in the late 1970s was designed to convince the Persian Gulf states to produce more and to moderate the Organization of Petroleum Exporting Countries prices; this increased U.S. dependence on Persian Gulf oil. Neither conservation nor strategic reserves were pushed hard enough.

The vast U.S. balance-of-payments deficits caused by increasing imports of oil and by the domestic expansion policies promoted by Carter in 1977–1978 led to further deterioration of the dollar. With the Iranian revolution, this resulted in additional massive increases in the price of oil. These proved far more difficult for Bonn and Tokyo to absorb than the earlier price shock of 1973. This had the triple effect of weakening West Germany's ability to provide for aid abroad and to pay for arms increases at home, of inciting Japan to an export drive that threatens the U.S. automobile industry and revives the danger of U.S. protectionism, and of worsening the prospects of bankruptcy for many oil-importing developing nations. As political scientist Robert Keohane was shown, the American loss of monetary and economic power since the late 1960s is largely the result of U.S. policies; this was as true under Carter as before. The turnaround of late 1978, when inflation became Carter's top priority, entailed a willingness to provoke a recession. The resulting combination of inflation and recession made the administration and the Congress highly reluctant to provide resources for developing countries, thus emptying of substance one of the major global policies announced earlier by Carter.

Therefore, as some commentators have pointed out, American policy makers were increasingly driven to sticks because they lacked economic carrots. A policy that can punish but not reward is in poor shape. This could be witnessed not only in U.S. relations with Moscow but also in Carter's human rights and nonproliferation efforts. Above all, the drying out of economic aid at a time of international economic turmoil and rising demands for

resource transfers from the richer to the poorer countries could not fail to foster the very radicalism and anti-American resentment or rhetoric that Carter had hoped to dissipate through his new approach to the North-South dialogue.

Here again, the administration was caught in basic contradictions it found difficult to manage. Abroad, confidence in the dollar as a reserve currency was dealt a blow by the decision to freeze Iranian assets. Here, two foreign policy goals collided. Domestic unwillingness to accept the energy crisis as a "moral equivalent of war" has led to a dissipation of U.S. monetary resources and to a weakening of the international monetary and financial system. Conversely, the administration's commitment to the dollar as the major reserve currency led, since 1978, to a domestic interest rate policy which, as political scientist Miles Kahler has noted, retards "increased industrial investment—one long-term solution to inflationary bias in the economy." And its commitment to trade liberalism conflicted with its addiction to traditional laissez-faire policies at home. Because of the reluctance of Congress and of the public toward an interventionist industrial policy that would go beyond ad hoc bailouts to firms in trouble, domestic support for a liberal trade policy may be undermined, as those firms lose their competitive edge with regard to their foreign competitors.

THE DECISIVE BATTLEGROUND

The last failure was Carter's inability to master the politics of foreign policy. One political task was to obtain the cooperation of Congress. Carter did achieve two major successes: a painful one, the Senate's consent to the Panama treaties, and a triumphant one, the management of the multilateral trade negotiations. Probably no administration could have prevented Congress from legislating its own frequently contradictory and fragmentary preferences and dislikes in areas such as nuclear proliferation and human rights. But the distant relations between Carter and congressional leaders, when their authority was weaker than in the days of the seniority system and of stabler coalitions, did not help provide the administration with enough support to save it from the obligation to fight and to rally a different mix of friends or clients on each issue.

Above all, the absence of a coherent strategy got the administration into trouble with Congress over the crucial question of Soviet-U.S. relations. The Senate's skepticism over SALT II did not receive sufficient attention in time. When a concerted administration counteroffensive developed at last, Carter's officials far too often seemed to fight on their adversaries' terrain and to defend the treaty as harmless rather than as beneficial, except insofar as it allowed the United States to undertake every needed and planned arms build-up. But more damaging was Carter's inept handling of the issue of the Soviet brigade in Cuba, which was allowed to delay consideration of the SALT treaty once more, this time fatally.

The decisive battleground was the public. If Congress, in 1979, seemed to listen more attentively to the champions of the new orthodoxy that finally prevailed on November 4, 1980, than to Carter, it was because a divided administration had allowed the opposition to gain control of the agenda and of the minds of the American people. The president and his top aides did not, as Brzezinski recognized, "adequately emphasize the importance of formal speeches, broadly conceptual-type statements which would convey to the American public on a continuing basis the sense of direction."[4]

There were such speeches, but they conveyed no such sense. Either they were no more than lofty sermons, or they juxtaposed but did not reconcile or integrate policies pointing in opposite directions, or they provided shopping lists rather than clear priorities. To Carter, politics seemed to mean the strategy and tactics of coming to power; government meant the management of issues. But the successful management of issues requires politics in the double sense of coalition building and educating. This is particularly indispensable when there is no clear consensus on a policy at the outset. When Carter took over, there was consensus on two points only: Idealism had to be revived, and new Vietnams avoided. The shocks of recent years have destroyed both, and the Carter administration failed to move the public and Congress beyond these points.

When the original cold war consensus was dissolved by the Vietnam war, Nixon and Kissinger did not attempt to fashion one by coalition building and by public education. They tried to obtain public assent through success and spectacle. It worked for a while, but not after 1974. The Carter administration chose to be resolutely unspectacular. Except for Camp David, its biggest successes were negative—troubles avoided—or atmospheric. Its fiascoes, real or apparent, were sensational—the Soviet airlift to Ethiopia, the convulsions of Iran, the invasion of Afghanistan.

Whoever wants to follow a complex course—a policy that is not merely one of suitably cautious confrontation, but a strategy of mixed relationships—must do a great deal of explaining. Carter needed to point out both that few failures must be fatal or definitive and that few successes are irreversible or decisive. He needed to clarify the rationale behind cooperation with foes or pressure on friends.

When there is no single cause to rally the nation, the politics of foreign policy become much more difficult, and more indispensable. In every policy area, the Carter administration failed to use the bully pulpit. It overestimated the degree to which renewed idealism could overcome a deeply ingrained inability to understand inexpiable class or power conflicts abroad or to sympathize with methods of change other than peaceful and gradual, even in countries where there is a choice only between repression and revolt. It misjudged the extent to which the memory of Vietnam would prevent a recurrence of the early postwar anguish of insecurity, if developments in the Third World and Moscow's relentless military buildup seemed to imperil U.S. pre-eminence.

Without a strategy and without skill in political maneuver and persuasion, the Carter administration left the domestic battlefield to its adversaries. They would not have prevailed if Soviet behavior had not appeared to vindicate the cold warriors. Even though Soviet behavior is objectively expansionist, it matters whether one interprets Moscow's moves as a necessary result of the essence of an imperial or of a revolutionary system or as the complex outcome of external ambitions, external frustrations, miscalculations, internal weaknesses, bureaucratic drives, and atavisms. Policy responses ought to be widely different, depending on the interpretation. But the new orthodoxy would not have prevailed either, if it had not had so many secret, or not-so-secret, sympathizers within the administration and if the president had not given the impression first that he did not always see the difference between his advisers' views, and

later, that Afghanistan had forced him, belatedly and somewhat abjectly, to recognize the error of his earlier ways.

NO ROAD MAPS OR PANACEAS

There are several lessons for the future. First, U.S. leaders must insure the unity of domestic and foreign policy. Reagan asserts he wants to do just that by reviving the U.S. economy as well as American military strength, and by restoring American productivity and self-confidence as well as U.S. leadership. But in an era of finite resources and protracted economic difficulties, tough decisions will have to be made. Some of the domestic transformations required for a sound foreign policy—a shift in industrial structures that would save the United States from the choice between protectionism and industrial disasters, an energy policy that would drastically reduce domestic consumption and dependence on imports—might require the kind of *dirigisme* that the Reagan ideology deems intolerable, indeed un-American. And an obsession with America's military might could lead to further inflation, or, if it is combined with drastic cuts in social services or results in dubious military interventions abroad, it could crack the very superficial consensus that swept Carter out of office and bring new convulsions to the body politic.

The second imperative for any U.S. administration is to erase from the minds of its leaders and from its public vocabulary any hyperbole and any illusion about the quick coming of that great American dream: the elimination or the moderation of conflict in international affairs, the advent of harmony. Three different visions of postwar U.S. diplomacy all nurtured such hopes, and even though such statesmen as Dean Acheson or Kissinger were too skeptical and realistic to harbor these hopes themselves, they were not above letting them slip into their rhetoric. The Cold War vision looked forward to the mellowing of a Soviet Union persuaded by external barriers and situations of strength that reasonable, responsible behavior would be in its interest. The détente vision promised a Soviet Union playing the game of stability in exchange for symbolic status rewards and material incentives, to the point of cooperating with the United States in management and resolution of third party conflicts. The Carter vision added to this the dream of convergence between U.S. deeds and Third World aspirations, of the acceptance of American political ideals by foreign regimes, and the miracle (or mirage) of a world in which nuclear weapons would be on their way out.

Political scientist Robert W. Tucker's charge of immoderate optimism is right, but Carter was not the first one guilty of it. What is needed is a vision of inevitable, but limitable, conflict; of unavoidable, but manageable, contradictions; of solutions leading to new problems; of no exit from competition with Moscow, from torment in regional disputes and in world economic issues, from potentially anti-American revolutions. Excessively high expectations lead to too many domestic vendettas and sudden reversals of course.

The third lesson, however, is about the difficulty of curing Americans of their seemingly congenital fondness for simplicity. Two of the three visions entailed complex policies. Kissinger moved from bipolar competition to a triangular game and tried to turn Soviet-U.S. relations into a mix of containment and cooperation. Carter tried to apply the notion of mixed relationships even to friends and allies. He attempted to move from a strategy centered on great power geopolitics to a policy that gave precedence both to regional realities and to global issues.

Both Kissinger and Carter found themselves attacked for reasons that had little to do with their conceptions—Kissinger for the secrecy of his methods and the amorality of his inspiration; Carter for his incoherence and clumsiness. Yet both men were also savaged by those who could not accept any vision more subtle than that of a cold war crusade. Kissinger was criticized either for consorting with communist regimes or for not playing the China card against the Soviets hard enough, and for making deals with Moscow that—since the Kremlin wanted them—could be only in the enemy's interest.

Carter was denounced for undermining "moderately repressive" but friendly regimes and replacing them with even more repressive and hostile ones, for making unilateral concessions to Moscow such as canceling the B-1 bomber and the neutron bomb, for geopolitical naiveté in general. Kissinger himself joined an offensive against the Carter administration that originated in circles that had first targeted him. By 1979 a divided government faced an opposition united behind a nostalgic dream of return to the pious simplicities of the age of U.S. preponderance.

It is as if two archetypes only were competing for American approval: the Popeye archetype of the United States as the guardian of law and order, insuring stability and general happiness through strength and toughness; and the archetype of the missionary United States helping the poor abroad and bringing its values to those who suffer in the dark. Today's world fits neither scheme. But the reactions of much of the American political class, of some in the intellectual establishment, and of a majority of the public reminds one of the behavior of a patient who, disliking what he reads on his thermometer, breaks it.

Instead of examining the reasons for the divorce between these archetypes and the real world, many Americans prefer to blame other Americans. The purists tend to indict a corrupt, militaristic, or capitalist establishment for the failure of America's missionary vocation to rid the world of political and economic diseases. Those in the grip of a High Noon vision of America's role abroad blame the naive idealists, the tiresome exponents of complexity, the liberals who do not understand power, the writers who may be soft on communism, or that famous McGovern wing of the Democratic party that supposedly captured the Carter administration. They have gone dangerously far in convincing not only themselves, and the American public, but even America's friends and perhaps its foes that America has been dragged into decline by their domestic enemies. Internal settlements of accounts substitute for an appraisal of the state of the world.

It is this craving for simplicity rather than, as sociologist Michael Crozier says in his book *Le mal américain,* an inability to recognize and cope with evil, that is distinctively American; and it may well be one of America's major forms of parochialism, even in an age of inevitable involvement. Isolationism is dead, but the insular spirit that bred both of these activist archetypes lives on. Indeed, the last lesson is that the most distinctive American belief, generated by America's origins and confirmed by so much of America's history, remains the most resilient: faith in American exceptionalism.

Kissinger, toward the end of his tenure

in office, said that America had to learn to behave as an ordinary nation. Carter, by his understated manner and his reluctance toward grand imperial moves, his apparent meekness toward the challenges of pygmies, his willingness to accept not only military equality but also certain kinds of inequality with the Soviet Union, made people believe that he too accepted decline as inevitable. In the process, he allowed them to forget how much of the missionary archetype could be found in his original approach to world affairs. The Reagan victory was a revenge of exceptionalist faith.

The idea of a world in which the United States would be merely one actor like any other, or even a great power like so many others in history, remains intolerable. But if the denial of complexity and the dogma of exceptionalism, of the "city on the hill," are so deep and tenacious, yet incompatible with external realities, can one be confident that the new administration will be capable of offering more than an atavistic display of axiomatic assertiveness? Will the new administration be able to devise anything more than a mere series of ad hoc responses once it becomes obvious that nostalgia provides no road map, and military strength no panacea?

NOTES

1. Marina v. N. Whitman, "Leadership without Hegemony: Our Role in the World Economy," *Foreign Policy* 20 (Fall 1975).
2. "A Conversation with Zbigniew Brzezinski" on "Bill Moyers' Journal," on WNET, November 1980.
3. Robert Legvold, "Containment without Confrontation," *Foreign Policy* 40 (Fall 1980), p. 92.
4. "Bill Moyers' Journal."

Section I–D. A REVIVAL OF THE COLD WAR CONSENSUS? THE REAGAN ADMINISTRATION

While the administrations of Presidents Richard Nixon and Jimmy Carter attempted to replace the shattered cold war consensus with new foreign policy approaches, the administration of President Ronald Reagan has tried—in large measure—to restore the foreign policy values of that earlier era. For this administration, the Soviet Union and the threat of international communism were to be at the center of America's foreign policy. That nation and its ideology were primarily responsible for global unrest; therefore, international problems were to be viewed mainly through the East-West prism. The essential goal for the United States must be to restore its national will and capabilities and lead other free nations against this Soviet challenge. In essence, then, the more differentiated view of international politics that the Nixon and Carter administrations had attempted to employ in the post-Vietnam years was to be abandoned in favor of one closely akin to that of three decades earlier.

The first two essays summarize the effort by the Reagan administration to restore the principal elements of this earlier approach by squarely placing the Soviet Union at the center of U.S. foreign policy. The first selection, a speech by President Reagan to the British Parliament in June 1982, is a stinging attack upon totalitarianism and Marxist regimes and a ringing defense of freedom and democracy. The philosophical roots of American policy for the Reagan administration are fully evident in this presentation. In tone and design, moreover, the speech bears a sharp resemblance to President Truman's speech to a joint session of Congress in March 1947 (cf. pp. 56–60 above) as it pits two ways of life against one another.

Totalitarianism, not democracy, President Reagan argues, is on trial today. "From Stettin on the Baltic to Varna on the Black Sea, the regimes planted by totalitarianism have had more than 30 years to establish their legitimacy. But none—not one regime—has yet been able to risk free elections." We are also witnessing a great revolutionary crisis in the world today, President Reagan continues, "a crisis where the demands of the economic order are conflicting directly with those of the political order. But the crisis is happening not in the free, non-Marxist West, but in the home of Marxist-Leninism, the Soviet Union." Further, although the Soviet Union is unable to meet the demands of its own society, yet it continues to provide assistance to "Marxist-Leninists in many countries," as it had done since 1917.

By contrast, the desire for freedom is increasing on a global scale and democracy continues to take root in various regions of the world. Nonetheless, if this process is to continue, President Reagan asserts, the free nations of the world must commit themselves to assist the development of democracy around the world. If this were done over the long term, moreover, the "march of freedom and democracy . . . will leave Marxism-Leninism on the ashheap of history."

The second essay, "A Strategic Approach to American Foreign Policy," was originally a speech by former Secretary of State Alexander Haig to the American Bar Association in August 1981. This speech reiterates the centrality of the Soviet Union to America's foreign policy and outlines some specific foreign policy goals for the Reagan adminstration. First of all, Secretary of State Haig identifies the building of four pillars as crucial to the Reagan approach to the world: "the restoration of America's economic and military strength," "the reinvigoration of our alliances and friendships," "our commitment to progress in the developing countries through peaceful change," and "a relationship with the Soviet Union marked by greater Soviet restraint and greater Soviet reciprocity." Despite this cataloging of these four pillars, Haig makes clear that the last one is the focal point of this new American approach, since the others often depended upon success in this area for their achievement. Thus, efforts must be made by the United States to restrain Soviet involvement in exploiting regional conflicts, means must be sought to stabilize and reduce the level of armaments, and changes must be made in America's economic relationship with the Soviet Union and Eastern Europe. By undertaking such initiatives, the United States would be able to "create barriers" to Soviet aggression and build "incentives for Soviet restraint."

The last two essays in this section provide critiques of the Reagan foreign policy approach by analyzing its application in two important areas. The first deals with U.S. policy in Central America, while the other deals with America's arms policy toward the Soviet Union. In the essay entitled "The Reagan Administration and Revolutions in Central America," Walter LaFeber provides an overview of American policy toward El Salvador, Nicaragua, and Honduras from 1981 to 1983. LaFeber begins his analysis by outlining how revolutionary change in Central America has been largely viewed through the prism of the cold war by the Reagan administration, with Cuba and the Soviet Union identified as largely responsible for the unrest in that region. Furthermore, the Reagan administration proceeded to embrace the distinction between "authoritarian" and "totalitarian" regimes articulated by former UN Ambassador Jeane Kirkpatrick to justify its policy in the region. Finally, American policymakers also attempted to apply the principles of "Reaganomics" to the region—through its Caribbean Basin Initiative (CBI)—as a strategy to foster economic development.

Throughout the analysis, LaFeber raises serious doubts about the wisdom of these approaches to confronting the problem of revolutionary change in Central America. The Reagan administration, for instance, has failed to appreciate sufficiently the indigenous factors that have contributed to these changes; it has relied too much upon the use of force to resolve the problems in the short run without anticipating the long-term consequences of this strategy; and it has failed to pursue negotiations at crucial junctures when

they were offered. LaFeber concludes that the Reagan administration's interpretation of events and its actions may make matters worse for the United
States in the region. More generally, the actions clash with our historical
support for democracy and change.

As the Haig selection made clear, another important part of the Reagan
administration's approach to foreign policy, and toward the Soviet Union in
particular, was the rebuilding of America's defense forces. The building of
the MX missile, the B-1B bomber, and the Trident II missile were integral
parts of this rearmament program. In addition, though, the Reagan administration also proposed a new missile defense system for the future. In a March
1983 speech to the nation, President Reagan called for the United States to
"embark on a program to counter the awesome Soviet threat with measures
that are defensive." Such a system "could pave the way for arms control
measures to eliminate . . . [nuclear] weapons themselves." Formally called
the Strategic Defense Initiative (SDI), but more commonly known as "Star
Wars"—after the popular motion picture—this proposal has generated a
considerable amount of controversy.

In the last essay in this section, "Stabilizing Star Wars," Alvin M. Weinberg and Jack N. Barkenbus critique this proposal and provide what they
judge is a more workable alternative. The problem with the original "Star
Wars" system, they contend, is that it is "extremely expensive" to develop,
"vulnerable to . . . Soviet countermeasures, and deployable only in the 21st
century." More importantly, Star Wars does not guarantee that there would
be a reduction of offensive nuclear weapons as these new defensive systems
are deployed.

The authors' alternative, dubbed the "defense-protected build-down (DPB),"
seeks to overcome these difficulties by using currently available defense
technology and by requiring "symmetrical reduction of offensive forces based
upon credible estimates of the defense's effectiveness." Furthermore, this
DPB system would only be put into place incrementally as a further incentive for offensive weapons reductions. While Weinberg and Barkenbus acknowledge that their proposed system has some uncertainties, they do see
it as a more workable proposal than the "Star Wars" program. In this sense,
their essay serves as an important point of contrast with the policy approach
of the present administration and advances the debate on this important
aspect of American foreign policy.

15. ADDRESS TO MEMBERS OF THE BRITISH PARLIAMENT, JUNE 8, 1982

Ronald Reagan

My Lord Chancellor, Mr. Speaker:

The journey of which this visit forms a part is a long one. Already it has taken me to two great cities of the West, Rome and Paris, and to the economic summit at Versailles. And there, once again, our sister democracies have proved that even in a time of severe economic strain, free peoples can work together freely and voluntarily to address problems as serious as inflation, unemployment, trade, and economic development in a spirit of cooperation and solidarity.

Other milestones lie ahead. Later this week, in Germany, we and our NATO allies will discuss measures for our joint defense and America's latest initiatives for a more peaceful, secure world through arms reductions.

Each stop of this trip is important, but among them all, this moment occupies a special place in my heart and in the hearts of my countrymen—a moment of kinship and homecoming in these hallowed halls.

Speaking for all Americans, I want to say how very much at home we feel in your house. Every American would, because this is, as we have been so eloquently told, one of democracy's shrines. Here the rights of free people and the processes of representation have been debated and refined.

It has been said that an institution is the lengthening shadow of a man. This institution is the lengthening shadow of all the men and women who have sat here and all those who have voted to send representatives here.

This is my second visit to Great Britain as President of the United States. My first opportunity to stand on British soil occurred almost a year and a half ago when your Prime Minister graciously hosted a diplomatic dinner at the British Embassy in Washington. Mrs. Thatcher said then that she hoped I was not distressed to find staring down at me from the grand staircase a portrait of His Royal Majesty King George III. She suggested it was best to let bygones be bygones, and in view of our two countries' remarkable friendship in succeeding years, she added that most Englishmen today would agree with Thomas Jefferson that "a little rebellion now and then is a very good thing." [*Laughter*]

Well, from here I will go to Bonn and then Berlin, where there stands a grim symbol of power untamed. The Berlin Wall, that dreadful gray gash across the city, is in its third decade. It is the fitting signature of the regime that built it.

And a few hundred kilometers behind the Berlin Wall, there is another symbol. In the center of Warsaw, there is a sign that notes the distances to two capitals. In one direction it points toward Moscow. In the other it points toward Brussels, headquarters of Western Europe's tangible unity. The marker says that the

Source: *Public Papers of the Presidents of the United States, Ronald Reagan 1982* (Washington, D.C.: U.S. Government Printing Office, 1983), pp. 742–48.

distances from Warsaw to Moscow and Warsaw to Brussels are equal. The sign makes this point: Poland is not East or West. Poland is at the center of European civilization. It has contributed mightily to that civilization. It is doing so today by being magnificently unreconciled to oppression.

Poland's struggle to be Poland and to secure the basic rights we often take for granted demonstrates why we dare not take those rights for granted. Gladstone, defending the Reform Bill of 1866, declared, "You cannot fight against the future. Time is on our side." It was easier to believe in the march of democracy in Gladstone's day—in that high noon of Victorian optimism.

We're approaching the end of a bloody century plagued by a terrible political invention—totalitarianism. Optimism comes less easily today, not because democracy is less vigorous, but because democracy's enemies have refined their instruments of repression. Yet optimism is in order, because day by day democracy is proving itself to be a not-at-all-fragile flower. From Stettin on the Baltic to Varna on the Black Sea, the regimes planted by totalitarianism have had more than 30 years to establish their legitimacy. But none—not one regime—has yet been able to risk free elections. Regimes planted by bayonets do not take root.

The strength of the Solidarity movement in Poland demonstrates the truth told in an underground joke in the Soviet Union. It is that the Soviet Union would remain a one-party nation even if an opposition party were permitted, because everyone would join the opposition party. [*Laughter*]

America's time as a player on the stage of world history has been brief. I think understanding this fact has always made you patient with your younger cousins—

well, not always patient. I do recall that on one occasion, Sir Winston Churchill said in exasperation about one of our most distinguished diplomats: "He is the only case I know of a bull who carries his china shop with him." [*Laughter*]

But witty as Sir Winston was, he also had that special attribute of great statesmen—the gift of vision, the willingness to see the future based on the experience of the past. It is this sense of history, this understanding of the past that I want to talk with you about today, for it is in remembering what we share of the past that our two nations can make common cause for the future.

We have not inherited an easy world. If developments like the Industrial Revolution, which began here in England, and the gifts of science and technology have made life much easier for us, they have also made it more dangerous. There are threats now to our freedom, indeed to our very existence, that other generations could never even have imagined.

There is first the threat of global war. No President, no Congress, no Prime Minister, no Parliament can spend a day entirely free of this threat. And I don't have to tell you that in today's world the existence of nuclear weapons could mean, if not the extinction of mankind, then surely the end of civilization as we know it. That's why negotiations on intermediate-range nuclear forces now underway in Europe and the START talks—Strategic Arms Reduction Talks—which will begin later this month, are not just critical to Americans or Western policy; they are critical to mankind. Our commitment to early success in these negotiations is firm and unshakable, and our purpose is clear: reducing the risk of war by reducing the means of waging war on both sides.

At the same time there is a threat posed to human freedom by the enormous power of the modern state. History teaches the dangers of government that overreaches—political control taking precedence over free economic growth, secret police, mindless bureaucracy, all combining to stifle individual excellence and personal freedom.

Now, I'm aware that among us here and throughout Europe there is legitimate disagreement over the extent to which the public sector should play a role in a nation's economy and life. But on one point all of us are united—our abhorrence of dictatorship in all its forms, but most particularly totalitarianism and the terrible inhumanities it has caused in our time—the great purge, Auschwitz and Dachau, the Gulag, and Cambodia.

Historians looking back at our time will note the consistent restraint and peaceful intentions of the West. They will note that it was the democracies who refused to use the threat of their nuclear monopoly in the forties and early fifties for territorial or imperial gain. Had that nuclear monopoly been in the hands of the Communist world, the map of Europe—indeed, the world—would look very different today. And certainly they will note it was not the democracies that invaded Afghanistan or suppressed Polish Solidarity or used chemical and toxin warfare in Afghanistan and Southeast Asia.

If history teaches anything it teaches self-delusion in the face of unpleasant facts is folly. We see around us today the marks of our terrible dilemma—predictions of doomsday, antinuclear demonstrations, an arms race in which the West must, for its own protection, be an unwilling participant. At the same time we see totalitarian forces in the world who seek subversion and conflict around the globe to further their barbarous assault on the human spirit. What, then, is our course? Must civilization perish in a hail of fiery atoms? Must freedom wither in a quiet, deadening accommodation with totalitarian evil?

Sir Winston Churchill refused to accept the inevitability of war or even that it was imminent. He said, "I do not believe that Soviet Russia desires war. What they desire is the fruits of war and the indefinite expansion of their power and doctrines. But what we have to consider here today while time remains is the permanent prevention of war and the establishment of conditions of freedom and democracy as rapidly as possible in all countries."

Well, this is precisely our mission today: to preserve freedom as well as peace. It may not be easy to see; but I believe we live now at a turning point.

In an ironic sense Karl Marx was right. We are witnessing today a great revolutionary crisis, a crisis where the demands of the economic order are conflicting directly with those of the political order. But the crisis is happening not in the free, non-Marxist West, but in the home of Marxist-Leninism, the Soviet Union. It is the Soviet Union that runs against the tide of history by denying human freedom and human dignity to its citizens. It also is in deep economic difficulty. The rate of growth in the national product has been steadily declining since the fifties and is less than half of what it was then.

The dimensions of this failure are astounding: A country which employs one-fifth of its population in agriculture is unable to feed its own people. Were it not for the private sector, the tiny private sector tolerated in Soviet agriculture, the country might be on the brink of famine. These private plots occupy a bare 3 percent of the arable land but account for nearly one-quarter of Soviet farm output and nearly one-third of meat products and vegetables. Overcentralized, with little or no incentives, year after year the Soviet system pours its best resource into the making of instruments of destruction. The constant shrinkage of economic growth combined with the growth of military production is putting a heavy strain on the Soviet people. What we see here is a political structure that no longer corresponds to its economic base, a society where productive forces are hampered by political ones.

The decay of the Soviet experiment should come as no surprise to us. Wherever the comparisons have been made between free and closed societies—West Germany and East Germany, Austria and Czechoslovakia, Malaysia and Vietnam— it is the democratic countries that are prosperous and responsive to the needs of their people. And one of the simple but overwhelming facts of our time is this: Of all the millions of refugees we've seen in the modern world, their flight is always away from, not toward the Communist world. Today on the NATO line, our military forces face east to prevent a possible invasion. On the other side of the line, the Soviet forces also face east to prevent their people from leaving.

The hard evidence of totalitarian rule has caused in mankind an uprising of the intellect and will. Whether it is the growth of the new schools of economics in America or England or the appearance of the so-called new philosophers in France, there is one unifying thread running through the intellectual work of these groups—rejection of the arbitrary power of the state, the refusal to subordinate the rights of the individual to the superstate, the realization that collectivism stifles all the best human impulses.

Since the exodus from Egypt, historians have written of those who sacrificed and struggled for freedom—the stand at Thermopylae, the revolt of Spartacus, the storming of the Bastille, the Warsaw uprising in World War II. More recently we've seen evidence of this same human impulse in one of the developing nations in Central America. For months and months the world news media covered the fighting in El Salvador. Day after day we were treated to stories and film slanted toward the brave freedom-fighters battling oppressive government forces in behalf of the silent, suffering people of that tortured country.

And then one day those silent, suffering people were offered a chance to vote, to choose the kind of government they wanted. Suddenly the freedom-fighters in the hills were exposed for what they really are—Cuban-backed guerrillas who want power for themselves, and their backers, not democracy for the people. They threatened death to any who voted, and destroyed hundreds of buses and trucks to keep the people from getting to the polling places. But on election day, the people of El Salvador, an unprecedented 1.4 million of them, braved ambush and gunfire, and trudged for miles to vote for freedom.

They stood for hours in the hot sun waiting for their turn to vote. Members of our Congress who went there as observers told me of a woman who was wounded by rifle fire on the way to the polls, who refused to leave the line to have her wound treated until after she had voted. A grandmother, who had been told by the guerrillas she would be killed when she returned from the polls, and she told the guerrillas, "You can kill me, you can kill my family, kill my neighbors, but you can't kill us all." The real freedom-fighters of El Salvador turned out to be the people of that country—the young, the old, the in-between.

Strange, but in my own country, there's been little if any news coverage of that war since the election. Now, perhaps they'll say it's—well, because there are newer struggles now.

On distant islands in the South Atlantic young men are fighting for Britain. And, yes, voices have been raised protesting their sacrifice for lumps of rock and earth so far away. But those young men aren't fighting for mere real estate. They fight for a cause—for the belief that armed aggression must not be allowed to succeed, and the people must participate in the decisions of government—[*applause*]—the decisions of government under the rule of law. If there had been firmer support for that principle some 45 years ago, perhaps our generation wouldn't have suffered the bloodletting of World War II.

In the Middle East now the guns sound once more, this time in Lebanon, a country that for too long has had to endure the tragedy of civil war, terrorism, and foreign intervention and occupation. The fighting in Lebanon on the part of all parties must stop, and Israel should bring its forces home. But this is not enough. We must all work to stamp out the scourge of terrorism that in the Middle East makes war an ever-present threat.

But beyond the troublespots lies a deeper, more positive pattern. Around the world today, the democratic revolution is gathering new strength. In India a critical test has been passed with the peaceful change of governing political parties. In Africa, Nigeria is moving into remarkable and unmistakable ways to build and strengthen its democratic institutions. In the Caribbean and Central America, 16 of 24 countries have freely elected governments. And in the United Nations, 8 of the 10 developing nations which have joined that body in the past 5 years are democracies.

In the Communist world as well, man's instinctive desire for freedom and self-determination surfaces again and again. To be sure, there are grim reminders of how brutally the police state attempts to snuff out this quest for self-rule—1953 in East Germany, 1956 in Hungary, 1968 in Czechoslovakia, 1981 in Poland. But the struggle continues in Poland. And we know that there are even those who strive and suffer for freedom within the confines of the Soviet Union itself. How we conduct ourselves here in the Western democracies will determine whether this trend continues.

No, democracy is not a fragile flower. Still it needs cultivating. If the rest of this century is to witness the gradual growth of freedom and democratic ideals, we must take actions to assist the campaign for democracy.

Some argue that we should encourage democratic change in right-wing dictatorships, but not in Communist regimes. Well, to accept this preposterous notion— as some well-meaning people have—is to invite the argument that once countries achieve a nuclear capability, they should be allowed an undisturbed reign of terror over their own citizens. We reject this course.

As for the Soviet view, Chairman Brezhnev repeatedly has stressed that the competition of ideas and systems must continue and that this is entirely consistent with relaxation of tensions and peace.

Well, we ask only that these systems begin by living up to their own constitutions, abiding by their own laws, and complying with the international obligations they have undertaken. We ask only for a process, a direction, a basic code of decency, not for an instant transformation.

We cannot ignore the fact that even without our encouragement there has been and will continue to be repeated explosions against repression and dictatorships. The Soviet Union itself is not immune to this reality. Any system is inherently unstable that has no peaceful means to legitimize its leaders. In such cases, the very repressiveness of the state ultimately drives people to resist it, if necessary, by force.

While we must be cautious about forcing the pace of change, we must not hesitate to declare our ultimate objectives and to take concrete actions to move toward them. We must be staunch in our conviction that freedom is not the sole prerogative of a lucky few, but the inalienable and universal right of all human beings. So states the United Nations Universal Declaration of Human Rights, which, among other things, guarantees free elections.

The objective I propose is quite simple to state: to foster the infrastructure of democracy, the system of a free press, unions, political parties, universities, which allows a people to choose their own way to develop their own culture, to reconcile their own differences through peaceful means.

This is not cultural imperialism, it is providing the means for genuine self-determination and protection for diversity. Democracy already flourishes in countries with very different cultures and historical experiences. It would be cultural condescension, or worse, to say that any people prefer dictatorship to democracy. Who would voluntarily choose not to have the right to vote, decide to purchase government propaganda handouts instead of independent newspapers, prefer government to worker-controlled unions, opt for land to be owned by the state instead of those who till it, want government repression of religious liberty, a single political party instead of a free choice, a rigid cultural orthodoxy instead of democratic tolerance and diversity?

Since 1917 the Soviet Union has given covert political training and assistance to Marxist-Leninists in many countries. Of course, it also has promoted the use of violence and subversion by these same forces. Over the past several decades, West European and other Social Democrats, Christian Democrats, and leaders have offered open assistance to fraternal, political, and social institutions to bring about peaceful and democratic progress. Appropriately, for a vigorous new democracy, the Federal Republic of Germany's political foundations have become a major force in this effort.

We in America now intend to take additional steps, as many of our allies have already done, toward realizing this same goal. The chairmen and other leaders of the national Republican and Democratic Party organizations are initiating a study with the bipartisan American Political Foundation to determine how the United States can best contribute as a nation to the global campaign for democracy now gathering force. They will have the cooperation of congressional leaders of both parties, along with representatives of business, labor, and other major institutions in our society. I look forward to receiving their recommendations and to working with these institutions and the Congress in the common task of strengthening democracy throughout the world.

It is time that we committed ourselves as a nation—in both the public and private sectors—to assisting democratic development.

We plan to consult with leaders of other nations as well. There is a proposal before the Council of Europe to invite parliamentarians from democratic countries to a meeting next year in Strasbourg. That prestigious gathering could consider ways to help democratic political movements. This November in Washington there will take place an international meeting on free elections. And next spring there will be a conference of world authorities on constitutionalism and self-government hosted by the Chief Justice of the United States. Authorities from a number of developing and developed countries—judges, philosophers, and politicians with practical experience—have agreed to explore how to turn principle into practice and further the rule of law.

At the same time, we invite the Soviet Union to consider with us how the competition of ideas and values—which it is committed to support—can be conducted on a peaceful and reciprocal basis. For example, I am prepared to offer President Brezhnev an opportunity to speak to the American people on our television if he will allow me the same opportunity with the Soviet people. We also suggest that panels of our newsmen periodically appear on each other's television to discuss major events.

Now, I don't wish to sound overly optimistic, yet the Soviet Union is not immune from the reality of what is going on in the world. It has happened in the past—a small ruling elite either mistakenly attempts to ease domestic unrest through greater repression and foreign adventure, or it chooses a wiser course. It begins to allow its people a voice in their own destiny. Even if this latter process is not realized soon, I believe the renewed strength of the democratic movement, complemented by a global campaign for freedom, will strengthen the prospects for arms control and a world at peace.

I have discussed on other occasions, including my address on May 9th, the elements of Western policies toward the Soviet Union to safeguard our interests and protect the peace. What I am describing now is a plan and a hope for the long term—the march of freedom and de-

mocracy which will leave Marxism-Leninism on the ashheap of history as it has left other tyrannies which stifle the freedom and muzzle the self-expression of the people. And that's why we must continue our efforts to strengthen NATO even as we move forward with our Zero-Option initiative in the negotiations on intermediate-range forces and our proposal for a one-third reduction in strategic ballistic missile warheads.

Our military strength is a prerequisite to peace, but let it be clear we maintain this strength in the hope it will never be used, for the ultimate determinant in the struggle that's now going on in the world will not be bombs and rockets, but a test of wills and ideas, a trial of spiritual resolve, the values we hold, the beliefs we cherish, the ideals to which we are dedicated.

The British people know that, given strong leadership, time and a little bit of hope, the forces of good ultimately rally and triumph over evil. Here among you is the cradle of self-government, the Mother of Parliaments. Here is the enduring greatness of the British contribution to mankind, the great civilized ideas: individual liberty, representative government, and the rule of law under God.

I've often wondered about the shyness of some of us in the West about standing for these ideals that have done so much to ease the plight of man and the hardships of our imperfect world. This reluctance to use those vast resources at our command reminds me of the elderly lady whose home was bombed in the Blitz. As the rescuers moved about, they found a bottle of brandy she'd stored behind the staircase, which was all that was left standing. And since she was barely conscious, one of the workers pulled the cork to give her a taste of it. She came around immediately and said, "Here now—there now,

put it back. That's for emergencies."
[*Laughter*]

Well, the emergency is upon us. Let us be shy no longer. Let us go to our strength. Let us offer hope. Let us tell the world that a new age is not only possible but probable.

During the dark days of the Second World War, when this island was incandescent with courage, Winston Churchill exclaimed about Britain's adversaries. "What kind of a people do they think we are?" Well, Britain's adversaries found out what extraordinary people the British are. But all the democracies paid a terrible price for allowing the dictators to underestimate us. We dare not make that mistake again. So, let us ask ourselves, "What kind of people do we think we are?" And let us answer, "Free people, worthy of freedom and determined not only to remain so but to help others gain their freedom as well."

Sir Winston led his people to great victory in war and then lost an election just as the fruits of victory were about to be enjoyed. But he left office honorably, and,

as it turned out, temporarily, knowing that the liberty of his people was more important than the fate of any single leader. History recalls his greatness in ways no dictator will ever know. And he left us a message of hope for the future, as timely now as when he first uttered it, as opposition leader in the Commons nearly 27 years ago, when he said, "When we look back on all the perils through which we have passed and at the mighty foes that we have laid low and all the dark and deadly designs that we have frustrated, why should we fear for our future? We have," he said, "come safely through the worst."

Well, the task I've set forth will long outlive our own generation. But together, we too have come through the worst. Let us now begin a major effort to secure the best—a crusade for freedom that will engage the faith and fortitude of the next generation. For the sake of peace and justice, let us move toward a world in which all people are at last free to determine their own destiny.

Thank you.

16. A STRATEGIC APPROACH TO AMERICAN FOREIGN POLICY

Alexander Haig

Americans admire law. At its best, it expresses our sense of justice, moderation, and fair play. It also reflects our national character—our enthusiastic idealism and our famous pragmatism. Uncoordinated, these traits could lead us in contradictory directions. Yet when they are in balance, they give us the strength, confidence, and skill that has made us great.

We have discovered that foreign policy, like law, must be rooted in the strength of our national character. A foreign policy that forsakes ideals in order to manipulate interests offends our sense of right. A foreign policy that forsakes power in order to pursue pieties offends our sense of reality. Only a vision with worthy ideals can capture our imagination. Only a practical program for achieving those ideals can be worthy of our support.

Despite the vicissitudes of history, Americans have always rallied to the vision of a world characterized by freedom, peace, and progress. President Reagan shares this vision. He also understands that progress toward such a world depends on the strength of the United States. More than money and arms, such strength comes from our willingness to work for our convictions and even to fight for them.

In the 1980s, these convictions will be put to a hard test. Familiar patterns of alliance and ideology are breaking down, and strategic changes have already occurred that demand a different approach to American foreign policy. Let us summarize these changes briefly.

- The Communist bloc, once the tightly disciplined instrument of Soviet power, has been shaken by the Sino-Soviet schism. Increasingly severe internal problems afflict the Soviet-controlled states. And chronic economic failure has eroded the appeal of Marxist-Leninist theories.
- At the same time, the Third World has emerged in all of its diversity. The fragile initial solidarity of the modernizing states has begun to fragment. Their internal stability is threatened by sudden social, political, and economic change. Simultaneously, the West has become increasingly dependent on their natural resources.
- The prospects for peaceful progress have been overshadowed, not only by regional conflict but also by the emergence of the Soviet Union as a global military power. The Soviets have chosen to use their power to take advantage of instability, especially in the developing world. They have become bolder in the promotion of violent change.
- The new Soviet military capability has not been offset by Western strength. The United States has gradually lost many of the military advantages that once provided a margin of safety for the West—in some cases

Source: *Department of State Bulletin,* September 1981, pp. 10–13.

by choice, in others through neglect and error. Our partnership with Western Europe and Japan has been shaken by quarrels over political and economic issues.

These strategic changes raise important questions about Western security in the decade ahead.

- Can the United States and its allies finance the rebuilding of their military strength? The answer is yes. Despite our economic troubles, we possess resources far exceeding those of potential adversaries. But this depends on popular support for defense policies and a diplomacy that encourages cooperation.
- Can the Atlantic alliance and other collaborative institutions survive in the new environment? The answer is yes. The cooperative impulse still exists. But this impulse may not survive another decade of relative military decline or sterile economic rivalry.
- Can the West and the developing countries find common interests? The answer is yes. The West alone offers the technology and know-how essential to overcoming the barriers to modernization. The developing countries, whatever their ideology, are beginning to recognize this fact. But a successful relationship also demands an imaginative approach on our part to both the economic and the security aspects of modernization.
- Can the United States hold together its allies and friendships, despite adverse strategic changes? The answer is yes. But our allies and friends must be confident of American leadership. They must also be confident that the security arrangements deterring the

Soviet Union are effective, and we are the linchpin of these arrangements. The American role remains unique and indispensable.

These crucial questions can all be answered in the affirmative if American foreign policy is sensitive to both American ideals and the changes in the strategic environment. President Reagan believes that the key to success lies in a strategic approach. The time is long past when we could pursue foreign, defense, and economic policies independently of each other. In today's world, the failure of one will beget the failure of the others. Instead, each of these policies must support the others if any is to succeed. And success in each makes for the success of all.

PILLARS OF SUPPORT

This strategic approach provides the support for a new foreign policy structure with four pillars: first, the restoration of our economic and military strength; second, the reinvigoration of our alliances and friendships; third, the promotion of progress in the developing countries through peaceful change; and fourth, a relationship with the Soviet Union characterized by restraint and reciprocity.

The first pillar of our foreign policy is the restoration of America's economic and military strength. The President understands that a weak American economy will eventually cripple our efforts abroad. His revolutionary programs of budgetary reductions, tax cuts, and investment incentives have earned the overwhelming support of the American people and the Congress. After years of persistent problems, American economic recovery will not be easy. But hope in a better future— a sounder dollar, more creative enterprise, and a more effective government— has been raised.

At the same time, the President is taking long overdue action to correct our military deficiencies. This includes modernization and balanced expansion of our existing forces. It also includes the improvement of our industrial base. These efforts will make it easier for the United States, our allies, and other nations to resist threats by the Soviet Union or its surrogates.

The American people's willingness to support this program, even in time of austerity, is the indispensable signal that we are prepared to defend our vital interests. But we should not delude ourselves. A beginning is not enough. If we fail to follow through on these forecast improvements to our defenses, then our foreign policy, our prosperity, and ultimately our freedom will be in jeopardy.

The second pillar is the reinvigoration of our alliances and friendships. We have been working toward a more effective Western partnership, sensitive to the concerns of our allies and built on a more sophisticated process of consultation. Already, we have taken action together on such issues as the Polish crisis and theater nuclear forces. We are also working on common approaches to the problems of southern Africa. Finally, the Ottawa summit has enabled the leaders of the West to deepen their understanding of each other's policies.

American leadership means cooperation with friends as well as with allies. Such cooperation is not a favor, it is a necessity. We need friends to succeed. And both we and our friends must be strong and faithful to each other if our interests are to be preserved. Our actions in the Far East, in Southwest Asia, and in the Middle East have demonstrated that the era of American passivity is over.

The third pillar of our policy is our commitment to progress in the developing countries through peaceful change. We want to establish a just and responsible relationship with the developing countries. This relationship will be based, in part, on our belief that our principles speak to their aspirations and that our accomplishments speak to their future. But it will also be based on our mutual interest in modernization. Western capital, trade, and technology are essential to this process.

The United States stands ready to assist the developing countries and to participate in the so-called North-South dialogue. President Reagan recognizes that the essence of development is the creation of additional wealth rather than the selective redistribution of existing wealth from one part of the world to another. Progress depends on both domestic economic policies and on the strength of the world economy. The governments of the developed and developing countries, along with the private sector, each have their special roles to play in establishing the close and constructive relationships that are crucial to success.

The United States has already begun to put this new approach into practice through a unique program with Jamaica. We are also acting with Mexico, Venezuela, and Canada to create a Caribbean Basin plan. And we are looking forward to the Cancun summit. We believe that this summit, free of a confrontational atmosphere, will facilitate the dialogue on problems of the developing countries.

Western assistance for development stands in stark contrast to the actions of the Soviet Union, which offers little economic aid. Instead, Moscow and its surrogates seek to exploit historic change and regional conflict to the detriment of peaceful progress. The United States and its allies are working with regional partners to arrest the trend toward violence and instability, and we have increased our security assistance in recognition of the crucial link between modernization and political stability.

The fourth pillar is a relationship with the Soviet Union marked by greater Soviet restraint and greater Soviet reciprocity. I want to discuss this pillar at length today because Soviet-American relations must be at the center of our efforts to promote a more peaceful world.

Over a century ago, Alexis de Tocqueville predicted that the United States and Russia were destined to become the world's most powerful states. This prophecy has come to pass in the nuclear age. Our unreconciled differences on human rights must, therefore, not be permitted to bring a global catastrophe. We must compete with the Soviet Union to protect freedom, but we must also search for cooperation to protect mankind.

This search has been both difficult and disappointing. Most recently, we invested extraordinary efforts in the decade-long search for detente. But even as the search for a reduction in tensions intensified, the instrument of tension—Soviet military power—was strengthened. This buildup gained momentum from a remarkably stable and prosperous period in Soviet history.

As the Soviet arsenal grew and the West failed to keep pace, Moscow's interventionism increased. The achievement of global military power, justified as parity with the West but exceeding it in several categories, assumed a more ominous role: the promotion of violent change, especially in areas of vital interest to the West. Today's Soviet military machine far exceeds the requirements of defense; it undermines the balance of power on which we and our allies depend, and it threatens the peace of the world. An international system where might—Soviet might—

makes right, endangers the prospects for peaceful change and the independence of every country.

Perhaps predictably, the Soviet attempt to alter the balance of power has produced a backlash. The American people have shown that they will not support unequal treaties; they will not accept military inferiority. The once-staunch Chinese ally has become an implacable opponent of the Soviet quest for hegemony. And Moscow has earned the enmity and fear of many nonaligned states through such actions as the occupation of Afghanistan and support for Vietnam's subjugation of Kampuchea.

This backlash comes at a time when Soviet prospects are changing for the worse. The economies of Moscow's East European allies are in various stages of decline. The Soviet economy itself may have lost its capacity for the high growth of the past. Ambitious foreign and defense policies are, therefore, becoming more of a burden. Perhaps most seriously, as events in Poland have demonstrated, the Soviet ideology and economic model are widely regarded as outmoded.

The decade of the 1980s, therefore, promises to be less attractive for Moscow. But the troubles and power of the Soviet Union should give pause to the world. Moscow's unusual combination of weakness and strength is especially challenging to the United States.

What do we want of the Soviet Union? We want greater Soviet restraint on the use of force. We want greater Soviet respect for the independence of others. And we want the Soviets to abide by their reciprocal obligations, such as those undertaken in the Helsinki accords. These are no more than we demand of any state, and these are no less than required by the U.N. Charter and international law. The rules of the Charter governing the international use of force will lose all of their influence on the behavior of nations if the Soviet Union continues its aggressive course.

Our pursuit of greater Soviet restraint and reciprocity should draw upon several lessons painfully learned over the past decade in dealing with the Soviet Union.

- Soviet antagonism toward Western ideals is deeply rooted. We cannot count upon a convergence of Soviet and Western political principles or strategic doctrines. Convergence should not be, and cannot be, a goal in negotiations. As a corollary, we should avoid dangerous optimism about the prospects for more benign Soviet objectives.
- The Soviet Union does not create every international conflict, but it would be dangerous to ignore Soviet intervention that aggravates such conflict. Even as we work to deal with international problems on their own terms, we must deal with Soviet interventionism. A regional approach that fails to appreciate the strategic aspect of Soviet activity will fail ultimately to resolve regional conflicts as well.
- A working relationship with the Soviet Union depends on a balance of alternatives and our ability to communicate to Moscow that such alternatives exist. We must indicate our willingness to reach fair agreements that speak to the legitimate interests of both the Soviet Union and the United States. But we must also be prepared to defend our interests in the absence of such agreements. Our ability to do so will be a major inducement for Soviet cooperation.
- Finally, the search for real reductions in tension with Moscow must cover the full spectrum of our relationship. We have learned that Soviet-American agreements, even in strategic arms control, will not survive Soviet threats to the overall military balance or Soviet encroachment upon our strategic interests in critical regions of the world. Linkage is not a theory; it is a fact of life that we overlook at our peril.

U.S. ACTIONS

Based on these guidelines, the United States has taken steps toward the achievement of a more stable and beneficial relationship with the Soviet Union. Our actions have been shaped both by the lessons of the past and by Winston Churchill's observation that the key to the Soviet riddle was Soviet national interest.

President Reagan has written President [Leonid I.] Brezhnev that we want a constructive and mutually beneficial relationship with the Soviet Union.

What, in turn, do we offer the Soviets? We offer a reduction in the tensions that are so costly to both our societies. We offer diplomatic alternatives to the pursuit of violent change. We offer fair and balanced agreements on arms control. And we offer the possibility of Western trade and technology.

But such a relationship can only be the consequence of a pattern of greater Soviet restraint. In the absence of such restraint, our military capability, our alliances, and our friendships will enable us to protect our interests.

Over the last 6 months, this message has been reinforced by over 50 direct contacts at senior diplomatic levels. And we have prepared a concrete agenda of the outstanding problems between us in these areas: geopolitical issues, arms control, and economic relations.

Geopolitical Issues. The most persistent troubles in U.S.-Soviet relations arise from Soviet intervention in regional conflicts, aggravating tensions, and hampering the search for peaceful solutions. Unless we can come to grips with this dimension of Soviet behavior, everything else in our bilateral relationship will be undermined, as we have seen repeatedly in the past.

The Soviet Union must understand that it cannot succeed in dominating the world through aggression. A serious and sustained international reaction will be the inevitable result, with greater dangers for everyone—including Moscow. The Soviet Government must recognize that such a reaction has finally occurred, provoked by the crises of Afghanistan and Kampuchea. And the international community has proposed ways and means for resolving those crises to the satisfaction of all legitate interests.

The people of Afghanistan overwhelmingly oppose the Soviet occupation and the Babrak Karmal regime. The vast majority of the world's nations are challenging the Soviets to come to the negotiating table, to agree to a political solution, to withdraw their forces, and to restore Afghanistan's nonaligned status. The proposal of the European Community for a two-stage conference is a sound step toward the achievement of these objectives. But the Soviet Union still prefers to promote a bizarre theme: that the United States is unwilling to negotiate about questions of critical international concern; that the United States wants a return to the cold war; that the United States is the source of the trouble in Afghanistan.

The Soviet Union must begin to understand that Afghan resistance and international pressure will be sustained. By supporting initiatives such as that of the European Community, we offer the Soviet Union the alternative of an honorable solution.

The same is true for Kampuchea. The U.N. conference and the attempts of the ASEAN [Association of South East Asian Nations] nations to find a political solution to the Soviet-supported Vietnamese occupation have won broad support. Here, too, the international community has been rebuffed by Vietnamese and Soviet refusal even to attend the conference. Here as well, we believe that patience and perseverance—and the design of sound diplomatic solutions—offer the Soviets and their surrogate the choice: international isolation and failure or international cooperation and a way out.

I have often mentioned the activities of the Soviet Union and its Cuban proxy in aggravating tensions from Central America to southern Africa. Can there be a greater contrast between their efforts and those of the West in trying to resolve the political, economic, and security problems of these regions?

It is time for those who preach peace to contribute to peace. The way to do it is through new restraint, both in Moscow and Havana.

Arms Control. Our past hopes for relaxation of tensions with the Soviet Union were eventually concentrated on the search for arms control. But we overestimated the extent to which arms control negotiations would ease tensions elsewhere. And we underestimated the impact of conflict elsewhere on the arms control process itself. The attempt to regulate and reduce nuclear weapons must remain an essential part of the East-West agenda, but we must focus on its central purpose: to reduce the risk of war.

Only balanced and verifiable agreements that establish true parity at reduced levels can increase our security. I have already addressed the broader principles that govern our approach. As we begin this part of the dialogue, it is essential to recognize that fair agreements can be reached with patience and perseverance. Above all, we must demonstrate that we can sustain the balance by our own efforts if agreements fail to do so. Indeed, if we do not cause the Soviets to believe that in the absence of arms control they face a more difficult future, they will have little or no incentive to negotiate seriously.

- On this basis, we have commenced discussions with the Soviets on theater nuclear forces, and we have proposed that formal negotiations open before the end of this year. We want equal, verifiable limits at the lowest possible level of U.S. and Soviet long-range theater nuclear weapons.
- We have also launched a frank discussion of compliance with existing arms control agreements.
- We have initiated the intense preparations and conceptual studies that must precede a resumption of progress in Strategic Arms Limitation Talks.
- We and our European allies have proposed an innovative new set of confidence-building measures in Europe, which could provide a valuable means to reduce uncertainty about the character and purpose of the other side's military activities.

It is now up to the Soviet Government to put its rhetoric of cooperation into action.

Economic Relations. East-West economic ties are also on our agenda with the Soviet Union. Over the past decade, these ties have grown rapidly, but they have not restrained the Soviet use of force. The time has come to refashion East-

West economic relations. We shall seek to expand those ties that strengthen peace and serve the true interests of both sides.

The Soviets have looked toward Western agriculture, technology, trade, and finance in order to relieve the pressing economic problems of Eastern Europe and of the Soviet Union itself. But the Soviet leaders must understand that we cannot have full and normal economic relations if they are not prepared to respect international norms of behavior. We must, therefore, work to constrain Soviet economic leverage over the West. Above all, we should not allow the transfer of Western technology that increases Soviet war-making capabilities.

SUMMARY

In sum, American strategy toward the Soviet Union is proceeding on two fronts simultaneously.

First, we are creating barriers to aggression. We are renewing American strength. We are joining with our allies and friends to protect our joint interests. And we are making strenuous efforts to resolve crises which could facilitate Soviet intervention.

Second, we are creating incentives for Soviet restraint. We are offering a broader relationship of mutual benefit. This includes political agreements to resolve outstanding regional conflicts. It encompasses balanced and verifiable arms control agreements. And it holds the potential benefits of greater East-West trade.

We are not under any illusion that agreement with the Soviets will be easy to achieve. The strong element of competition in our relations is destined to remain. Nonetheless, we believe that the renewal of America's confidence and strength will have a constructive and moderating effect upon the Soviet leaders. By rebuilding our strength, reinvigorating our alliances, and promoting progress through peaceful change, we are creating the conditions that make restraint and reciprocity the most realistic Soviet options. The Soviets will eventually respond to a policy that clearly demonstrates both our determination to restrain their continued self-aggrandizement and our willingness to reciprocate their self-restraint.

The four pillars of foreign policy that I have described today will not be easy to build. International reality tells us that the hazards are great and the tasks enormous. We can expect disappointments. We should be prepared for reverses. Some will tell us that we are dreaming of a world that can never be. Others will tell us that the reassertion of American leadership is out of tune with the times.

An American foreign policy of cynical *realpolitik* cannot succeed because it leaves no room for the idealism that has characterized us from the inception of our national life. An America that accepts passively a threatening strategic environment is not true to itself or to the world. The test of our foreign policy is ultimately the test of our character as a nation.

Winston Churchill once said: "The only real sure guide to the actions of mighty nations and powerful governments is a correct estimate of what they are and what they consider to be their own interests." Our foreign policy must partake of what we are, what we represent to ourselves and to the world. Surely, the secret of America's ability to renew itself is our fundamental confidence in the individual. We stand for the rights, responsibilities, and genius of the individual. We rely on the individual's capacity to dream of a better future and to work for it. This is the conscience, even the soul of America. Ultimately this is what America is about. Ultimately, we must be prepared to give our fortunes, lives, and sacred honor to this cause.

17. THE REAGAN ADMINISTRATION AND REVOLUTIONS IN CENTRAL AMERICA

Walter LaFeber

Recent U.S. presidents have won office less for having proved their talent in governing than for an ability to soothe. These presidents have resembled the clergy welcomed by a tragedy-stricken family. Richard Nixon's mysterious "plan" for peace helped him defeat the Vietnam-tarred ticket led by Hubert Humphrey. Jimmy Carter's non-Washington background seemed a welcome relief after the chicanery of Watergate and the Nixon pardon. Ronald Reagan offered both congeniality (a welcome contrast to Carter's up-tight insecurity) and a soothing traditionalism that promised the triumph of the nation's past over the complexities of its future.

In no foreign policy area has Reagan's traditionalism been more apparent than in Central America. And no area needed more attention. His ambassador to the United Nations, Jeane Kirkpatrick, warned in early 1981 that "Central America is the most important place in the world for the United States today." Many North Americans seemed to share that view, at least in 1980. Reagan consequently ran on a Republican platform that deplored "the Marxist Sandinista takeover of Nicaragua and the Marxist attempts to destabilize El Salvador, Guatemala, and Honduras." The plank condemned Carter's offer of aid to the Nicaraguans.

The platform then warned of possible future action: "However, we [Republicans] will support the efforts of the Nicaraguan people to establish a free and independent government."[1] Arguing that foreign devils and ideologies were to blame for Nicaraguan troubles, these words ignored reality. If Central America had suddenly become "the most important place in the world" for U.S. security, Washington officials had made it so through a century of North American involvement, and particularly by their post-1954 military and economic policies. The overwhelming number of Central Americans were in rebellion because their children starved, not because they knew or cared anything about Marxism.

Reagan's closest advisers elaborated the platform's themes. Richard Allen, soon to be the president's national security adviser, reassured frustrated voters during the campaign that the new administration would stop "Fidel Castro's Soviet-directed, armed and financed marauders in Central America." Allen urged the use of military force. In a fascinating interpretation of the past century of U.S. interventions in the Caribbean region, Allen added: "U.S. military power has always been the basis for the development of a just and humane foreign policy." He played to a large number of North Americans who felt that, in the words of one irate citizen, "What we need is another Teddy Roosevelt."[2] The halcyon days of empire building could be recaptured, if only North Americans thought positively, acted militarily, and rewrote history.

Source: *Inevitable Revolutions, The United States in Central America*, by Walter LaFeber, by permission of the author and W. W. Norton & Company, Inc. Copyright © 1984, 1983 by Suzanne Margaret LaFeber.

196

REAGAN AND THE COLD WAR PRISM

The rewriting of history was of special importance. After the experiences of Vietnam, many North Americans were reluctant to become involved in another indigenous revolution. The new administration and its supporters tried to circumvent that problem by declaring, in the president's words, that the Vietnam conflict was "a noble cause," and—more important—that the problems in Central America were not indigenous but caused by Castro and the Soviet Union.

Within a month after taking office, Secretary of State Alexander Haig warned North Atlantic Treaty Organization (NATO) delegates that "a well-orchestrated Communist campaign designed to transform the Salvadoran crisis from the internal conflict to an increasingly internationalized confrontation is underway." In mid-March, a "senior official"—obviously Haig—declared the revolutions were part of "a global problem," so "we have to talk to the Russians about them."[3] The mistakes in Vietnam would not be repeated; instead of trying to resolve the problem within only Central America, the administration intended to "go to the source" of the problem. The phrase meant a possible attack on Cuba, since Castro's regime, in the words of Assistant Secretary of State for Inter-American Affairs Thomas Enders, "is a Soviet surrogate."[4]

Reagan then raised tensions with Cuba to the highest pitch since the 1962 missile crisis. Some officials demurred. The top U.S. official in Havana, Wayne Smith, told the State Department that Castro's aid to the revolutionaries had been greatly overestimated, and the Cuban leader wanted to negotiate with—not confront—the United States. Enders nevertheless repeatedly accused Castro of uniting revolutionary factions so that, as they had in Nicaragua, the rebels could establish "more Marxist-Leninist regimes in this hemisphere." At best this was a partial truth. Not Castro, but the Catholic church and professional groups had been most critical in creating a united front against Anastasio Somoza in 1978 and 1979. But that interpretation threatened the administration's simpler views about Central American revolutionaries. Enders was correct in claiming that Cuban arms helped the Sandinists. He neglected to add, however, that they received more weapons from other sources, including Venezuela and the U.S. Mafia.[5]

The major administration effort to sell its version of Central American history came in mid-February 1981, when the State Department issued a long "White Paper" on Cuban and Soviet involvement in El Salvador. Within four months, the White Paper came under scathing attacks from correspondent John Dinges of the *Los Angeles Times* and Latin American expert James Petras in *The Nation*. In June they were joined by the *Washington Post* and, most remarkably, by the usually pro-administration *Wall Street Journal*. These attacks shredded the White Paper's claim that Cuban and Soviet officials guided the revolutionaries, and that large Soviet bloc arms shipments enabled the rebels to expand their control. The State Department then issued a second White Paper that acknowledged errors in the first, but reasserted claims about Soviet and Cuban involvement.[6] The second paper convinced few more readers than had the first. No serious observer doubted that Castro and Russian officials were deeply interested in the revolutions and worked to encourage them. But few outside the administration believed that the Soviet bloc provided most of the arms (which came largely from the immense private international arms market or from dead or captured government soldiers), or that international communism rather than nationalism actually fueled the revolutions.

By late March 1981, the administration's policy was in trouble. Despite Reagan's obvious talents as a communicator, public opinion polls showed North Americans overwhelmingly opposed to any U.S. military involvement in Central America; they were highly skeptical of the Reagan-Haig approach.[7] A State Department expert on Latin America declared anonymously that perhaps the crisis had been overblown by the media. In this case, however, the media had only avidly followed the administration's lead.[8]

The White House staff tried to deflate the crisis because of fear that the Central American fireworks distracted North Americans from supporting Reagan's domestic economic measures, which were approaching decisive action in Congress. But the president was also bitter. Asked on March 27 about his foreign policy problems, he blamed them on a worldwide conspiracy: "We have to recognize that the campaign against what we're doing, the helping of El Salvador, is a pretty concerted and well-orchestrated thing." The propaganda, he went on, has "been world-wide. And you find the same slogans being used in demonstrations in European countries about the United States in El Salvador. You find it here." That explanation failed to explain why the Roman Catholic church, Mexico, and Venezuela, among many other anti-Communists, opposed the Reagan-Haig definition of—and a military solution for—the Central American crises.

The president's words closely resembled the "paranoid style," as historian Richard Hofstadter had noted during the 1960s, that frequently afflicted North Americans. But the administration kept at it. After examining these explanations and the release of documents to support the explanations, the authoritative *Latin America Weekly Report* of London claimed that "the administration has been grossly inept, misusing, manipulating, and inventing evidence. This has meant that even when it does have a case, few believe it."[9]

In view of these failures, why did the Reagan administration persist in following its policies? A number of reasons can be offered. The president and his closest White House advisers were inexperienced and ignorant of foreign policy. Their background and ideology led them sincerely to believe that the Soviets caused most of the world's problems, even in Central America. Their approach, moreover, promised sweet political rewards. By fixing on the areas as the first arena for confrontation with the Soviets, the administration could win in its own "backyard." The world could see then that Carterism had given way to tough Republicanism. Reagan thus escalated a regional conflict into a global confrontation between the superpowers. Knowing little about Central America, and—ironically—actually underestimating the power of the revolutionaries, the president refused to pursue a possible political settlement in El Salvador after the rebel offensive failed in early 1981. He decided instead to display U.S. power.

His advisers had little idea of how to deal with Communists or revolutionaries outside of using force. Lacking the Richard Nixon-Henry Kissinger subtlety in using China and economic leverage to contain the Soviets, or anything resembling Carter's policy of employing human rights as a diplomatic weapon, the new administration could not think creatively in political and diplomatic terms. Any tendency to think politically was short-circuited by a purge in the State Department that removed many of the Foreign Service officers who were most experienced in Latin American affairs and whose places were taken by military officers appointed by Haig. The most notable were General Vernon Walters, former deputy director of the Central Intelligence Agency (CIA), who long had intimate ties with Latin American dictators; Robert McFarlane, a former Marine Corps officer whom Haig named as State Department counselor; and Lieutenant-General Gordon Sumner.[10]

Some of the strongest opposition to Haig's policies, however, came from the Pentagon. In a reversal of the usual textbook version of how bureaucratic politics are supposed to work, the State Department argued for a military approach (even a blockade) in Central America, while the military leaders in the Pentagon opposed it. The Pentagon's reasoning was not complex. Reagan had promised the largest peacetime military budget in history. The generals and admirals did not want to lose those billions by sinking into an unpopular war. Because of this internal opposition, the administration's policy did not go decisively in any new direction. It was unable to move ahead militarily and incapable of moving politically.[11] The policy resembled an antique clock that could no longer tell time; it was largely useless, but the family could not bear to discard it and lacked the capacity to fix it.

JEANE KIRKPATRICK AND THE "AUTHORITARIANS"

Besides looking at Central America through the prism of the cold war, the administration formulated another theo-ry about the revolutions. It had appeared before, in the 1940s, to support the elder Somoza's dictatorship. Now the theory surfaced in a 1979 essay by Jeane J. Kirkpatrick. She had been a professor of political science at Georgetown University in Washington, D.C., before this essay caught Reagan's eye and he appointed her U.S. ambassador to the U.N. in 1981.[12]

Kirkpatrick based her argument on a sharp distinction between "authoritarian" and "totalitarian" governments. Authoritarians sought to preserve "traditional" societies, she argued, and maintained open capitalist economies. Totalitarians, however, sought to control every part of society, including the economy. Good authoritarians included Somoza and the Shah of Iran. Bad totalitarians were exemplified by Josef Stalin and Adolf Hitler. An expert on South America, Kirkpatrick attacked Carter for opposing authoritarian governments merely because they violated human rights. Somoza, she believed, had established little more than "an efficient, urban political regime."

Certain conclusions followed from this formulation. Human rights dropped precipitously in importance. A government's degree of anti-communism and its warmth towards foreign investment became the major measuring sticks in any U.S. decision to help or hinder that government. In a major speech of 31 March 1981, Haig adopted the Kirkpatrick rationale and, presumably, the policy results. He announced a preference for authoritarians because they "are more likely to change than their totalitarian counterparts." Kirkpatrick's reading of history was triumphant, at least in Reagan's Washington.

Some observers doubted the accuracy of Kirkpatrick's reading. True, authoritarian societies had changed, but sometimes for the worse—as when the tsar of Russia gave way to the Communist party. Authoritarians in Latin America (and the Middle East), moreover, did not always preserve traditional societies. Somoza, the Salvadoran oligarchs, and the Guatemalan generals had destroyed the bonds that held their societies together. If authoritarians had been as beneficent and flexible as Kirkpatrick claimed, the professional elite and the Catholic church (certainly the most "traditional" institution in Latin America), would not have become revolutionaries. Authoritarians had exploited and divided their societies until radical revolution became the last hope of the masses and the middle class.

Against Kirkpatrick's and Haig's hopes, moreover, their authoritarians did not even turn out to be good anti-Communists. Both officials had focused on the Argentine military regime as a linchpin of anti-communism in the hemisphere. Haig and General Walters worked hard to involve the Argentine generals in Central America so they could help train Salvadoran and Guatemalan soldiers. In early 1982, however, Argentina went to war with Great Britain over the Falkland Islands. The United States supported the British position. Deeply angered, the Argentine military immediately moved closer to the Soviet Union (to whom they annually sold vast amounts of wheat), and publicly lined up with Castro on important Third-World issues.[13]

Within a year after the Reagan administration adopted the authoritarian-totalitarian distinction, the policy was paralyzed. The authoritarians could not handle modernization. They responded to change with violence. They cozied up to the Soviet Union. Kirkpatrick's thesis failed even to offer a coherent criticism of Jimmy Carter. She had labeled his policies, especially in the human rights area,

as largely responsible for Somoza's defeat. Actually, Carter had supported Somoza and then the National Guard until nearly the moment of the Sandinist victory. Finally, her claim ignored the revolution's causes. More accurate was the historical summation of a fearful National Guard officer as Somoza fled for his life: "I'm going too. There is no way we can defend ourselves against the people. It's not the guerrillas I'm afraid of but the people. I know they hate us and they could overwhelm us."[14]

REAGANOMICS FOR LATIN AMERICA

By late 1981, as the president's initial policies had hit dead ends, the administration tried to regroup and develop a three-pronged approach. First, it stepped up military aid to El Salvador and reopened the pipeline for such assistance to Guatemala. (That pipeline had been closed since 1977 because the Guatemalan generals refused to meet Carter's requests to reduce the shootings, beheadings, and torturing of political opponents. By 1981 the generals had not changed, but the U.S. government had.)[15] Second, the president approved a plan to destabilize and overthrow the Nicaraguan government through a range of indirect and direct pressures, a policy examined below. Reagan and Haig attempted to keep these first two steps out of public discussion. But they and Enders trumpeted their proposed third policy: a Caribbean Basin Initiative (CBI) that Reagan promised would revitalize friendly Central American and Caribbean countries through $350 million of U.S. aid and a major application of free-market principles.

No one doubted the need for a new economic approach. In 1980 the region's economic growth fell below population growth. Unemployment shot upwards as trade collapsed. Without major revolutionary problems, even Costa Rica endured a 60 percent inflation rate and a 200 percent devaluation of its currency.[16] The only Central American democracy edged towards bankruptcy. Reagan responded with $350 million, but gave $128 million of it to El Salvador. Even if the funds had been equitably distributed, the amount could have made no more than a tiny start in slowing the capital outflow. The president was mainly urging Latin Americans "to make use of the magic of the marketplace, the market of the Americas." In this spirit of Reaganomics, he proposed lower trade barriers for interregional commerce and open doors for North American investors.

The best rationale for such an approach came from Michael Novak. A Roman Catholic and a Democrat, Novak had turned to neoconservatism in the late 1970s. He worked at the American Enterprise Institute, a major "think tank" for the neoconservative movement, and in 1981 Reagan named him to head the U.S. delegation on the U.N. Human Rights Commission.

In his thoughtful essay, *The Spirit of Democratic Capitalism,* Novak rightly observed that Latin American growth rates since 1945 had risen at a pace seldom matched anywhere in the world.[17] The southern nations, however, lacked "the political will and the economic techniques" to use the new wealth equitably. Novak understood that oligarchs and militarists were the guilty parties; he did not try to defend them. He called instead for business people to copy the North American example by developing a pluralistic, marketplace economy where capital could become "creative" and individual freedom prosper. If better times did not quickly appear, he worried, "Liberation Theology" could win the day.

Novak saved his sharpest knives for the radical priests and bishops who used dependency theory to explain the crisis, and who urged greater state involvement to break Latin American dependence on capitalist powers. He warned that their approach could lead to a "new union of Church and state (this time on the left)" that might well end in "economic decline" and the suppression of individual freedom. Novak criticized the church for giving "too little encouragement to economic activism," but "much to political activism."

He countered by emphasizing "the role that business corporations—especially domestic ones—might play in building up structures of middle-class democracy." When that was accomplished the three strong Latin American institutions—clergy, military, and large landowners—"may be checked by the growth of a new middle class based in commerce and industry." Novak thus justified the use of marketplace economics much as Kirkpatrick justified Reagan's support for Latin American dictators. Each policy rested on a certain reading of history.

Novak's analysis, however, had little in common with Central American history after 1900. Contrary to his claim, "business corporations," including domestic firms, had been in the forefront of the region's development, but had never seen the need to build a "middle-class democracy." For their own reasons, they preferred cheap, docile labor to a more expensive, aggressive, middle class. The foreign-owned banana and mining companies, the banks, and the huge agribusinesses that flourished in the 1960s wished to maintain the status quo, support slow (usually imperceptible) reform, and ally themselves to the oligarch-military complex. The wealthy and powerful Central Americans, not unnaturally, cooperated.

Novak erred in believing Central Americans bore major responsibility for their economic dilemmas. At nearly every opportunity, North American firms had tried to fix the marketplace instead of allowing it to operate freely. They had used their great political power in exactly the manner Novak condemned—that is, by controlling or eliminating political and economic competition. They often did so, moreover, with the help of the U.S. government.

Novak missed the main theme in post-1900 Central American history. The United States, which he believed served as an example for Latin Americans, repeatedly used its political, economic, and military power to fix the marketplace, and so the "magic of the marketplace" never worked. U.S. officials and business executives believed in *realpolitik,* not magic. Novak, moreover, failed to mention that Central and South Americans repeatedly tried to break free of this system so they indeed could, as he noted, creatively check the power of the church and the military and overcome "state tyranny." But each time they tried—in Nicaragua during the 1920s or after 1977, in Guatemala during the early 1950s, in El Salvador during the early 1980s—they ran up against the power of the United States government.

One cannot use force to prevent a people from controlling their own resources and political processes, then condemn that people for failing to do so. Novak emphasized that "liberty" was the "key" to having enough "bread." Neoconservatives in the United States raised that formula into an article of faith. But the formula had not worked in Central America. The people had the "liberty" only to starve until many concluded that control over "bread" might give them some "liberty."

The irony of Novak's position became apparent in 1982 when Reagan's Caribbean Basin Initiative (CBI) proposal ran aground on North American—not Central American—refusals to play by marketplace rules. After intense lobbying by U.S. business and labor groups, the House of Representatives threw out the CBI's free-trade provisions for footwear and leather goods imported from Latin America. The president then weakened his own plan by bowing to domestic pressure and imposing import quotas on sugar. The plan had little effect on other Central American exports because most (such as coffee and bananas) did not compete with U.S. products, and so already entered under favorable tariffs. Many Latin American executives also opposed key parts of the CBI, including tax breaks to foreign businesses and more rewards to foreign investors. These business people understood full well that once foreign investors entered their market, U.S., Japanese, and West European multinational corporations would control it.[18] The CBI would thus merely strengthen the economic dependency that had plagued the region's past.

Novak's analysis did not recognize the huge role government would have to play in Central America before U.S. business virtues could be safely installed. But recognizing that problem would only have led Reagan and Novak into another sticky issue for free-marketeers: Who would control the government? If the Central American conservatives so favored by the Reagan administration held power, the status quo would surely continue. But removing those conservatives could require revolutionary tactics.[19] Reaganomics could believe that the larger capitalists deserve favor because they create wealth, but in Central America that view continued to be a prescription for economic and political disaster. Reagan,

Novak, and other neoconservatives cannot have both a freer market in the Caribbean and also more equal distribution of wealth. Such a feat is impossible until a fundamental restructuring occurs, a change that will take decades and require revolutionary tactics. No one around Reagan advocated such change. Novak did not even discuss the problem.

The CBI became a channel for sending aid to such right-wing regimes as El Salvador's. But in none of its forms did CBI bridge the chasm that separated Reaganomics from historical realities in Central America. Some U.S. business people deeply involved in Latin America understood the intellectual problems that bedeviled the Reagan administration. One such group listened without enthusiasm to speeches by Enders, NSC (National Security Council) adviser William Clark, and other top officials who again elaborated on the Cuban and Soviet evils. One executive later commented: "So we're going to fight the Commies. What else is new?"[20]

Reagan received little help from allies in resolving his dilemmas. Enders claimed that Canada, Mexico, and Venezuela "have almost precisely the same approach" to Central America.[21] The generalization was questionable. Despite their own massive economic problems, the Mexicans continued to support the Sandinist government and insisted that Castro be brought into negotiations for a settlement. Even Venezuela, wary of the revolutionaries, followed suit and tried to find some political arrangement before radicalism, and perhaps armed conflict, struck the entire area.[22]

A split in the Atlantic Alliance was equally serious. West German Social Democratic officials worked so closely with the Sandinists and the Salvadoran revolutionaries that Reagan finally sent Enders to tell them to stop interfering in Central American affairs. Dependent on U.S. military power for their security, the West Germans complied.[23] The French Socialist government of President François Mitterrand, however, stood fast. Mitterrand sent $15 million worth of arms to the Sandinists just as Reagan attempted to isolate them. French Foreign Minister Claude Cheysson listened to Haig's displeasure, then declared: "The worst error we could make would be to follow the policy adopted by the United States."[24]

EL SALVADOR: RECYCLING HISTORY

When Reagan entered office, the Salvadoran rebel offensive launched in early January 1981 had failed. He had a sudden opportunity to negotiate a settlement of the bloody revolution. But the president remained true to his ideology. Instead of seizing the moment for discussions, he drove for total military victory. U.S. officials assumed they were pursuing a new, tougher approach when they were actually continuing a decades-old policy that had helped cause the revolution. The Reagan administration sought to fight fire by pouring on gasoline. But with approximately 4,000 rebels facing 17,000 U.S.-trained and supplied army and security forces in a tiny country, Washington's wager on military victory seemed sound. Within two months, however, the war stalemated. A Pentagon study concluded that the Salvadoran army, despite U.S. training, resembled a nineteenth-century force incapable of fighting any kind of war, conventional or guerrilla.[25]

The administration panicked. Having announced that he intended to restore U.S. military credibility in a vital East-West conflict, the president watched victory move out of reach. When Haig dispatched top officials to plead with West Europeans and Latin Americans for cooperation, they returned emptyhanded. Particular embarrassment occurred when Haig reprimanded Panama for funneling arms to the Salvadoran rebels. Since 1903 the United States had controlled Panama as a virtual colony. But the Panamanian president denied any role, adding: "The only country that uses our territory against our will to interfere in El Salvador is the United States." General Omar Torrijos, Panama's strongman, told the U.S ambassador: "This message has come to the wrong address. It should have been sent to Puerto Rico."[26]

Reagan had little better luck at home. Despite his use of tried-and-proven cold war rhetoric, despite the media's failure to show the complexities and causes of the Salvadoran revolution, the White House admitted in March 1981 that public opinion opposed the president's policy.[27] A Reagan spokesman noted that Roman Catholics especially condemned the policy, and did so in thousands of letters sent directly to the White House.[28] The State Department then tried to reverse the opinion by issuing the "White Paper," but as noted above that attempt boomeranged. One knowledgeable observer, Jiri Valenta, even argued that Reagan helped the Soviets; the Russians were militarily tied down in Afghanistan, and could become involved directly in Poland, so they doubtless hoped that Reagan would likewise become bogged down in his own "backyard."[29]

In Salvador, meanwhile, the death-squads worked efficiently, even if the army did not. The remains of 300 to 500 civilians were found each month, on average. Over forty mayors and local councilmen who belonged to President José Napoleon Duarte's Christian Democratic party

were killed during the year ending April 1981. The party's secretary general had no love for the guerrillas, but he warned that if the right wing won the military victory sought by Reagan, "we may all end up in exile in Venezuela, or"—he drew his finger across his throat. One leading government official admitted in April that "right-wing violence had gotten out of hand. . . . We can't control the Treasury Police and the National Guard."[30]

In October 1981, the revolutionary spokesmen again offered to negotiate "without preconditions." The State Department flatly rejected the overture. It argued that captured documents proved the revolutionaries hoped to use the mediation effort throughout 1981 only to stall for time and split the United States from the Salvadoran government. A revolutionary spokesman did not disavow the documents. He did emphasize, however, that the program in the documents was optional, and that the issues could be negotiated. The State Department apparently did not press to test the spokesman's sincerity. U.S. policy precluded such negotiations.[31]

The policy only intensified the war. U.S. military aid that amounted to $6 million in 1980 leaped to $35.5 million in 1981 and $82 million in 1982. Some 1,500 Salvadoran soldiers received special training in North American camps. Economic aid tripled from $58.5 million in 1980 to $189 million in 1982. The United States sent more aid to El Salvador in 1981 and 1982 than to any other Latin American nation. The assistance could not do the job; it could not, for example, begin to offset the $1.5 billion of capital that fled the country for U.S. and Swiss banks during those years.[32]

If the military victory moved out of sight, a second objective appeared more attainable. Reagan began to base his entire policy on an election scheduled for March 1982. He hoped that it would bring to power a regime that could draw off support from both the reactionary military and the revolutionaries. The election's purpose was important—to choose a constituent assembly that would write a new constitution and choose an interim president to govern until new elections were held in 1983 or 1984. Going along with carefully worked-out policy, Duarte's government offered the rebels a place on the ballot if they would lay down their arms and play by the new political rules. The revolutionaries, however, understood that such an approach could mean their physical as well as political death. Their suspicions were confirmed when the security forces' death-squads circulated a list of over one hundred rebels to be shot on sight. Five leading leftist leaders, representing a spectrum of the most revolutionary groups, instead appealed to Reagan for talks "without preconditions by any of the parties to the conflict."[33] U.S. officials again quickly rejected the offer.

On 28 March 1982, elections were held throughout El Salvador, except in a few rebel-controlled areas. The revolutionaries warned Salvadorans not to vote, but the turnout, announced by the government to be 1.5 million voters, was enormous. (Later investigation concluded the turnout was closer to one million or 1.2 million, but that level was impressive nevertheless.) Assistant Secretary of State Enders lauded the voters for repudiating "the claim of the violent left that it has the people behind it."[34] Unable to win its military victory, U.S. officials brandished the March election results as if they were waving a talisman to drive off the forces of darkness.

The talisman possessed few supernatural powers. Central American leaders, particularly those in El Salvador, had too long made mockeries of such elections. A Latin American expert at the conservative American Enterprise Institute in Washington stated the problem in moderate terms: "Elections in Central America, with Costa Rica being the major exception, have generally been peripheral to the main arenas of politics."[35] Without a democratic tradition, but burdened by a bloody history of corrupt elections and military death-squads, El Salvador was supposed to move overnight from feudalism to a workable democratic system.

Unsurprisingly, feudalism triumphed. As peasants voted, their identity cards were marked and their thumbs stamped with ink. Authorities claimed these measures were aimed at eliminating vote fraud, but rumors warned of ugly consequences for those lacking these receipts. Ballots were numbered and ballot boxes transparent. Salvadorans felt they cast their votes in full view of the government.[36] Given the peasants' fear of the military, a fear warranted by the bodies left in streets or piled up at the bottom of ravines, the election results did not surprise. Major Roberto D'Aubuisson led a coalition of right-wing groups that won thirty-six seats of the sixty in the constituent assembly.

It was a stunning victory for the forces of darkness. D'Aubuisson's ARENA (National Republican Alliance) party turned out to be the best organized in the campaign, even though it had been hurriedly put together by exiled oligarchs and reactionary military officers. Duarte's Christian Democrats won only twenty-four seats, despite strong U.S. support that included rumored financial contributions. Part of the aid came from the CIA, whose director, William Casey, acknowledged that the intelligence agency had been involved in the election, and had provided "information and capabilities" to the Duarte government before the voting.[37] D'Aubuisson, on the other hand, received help from McCann-Erickson, the largest U.S. public relations agency operating abroad. In a well-run advertising campaign, McCann-Erickson spent $200,000 to sell the right-wing terrorist's brand of electoral politics. Most of the money probably came from Miami-based émigrés, who counted on D'Aubuisson to restore the old order.[38] The CIA proved no match for Madison Avenue.

Reagan's policy lay in ruins. Before the election, State Department officials had claimed that only Duarte could restore the nation, and denounced D'Aubuisson as the reported leader of "a right-wing terrorist group."[39] After the election the United States had to accept D'Aubuisson as the country's legislative leader—and elected by the process the Reagan administration had devised. The respected *Economist* of London concluded that after Reagan spent months trying to civilize them, "he saw a majority of voting Salvadorans apparently plumping for savagery."[40]

Having made the election the centerpiece of his policy, Reagan now moved to destroy its results. When D'Aubuisson threatened to put a friend in the presidential chair, U.S. officials brought pressure on the Salvadoran army, which still held ultimate power, to appoint a moderate. The military, faced with possible cutoff or reduction of U.S. arms, complied. But then the D'Aubuisson-led assembly stopped the land reform program, the program with which the United States had planned to win the hearts and minds of the masses away from the revolutionaries. D'Aubuisson was not about to hand out the wealth of those who had helped him to power. Pushed by U.S. congres-

sional demands that the land reforms continue, the State Department attempted to put the program back on track. The result was a standoff. U.S. officials could not undo the results of an election they had made their own. Meanwhile, leaders of the land reform charged that as much as $30 million had been lost because of theft and corruption.[41]

U.S. pressure to reverse the election results finally created an anti-American backlash. D'Aubuisson declared that Salvadorans had to organize so they could refuse Washington's continual demands. The nation's second-largest newspaper claimed that U.S. reform programs threatened the country with "total bankruptcy." A liberal Salvadoran complained that it was "preposterous the way the United States stomps through here."[42] The nation's dislike of foreigners had sturdy roots in history, so such attitudes were not surprising to those who knew that history.

Another election result was more grim. Within four months after the balloting a number of Christian Democratic leaders were murdered, including six mayors. Witnesses blamed military-controlled death-squads.[43] The country's defense minister, General José Guillermo Garcia, held the most power and had become Reagan's main hope, but Garcia could not control the death-squads. Nor could he control his own more moderate military officers. The officer corps deeply divided along generational and ideological lines. One popular officer caused a crisis in early 1983 by threatening to rebel against Garcia unless the defense minister fought more vigorously against the revolutionaries. With U.S. support, the uprising was put down, but Garcia was forced out and army morale was shattered. Other younger officers talked of possible discussions with the revolutionaries. In May 1983, the military fell under the control of extreme right-wing officers who had been linked to terrorism and the murder of North Americans.[44]

The revolutionaries also suffered from dissension. The traditional divisions between the moderate Left and hard-line Marxist guerrilla fighters intensified after the election. In early 1983, one rebel group killed the leader of another revolutionary fraction. Ill and disillusioned, Cayetano Carpio—the father figure of the rebellion—committed suicide. It seemed that the revolutionaries were held together only by U.S. opposition to negotiations and the bloodthirstiness of the right-wing death-squads. (A Salvadoran tourist official explained the sharp drop in foreign visitors by noting the 35,000 civilians who had been slaughtered in the three years after 1978, and then admitting, "we have an image problem.")[45]

In February 1983, Jeane Kirkpatrick announced victory. "The guerrillas are not winning anything," she said on a visit to El Salvador. "They do not even expect it." She applauded the country's "legitimate democratic government," an apparent reference to D'Aubuisson. But within a month Kirkpatrick had caused a major crisis within the Reagan administration and brought Salvador back to the newspaper headlines. She returned from her trip to tell Reagan that unless U.S. military aid rapidly increased not only El Salvador would fall to the revolutionaries, but all of Central America could soon come under control of Cuban-oriented regimes. Reagan began making public statements that unless Congress at least doubled military aid to Salvador, Mexico could ultimately be affected and Soviet-supported governments would then be on the doorstep of the United States.[46] ("As San Salvador goes so goes Nutley, New Jersey," was the way skeptical critics rephrased the president's domino theory.)

Kirkpatrick triggered the panic for several reasons. In early 1983 the revolutionaries so effectively regrouped that they successfully struck and briefly controlled new areas of El Salvador. They demonstrated military capabilities that the U.S.-trained Salvadoran troops could not handle, and that further dispirited and divided Garcia's officer corps. The revolutionary Farabundo Martí Liberation Front (FMLN) began to predict military victory within a year. But Kirkpatrick had another concern closer to home. Under Enders's quiet leadership, the State Department had begun to explore a "two-track" proposal that would lead to negotiations with the rebels while the fighting continued. Enders had taken over control of policy when Secretary of State George Shultz (who had replaced Haig in mid-1982) displayed little interest in Latin America. Kirkpatrick was appalled at Enders's "Lone Ranger" policymaking and went directly to Reagan to stop the two-track approach. She was joined by Reagan's NSC adviser, William Clark, who had little experience in foreign policy (although he and Shultz were the president's two closest advisers in the area). Clark was fully committed to a hard-line, military approach to Central American problems. Kirkpatrick and Clark succeeded in seizing the policy from the State Department.[47] In May 1983, Reagan fired Enders.

The immediate result was a vastly enlarged U.S. military involvement in the Salvadoran bloodbath. Reagan urged Congress to double military assistance to at least $110 million per year, vastly expand the training of Salvadoran troops by U.S. advisers, and possibly raise the number of those fifty-five advisers already stationed in the country. Meanwhile the president publicly portrayed the situation in stark terms, and shrewdly moved to blame revolutionary victories on his congressional critics who refused to give him all the money he wanted to pour into Salvador. Kirkpatrick added to the pressure when she suggested the need for hundreds of millions of dollars for a Central American "Marshall Plan" that would create a new economic infrastructure (highways, utilities, and schools). Finally, Reagan's advisers resorted to the old standby—elections. They demanded that the March 1984 presidential elections be moved to late 1983. The advisers believed the voting would undercut the growing political attractiveness of the revolutionaries—who, sensing military victory and knowing their candidates' lives could not be made secure from D'Aubuisson's assassins, refused to join the election process.[48]

Although these proposals caused furious political debate in early 1983, they of course offered little that was new. The Kirkpatrick-Clark policy only enlarged an approach that had already failed, an approach that was based on U.S. military aid and advisers. The more they North Americanized the war, the more the revolutionaries could claim to be fighting against a foreign invader and the more the Salvadoran government became dependent on the United States. Indeed, the Salvadoran military was already so dependent and weak that the very mention of U.S.-rebel negotiations had terrified Garcia's officers and threatened to paralyze their operations in the field. Many of them feared they were following the same dead-end path trod in 1979 by Somoza's National Guard in Nicaragua. As for the election proposal, it was—in the words of a State Department official—a symbolic gesture to please North Americans who continued to have a touching faith in national balloting, even when that balloting occurred in the middle of a violent revo-

lution that wracked a country having no tradition of democratic elections. The suggestion for a new Marshall Plan (or "Kirkpatrick Plan," as it came to be known) was more interesting. It, however, immediately raised the questions posed by Thomas Mann to Eisenhower's cabinet in 1959: Are we certain, Mann asked, that U.S. politicians and taxpayers will carry through on such a long-term commitment, and that the Latin Americans will carry through on their responsibilities for reforms and administration? The Alliance for Progress had answered those questions with a resounding, tragic negative.

By the spring of 1983 Reagan had three general alternatives in Salvador. He could withdraw U.S. support of the makeshift, uneasy right-wing coalition and allow the revolution to take its course. This alternative would probably lead to a breakup of the military government, an all-out terrorist campaign conducted by D'Aubuisson's forces, and then a victory by either the revolutionaries or by a group made up of the more moderate FDR (Revolutionary Democratic Front)-FMLN leaders and the more liberal military officers. A second alternative would be a negotiated settlement in which the United States would work closely with Venezuela, Mexico, and perhaps Spain. Meaningless elections would have no place in this alternative. Instead, the United States would work with its military allies in Salvador while the other powers would deal with their contacts among the revolutionaries. The objective would be to split off both the far-Left and far-Right and create power sharing between those on both sides willing to compromise. The United States and the other powers would then be responsible for enforcing the compromise.

Reagan showed no sign of following either of these alternatives. One wing of the Republican party, which included Kirkpatrick and Clark on foreign policy issues, posed a major obstacle. It would brook no compromise with leftist forces. Reagan agreed with those Republicans. On the political level, he had no intention of compromising (nor did he have any idea about how to go about it). On the ideological level, he delivered several remarkable speeches in March 1983 that called for a virtual holy war against communism. There seemed little chance that he would either withdraw or pursue a meaningful negotiated settlement. That left the third alternative—to pursue traditional policies and further commit the U.S. military to the war. While promising that no U.S. combat troops were to be involved in the fighting, Reagan prepared to send ever-larger numbers of military and economic advisers. That North American power could ultimately "win" the war could not be doubted. Reagan could win much as William Howard Taft, Woodrow Wilson, and Calvin Coolidge had won against revolutionaries in Nicaragua between 1911 and 1933. But neither could it be doubted that such a victory would require a continuing bloodbath in Central America, further polarize the area and thus turn the initiative to the extremists on both sides, divert U.S. attention and resources from more important domestic and foreign problems, and result in a running argument with allies who feared the president's policy.

And after Reagan or his successor won such a victory, conservative forces would necessarily govern repressively while the remnants of the revolutionaries regrouped to fight again. Salvadoran history would simply be recycled back to early 1981.

NICARAGUA AND HONDURAS: TRANSFORMING INTERNATIONAL CONFLICT INTO REVOLUTION

Policy in Salvador fulfilled Kirkpatrick's hope that the United States would side with authoritarian regimes. Policy towards the Nicaraguan Sandinist government displayed the reverse side of the Kirkpatrick thesis. The approach fit a longer North American view, originating as early as the 1790s—revolutions of the Left were inherently dangerous to U.S. interests and were to be met with displeasure or force.

The Reagan administration moved quickly to weaken the Sandinists' hold on power The 1980 election results in the United States made little difference in this regard; a high Nicaraguan official declared privately that if Carter had remained in office, "we would still be at loggerheads."[49] The problem was historical and ideological, not personal or partisan. Reagan only turned the screws more rapidly and tightly. By late February 1981 economic aid was turned off. In the summer Washington officials accused the Sandinists of moving close to the Soviet bloc. By the end of the year the president endorsed a CIA plan that aimed at destabilizing the Nicaraguan government. He also accepted a Pentagon program for rapidly building up Honduran forces. Those troops, aided by more than 100 U.S. military advisers and as many as 5,000 ex-Somoza supporters, were poised to wage war against the Sandinists.

Two particular issues pushed Reagan's policy so far so fast. One was Sandinist military aid to the Salvadoran revolutionaries. The other was the Nicaraguan regime's tightening of internal controls that drove out private business and threatened to turn the country into a consolidated socialist state. In 1981 the two issues were closely related. Broken by the Somozas' forty-year-long robbery, tied by terms negotiated with the international bankers in 1979 and 1980, and saddled with an economy devastated by the civil war, the Nicaraguans needed U.S. economic help above all else. Only the United States could provide the $3 million a day that one top Nicaraguan official estimated his country needed to survive. Only U.S. approval could open doors to international lending agencies or encourage other nations to help. "We need 10 years to regain the 1977 gross national product," the Nicaraguan official declared.[50] Without Washington's aid the Sandinists would not accomplish even that goal.

Holding the high cards, U.S. officials demanded in late January 1981 that Nicaragua stop helping their "revolutionary brothers" in El Salvador and pull back from a growing relationship with Cuba and the Soviet bloc. Haig announced he was stopping $15 million of economic aid headed for Managua, as well as nearly $10 million of wheat, for thirty days to test whether the Sandinists would stop helping the Salvadoran rebels. Bread lines appeared in Nicaraguan cities. One of Reagan's National Security Council officials warned a Nicaraguan: "The question is not whether U.S.-Nicaraguan relations are good or bad, but whether there will be any relations at all."[51]

In early April, the State Department announced good news: the Nicaraguan "response has been positive. We have no hard evidence of arms movements through Nicaragua during the past few weeks, and propaganda and some other support activities have been curtailed." But then came the non sequitur: because "some arms traffic may [sic] be continuing and other support very probably continues," aid would be cancelled anyway.[52]

The announcement was illogical. Politically, however, it made sense because it appeased the extreme right-wing of the Republican party led by powerful Senator Jesse Helms of North Carolina. Helms, who chaired the Foreign Relations Subcommittee on Latin America, had demanded an end to the assistance. Diplomatically, moreover, it demonstrated to the administration's satisfaction a toughness that failed to appear in the confusion and failure that marked Reagan's foreign policy elsewhere, including El Salvador.

With its economic leverage gone, the United States could no longer use it to discipline the Sandinists as they reopened the arms flow to El Salvador and employed Communist-bloc equipment and advisers to build a 25,000-man army (the largest in Central America) and a 30,000-strong militia. The Sandinists wanted to develop a 50,000-man force if they could find the resources. They did find help behind the Iron Curtain, and obtained tanks, helicopters, heavy artillery, and surface-to-air missiles. They also sent seventy men to Bulgaria for jet training. ("Yes, they are there," a high Nicaraguan official admitted privately, "but don't worry. They are flunking the course." His North American listeners were not amused.)[53]

But if the United States had lost some leverage, the Sandinists had lost most of their alternatives for development. As a member of their three-man governing junta, Sergio Ramírez Mercado, noted in early 1982: "We know that we cannot produce the profound social gains we want if we are in confrontation with the United States." To accomplish such gains, the Sandinists believed they had to dismantle the system inherited from Somoza. They intended to develop light industry and agriculture for internal consumption as well as export. Sandinists planned to rebuild by controlling capital movement, and by combining state controls with a private sector that accounted for over 60 percent of the economy. Political pluralism had to be limited. National efforts could not be spent on political struggles. North Americans, however, viewed this particular kind of one-party state with alarm.

By mid-1981 all U.S. aid had stopped. The revolution moved sharply to the left. Businessmen who criticized the government were arrested or exiled. (The regime carefully tried to maintain the appearance of balance by simultaneously jailing several Communist party members.) Cut off from U.S. money, Sandinists found help not only in Western Europe and Mexico, but in the Soviet bloc and General Muammar Qaddafi's Libya. But the aid was insufficient. The Russian promise of $166 million over five years, with perhaps more to come, hardly touched Nicaraguan needs. The Sandinists tightened up at home. Aid to the private sector dropped. Incentives for foreign investors disappeared. State controls and nationalization spread. But without U.S. aid, little seemed to help. Inflation and unemployment rose. "We have failed so far economically," a high Nicaraguan official admitted in late 1981.[54]

Political repercussions quickly followed. The three-man junta and the nine-person directorate (which theoretically held ultimate power) divided between pragmatists who wanted to slow down use of state controls and self-styled Marxist-Leninists who pushed for rapid centralization. Officials who tried to restrain the Marxist-Leninists began to quit or were expelled from the regime. Many who left, however, continued to plead for U.S. help. Alfonso Robelo, for example, warned that U.S. hostility played into the

hardliners' hands. Arturo Cruz, a respected banker, revolutionary, and ambassador to Washington before he quit the Nicaraguan government, remarked as he left his home country that although he disagreed with the Sandinists, he would do all in his power to support them rather than have the regime fall because of U.S. pressure or internal opposition.[55]

The moderates were trapped. As the Roman Catholic leaders cooled towards the revolution, unsympathetic clergy were picked out for political attack and humiliation by the Sandinists. Church leaders became more hostile and the Sandinists responded in kind. The regime cracked down on 50,000 Miskito Indians in distant provinces along the Atlantic Ocean and the Honduran border. Never hispanized, the Miskitos had historically opposed attempts by Managua to control them. They had become fertile ground for ex-Somoza supporters. Some 10,000 of the Indians moved into Honduras for refuge. As they did so, their village priests also turned against the government. A large, rebellious force had developed, and in turn the radical Sandinists urged further centralization of power and aid from the Soviet bloc to deal with that force.[56]

Reagan's hope of slowly strangling the Managua regime appeared to be working. Caught in what one Sandinist leader called "a vicious circle," the more the government extended its control to protect itself, the more it alienated key segments of the population. Ex-Somoza henchmen and disaffected Sandinists found support among the Indians and from the Salvadoran military. They also found friends in Florida and California, where the United States government allowed anti-Sandinist troops to drill, although most former Sandinists would have nothing to do with these remnants of the hated National Guard. Reagan did little to stop the old Somoza supporters. "Under the Carter and Nixon administration, what we were doing was a crime," said the leader of one private army. "With the Reagan administration no one has bothered us for ten months."[57]

In November 1981, Reagan approved a $19 million CIA plan to undercut the Sandinist regime. In December, Haig refused to rule out a U.S. blockade of Nicaragua or the mining of harbors. Enders told the Senate that plans had been drawn up, but not yet approved, for military action against both Cuba and Nicaragua.[58]

Reagan's advisers planned to use Honduras as a staging area for the attacks. The choice was not surprising. If Somoza's Nicaragua had been the most cooperative of all Latin American countries in supporting U.S. policies, Honduras had run a close second. The Hondurans had long been more fully controlled by North American capital than even Nicaragua. Their new professional army had been produced by U.S. advisers and training schools. As many as 5,000 Somoza followers made Honduras home base. Honduras once again became what it had frequently been since its independence 150 years earlier, a launching area for attacks on neighboring regimes. Eisenhower had used Honduras for this purpose when he overthrew the Guatemalan government in 1954.

Once again, U.S. policy began to turn during the final months of the Carter administration. It nearly doubled military aid for Honduras to $5 million in 1980. Reagan again doubled military assistance, then raised it to $15 million for 1982. He also dispatched a team of Green Berets to operate along the Salvadoran border. In mid-1982 and again in early 1983, U.S. troops went through maneuvers with the Honduran army (merely to test "communications procedures," said one U.S. officer), and built a large base camp located just forty-five miles from a major Nicaraguan military station. Honduras possessed a 20,000-man army and the largest, best-equipped air force in Central America. The United States sent in even more transport planes and large helicopters to increase the army's mobility. In mid-1982 skirmishes broke out in which Nicaragua claimed forty soldiers died.[59]

A war between Honduras and Nicaragua could involve El Salvador and Guatemala. The latter two countries could not pass up the opportunity to attack their rebels who found sanctuary in Honduran jungles or obtained help from Nicaragua. The entire region could ignite. Another, more immediate danger also loomed. U.S. policy could push Honduras into its own revolution. For once again the United States threatened to destabilize a friendly government by using it to fight a battle in the cold war.

At first glance, Honduras appeared to be as compliant to U.S. wishes as the stereotypical banana republic was supposed to be. When Washington officials demanded an end to the long-lived, thoroughly corrupt military government, the Hondurans held elections in 1981 and 1982 that brought a respected lawyer, Roberto Suazo Córdova, to the presidency. Delighted State Department officials lauded the results as a vindication of U.S. policy in the area. They celebrated too soon, and, perhaps, knowingly. Suazo Córdova, by constitution and by fact, did not rule the country. The army commander-in-chief held that power. Only he, not the president, could constitutionally give marching orders to the army, and he held veto power over the president's appointment of cabinet members and their subsequent actions. The professional, self-dedicated army officer corps had become the most coherent institution in an increasingly fragmented country.[60]

In 1981 and 1982, the military came under the control of certain army officers (known respectively as the "iron circle") who were led by General Gustavo Alvarez Martinez. General Alvarez hated anything that he thought might be associated with communism, and he particularly detested Nicaragua. Trained in Argentine military methods, Alvarez quickly cultivated U.S. officials. After Honduran troops helped the Salvadoran army massacre guerrillas and peasants during late spring of 1982, the FMLN revolutionaries darkened much of Honduras by blowing up electrical power stations. An infuriated Alvarez flew to Washington seeking more help. He returned with $23 million of military aid.[61] Alvarez fit well into Reagan's plans, even if the general did not gain power through democratic elections.

But the United States was crossing a deep ravine on a tottering bridge. Despite Alvarez and a long history of U.S. ties, Honduras remained a country that had endured 126 changes of government, 16 constitutions, and 385 coups since gaining independence. Life expectancy was under fifty years. Peasants in rural areas earned $150 annually, 30 percent had no land at all, and nearly half their children died before the age of five. The country carried a $1.7 billion debt, but its foreign currency reserves sunk below $20 million in 1981, and capital started to exit. Most ominously, given Reagan's plans, the military appeared hollow. Top officers who opposed Alvarez's militancy warned that the army might dominate Hondurans, but it had no chance against the battle-tested, dedicated Sandinists—at least not unless the United States provided massive support. As one former Hon-

duran officer warned; "Here soldiers are rounded up into the army from . . . movie houses and concerts. And you have a high command that would send them out to fight, then take off for Miami the minute things got bad."[62]

As the pressure built in 1981 and 1982, Honduras began to crack. For the first time in recent history, politicians and labor leaders disappeared or were found murdered. "Clandestine cemeteries" appeared. Death-squads and torture became more widespread. Left-wing guerrillas kidnapped, robbed banks, murdered, and hijacked. Mass demonstrations of as many as 60,000 people protested repression by security forces. Two U.S. military advisers were shot and the Honduran Congress was bombed.[63] The country slid towards terrorism precisely as Reagan was developing it into a base for military action against the Sandinists and Salvadoran revolutionaries.

As regional conflict impended, Nicaragua moved to the left. One Western diplomat observed that Reagan's intentional radicalization of the Managua government "only makes sense if you think that the radicalized state will be of short duration."[64] The polarization of Honduras, however, made sense only in the long sweep of U.S. involvement in Central America. Each time Washington officials had used one of the southern nations for the sake of U.S. interests, it seemed that North Americans won in the short run and Central Americans lost in the long run. An observer with perspective could conclude that Honduras in the 1980s resembled Nicaragua in the early 1970s.

CONCLUSION

By the 1980s, the U.S. system in Central America had turned full circle. It had opened the twentieth century by using military force to fix North American control over the area. Given its armed might and economic power, no one could doubt that the United States would dominate the area at will. Even in El Salvador, whose oligarchs had a proud history of keeping foreigners at bay, North American influence developed until by the 1920s, in the words of one horrified diplomat, the U.S. minister bragged "that he made the native police kneel down when he passed."[65]

By the 1930s such kowtowing, not to mention landing the U.S. Marines, had become too costly. Nor were such blatantly imperialist gestures any longer needed. The blunt instruments were replaced with the Good Neighbor's economic leverage. That leverage had been maturing since the United States checked the British entrepreneurs and gained economic supremacy in the region before World War I. The Good Neighbor was reinforced by the common effort of World War II, although that effort did not produce equal benefits for all the countries involved. Using government controls during the conflict and freer-market principles afterward, the United States built an economic empire at the expense of its Latin American neighbors.

By the 1950s, the Good Neighbor had lost its power. It did so at the moment U.S. economic hegemony was besieged by West Europeans and Japanese, and Washington's political hegemony was embarrassed by Fidel Castro's survival. The Alliance for Progress attempted to modernize and extend Good Neighbor principles, but updated New Deal remedies no longer worked. Indeed, they weakened the system by raising both the expectations of the masses and the wealth and power of the oligarchs. Revolutionary groups multiplied, the United States

responded with increased military commitments. That response reached a high point in the Reagan administration. Having helped create a fertile ground for revolution, the United States helped it grow with military confrontation. Such a policy was logical only if North Americans were willing massively to intervene in, and perhaps occupy, Central America (much as they did between 1911 and 1933), or if their local allies in the area were trustworthy and stable. Neither condition existed.

Nor could U.S. officials square their policies with Thomas Jefferson's theory of self-determination. The contradiction between Jefferson's ideals and North American actions in Central America appeared in his lifetime; by the time of Theodore Roosevelt the United States explicitly defined such self-determination unilaterally and in its own interest. If Central Americans hoped to determine their own futures, for better or worse, they could not do so through election processes (which had long been corrupted and made meaningless everywhere except Costa Rica), or through their elites (who prospered by exploiting their own people). Outside Costa Rica, no peaceful means for needed change existed. As poverty accelerated, revolution erupted. In 1983, Secretary of State George Shultz told Congress that the United States would not tolerate "people shooting their way into power."[66] But other secretaries of state had not taken that view when oligarchs and generals shot their way into power in Salvador in 1932, Nicaragua in 1934 to 1936, Guatemala in 1954, or Honduras in 1963. (Fortunately, Shultz's rule was also not applied in 1776.)

Unable to deal with the products of its own system, reconcile the contradiction between its professed ideals and its century-old foreign policy, or work with other powers to resolve these dilemmas, the United States, from Eisenhower to Reagan, resorted to force. The result was more revolution.

In 1926, Stokely W. Morgan, assistant chief of the Division of Latin American Affairs in the State Department, told graduating Foreign Service officers that their government was enduring rough times in Central America, but as that region matured, the relationship would change:

If the United States has received but little gratitude, this is only to be expected in a world where gratitude is rarely accorded to the teacher, the doctor, or the policeman, and we have been all three. But as these young nations grow and develop a greater capacity for self-government, and finally take their places upon an equal footing with the mature, older nations of the world, it may be that in time they will come to see the United States with different eyes, and to have for her something of the respect and affection with which a man regards the instructor of his youth and a child looks upon the parent who has molded his character.[67]

By the 1980s, however, too many of the youths viewed the teacher with neither respect nor affection, but as a presence that could be removed only with force. North Americans consequently faced revolutionary crises in Central America. The explanation for that confrontation lay not in Ronald Reagan's belief that "the Soviet Union underlies all the unrest that is going on."[68] It lay in the history of how the class-ridden remains of the Spanish empire turned into the revolution-ridden parts of the North American system.

NOTES

1. The text is found in the *New York Times,* July 13, 1980.

2. The Allen quotes are in *Latin America Weekly Report,* December 4, 1981, p. 1; and Penny Lernoux, "El Salvador's Christian Democrat Junta," *The Nation,* December 13, 1980, p. 633; *Washington Post,* October 7, 1977.

3. Text is in *New York Times,* February 21, 1981, p. 6; also quotes in *Washington Post,* March 9, 1981; *New York Times,* March 14, 1982.

4. U.S. Department of State, "Cuban Support for Terrorism and Insurgency," *Current Policy,* no. 376, March 12, 1982, p. 3. The first time the "go to the source" phrase was used was probably by William Clark, deputy secretary of state and later Reagan's national security adviser; his quote is in *Washington Post,* March 9, 1981.

5. Jiri Valenta, "The U.S.S.R., Cuba, and the Crisis in Central America," *Orbis* 25 (1981), pp. 736-38; Wayne Smith, "Dateline Havana...," *Foreign Policy* no. 48 (Fall 1982), p. 157; Enders's statement is in U.S. Department of State, "Cuban Support for Terrorism and Insurgency," p. 1; and in Enders's essay in Howard J. Wiarda, Ed., "The Crisis in Central America," *AEI Foreign Policy and Defense Review* 4 (1982), pp. 7-8.

6. Mark Falcoff, "The El Salvador White Paper and Its Critics," in ibid., 18-24, is a good defense of the "White Paper," and gives some of the key criticisms offered by James Petras in *The Nation,* March 28, 1981; *Los Angeles Times,* March 17, 1981; Robert Kaiser, "White Paper on El Salvador Is Faulty," *Washington Post,* June 9, 1981; and *Wall Street Journal,* June 8, 1981. The original "White Paper" was U.S. Department of State, *Communist Interference in El Salvador; Documents Demonstrating Communist Support of the Salvadoran Insurgency,* February 23, 1981 (author's possession).

7. A good summary is in Cynthia Arnson, *El Salvador: A Revolution Confronts the United States* (Washington, D.C.: Institute for Policy Studies, 1982), p. 73.

8. An analysis is in *New York Times,* March 14, 1981.

9. *Latin America Weekly Report,* March 26, 1982, pp. 10-11; the Reagan quote is in *Washington Post,* March 29, 1981.

10. *Boston Sunday Globe,* September 6, 1981; Carla Anne Robbins, "A State Department Purge," *New York Times,* November 3, 1981.

11. See also *Latin America Weekly Report,* November 13, 1981, p. 10.

12. The Kirkpatrick essay and other essays she has written on Latin American and U.S. politics can be found in Jeane J. Kirkpatrick, *Dictatorships and Double Standards: Rationalism and Reason in Politics* (New York: Simon & Schuster, 1982), especially pp. 23-90. Haig's speech is excerpted in *New York Times,* April 21, 1981.

13. Critiques can be found in Theodore Draper, "The Ambassador's Theories," *New York Times Book Review,* July 25, 1982, p. 1; Thomas J. Farer, "Reagan's Latin America," *New York Review of Books,* March 19, 1981, pp. 12-13; Robert E. White, "Central America: The Problem That Won't Go Away," *New York Times Magazine,* July 18, 1982, p. 22.

14. Quoted in Bernard Diederich, *Somoza and the Legacy of U.S. Involvement in Central America* (New York: E. P. Dutton, 1981), p. 327.

15. *Latin America Weekly Report,* November 13, 1981, p. 11.

16. Enders essay in Wiarda, Ed., "Crisis in Central America," p. 8; *New York Times,* February 1, 1982.

17. Michael Novak, *The Spirit of Democratic Capitalism* (New York: Simon & Schuster, 1982), especially pp. 287-314.

18. *Latin America Weekly Report,* May 28, 1982, p. 4; Michael Kryzanek, "President Reagan's Caribbean Basin Formula," in Wiarda, Ed., "Crisis in Central America."

19. See Richard R. Fagen, "A Funny Thing Happened on the Way to the Market...," *International Organization* 32 (1978), pp. 292-93.

20. *Latin America Weekly Report,* July 2, 1982, p. 6.

21. Ibid., September 18, 1981, p. 5, has the Enders quotation.

22. Ibid., August 13, 1982, p. 5; *New York Times,* March 11, 1981.

23. *Latin America Weekly Report,* September 18, 1981, p. 2.

24. Ibid., July 16, 1982, p. 11.

25. *New York Times,* February 21, 1981.

26. Quoted in Penny Lernoux, "They're *Our* S.O.B.s...," *The Nation,* March 28, 1981, p. 363.

27. See the study by the Columbia University School of Journalism, summarized in *Latin America Weekly Report,* February 20, 1981, p. 5.

28. *New York Times,* March 14, 1981; *Washington Post,* March 10, 1981.

29. Valenta, "U.S.S.R., Cuba and the Crisis in Central America," pp. 738-40.

30. Quoted in *Washington Post,* March 21, 1981; also see ibid. March 9, 1981.

31. The documents are declassified; copies in author's possession, for which the author is indebted to Alex Singer of Cornell University. See the analysis in *New York Times,* November 5, 1981.

32. U.S. Department of State, "El Salvador," *Gist* (June 1982); U.S. Department of State, "Latin America and the Caribbean Bilateral Assistance," *Current Policy,* no. 269 (March 23, 1981); *Latin America Weekly Report,* January 30, 1981; U.S. Department of State, "El Salvador," *Gist,* February 1983.

33. Quoted in *New York Times,* January 28, 1982.

34. U.S. Department of State, "Commitment to Democracy in Central America," *Current Policy,* no. 386 (April 21, 1982), pp. 1-2.

35. Wiarda, Ed., "Crisis in Central America," pp. 5-6.

36. *Latin America Weekly Report,* February 19, 1982, p. 7; White, "Central America: The Problem That Won't Go Away," p. 25.

37. *Wall Street Journal,* July 16, 1982; *Latin American Weekly Report,* August 6, 1982, p. 3; *New York Times,* July 30, 1982.

38. Wayne Biddle, "The Selling of D'Aubuis-

son," *The Nation,* July 24-31, 1982, pp. 72-73.

39. Excerpts of statement in *New York Times,* March 14, 1981; State Department letter to Congressman Lee H. Hamilton, May 12, 1981, quoted by White, "Central America: The Problem That Won't Go Away," p. 25.

40. *Latin America Weekly Report,* April 2, 1982, p. 1; *The Economist,* May 1, 1982, p. 14.

41. A good summary of the land reform program at that point is in two stories in the *Washington Post,* May 31, 1982; also *Latin America Weekly Report,* April 30, 1982, p. 4; and Oxfam America's *El Salvador Land Reform 1980-1982 Impact Audit* by Laurence R. Simon and James C. Stephens, Jr., with 1982 Supplement by Martin Diskin (Boston: Oxfam America, 1982); *Latin America Weekly Report,* July 30, 1982, p. 12.

42. Quoted in the *New York Times,* June 20, 1982.

43. Ibid., June 1, 1982, August 5, 1982.

44. Gino Lofredo, "In Salvador, Discontented Officers," *New York Times,* May 24, 1982; *Washington Post,* July 7, 1982; ibid., June 1, 1983.

45. Quoted in *Latin America Weekly Report,* February 26, 1982, p. 3, which considered the explanation a strong candidate for "the understatement of the year award"; *New York Times,* July 27, 1982; *Washington Post,* July 31, 1982.

46. *New York Times,* February 10, 1983; see especially *Washington Post,* March 6, 1983. Reagan's speech is analyzed in ibid., March 11, 1983.

47. *Washington Post,* March 6, 1983; author's interviews in Washington, D.C., March 1983.

48. Ibid.; *New York Times,* March 6, 1983.

49. Author's interview with an anonymous Nicaraguan official in Ithaca, New York, October 29, 1981.

50. Ibid.

51. Quoted in *New York Times,* February 13, 1981.

52. Quoted in ibid. April 2, 1981.

53. Ibid., January 14, 1982; author's interview with Nicaraguan official, October 29, 1981; *Washington Post,* January 31, 1981; *New York Times,* February 12, 1981.

54. A good brief discussion is in *Latin America Weekly Report,* June 25, 1982, p. 9; the quote is from author's interview with Nicaraguan official, October 29, 1981; see also *New York Times,* May 8, 1981; and Thomas W. Walker, "The Sandinist Victory in Nicaragua," *Current History* 78 (1980), p. 61.

55. Quoted in *Washington Post,* November 16, 1981.

56. *New York Times,* May 29, June 18, 1981, August 18, 1982.

57. Quoted in ibid., December 28, May 2, 1981.

58. Enders's quote is in *Latin America Weekly Report,* December 18, 1981, p. 12; other reports on the destabilization plan are in Loren Jenkins, "Honduras on the Edge," *The Atlantic* 250 (1982), pp. 16-20; *New York Times,* December 6, 1981.

59. The U.S. officer is quoted in *New York Times,* August 5, 1982. A good background on the buildup is in Jenkins, "Honduras on the Edge," pp. 18-20; see also U.S. Department of State, "Latin America and the Caribbean Bilateral Assistance," *Current Policy,* no. 269 (March 23, 1981); *Washington Post,* May 5, 1981; *New York Times,* August 9, 1981; *Latin America Weekly Report,* July 30, 1982, pp. 1-2.

60. The best account is James A. Morris and Steve C. Ropp, "Corporatism and Dependent Development: A Honduran Case Study," *Latin American Research Review* 12 (1977): 27-68; Anne Nelson, "Honduran Choice," *The Nation,* December 12, 1981, p. 629.

61. *Latin America Weekly Report,* July 23, 1982.

62. Quoted in *Washington Post,* May 5, 1981; also *New York Times,* September 1, 1982; Jenkins, "Honduras on the Edge," p. 18; Catholic Institute for International Relations, *Honduras: Anatomy of a Disaster* (London: Catholic Institute for Interna-

tional Relations, undated but probably 1975), pp. 3-5.

63. *New York Times,* September 25, 1981; *The Economist,* September 4, 1982, pp. 33-34.

64. *Washington Post,* July 26, 1982.

65. Francis White to Joseph Grew, October 11, 1924, decimal file 121.4/12, Record Group 59, National Archives, Washington, D.C.

66. Senate Appropriations Committee, "Testimony of Secretary of State... Shultz before the Subcommittee on Foreign Operations, Senate Appropriations Committee, March 22, 1983," typescript in author's possession, p. 32.

67. Lecture delivered before the Foreign Service School, January 29, 1926, in Joseph C. Grew to American Diplomatic Officers..., decimal file 120.3, Record Group 59, National Archives, Washington, D.C. I am indebted to David Langbart for pointing out this document in the Department of State Archives.

68. *New York Times,* October 20, 1980.

18. STABILIZING STAR WARS

Alvin M. Weinberg and Jack N. Barkenbus

For more than three decades the arms race has spiraled upward because neither the United States nor the Soviet Union will accept anything less than strategic parity with its rival. Clearly, traditional arms control efforts show little promise of reducing the nuclear stockpiles even though deterrence with much smaller arsenals is desirable and theoretically possible. Suggestions to speed up the arms control process with unilateral actions fail to take into account the political realities of today's world. Given prevalent strategic doctrines and the current climate of tension and distrust, no leader will order a serious reduction in nuclear weapons without an equivalent and verifiable reduction by the other side.

But by exploiting an unfolding change in U.S. doctrine, unilateral measures with a real chance of prompting a positive Soviet response might be politically feasible. Unilateralism can work if the United States dismantles some offensive weapons at the same time it deploys ballistic missile defense (BMD). The dangerously high number of offensive strategic missiles in the world can be reduced if Washington embarks on such a "defense-protected build-down" (DPB).

Although most analysts agree that in theory a defense-oriented world is safer than and preferable to an offense-oriented world—that mutual assured survival is better than mutual assured destruction (MAD)—defensive weapons

Source: *Foreign Policy* 54 (Spring 1984), pp. 164–70.

systems are widely opposed for three reasons. First, many arms control experts fear that deployment of these weapons will touch off yet another expensive round of U.S.-Soviet technological competition, leading eventually to new offensive weapons systems that can overwhelm the defense. Second, even if this renewed competition for offensive superiority does not occur, it is argued, any defense that is not totally effective against awesomely destructive nuclear weapons is not worth deploying. Finally, the transition from an offense-oriented world to a defense-oriented one is generally seen as fraught with risks. At worst, the deployment of defensive weapons by the United States might compel the Soviet Union to deploy its own defensive system and expand its offensive forces—or even attack the United States before its own forces could be neutralized.

An orderly transition to a defense-oriented world, however, can be achieved by combining deployment of defensive weapons with a concomitant and compensating reduction of offensive weapons. By destroying a certain percentage of its missiles in the process of deploying defensive weapons systems, Washington would clearly signal Moscow that the United States was not seeking a strategic advantage but simply exchanging one kind of parity for another.

A NEW INTERNATIONAL NORM

The DPB scheme is quite different from the vision President Ronald Reagan conjured up in his Star Wars speech of March 23, 1983, of an America—and ultimately a world—free of the threat of nuclear destruction. That vision is an illusion. Science and technology cannot rid the world of nuclear weapons. Even if a perfect missile defense were possible, other delivery systems for nuclear weapons would still endanger millions of Americans. The real issue, therefore, is not whether the world can return to an era free from the possibility of a nuclear holocaust, but whether political leaders can significantly reduce the level of destruction that can be wreaked on the Earth—that is, reduce the force level at which MAD operates.

The Star Wars speech called upon the scientific community to devise a network of exotic space- and land-based systems capable of intercepting and destroying Soviet strategic ballistic missiles during various stages of their flights. No one not privy to the classified scientific literature on these systems can definitively judge the feasibility of these programs. It appears abundantly clear, however, that BMD systems using devices such as lasers and particle beams would be extremely expensive, vulnerable to much less expensive Soviet countermeasures, and deployable only in the 21st century.

DPB, however, does not depend on the success of this costly technological gamble. Instead, it is based on the development of BMD systems using interceptor missiles, which has progressed steadily over the last decade. Short-range interceptors capable of defending offensive missile sites—not population centers— by attacking Soviet warheads as they reenter the atmosphere can probably be deployed in the 1980s. The uncertainties are great, but at this point the best evidence suggests that such systems could destroy between two and eight re-entry vehicles for every one that gets through.[1]

Although many strategic defense en-thusiasts bemoan the fact that current BMD systems could only provide marginal improvements in U.S. defenses, this characteristic is actually a major advantage of DPB. Its incomplete effectiveness requires policy makers to move incrementally, thereby preventing a sudden destabilization of the strategic balance. The importance of DPB in the beginning resides not in the level of protection provided but in its ability both to initiate a winding-down process and to establish a new international norm of behavior based on offensive arms reduction rather than expansion. DPB should therefore be limited initially to the construction of silo-defense systems and concomitant reductions in very accurate U.S. land-based intercontinental ballistic missiles (ICBMs) that, because they threaten Soviet forces, raise the specter of a first strike.

The call for simultaneously deploying defensive systems and freezing offensive weapons levels—for creating a lightly armed, heavily defended world—is not new, since strategic planners have long recognized that the unlimited use of offensive weapons can invariably overcome defensive systems. What is new about the DPB proposal is the symmetrical reduction of offensive forces based upon credible estimates of the defense's effectiveness.

Assume that initially, without defensive systems, both the United States and the Soviet Union deploy an equal number of offensive weapons. A BMD system deployed by the United States would reduce the number of Soviet weapons able to reach their targets, upsetting the strategic balance. Under DPB, the United States would restore this balance by reducing its stockpile of offensive weapons enough so that the two sides would be again evenly matched in warheads that can hit their targets.

Here is a simplified example of how DPB might work. Assume that the United States and the Soviet Union have achieved parity with 1,000 weapons each. A U.S. BMD system capable of destroying 10 per cent of these warheads in an all-out Soviet attack would leave Moscow with only 900 deliverable weapons. This situation would permit Washington to dismantle 100 of its warheads and still maintain the offensive balance. If the Soviets followed suit by deploying a BMD they believed would be twice as effective—which would have double the kill probability of its U.S. counterpart— Moscow would have to reduce its nuclear arsenal to 800 warheads. These measures would leave each side with 720 deliverable warheads in each other's estimation, since the United States would consider itself able to destroy 10 per cent of the Soviets' 800-warhead arsenal, and the Soviet Union would consider itself able to destroy 20 per cent of America's 900-warhead arsenal.

The reduction in American offensive weapons would give the Soviet Union a powerful incentive not to increase its offensive forces or deploy a BMD without scrapping any missiles. If Moscow tried to take advantage of the situation, the United States would be forced to restore some or all of its destroyed offensive weapons. Hence, the traditional argument against defensive systems—that they would cause the offensive arms race to escalate—would no longer hold. Under DPB the pressure to catch up would be eliminated because the deployment of defensive weapons and the concomitant destruction of a certain number of offensive weapons would maintain the strategic nuclear balance.

The difficulty in estimating the effectiveness of a defensive system is a serious shortcoming of the DPB strategy. The United States will prudently tend to underestimate the effectiveness of the American defensive system and thus dismantle as few of its offensive weapons as pos-

sible. The equally prudent Soviet Union, in responding to the deployment of a U.S. BMD system, could be expected to overestimate the effectiveness of American defenses.

To overcome this difficulty, DPB should be implemented in very small stages. If the initially deployed American BMD system were judged capable of neutralizing one-tenth of the Soviet force, the United States would have to reduce its own warhead arsenal by only 10 per cent. Thus even large errors in the kill probability calculation would affect the weight of a delivered Soviet attack only marginally.

Therefore, the United States could afford to implement unilaterally a DPB policy and assess the Soviet response. There are risks and expenses involved in dismantling a small fraction of U.S. offensive arms should the Soviets choose to bolster their offensive capabilities in response to DPB. But the risks would at worst be temporary. The United States would not continue to build down if the Soviets reacted negatively.

A DEFENSE-ORIENTED WORLD

Although DPB should be implemented incrementally, over time these increments could add up to substantial protection. Each reduction in the adversary's offensive warheads would invite a corresponding reduction in the other side's offense without requiring a formal treaty. The scheme should lead to a downward rather than an upward spiral, provided each side takes its own defensive potential seriously and actually reduces offensive forces as defensive systems are put into place. The actual attrition of the offensive force could produce a world that, while still dependent on MAD to keep each side honest, would be threatened by far less astounding force levels. Yet there is no magic force level above which MAD holds and below which it loses its potency. Even one 100-kiloton bomb aimed at each of the 10 largest cities in the United States and the Soviet Union would be a very formidable deterrent. The attractiveness of disarming through defense is its potential to shrink force levels in terms of both weapons launched and weapons delivered. And if one views the primary purpose of the defensive weapons to be the creation of a situation that allows political leaders to reduce their own arsenals of offensive weapons rather than to neutralize an attack totally, the demands on the system were correspondingly reduced.

Implementing DPB would require withdrawing from the 1972 U.S.-Soviet antiballistic missile (ABM) treaty—a step that should be taken only with the greatest forethought. Abrogating this treaty would heighten superpower tensions if it were done precipitously and without regard for creating a better substitute. But if the ABM treaty were amended to allow for gradual, explicitly defined phasing in of BMD systems together with DPB, the agreement would stabilize the builddown process. Moreover, if the administration's strategic defense policies proceed much further, they may violate the ABM treaty anyway. DPB could help assure that the treaty's termination has constructive, not destructive, consequences. Indeed the expensive ABM research Reagan favors can be justified only if the eventual deployment would diminish, not exacerbate, superpower tensions and slow the offensive arms race.

Recent frustrations in arms control negotiations emphasize the advantage of a defense-oriented strategy. Arms controllers have always realized that a two-party MAD confrontation is theoretically stable, for parity is achieved when both sides have the same number of missiles. But a three-party MAD confrontation is theoretically unstable since each party will seek as many offensive weapons as its two adversaries combined. A lasting parity is possible only if no parties have any missiles or if each party has an infinite number of missiles. This problem beset the now-suspended intermediate nuclear force negotiations; the Soviets insisted on deploying enough medium-range missiles to counter French and British as well as U.S. forces, while the United States demanded parity based on the superpowers' medium-range arsenals alone. By contrast, a defense-oriented world would be less prone to this instability, since defense without offense is not threatening. And if eventually both superpowers were armed to the teeth with defensive systems but all nuclear powers had only a few offensive weapons, nuclear war would not necessarily lead to nuclear annihilation.

Ballistic missile defense has until now been attacked as a costly, unworkable, and destabilizing pipe dream, advocated only by recalcitrant hawks intent on building a Fortress America. DPB provides a way of using today's imperfect defense technology to reduce the superpowers' arsenals and the extent of the catastrophe that would result should deterrence fail.

The world will never again be free of the weapons of mass destruction. Disarmament alone can never be a practicable mechanism to achieve this world, a world that is not hostage to these devices. But by committing itself to both offensive disarmament and the deployment of defensive weapons, the United States can begin to put an end to the senseless, perilous, and seemingly interminable arms race.

NOTES

1. Ashton B. Carter, "ABM Update: An Assessment of Missile Defense in the 80s," given at the American Physical Society meeting on January 25, 1983.

SUGGESTED READINGS—PART I

Brown, Seyom. *The Faces of Power: Constancy and Change in United States Foreign Policy from Truman to Reagan.* New York: Columbia University Press, 1983.

Carter, Jimmy. *Keeping Faith.* New York: Bantam Books, 1982.

Crabb, Cecil V., Jr. *Policymakers and Critics: Conflicting Theories of American Foreign Policy.* New York: Praeger Publishers, 1976.

Dallek, Robert. *The American Style of Foreign Policy: Cultural Politics and Foreign Affairs.* New York: Alfred A. Knopf, 1983.

Gaddis, John Lewis. *Strategies of Containment.* New York: Oxford University Press, 1982.

Morgenthau, Hans J. *In Defense of the National Interest.* New York: Alfred A. Knopf, 1952.

Osgood, Robert E. *Ideals and Self-Interest in America's Foreign Relations.* Chicago: The University of Chicago Press, 1953.

Perkins, Dexter. *The American Approach to Foreign Policy.* Rev. ed. Cambridge, Mass.: Harvard University Press, 1962.

Yergin, Daniel. *Shattered Peace: The Origins of the Cold War and the National Security State.* Boston: Houghton Mifflin, 1977.

The Policymaking Process and Competing Value Systems

The president proposes an increase in military aid to the Salvadoran government in its efforts to control guerrilla activities; the Congress cuts off funding of the *contras* in Nicaragua; the Department of State and the Department of Defense differ on the role of negotiation and force in Central America; several religious groups protest at the White House and on Capitol Hill over increased military activity by the United States in Central America; the latest public opinion poll shows a reluctance to support President Reagan's policy in Central America, although support for his handling of foreign policy generally remains high.

Such descriptions aptly depict the many actors that participate in the foreign policy process and also reflect the difference in values and beliefs about foreign policy among various institutions, individuals, and groups. By their efforts—and in their own way—all of these foreign policy participants attempt to influence the policy of the United States abroad. The increased competition among a variety of sources is an important characteristic of American foreign policymaking today.

While presidents and their advisers usually come to office with particular foreign policy approaches, the Congress has increasingly sought to imprint its own stamp on American foreign policy. Similarly, the president is often confronted by foreign policy bureaucracies that have their own institutional view of the direction of foreign policy. The Department of State, the Department of Defense, and the intelligence community, for instance, are likely to view a foreign policy problem from different perspectives and thus offer different policy options to the president. This "bureaucratic politics" of the executive branch can often take on a life of its own and can be very instrumental in shaping the ultimate actions of the United States abroad.

In addition to these formal political institutions and participants, other groups and interests also compete to influence the foreign policy process. Various ethnic, religious, ideological, and economic interest groups often attempt to shape policy in a manner consistent with their own views on foreign affairs. While such interest groups obviously are unable to affect policy as directly as the president, the Congress, or the bureaucracies, they can be especially important to policy formulation when their activities are focused on particular issues (e.g., aid and trade issues) and directed at U.S. policy toward particular nations and regions.

Finally, the public at large can also affect the foreign policy process through the values and beliefs that it expresses over the policy course followed by the government. The public can use its ultimate weapon—the electoral process—to defeat a candidate over his or her foreign policy position. But prior to the use of that decisive measure, the public can express its value preference through the public "mood" that it creates. The public mood refers to the aggregate set of values and beliefs that the public expresses on foreign policy. Moreover, such a mood set limits on what policymakers ultimately do. Elected officials are sensitive to these views and usually do respond to the public wishes—at least in the broad designs of policy, if not always in every decision.

Part II of this reader provides a series of readings that illustrate the role of these various policy participants and that demonstrate the value conflicts that often arise among these groups as they seek to shape American foreign policy.

Section II–A. PRESIDENT VERSUS THE CONGRESS

The most important participants in the foreign policy process are the president and the Congress. While each branch of government has constitutionally prescribed power over particular aspects of the formulation and conduct of foreign policy, each also shares responsibilities shaping America's foreign policy. The very fact that these two political institutions share foreign policy responsibilities inevitably leads to conflict over who should hold sway over the process. While this conflict between these two branches has received the greatest amount of attention in the post-Watergate and post-Vietnam periods, students of executive-congressional relations note that this tension between the two branches has been evident throughout the history of the Republic.[1] Some have asserted, for example, that there is really a cyclical or "pendulum swing" pattern in the dominance of one branch over the other in the foreign policy arena. The three selections chosen for this section highlight this struggle imposed by the Constitution, the recent pattern of one branch dominating the other, and two alternate views of resolving this political dilemma for the American foreign policy process.

The first selection, "The Constitution and Foreign Affairs," by congressional-executive scholar, I. M. Destler, surveys the constitutional and procedural conflicts that the Congress and the executive have faced over the conduct of foreign policy. Drawing from political scientist Richard Neustadt, Destler contends that the structure of the Constitution provides for "separate institutions sharing powers" and notes that this characterization fully applies to foreign policy. The result has been a foreign policy process that has not always run smoothly. Instead, each branch of the government has attempted to gain dominance both historically and in the more recent period. For the last four decades, for instance, Destler has divided the struggle between the two branches into two phases: the period between World War II and the Vietnam involvement by the United States, and the period from the Vietnam War to the present. In the earlier period, Congress yielded "key domains" to the president and the executive branch in the formulation and execution of foreign policy. What emerged in the view of a number of critics was the "imperial presidency" in which the president was able to gain the vast majority of his foreign policy agenda. Bipartisanship and presidential leadership were the key phrases in describing the conduct of foreign policy. Much as the cold war has produced value consensus among the American public, it largely produced value consensus between the executive and legislative branches.

Beginning with the 1970s, however, the Congress began to "reclaim" and to "innovate" in its role in foreign policymaking through such important measures as the War Powers Resolution of 1973, the Hughes-Ryan Amendment of 1974, and the Trade Act of 1974, among others. This resurgence by the Congress has in turn caused both congressional and executive participants and political analysts to inquire whether a balance has really been restored between the two branches or whether the Congress had gone too far in its efforts to play a larger role in the policy process. Clearly by the mid-1970s, a conflict has been joined between the two branches.

What should be done about this political struggle between the Congress and the president over the control of foreign policy? Destler's essay suggests alternate strategies, two of which are explored here. Former Senator John Tower of Texas and former Deputy Secretary of State Warren Christopher provide different perspectives on this continuing contest between the two branches. The second reading is "Congress versus the President: The Formulation and Implementation of American Foreign Policy" by John C. Tower. Although Tower's perspective is not unique among members of Congress, he argues somewhat ironically that the traditional division of labor between the Congress and the president should be restored: the Congress should once again play a subordinate role to the executive in the foreign policy arena. Because the Congress "often represents competing regional and parochial interests, it is almost impossible for it to forge a unified national foreign policy strategy and to speak with one voice in negotiating with foreign powers." Further, Tower sees much of the effort by the Congress to legislate on foreign policy as "ill conceived" and "detrimental to the national security and foreign policy interests of the United States."

By contrast, Warren Christopher in "Ceasefire between the Branches: A Compact in Foreign Affairs," seeks the resolution of the contest between the two branches more through the mechanism of a new "compact" than through the dominance by either branch. While Christopher acknowledges that advocates for both branches can make their case through constitutional or legal decisions, a better way for the nation to proceed is to join in this new compact in which "each branch [would] respect and defer to the unique capabilities of the other . . . " and would "complement each other." He then outlines five major principles to shape this new covenant between the Congress and the president. Note that these principles deal more with procedural and substantive measures to forge this relationship rather than constitutional or statutory revisions.

NOTES

1. See Arthur Schlesinger, Jr., "Congress and the Making of American Foreign Policy," *Foreign Affairs* 51 (October 1972), pp. 78–113, and Thomas M. Franck and Edward Weisband, "Congress as a World Power," *Worldview* 22 (October 1979), pp. 4–7.

19. THE CONSTITUTION AND FOREIGN AFFAIRS

I. M. Destler

J. W. Fulbright once called it "American Foreign Policy in the Twentieth Century Under an Eighteenth Century Constitution."[1] In no other policy sphere has our governing charter generated as much anxiety about its suitability to the modern world. Can a system with divided authority, with two major foreign policy decisionmaking institutions, meet the need for united national action on life-or-death matters like, for example, the control and deployment of nuclear arms?

There are those who would deny the problem through simple assertion of presidential predominance. Citing authorities from John Marshall (as federalist Congressman)[2] through Woodrow Wilson (as Constitutional scholar)[3] to Edwin Meese (as presidential counselor)[4], executive branch practitioners and even scholars assert repeatedly that, on foreign policy, the president reigns supreme (or at least ought to). He doesn't. The Constitution grants to him just a handful of powers of particular relevance to foreign policy: negotiating treaties, appointing and receiving ambassadors, and commanding the armed forces. The Congress had a longer specific list: ratifying treaties, confirming ambassadors, declaring war, maintaining armed forces, and regulating foreign commerce. And if one moves to more general authorities, the legislative branch again appears to have the advantage: the right to sign or veto laws pales before the power to write them, particularly those laws

Source: News for Teachers of Political Science (Washington, D.C.: American Political Science Association, Spring 1985), pp. 14–16, 23.

which appropriate money. When the legislative branch insists on blocking an action, it generally has the capacity to prevail. A contemporary example is the congressional cutoff of CIA funds for the "contras" fighting the government of Nicaragua.

In foreign policy also, therefore, the Constitution sustains Richard Neustadt's apt characterization: it establishes a government of "separate institutions sharing powers."[5] Or to cite the older, classic aphorism of Edwin S. Corwin, the Constitution is "an invitation to struggle for the privilege of directing American foreign policy."[6]

To the degree that presidents have the upper hand in that struggle—and they do today on most issues, most of the time—the reasons are circumstantial. One is that members of Congress don't always accept the Constitution's invitation: often they don't struggle for actual policy control because they like having the buck stop at the other end of Pennsylvania Avenue. This leaves them free to criticize, and free of responsibility when things go badly overseas. A second source of presidential advantage is the nature of foreign policy action. Although much of U.S. international activity today is programmatic in character, and thus susceptible to the same general statutory and spending controls which Congress applies to domestic programs, a crucial component of foreign policy is country-specific or situation-specific actions that cannot be regulated through general statutes or fiscal controls. These require, as Alexander

Hamilton put it in *The Federalist,* "decision, activity, secrecy, and dispatch,"[7] characteristics of executive rather than legislative institutions. Hence when a freshman Republican Congressman once asked President Dwight D. Eisenhower which committee he should join, Ways and Means, or Foreign Affairs, Ike responded he should pick the former. The reason: "that on taxes Ways and Means was king, but that on foreign relations he was."[8] Eisenhower exaggerated, but the distinction is real. Taxes are susceptible to general statutory regulation. Diplomacy is not.

The strongest congressional foreign policy tools are clumsy and blunt: to reject a treaty, for example, or deny funding for a program, a country, or a war. What most members of the Senate wanted Richard Nixon to do on Vietnam during his first term was something more subtle: to take a more flexible negotiating line. He didn't want to, and they couldn't make him. They were unwilling to brandish the club of appropriations to force cessation of specific military actions until summer 1973, *after* the peace agreement was initialed and the troops were home.

Over the Constitution's first 150 years, the two branches fashioned a crude if shifting balance. Presidents piled up precedents for deploying military force without prior legislative sanction, albeit almost always in the Western Hemisphere or against non-governmental adversaries like pirates. At the same time, Congress asserted its authority regularly, especially through rejection or amendment of treaties.[9] This culminated, of course, in the Senate's failure to ratify Woodrow Wilson's Treaty of Versailles.

But World War II brought Americans into an era of global foreign policy engagement unprecedented in scope and duration. So in the 40 years since that war,

our political system has had to find new ways to reconcile the demands of activist diplomacy with the constraints (and values) of constitutional, democratic government. This period has brought substantial adaptation, the development of extra-constitutional mechanisms to make divided domestic powers compatible with perceived international needs. In the early postwar years, these typically involved Congress acquiescing in its own circumvention: new authorities and practices and institutions were developed to enhance presidential (and executive branch) flexibility. Then, in reaction to Vietnam, there developed a different sort of institutional adaptation. Mechanisms were imposed by Congress on resistant presidents, designed to constrain them and to recoup legislative authority, but in ways consistent, at least potentially, with ongoing presidential foreign policy leadership. Over this same period, moreover, parallel changes were developing in a different sphere of executive-congressional power sharing, that concerning the regulation of foreign commerce.

EARLY ADAPTATION: CONGRESS YIELDS UP KEY DOMAINS

The years between World War II and Vietnam are often depicted as a period of popular consensus and executive branch dominance. This is a substantial oversimplification. There was constant foreign policy debate, and presidents did not always win on Capitol Hill: foreign aid, for example, was regularly cut, sometimes by 20 percent or more. It was, after all, during the Kennedy administration that Fulbright offered the critique whose title opens this essay. He worried about how the United States could possibly cope with "today's aggressive revolutionary forces by continuing to leave vast and vital decision-making powers in the hands of a decentralized, independent-minded, and largely parochial-minded body of legislators."[10]

But in certain key domains, the president did reign supreme, and Congress was present at this coronation. Most important were decisions to deploy American troops in foreign combat. There had been, of course, "abundant historical precedent" for presidents "send[ing] the Army or Navy into combat without benefit of Congress."[11] They had been cautious, however, on actions outside this hemisphere, and Franklin Roosevelt was *very* cautious in the approach to World War II.

But that conflict vindicated the interventionists, who drew the lesson of Munich: the longer one waited to fight aggression, the higher the cost. So when North Korean forces crossed the demarcation line in that country, Harry S Truman responded quickly. Without any congressional sanction whatsoever, he ordered American forces to enter what would be, until Vietnam, our fourth-bloodiest war. And "enlightened" Americans applauded.

Truman's action ended up costing him politically: when the war turned sour, there was no one who shared responsibility. Perhaps learning from Truman's plight, Eisenhower took care to obtain general authorizing resolutions from Congress when he wished to threaten military action in the Taiwan straits, or the Middle East. Kennedy and Johnson followed this precedent of obtaining broad congressional resolutions sanctioning possible future resort to force: to counter Cuba in 1962; and to respond to the incidents in the Tonkin Gulf in 1964.

The legal necessity for such resolutions was never clear. In response to Senate Foreign Relations Committee questioning three years later, Under Secretary of State Nicholas Katzenbach would characterize the Tonkin resolution (in combination with the SEATO Treaty) as "the functional equivalent" of the action the Founding Fathers had intended when they gave Congress the power to declare war. But "it would be my view," he later added, that President Lyndon Johnson could have sent ground forces to Vietnam without it.[12] That same month, Johnson told a press conference that the resolution was "desirable," but not "necessary to do what we did and what we are doing."[13] In fact, presidents generally, as Eisenhower put it in his memoirs, insisted they had the "Constitutional authority to act" without such congressional authorization; the purpose of broad authorizing resolutions was simply "to make clear the unified and serious intentions" of the American people.[14] On matters of war and peace, it was broadly accepted that the president made the basic decisions and the role of Congress, at the time of those decisions, was to stand behind him.

If the war power was, in the large cases, the most critical sphere of constitutional adaptation, there was another that was operationally at least as important, year in and year out. This was in the broad field that acquired the label of "intelligence activities." The Central Intelligence Agency was established by statute in the National Security Act of 1947, but for twenty years thereafter its programmatic activities went basically unconstrained, whether they be covert paramilitary actions, engagement in foreign politics, subsidies to a range of domestic and foreign groups, or simply the gathering and analysis of information on a global scale. Of course, small subgroups of the Senate and House armed services and appropriations committees were informed of its budget and certain activities. But they seldom wanted to learn much more, even though the activities of the CIA and its sister agencies overlapped, and sometimes dwarfed, a wide range of "overt" programmatic actions by State, Defense, and other executive agencies subject to detailed congressional monitoring. So while House appropriations subcommittees nitpicked the State Department and foreign aid budgets, the CIA—a talented, elitist, extra-democratic organization— was free of serious Capitol Hill constraints.[15]

Arms sales were another category of recurrent foreign policy operations which grew beyond congressional reach. Originally they were under statutory discipline as a component of the military aid program, but as countries became able to pay hard currency for their weapons, Congress lost this handle.

Over this same period, Congress was also yielding up substantial power over international trade, a sphere where the Constitution granted it clear primacy. The tariff, "more than any other single topic, had engrossed its energies for more than a hundred years."[16] But beginning with the Trade Agreements Act of 1934, power to set tariff rates was delegated to successive presidents, as long as they did so through negotiation of "reciprocal" barrier-reducing agreements with other nations. Unlike war powers or intelligence, Congress set real limits on this authority—on each time period for negotiations, and on how much tariffs could be reduced during that time period. But the delegation of tariff powers was, nonetheless, a substantial departure from previous congressional practice. And it led, cumulatively, to a reduction of U.S. duties from the 60 percent of 1931 to under 5 percent today.

These constitutional adaptations, whose common element was Congress yielding

up power, endured through the nineteen-sixties. The seventies brought a new pattern. For security issues, the cause was Vietnam and the domestic strife it generated. For trade, the prime impetus was the declining importance of the tariff. In both, Congress took the lead in fashioning new mechanisms for power sharing that could increase its influence without making coherent foreign policy impossible for the nation as a whole.

THE SEVENTIES: CONGRESS RECLAIMS AND INNOVATES

As everywhere recognized, the Vietnam war brought an end to congressional deference on national security issues. Though legislators never mustered the will to confront the president on that issue until after the peace agreement was signed and combat forces were withdrawn, Congress did override Presidents Nixon and Ford on several highly-visible operational issues. Legislation enacted in August 1973 barred further bombing of Indochina. Arms sales to Turkey were embargoed by statute in December 1974. A year later, Congress outlawed covert aid to a CIA-backed faction fighting Soviet-supported forces in Angola.

These direct rebuffs of presidential actions won most of the headlines, but many legislators saw them as cases of foreign policy failure, not success. If one branch undercut the other, U.S. influence in the world could only decline. So senators and representatives searched for means by which Congress could assure itself influence over presidential foreign policy-making, but limit the occasions of explicit repudiation. They wanted to push presidents and their advisers to consult in advance, to listen to congressional sentiment before they committed themselves, and to modify their course, actual or projected, if negative political winds blew too strong. And they wanted also to force congressional attention, in the phrase of the day, to the policy takeoffs, not just the crash-landings.

The most visible, and potentially important, fruit of this effort was the War Powers Resolution passed over Nixon's veto in the fall of 1973. Senate sponsors of the bill, led by Jacob Javits (R-NY), had originally wanted to specify, substantively, exactly what sorts of situations justified presidential troop deployment without congressional sanction. To their House counterparts this posed serious practical and constitutional difficulties, and the law as enacted made only a weak, non-binding effort to define or delimit the substance of presidential war powers. Instead, the resolution established procedures governing the sending of U.S. troops into foreign battle. Its core sections provided that the president was to "consult with Congress," in "every possible instance," before "introducing United States Armed Forces into hostilities or into situations where imminent involvement in hostilities is clearly indicated by the circumstances." (Sec. 3) He was to notify congressional leaders in writing, within 48 hours, when he did so. (Sec. 4) And, in the only provisions that had real bite, he was to withdraw them within sixty days unless Congress took affirmative authorizing actions, and sooner "if the Congress so directs by concurrent resolution." (Sec. 5)[17]

Congress took a somewhat similar approach on intelligence activities, seeking to enforce consultation and a degree of what two experts have labelled "co-determination."[18] A crude beginning was the Hughes-Ryan amendment of 1974, which forbade the Central Intelligence Agency from undertaking covert activities "unless and until" the president no-

tified "appropriate" congressional committees of their nature and scope. In response to complaints that the total membership of such committees added up to over a hundred, a rather large group for keeping a secret, each house centralized oversight responsibilities through establishment of an intelligence committee. And after an effort to negotiate a broad congressional "charter" for the CIA broke down in early 1980, a short bill was enacted that October replacing Hughes-Ryan with a broader statutory requirement: that the two intelligence committees be "kept fully and currently informed of intelligence activities" (not just covert actions, not just CIA), with a carefully drafted exception to the prior notice requirement for covert actions in "extraordinary circumstances."[19] There was no provision for Congress having to approve such actions: it was recognized that intelligence activities required secrecy, and committee-based consultation had to serve as a surrogate for the broader democratic process. But the aim nonetheless was to establish a degree of *de facto* power-sharing and congressional constraint.

On arms sales, Congress responded to the executive challenge with a device it had employed increasingly since the thirties: it instituted a legislative veto. Over the protest of President Ford, it enacted the Nelson-Bingham amendment to the Arms Export Control Act in 1974, and strengthened it in 1976. Plans for arms sales above a certain size, to nations other than major allies, now had to be reported to Congress in advance and were to be abandoned if a majority in each house voted against them.

A final process innovation, perhaps the most important in its impact and broader potential, was developed for trade policy. The Nixon-Ford administration, preparing to enter the "Tokyo Round" negotiations on reducing nontariff barriers to trade, needed to persuade skeptical foreign governments that the agreements our negotiators signed would, in fact, be implemented through changes in U.S. law. But unlike on tariffs, Congress could not authorize such changes in advance through a quantitative formula setting limits to American concessions.

Senate Finance Committee members rejected, as unconstitutional, an administration formula providing broad, advance statutory authorization for the president to decree changes in trade-related laws. But negotiations among executive branch and congressional trade specialists yielded agreement to employ an expedited legislative procedure for any bill implementing an agreement reached in the authorized trade negotiations. Section 151 of the Trade Act of 1974 guaranteed an up-or-down vote, within 90 days, on such a bill. And amendments were prohibited; members had to vote on the legislation *as submitted by the president.*

This mechanism became known as the "fast-track procedures." And like the power-sharing adaptations for security policy, their aim was to make coherent, Executive-led U.S. action possible in the foreign realm, but with constraints that pushed the president and his senior advisers toward consultation, toward taking congressional concerns and priorities into account. This procedural innovation proved a smashing success when Jimmy Carter's Special Trade Representative, Robert Strauss, concluded the Tokyo Round negotiations in 1979. The president's implementing bill, drafted in fact on Capitol Hill by a team of congressional and executive branch aides, won quick and overwhelming approval, with only seven negative votes in the House and four in the Senate. From that time onward, the new process has been broadly accepted as *the* means of handling comprehensive trade agreements.[20]

Unfortunately, no comparable acceptance has come to the power-sharing mechanisms in the security sphere. Presidents have continued to challenge the War Powers Resolution in concept even as they grant it grudging acceptance in practice. The eleven-plus years since its enactment have brought, of course, no U.S. military involvements remotely comparable to Korea or Vietnam, and presidents have generally reported hostility-connected troop deployments as required, though in language that hedges on whether it binds them.[21] None have kept U.S. troops in overseas hostilities in clear-cut violation of its time limits. Ronald Reagan balanced, in the fall of 1983, a denunciation of the resolution with his approval of the most significant congressional action it has yet triggered: legislation authorizing and constraining deployment of U.S. peacekeeping forces in Lebanon. And even while denying its legal necessity, Reagan pledged he would abide by its provision.[22] He dispatched troops to Grenada shortly thereafter but combat consumed only a fraction of the sixty days that the Resolution allowed.

It is hard to find any case of a president who has suffered a foreign policy defeat *because of* the War Power Resolution, the complaints of Secretary of State George Shultz on Lebanon notwithstanding. And it is hard to conceive of a formula better crafted to balance the need for presidential capacity to respond quickly to foreign emergencies and the need—as a matter of right *and* effective policy—for a democratic judgment on the deployment of troops in combat.

But the War Powers Resolution suffers from its history: it was a measure forced by Congress on a president at a time of political weakness. This undercuts its legitimacy in the executive branch, and among those prone to favor the military instrument. The prior history of presidential warmaking undercuts it as well. The resolution is fully consistent, in this analyst's view, with the letter of the Constitution, and the Supreme Court certainly *could* find a basis for affirming it should it one day rule on the issue. But it could also cite post-1787 experience if it decided to come down the other way.

The other congressional security innovations have similarly weak political foundations. The intelligence consultation process worked reasonably well under Carter, whose CIA chief concluded that, on balance, "congressional oversight strengthens intelligence capabilities."[23] It has grown badly frayed under Reagan, whose Director of Central Intelligence has displayed a very different attitude. Thus, though in design and in general practice the new congressional process has supported a broad U.S. intelligence effort, and created power centers on Capitol Hill with a positive stake in that effort, the branch that crafted it remains dependent on its counterpart's cooperation to make the power-sharing work. The current lack of such cooperation renders more likely the sort of direct rebuff that Congress has applied to the Nicaraguan "contra" operation.

Finally, the legislative veto for arms sales was designed to prevent politically-imprudent presidential action, not to overturn it. Its basic weakness, of course, is the bluntness of the instrument: if exercised, it repudiates presidential—and hence (for the world audience) American—foreign policy. But no legislative veto has even been exercised on an arms sales, or on any other postwar presidential foreign policy action. The device works rather as a club in the closet, giving executive branch leaders a compell-

ing reason to take congressional soundings in advance. Only when an administration egregiously fails to take or heed such soundings, as on the Reagan sale of advanced radar aircraft (AWACS) to Saudi Arabia—has Congress come even close to employing the weapon.[24]

But the Supreme Court found the legislative veto unconstitutional in June 1983, in an opinion dubious in its logic but undeniable in its impact.[25] Like the other executive-congressional power-sharing devices, it arguably served executive branch as well as legislative branch interests. But it was, on arms sales and most other cases, imposed by the latter on the former, so Justice Department lawyers argued against it before the high tribunal. The resulting decision leaves legislators with less efficient ways of trying to retain strings on the powers they delegate to the president.

A review of postwar experience in executive-congressional power-sharing, then, reveals a complex past and an uncertain future. On trade agreements we have had successful procedural adaptation; on political-military matters there has been stalemate. A return to the pattern of the forties and fifties is most unlikely; there is consensus on neither the substance of foreign policy nor the superiority of presidential wisdom. But the congressional innovations of the seventies have not, in general, found executive branch acceptance.

This has rendered them fragile vehicles for bridging the gap between the branches. For procedures aimed simultaneously at institutionalizing and constraining congressional policy influence are anything but automatically effective: they require that both branches accept the reality and legitimacy of shared power and agree to play by certain rules of the game. Presidents and their senior advisers are often reluctant to do so whenever they feel strong enough to do otherwise. They see legislators as part-time players in a full-time game. They feel enough constraints on their freedom of action without readily accepting more. In the short run, Congress often reinforces such behavior, responding to executive assertiveness by retreating, and to executive hesitation by moving to fill the void. Thus, at times Jimmy Carter invited more congressional pressure by compromising, and Ronald Reagan has sometimes won respect by sticking to his course despite Capitol Hill resistance.

But in the longer run, executive leaders have reason to regret it when they have not built a strong political base for foreign policy actions, particularly in controversial domains. For all his troubles, Carter never sustained a direct congressional foreign policy rebuff like that administered to Reagan on "covert" Central American operations.

What then can be done? At the most general level, one finds among scholars and practitioners four basic prescriptions.

The first is to *accept the current system,* perhaps even applauding the virtues of our variant of democracy, of divided powers. Those who advocate this course tend to be persons whose bent is domestic politics more than foreign policy, or persons who fear that purposive American international action will have unfortunate consequences and therefore like a system which offers multiple opportunities for impeding such action.

The second option is to *overturn the current system,* to amend the Constitution so that the United States can, in Lloyd Cutler's phrase, "form a government"[26] that can take coherent and purposive central action. Such proposals typically seek changes which would make our system function more like a parliamentary regime, with a closer linking of the electoral fates of senators, representatives, and the president.

A third proposal, advanced in particularly pure form by Senator John Tower (R-Texas), is that Congress should recede. Tower advocates "a return to the situation that prevailed in the 1950s and 1960s," admonishing us that "chess is not a team sport."[27]

Finally, there is a variety of proposals for institutional adaptation, for accepting the structure of the current constitutional system but seeking to build bridges for cooperative foreign policymaking between the two branches. Warren Christopher for example, calls for a "compact" between them that "would affirm the President's basic authority to articulate and manage our foreign policy," with the executive in turn sharing information, providing consultation, and obeying those (hopefully broad) policy constraints that the Congress does impose.[28]

Though this is not the place to assess these approaches in detail, or to offer alternatives,[29] this analyst finds himself most comfortable with the fourth general approach. But its successful pursuit will require executive acceptance of measures not greatly different, in effect if not in form, from those that past administrations have found so hard to swallow.

NOTES

1. This was the title of a Fulbright speech and article published in *Cornell Law Quarterly,* Fall 1961.
2. "The President is sole organ of the nation in its external relations, and its sole representative with foreign nations." John Marshall, 1800. Quoted in Louis Henkin, *Foreign Affairs and the Constitution* (Mineola, N.Y.: The Foundation Press, 1972), p. 45.

3. "One of the President's powers is . . . his control, which is very absolute, of the foreign relations of the nation." Woodrow Wilson, 1908, quoted ibid., p. 304.

4. "It is the responsibility of the President to conduct foreign policy; limits on that by the Congress are improper as far as I'm concerned." Edwin Meese III, quote in *The Washington Post,* April 15, 1983.

5. Richard Neustadt, *Presidential Power* (New York: Signet, 1964), p. 42.

6. Edwin S. Corwin, *The President: Office and Powers* (New York: New York University Press, 1940), p. 200.

7. *The Federalist* (New York: Random House, Modern Library, 1980), p. 454.

8. Quoted in Richard F. Fenno, Jr., *Congressmen in Committees* (Boston: Little, Brown, 1973), p. 30.

9. See especially Arthur M. Schlesinger, Jr., *The Imperial Presidency* (Boston: Houghton Mifflin, 1973), chs. 3 & 4.

10. "American Foreign Policy in the Twentieth Century . . . ," p. 7.

11. Schlesinger, *Imperial Presidency,* p. 51.

12. *U.S. Commitments to Foreign Powers,* Hearings before the Senate Committee on Foreign Relations, August 17 and 21, 1967, pp. 82, 141.

13. News Conference of August 18, 1967, reprinted ibid., p. 126.

14. Dwight D. Eisenhower, *Mandate for Change* (Garden City, N.Y.: Doubleday, 1963), pp. 468-69.

15. See Harry Howe Ransom, *The Intelligence Establishment* (Cambridge, Mass.: Harvard University Press, 1970).

16. James L. Sundquist, *The Decline and Resurgence of Congress* (Washington, D.C.: The Brookings Institution, 1981), p. 99. Sundquist provides a thorough account of the ebb and flow of congressional foreign policy engagement in chapters V, X, and XI.

17. Quotations are taken from the War Powers Resolution, Public Law 93-148. The text and comprehensive history of its enactment and application appear in *The War Powers Resolution: A Special Study of the Committee on Foreign Affairs* by John J. Sullivan, 1982.

18. Thomas M. Franck and Edward Weisband, *Foreign Policy By Congress* (New York: Oxford University Press, 1979), pp. 61-162.

19. For a contemporary discussion of the Intelligence Oversight Act of 1980 and the broader problems of power-sharing on covert operations, see Loch K. Johnson, "The CIA: Controlling the Quiet Option," *Foreign Policy,* Summer 1980, pp. 143-53.

20. On the enactment of the "fast-track" procedures, see I. M. Destler, *Making Foreign Economic Policy* (Washington, D.C.: The Brookings Institution, 1980), pp. 170-78. On their implementation in 1979, see Robert Cassidy, "Negotiating about Negotiations," in Thomas M. Franck, ed., *The Tethered Presidency* (New York University Press, 1981), pp. 264-82; Destler and Thomas R. Graham, "United States Congress and the Tokyo Round: Lessons of a Success Story," *The World Economy,* June 1980, pp. 53-70; and Destler, "Trade Consensus; SALT Stalemate: Congress and Foreign Policy in the Seventies," in Thomas E. Mann and Norman J. Ornstein, eds., *The New Congress* (American Enterprise Institute, 1981), pp. 319-59.

21. Ford on evacuation of U.S. citizens from Vietnam in 1975: "In accordance with my desire to keep the Congress fully informed . . . and *taking note of* the provision of section 4 of the War Powers Resolution"; Carter on the Iran rescue mission: "Because of my desire that Congress be informed and *consistent with* the reporting requirements of the War Powers Resolution"; Reagan on U.S. participation in the force monitoring the Egyptian-Israeli Sinai agreement: "*consistent with* Section 4(a)(2) of the War Powers Resolution" (emphasis added). See House Committee on Foreign Affairs, "The War Powers Resolution: Relevant Documents, Correspondence, Reports," Committee Print, December 1983, pp. 43, 47, 57.

22. For a fuller analysis of the Lebanon epi-

sode, see I. M. Destler, Leslie H. Gelb, and Anthony Lake, *Our Own Worst Enemy: The Unmaking of American Foreign Policy* (New York: Simon & Schuster, 1984), pp. 159-62.

23. Stansfield Turner and George Thibault, "Intelligence: The Right Rules," *Foreign Policy,* Fall 1982, p. 130.

24. See I. M. Destler, "Congress and Foreign Policy Operations: The AWACS Sales to Saudi Arabia," paper prepared for Executive Legislative Relations Project, Georgetown University Center for Strategic and International Studies, publication forthcoming.

25. For an analysis and prognosis on the congressional veto in general, including broad reference to other writings on the subject, see Joseph Cooper, "The Legislative Veto in the 1980s," in Lawrence C. Dodd and Bruce I. Oppenheimer, eds., *Congress Reconsidered,* Congressional Quarterly Press, 1985, pp. 364-89. For a foreign policy-specific reaction to the Court's *Chadha* decision see, I. M. Destler, "Dateline Washington: Life after the Veto," *Foreign Policy,* Fall 1983, pp. 181-86.

26. Lloyd N. Cutler, "To Form a Government," *Foreign Affairs,* Fall 1980, pp. 126-43.

27. John G. Tower, "Congress versus the President," *Foreign Affairs,* Winter 1981/82, pp. 234, 243.

28. Warren Christopher, "Ceasefire between the Branches: A Compact in Foreign Affairs," *Foreign Affairs,* Summer 1982, pp. 999ff.

29. For some of this author's prescriptive thoughts, see: "Executive-Congressional Conflict in Foreign Policy: Explaining It, Coping with It," in Lawrence C. Dodd and Bruce I. Oppenheimer, eds., *Congress Reconsidered,* 3d ed., 1985, pp. 351-60; "Congress," in Joseph S. Nye, Jr., ed., *The Making of America's Soviet Policy* (New Haven, Conn.: Yale University Press, 1984), pp. 54-61; "Dateline Washington: Congress as Boss?" *Foreign Policy,* Spring 1981, pp. 176-80; and "Trade Consensus, SALT Stalemate" (fn. 20), pp. 354-59.

20. CONGRESS VERSUS THE PRESIDENT: THE FORMULATION AND IMPLEMENTATION OF AMERICAN FOREIGN POLICY

John G. Tower

The President is the sole organ of the nation in its external relations, and its sole representative with foreign nations.

John Marshall

One of the oldest conflicts in the American system of government is that between Congress and the President over the right to formulate and implement foreign policy. Is the President solely responsible for the conduct of external relations? Is the Congress an equal partner? Or does Congress have the right to shape U.S. policy by enacting legislation which proscribes a President's flexibility? These are not just debating points for historians and constitutional lawyers, but critical issues which need to be addressed if we are to see the successful exercise of American diplomacy in the 1980s. Our effectiveness in dealing with the problems ahead, especially U.S.-Soviet competition in the Third World, will depend to a significant degree on our ability to resolve the adversary relationship between the President and Congress.

The struggle for control of foreign policy came to the fore in the twentieth century, with America's reluctant entry into world affairs, two World Wars, and a smaller, but more complex, postwar bipolar world characterized by the increasing interdependence of nations. The first significant Congressional challenge to the

Source: Reprinted by permission of *Foreign Affairs* Winter 1981/1982, pp. 229–46. Copyright 1981/1982 by the Council on Foreign Relations, Inc.

Executive's foreign policy prerogative occurred during the interwar years. After the Senate rejected President Wilson's Versailles Treaty in 1920, Congress continued to assert itself in the formulation of foreign policy. By the 1930s, a strong Congress was able to prevent presidential initiative in the critical prewar years. The almost universal consensus today is that this Congressional intrusion had been a disaster and had inhibited the United States from playing a useful role in Europe that might have prevented World War II.

Following the Japanese attack on Pearl Harbor and our entry into the Second World War, Congress and the President stood in agreement over the direction of American foreign and military policy. Congressional intervention all but ceased.

The post-World War II period was marked by a reasonable balance between Congress and the President in the foreign policy decision-making process. In fact, Presidential foreign policy initiatives were generally accepted and reinforced by bipartisan support on Capitol Hill. American foreign policy was fairly coherent and consistent through changing complexions of the body politic. The United States was perceived as a reliable ally and its leadership generally accepted with a high degree of confidence by the non-communist world. But the relative stability between Congress and the President began to erode in the early 1970s with Congressional disenchantment over the Vietnam War. By mid-decade the two branches were locked in a struggle for control of American foreign policy. To a certain extent Congress won, and the balance between Congress and the President has swung dangerously to the legislative side with unfavorable consequences for American foreign policy.

If the balance is not soon restored, American foreign policy will be unable to meet the critical challenges of the 1980s. We are entering an era of fast change and increasing volatility in world affairs. Political instability and regional conflict are on the rise, especially in the Third World. Developing nations in many parts of the world are being torn apart by civil wars between pro-West and Soviet-supported factions, subverted by externally supported insurrection, or subjected to radical or reactionary anti-Western pressures. The industrialized economies of the West are ever more dependent on a lifeline of resources from an increasingly vulnerable part of the world. The Soviet Union has pursued an aggressive interventionist policy on its periphery and abroad, supported by its emerging global force projection capability and its successful use of less direct means of projecting power.

We may well be in a situation today which is analogous to that of the late 1930s, when America's inability to play a more active role in world affairs helped permit the Axis to realize its objectives without serious challenge. During this period Congress tied the President's hands, with disastrous consequences. Now we are back in the same situation, and risk making the same mistakes. If the United States is prevented from playing an active role in countering Soviet and Soviet

proxy involvement in the Third World, the 1990s could well find a world in which the resource-rich and strategically important developing nations are aligned with the Soviet Union.

What is the proper balance between Congress and the President in the formulation and implementation of foreign policy? Although the bulk of opinion argues for strong Executive authority in the conduct of external relations, the Constitution itself offers no clear definition as to where legislative authority ends and Presidential prerogative begins. The Constitution would appear to have vested war powers in both the Executive and Legislative branches. Although it conferred the power to declare war and raise and support the armed forces on Congress (Article I, Section 8), the Constitution also made the President Commander-in-Chief of the armed forces (Article II, Section 2). Nowhere in the Constitution is there unambiguous guidance as to which branch of government has the final authority to conduct external relations. Nonetheless, there is the strong implication that the formulation and implementation of foreign policy is a function of the Executive Branch, both as a practical necessity and as an essential concomitant of nationality.

John Jay argues this point in the *Federalist Papers* (Number 64, March 5, 1788):

The loss of a battle, the death of a Prince, the removal of a minister, or other circumstances intervening to change the present posture and aspect of affairs, may turn the most favorable tide into a course opposite to our wishes. As in the field, so in the cabinet, there are moments to be seized as they pass, and they who preside in either, should be left in capacity to improve them. So often and so essentially have we heretofore suffered from the want of secrecy and dispatch, that the Constitution would have been inexcusably defective if no attention had been paid to those objects. Those matters which in negociations usually require the most secrecy and the most dispatch, are those preparatory and auxiliary measures which are not otherwise important in a national view, than as they tend to facilitate the attainment of the objects of the negociation. For these the president will find no difficulty to provide, and should any circumstance occur which requires the advice and consent of the senate, he may at any time convene them.

The Supreme Court has forcefully upheld Executive authority in foreign relations. In 1935 Justice Sutherland, in the case of *U.S.* v. *Curtiss-Wright Export Corporation et al.* (299 U.S. 304), cited a series of previous Court decisions in arguing that the powers of "internal sovereignty" lay with the individual states, but those of "external sovereignty" were with the national government.

[There are fundamental differences] between the powers of the federal government in respect to foreign or external affairs and those in respect to domestic or internal affairs. ... Not only ... is the federal power over external affairs in origin and essential character different from that over internal affairs, but participation in the exercise of the power is significantly limited. In this vast external realm, with its important, complicated, delicate and manifold problems, the President alone has the power to speak or listen as a representative of the nation. He *makes* treaties with the advice and consent of the Senate; but he alone negotiates. Into the field of negotiation the Senate cannot intrude; and Congress itself is powerless to invade it.

It is quite apparent that if, in the maintenance of our international relations, embarrassment—perhaps serious embarrassment—is to be avoided and success for our aims achieved, congressional legislation which is to be made effective through negotiation and inquiry within the international field must often accord to the President a degree of discretion and freedom from statutory restriction which would not be admissible were domestic affairs alone involved.

In addition to the constitutional, judicial and historical arguments against Congressional intervention in foreign policy, there is an even more clear-cut issue of the efficacy of Congressional involvement in foreign policy. To the extent that Congress often represents competing regional and parochial interests, it is almost impossible for it to forge a unified national foreign policy strategy and to speak with one voice in negotiating with foreign powers. Because of the nature of the legislative process a law may be passed in response to a certain set of events, yet remain in effect long after the circumstances have changed. The great danger of Congressional intervention in foreign affairs is that enacted legislation becomes an institutional rigid "solution" to a temporary problem.

The President, along with the Vice President, is the only officer of government who is elected by and responsible to the nation as a whole. As such, only he possesses a national mandate. As head of the Executive Branch, the President can formulate a unified foreign policy, taking into consideration how each aspect of it will fit into an overall strategy. He and his advisers can formulate their strategy with the necessary confidentiality not only among themselves, but between the United States and foreign powers. The President has the information, professional personnel, operational experience, and national mandate to conduct a consistent long-range policy.

The legislative body, on the other hand, is elected to represent separate constituencies. Congress must of necessity take a tactical approach when enacting legislation, since the passage of laws is achieved by constantly shifting coalitions. This serves us well in the formulation of domestic policy, where we proceed by voting on one discrete piece of legislation at a time. Although many of us may have our own long-term strategies in mind as we vote on specific legislative matters, the overall effect is a body of legislation passed piece by piece by a changing majority of legislators. We build domestic policy one step at a time to the end that the final product of domestic legislation is reflected in a consensus of various coalitions. If we later find out we have made an error in a specific piece of domestic legislation, we can change it. For example, if we determine that we have underfunded housing subsidies we can increase them the next year. But the process by which generally accepted domestic policy is arrived at does not lend itself to the formulation of a long-term, coherent, foreign policy. Once we alienate a friendly government, perhaps through shortsighted legislation, it may take years for us to rebuild that relationship and recoup the loss.

A foreign policy should be an aggregate strategy, made up of separate bilateral and multilateral relationships that fit into a grander scheme designed to promote the long-term national interests. With a comprehensive design in mind, those who execute foreign policy can respond to changes in the international environment, substituting one tactic for another as it becomes necessary, but retaining the overall strategy.

In 1816, the Senate Foreign Relations Committee put the argument this way:

The President is the constitutional representative of the United States with regard to foreign nations. He manages our concerns with foreign nations and must necessarily be most competent to determine when, how, and upon what subjects negotiation may be urged with the greatest prospect of success. . . . The Committee . . . think the interference of the Senate in the direction of foreign negotiations are calculated to diminish that responsibility and thereby to impair the best security for the national safety. The nature of transactions with foreign nations, moreover, requires caution and unity of design, and their success frequently depends on secrecy and dispatch.

Five hundred and thirty-five Congressmen with different philosophies, regional interests and objectives in mind cannot forge a unified foreign policy that reflects the interests of the United States as a whole. Nor can they negotiate with foreign powers, or meet the requirement for diplomatic confidentiality. They are also ill equipped to respond quickly and decisively to changes in the international scene. The shifting coalitions of Congress, which serve us so well in the formulation and implementation of domestic policy, are not well suited to the day-to-day conduct of external relations. An observer has compared the conduct of foreign relations to a geopolitical chess game. Chess is not a team sport.

The 1970s were marked by a rash of Congressionally initiated foreign policy legislation that limited the President's range of options on a number of foreign policy issues. The thrust of the legislation was to restrict the President's ability to dispatch troops abroad in a crisis, and to proscribe his authority in arms sales, trade, human rights, foreign assistance and intelligence operations. During this period, over 150 separate prohibitions and restrictions were enacted on Executive Branch authority to formulate and implement foreign policy. Not only was much of this legislation ill conceived, if not actually unconstitutional, it has served in a number of instances to be detrimental to the national security and foreign policy interests of the United States.

The President's freedom of action in building bilateral relationships was severely proscribed by the series of *Nelson-Bingham Amendments,* beginning with the 1974 Foreign Assistance Act (P.L.

93-559). This legislation required the President to give advance notice to Congress of any offer to sell to foreign countries defense articles and services valued at $25 million or more and empowered the Congress to disapprove such sales within 20 calendar days by concurrent resolution. In 1976, the Nelson-Bingham Amendment to the Arms Export Control Act (P. L. 94-329) tightened these restrictions to include advance notification of any sale of "major" defense equipment totaling over $7 million. Congress is now given 30 days in which to exercise its legislative veto.

The consequence of these laws is that for the past seven years every major arms sale agreement has been played out amidst an acrimonious national debate, blown out of all proportion to the intrinsic importance of the transaction in question. Often the merits of the sale and its long-term foreign policy consequences are ignored, since legislators are put into the position of posturing for domestic political considerations. The debate diverts the President, the Congress and the nation from focusing on vital internal matters. Finally, because arms sales debates command so much media attention, legislators are inclined to give impulsive reaction statements before they have an opportunity for informed deliberation. They thereby often commit themselves to positions that, on cool reflection, they find untenable but difficult to recant.

The recent debate over the sale of AWACS (Airborne Warning and Control System) surveillance aircraft to Saudi Arabia is a classic case in point. Under such circumstances, it becomes extremely difficult for elected legislators to ignore constituent pressures and decide an issue on its merits. For example, Congressman Dan Rostenkowski (D-Ill.) said following the House vote to reject the AWACS sale that he voted against selling AWACS to Saudi Arabia for political reasons, despite his view that the sale should go through on its merits.

Such a situation raises the possibility that should the Congressional decision do ultimate violence to our national interest, the nation whose perceived interests have been sustained by successful lobbying will pay a price later. My colleague, Senator William Cohen (R-Maine), who opposed the sale on its merits, felt compelled to vote for it because he feared its defeat would precipitate an American backlash against Israel:

If the sale is rejected, [Israel] . . . will be blamed for the dissolution of the peace process . . . when the crisis comes, . . . when everyone is pointing an accusatory finger looking for a scapegoat, I do not want to hear any voices in the United States say—if only they had not been so intransigent, if only they had agreed not to interfere, if only they had not brought this mess—this death—upon themselves.

In some cases Congress allows a sale to go through, but only after a series of trivial and humiliating restrictions are placed on the purchasing nation. This tends to negate whatever goodwill the sale was designed to achieve. For example, in 1975 the President agreed to sell HAWK surface-to-air mobile missiles to Jordan. After a national brouhaha filled with many insults to King Hussein and questions about the stability of his regime, the sale finally went through, but only in "compromise" form—we took the wheels off. Presumably, HAWK missiles without wheels would allow the Jordanians to use them in fixed positions to protect the capital and key military locations, but prevent them from moving the missiles to the front line to be used against Israel. King Hussein later asked then Secretary of State Henry Kissinger why Congress had insisted on such a trivial point. It was never a question of whether the HAWKS would be mobile or not—we knew the Jordanians would be able to buy the wheels on the international market if they decided to violate the terms of the sale. The end result was that rather than cement our friendly relations with Jordan, we succeeded in humiliating a longtime friend.

Such actions are not soon forgotten. In his recent visit to Washington, King Hussein indicated that Jordan is considering turning to the Soviet Union for its new air defense missiles. This attitude clearly stems in part from his unhappiness over Congressional restrictions on U.S. arms sales to Jordan. According to a State Department spokesman, the 1975 HAWK missile sale "still rankles" in Jordan.

The *Turkish Arms Embargo* was a case where Congress tied the President's hands in negotiations. After the Turkish invasion of Cyprus on July 19–20, 1974, the Administration became involved in negotiations aimed at reconciling our two NATO allies, Greece and Turkey. After two days, a cease-fire was achieved, with Turkey controlling 25 percent of Cyprus.

Yet Congress was moving on a path of its own. On August 2, the House introduced two measures demanding the immediate and total removal of Turkish troops from Cyprus. After the second Turkish assault on August 14, the Senate Foreign Relations Committee prompted a State Department inquiry into possible Turkish violations of U.S. arms restrictions.

At one point, Prime Minister Ecevit of Turkey privately communicated his willingness to settle on terms representing a significant improvement over the status quo. The Administration was concerned that Congressional action would make it harder for Turkey to follow a conciliatory policy and thus destroy any hopes of a negotiated settlement. In an attempt to discourage a Turkish embargo, the White House invited several of my colleagues to attend briefings on the possibility of negotiations. Even after being shown evidence that a negotiation likely to improve Greece's position was in the making, the Congressmen continued to call for an arms embargo; soon, all hopes for a negotiated settlement vanished. On September 16, Ecevit's moderate government collapsed, and on October 17, the Congress imposed a Turkish arms embargo on a "very, very reluctant" President Ford. The embargo began on February 5, 1975; by that time, Turkey controlled 40 percent of the island. On June 17, 1975, Turkey responded to the embargo by placing all U.S. bases and listening posts on provisional status. On July 24, 1975, the House rejected a motion to partially lift the embargo; two days later, Turkey announced it was shutting down all U.S. bases and posts on its territory.

Thus, instead of reaching an agreement with a moderate Turkish government that controlled one-quarter of Cyprus, the United States had severely strained relations with an angry Turkish government that controlled two-fifths of the island. Furthermore, the aid cutoff weakened Turkey militarily, jeopardizing the southern flank of NATO and putting at risk our strategic listening posts in that country.

In a society such as ours, with its heterogeneous mix of various national and ethnic groups, strong lobbies are inevitable. But to submit American foreign policy to inordinate influence by these groups —often emotionally charged—is to impair a President's ability to carry out a strategy which reflects the interests of our nation as a whole. The Nelson-Bingham Amendments and the Turkish Arms Embargo were two pieces of legislation conducive to such a situation.

A second major area where Congressional intervention contributed to foreign policy disasters was the series of anti-war amendments. Throughout the early 1970s Congress proposed a series of acts aimed at forcing the United States into early withdrawal from Southeast Asia and cutting off American aid to Vietnam, Laos and Cambodia. The *Cooper-Church Amendment,* which became law in early 1971, cut off funds for U.S. troops, advisers and air support in and over Cambodia. The *Eagleton Amendment* (1973) called for American withdrawal from Laos and Cambodia. The *McGovern-Hatfield Amendment* (1970-71) set deadlines for American withdrawal from Indochina. Even though these two latter anti-Vietnam amendments did not become law, the pattern was clear by the early 1970s. My Senate colleagues would introduce one amendment after another, making it clear to the North Vietnamese that we would eventually legislate ourselves out of Vietnam. The Administration lost both credibility and flexibility in the peace negotiations. By making it clear to the North Vietnamese that Congress would prevent the President from further pursuing the war, or from enforcing the eventual peace, Congress sent a clear signal to our enemies that they could win in the end. The North Vietnamese were encouraged to stall in the Paris Peace Talks, waiting for American domestic dissent to provide them with the victory their military forces had been unable to achieve. After the Paris Agreements, aid to South Vietnam was throttled.

Finally, on July 1, 1973, we destroyed any hope of enforcing the Paris Peace Accords. The *Fulbright Amendment* to the Second Supplemental Appropriations Act for FY 1973 prohibited the use of funds "to support directly or indirectly combat activities in . . . or over Cambodia, Laos, North Vietnam and South Vietnam." As I said in Congressional debate over the Eagleton Amendment, the forerunner to the Fulbright Amendment:

It has tremendous significance because it marks the placing on the President of an . . . inhibition in the conduct of foreign relations, in the negotiating of agreement and treaties, and in the implementation and enforcement of those agreements once arrived at. . . . What we have in effect done in the Eagleton Amendment is said to [the North Vietnamese]: 'You may do whatever you please. Having concluded this agreement, we intend to walk away from it, and we don't care whether you violate those provisions or not.'

I believed then and still believe that our failure to enforce the Paris Accords was a principal contributor to Communist victory in Indochina and the resulting horrors we have seen since in Laos, Cambodia and Vietnam. Reasonable men may argue whether or not we were right in being in Vietnam in the first place. I remain convinced that we made many mistakes that led us there, and that our direct involvement was ill conceived. But to deny a President the military means to enforce a negotiated agreement guaranteed that all the sacrifices that came before it would be in vain. Just because a peace agreement is signed or a cease-fire agreed to is no guarantee that both sides will live up to it. After World War II we enforced the peace with Germany and Japan by occupation forces. We guaranteed the Korean cease-fire by the continued presence of U.N. troops at the Demilitarized Zone. The Fulbright Amendment prohibited our enforcing the Paris Accords. We bought a settlement in Vietnam with 50,000 American lives that gave South Vietnam, Cambodia and Laos a chance to survive—a chance that was thrown away when we refused to be guarantors to that settlement.

The *War Powers Act* (P.L. 93-148) is probably the most potentially damaging of the 1970s legislation, although we have yet to experience a crisis where its effects are felt. The War Powers Act (1973) grew out of Congress' frustration with the war in Vietnam and its desire to prevent such a situation from ever happening again. Although President Nixon vetoed the Act on October 24, 1973, terming it "unconstitutional," his veto was overridden two weeks later by the House and Senate.

The act provides that before American troops are introduced "into hostilities or into situations where imminent involvement in hostilities is clearly indicated by the circumstances" the President is to consult with Congress "in every possible instance." The President must notify Congress and submit a report within 48 hours after armed forces are sent abroad, "setting forth the circumstances necessitating the introduction of U.S. forces" and the "estimated scope and duration of the hostilities or involvement." After this initial two-day period, the President has 60 days to withdraw those forces or receive Congressional authorization for an extension, or a declaration of war.

This act jeopardizes the President's ability to respond quickly, forcefully and if necessary in secret, to protect American interests abroad. This may even invite crises. Although the Act does not specify whether the report to Congress must be unclassified, there remains the possibility that a confidential report would become public knowledge. In many cases the more urgent the requirement that a decision remain confidential, the greater the pressures for disclosure. Thus, by notifying Congress of the size, disposition and objectives of U.S. forces dispatched in a crisis, we run the risk that the report

may get into the public domain. If this information becomes available to the enemy, he then knows exactly what he can expect from American forces and thus what risks he runs in countering American actions. This removes any element of surprise the U.S. forces might have enjoyed and eliminates any uncertainties the adversary might have as to American plans.

It is interesting to speculate on just how damaging the legislation could prove to be at some future point. For that matter, what if the Iranian rescue attempt had gone somewhat differently? On April 26, 1980, President Carter reported to Congress the use of armed forces in the unsuccessful attempt to rescue American hostages in Iran on April 24, in full compliance with the 48-hour notification requirement of the War Powers Act. In this case, the rescue operation was over by the time the report was submitted, so there was no longer a need for secrecy nor a need for Congress to consider whether forces should be authorized or withdrawn. But what if the rescue attempt had bogged down or been planned as a longer effort? No doubt the details would have gotten out almost immediately, leaving little doubt in the minds of the Iranians just what the Americans were up to. While the framers of the War Powers Act intended it to prevent another Vietnam, their legislation has the effect of severely limiting the President's ability to respond quickly, forcefully and in secret to a foreign crisis.

In addition to the questionable wisdom of the reporting and consulting requirements of the War Powers Act, there are also doubts as to whether the legislative veto contained in the act is constitutional. Section 5 of the Act allows Congress the right to terminate any use of force, at any time, that has not been specifically authorized by either a declaration of war or similar legislation, by a concurrent resolution passed by a simple majority of both Houses. The legislative veto contained in the War Powers Act would appear to be in violation of Article 1, Section 7 of the Constitution. This so-called presentation clause clearly stipulates that an act can become law only if it is passed by a majority of both Houses of Congress followed by the President's assent, or by a two-thirds vote in each Chamber to override the President's veto. [Editor's Note: The *Chadha* decision of 1983 ruled that the legislative veto was unconstitutional.]

After the Indochina debacle, there was a raft of Vietnam-syndrome legislation that sought to prevent the President from getting us involved in "future Vietnams." The *Tunney Amendment* to the Defense Appropriations Act of 1976 (P.L. 94-212), which passed the Senate on December 19, 1975, prohibited the use of "funds appropriated in this Act for any activities involving Angola other than intelligence gathering."[1] My colleagues feared that President Ford's attempts to offer minimal assistance to the pro-West UNITA (National Union for the Total Independence of Angola) and FNLA (National Front for the Liberation of Angola) factions would somehow embroil us in "another Vietnam." The domestic debate over whether we should become involved in Angola sent a clear signal to the Soviets and their Cuban proxies. They knew that the risk of U.S. intervention was low, and the possibility of continued U.S. assistance to the pro-Western factions slim.

Although the Soviet-Cuban airlift halted temporarily in December with President Ford's stern warning to the Soviet Ambassador, the airlift resumed with a vengeance following passage of the Tunney Amendment on December 19, 1975. The number of Cubans in Angola doubled as they began flying in fresher troops for what was to become an all-out offensive against pro-Western forces. By January the Soviet Union had increased its military assistance to the MPLA (Popular Movement for the Liberation of Angola) and stationed Soviet warships in the vicinity of Angola. They began extensive ferrying operations for Cuban troops. It was clear that the United States had lost whatever leverage it might have had to persuade Soviet leaders to reduce Soviet and Cuban involvement in Angola.

With Angola the Soviet Union entered a new phase; never before had it or its surrogate Cuban army attempted such large-scale operations in Africa or anywhere else in the Third World. Their successful intervention in Angola bestowed on the Soviet Union and Cuba the image of dependable allies and supporters of radical movements in southern Africa. The United States by contrast was portrayed as having lost its taste for foreign involvement after Vietnam, and as being domestically divided over a foreign policy strategy. The moderate black African states lost confidence in America's willingness to stem the tide of Soviet involvement in the region.

After being reduced to sporadic guerrilla engagements for over a year, in July 1977 the pro-West UNITA faction declared its intention to renew the fight. Following this announcement, the Soviets and Cubans increased their efforts. As of late 1979, there were some 19,000 Cuban troops, 6,000 Cuban civilian technicians and 400 to 500 Soviet advisors in Angola. Although the guerrilla war continues, the Clark Amendment prohibits the United States from offering any aid to the pro-Western faction. The Clark Amendment prevents us from responding to Soviet and Cuban involvement in Angola, and leaves open to them the mineral-rich, strategically important region of southern Africa. [Editor's Note: The foreign aid bill passed in the summer of 1985 repealed the Clark Amendment.]

Finally, two of the most damaging Congressional intrusions into national security policy were the Senate Select Committee to Study Governmental Operations with Respect to Intelligence Activities (the so-called *Church Committee*) and the *Hughes-Ryan Amendment* to the Foreign Assistance Act (P.L. 93-189). As vice-chairman of the Church Committee (1975-76) I sought to limit the damage to our intelligence community, although to little avail. By conducting a public inquiry into the CIA we exposed not only its supposed blunders and malfeasance but also important information as to how the CIA is organized, how it gathers intelligence and what kinds of sources and methods it uses.

The Hughes-Ryan Amendment, which became law on December 30, 1974, prohibited any CIA activities abroad that are not directly related to intelligence gathering, "unless and until the President finds that each such operation is important to the national security of the United States and reports, in a timely fashion, a description and scope of such operations to the appropriate committees of Congress." By 1977 information about covert intelligence activities was available to eight Congressional committees, for a total of 200 members or roughly 40 percent of Congress.[2]

This, plus the Church Committee hearings, confirmed to our adversaries that clandestine operations would be severely curtailed in the future. It sent a signal to our adversaries that they could proceed with impunity in the "back alleys of the world." These actions also shook the confidence of those friendly states which had cooperated with us in intelligence gathering, and caused many of them to reassess their relationship with the U.S. intelligence community. They feared Congressional investigations of the CIA would expose their own intelligence sources and methods. In private conversations with officials of friendly intelligence agencies, I have been told that the Church Committee raised doubts about the wisdom of their cooperating with the United States in the future. This has also adversely affected our cooperation with countries that for political reasons take a publicly hostile attitude toward the United States, but who privately cooperate with us on some matters of mutual interest. They fear the publicity generated by a Congressional investigation would expose what is essentially a private relationship, and lead to unfavorable domestic political consequences for them. Finally, either through leaks or publicly released data, the Church Committee titillated the press with daily helpings of some of our nation's most treasured secrets.

If we are to meet the foreign policy challenges facing us in the 1980s, we must restore the traditional balance between Congress and the President in the formulation and implementation of foreign policy. To do so, much of the legislation of the past decade should be repealed or amended.

Many in Congress are coming to this conclusion and are working toward a reversal of the imbalance. The 1980 modification of the Hughes-Ryan Amendment to require notification of covert actions to only the two Intelligence Committees is one such step, as is the Senate's October 22, 1981, vote to repeal the Clark Amendment. Further efforts in this direction are essential if we are to have the maximum flexibility required to respond to a fast-changing world.

In addition to reversing much of this legislation, we should also look at new legislation which may be appropriate. There are strong arguments in favor of creating an unspecified contingency fund for economic and military assistance. One of the consequences of the 1970s legislation was that such funds which had previously existed were either abolished or severely curtailed. Reestablishment of such funds would grant the President the flexibility he needs to be able to respond quickly to help new friends that emerge unexpectedly, or old friends who are suddenly endangered. While disbursement of these funds should be made with appropriate notification to Congress, the inevitable delays involved in waiting for new Congressional authorization should be avoided.

For example, when Zimbabwe became independent on April 18, 1980, the new government was strongly anti-Soviet, pro-West and in need of economic assistance. On the day he took office, President Mugabe invited the United States to be the first nation to establish diplomatic relations with and open an embassy in Zimbabwe. We responded with a pledge of economic assistance, but due to the lack of funds for such contingencies, were able to grant only $2 million. We had to wait almost ten months, until the next appropriations cycle could be completed, to grant Zimbabwe the amount of economic assistance it needed.

We face a similar situation in northern Africa today. In the confusion cast over the area in the wake of the Sadat assassination, Libyan President Qaddafi has heightened threats against the anti-Soviet government of Sudan. The Libyan army appears to be on an alerted posture. Were Libya to attack Sudan tomorrow, there is very little the United States could do right away to assist President Nimeiry.

As legislation now stands the President has certain limited flexibility to grant military assistance to respond quickly to unplanned situations. The Foreign Assistance Act of 1961, as amended, permits the President, in the interests of national security, to draw on U.S. military stocks, defense services, or military education and training, up to $50 million in any fiscal year for foreign use. In 1981 the Reagan Administration requested that new contingency funds totalling $350 million be established for emergency economic and military assistance. As of mid-November 1981 Congressional action on this request is still pending, although it appears that both Houses are moving to reduce significantly the size of these contingency funds.

In supporting such discretionary authority and appropriations, and urging the repeal of the excessively restrictive legislation of the 1970s, I am in effect proposing a return to the situation that prevailed in the 1950s and 1960s.

At that time the Congress did provide discretionary authority and substantial contingency funds for the use of Presidents Truman, Eisenhower, Kennedy and Johnson. Each of these Presidents employed his authority to act quickly and decisively in ways which, on balance, served the national interest—especially in new and unforeseen situations emerging in what we now call the Third World. The basic authority of the Congress to appropriate funds for the armed forces and foreign activities remained constant. Indeed, the Congress from time to time expressed its views forcefully as to the desirability of support for nations that acted in ways prejudicial to American interests. (An early example of such legislation was the Hickenlooper Amendment, which for many years expressed Congress' general opposition to continue aid to countries that nationalized private American companies without adequate compensation.) The crucial difference is that such expressions of Congressional sentiment almost invariably contained a saving clause that permitted the President to go ahead if he certified to the Congress that the action was necessary for overriding national security reasons. This is a perfectly sound and reasonable practice, and one that avoids the immense complications and possible unconstitutionality of the legislative vetoes introduced by the various amendments of the 1970s.

In short, what I propose above is vastly more effective than the present situation, sounder from every constitutional standpoint, and fully in keeping with past precedents.

Finally, in reconsidering the legislation of the 1970s, it is useful to reexamine it and its causes in a more dispassionate light than that of the period. At the time, much of this legislation was considered a necessary response to counter the excesses of the presidency. Since the Vietnam War had never been formally declared by Congress, it was seen as the President's war. Watergate, along with the war, was considered to be the result of a Presidency grown too authoritarian. If the war were ever to end, and if future Vietnams were to be prevented, the President's foreign policy authority would have to be proscribed. As Arthur Schlesinger put it, the theory "that a foreign policy must be trusted to the executive went down in flames in Vietnam.... Vietnam discredited executive control of foreign relations as profoundly as Versailles and mandatory neutrality had discredited congressional control."[3]

If this legislation was motivated by an "Imperial Presidency," whose ultimate manifestation was an undeclared war, then the motivation is flawed. Blame for Vietnam can be laid at many doors: a series of American Presidents, and those in the civilian leadership who advocated gradual escalation and limited rules of engagement. But Congress was not blameless. The war in Vietnam, while undeclared by Congress in a formal sense, had de facto Congressional support. Beginning in the mid-1960s the Administration sent defense authorization and appropriations bills to Congress—legislation which clearly designated certain men and monies for the war effort. Year after year Congress acquiesced in the Vietnam War, by authorizing and appropriating resources for it. As former Senator J. William Fulbright remarked, "It was not a lack of power which prevented the Congress from ending the war in Indochina but a lack of will." With waning public support for a war which seemed to drag on forever, many in Congress and the media looked to a single explanation—for a scapegoat who could be held accountable for an unpopular war. Blame for the war in Vietnam was attributed to the usurpation of power by the President.

In the early 1970s Congress reversed itself and belatedly attempted to use its appropriation authority to end the war. While this was certainly within its prerogative, the timing was of questionable wisdom. Our efforts to disengage from Vietnam and to negotiate with the North Vietnamese were made more difficult by Congressional intervention. Congressional action made a settlement all the more difficult to achieve and, ultimately, impossible to enforce. The view that the Vietnam War discredited forever Executive control of foreign policy was an emotional reaction, driven by the passion of the moment. Because of it, Congress embarked on a course to limit not only President Nixon's flexibility, but also that of future Presidents. Congress prescribed a cure for a nonexistent disease. The lasting effect was that Congress institutionalized its foreign policy differences with the President by legislating permanent solutions for a temporary situation.

As Cyrus Vance said at the 1980 Harvard commencement, "Neither we nor the world can afford an American foreign policy which is hostage to the emotions of the moment." The authority to conduct external relations should not vacillate between Congress and the President as a result of failed or unpopular initiatives. The whole point of a written constitution and body of judicial opinion is to establish a consistent mechanism for apportioning authority. Whereas the Constitution confers on the Senate the duty of advice and consent in the making of treaties, on the Congress the power to appropriate monies for armed forces and to declare war, and special authority in the field of trade, it confers on Congress no other special rights in the field of external affairs.

The cumulative effect of this legislation is that, as the United States enters a period when the greatest flexibility is required of an American President to deal with fast-changing situations in the world, Congress has inhibited the President's freedom of action and denied him the tools necessary for the formulation and implementation of American foreign policy. We know that the Soviet Union maintains clandestine operations which are well organized, well disciplined, well financed, well trained and often well armed, in virtually every Third World country. They are in a position to exploit many restive

political situations which they may or may not originate. To inhibit the United States in its ability to conduct covert operations, to provide military assistance to pro-West governments or groups, and to respond quickly to military crises is to concede an enormous advantage to the Soviet Union and its proxies.

It is my sincere hope that Congress will reexamine its role in the conduct of foreign policy and repeal or amend, as necessary, the legislation of the 1970s. The end towards which we should work is to do whatever is necessary to strengthen America's ability to formulate and implement a unified, conerent and cohesive foreign policy to face the challenges of the 1980s.

NOTES

1. The Clark Amendment to the Arms Export Control Act of 1976 (Sec. 404, P.L. 94-329), which became law on June 30, 1976, further tightened the restriction by prohibiting "assistance of any kind . . . for the purpose, or which would have the effect, of promoting or augmenting, directly or indirectly, the capacity of any nation, group, organization, movement, or individual to conduct military or paramilitary operations in Angola."
2. In one of the few reversals of the 1970s legislation, in October 1980 the President signed into law an amendment to the National Security Act (P.L. 96-450), which stipulates that he must report covert operations to only two Congressional Committees, the House and Senate Select Committees on Intelligence.
3. Arthur M. Schlesinger, Jr., *The Imperial Presidency* (Boston: Houghton Mifflin, 1973), pp. 282-83.

21. CEASEFIRE BETWEEN THE BRANCHES: A COMPACT IN FOREIGN AFFAIRS

Warren Christopher

Those who serve in government, especially when under attack, are likely to be conscious—somewhat defensively perhaps—of the spirit of the old Spanish proverb: "It is not the same to talk of bulls, as to be in the bullring." The memory of that sentiment has had some bearing on my observations from the safe distance of private life. It has commended a focus on institutional problems—those that transcend partisanship.

One such issue deserves special, constant attention. It is the distribution within our government of authority for foreign affairs.

The country has already struggled at length with this issue. The ordeals of Vietnam and Watergate exposed grave perils to our constitutional structure—an accumulation of vast power in the President's hands, and room for enormous abuse. Congress responded by passing a great deal of legislation, and some might think the issue settled.

I think otherwise. On the basis of four years in the Department of State, I believe the methods of operation now in place leave us poorly equipped to conduct the kind of foreign policy our country requires in a complex, turbulent, dangerous world. We have not yet resolved the dilemma posed by our need to reconcile the imperative of democracy at home with the demands of leadership in the world.

So it is encouraging that the issue is being reopened. Specifically, two leaders in the Congress, the Chairman of the Senate Armed Services Committee, Senator John Tower, and the Chairman of the Senate Foreign Relations Committee, Senator Charles Percy—writing respectively in *Foreign Affairs* and *Foreign Policy*—have raised questions about the existing equation.[1]

As it happens, both Senator Percy and Senator Tower belong to the same party as the President. While they achieved a significant degree of impartiality, the truth is that we have not yet been able to exclude political considerations from these discussions. As a wise man once said, "Where you stand often depends on where you sit."

Thus, it would be quite ordinary for a Democrat to have advocated a stronger presidency for Mr. Carter, while now endorsing greater restraints upon President Reagan. After all, President Carter needed enough power to do what was "right"; President Reagan, on the other hand, needs to be kept from "mistakes."

But as Americans as well as partisans, it is important to think institutionally as well as politically. Perhaps that process will be advanced if people who are no longer in office speak out about how power should be shared. So I propose to downplay, for the moment, my doubts about where President Reagan is leading us, and to concentrate instead on the means by which our course is set—on what role the Executive, the Congress and the courts

Source: Reprinted by permission of *Foreign Affairs,* Summer 1982, pp. 989–1005. Copyright 1982 by the Council on Foreign Relations, Inc.

should play to preserve a rational system of balances and checks among the three branches.

I do this in these pages less to declare conclusions than to invite further discussion—to share some experiences and thoughts on the distribution of power in foreign affairs, and to suggest that all who have been concerned with the issue should now devote additional, careful attention to it.[2]

Before turning to some thoughts for the future, it is worth looking at the way the courts and the Congress have recently related to the Executive on international matters.

As to the courts, Alexis de Tocqueville once said that, "Scarcely any political question arises in the United States that is not resolved, sooner or later, into a judicial question." That was true of the major issues of presidential power faced in the four years of the Carter Administration. It is quite stunning that five significant foreign policy decisions of that period were challenged in the courts—and were brought to final decisions within President Carter's term or shortly after it ended. The resolution of those issues brought the basic judicial doctrines on foreign affairs authority into sharp focus.

In the early part of his Administration, President Carter spent a great deal of his political capital—which, given his narrow electoral margin, was already in short supply—on gaining approval of the two Panama Canal Treaties and of legislation to carry them out. Indeed, Clark Clifford, perhaps our most sophisticated observer of presidential power, thought he spent too much. The constitutional requirement for ratifying treaties—two-thirds of those present, or as many as 67 out of 100 Senators—is a difficult standard, and the Administration had to struggle for almost every vote. In all, some 21 reserva-

tions, conditions or amendments were affixed to the Treaties before they were approved.

Among other things, the ratification struggle required negotiation, with the active involvement of the Senate leadership, of the so-called DeConcini condition, named for the Senator from Arizona. That condition gave the United States the right to take in Panama whatever steps it deemed necessary to reopen the Canal if it were closed. The DeConcini condition inflamed Panamanian nationalism, and it was necessary to work out additional language in the second Treaty providing that the rights reserved to the United States did not allow intervention in Panama's internal affairs.

But even after the Treaties were ratified, the battle was not over. Sixty members of the House of Representatives filed suit challenging the constitutionality of the transfer of the Canal. The Congressmen based their argument on Article IV, Section 3, clause 2 of the Constitution which provides that the Congress "shall have Power to dispose of . . . Territory or other Property belonging to the United States." They contended that this clause proscribes dispositions of U.S. property by self-executing treaties, which are ratified by the Senate only. Rather, they said the action of both Houses of Congress is required.

In upholding the transfer, the Court of Appeals for the District of Columbia Circuit distinguished the property clause from those provisions of the Constitution which are by their terms exclusive, such as the grant to Congress of the power to appropriate funds.[3] The court concluded that in the international setting, the treaty power is another constitutionally permissible means of transferring property owned by the United States to other countries. The Supreme Court declined to hear the case.

President Carter's decision in December 1978 to downgrade our relations with Taiwan and recognize the People's Republic of China provided another significant test of presidential power. The President's termination of the Mutual Defense Treaty with Taiwan was challenged on constitutional grounds by Senator Barry Goldwater and others. Their lawsuit contended that since a treaty cannot go into force without the consent of the Senate, the termination of a treaty should also require either the same two-thirds majority of senators present, or else the concurrence of majorities in both the House and the Senate.

The U.S. District Court for the District of Columbia agreed with the Senators,[4] but their theory fared badly on appeal. The Court of Appeals for the District of Columbia Circuit held that President Carter acted within his powers. Though citing a variety of factors in its decision, the court relied heavily on the fact that the treaty itself contained a termination clause, which was without conditions or designation as to who could exercise it. The court said the "President's authority as Chief Executive is at its zenith when the Senate has consented to a treaty that expressly provides for termination on one year's notice."[5]

This "on-the-merits" analysis was rendered unnecessary by the Supreme Court, which ordered that the original complaint be dismissed.[6] Four Supreme Court Justices concluded that the case presented a "non-justiciable" political question and a fifth concluded that the case was not "ripe" for review because Congress had not formally challenged the President's action. A sixth Justice concurred in the result, and a seventh dissented from the view that the issue was non-justiciable, agreeing with the Court of Appeals that the President clearly had power to act.

A third court test of presidential power raised the issue of distinguishing between treaties, which require Senate approval for ratification, and executive agreements, which do not. The challenge was to President Carter's 1977 decision to return to the people of Hungary the "Holy Crown of St. Stephen." The crown had been given to Stephen by Pope Sylvester in 1000 A.D., when Hungary became a state in the international system of Europe; thus, it had great symbolic importance to the people of Hungary. In 1945, lest it fall into other hands, the Hungarian Commander of the Crown Guards entrusted the crown to the United States for safekeeping. President Carter's decision to return it prompted opposition from a number of Hungarian nationals and a lawsuit by Senator Robert Dole, who contended that the agreement was either a modification of an old treaty, or else a new treaty, and therefore required approval by two-thirds of the Senate.

In rejecting Senator Dole's action, the District Court for Kansas concluded that this particular transaction "has the indicia of an Executive Agreement."[7] On appeal, however, the Court of Appeals for the Tenth Circuit, relying on *Baker* v. *Carr,* the landmark case on "political questions," held that the controversy was of a political character not susceptible to judicial handling.[8] It said the court had "no way of ascertaining the interests of the United States, or of its people, in the controversy." The Supreme Court did not hear the case.

A fourth case involved the Iran hostage settlement agreements, the Declaration of Algiers, and the disposition of billions of dollars in Iranian assets which had been frozen by President Carter in November, 1979, after the American Embassy in Tehran and the Embassy's personnel were seized. The hostage settlement provided that a portion of those assets would be returned to Iran, and that the underlying claims asserted against those assets would be settled by an Iran-U.S. Claims Tribunal, out of a replenishable security fund provided by Iran for that purpose.

In formulating the hostage agreements, the U.S. negotiators had been very conscious of the limits of presidential power. Yet the negotiating situation and the time constraints seemed to rule out action by the Congress. Therefore, it was vital to cast the agreements in a way that would permit action by the President alone. But a company that had perfected a claim against Iran subsequently challenged the President's action, claiming it exceeded his powers.

The President was upheld unanimously by the Supreme Court.[9] The central questions were whether the President could, on his own, nullify attachments, order the transfer of Iranian assets, and suspend the enforcibility of claims against Iran in U.S. courts. While the Court found specific statutory authorization for the President's treatment of the assets, it found none for the suspension of claims in U.S. courts. Nevertheless, it said that the statutes indicated Congressional acceptance of wide leeway for the President to settle claims against foreign countries. It was crucial that "Congress has implicitly approved the practice of claim settlement by executive agreement" by, among other things, adopting the International Claims Settlement Act of 1949 to allocate and distribute funds resulting from such settlements. This was part of a long history of Congressional acquiescence in such settlements without the advice or consent of the Senate.

It also was important that the hostage settlement agreement provided an alternative channel, the Iran-U.S. Claims

Tribunal, for settling the claims. And, significantly, the Court noted that the settlement was "a necessary incident to the resolution of a major foreign policy dispute between our country and another."

The fifth case involved Philip Agee, a former employee of the Central Intelligence Agency. It is widely known that members of the CIA operate abroad "under cover." Mr. Agee adopted the practice of publishing the names of Americans abroad who, he said, are employees of the CIA. Every person so identified became a candidate for expulsion and sometimes a target for assassination. After much deliberation Secretary of State Cyrus Vance revoked Agee's passport, and Agee challenged his power to do so.

Agee contended, first, that the regulation under which his passport was revoked exceeded the power delegated by the Congress in the Passport Act of 1926. He also maintained that the revocation of his passport impinged upon his constitutional rights, in particular his Fifth Amendment due process right and right to travel and his First Amendment right of free speech.

In 1980 the lower courts agreed with Agee's contention; in 1981, however, the Supreme Court reversed.[10] It noted a long history of Executive discretion in granting, withholding or revoking passports, and relied on subsequent Congressional enactments in the passport area as evidence that Congress had approved regulations asserting authority to withhold passports on national security or foreign policy grounds. On the constitutional claims, the Court held that the right to hold a passport—involving "the freedom" of international travel as opposed to the different "right" to travel domestically—is subordinate to national security and foreign policy considerations and thus subject to reasonable governmental regulation. And the Court held that Agee's campaign against the CIA involved not only speech, but also conduct, which is not afforded First Amendment protection.

In all five of these cases, the validity of an action of the Executive Branch in a foreign policy matter was challenged. And in each case, the challenge was rejected by the courts. While the judicial reasoning differed from case to case, the outcome in all instances was to let the President have his way.

It is evident that cases involving foreign affairs raise, in the words of Justice Rehnquist in the hostage settlement case, searching questions about "the manner in which our Republic is to be governed." They remind us that we have a government characterized by what Alexander Hamilton called "vibrations of power." The cases came to the courts for decision precisely because the distribution of authority in our government is not exactly defined.

The results reflect the tradition of judicial deference to Executive action in the field of foreign affairs. As Chief Justice Burger said in the *Agee* case, "Matters intimately related to foreign policy and national security are rarely proper subjects for judicial intervention." When a foreign policy action is challenged, courts exhibit an almost instinctive wariness. They readily question the "standing" of the parties, resort to the "political question" or "ripeness" doctrines, or search for an indication of Congressional authorization.

Courts may be particularly hesitant to intervene where, as in three of the cases mentioned, the suits are commenced by individual Congressmen or small groups of members, rather than by Congress as a whole. In such circumstances, judges may feel that the lawsuits reflect the failure of those bringing the actions to sustain their viewpoint in the Congress.

On foreign policy matters, the deference of the courts to the President is, I think, healthy. We should expect, and welcome, somewhat closer judicial scrutiny of the other branches when, as in the Agee case, First Amendment issues are involved. But as a general proposition, the judicial system is not well suited for a major role in the foreign policy realm.

However, looking at the relationship between the President and the courts scarcely begins the analysis. It is revealing that all of the five court cases involved the allocation of power between the President and the Congress. And that is where the real fight has been.

Advocates of Congressional predominance on the one hand, and of Executive preeminence on the other, generally have found the Constitution to be clear and unambiguous on the issue. Each side has found the Constitution unmistakably in favor of its own view.

Congress, after all, has the authority under Article I, Section 8, of the Constitution to declare war, raise and support armies, and provide and maintain a Navy, as well as having the ultimate power of the purse under Article I, Section 7.

But, on the other hand, Article II, Section 2, denominates the President Commander-in-Chief of all the armed forces. And only the Executive can negotiate with foreign countries—even if the Senate must "advise and consent" when formal treaties are reached.

The reality, in fact, is much like Ambrose Bierce's definition of politics—"a strife of interest masquerading as a contest of principles." For the Constitution is, in fact, ambiguous. Reference to the text—even to the framers' descriptions— cannot fully settle the matter. The framers left a great deal of room for their successors to adopt methods and apply values of their own.

Therefore what we really face is not a quarrel about what the Constitution means, but about what, within a broad constitutional framework, our national interest requires. We cannot simply interpret; we have to think. And we have to respond to experience.

For most of our history those processes—together with healthy dollops of inertia and accident—led to a steady accumulation of power in the President's hands. Prior to World War II, for example, the major Congressional interventions in foreign policy—the repudiation of the Treaty of Versailles, and the neutrality laws—raised lasting concern about Congressional competence in this realm. With some prominent exceptions, members of Congress tended to think parochially; they found it hard to think globally.

Then after the war, the mantle of global leadership descended on us, and under unprecedented international conditions. Now we teetered perpetually on the edge of crisis. Our new role clearly required more international activity than Congress could closely supervise, clearer articulation than hundreds of separate voices could provide, more coherence than hundreds of independent thinkers could muster. Quick decisions and prompt policy adjustments often were required—hardly the specialties of deliberative bodies such as the Congress.

We also saw that we faced adversaries with unitary systems, apparently unfettered by any need to consult or concur. The Soviets, it seemed, could move quickly, ruthlessly, and in secret. At home, Congressional involvement risked delay, uncertainty and leaks.

Thus formed our dilemma. Many asked whether we could any longer afford to have the Congress, or the public, fully informed and routinely involved in national security decisions. The deeply disturbing implication of that perspective, however, was that it impinged upon our system itself. For neither absolute secrecy nor unfettered Executive supremacy, in any area, is consistent with democratic ideals.

Nor, we soon discovered, do they necessarily produce good policy. We uncovered that particular reality in the jungles of Vietnam—in a long, costly, divisive, frustrating conflict that led to an abrupt reversal of the historic trend toward Executive power. As the war dragged on, members of Congress felt themselves to be deceived on central issues—such consequential matters as the Gulf of Tonkin Resolution, presidential intentions to escalate, the estimated cost of the war and taxes to pay them, bombing in Cambodia and Laos, enemy troop strengths and body counts, the dependability of our South Vietnamese ally, and our chances for success.

The division between the Executive and the Congress was worsened by the fact that the war effort was commanded by two Presidents who were uncommonly given to secrecy, jealous of their power, and impatient with dissent. Perhaps largely as a result of these aspects of presidential character, even many members of Congress who supported the war also simultaneously supported broad steps to curb the President's power.

Finally, the rivalry gained intensity as a consequence of expansive constitutional premises originating in the Executive Branch—the Johnson Administration's notion of a shrunken world, giving the President the right to order troops into battle literally anywhere without looking to Capitol Hill; and President Nixon's theory that the President, as "Commander-in-Chief," could continue an existing war indefinitely, and even extend it geographically, so long as the purpose was to protect troops already engaged.

It was in response to such trends that the Congress moved forcefully in the 1970s to reassert its prerogatives and reclaim its power. Specific steps included a right to veto arms sales above a certain size; country-specific prohibitions on aid; limitations on CIA operations abroad; a requirement that executive agreements with other countries be fully reported on Capitol Hill; and the War Powers Resolution of 1973, under which, among other things, Congress must be informed within 48 hours when U.S. troops are sent into hostile situations, and the President must then gain Congressional approval within 60 days or else withdraw the troops.

Along with all the new procedures and prohibitions, Vietnam and related abuses left behind a new ethic on Capitol Hill. The Executive, it says, is not to be trusted. Deference is outdated. In the new ethic, the Congressional role must be one not simply of oversight or advice or basic design, but of active engagement at every stage.

Thus major arms transactions—such as those in the Middle East—routinely are fought out on Capitol Hill. The Congressional veto, reversing the traditional roles of Congress and the President, is imposed with greater frequency. Policy and plans in troubled areas are constantly ventilated, and our involvement is probed, publicized and pared down by Congressional resolutions. Major treaties—such as the Panama Canal Treaties and SALT II—are not only analyzed and debated, but renegotiated in the Senate.

Adverse consequences litter the foreign policy landscape. For example, when treaties are negotiated, what confidence can the other side have that compro-

mises it makes will not be reopened in the Senate, and further demands made? Some would say the logical next step is for our negotiating partners to hold back some concessions in negotiations with the Executive, so they have something to trade away in negotiations with the Senate.

In granting aid, to take another example, Congress often delays so long and then imposes so many restrictions as to assure that its objectives will be unachievable and its fears self-fulfilling. In the case of Nicaragua in 1979, when there was still a chance that we could influence the direction of the Sandinista government, it took months to gain authority from the Congress for a modest aid program, and even then it was hedged with debilitating conditions. Educators, medical personnel and others from Cuba, meanwhile, were on the scene within hours.

My concern is that a great nation simply may not be able to operate in the way we have and still advance its interests successfully in a complex, disorderly, dangerous world.

Based upon these general observations, I have been drawn to the conclusion that we would be well-served by a new "compact" between the Executive and the Congress on foreign policy decision-making, based on mutually reinforcing commitments and mutually accepted restraints.

The premise of such a compact would be that the separate branches have differing characteristics, and thus distinct capacities. And the compact's purpose would be to have each branch respect and defer to the unique capabilities of the other, so that instead of magnifying the weaknesses of each, we would embrace the strength of the whole. The arrangement would recognize that the Presidency and the Congress were not designed to mirror each other, or to compete over the same functions, but to complement each other, each bringing unique qualities to bear on the decisions they were expected to share.

The compact would embrace a number of principles.

First it would affirm the President's basic authority to articulate and manage our foreign policy.

As a fundamental precept, the compact would call for restraint on the part of the Congress—for Congress to recognize and accept the responsibility of the Executive to conduct and manage foreign policy on a daily basis. To other nations, it is exasperating and at times even incomprehensible that our system permits, even encourages, contests over the President's power to manage in the foreign sphere. Even when such challenges are ultimately defeated, they risk misunderstandings here and abroad about the dependability of actions by the United States. Our reputation for reliability is squarely at stake.

The growing complexity of the global agenda makes it increasingly important that the Executive have the authority to make and implement a coherent foreign policy. The simple truth is that if the Executive is immobilized in rancorous debate and struggles over power, that circumstance comforts our adversaries, confuses our friends, and cripples our country.

Vietnam and Watergate demonstrated that the Executive can act imprudently and dangerously, and can overreach its authority. However, those episodes did not, in the process, obviate the inherent limitations on the capacity of the Congress for the day-to-day management of foreign policy. The limited time members of Congress can devote, the influence of short-term political pressures, the delays associated with collective decisions,

the multiplicity of voices and purposes—all of these factors do still exist on Capitol Hill. So the answer to presidential error and abuse is to straighten out the Executive, not to substitute the Congress.

What is needed most of all is a new operative attitude on Capitol Hill. It is essential that Congress recognize that while full information and consultation are essential and broad policy should be jointly designed, attempts to dictate or overturn Executive decisions and actions are extraordinary and costly remedies. They should be employed rarely, in extreme circumstances, and not routinely—for they have consequences far beyond the immediate issue at hand.

In carrying out its part of the compact, the Congress might also move to consolidate its foreign policy jurisdictions. Secretary Vance and I estimated that we spent at least 25 percent of our time testifying, preparing to testify, or otherwise engaged in relations with Congress. Perhaps that could be scaled back—not to withhold information, but to limit the number of times it has to be retold before various committees and subcommittees in each House.

In this context, it is pertinent to note another source of controversy on foreign policy decision-making: that is, the recurrent struggles within the Executive Branch between the State Department and the National Security Adviser. (This controversy spills over into the Executive—Legislative struggle because the National Security Adviser is not confirmed by the Senate and, as a personal assistant to the President, cannot be called to testify on Capitol Hill.)

In my view, the Secretary of State and the National Security Adviser play vital but markedly different roles, which should be complementary and not competitive. The Secretary of State should be the architect of our foreign policy and sole authoritative spokesman other than the President. The National Security Adviser should play an inside role, coordinating the many Cabinet agencies which are involved in foreign affairs decisions, obtaining prompt resolution of conflicts between the agencies, and insuring effective follow-through on decisions once they are made by the President. He should be able to offer his substantive advice privately to the President, but the Secretary of State should be kept informed of the advice the President is getting. The National Security Adviser should shun public attention, eschewing television appearances, press briefings and diplomatic missions abroad.

Second, the compact would require that the Executive cooperate fully with the Congress and assist it in fulfilling its legitimate role.

In practice, the foreign policy compact should reflect the distinct functions of the branches. The Congress, through the authorization and appropriations process, has and must retain a role in setting the basic direction of policy, and in apportioning funds among various international functions and different capabilities.

Moreover, the Congress often is more able than the Executive to sense and reflect changes in popular thinking, and to identify both the congruities and the disparities between directions in national policy and trends in public opinion.

Congress can be an effective forum for testing ideas. Through hearings, as well as through the mails, it is a route of access for the public to the government. And since it is broadly and continuously representative of the nation as a whole, the Congress is ideally situated to help design the broad outlines of foreign and security policies that will be able to sustain public support.

These functions are distinct, it seems to me, from the Executive's responsibility to manage. Under the compact I envision, along with his managerial function, the President would be obliged to cooperate fully with the legitimate functions of the Congress. As part of that, the Executive would also recognize its vital responsibility to assure that Executive actions comport with the laws Congress enacts.

That is only common sense in any case. As we have seen, a distrustful Congress has ample weaponry in any conflict between the branches—the power to withhold funds, to circumscribe Executive discretion, to hold harassing hearings, to reject or rewrite treaties or to deny confirmations, and in various other ways to undercut the Executive's authority.[11] Therefore, out of self-interest, the President should be sensitive not only to what the Constitution permits, but to what comity requires. It is in the interest of both branches to avoid the use of blunt instruments.

The obligation of comity holds especially for sharing information and for consultation, so that Congress can share in the broad design of policy and oversee its execution. There are cases, of course, where Executive privilege is appropriate, and where sensitive information must be closely guarded. But they should be understood as rare exceptions to the rule. In my own experiences, I recall very few instances in which the added risk of a leak on Capitol Hill outweighed the potential damage that excessive secrecy would cause. During the 444 days the hostages were held, I provided periodic secret briefings on Iran and Afghanistan to the Senate and House leadership—sometimes daily, usually twice a week—and there was never a significant violation of the confidential relationship that was established.

The President's responsibilities for scrupulous adherence to the law are heightened, not lessened, by judicial deference in foreign policy. Irrespective of the courts, it is the President's duty, under Article II, to "take care that the laws be faithfully executed." It is also worth remembering that, while the courts have established doctrines which permit deference in foreign affairs, those same doctrines are flexible enough to permit judicial interventions if the Executive overreaches. The President owes an obligation to the institution of the presidency, and to the country, to build and preserve the kind of trust and common purpose that will permit the Executive to function—to lessen the rationale for the other branches to intervene through legislation or lawsuits.

El Salvador provides a current example. As a rule I am highly skeptical of country-specific restrictions on aid—even for the best of purposes. They cannot account for changed circumstances, and in a world where events happen with breathtaking speed, that may be a disqualifying flaw.

But doubts about such restrictions do not justify the Executive in being less than faithful to what a country-specific law requires—as was the case when President Reagan certified human rights progress in El Salvador which, by all other accounts, simply had not taken place. Our Ambassador to El Salvador, Deane Hinton, a career diplomat, reportedly told an audience of businessmen in El Salvador in February that the certification requirement was "tonto," which translates as "foolish" or "stupid." *The New York Times* report on that remark then quoted an unidentified embassy official as confirming that the presidential certification was not exactly true—that the certification requirement "forces the President to overstate things in order to get

the aid that must be sent. What choice did we have?"[12]

At least two other choices suggest themselves—either to observe the law, or to seek to have it changed. For a questionable certification strains credibility, mocks the Congress, and invites a return to disabling war between the branches. It violates the foreign policy compact I believe is so vital.

Along with the functional approach discussed above, the depth of Congressional involvement and the intensity of its oversight might also be varied depending upon the nature and the gravity of the issue. At the most fundamental level, a government makes no more fateful decision than the decision to go to war. The President should want to share that decision with the Congress. When the President and the Congress stand together, the nation's commitment is clear.

On the other hand, steps short of war ought to require less collaboration and permit more Executive discretion. To be sure, a decision to provide arms to a country could lead, as in Vietnam, to a combat involvement. But it is not inevitably the same thing. Military aid or sales and other steps short of combat can be considered on their own terms—managed by the President, within general policy guidelines jointly designed. Indeed, after Vietnam, both the Executive and the Congress are probably more inclined to treat our security relationships not as slippery slopes, but rather as staircases, with delineated landings from which we must choose, deliberately, either to deepen or lessen our involvements.

Third, the compact should be accompanied by a renewed spirit of bipartisanship in foreign affairs.

Over the last three decades we have seen a steady and dangerous erosion of the bipartisanship of the period immedi-

262 / The Policymaking Process and Competing Value Systems

ately after World War II. More and more, Democrats may be tempted to find satisfaction in a Republican foreign policy going awry, or vice versa. Yet the "outs" bear the practical consequences, if not the political ones, along with everyone else.

Unbridled partisanship is unwise under any circumstances; it is especially risky when, as now, one party controls the White House and another controls at least one House of the Congress. This had been recognized as an element in the potential "deadlock of democracy."

The immediate post-World War II period was a high point for bipartisanship. The formulation of the earlier era, "Politics stops at the water's edge," may sound utopian now, and certainly we cannot exclude foreign policy from our political debates. We can, however, temper them with a recognition that in this arena careless words or obstructionist tactics can have widespread repercussions. As Senator Percy has said, "despite the obstacles to strengthening bipartisanship, it must be achieved if the United States is to maintain a leadership role in the world."[13]

Fourth, the compact should recognize the essential role of sufficient resources in an effective foreign policy.

No matter how free the Executive hand to manage foreign policy, the compact will be disserved, and our diplomacy will be hamstrung, if the necessary funds are denied. Over the past 20 years, for example, while our stake in orderly worldwide economic development has grown, our expenditures for foreign assistance have been cut roughly in half in real terms. The urgency of this problem is manifest in the fact that in fiscal 1980 and 1981 no foreign aid appropriations at all were passed. Continuing resolutions, at frozen and inadequate funding levels, had to be used instead.

Diplomatically, meanwhile, we deal with 53 more countries than we did in 1960, and we work on more and harder issues—but with fewer professional diplomats than we had in 1960. We currently budget, for our entire diplomatic establishment, less than one percent of what we spend on defense. Yet our security depends increasingly upon our diplomacy, as well as upon our capacity to employ force.

Our diplomacy would be further disabled by the current effort to slash the educational exchange programs that have fostered so much understanding of our country among national leaders, journalists, educators and others in foreign lands. In my own experience in diplomacy, I recall many times being impressed by the depth of a foreign counterpart's grasp, if not necessarily acceptance, of the U.S. position, only to learn that he or she had participated in one of our exchange programs.

When we shortchange our diplomatic programs we undercut our foreign policy every bit as effectively as binding the President up in a procedural straitjacket. We increase the probability that instead of celebrating successes in foreign affairs, we will have to keep assigning blame for the failures. And a big share of the blame lies in expecting a global, great-power foreign policy for a third-rate price.

Fifth, as we proceed with the compact, we must nevertheless be realistic enough to recognize that even if we can reach a more effective and agreeable arrangement, we will not match the alleged efficiency of undemocratic regimes.

We should not try. Rather, we should celebrate our democratic traditions, and resolve to make them work better.

The fact that we make many of our national decisions by voting, by the choices of our people and their elected representatives, unquestionably does leave us at some disadvantage in facing adversaries ruled by decree. Democracy can be cumbersome. It can mean delay, and there can be discontinuity when the people change their leaders.

Though we can adjust our system to make it work more smoothly, some inefficiencies are plainly inherent. But they are also important. For they guarantee to our own people and exemplify to the world our commitment to the ideals which are the aspiration of most of the world's people—in particular, the ideal that the people should share in decisions affecting their lives.

Despite its random elements, our system was not randomly designed. The tensions among the branches were quite deliberately incorporated, in large measure to protect the people and safeguard popular rule. The discretion, the tensions, the "vibrations," are the hallmarks of a system of government that could endure, evolve and thrive for almost two centuries.

The best time to bring such a compact into operation would be the commencement of a new Administration after a national election, or perhaps after a Congressional election. The sense of unity and national purpose which usually marks such periods would provide the best environment for seeking the mutually reinforcing commitments and mutually accepted restraints described above. The forum for confirming such undertakings could be a meeting between a broad range of Congressional leaders and the President and key national security officials, perhaps somewhat comparable in composition to the day-long meeting held by President Carter at the Smithsonian Institution in December 1976. Thereafter, a small group (perhaps the Secretary of State and bipartisan leaders from both

Houses) could be charged with monitoring observance of the compact and identifying potential violations.

If the general concept of the compact is thought to have merit, it could usefully be ventilated by a special hearing of the Senate Foreign Relations Committee or the House Foreign Affairs Committee. Or one of the many institutes dedicated to foreign affairs might draw together a group of scholars and public officials to probe its premises and discuss implementation.

Whatever the next step, I believe such a new compact is needed, not to rearrange our system, but to refine it slightly, so that the framers' ingenious plan may continue to both embrace democracy and effectively defend it.

NOTES

1. John G. Tower, "Congress versus the President: The Formulation and Implementation of American Foreign Policy," *Foreign Affairs*, Winter 1981/82; and Charles H. Percy, "The Partisan Gap," *Foreign Policy*, Winter 1981/82.

2. The distinct perspectives of the Executive and the Congress have been amplified in a number of important articles including Lee H. Hamilton and Michael H. Van Dusen, "Making the Separation of Powers Work," *Foreign Affairs*, Fall 1978; Douglas J. Bennet, Jr., "Congress in Foreign Policy: Who Needs It?" *Foreign Affairs*, Fall 1978; Lloyd N. Cutler, "To Form a Government," *Foreign Affairs*, Fall 1980; and Charles McC. Mathias, Jr., "Ethnic Groups and Foreign Policy," *Foreign Affairs*, Summer 1981.

3. *Edwards* v. *Carter*, 580 F. 2d 1055 (D.C. Cir. 1978) cert. denied, 436 U.S. 907 (1978).

4. *Goldwater* v. *Carter*, 481 F. Supp. 949 (1979).

5. *Goldwater* v. *Carter*, 617 F. 2d 697, 708 (D.C. Cir. 1979).

6. *Goldwater* v. *Carter,* 444 U.S. 996 (1979).

7. *Dole* v. *Carter,* 444 F. Supp. 1065, 1070 (1977).

8. *Dole* v. *Carter,* 569 F. 2d 1109 (10th Cir. 1977). See *Baker* v. *Carr,* 369 U.S. 186 (1962).

9. *Dames & Moore* v. *Regan,* 453 U.S. 654, 680, 688 (1981).

10. See *Agee* v. *Vance,* 483 F. Supp. 729 (1980), affirmed in *Agee* v. *Muskie,* 629 F. 2d 80 (1980); reversed in *Agee* v. *Haig,* 453 U.S. 280 (1981).

11. For example, in 1975, given Soviet support for one faction in Angola, there was a strong Executive Branch impulse to intervene in that former Portuguese colony in Africa. With memories of Vietnam still so fresh, however, there was not much prospect that Congress would approve. To bypass that obstacle, a major covert operation was planned. The sequel was a flat Congressional ban on any involvement in Angola—and more impetus for strict limits on, and broad Congressional review of, covert operations anywhere in the world.

12. *The New York Times,* February 26, 1982, p. A6.

13. Percy, op. cit., p. 45.

Section II–B. BUREAUCRATIC POLITICS AND FOREIGN POLICY

Beyond the Congress and the president, the role of the bureaucracy has been increasingly a focal point of analysis in explaining American foreign policy. One reason for this new emphasis on the bureaucracy in foreign policymaking is undoubtedly related to the growth of executive institutions associated with foreign affairs and with the expansion of policy activities by other bureaucracies, not traditionally seen as participants in foreign policymaking. With the passage of the National Security Act of 1947, for example, a large national security apparatus came into existence with the formation of the National Security Council, the Central Intelligence Agency, and the National Military Establishment (later the Department of Defense). These institutions emerged to complement the principal foreign policy bureaucracy, the Department of State. In addition, other bureaucracies began to assume a role in the foreign policy process and have been used increasingly by presidents to shape policy. The Department of Treasury, the Department of Commerce, the Department of Agriculture, and the Department of Energy, among others, have assumed a larger role in foreign policymaking. In short, then, the very existence of numerous bureaucracies has become an important source of increasing their role in foreign affairs.

A second reason for this emphasis upon bureaucracies has been the emergence of *competition* among them. As these new bureaucracies developed, and as others expanded their activities, conflict over policy and over "turf" (i.e., areas of expertise of a bureaucracy) inevitably developed. Increasingly, various bureaucracies (and the individuals within them) staked out their positions on issues and then sought to prevail in the bargaining process that resulted. The consequence was a foreign policy that was increasingly less the decision of any one or even a set of key individuals and more the result of the "pulling" and "hauling" among the competing bureaucracies.[1] This perspective, aptly named "bureaucratic politics," has emerged in the view of some analysts as a particularly useful way to understand how American foreign policy is made.

Yet a third reason for the importance of bureaucracies in foreign policy is related to the control of them by the executive branch, the Congress, and the public at large. As some bureaucracies have grown and gained a prominent place in the policy process, the ability of other institutions to control their effect on policy has become an issue of concern. Two foreign policy bureaucracies in particular have received attention over the last decade as organizations that have seemingly exercised too independent an effect on foreign policy. One was the Central Intelligence Agency, the other was the National Security Council. As the Church Committee investigations revealed, the lines of accountability of the CIA to the president were not always operating and the agency sometimes carried out covert operations without the knowledge of the rest of the government.[2] In a similar way, the National Security Council, and especially the assistant for national security affairs (the National Security Adviser), has assumed a greater portion of the key foreign policymaking at the expense of the Department of State and the secretary of state.

The next three selections illustrate these reasons for examining foreign policy bureaucracies and the value conflicts that have resulted among them and the other institutions of government in making foreign policy. The first essay examines several key foreign policy bureaucracies and the competition among them for the overall control of foreign policymaking. The second essay illustrates the nature of this "bureaucratic politics" through the use of a recent important foreign policy decision, the choice of a bargaining position for arms control talks with the Soviet Union. The third essay discusses the types of controls existing on one important foreign policy bureaucracy, the intelligence community, and criticizes recent efforts to change those controls.

Specifically, the first essay, "How Important Is National Security Structure to National Security Policy?" by Arthur Cyr discusses the conflict that has developed between the National Security Council and the Department of State and between the National Security Adviser and the secretary of state. These clashes have been the most evident bureaucratic foreign policy conflict in recent years and have generated considerable debate over the proper role of these two bureaucracies and these key individuals in policy formulation.

Cyr identifies three different approaches to describe the organizational structure of the key foreign policy bureaucracies: the administrative approach, the theoretical approach, and the centralized dominance approach. He then uses these approaches to interpret the national security structures of the various administrations from Truman to Reagan. What should be particularly evident from this reading is that Cyr identifies a particular structural and procedural arrangement that he thinks is best for foreign policymaking. This preferred approach, moreover, would require more presidential leadership and allow the secretary of state a larger role in the policy process than in the past. Do you agree with Cyr's preferred approach? What are its strengths and weaknesses? What are some problems with the other approaches that he identifies?

The second reading, "Shades of Zero," drawn from Strobe Talbott's *Deadly Gambits,* discusses the "bureaucratic politics" involved in arriving at the "zero option" position by the United States to begin the intermediate arms control talks with the Soviet Union in November 1981. These talks were aimed at controlling the level of intermediate range or theater nuclear weapons that would be placed in Central Europe by the two superpowers. The talks themselves were the outgrowth of the Dual Track decision taken by the NATO nations in December 1979. That decision called for the deployment of 572 cruise and Pershing II missiles by the United States in Western Europe to counterbalance the SS-20 intermediate range missiles which the Soviet Union had deployed *if* arms control negotiations on these types of nuclear weapons were not successful by December 1983.

In this selection, Talbott recounts the bureaucratic bargaining that went on over this initial negotiating position. Notice how the Department of State and the Department of Defense wanted to define the meaning of "zero" in different ways. How much did each side modify its position through the course of the discussions? Notice the role of the interagency group (the principal decision unit that tries to coordinate policymaking among the foreign policy bureaucracies) in this process. How important were such key "players" as Secretary of State Alexander Haig, Secretary of Defense Caspar Weinberger, the Joint Chiefs of Staff, the Assistant Secretary of Defense Richard Perle, Richard Burt, the director of the State Department's Bureau of Politico-Military Affairs, and the Arms Control and Disarmament Agency? What does this selection tell you about how policy is made within a bureaucratic setting?

The third essay, "Intelligence: The Right Rules," by former CIA Director Stansfield Turner and his assistant, George Thibault, assesses four types of controls placed upon the intelligence community, ranging from those internal to the intelligence agencies, those imposed by the president and Congress, and those exercised by the public at large. Turner and Thibault offer a useful assessment of each of these types of controls and analyze the recent changes in these controls, as set forth in an executive order issued by the Reagan administration in 1982. They also suggest the enactment of a charter for the intelligence community, an idea originally suggested by the Church Committee in its final report in the mid-1970s. In their judgment, such a charter would specify the duties and restraints on the entire community and would help bridge the gap between the need for secrecy in foreign policymaking with the need for accountability in a democracy.

NOTES

1. For a description of the "bureaucratic politics" approach to understanding foreign policy, see Graham Allison, *Essence of Decision: Explaining the Cuban Missile Crisis* (Boston: Little, Brown, 1971), pp. 144–84. The use of the "pulling" and "hauling" characterization is at p. 144. It is also at p. 158 in which Allison quotes from Roger Hilsman's *To Move a Nation* (Garden City, N.Y.: Doubleday Publishing, 1964), p. 6.
2. See "Foreign and Military Intelligence," Book I, Final Report of the Select Committee to Study Governmental Operations with Respect to Intelligence Activities, U.S. Senate, April 26, 1976 (the Church Committee Report, after the Chair of the Committee, Senator Frank Church).

22. HOW IMPORTANT IS NATIONAL SECURITY STRUCTURE TO NATIONAL SECURITY POLICY?

Arthur Cyr

In ancient times alchemists believed implicitly in the existence of a philosopher's stone which would provide the key to the universe and, in effect, solve all the problems of mankind. The quest for coordination is in many respects the twentieth century equivalent of the medieval search for the philosopher's stone.

Harold Seidman[1]

The conflict between the president's assistant for National Security Affairs and the secretary of state, and more broadly between the National Security Council staff and the State Department, has been one of the most persistent, contentious organizational problems afflicting the United States government. Since the beginning of the Kennedy administration in 1961, when McGeorge Bundy brought into play a more informal and, in some ways, more assertive NSC staff structure, there has been a perception of tension between the two foreign policy centers. Some might argue that the competition reached a destructive height of intensity during the Carter years, with the open rivalry between Secretary of State Cyrus Vance and Security Assistant Zbigniew Brzezinski. Vance and Brzezinski have followed the contemporary style, not only by clashing while in power but also through their publication of very revealing books soon after leaving government, which lay out in considerable detail their disputes over how to handle the Iran crisis, security and other relations with the Soviet Union, and a range of other matters. Reviewers have sometimes, not sur-

prisingly, considered the books in tandem, given the wealth of opportunity for comparison and contrast.[2]

Yet if the subject is both timely and of continuing importance, there seems to be remarkably little agreement among analysts on how best to provide a remedy for organizational disarray. This perhaps relates in part to a situation in which informed people have varied in their perceptions of the standing role of the security assistant over time. For Louis W. Koenig, the past is revealing in that the job has had de facto cabinet rank at least since the early 1960s: "President Johnson continued to employ Bundy as national security assistant at a level of influence equal to that under President Kennedy. In the Washington community, Bundy, in both presidential administrations, was widely regarded as the virtual equal of Secretary of State Rusk and Secretary of Defense McNamara." Brzezinski sees things differently: "Carter . . . at the very first cabinet meeting gave me cabinet status—unlike my predecessors and my successor."[3] Brzezinski suggests in forthright fashion that the security assistant's post be formalized in statute as the significant job that it has become. He argues that this will mean recognition that the White House will be the center of

Source: *World Affairs* 146, no. 2 (Fall 1983), pp. 127-47, a publication of the Helen Dwight Reid Educational Foundation.

policy formulation, with the State Department given the mission of implementation.[4]

Henry Kissinger, on the other hand, now states that he and Nixon made a mistake in trying to centralize policy control in the White House. He argues that the traditional approach of a strong secretary of state is best. Most formal studies of foreign policy organization have concurred with his present view, though with many variations and permutations. There has hardly been unanimity on recommendations. One major study even suggested a new "secretary of foreign affairs," to have authority over the State Department but also to have wider substantive and coordination responsibilities at the very top, a notion echoed at least vaguely in the effort of the Reagan administration to assign George Bush the task of general "crisis manager."[5]

The thesis of this paper is that the ideal approach to American foreign policy organization does not exist, not least because structure inevitably changes as a function of presidential style and authority, but that overall the best direction is for the State Department to have as much initiative as possible in policy formulation, including conceptual interrelation of tasks of different departments, while the assistant for national security affairs has the role primarily of administrator rather than policy planner. This organizational approach is not perfect but is less likely than others to lead to unclear, conflicting policy declarations at the top or confusion or outright competition in actually carrying out decisions. The best examples of the *Administrative approach,* as this style will be termed throughout, are current and comparatively early post-war administrations— perhaps the Reagan administration (though not at the start), and the Kenne-

dy, Eisenhower and Truman regimes. Security assistants who seem to exemplify the administrative style are Robert Cutler and Gordon Gray under Eisenhower, McGeorge Bundy under Kennedy, and perhaps William Clark under Reagan. The Truman administration defined this basic approach to foreign policy coordination and implementation, and arguably there was considerable continuity until the Johnson administration, which in this area as in a number of others, foreign and domestic, represented a break with the past.

President Truman and his senior foreign policy colleagues were committed to institutional and organizational changes that would reflect the political—and indeed philosophical—shift in attitude from American isolationism to broad international commitment and involvement. The armed services organization was rationalized, with the air force given an identity separate from the army, and a symbolic Pentagon was constructed as the nation changed course in a fundamental way with the decision to maintain a large peacetime military establishment. The National Security Council was created by statute in 1947 in order to provide foreign policy coordination in a manner that was seen to be impossible through reliance on the State Department alone. The Council was comprised of the president, vice president, secretaries of state and defense, head of the CIA and director of the Office of Civilian and Defense Mobilization. President Truman, who had no formal graduate training, cultivated a keen interest in history; likewise, though not a professional public or private sector executive, he was apparently very much aware of the importance of structure to policy. The former avocation has been much discussed; the latter insight has not been addressed nearly so often, perhaps because we are inclined to take presidential interest in organization for granted, though Dean Acheson, in his memoirs, does stress his own appreciation for this talent of a superior to whom he was most sympathetic.[6]

One important feature of Truman's style was emphasis on the process by which decisions are made; another was the clear use of the NSC structure for policy implementation. Acheson notes the fact that Truman was careful to ensure that major decisions were set down as soon as possible in writing. In this he reflected the lawyer's appreciation for essential clarity; he also demonstrated the lawyer's shrewdness in seeing that collective decisions can be and are misinterpreted by the participants, sometimes because perceptions honestly vary and at other times because people consciously calculate that misinterpreting what happened will further their own bureaucratic interests. Also noteworthy is the exclusion of trade and finance departments from the NSC structure in formal terms. The post-war world was enormously challenging for Washington policymakers. They had to cope with recent enemies which were totally devastated, emerging conflict with the Soviet Union, and the horror of atomic weapons. Yet in important ways the international system was clearly simpler. Truman's failure to include Treasury or Commerce in the NSC speaks directly to the revisionists who argue that economic drives, especially to open overseas markets, were the main or only ones in post-war American foreign policy.

For Truman, the main policy definition in the international arena was to be with the secretary of state after the president, a point reflected in the personalities and authority of the secretaries with whom he worked most closely, George Marshall and Acheson. The NSC staff was clearly administrative in nature.[7]

The hallmark of what can be termed the administrative approach is the principal emphasis on handling day-to-day business, with special emphasis on coordination and ensuring that presidential directives and NSC decisions are carried out. Making the translation from concept to implementation, from declaration to operations, is the key approach. The test of effectiveness is not necessarily successful policy but coherent policy largely defined elsewhere. Obviously specific structures have changed dramatically, depending on the needs and interests of particular presidents. For this reason among others, the contrast between the Eisenhower and Kennedy administrations has usually received more attention than the elements of continuity. Eisenhower operated with a very large, rather formal national security structure centered around very frequent meetings of the large Planning Operations Coordinating boards. Kennedy, by contrast, did away with most of Eisenhower's formal committees, including a range of standing interdepartmental groups, following the rationale that in many cases meetings of these groups had become ends in themselves without having cutting edge impact on actual policy. Such criticism of the Eisenhower administration had become quite common by the time Kennedy ran for president and went beyond purely partisan political calculations. The new president clearly had a desire to be actively—and visibly—engaged in the policy process in detailed, continuous terms.[8]

Yet in the broad outlines, beyond specific organizational differences, there was considerable similarity in the ways the two presidents viewed the foreign policy process. Each had different attitudes toward the structure and schedule of the National Security Council and closely related formal bodies, but both saw the NSC staff as largely administrative. Eisenhower appears to have been pleased, and perhaps somewhat surprised, when the newly elected president came to see him in December 1960 (alone, without entourage) to discuss the transition and expressed a strong desire to retain Andrew Goodpaster, then performing some of the tasks of the national security assistant, for at least a time in the new administration.[9]

Kennedy and Eisenhower may have differed on the relative importance of particular posts and personalities but again this did not happen in a manner which changed the locus of foreign policy decision-making on key issues away from the State Department and toward the White House. In 1962, when Bundy was offered the presidency of Yale University, Kennedy was adamant in stressing the invaluable contribution of his security assistant and the need for him to stay where he was; Eisenhower's high regard for John Foster Dulles, his secretary of state, is well known and was often demonstrated, most touchingly during the latter's fatal illness. Yet Dulles, who brooked no challenge to his role as main deputy to the president on foreign policy, was never given complete independence and certainly not on basic decisions affecting the use of military force. The president was clear in keeping ultimate authority; Eisenhower originated the post of special assistant for national security affairs to facilitate White House involvement. Bundy was professionally close to Kennedy but was essentially a summarizer of issues and "options." Even on Vietnam, he was not so clearly an advocate until the Johnson administration. By all accounts he served mainly as a facilitator of decisions rather than as one who pressed a particular position or viewpoint. He in no way tried to centralize foreign policy in the White House; defense policy in particular was left to the cabinet officer responsible. Structure can change drastically in the administrative model; function is key.[10]

The second basic style of national security policy formulation and implementation can be termed the *Theoretical approach*. In this system, the national security assistant and his staff are engaged essentially in policy discussion and analysis, not mainly administration. Examples of this style are Walt W. Rostow in the Johnson administration, Zbigniew Brzezinski in the Carter administration and Richard Allen in the first part of the Reagan administration. Again, particulars of personality and structure differ from one case to another. Rostow's staff was comparatively small, Brzezinski was consistently visible in the public eye as a direct challenger for the role of secretary of state, and Allen's tenure was in some ways the most controversial. A consistent element from various sources is that these security assistants were more given to planning and conceptualization than to the details of implementation. Both Rostow and Brzezinski arguably are especially adept at defining comprehensive, imaginative world views, symbolized in such phrases as "the takeoff stage" and "arc of crisis," terminology for respectively the crucial point where a country begins rapid industrialization and modernization, and the widespread national political instabilities of South and Southwest Asia. Allen's national security staff concentrated on the generation of a large number of policy planning studies, undertaking a function that in earlier times was much more associated with the policy planning staff of the State Department.[11]

I.M. Destler describes the approach well in his characterization of Rostow as Johnson's assistant:

...Rostow seems not to have had as strong a mandate as Bundy under Kennedy. He was also a very different type of person. Bundy was a pragmatist who seldom allowed his personal views on policy to prejudice his presentations of alternative viewpoints and balanced analyses to the President. He was also an exceptional administrator-operator. Rostow, by contrast, was primarily a thinker and more than a bit of an ideologue, who tended to view particular events in terms of the broader theoretical constructs he was most adept at developing.[12]

Brzezinski himself notes the importance of abstract analysis in his policy thinking and his own approach to the job:

Vance was also not predisposed to engage in wide-ranging doctrinal and strategic dialogues about historical trends or in the kinds of sharp debates which are needed to rebut the arguments of our adversaries. And yet, in my judgment, even to reach an accommodation with the Soviets required us to engage them in a historical-philosophical dialogue. . . .[13]

The third and final approach to national security policy is *Centralized Dominance,* best represented—indeed only represented—by the Nixon administration. President Nixon at the start of his first term apparently had preliminary thoughts along the lines of establishing some competition between Secretary of State William Rogers and Assistant for National Security Affairs Kissinger. One reason for naming Rogers as secretary reportedly was his personal rapport with Nixon. Soon, however, preliminary moves toward a balanced State-NSC relationship were abandoned in favor of centralization of fundamental power in the hands of the president and his assistant. The professional bureaucracy was made exceptionally busy with requests for an inclusive series of policy reports, the main incentive for which was to keep the existing machinery totally preoccupied. The president was clearly encouraged in his natural suspicion of the State Department by a security assistant anxious to make his role central and predominant. Henry Kissinger argues that this was not his original intention, that the goal rather was to return to something resembling the Eisenhower model. Early in his memoirs, he describes visiting the former president in the hospital and coming away impressed with the insights and advice received.[14] In practice, however, he was clearly in tune with his own president in establishing policy dominance in his White House office, serving as the aide who handled the most pressing and important foreign policy problems, accommodating the many requirements of his chief, deftly cutting out not only the State Department but also his own staff from an approach that was highly personalized and secretive.[15]

There are a range of shortcomings inherent in both the Theoretical and Centralized Dominance approaches—already hinted at—which hamper effectiveness, at least over the longer term. One is almost tempted to describe them in some ways as polar extremes, the former placing neat reflecting intellectual activity over policy effectiveness, the latter stressing control and power to such an extent that across the board coordination of policy is ultimately undermined. In both cases there is a clear departure from the role originally defined for the National Security Council staff. The Rostow and Brzezinski years provide comparable examples of the sacrifice of coordination in the functioning of a highly informal policy process. The "Tuesday lunch" of the Johnson administration addressed Vietnam war policy in a manner limited to the president, the secretary of state, the secretary of defense, the security assistant, personal aide Bill Moyers and occasional others. One result was that major decisions were taken without wide coordination. In December 1966, for example, a major peace initiative from Washington toward North Vietnam via Poland was overcome by the bombing of Hanoi, which had been decided upon two weeks earlier and then very likely forgotten by the principals at the top. William Bundy, a senior State Department official under Johnson, reflected later that the president ". . . was very difficult to pin down on where he *had* come down on a thing. I think his style generally carried lack of system and structure way too far." Likewise, the weekly informal breakfasts and lunches among top foreign policy officials of the Carter administration—the former including the president and various others, the latter limited to Vance and Brzezinski plus Defense Secretary Brown, did not prevent policy inconsistencies. Clearly the approach did not result in concord. Vance, in his memoirs, is quite positive about the practice, mainly because it permitted senior officials to interact without the constraints or complications of their staffs or customary bureaucratic behavior. The meetings did not prevent many differences with his colleague in the White House, however, including Brzezinski's alleged effort to open and maintain his own policy "channel" to the government in Iran.[16]

The Theoretical approach also generally fails to ensure regular attention to policy areas which do not immediately grip top policymakers, and here the problems join with those of too much centralization. In neither the Johnson nor the Carter administrations was there systematic policy review. In the former, Vietnam again came to occupy senior officials to such an extent that other parts of the world were ignored. Kissinger has argued, presumably not entirely facetious-

ly, that this was not too disheartening since the result in European affairs was that there was less mischief, tension and interference from American initiatives than would otherwise have been the case. Postponement of consideration of economic and security concerns, however, does not really provide solutions and conceivably earlier attention to developing inflation, strains in currency relationships and the effects of the real diminution of American defense efforts vis-à-vis the Soviets *and* vis-à-vis our European allies would have mitigated later problems.[17]

Concerning the Carter administration, intensive concentration on the Middle East and the Gulf, first in the context of Camp David and then in regard to Iran, drew attention away from other parts of the globe because the only attention that really counted was at the top of the government. The president was most anxious to be involved in a very detailed manner, lines of authority were complicated and confused by the competition between Vance and Brzezinski, and as a result there was apparently no orderly process for bringing many different sectors of the bureaucracy into play in an effective manner. One important shortcoming under both Johnson and Carter was an absence of effective balance in policy formulation and implementation among presidential attention/involvement, the activities of other top players in the administration, and the myriad initiatives and efforts within the wider foreign policy bureaucracy. As indicated, Vance was very positive about the absence of foreign policy professionals from the weekly discussions over meals, yet this lack of involvement surely hampered both coordination and implementation. To be sure, there were no apparent blunders resulting only from the obvious lack of coordination, yet arguably the policy inconsistencies of the Carter administration would have been mitigated by more of the sort of staff work emphasized by Eisenhower. There will be more below contrasting these two presidents, given their striking differences in approach both to leadership and administration.[18]

The early phase of the Reagan administration suffered from the different combination of specific problems, and if anything even greater disarray and competition among senior officials. This reflected the presence in office of a president who apparently is less interested and engaged in the policy process, especially regarding foreign affairs, and in Richard Allen, a security assistant, who was at the least less ambitious than his immediate predecessors (save the special case of Brent Scowcroft) to control decision making and access to the president. His emphasis again was on analysis rather than implementation. An immediate problem for Allen, as for domestic adviser Martin Anderson, was the need to go through Counsellor Edwin Meese to reach the president. Cabinet officers in turn began to deal directly on international matters with Meese, James Baker and Michael Deaver in the White House. The lack of direct access by the security assistant was a marked change from past practice that well predated Bundy. The conflicts over personality and foreign policy control that took place within the Reagan administration's first months seem to have involved the secretary of state much more directly with Baker, Meese and Deaver. In turn, the events that led to Allen's departure from his post appear to have involved others in the White House rather than Secretary Haig.[19]

Judge Clark has brought a different style as well as set of priorities to the security assistant's tasks. His emphasis has been on administration rather than policy analysis, although he has intervened directly in the policy process, apparently with increasing confidence. His opposition to Assistant Secretary of State for Latin American Affairs, Thomas Enders, was reportedly based on both policy differences and concern about administrative procedures and effectiveness. Clark does have a willingness to press his own hard-line views, but after resolution of specific disputes is inclined ". . . to roll control back to the agencies."[20]

The Centralized Dominance approach suffers from the fact, which is clearly unavoidable, that even exceptionally talented and driven individuals have their limitations. Kissinger expanded the NSC staff from twelve to fifty-four—among those acknowledged in formal organizational terms—yet was still not completely able to control or even oversee all policy processes. In this sense, there is a parallel with the Theoretical model in terms of the band of ineffectiveness. Inevitably, only a few policy areas receive sustained attention at the top, and the top is all that really matters for decisive policy action. Not all interested individuals are included in even major decisions. Effectiveness inevitably suffers, from the beginning with the Theoretical approach, over time with Centralized Dominance. Kissinger announced with fanfare that boomeranged that 1973 would be the Nixon administration's "Year of Europe," which was a backhanded way of recognizing that the two leaders' preoccupation with the triangular relationships among the United States, the Soviet Union and China had led to serious neglect of our allies. Policies toward parts of the world viewed as secondary, notably Africa and Latin America, gyrated between inattention and very intensive concentrated efforts, depending upon whether those at the top

were involved elsewhere (which was usually the case and reminded professionals
in the foreign service that they did not
count for much) or were focused on one
of these regions (which was not usually
the case and so inevitably created great
tensions among the professionals and others involved).

Destler has elaborated on the domestic
constraints which frustrate total control
from the top. Tying policy so closely and
clearly to the White House can restrict
freedom of action and inhibit initiative:

... the Nixon-Kissinger system of closed policy-making is limited by the limits of presidential power at home. Spurning broader
bureaucratic or domestic alliance-building, it
tends to work only on those issues where the
president can personally assure the official or
unofficial U.S. action which is at issue. Usually this reinforces the Nixon-Kissinger bias toward political-military instruments and issues.
It is easier to deliver a B-52 bomb load on
Hanoi than to win Congressional approval of
a piece of trade legislation.[21]

The committee structures of the NSC
are one interesting analytic tool to use in
trying to understand both change and continuity over time. Focusing on them can
exemplify important analytic points.
Brzezinski stresses the suppleness of the
mechanism: "Few people outside the
upper levels of government realize the
extent to which there is institutional
flexibility and inherent ambiguity in the
way foreign policy is made."[22] Use or
avoidance of committees, therefore, can
give broader insight because leaders have
so much freedom; they do not need to be
highly attentive to legal prescriptions beyond those defining the NSC itself.

Presidents in fact have demonstrated
great diversity in the ways they have approached and appointed committees. Eisenhower and Truman both had faith in
formal processes, and the organization

upon which they relied reflected that fact.
Kennedy's approach, as indicated here
and frequently elsewhere, was much more
informal, although not necessarily disorderly. His cabinet rarely met as a group,
the large formal foreign policy coordinating committees of the Eisenhower years
were abolished, and there was more reliance on smaller groups tailored to specific
cases and needs. Bundy served as a main
coordinator, keeping schedules on track.

Whether Kennedy would have moved
to a more formal set of arrangements had
his tenure been longer is moot, but clearly
the combination of personalities in the
Johnson administration who dealt with
foreign policy in broad terms resulted in
pressures for more structure. Johnson
therefore instituted the Senior Interdepartmental Group (SIG) and the Interdepartmental Regional Groups (IRGs) in an
effort to improve coordination. The
former was chaired by the undersecretary of state, the latter by assistant secretaries. The SIG was designed to address
very important foreign policy problems,
while the IRGs tackled primarily more
specific regional concerns. In addition to
the State Department, agency representation on both types of committee included the Department of Defense, Office
of the Secretary of Defense, the Joint
Chiefs of Staff, the Central Intelligence
Agency, the Agency for International Development, the U.S. Information Agency,
the National Security Council staff, and
other agencies. To quote Destler:

The committees were given broad mandates,
including jurisdiction over agency programs
"of such a nature as to affect significantly the
overall U.S. overseas program in a country or
region." Problems could come before them
on appeal from lower-level officials, or assignment from the Secretary, or through their
own initiative. The SIG, for example, was
specifically mandated to conduct "periodic surveys" on "the adequacy and effectiveness of

interdepartmental overseas programs and activities."[23]

The SIG/IRG system, established by Johnson in March 1966, was clearly an effort to provide a counterpoint to the informal policy process which the president preferred, but equally significant as the formation of the groups is the fact that they did not survive under the successor Nixon/Kissinger regime. Kissinger states that he was guided, at least in part, by the views of former President Eisenhower in the decision to abolish the structure:

Eisenhower insisted that the SIG structure had to be ended because the Pentagon would never willingly accept State Department domination of the national security process. It would either attempt end-runs or counterattack by leaking. He had been fortunate to have a strong Secretary of State, but Dulles's influence had derived from the President's confidence in him and not from the State Department machinery. And for all his admiration for Dulles, he had always insisted on keeping control of the NSC machinery in the White House.[24]

We already have a clear set of pictures—biased but informative—of the approaches to foreign policy structure taken by the Nixon and Carter administrations. According to Kissinger, he was essentially sympathetic to the status quo and traditional approaches at the start of his time in power. Favoring retention of the ISG/IRG system (only later did he come to appreciate Eisenhower's comments), he was overruled by a president highly suspicious of the State Department. Kissinger then moved to advocate basically ". . . the Eisenhower NSC system, weighted somewhat in favor of the State Department by retaining the State Department chairmanship of the various subcommittees."[25] Kissinger discusses with emphasis his chief's abiding mistrust of the professional foreign service, which severely handicapped opposition of new Secretary of State William Rogers and Under Secretary for Political Affairs U. Alexis Johnson. Less stressed is the point that Nixon's sentiments were no doubt congruent with Kissinger's own desires. While the State Department personnel would participate in the new system, including chairing the interdepartmental groups, final policy review would be under White House direction. Kissinger stresses that this was the practice under Eisenhower, without noting as well that the regime would be considerably less open and more driven than had been the case earlier. Technical directives under Nixon and Kissinger were termed National Security Study Memoranda (NSSM) and National Security Decision Memoranda (NSDM).[26]

The Carter administration in foreign policy terms reflected from the start the balance of power competition between Vance and Brzezinski, rather than the earlier dominance of Kissinger and Nixon (and, in effect, Kissinger alone after Ford succeeded Nixon). Vance describes the developing situation in his memoirs. Brzezinski proposed in a detailed memorandum to Carter an NSC system that generally kept the existing style of specialized committees but distributed chairmanships among the different departments involved—that is, the secretary of state would chair the "Policy Issues Committee," the secretary of defense the "Defense Issues Committee" and so on. Reflecting the control achieved by Kissinger, and hinting at his own uneasiness, Vance notes that during ". . . the previous administration such committees had been chaired by Kissinger or, after he became secretary of state, his deputy and successor as national security advisor, General Brent Scowcroft." Brzezinski makes clear his own appreciation of the important role of committees and who sits where on them: "In the end, Kissinger came to exercise control by chairing a series of sub-cabinet committees, attended by sub-cabinet level senior officials."[27]

The president was critical of the complex Brzezinski committee formulation, which he regarded as being too much like the Nixon/Kissinger approach, and so a simpler structure was developed. This latter, successful proposal shrank the structure from seven committees (three of which would be chaired by the security assistant) to only two. The Policy Review Committee (PRC) was to be concerned with military, economic and other basic foreign policy matters and chaired by the appropriate cabinet department head—State, Defense or Treasury. The Special Coordination Committee (SCC) would address intelligence policies, arms control and "crisis management," and would be chaired by the assistant for national security affairs. Brzezinski writes about the latter: "I stated that all of these matters not only posed potential jurisdictional conflicts but in one way or another touched upon the president's own political interests. It followed that the assistant for national security affairs should chair the Special Coordination Committee and that this committee ought to be the decision-making framework for the three types of issues mentioned above." The transition of the new administration also included a change in symbols and titles: the NSSM and NSDM were changed to Presidential Review Memoranda (PRM)/NSC, and Presidential Directives (PD)/NSC.[28]

Brzezinski more than Vance stresses the secretary of state's peripheral role in setting up these new structures. Vance describes himself as relatively satisfied with the SCC ("I did not want to get bogged down in the minutiae that attended crisis management problems"), while Brzezinski observes the secretary was rather displeased (". . . Vance first registered his unhappiness with the assignment of SALT to the SCC. . . . He then focused on crisis management, saying that this was properly the responsibility of the secretary of state . . .").[29] Vance does complain, understandably, about the fact that the security assistant had the authority to prepare a summary for the president when no consensus emerged from SCC or PRC sessions, and to prepare a Presidential Directive when a clear choice had been made. These papers were sent directly from Brzezinski to the president, without review by other meeting participants. The secretary states his opposition clearly:

I opposed this arrangement from the beginning, and I said so to the president. He told me he preferred this procedure because he was afraid of leaks if these sensitive documents were circulated before they reached his desk. . . In retrospect, I made a serious mistake in not going to the mat on insisting that the draft memoranda be sent to the principals before they went to the President, whatever the risk.[30]

The Reagan administration has hardly been free of the same serious problems that divided the White House and State Department during earlier administrations. This has been true despite the fact that President Reagan, in his quest for office, was caustic in describing the debilitating nature of the Brzezinski/Vance conflict. At the very start of the new administration, Secretary of State Alexander Haig presented the president with a memorandum that would have drastically centralized foreign policy authority. The White House summarily rejected the plan and ploy, which was followed by a running conflict that continued until the secretary left the administration. His successor, George Shultz, a much more collegially minded secretary, has nonetheless not avoided conflict with the White House. Throughout, the administration has continued to rely on interdepartmental committees in a comparatively complex organizational structure.[31]

There are several major lessons that emerge from reflection on the national security policy process. Among them are the need to accommodate structures to particular presidential styles and techniques. At the same time, some presidential approaches are better than others. A basic thesis argued here is that things have indeed gotten worse rather than better, and that this reflects leadership shortcomings along with a more complicated policy environment. In practical terms, the case is for strong presidential leadership in foreign policy, complemented by a secretary of state who is the principal policy deputy and the administration model of overall national security policy organization. If this seems a vote for the past and conventionalism, that is because past approaches were better than recent ones; if not perfect, they were at least less confused.

The need for strong presidential leadership in foreign policy used to be a truism but now is almost a novelty. One reason for infighting between the State Department and the White House is lack of assertiveness at the very top, an absence of a clearly defined leadership posture. A high official in the Kennedy Administration once noted that his president was not too troubled by senior people saying somewhat different things about major foreign policy issues; there was no doubt about where the last word would come from. By contrast, more recent administrations have been seriously troubled by a lack of strong Presidential direction of personalities or policies. Both Presidents Carter and Reagan have lacked sophistication concerning foreign policy, a situation in each case related to lack of experience in the international as opposed to the domestic milieu, and in the latter case perhaps to basic lack of interest as well. Arguably both presidents have been highly domestic in basic policy interest and orientation compared with Eisenhower, Kennedy, Nixon or even Johnson. The point has been made that President Reagan may be the most domestically focused President since before the Second World War.[32]

One result of lack of interest plus lack of leadership is that conflicts among subordinates are permitted to become more disruptive than would otherwise be the case. Carter's significant diplomatic achievements, notably Camp David, were overshadowed by the conflict between the secretary of state and the security assistant, a conflict which was not controlled, only mitigated, by the president. Likewise, there is no impression that the feuding between Secretary Haig and the White House, as well as various other cabinet members, during the first part of the Reagan administration, was addressed in a decisive way by the man at the top until the very end.

An appropriate complement of strong presidential leadership is a prominent role for the secretary of state as principal deputy in the formulation as well as conduct of foreign policy. Henry Kissinger established his dominance of policy in part through carrying out foreign policy negotiations that had previously been the responsibility of the secretary. The only example of someone besides the secretary establishing centralized control is also Kissinger, and then only after considerable effort and time and with presidential support. The more usual alternative has been civil war within the foreign policy sectors of the government. The secretary has cabinet seniority, a broad policy mandate and independence of particular substantive concerns to provide overall definition and direction.

There is no necessary tension between a strong secretary and presidential leadership, despite some examples of more recent years; indeed, if the system works well the two roles, domains and personalities should reinforce one another, not undercut one another or exclude one another. Truman was able to delegate to Marshall and Acheson without diluting his ultimate authority. The newer picture of Eisenhower which is emerging indicates that he was not nearly as passive as most sophisticated observers imagined earlier. James David Barber, in his analysis of presidential styles, describes Eisenhower in the generally pejorative terms of "passive-negative," although he also concedes (in a book that is remarkably friendly to Kennedy's personality) that Eisenhower's " . . . case presents certain difficulties." Fred Greenstein, an Eisenhower revisionist, argues that the president in the foreign policy field and others was in fact an activist, hard working and attentive to major decisions.[33]

There are, in fact, striking contrasts between Eisenhower and Carter. The former could be in charge on major decisions—which included during his tenure several directly confronting war or peace—partly because he delegated less important decisions, along with control over day-to-day operations, to others. Carter, in the eyes of critics, failed to assert control from the top on major issues precisely because he had difficulty delegating any authority or independence, insisting on involving himself in the endless details of policy analysis and operations. Revealing comments

by both presidents help to make this point. Eisenhower left no ambiguity concerning how he wanted cabinet relationships to be handled, when he told his defense secretary at one point: ". . . I want *you* to run Defense. We *both* can't run it, and I *won't* run it. I was elected to worry about a lot of things other than the day-to-day operations of a department." Carter on the other hand stresses in his memoirs that, ". . . the final decisions on basic foreign policy would be made by me in the White House." In actual practice, he seems to have gone well beyond concern only with "basic" decisions. Carter was well aware of the likelihood of conflict between Vance and Brzezinski, but felt the arrangement he was putting in place would facilitate his own control. He adds that, ". . . I find it interesting that Vance recommended Brzezinski for this job, and Zbig recommended Cy for secretary of state. Both were good suggestions." Eisenhower apparently agreed strongly with Arthur Krock's criticism of Lyndon Johnson's similar compulsion to be visibly involved in all aspects of policy—his "ubiquity"—as a fatal flaw that brought down his presidency.[34]

If the best approach is strong presidential leadership and strong direction by the secretary of state, a basic corollary is that the job of security assistant should be much more explicitly and purely an administrative position. To follow up on National Security Council and presidential decisions, schedule meetings and move papers, ensure that the various sectors of the bureauracy are consulted and informed—these are tasks which are essential yet have not been the main focus of the job since the Kennedy administration. The jury in effect is still out on the record and effectiveness of the Reagan administration. As indicated, the administrative approach did not characterize

Richard Allen's tenure as security assistant. Judge Clark does appear to be primarily an administrator—certainly by his own admission his skills are not primarily theoretical. Yet he does have apparently very strong political views, despite only very recent international experience, and as indicated is ready to inject them in Latin American and other policy areas. His tenure so far has been too short, and information on the functioning of the NSC staff insufficiently complete, for a definitive judgment.[35]

Personality clashes and conflict of ambitions between the secretary of state and the security assistant have been important but hardly explain all the problems of policy coordination. Examining the functioning of interdepartmental committees not only highlights the approaches to policy formulation and implementation taken by different leaders, the exercise also leads into consideration of the limitations of the National Security Council as a statutory body. As described earlier, the formal members are very small in number. Other senior officials have been included, as desired by the president; this has often reflected more personal relationship than formal foreign policy authority or expertise, represented for example by the reported active participation of Attorney General John Mitchell during the Nixon years. But this flexibility does not appear to have been used by recent presidents even though the plate of "high politics" issues has become increasingly full with trade, finance and other economic and technical matters. Although Mitchell was involved, Nixon's NSC meetings, not surprisingly, apparently included far fewer people than had been the case under Eisenhower; and Kissinger has been described as especially anxious to exclude subordinates from sessions. Brzezinski mentions that there was involvement by the secretary of the treasury in the PRC but adds that the official chaired meetings of the group [numbered] only two or three times.[36]

Given the complexity and wide range of major current international relations issues, the challenge of coordination and the importance of form to function—this last point appreciated by the State Department in the effort to retain the SIG/IRG system—there are persuasive reasons for formal expansion of the NSC to include cabinet departments which have come to be much more substantially involved in international concerns. These would be the departments of Agriculture, Commerce, Labor and the Treasury. The practice of temporary participation should be employed to cast the net even more widely, to include such departments as Education, Housing and Urban Development, Health and Social Services, and Transportation. This would tend to underscore the role of security assistant as coordinator in terms of daily business, while opening the door for a strong secretary of state to provide the forceful and imaginative efforts at conceptual and policy integration required. The proper sort of presidential guidance would ensure the standing of the secretary of state as first among equals. More senior participants in the NSC in formal terms would tend to underline the great scope of contemporary "high politics."

There are some important further organizational implications to this approach to foreign policy coordination, most of which have been discussed elsewhere by a variety of different analysts of the subject. A system of a larger NSC, with more explicit recognition in governmental structure at the very top of the diversity of the foreign policy agenda, implies among other things a large number of interdepartmental committees active in concrete terms. Congruence with the organizational approach discussed here argues that the secretary of state and his deputies should chair as many of these as possible; the security assistant should chair literally none. Formal expansion of the NSC should also help to breathe new life into many such committees which exist only on paper, have not really been employed with energy and interest for a number of years, yet retain the potential to help integrate different policy areas and domestic into international concerns.

This in turn calls attention to the importance of the assistant secretary post within the State Department. More emphasis on the importance of these positions, perhaps in part through efforts by the president and secretary of state to give them great public and intragovernmental visibility, would encourage more orderly and thorough policy. Destler uses the phrase "lines of confidence" to describe the importance of good working relationships between the president and secretary on the one hand and each assistant secretary on the other. He quotes Dean Rusk, whose own experience gives him much weight as a witness, that these ties are "the real organization of government at higher echelons." Destler emphasizes the significance of the regional assistant secretaries, but the point applies perhaps even more to the less influential roles of the functional assistant secretaries. His point is well taken that the status of assistant secretaries could be helped by a specific presidential declaration that they are of cabinet importance in his eyes.[37]

Two other structural points bear on strengthening the central foreign policy role of the State Department. One important way to keep the NSC staff on the track of implementation, practical coordination and administration is through enhancement of the Policy Planning Staff of the Department. The staff has not always been in the background in recent years; certainly during Kissinger's tenure as secretary the planning group was visible through the appointment of his deputy, Winston Lord, as director. Yet that has not been the norm, and at time the NSC, for instance most notably under Rostow and Allen, has taken over functions that really should be handled more appropriately by the "planning" arm of the State Department. Another avenue for trying to enhance the overall role and impact of the Department would be closer coordination with the Office of Management and Budget. This would be different from the effort in the 1960s to use a variation of the Planning Programming Budgeting approach of McNamara's Pentagon for foreign policy analysis more generally. This suggestion was contained in the report of a comprehensive evaluation of the foreign policy process carried out during the Carter administration, but the emphasis there was much more on closer ties between the budget office and the NSC for analysis purposes. In fact the Pentagon has, not surprisingly, been in the lead in working with OMB for policy planning purposes. Traditionally, the foreign service ideal has not been an individual steeped in financial analysis. That attitude is probably quite correct insofar as good diplomacy requires other primary measuring rods, and foreign policy in any case—meaning the budget of the State Department—is not a costly enterprise when considered alone. But at the same time foreign service personnel would probably benefit somewhat from more expertise in quantitative skills, just as OMB civil servants would likely gain through more extensive interaction with their colleagues on the diplomatic side.[38]

This is, finally, a backward looking analysis which attempts to make a case for changing our practical approach to foreign policy making to one which much more resembles those of administrations which held office two decades ago and more. The assumption and conclusion is not that they always functioned smoothly or in every case of decision effectively. Rather, there are persuasive reasons for believing that they were able to handle major, often complex, decisions in a reasonably orderly manner. The fact that the international environment is much more complex now, in terms of number of actors and kinds of important issues, is evidence for the paramount importance of making policy as orderly as possible. Certainly the current policy agenda and the records of the past several administrations do not argue for continuation of the divisive, often highly uncoordinated approaches of either White House dominance or bickering between NSC staff and State Department. Nixon and Kissinger had dramatic foreign policy successes in relations with other great powers, China and the Soviet Union, and these did result from a process which Stanley Hoffmann has analyzed in detail as involving ". . . on a grand scale maneuver, shock tactics and surprise—the opposite from what one had come to expect from the highly predictable and heavy diplomacy of the sixties."[39] Yet there is no reason in logic or in practice why the approach had to be so secretive and isolated. More collegiality might have kept relations with Europe and Japan from growing worse, and might have—indeed almost certainly would have—resulted in more consistent and orderly policy attention to Africa, Latin America and South Asia.

Perhaps an emphasis on collegiality is the most important factor of all in effective and consistent foreign policy. Earlier administrations and leaders should not be idealized. Yet Truman and Eisenhower did have a general respect for procedure and the importance of delegation of authority. Likewise, while Bundy may have been accorded de facto Cabinet standing, he did not press to have this de jure and generally does not appear to have confused his role with those of others at the top of the government. These are virtues we seem to have lost in our foreign policy planning and implementation in three more recent administrations which represent, in organizational terms, an unfortunate combination of two examples of Theoretical and one of Centralized Dominance approaches.

NOTES

1. Harold Seidman, *Politics, Position and Power—The Dynamics of Federal Organization* (New York: Oxford University Press, 1970), p. 164.
2. See, e.g., Walter Goodman, "The War of the Memoirs," *The New York Times Book Review,* May 29, 1983, p. 23.
3. Louis W. Koenig, *The Chief Executive* (New York: Harcourt, Brace, Jovanovich, 1981, 4th ed.), p. 224; Zbigniew Brzezinski, *Power and Principle: Memoirs of the National Security Adviser 1977-1981* (New York: Farrar, Strauss, Giroux, 1983), p. 60.
4. Brzezinski, Chapter 15.
5. I. M. Destler, *Presidents, Bureaucrats and Foreign Policy—The Politics of Organizational Reform* (Princeton, N.J.: Princeton University Press, 1974), pp. 26ff. Reference is specifically to a 1960 Brookings Institution study; proposals have been made in the past by Herbert Hoover, Nelson Rockefeller and other prominent leaders for in effect a second U.S. vice president.
6. Dean Acheson, *Present at the Creation* (New York: W. W. Norton, 1969), p. 733.
7. Ibid.

8. Arthur Schlesinger Jr., *A Thousand Days—John F. Kennedy in the White House* (Boston: Houghton Mifflin, 1965), p. 210.

9. Robert H. Ferrell (ed.), *The Eisenhower Diaries* (New York: W. W. Norton, 1983), passim.; during the last part of the Eisenhower administration, Gordon Gray handled long-range planning by the NSC (not the staff alone), while Gen. Goodpaster handled routine daily business, as described in Dwight D. Eisenhower, *Waging Peace* (Garden City, N.Y.: Doubleday Publishing, 1965), p. 319.

10. Destler, *Presidents, Bureaucrats and Foreign Policy*, pp. 100-104, 107.

11. Interviews.

12. Destler, *Presidents, Bureaucrats and Foreign Policy*, p. 107.

13. Brzezinski, *Power and Principle*, p. 43.

14. Henry Kissinger, *White House Years* (Boston: Little Brown, 1979), p. 43.

15. See, e.g., Destler, *Presidents, Bureaucrats and Foreign Policy*, pp. 118-153.

16. William Bundy is quoted in Fred Greenstein, *The Hidden-Hand Presidency—Eisenhower as Leader* (New York: Basic Books, 1982), p. 243; David Kraslow and Stuart H. Loory, *The Secret Search for Peace in Vietnam* (New York: Vintage Books, 1968), pp. 83-84; Cyrus Vance, *Hard Choices—Critical Years in America's Foreign Policy* (New York: Simon & Schuster, 1983), p. 39.

17. See, e.g., Kissinger, *White House Years*, pp. 17–19 on the Johnson administration and Chapter 11 on his and Nixon's own efforts to attend early to Atlantic Alliance matters.

18. Greenstein, *The Hidden-Hand Presidency*, is probably the most thorough and persuasive of the recent positive studies of Eisenhower's leadership style in the White House.

19. Interviews.

20. Morton Kondracke, "White House Watch: Enders's End," *The New Republic*, June 27, 1983, pp. 7-10.

21. Destler, pp. 303-304.

22. Brzezinski, p. 57.

23. Destler, p. 208.

24. Kissinger, p. 43.

25. Ibid., p. 44

26. Ibid., pp. 45-46.

27. Vance, *Hard Choices*, p. 36; Brzezinski, p. 58.

28. Brzezinski, pp. 61-62.

29. Brzezinski, p. 62; Vance, p. 36.

30. Vance, p. 37.

31. Interviews.

32. Interviews.

33. See Koenig, *The Chief Executive*, p. 349; Greenstein, passim.

34. Koenig, p. 348; Greenstein, p. 91, describes Eisenhower's underlining of the passages in Krock's memoirs about the Johnson administration; Jimmy Carter, *Keeping Faith—Memoirs of a President* (New York: Bantam Books, 1982), p. 52.

35. Interviews.

36. Destler, pp. 123-124; Brzezinski, p. 59.

37. Destler, pp. 263ff.

38. *National Security Policy Integration* (Washington: President's Reorganization Project, September 1979).

39. Stanley Hoffmann, *Primacy or World Order—American Foreign Policy Since the Cold War* (New York: McGraw-Hill, 1978), p. 50.

23. SHADES OF ZERO

Strobe Talbott

It was Helmut Schmidt's Social Democratic party that originally came up with the concept of the *Null-Lösung,* the "zero solution." The idea was that the removal of all the offending weapons on the Soviet side would make the American deployment unnecessary. The concept was originally floated as a means of dampening internal strife within the party and gaining West German public support. It caught on quickly elsewhere on the continent, but not in Washington. To many in the U.S., the very phrase "zero option" was suspect. Like "ban the bomb," "zone of peace," or "a nuclear-free Europe," it was one of those distinctly and distastefully European euphemisms for avoiding unpleasant political realities.

In early and mid-1981, while the new Administration was wrestling with various options in Washington, hundreds of thousands of West Europeans were taking to the streets in a movement protesting the spread of nuclear weapons. A new and disagreeable stereotype appeared on American television screens: disorderly legions of students, joining hands with clergymen, burghers and housewives, marching along the boulevards of Brussels, Nottingham, and Düsseldorf. Most of their chanted slogans and banners were impartial in denouncing nuclear weapons of both superpowers, but the overall tone and the accompanying message to their elected representatives in various parliaments were distinctly more anti-American than anti-Soviet. The crude caricatures of Reagan as a cowboy with rockets in his holsters made Brezhnev and his bushy eyebrows look grandfatherly by comparison. The Soviet rockets at issue were at least deployed on Soviet territory and thus easier to regard as defensive, while the American weapons would be far from home on West European soil. Besides, the Soviet missiles were familiar fixtures on the political landscape, part of the status quo; the American ones were something new, menacing, in prospect—and therefore might be stopped. The demonstrators were for peace and an "end of the madness" of the arms race. They were against a "new round" to that race, which meant the Pershing IIs and the Tomahawks.

Officials of the Reagan Administration described what was happening in Europe as appeasement, pacifism, or neutralism, and the zero option seemed to be part of its vocabulary. In a speech before the Conservative Political Action Conference on March 22, Richard Allen observed that only "pacifist" elements in Europe "believe that we can bargain the reduction of a deployed Soviet weapons system for a promise not to deploy our own offsetting system. Common sense tells us this is illusory." Allen succinctly expressed the Administration's contempt for the zero option, but his statement also contained an unintentional preview of the proposal that Reagan would make to the Soviet Union nine months later, in November 1981.

Source: From *Deadly Gambits,* by Strobe Talbott, pp. 56-70. Copyright © 1984 by Strobe Talbott. Reprinted by permission of Alfred A. Knopf, Inc.

Those nine months saw the Administration come a long way. The State Department and Pentagon both ended up endorsing the zero option, although their preferences were for significantly different versions. Alexander Haig wanted to accommodate the Europeans by adopting the spirit of the zero option, but modifying it in a way that would make deployment politically more palatable within the alliance. In that sense, Haig wanted to maintain the dual-track approach on which NATO had embarked in 1979.

Richard Perle, by contrast, had never had any use for the NATO decision, and he felt no compulsion to see it vindicated or implemented. He had no particular quarrel with the analysis on which Allen had based his rejection of the zero option back in March: the zero solution was indeed, as Allen had said, "illusory." But then, in Perle's view, so was arms control, at least as it had traditionally been practiced. Yet it was an illusion that many Europeans, and many Americans, too, insisted on keeping alive. Many Europeans were calling for the zero solution. So why not give it to them? Then, when it failed, they would be party to the failure, just as they had been party to what Perle saw as the folly of the December 1979 decision.

THE STATE DEPARTMENT: UP FROM ZERO

Alexander Haig was acutely conscious of his vulnerability to the charge that he was too solicitous of the Europeans. He heard that Weinberger had told James Baker, one of the President's closest aides: "Al seems to think that every time Schmidt's got a problem, it's automatically our problem." Weinberger also complained to Reagan about "Al's automatically siding with the West Europeans all the time." As he began to think about the

way to approach the European nuclear arms negotiations, Haig wanted, if possible, to avoid playing into the hands of his critics. He was, therefore, not in the least predisposed to embrace the zero option—a European idea—when he set off for West Germany in September 1981.

In Bonn, he was asked what the Soviet Union would have to do to make the zero option possible. "I think," replied Haig, "clearly it is rather ludicrous to debate an issue in which we are faced with some thousand warheads already deployed in SS-20 missile systems versus some contemplated and less numerous corresponding systems on the part of the West." Amidst all this forbidding syntax, the word "ludicrous" leaped out in the German press. Haig was widely reported as having dismissed the zero option itself as "ludicrous." His hosts, Chancellor Schmidt and Foreign Minister Hans-Dietrich Genscher, were acutely unhappy with the misquote and were eager for their guest to correct the record. At a farewell press conference, Haig said that while it would be "premature" to make a definitive statement, "I think I can affirm that we have not rejected this zero option proposal, and under ideal conditions, such a proposal might be very worthy of exploration and consideration."

Haig intended the comment as a gesture of support for Schmidt and Genscher rather than a blessing on the zero option. Still, some of his aides back in Washington felt it made their work easier as they set about developing a proposal that would accomplish the twin goals of getting negotiations started with the Soviets and bolstering support for U.S. policies in Europe. By paying lip service to the ideal solution of zero, the U.S. could hold the high ground in the propaganda war with the Soviets even as it set about negotiating toward a realistic goal—perhaps something in the neighborhood of 600 American warheads against the same number of Soviet ones.

If the Soviets could be squeezed down to, say, 200 triple-MIRVed SS-20s and held there, they would have 600 warheads. That would mean deploying approximately 600 new American warheads. In these calculations, the figure 572 single-warhead Pershing IIs and Tomahawks that had been established by NATO in December 1979 made sense. The original dual-track decision, after all, had rested on the assumption that some new Western deployments were going to be necessary in any event, no matter what the outcome of the negotiations. A true zero solution, if it was attainable, would actually be inconsistent with the December 1979 decision, for the new NATO missiles were not intended to match the SS-20s on a warhead-for-warhead basis. Rather, they were meant to enhance the credibility of NATO's deterrence of a Soviet conventional attack.

Before Haig's visit to West Germany, his aides had not cared so much whether U.S. declarations actually mentioned zero, so long as U.S. policy implicitly left open that possibility as a sop to the West Europeans. The phrase that had gained currency within the State Department by late summer of 1981 was "reductions to the lowest possible equal level." However, once Haig had, in Berlin, publicly endorsed the lowest of all possible equal ceilings—zero—"under ideal circumstances," and thereby cheered his German hosts by saying the magic word, Haig's deputies realized that now zero had to figure explicitly in the American proposal.

Burt, Eagleburger, and Gompert amended their phraseology accordingly. They added references to zero in their deliberations and memos. The new stock language became "lowest possible equal ceilings, including, ideally, zero," or "with the ultimate goal of zero."

THE PENTAGON: DOWN TO ZERO

Weinberger was convinced that, however much the U.S. might regret the impulses toward drastic disarmament then throbbing in Europe, it had to take them seriously. What was needed was a negotiating position that would redirect those impulses from defeatist panic into support for American policy and deployments. Unlike Haig, Weinberger was not especially sympathetic to the West Europeans. In private, he spoke of being fed up with European "hangups" and "moaning and groaning." He sometimes described the task facing the U.S. as a combination of therapy and trickery: "We've got to make them think that what we're doing is good for them. Not just that, but we've got to make them think that they're going to *like* it, and that it's what they've been asking us to do."

How to do that was a matter that Weinberger delegated to Richard Perle, who began to formulate a version of the zero option that differed importantly from the one then taking shape at the State Department. Perle decided to treat the option not just as an ideal but as the true, sole, and immutable goal of the negotiations, and to settle for nothing else. If anyone told Perle that the zero option was a gimmick designed to deal with a short-term political problem within the alliance, he would reply that the same was true of what the allied ministers had done in 1979. Only they had had less excuse. They had been starting from scratch. They had had real choices. He was simply trying to make the best of a bad inheritance, to limit the damage caused by his predecessors—and his colleagues at the State Department had compounded that damage by arranging for Reagan to endorse the dual-track decision during Margaret Thatcher's visit in February.

Perle was co-chairman, along with Richard Burt, of the Interagency Group charged with preparing for the talks. At a meeting in late August, Burt made a presentation, the nub of which was that the State Department was closing ranks behind a U.S. proposal for lowest possible equal ceilings on warheads. Perle did not like what he was hearing. He could see that the State Department position was intended to point the negotiations in the direction of an agreement whereby the West would end up with approximately 600 new warheads to compensate for the Soviet's being allowed to keep at least that many SS-20 warheads. Perle went home that night and sat up late in his study drafting a memo to Weinberger laying out his misgivings.

At Perle's direction, the Pentagon's analysts had been running studies for some time about the probable impact of various permutations and combinations of Pershing IIs, Tomahawks, SS-20s, and other missiles on the military balance in Europe. Those studies concluded that there were 250-300 vital military installations in Western Europe—air bases, nuclear storage sites, and ports. Thus, even if the Soviets had only 100 SS-20s, each triple-MIRVed, that would give them 300 warheads, or enough to cover all the important NATO targets. A deal that let the U.S. go ahead with its Pershing IIs and Tomahawks in exchange for leaving the Soviets not 100 but 200 SS-20s, with 600 warheads, hardly seemed to Perle like a bargain. That would be twice as many warheads as the U.S.S.R. needed to threaten a comprehensive strike against the alliance. "Only as you approach zero," Perle concluded, "do you reduce the Soviet threat to those targets."

In his memo to Weinberger, Perle argued that the State Department's position was based on sloppy analysis. It failed to consider the military consequences of the diplomatic initiative then taking shape. "Considerably more work needs to be done," he warned. The interagency process to date had turned up "too many questions and too few answers." This was to become a standard Perle ploy: accuse the rest of the Administration of shortsighted impatience; warn against being "stampeded" into hasty decisions; call for more work, which would naturally take more time; encourage delay in the name of thoroughness.

Perle challenged the State Department's conviction that the Soviets would not give up all their SS-20s, or at least significant numbers of them. "The easy assumption that the Soviets would resist reductions is imprudent in the extreme," he wrote. "They might actually propose such cuts." Since the Soviets had far more SS-20 warheads than there were major targets in NATO, a large number of those warheads were "surplus to their military needs and can therefore be expended to achieve political needs." (On this point, Perle was prescient. The Soviets did probably deploy more SS-20s than their original program called for; and they did eventually offer to trade down on the surplus—although not, of course, to zero.) So, he concluded, instead of seeking an agreement that did little or nothing to improve NATO defenses—and instead of leaving the Soviets an opportunity to surprise everyone by proposing a cutback in SS-20s on their own—why not come forward with a bold, simple American initiative that would solve both the military and political problems at hand?

Perle saw another, strictly political advantage in what he was proposing. A no-nonsense, all-or-nothing American embrace of the zero option would steal a march on the Soviets in the propaganda campaign. Much more than the State Department's half-hearted acknowledgment of zero as the ideal outcome, an American commitment to achieving zero as the only acceptable outcome would "put the Soviets on the defensive" and keep them there. To judge from public-opinion polls, parliamentary debates, and demonstrations in the streets, the Soviets had been achieving alarming success with claims that their proposal for a moratorium proved their commitment to disarmament, while the U.S. was hellbent on loading the continent up with new missiles and starting a new arms race. Now the U.S. would be able to shift the onus back onto the Soviets: if they were serious about halting the arms race and easing the anxieties of their neighbors, why shouldn't they do away with precisely those weapons that had forced NATO to move toward modernization?

The next day, Perle sent his memo, under the heading "A Defense Proposal," to Weinberger by way of his immediate superior, Fred Iklé, who welcomed the idea. Iklé had commented on a number of occasions when the subject of the Europeans' advocacy of the zero option came up, "We already chose a 'zero option' as our own deployment mode in Europe back when we took out our Jupiters and Thors in the early sixties. Anything above zero is forced upon us by the other side."

Iklé was also one of those in the new Administration who advocated arms-control agreements that were simple—easy to explain, easy for audiences at home and abroad to understand. One complaint about SALT II, from some liberals as well as conservatives, had been that it was too complicated. Iklé felt that the goal of effective presentation was best served by the zero option in its simplest, starkest, most straightforward form. He also believed that Perle's approach would be "more responsive to, and in harmony with, what our allies wanted," since they are looking for an excuse to get out of accepting the new American missiles, and here was a proposal that held out that possibility.

ZERO PLUS VERSUS ZERO ONLY

But the allies were not likely to take comfort from a proposal like that forever, or even for long. As soon as a zero proposal was made, everyone would see that achievement of the zero solution was an impossibility. If observers in the West were slow to come to that realization, the Soviets could be counted on to make the proposal's unacceptability to them quite plain. Then everyone would start asking what other solution the U.S. might settle for. It was partly in anticipation of a Soviet rejection that the State Department argued against letting the Administration get "locked in" to the zero solution. State called its position "zero plus," as opposed to the Pentagon's advocacy of "zero only."

By early October, this argument, refined and intensified, had acquired a ritualistic quality and had come to dominate the discussions of the Interagency Group. The debate was carried on primarily between Burt and Perle. The disagreement boiled down to whether the U.S., in its opening move, should assert not only its preference for zero but also its willingness to consider a negotiated compromise higher than zero. Burt felt it should; Perle felt it should not.

Burt was now the key figure in the State

Department's handling of arms control. He had more expertise and interest in it than Eagleburger. On the question of how to make the best of the December 1979 dual-track decision he was not just skeptical about the chances of reaching an agreement before deployment; he was absolutely certain that there was no chance at all. The military imbalance in favor of the U.S.S.R. made a diplomatic solution in the interests of the West impossible. The task facing the Administration was what he called "alliance management." That phrase connoted a combination of therapy and trickery not unlike what Weinberger and Perle were after. The object of making a proposal and undertaking negotiations was damage limitation, public relations, and getting the new NATO missiles deployed with a minimum of anguish and recrimination inside the alliance. Burt's disagreement with Perle over the zero option was a matter of how to attain that goal.

Burt kept reminding his colleagues that "the purpose of this whole exercise is maximum political advantage." The zero option would serve that end only if it was flexible and perceived to be so. By telling the Soviets and the world that the U.S. would like to eliminate, or "zero-out," missiles in Europe but would listen to proposals for other ways of achieving a balance of nuclear power, said Burt, "we can have our cake and eat it, too; we'll get credit for a breathtaking initiative while avoiding the connotation of refusal to entertain other possibilities for significant reductions."

Perle turned that argument on its head. He contended that the State Department was recommending a recipe that would spoil the cake altogether. If followed, the recommendation would deprive the U.S. of both the political and the military benefits everyone agreed were desirable.

By making it obvious to the Soviets that the U.S. was not serious about zero and would settle for something higher, the Administration would be guaranteeing that the Soviets would ignore zero, insofar as it figured in the American proposal at all, and set their sights very high indeed— high enough to preserve all their current deployments and future plans.

Perle cited the Pentagon studies that he had designed to prove his contention that any significant number of SS-20s at all, even if they were matched by Pershing IIs and Tomahawks, left Western Europe in jeopardy and undercut the credibility of NATO deterrence. His reasoning was that the SS-20s were far more potent and menacing weapons than the still undeployed American weapons. For the U.S. to assume in advance that zero was unacceptable would be to bow to the Soviets as arbiters of what was acceptable. By pressing this point every chance he could, and by pressing it with his own special blend of righteous wrath and sweet reason, Perle managed to make it seem like an act of political and intellectual cowardice for anyone to mention negotiability as a criterion.

Carried to an extreme, Perle's position would preclude genuine and productive negotiation. The key officials of the State Department's European Bureau and, to a lesser but growing extent, of its Politico-Military Bureau believed that was just what Perle intended.

Paul Nitze, meanwhile, was keeping his mind open and his powder dry. He agreed that "zero only" had the advantage of simplicity, of giving the Europeans what they professed to want, and of shifting the propaganda onus back onto the Soviets. Nitze shared another concern of Perle's: that zero plus had the political liability of looking to the West Europeans like a trick to proceed with deployment of the 572 American missiles in NATO. He also found the State Department's formulation fuzzy. Nor did Nitze have any patience with Burt's talk about "alliance management" as the sole purpose of the negotiations. Nitze had not taken the job simply "to be part of a charade." He did not intend to prejudge the possibility of reaching an agreement. He wanted an opening position that was clear and simple.

At the same time, Nitze had long been a believer in leaving a delegation considerable flexibility for exploring areas of compromise. One of his many criticisms of Henry Kissinger, from his experience as a member of the SALT delegation a decade earlier, was that Kissinger insisted on trying to run negotiations taking place in Vienna and Helsinki by remote control from Washington. This, Nitze believed, had led to mistakes and missed opportunities. Rostow had persuaded Nitze to accept the job as negotiator for the European arms-control talks with repeated promises that he would have a strong hand in writing his own initial instructions and in amending them as the negotiations progressed.

So Nitze remained above the fray, taking the attitude that whatever decision the interagency process in its wisdom produced he would dutifully accept and try to make work. He appeared content to go along with Perle on the opening position and hold his own fire for fights later on over how that opening position might have to evolve during the course of the negotiations.

A QUESTION OF RANGE

No sooner did State and Defense square off against each other over the most presentable version of the zero option than they plunged into a thicket of subsidiary disputes. One concerned the "scope" of the proposal. What weapons were to be covered by the proposed agreement? The Soviets, not surprisingly, included in their calculation of the nuclear balance in Europe every NATO weapon that they considered capable of reaching the U.S.S.R. This meant counting existing weapons, like carrier-based aircraft and British and French forces, as well as new weapons like the Pershing II and the Tomahawk. The Reagan Administration was solidly committed to the proposition that the only weapons on the NATO side that were eligible for limitation were the new American missiles. But the Administration was divided over what to count on the Soviet side. The division was predictable: State wanted a proposal of narrower scope that would concentrate on SS-20s, while Perle wanted to broaden the scope to include other Soviet missiles.

Burt made his case on the grounds that a less comprehensive proposal would be more "plausible" to the Europeans. Plausibility had replaced the more traditional, but now discredited, criterion of negotiability. A plausible proposal was one that would appear negotiable to those who were naïve enough to think that an agreement was possible (or, for that matter, desirable).

Perle argued his maximalist position on grounds of logic and history. Logic told him that mobile, land-based Soviet missiles with ranges shorter than that of the SS-20 were potentially as dangerous as SS-20s themselves and should, accordingly, be limited by an agreement. He did not accept the distinction between long- and shorter-range Soviet missiles if their launchers could be moved. He felt their very mobility should be figured into any calculations of range. A missile whose launcher could be rushed forward in a crisis had an effective range much greater than the distance it could actually fly. History told him that past arms-control agreements had been flawed by the American penchant for arbitrarily exempting Soviet weapons that should have been limited. The classic examples were the Backfire bomber and the SS-20 itself, which Perle felt had come to haunt the U.S. because of the failure of SALT to achieve real arms control.

The SS-20 had a number of short-legged cousins. Of these, the most important were the SS-12 and SS-22. There was also yet another missile just coming into service, the SS-23. The SS-22 was a modern version of the SS-12, much as the SS-20 was a modernization of the SS-4 and -5. The SS-20 and SS-22 were both technologically advanced, relatively accurate, mobile missiles, but the SS-20 had multiple warheads and a nearly intercontinental range of as much as 5,000 kilometers, while the SS-22 was a single-warhead weapon with a range of less that 1,000 kilometers.[1]

Perle's original memo to Weinberger setting forth the hard-and-fast zero option had urged that the U.S. present at the outset of the negotiations a plan whereby both sides would reduce to zero the number of missiles with ranges greater than 800 kilometers. This would preclude deployment of the Pershing IIs and the Tomahawks on the American side while forcing the Soviets to eliminate all their SS-20s, plus the older, single-warhead SS-4s and SS-5s that the SS-20s were meant to replace, plus the shorter-range SS-12s and SS-22s (Perle was using the Pentagon's maximum estimate of their ranges). In congressional testimony later in the year, Perle warned that "a failure to limit" shorter-range Soviet missiles "would leave an agreement eliminating the Soviet SS-4, SS-5 and SS-20 missiles hopelessly vulnerable to circumvention;

for the fact is that the Soviets can cover some 85% of the NATO targets assigned to the SS-20 with the shorter-range SS-22 if they are deployed in sufficient numbers and moved forward on Warsaw Pact territory." The Pentagon believed that, once the SS-23 was in service, it could strike "as much as 50 percent of European NATO."

Almost everyone saw the technical logic in Perle's position, and opposed him nonetheless on grounds of intra-alliance politics. The documents amplifying the December 1979 two-track decision referred to long-range Soviet missiles—i.e., the SS-4, -5, -20 series—as the principal disruptive factor in the European strategic balance, and therefore the principal items on the agenda for the proposed negotiations. The NATO ministers had made it clear they would not back any proposal that seemed to go significantly beyond the guidelines set in December 1979.

At meetings of the NATO Special Consultative Group in Brussels in the late summer and fall, Lawrence Eagleburger notified his foreign-ministry counterparts that the Administration was concerned about the shorter-range systems and hoped to find a way of dealing with them in the talks. The allies were not willing to go as far as Perle in subjecting shorter- and longer-range missiles to equal treatment. Rather, they wanted to treat shorter-range systems as separate from, and less important than, the longer-range ones. The SS-20s would be counted and limited under the "central aggregate" established by the agreement, and there might be accompanying, less-stringent rules, called collateral restraints, that would prevent the Soviets from deploying additional SS-12s and -22s which might be able to cover some of the same targets as the SS-20s. The State Department, the Arms Control and Disarmament Agency, Paul Nitze, and the Joint Chiefs of Staff all lined up with the Europeans, against Perle.

The Chiefs had their own very characteristic reason for opposing the inclusion of shorter-range Soviet weapons with the zero option proper: they were afraid that, if the U.S. insisted on treating SS-12s and -22s along with the SS-4s, -5s, and -20s, the Soviets might have a stronger case for including shorter-range Western missiles, notably the Pershing Is already deployed in West Germany, in whatever limits or bans were finally negotiated to cover the Pershing IIs and Tomahawks. Here was an instance of what had long been, and would now again become, a recurring tension within the U.S. government and within the Pentagon itself. On the one hand, there was a desire, personified by Perle, to include as many Soviet weapons as possible in whatever restrictions were to be proposed. On the other hand, there was anxiety about what one member of the Joint Staff called "the boomerang effect: if we throw at the Soviets a proposal aimed at limiting a maximum of their stuff, they get all the greedier in trying to limit ours—and by the logic of our own position, it's that much harder for us to resist them." The Chiefs had a tendency to worry about what would happen if the U.S. proposal was ever accepted. That was not a big concern of Perle's. He saw his proposal not as a means to an end but as an end in itself.

A WHIFF OF BLACKMAIL

The Chiefs were also worried that the more comprehensive a proposal the U.S. put forward in the talks, the harder it would be to fend off the inevitable Soviet counterproposal covering American aircraft. The Soviets had always maintained that limits on aircraft must be included in whatever agreement was finally reached. What they had in mind was limits on American bombers that were not covered by SALT but that could drop nuclear bombs on the Soviet Union from "forward bases" in Western Europe. These were primarily F-111s in England and FB-111s back in the U.S. that could be moved to Europe on short notice, as well as F-4 Phantom fighter-bombers and A-6 and A-7 attack bombers on aircraft carriers in the Mediterranean and North Atlantic. Keeping aircraft off the agenda of arms-control negotiations was an obsession with the Chiefs. They would examine almost any option advanced within the bureaucracy, not to mention any proposal likely to be advanced by the Soviets at the negotiations, with a keen and suspicious eye for some hidden, delayed-action feature that might require them later to accept limits on aircraft.

Their resistance to any such limits was not as parochial or as unreasonable as their civilian detractors sometimes made it seem. Aircraft were a tricky subject for arms-control negotiations because of their versatility. Versatility carries with it ambiguity. Whereas almost all ballistic missiles were nuclear-armed, bombers could just as well be armed with conventional weapons as nuclear ones. The same plane could be used in a relatively restricted geographical area, or it could operate over great distances. For example, during the Vietnam War, B-52s based in the Philippines flew a short way to drop conventional bombs on North Vietnam; yet the same aircraft, with modifications, could also serve the Strategic Air Command as intercontinental "delivery vehicles" for attacking the Soviet Union with thermonuclear weapons.

Perle was well aware of the intensity of the Chiefs' concern and considered it legitimate, up to a point. In his August memo to Weinberger, when he first advanced the zero-only option, Perle had warned that extending the negotiations from missiles to bombers would at some point raise the question "Do we want to count F-15s in St. Louis when we get around to counting aircraft?" But he also knew that the Soviets had more "aircraft of comparable characteristics" than the U.S. and therefore would feel more of a pinch if aircraft were added to the negotiations. Widening the talks to include aircraft would be a way to call the Soviets' bluff. Soviet fighter-bombers were generally less capable than American ones, but they were more numerous, and presumably any agreement that limited U.S. fighter-bombers like the F-111 and the Phantom might also very well constrain the Soviet Sukhoi-24, code-named Fencer by NATO, and the MiG-27 Flogger. More important, it would constrain the Soviet Backfire bomber, which had so bedeviled the previous Administration's attempts to negotiate and ratify SALT II.

But, as with shorter-range missiles, the Chiefs worried what would happen if the U.S. proposal ended up being accepted in some form. They knew American aircraft were better fighting machines than Soviet ones, and they did not want to see Phantoms being traded off in simple-minded numbers games against Fencers or even FB-111s against Backfires.

Perle was prepared to indulge his uniformed colleagues at the Pentagon in their reflexive and obsessive opposition to any limits on aircraft, but only for something in exchange. He made no bones about the Chiefs' obligation, as he saw it, to him. He would let the Chiefs have their way on aircraft only if they supported him on the zero-only option. At a series of meetings with military officers, including Rear Admiral Robert Austin, the

Chiefs' representative on the Interagency Group, Perle stressed the need for "a coordinated position in this building." He made clear that, while he would like the Defense Department to present a united front against the State Department on every issue, he absolutely insisted on it with regard to the zero-only option. Just to make sure this message got across at the highest level, Perle had Weinberger lay down the law to General David Jones, the chairman of the Chiefs.

Yet the Chiefs hesitated. At an Interagency Group meeting in early November, Richard Burt reviewed the various points that had been agreed by the group, including exclusion of aircraft, and then mentioned the two principal points of contention that remained—zero plus versus zero only and whether shorter-range Soviet missiles should be covered by zero. Admiral Austin spoke up in a way suggesting he and the Chiefs were leaning toward the State Department's zero-plus option.

Perle had thought the Chiefs were with him, and he countered Austin's unpleasant surprise with one of his own. "Well," he said, "maybe we should revisit aircraft."

Burt was incredulous. "What do you mean 'revisit aircraft'?"

Austin knew exactly what Perle meant: he was prepared to reopen an issue that everyone thought had been closed, and argue once again for inclusion of bombers in the U.S.'s opening position at the talks. Austin sensed a whiff of blackmail in the air. Perle, a third-level civilian official, could make this threat credible to Austin by invoking both of their bosses and by implying strongly that he was underscoring a threat that Weinberger had made to General David Jones. As the meeting was breaking up, Perle took Austin aside and told him that any "backsliding" by the Chiefs in their support for the zero-only option was "unacceptable," since it contravened "what has been worked out by the Secretary [of Defense] with the Chairman [General Jones]."

In the days following, Perle and Weinberger met separately with Jones and the other Chiefs to make sure there was no lingering misunderstanding: if the Chiefs failed to support them on the zero-only option, Perle and Weinberger would "reserve judgment" on the issue of aircraft. Just to show how serious they were, they added the issue of aircraft to the agenda for an upcoming National Security Council meeting.

What the tactic lacked in subtlety it made up for in effectiveness. General Jones broke the news to Eagleburger and Burt that the Chiefs would not be joining the State Department in support of zero plus. The Chiefs were the Administration's only high-level holdovers from the Carter period; they had endorsed SALT II; they were acutely conscious of being the odd men out, relative doves in an extremely hawkish Administration. By backing Weinberger and Perle on the zero option, they thought they might be able to build a better working relationship with the civilian side of the department. They were to be disappointed. Perle came away from the episode convinced that the Chiefs were not only living in the past in their devotion to old-fashioned arms control, but that they were, as he put it to a colleague, "push-overs and patsies for whoever leans on them the last, the longest and the hardest." He resolved to do the decisive leaning himself in the months to come.

A GLOBAL PROBLEM

The mobility of Soviet missiles raised questions not just of which ones to count

but of where to count them and how to make sure that all were accounted for. An SS-20 launcher set up in Siberia or Central Asia and aimed against a target in China could be loaded on the Trans-Siberian Railway, moved west of the Ural Mountains, and pointed at Britain or Italy. Therefore every SS-20 launcher, no matter where it was deployed, represented a potential threat to NATO. Yet the Soviets contended that only those SS-20s actually deployed as part of their defenses against NATO should be discussed in the negotiations and covered by whatever agreement was reached.

At the preliminary round of negotiations in October-November 1980, the U.S. delegation had made a vague proposal for limits that would be "world-wide in scope," thus covering all SS-20s wherever they were deployed, but that would "consider the regional aspects [of deployment] as well." When the Reagan Administration came into office, the Interagency Group chaired by Burt and Perle decided that the only way to tackle the problem of mobility was head-on—with a "global" limit covering all of the Soviet Union, and, as Perle put it, "none of this nonsense about regional sublimits." The idea of such a global limit had much to recommend it in the atmosphere of the new government. For one thing, it was simple, straightforward, bold—all virtues to which the Administration aspired for its arms-control proposals.

As in so many other instances, however, boldness was inversely proportional to negotiability. If anything was more important to the Soviets than fortifying their western flank against NATO, it was defending themselves against China. It was almost surely easier for the Soviets to imagine the U.S.S.R. under attack from the East than from the West. The notion of the West Europeans invading Russia must have strained the credulity of even the most paranoid worst-case planners in Moscow; the danger that China might, in some future xenophobic frenzy, hurl its huge army against the Soviet Union was less farfetched, at least from the Soviet standpoint.

Also, the Soviet Union feared an eventual Asian military alliance joining China, the U.S., and perhaps Japan and South Korea as well. One way to head off that possibility was for the U.S.S.R. to keep its European and Far Eastern options open and independent of each other. The Kremlin wanted to take advantage of diplomatic and arms-control opportunities in the West without letting down its guard in the East. Not only would that approach ensure maximum military flexibility, but it had the political benefit of sowing discord and distrust between the U.S. and the most important countries in Asia. Neither China nor Japan was happy about the possibility that Soviet-American arms-control agreements might have the effect of freeing Soviet weapons from Europe so they could be deployed in the Far East. It was very much in the Soviet interest to keep the Chinese and Japanese unhappy on just that score. If the Kremlin should ever agree to an American insistence on global ceilings, it would be enabling the U.S. to go to its Chinese and Japanese partners and say, "See? We've been looking out for your security as well as that of our European allies in this negotiation of ours with the Soviets." That was a boast the Soviets did not want the U.S. to be able to make.

RESTRICTING REFIRE

U.S. intelligence had concluded that the Soviets were manufacturing twice as many SS-20 rockets as launchers. That meant there was a powerful presumption that the system was meant to have a "rapid reload/refire capability." On the grounds that the Soviets would not waste such a capability, Perle and others felt prudence required assuming that each launcher in the field could have a refire missile in a camouflaged vehicle nearby or perhaps even stored within the body of the launcher itself. If the zero option was accepted, refires would not be a problem, since all Soviet launchers would have to be destroyed. But if the State Department got its way and some Soviet SS-20s were permitted under the American proposal, Perle wanted that proposal to include a ban on refires. The only way to verify such a ban would be by frequent on-site inspection of Soviet missile factories and storage areas. That meant knowing the location of all those sites and securing Soviet agreement to station inspectors at each one, or at least being able to have a look at short notice. Few believed the Soviets would accept on-site inspection of their most sensitive military production and storage facilities.

Perle seemed to be staking out a position that would serve at least two broader purposes: it would make the overall American proposal more resistant to internal U.S. pressures for compromise; and it would strengthen the case he was simultaneously making on the unresolved question of which version of the zero option to propose. In his original memorandum to Weinberger laying out the zero-only option, Perle wrote that it would have the advantage of "simplifying verification problems, which at levels higher than zero are probably insurmountable," and it would "simplify the problem of refire, which at levels higher than zero will perpetuate." An absolute ban would be easier to monitor and enforce, since to discover so much as a single SS-20 rocket or launcher would be to catch the Soviets in a violation of the treaty. In addition, the Soviets would not be able to carry out any tests on a weapon that was prohibited rather than merely limited; and flight tests of ballistic missiles are virtually impossible to conduct clandestinely, so compliance with the ban would be easy to monitor.

Perle's proposal was not just internally consistent but also internally self-reinforcing. The arguments for zero buttressed those for a ban on refires, and vice versa. Thus, on every issue he had taken a position that was extreme, but that was also simple and compelling as long as one did not dwell on the question of negotiability.

On the big question, whether to go with the zero-plus or zero-only version of the zero option, the interagency process had not been able to generate an agreed Administration position. On other questions, the maneuvering and horsetrading back and forth across the Potomac had yielded uneasy truces that produced the illusion of a united position for the moment but would lead to ambushes, skirmishes, and pitched battles months later, when negotiations with the Soviets were underway.

plicated subject all the more difficult to follow. The SS-4, -5, -20 series has a considerably greater range than the SS-12, -22, while the SS-22 has a greater range than the SS-23. SS stands simply for surface-to-surface. The numbers 4, 5, 12, 20, 22, and 23 indicate the order in which Western intelligence saw various weapons emerge; they do not represent a comparative assessment of how large or formidable the weapon is, and they have nothing to do with range. To give the whole problem yet another twist, the Soviets often dispute Western designations and data. For example, NATO differentiated between the SS-12 and -22, attributing to the latter a somewhat longer range, greater accuracy, and a smaller warhead. NATO claimed that there were about a hundred deployed launchers for the SS-12, -22 series. The Soviets admitted to only about half that number and denied that there were two separate types of missile at all. What the U.S. called the SS-22 the Soviets said did not exist as such. They considered it a variation, or test model, of the SS-12. The SS-23 was the latest addition and was often labeled by NATO the SS-X-23, "X" standing for experimental.

NOTE

1. Here, as so often, the NATO system for designating Soviet missiles makes a com-

24. INTELLIGENCE: THE RIGHT RULES

Stansfield Turner and George Thibault

The Israeli raid at Entebbe, the hostage rescue mission to Iran, and the rescue of Brigadier General James Dozier had one thing in common: No one in the public and few in the governments concerned knew anything about these actions beforehand. The need for secrecy in such military operations seems obvious. Less clear, but equally vital, is the importance of secrecy in other government activities such as intelligence operations during peacetime. This need has not changed significantly since 1777 when George Washington wrote: "The necessity of procuring good intelligence is apparent and need not be further urged—all that remains for me to add is that you keep the whole matter as secret as possible."

America's first president perhaps did not anticipate how difficult it would later become to reconcile the necessity for secrecy in intelligence activities with the constitutional provisions for open government and the guaranteed rights of Americans. The secret work of intelligence agencies inherently conflicts with the idea of openness; such secrecy can easily undermine individual rights in the name of protecting them. Consequently, every American administration has had to seek a balance between secrecy and openness.

From Washington's day until World War II, U.S. intelligence activities did not arouse significant concern because they were sufficiently limited. But in 1947, re-

calling the government's inability to bring together available intelligence that might have alerted the country to the impending attack on Pearl Harbor, President Truman centralized American intelligence activities. The president established the position of director of central intelligence (DCI) to coordinate the various foreign intelligence efforts spread across the Department of Defense, the Department of State, the Federal Bureau of Investigation (FBI), and elsewhere. The director would also head a new Central Intelligence Agency (CIA) through which all foreign intelligence data would flow.

The concentration of power in a single director and the creation of a new intelligence agency clearly increased the amount of secret government activity and thus the probability of conflicts between secrecy and open democracy. In the climate of concern for the adequacy of U.S. intelligence operations, the CIA opened mail to and from the Soviet Union, infiltrated domestic organizations suspected of threatening national security, and tested on unsuspecting Americans drugs that it thought might be used on its own agents. When these activities came to light in the mid-1970s, the executive and legislative branches of the U.S. government moved quickly to tighten controls on intelligence operations and to restore traditional guarantees of personal rights. The destructive criticism of all secret intelligence activity during this period demonstrated how far the national attitude had shifted toward a concern for individual rights and high standards of

Source: *Foreign Policy* 48 (Fall 1982), pp. 122–38.

legality even at the cost of national security.

In February 1976 President Ford issued an executive order governing the conduct of intelligence activities. In particular, the order laid down rules severely limiting intrusions into the lives of Americans. In January 1978 President Carter revised the Ford executive order, making minor changes in existing domestic constraints and establishing new procedures requiring the CIA director to clear sensitive collection activities in advance with the National Security Council (NSC). Congress established a requirement to review certain intelligence operations and set up two permanent committees to oversee intelligence activities.

But four years after the Ford executive order, concern that intelligence agencies might abuse secrecy began to diminish. The country was shaking itself free of the inhibiting consequences of its debacle in Vietnam and was ready to acknowledge once again the need to deal more effectively with a world often hostile to American interests. In the 1980 presidential campaign, Ronald Reagan charged that the Ford and Carter executive orders, undue criticism from the public and media, and excessive congressional oversight had hobbled intelligence capabilities. Once elected, President Reagan set out to correct these problems by loosening many of the controls on U.S. intelligence activities.

There are four types of controls and oversight:

1. internal controls created and enforced within the intelligence agencies themselves;
2. presidential controls such as the executive orders;
3. controls that come from Congress in its role as overseer of intelligence; and
4. controls that flow from public scrutiny of intelligence activities.

The internal controls that intelligence agencies impose on their own activities generally are easy to devise, involve only minimal risks to intelligence operations, and can be very effective. The control most widely used is the practice called compartmentation, which severely limits the number of people who know about a sensitive project to sometimes as few as a dozen. Compartmentation not only limits access to information, but also segregates the files relating to the project. No single document reveals every initiative an agency undertakes.

But protections such as compartmentation have their costs. By the time of the intelligence investigations in the mid-1970s, compartmentation within the CIA had become excessive and dangerous. The few individuals who had the most knowledge of sensitive programs had accumulated undue power. CIA directors learned about some operations only after they took place. Sometimes the lack of adequate coordination permitted conflicting or duplicative activities. There is no foolproof way to guard against these kinds of problems, but directors can help the situation by establishing an internal system of checks and controls.

Between 1977 and 1981, for instance, we adopted a corporate decision-making style in the CIA. Previously, the originating office forwarded important proposals to the director; the decision process included only those other offices with a direct interest in the proposal. To reduce the liabilities of extreme compartmentation, we began to involve a small, regular group of offices in most major decisions. We established specific levels of approval for various degrees of risk, encouraged the agency's inspector-general to probe widely, and sought to inculcate by example a tone of high ethical standards. Even with these steps to make internal procedures more open, the danger of leaks remained small because intelligence agencies in general are highly conscious of security. The most significant danger of such steps is rather that they may encourage undue caution in an organization that must take risks. A director has to counter this inclination toward excessive caution by encouraging subordinates to present bold and imaginative proposals when the results may justify taking high risks.

NSC REVIEW

At the presidential level two major types of formal external controls have been exercised: constraints on the authority of intelligence agencies to intrude on the privacy of Americans, and a requirement that the DCI clear sensitive intelligence collection operations with the NSC and present the council with an annual review of those activities. Regular NSC review may dull the effectiveness of intelligence operations, especially those involving high risk but also high payoff. Since NSC members are not as familiar with intelligence operations as the director, sometimes they do not appreciate the potential benefits of high-risk operations, especially when the benefits may be realized only in the long run. Timidity and parochial interests may supplant sound judgment.

There is a compensating advantage in reviewing and clearing sensitive collection operations through the NSC: It strengthens the DCI's control in an area where decisions are not black or white and where there exist enormous pressures to take high risks. Deciding which risks are worth taking is perhaps the most difficult decision a director must make.

The historical record is replete with schemes that might have endangered American lives, money, and prestige with little prospect of a commensurate return. Yet in general, risk taking is essential in intelligence work and must be encouraged when the potential payoff is worth it.

All techniques for collecting intelligence become compromised to some degree over time. Only constant innovation will keep the art of collection ahead of the art of counterintelligence. But innovation means trying something that has never been tried before. A brilliant and original idea may at first seem unorthodox and untenable. The director, then, must separate the wheat from the chaff among the many proposals that cross his desk. At times it is useful for the director to solicit outside advice. Like the head of any bureaucracy, he feels pressure to support his subordinates, to demonstrate his confidence in them and to encourage them to exercise initiative. If the director does not support enough innovative proposals, subordinates will stop offering them and initiative will wane.

The requirement of an NSC review provides a useful exercise for both the director and his subordinates. Those presenting the new ideas must do their homework better than they might otherwise because a rejection from the NSC is more difficult to appeal than one from the director. The requirement also forces the director, who must be able to present the scheme persuasively to an outside review board, to think the proposal through rigorously. The line between acceptable and unacceptable risks is a fine one. To determine what risks are acceptable, the DCI must look beyond the short-term success or failure of an isolated intelligence operation to the long-term effect on U.S. foreign policy if the operation fails. An example of this distinction is the question of spying on allies. The United States had to balance the potential value of information it could gain by, for example, spying on the regime of Shah Mohammad Reza Pahlavi in Iran with the risk of damaging Iranian-American relations if the operation were exposed. In most cases, the United States deems such risks unacceptable. The filter of an NSC review helps the DCI make this kind of judgment.

The NSC review procedure used to work as follows: Each year the DCI would provide a list of the sensitive operations approved by the NSC in the past year and a second list of the next 10 most sensitive operations for which he had thought NSC approval unnecessary. If the NSC did not agree with the DCI's judgment on where he drew that line, it could instruct him to seek its approval more frequently in the future. This process also provided the DCI with a check on his subordinates' judgments of what to approve on their own and what to bring to him for approval. This is part of an important system of small checks insuring that as operations become more significant, approval and supervisory authority automatically move upward.

Interaction with the NSC can also insure that intelligence collection activities do not endanger ongoing foreign policy actions. It may be desirable, for example, to recruit an informer who can tell what the negotiators from another country will present at the next negotiating session. Yet if the informer is uncovered, the negotiations may be ruptured. The American negotiator, who participates in the NSC decision, can best judge whether the potential value of the information is worth the risks.

The new Reagan executive order drops the requirements both for clearing sensitive collection operations with the NSC and for conducting an annual NSC review. A new subordinate directive providing for these procedures does not require the director to submit all proposed sensitive operations to the NSC; he now has considerable discretion in deciding what to submit for review. This difference may well be simply a matter of style, insignificant in practice. But it is difficult to understand why the DCI's obligations should not be spelled out explicitly. What is worrisome is that behind these changes may lie the belief that a less rigorous process of clearance would unshackle the DCI and permit him to conduct better intelligence. If the Reagan administration believes this, it does not understand the benefits of the review process and is likely to neglect it over time with potentially serious consequences.

A second type of presidential control sought to constrain intrusions into the lives of Americans. The Reagan executive order relaxes these constraints. The new order, for example, allows intelligence agencies other than the FBI to collect intelligence in the United States when significant foreign intelligence is involved; it permits physical surveillance of Americans abroad to collect significant information that cannot reasonably be obtained by other means; and it authorizes covert actions within the United States in support of foreign policy objectives as long as the actions are not intended to influence U.S. opinion. These changes are undoubtedly intended to take advantage of every opportunity for the CIA to gather useful foreign intelligence. Americans do become involved with foreigners in activities that have implications for intelligence, ranging from legal commercial relations to illegal narcotics smuggling and international terrorism. The CIA has always been authorized to inquire into such activities in an open manner—for example, by talking with travellers who have been abroad. But when Americans have preferred not to share their information, the CIA has not previously been authorized to collect that information covertly, except in very specific circumstances.

There is little evidence that spying on Americans in the United States would produce significant intelligence. And whatever intelligence is available the FBI can acquire. The FBI and the CIA already work together closely in counterintelligence work. The CIA watches foreign agents overseas; if an agent comes to the United States, the CIA hands the case over to the FBI. This concept of shared responsibility takes advantage of the best capabilities of the two agencies. The CIA is trained to operate overseas while the FBI is trained to operate in the United States where national and state laws apply. If the CIA begins to operate alongside the FBI in the United States, counterproductive competition would inevitably arise for dollars and territory; responsibility between the two agencies could be blurred; and resentment could build up over large and small bureaucratic issues. The FBI can expand its foreign intelligence collection in the United States if that seems necessary, rather than drawing the CIA into domestic work.

One other presidential control is the Intelligence Oversight Board (IOB). Instituted by the Ford Executive order, the board is a three-person panel that reports directly to the president. Ford and Carter empowered it to review intelligence activities that "raise questions of legality or propriety." Anyone, including agency employees, could use this unique channel to report known or suspected wrongdoing. Reagan has considerably weakened the IOB, limiting it to advising the president on matters of legality but not matters of propriety. Yet the investigations of 1975-1976 questioned the propriety of some of the CIA's actions as much as their legality. Again, apparently an impression exists that less scrutiny will somehow result in better intelligence.

CONGRESS'S JOB

Congress exercises the third major set of controls over intelligence. Since their establishment in 1976 and 1977, the Senate Select Committee on Intelligence and the House Permanent Select Committee on Intelligence have reversed the tradition of perfunctory oversight by two or three congressional leaders who preferred not to know the ungentlemanly details of intelligence activities. Instead, the two committees have acted as aggressive and responsible overseers while at the same time providing valuable advice and guidance for the intelligence agencies.

Nonetheless, congressional oversight does present considerable dangers. To a greater extent than with executive branch oversight, the fear that information will leak may inhibit the agencies from taking risks. The danger of leaks is particularly high because the committees are larger than necessary; sensitive material cannot be restricted to only a few committee members. Moreover, secrecy goes against the grain of most politicians. And even with the best of intentions, it is seldom easy to keep classified information separated in one's mind from unclassified information. Consequently, although the committee members seem to realize the need for security and have a good record of preserving secrecy, the requirement of disclosing information to Congress inhibits intelligence officers. In particular, the intelligence agencies fear leaks about highly controversial activities such as plans for covert action to influence political events in a foreign country.

The other danger of congressional oversight comes from the impulse of congressional committees to manage rather than just oversee. The distinction is easily blurred over such issues as whether the intelligence committees must always be informed of covert actions before they take place. It is not the job of Congress to dictate how the president should exercise his executive authorities, which include the use of covert action. It is, however, Congress's job to judge how well the president has used his authority in the past and, if necessary, to enact legislation that enlarges or limits that authority. This distinction is central to the constitutional balance of powers.

These dangers notwithstanding, congressional oversight strengthens intelligence capabilities. To a large degree, the widespread impression that congressional oversight has hobbled intelligence can be attributed to the 1980 battle over modifying the Hughes-Ryan amendment to the Foreign Assistance Act. This amendment, passed originally in 1974, required that the president report all covert actions to "the appropriate committees of Congress." Congress interpreted this to include the appropriations, armed services, intelligence, and foreign affairs committees in both the House and Senate. This interpretation allowed far too much disclosure, although sensitive covert actions constitute only a relatively small portion of the work of the intelligence community. The publicity surrounding the debate to repeal the amendment led the public to believe that all intelligence secrets were shared with the eight congressional committees and that as a result U.S. intelligence was crippled.

But the Hughes-Ryan amendment was modified in 1980. Now the president reports intelligence information to the Congress's two select intelligence committees. The change has not weakened congressional oversight since the select committees draw some of their membership from the other six committees that previously received intelligence information. Intelligence officials no longer have to respond to questions from other committees regarding how intelligence was gathered or whether covert actions are taking place. Such questions fall under the jurisdiction of the select committees. The members of these two committees understand intelligence matters better than do other congressmen; the former can cite this expertise to generate vital support among their colleagues when needed.

Perhaps the least recognized benefit of congressional oversight is that it can strengthen the control of the DCI. Directors have sometimes uncovered situations where their orders had been overlooked or ignored. While in the past some subordinates may have sought to hold back information from the DCI, today they know they may be called to testify before Congress where they would face the choice of disclosure or perjury. Few intelligence officials would care to explain why the director had to learn from a congressional hearing what he should have learned from his staff. There has been no evidence of deliberate withholding of information since the Ford executive order established the emphasis on checks and controls; still, inhibiting pressure from Congress in this area benefits everyone.

Finally, all intelligence officials who testify before the congressional intelligence committees benefit from the exchange. Like any specialists, intelligence officers can become too narrow in their outlook. Past mistakes have frequently resulted from insularity and from an absorbing dedication to getting the job done. The members of the two intelligence committees are detached enough from the intelligence process to offer a valuable perspective.

On balance, congressional oversight is beneficial. The Ford and Carter executive orders acknowledged this by designating the DCI the intelligence community's spokesman to Congress. The Reagan executive order, however, includes no such designation. In addition, the CIA's congressional liaison office has been downgraded. If the Reagan administration places less emphasis on congressional oversight and if an attitude develops that congressional oversight hobbles intelligence, Congress could lose its enthusiasm for playing this vital role. Politicians receive little thanks for membership on a committee whose actions are largely secret. So far, members on both committees have been conscientious and interested in their work. It is important to maintain this high level of congressional involvement by assuring present and future committee members that the executive branch values their role.

THE SAFE COURSE

The fourth type of controls are those exercised by the public. They go to the heart of the conflict between secrecy and open democracy. These controls are certainly the most controversial and the least understood. The Reagan administration has eliminated the provision of previous executive orders making the DCI the intelligence community's spokesman to the media. It has also drastically curtailed the release of unclassified intelligence reports to the public. Such attempts to hide intelligence activities from the public or simply to ignore the public are undesirable. They deprive Americans of a valuable source of information on national issues without good reason and deprive the intelligence community of a valuable source of outside stimulus and dialogue.

Many of the intelligence community's analyses are, or can be, declassified. Releasing them to the public can contribute to a well-informed citizenry. Two arguments are often made against providing sanitized analyses to the public. One is that preparing information for the public involves a significant additional burden for analysts, detracting from their ability to do their primary job of providing classified intelligence to the executive branch. This argument is spurious. Intelligence officials can sanitize most reports of interest to the public with minimal deletions and editing. And distribution is handled by other agencies.

The other argument, though not compelling, is more reasonable: It is difficult to determine what should be released. On the one hand, if intelligence information supports an administration's policy, it will be criticized as slanted to that purpose. On the other hand, if information appears to undercut policy, the administration will not appreciate its release. Good policy should be able to withstand objective criticism. But sometimes difficult situations will arise when the analysis that supports the current policy cannot be declassified while the analysis that undercuts the policy can.

One answer is to take no risks and publish nothing. This approach, however, is clearly unacceptable. The Defense and State departments continually publish intelligence analyses and information. Even with the purest intentions, there is a danger that these departments will release only selective information favoring their policy objectives. A better answer is for the DCI to take the initiative by releasing whatever will be useful to the public. The director should not let himself be pressured into supporting administration policy or intimidated into withholding information when policy makers do not like his news. In 1977 the CIA published an intelligence estimate on the world energy situation. Even though the CIA had begun preparing the estimate well before the Carter administration took office, we were criticized for supporting the president's energy program. Since it was released, that estimate has provided a valuable reference point for the public. Similarly, in 1978 we published an appraisal of the Polish economy showing that Poland was a potential credit risk. This report enraged policy makers who at the time were then encouraging investment in Poland. Today some bankers wish they had read the report more carefully.

The greatest payoff from public release lies in the area of economic intelligence. The U.S. business community, facing intense competition from foreign producers, can greatly benefit from intelligence information on trends in research and production, pricing mechanisms, and other areas. There is little doubt that other nations use their intelligence capabilities to support their international businesses; it is shortsighted for the United States not to do the same.

The past six years have witnessed major experimentation and change in the U.S. intelligence community. It has shifted away from an environment of maximum secrecy and begun to address the inherent problem of secrecy in a democracy. No change of such proportions comes easily to a large bureaucracy where traditions run deep and dialogue is constrained. It is no surprise, therefore, that some real damage to U.S. intelligence capabilities occurred during this transitional period.

Three significant causes of damage arose: a wave of public criticism, numerous leaks of security information, and some excessively detailed and restrictive procedures for conducting intelligence operations. Harsh public criticism followed the revelations of the Rockefeller Commission and of the investigative committees led by then Senator Frank Church (D-Idaho) and then Representative Otis Pike (D.-New York). The criticism fed the media's post-Watergate appetite to uncover malfeasance in government. The impact of this criticism on the CIA has generally been portrayed as a blow to morale. In the long term, however, that effect was minor. The more serious damage was to diminish enthusiasm within the agency for taking risks. The vast majority of intelligence professionals was unaware of the reported transgressions when they were occurring. In response to public criticism, these officials began avoiding activities that might expose the agency to further censure. Officers in the field feared punishment if they accepted risks and failed, or if they undertook what might later be judged the wrong risks. Because of a conscientious desire to protect the CIA, intelligence officers often chose the safe course. The CIA as a whole retrenched its activities lest it do anything that would bring on more criticism.

Fortunately, by late 1978 the media's eagerness to criticize the CIA began to diminish. At the same time, the public attitude toward national defense and intelligence was becoming more supportive. For the moment the nightmare of the mid-1970s seems over. The new concern, however, is whether the Reagan administration, by loosening controls on intrusions into the lives of Americans, risks damaging the public confidence that the intelligence community has earned over the past few years.

Leaks of security information were the second cause of damage during the 1970s.

These leaks have generated an impression that U.S. intelligence agencies cannot be trusted with sensitive information. Since Watergate and Vietnam, American society has virtually enshrined the so-called whistle blowers as heroes. Some of them may have done great service for their country. But others are simply self-serving individuals promoting their own special causes. Fortunately, while several leaks about actual espionage in the past six or seven years have involved serious breaches of security, very little information harmful to U.S. intelligence interests has been revealed. In short, the impression that intelligence agencies cannot keep secrets is highly exaggerated.

The problem of leaks has another dimension: the many books and pamphlets written by insiders in recent years. These authors include former CIA professionals who write about their past experiences and irresponsible individuals who deliberately disclose classified information. The writings of former professionals usually complain about perceived problems, past and present. The Supreme Court decision in the case of *Snepp v. United States* has put these people on notice that they must fulfill their contractual obligation to permit the CIA to review their manuscripts for legitimately classified information. Frank Snepp, the CIA's chief strategy analyst in Saigon from 1973 to 1975, published a book in 1978 entitled *Decent Interval* recounting the last years of U.S. involvement in the Vietnam war. The Court voted to deprive Snepp of the profits from his book about intelligence experiences not because he criticized the CIA but because he did not fulfill the contract he signed of his own volition to submit his manuscript for a security review prior to publication.

The CIA has a responsibility to protect classified information; therefore it must insist on controlling the dissemination of security information acquired while individuals are in its employ. Others who cannot be held to a contractual obligation, either because they are beyond the reach of U.S. law enforcement agencies or because they never worked in the CIA, still pose a problem. The most notable example is Philip Agee, who has published two books exposing CIA agents and activities.

The third cause of damage was a set of detailed procedures created in recent years to implement the provisions of executive orders. In some cases these established tighter controls than the order required. Overseas operations to detect the flow of narcotics to the United States, for example, were curtailed if intelligence officers had to invade the privacy of a known American smuggler. The new Reagan executive order revises these procedures and creates a better balance between the DCI and the attorney general by having them jointly set the rules and procedures for intelligence agencies. Although the attorney general plays a key role in controlling and regulating intelligence, it is unwise to give him final authority over operating procedures. Since the attorney general's office is not a principal user of foreign intelligence, it has an institutional inclination to tighten controls and to curtail intelligence activity rather than to let the CIA take risks.

A NEW CHARTER

Thus the United States has made substantial progress in removing the obstacles inhibiting intelligence capabilities in recent years. Three areas, however, still require attention. First, the public must continue to recognize the importance of good intelligence. Of course, the intelligence community has to merit public support by avoiding the mistakes of the past and by providing the anticipatory and objective reporting that the nation needs. The intelligence agencies can further help the public appreciate good intelligence by providing it with a greater understanding of their unclassified activities.

Second, the United States should enforce legislation to curb people like Agee who publish the names of U.S. intelligence agents. The bill passed by Congress in June 1982 making it a crime to identify covert agents represents a major step in the right direction. The media reflexively oppose any limits on what can be written or said; but this represents a parochial and unrealistic viewpoint. The new legislation can protect U.S. intelligence officers without jeopardizing the fundamental freedom of the press.

Third, Congress can prevent the pendulum from swinging too far in the direction of letting the CIA spy on Americans and relaxing executive and congressional oversight. Congress can insure continuing awareness of the value of controls and accountability by keeping its two intelligence committees alert and active. These committees must maintain a relationship with the intelligence agencies that is supportive but at the same time adversarial. Each committee, for example, might probe into one area of intelligence activity each year. The uncertainty about the subject of the next probe would reinforce the idea of accountability.

Congress can also decide whether the new rules on intrusions into American lives reflect the national consensus on the balance between good intelligence and the right of privacy. Since the problems must be discussed publicly and the American people must have a voice in the decision, Congress is better suited to resolve this issue than the president. There are, of course, some considerations that cannot

be discussed in public and some assessments that only those with a good understanding of the intelligence profession can make; these can be handled by the two congressional intelligence committees, whose members are well qualified to act as surrogates for the public.

The two committees should also work to codify the national consensus on intelligence into a basic charter for the intelligence community. The legal charter that was adopted in 1949 is now badly outdated; it does not describe the constitution or the operations of the intelligence community as it exists today. That is why U.S. intelligence activities are governed by executive orders that each administration can alter or discard. A congressional charter setting specific guidelines on how the government wants the CIA to operate should come first. Periodic changes in executive orders are inevitable. But a permanent charter can insulate the intelligence community from the seasonal vogues of domestic politics. Without a charter defining its mandate, the CIA cannot resist pressure from an administration to undertake potentially questionable activities.

During 1979-1980 the Senate Select Committee on Intelligence and the Carter administration worked assiduously to develop a charter satisfactory to both branches. There were numerous thorny issues such as whether to preclude the CIA's use of newsmen to collect intelligence. While we came close to agreeing on a reasonable charter, time ran out before we could resolve every difficult issue. A new attempt to devise a charter does risk opening another broad examination of intelligence. Yet the climate in the country and in Congress is quite different today. Prospects for a balanced judgment are considerably better than they were three years ago. And Congress could minimize the risks of reopening the charter issue by establishing in advance that the major issue to resolve is the degree of intrusion the public must accept. Instead of trying to construct a list of activities that the CIA would not be allowed to conduct, Congress should devise a set of positive guidelines on what the CIA should do and how it should act.

In taking on the difficult task of devising a new charter, Congress should understand the great danger the Reagan administration's new rules have created for U.S. intelligence capabilities. The United States cannot afford to ignore once again the inherent conflict between secrecy and democracy. A consistent and stable system of controls and oversight for intelligence is needed, for the sake of intelligence professionals who have been trying to do their jobs while never knowing exactly what they were authorized to do, and for the sake of the American people who discovered a few years ago that their blind trust in the intelligence community had been unwise. If the CIA ever again were to overstep its bounds and violate the rights of Americans and if another wave of intense public criticism were to follow, the agency could be mortally wounded.

Section II–C. INTEREST GROUPS AND PUBLIC OPINION IN FOREIGN POLICYMAKING

The final two participants in the foreign policy process are interest groups and public opinion. Both of these participants attempt to influence foreign policymaking, rather than directly control it as has been the case with the president, the Congress and the bureaucracy. Interest groups refer to segments of the population who are organized, have strongly held values and beliefs on political issues, and are unable to gain those values on their own.[1] Public opinion refers to the values and beliefs of the public at large on a variety of foreign policy issues and how it affects the decision process.

Foreign policy interest groups are varied and numerous. These interest groups, as with domestic American politics, are drawn from key segments within American society, such as large corporations (e.g., National Association of Manufacturers, U.S. Chamber of Commerce, Business Roundtable), labor unions (e.g., AFL-CIO and United Auto Workers), and farm organizations (e.g., American Farm Bureau Federation, the National Farmers Union, and the National Farm Organization). Increasingly, though, foreign policy interest groups have been drawn from other segments of society as well: religious organizations (e.g., National Council of Churches, American Friends Service Committee, National Conference of Catholic Bishops); veterans groups (e.g., American Legion, Veterans of Foreign Wars); ideological groups (e.g., Americans for Democratic Action, Heritage Foundation); ethnic groups (e.g., Greek, Irish, and Jewish lobbies); single-issue groups (e.g., the nuclear freeze movement); and foreign lobbies (e.g., South Africa, El Salvador, Saudi Arabia).[2]

While the number of these groups is increasing, their overall success in shaping policy is usually questioned for at least two reasons.[3] First, interest groups may have difficulty in gaining ready access to key foreign policy participants. Because the most important foreign policy crisis decisions are often made solely in the executive branch and because the executive branch is particularly difficult to lobby, the effectiveness of interest groups is immediately reduced. Second, countervailing interest groups may neutralize any lobbying effort on a specific issue. Increasingly as an interest group forms to lobby the Congress or the president on a foreign policy issue, another group might also develop to challenge that group. On the effort to ratify the SALT II treaty, for instance, groups quickly developed on both sides of that issue and worked to lobby the U.S. Senate. More recently, proponents and opponents of protectionist legislation have been actively engaged with the two key branches of government.

Despite these problems, however, at particular times and under particular conditions, interest groups do affect policy, and some are more successful than others. On issues that require congressional rather than just presidential action and on issues that involve budgetary and long-range policy direction, foreign policy interest groups can be effective. Similarly, economic and ethnic interest groups seem to have enjoyed more policy success than some of the other interest groups because of the resources—both material and human—that they can bring to any lobbying effort.[4] Economic groups have sufficient resources to engage in the direct lobbying of policymakers and the indirect lobbying of the public to support their position, while ethnic groups bring the strong commitment and zeal of their adherents to any lobbying effort.

The first two readings in this section focus on these two kinds of interest groups and assess their role in policymaking. The first reading, "Ethnic Groups and Foreign Policy," by Senator Charles McC. Mathias, Jr. (Rep., Md.), examines and evaluates the impact of ethnic interest groups on American foreign policy. The second reading, "The Petrodollar Connection," by Steven Emerson illustrates the lobbying efforts of several American corporations to influence the U.S. Senate to approve the sales of Airborne Warning and Control Systems (AWACS) aircraft to Saudi Arabia in 1981. Both essays illustrate the impact of these kinds of groups on U.S. foreign policy.

Senator Mathias begins his analysis by noting the difficulties in policymaking in which ethnic identities influence the policy positions that one supports. America, with its immigrant tradition, has been particularly susceptible to this problem. While ethnic identities among the American public regarding foreign policy have developed only gradually (although especially in the post-World War II period), this attachment for the land of their origin or that of their family has created at least two problems: an imbalance in the strength of some groups at the expense of others and, more importantly, "the loss of cohesion in our foreign policy." Too often the narrow interests of an ethnic group are misperceived as serving the national interest; foreign policy in that wider national interest becomes the casualty.

Senator Mathias supports this argument through several case examples of how those of Irish, East European, Greek, and Jewish heritage have tried to shape American policy. In particular, the Greek and Jewish lobbies have proved successful most recently. Yet, as he makes clear in his conclusion, this interest group success is not something he admires by noting that "ethnic politics . . . have proven harmful to the national interest." Interestingly, he argues that the president and the Congress must take steps to "strengthen our sense of common American purpose."

In early 1981, the Reagan administration informed Congress that it planned to conclude an $8.5 billion arms sales to Saudi Arabia.[5] The sale would include five AWACS planes, larger fuel tanks for its F-15 aircraft, new refueling tanker aircraft, and over 1,000 Sidewinder air-to-air missiles. Under the 1976 Arms Export Control Act of 1976, the Congress had the right of *disapproval* of any arms sale totaling more than $25 million. The House of Representatives overwhelmingly passed such a resolution of disapproval on October 14, 1981 by a vote of 301 to 111. On October 28, 1981, the Senate narrowly failed to pass this resolution by a vote of 52 to 48.

Emerson's analysis focuses on the concerted lobbying effort by various economic interest groups and Saudi Arabia to secure this Senate vote. What is important to note from his analysis is the large number of interest groups involved (ranging from oil-producing companies, airlines, health care firms, and banks to construction companies, farm groups, and defense contractors, among others), the variety of lobbying techniques both direct and indirect measures employed, and the use of professional lobbyists to represent a foreign government. Whether one wholly accepts Emerson's interpretation of the meaning of events in this instance is perhaps less important than to recognize the powerful potential role of foreign economic interest groups.

The last reading in this section focuses on public opinion and current U.S. foreign policy issues. While such opinion has not been successful in directing each and every policy decision that is taken by the political leadership, it can set the "mood," or the broad limits within which decision makers must act. Political leaders, moreover, are acutely aware of such public moods, and it does affect the actions that they take. Former Secretary of State Alexander Haig reports in his recent book, *Caveat,* that President Reagan's advisers "were intensely sensitive to the public mood and reluctant to take any action that might alter it in the President's disfavor."[6] Thus, by understanding the present public mood, the reader is once again able to appreciate the role of this participant in the foreign policy process.

In "American Opinion: Continuity, not Reaganism," John E. Rielly presents the results of the most recent comprehensive survey of American foreign policy beliefs. By taking the results as a whole, the public mood can be discerned. The survey results reported in this reading come from the third comprehensive analysis of foreign policy attitudes conducted by the Chicago Council on Foreign Relations. In 1974, 1978, and again in 1982, the Chicago Council commissioned the Gallup Organization to conduct a nationwide, random sample of public attitudes on foreign policy. Because of the continuity in this surveying, Rielly is able to make ready use of their earlier surveys to discern exactly how much the current public mood has stabilized and how much it has changed. In addition, since the Chicago Council on Foreign Relations also includes a "leadership sample" within its analysis, the similarities and differences between the public at large and this leadership sample are discussed.

Several key findings result from Rielly's analysis. First, there has been a remarkable continuity in the foreign policy attitudes of the public, despite the great differences in approach between the Carter and the Reagan administrations. Second, the public and their leaders are at odds on a number of key issues ranging from the role of the United States in foreign affairs to eliminating trade tariffs and restrictions to providing military and economic assistance to other nations. Third, although the public remains concerned with the Soviet Union, they strongly favor U.S. cooperation with that nation.

What has been the impact of the public mood summarized in this reading on the conduct of American foreign policy? How has it affected the Reagan administration's policy over the past few years? Once again the discerning readers should take the opportunity to compare this mood with the recent American foreign policy actions. By doing that, the impact of public opinion on U.S. policy will be more readily observed.

NOTES

1. For a definition of interest groups, see L. Harmon Ziegler and G. Wayne Peak, *Interest Groups in American Society*, 2d ed. (Englewood Cliffs, N.J.: Prentice-Hall, 1972), p. 3.
2. For an excellent discussion of interest groups, see Barry Hughes, *The Domestic Context of American Foreign Policy* (San Francisco: W. H. Freeman, 1978), pp. 157-71. Also see Thomas L. Brewer, *American Foreign Policy: A Contemporary Analysis* (Englewood Cliffs, N.J.: Prentice-Hall, 1980).
3. For these and other arguments, see Hughes, *The Domestic Context of American Foreign Policy*, pp. 198-202.
4. On the success of economic and ethnic groups, see Bernard Cohen, *The Public's Impact on Foreign Policy* (Boston: Little, Brown, 1973), p. 96. This judgment is drawn largely from interviews with executive branch officials.
5. On the AWACS sale, see *Congressional Quarterly Almanac 1981* (Washington, D.C.: Congressional Quarterly, Inc., 1982), pp. 129-40.
6. Alexander M. Haig, Jr., *Caveat: Realism, Reagan, and Foreign Policy* (New York: Macmillan, 1984), p. 130.

25. ETHNIC GROUPS AND FOREIGN POLICY

Charles McC. Mathias, Jr.

It is doubtful that there has ever been a democratic society—from Periclean Athens to modern America—that lived untroubled by conflict between the preferences and aspirations of groups within the society and the requirements of the general good. If the problem has been more constant and intense in the United States than in other democracies, it is because of the nature of American society—diverse and heterogeneous, a nation of nations, a melting pot in which the constituent groups never fully melted—and because of the American constitutional system with its separated power and numerous points of access thereto.

Whether ethnic diversity and its attendant foreign attachments have been, on the whole, a good or bad thing for the nation has been debated since the birth of the Republic. An obscure Frenchman who came to live in the new nation in the eighteenth century perceived among the "western pilgrims" who had come to America from all over Europe "one of the finest systems of population which has ever appeared." "Here individuals of all nations are melted into a new race of men," he wrote, "whose labors and posterity will one day cause great change in the world."[1] But a more famous Frenchman of the nineteenth century wrote in his classic study of American democracy that, although democratic liberties applied to the internal affairs of a nation as diverse as the United States bring "bless-

Source: *Foreign Affairs,* 59 (Summer, 1981), 975–98. Senator McC. Mathias' article is in Public Domain.

ings greater than the ills," this was assuredly not the case in the conduct of foreign relations. "Almost all the nations that have exercised a powerful influence on the world's destiny by conceiving, following up and carrying to completion great designs," Tocqueville wrote, "from the Romans down to the English, were controlled by an aristocracy. . . ."[2]

The case for ethnic political activities—or for the play of "factions," in the terminology of earlier times—is usually made in terms of the evils of suppressing free expression rather than any positive benefits accruing from the influence of the special interests. Lobbying, it is pointed out, is the exercise of the right of petition, sanctified in Anglo-American usage since the time of Magna Carta in 1215, and specifically named as one of the rights for which this nation was founded. In the Resolutions of the Stamp Act Congress in 1765 it was asserted that "it is the right of the British subject in these colonies to petition the King or either House of Parliament." The principle was reaffirmed by the First Continental Congress and in the Declaration of Independence—"our repeated petitions have been answered only by repeated injury"—and finally codified in the First Amendment to the Constitution, protecting the right of the people "peaceably to assemble, and to petition the Government for a redress of grievances."

The affirmation of a right, and of the dangers of suppressing it, does not, however, in itself assure that the right will be exercised responsibly and for the general good. Without challenging the right of petition, Presidents and political thinkers since the Founding Fathers have warned against the evils of the politics of factions, especially in the conduct of foreign relations. In *The Federalist,* Paper Number 10, Madison warned against the dangers of "faction," defined as a combination of citizens "who are united and actuated by some common impulse of passion, or of interest, adverse to the rights of other citizens, or to the permanent and aggregate interests of the community." Madison argued that redress against those who would practice such "vicious arts" would come from representative government itself, which would "refine and enlarge the public views, by passing them through the medium of a chosen body of citizens, whose wisdom may best discern the true interest of their country, and whose patriotism and love of justice, will be least likely to sacrifice it to temporary or partial considerations."

Whereas Madison took hope in the rationality and public-spiritedness of representative majorities, Washington in the Farewell Address stressed the power of artful minorities to do mischief. At a time when rival factions within the new nation were pulling, one toward England, the other toward France, Washington warned against the twin evils of excessive animosity and excessive attachment to particular foreign nations, especially the latter, "facilitating the illusion of an imaginary common interest, in cases where no real common interest exists. ...."

By the beginning of the twentieth century, the nation had been transformed from a vulnerable fledgling to a world power and, in the wake of the great immigration, from a predominantly Anglo-Saxon society to a potpourri of diverse, only partially absorbed ethnic groups and cultures. Under these altered conditions Presidents from Wilson to Carter have confronted the dilemma (as will Reagan too, no doubt, soon enough) of citizens who couple loyalty to America with bonds of affection for one foreign country or another.

President Wilson in 1914 proposed as an "infallible test" for the hyphenated American that, although he might retain "ancient affections," "when he votes or when he acts or when he fights his heart and thought are centered nowhere but in the emotions and the purposes and the policies of the United States."[3] President Carter, still fresh from the buffetings of office, and concerned apparently with domestic no less than foreign policy pressure groups, stated the problem bluntly in his farewell address: "We are increasingly drawn to single-issue groups and special interest organizations to ensure that whatever else happens, our own personal views and our own private interests are protected. This is a disturbing factor in American political life."[4]

Lest these pages be read as criticism of our country's ethnic groups, the distinction must be drawn between ethnicity, which enriches American life and culture, and organized ethnic interest groups, which sometimes press causes that derogate from the national interest. From the earliest migrations of West Europeans to the later arrivals from Eastern Europe and Asia, from emancipated blacks to recently arrived Hispanics, from famine-driven Irish to refugees from Hitler's tyranny, America has been repeatedly strengthened and enriched by the infusion of new talents and energies. The tired and poor, the homeless and tempest-tossed, the "wretched refuse" who pass through the "golden door," became within a generation or two, and sometimes less, the scientists and entrepreneurs, the farmers and the skilled laborers, the artists and writers who have made America the model and envy in so many respects of the whole world. It was hardly rhetorical excess when President Wilson said: "We have brought out of the stocks of all the world all the best impulses and have appropriated them and Americanized them and translated them into the glory and majesty of a great country."[5]

No less critical than the distinction between ethnicity and ethnic interest groups is that between foreign and American-based ethnic lobbies in the field of foreign policy. Although a good deal of attention and publicity are periodically attracted by the activities of foreign lobbyists or agents, a close examination of their activities shows that those lacking strong indigenous support acquire only limited or transient influence on American foreign policy. Influence-peddling by South Korea under the reported direction of Tongsun Park gave rise to extensive investigations in both the House and the Senate in 1978, which exposed important breaches of law and ethics, but whatever improper influence the "Koreagate" scandal involved, the South Korean government, for all its exertions, was unable to effect major changes in American policy or to acquire a solid base of influence within the Congress.

To state the matter bluntly: foreign bribes and gifts may suborn individual legislators and win specific favors, but they are no substitute for indigenous interest groups capable of aiding or threatening a member's reelection. Similarly (although the issue involved no known illegalities) the once formidable "China lobby," now a Taiwan lobby, failed to mount an effective campaign against the Carter Administration's decision in late 1978 to transfer American recognition from the Republic of China on Taiwan to the People's Republic of China. The efforts of American conservative groups (who complained of Taiwanese acquiescence in the change) were ineffective, although they might have have been highly effective if these groups had won the united support of an aroused Chinese-American community.

Other foreign lobbies whose influence, although well publicized, has in fact been limited and transient, have been those of the white minority states of southern Africa. Although the 1971 Byrd Amendment permitting the import of Rhodesian chrome remained on the books for some years, supporters of Rhodesia and South Africa within the United States have been unable to reverse the long-term direction of American policy toward black majority rule in Zimbabwe and Namibia. The dominant influences upon our African policy, I believe, have been the American tradition of support for the self-determination of peoples, along with a commitment to racial justice that is in large part an expression of respect and responsiveness toward our own black population.

As a general proposition it can be said that foreign lobbies that lack significant domestic support exert only limited influence on American foreign policy—more limited perhaps than is generally recognized. Further, those who command such support but then lose it—like the old China lobby—soon run out of steam. Nor are resources, however ample, a substitute for a domestic base. The Arabs are unequal competitors with an aid-dependent Israel for influence on American policy, not for lack of resources but for lack of an Arab-American community comparable in size, unity or motivation to the Jewish community of the United States. The real powerhouses of foreign influence are homegrown.

None of the ethnic groups that have wielded significant influence on American foreign policy acquired political clout on the day its members disembarked, even when they disembarked in considerable numbers. They had first to make the unpleasant discovery that the streets of the fabled land were not, as reported, paved with gold; and then, in the course of a generation or so, to learn the ropes and make their way, to become acculturated if not assimilated to American attitudes and practices. This most of the new arrivals did rapidly and well, first forming themselves into voting blocs to be cultivated by those in the existing power structures, then joining the power structure themselves. One ethnic group after another became assimilated into the American political mainstream, the difference between the later and the earlier immigrants being that, unlike the West Europeans who came in the earlier period and by and large became submerged in the larger American culture, the South and East Europeans who came later retained and often strengthened their ethnic identity while becoming Americans in all other respects, including political attitudes and practices. As the self-aware ethnics acquired knowhow and influence and power as Americans, they found they could not only make their way in the new land but that they could bring influence to bear on their countries of origin as well, and on American policies toward those countries.

So far had the process advanced by the mid-1970s—with Jews and Greeks exercising well-proven clout, blacks bringing increasing influence to bear on American policy toward Africa, and Hispanics (including many illegals) looming as the next prospective major ethnic political force— that by 1975 it could be plausibly argued, as it was by Nathan Glazer and Daniel P. Moynihan, that the immigration process could be considered "the single most important determinant of American foreign policy." Foreign policy, they wrote, "responds to other things as well, but probably first of all to the primal facts of ethnicity."[6] A leading journalist, less sanguine about the consequences of ethnic politics, wrote in 1979 of "pluralism gone mad,"[7] bringing to mind Ambrose Bierce's definition of politics as "a strife of interests masquerading as a contest of principles."

One of the ironies of American ethnic politics is that, just as immigrant groups acquire power and influence only in the new land, it was here too that many acquired an affection for and awareness of the old country that they probably had not felt when they lived there. Most, after all, came to the United States because they did not like their lives in the countries where they were born. If life had been idyllic at home, they would, presumably, have stayed there. Most of the later immigrants—the great waves of the late nineteenth and early twentieth centuries—came to America because they were poor or oppressed or both. Many too, when they arrived, were unskilled and lacking in education—the strata of societies least likely to be politically aware and active. As the saying went, dukes did not emigrate.

A number of factors fostered ethnic self-awareness in the new land. One was freedom—the opportunity to practice customs and religions and even speak languages that had been restricted or suppressed in the immigrants' homelands. Another was disappointment— the poverty of crowded urban ghettos, exploitation by employers and politicians, the prejudice of natives and the hostility of rival immigrant groups, the difficulties and dangers of life in the "mean streets." Thus beset, the immigrant ethnics sought security and solace in their special neighborhoods—"little Italies," "little Polands," Jewish "ghettos" and "Chinatowns." In these enclaves national consciousness was awakened and myths about native villages were born, if not as lost Edens then as safe and serene havens compared to the strange, vast, confusing, and in many respects inhospitable surroundings of America.[8]

Seeking votes and power among the strategically concentrated immigrant groups, politicians and party organizations played to and encouraged the ethnic consciousness of the bewildered newcomers and competed to prove their sympathy for it. Thus began the dubious political tradition, which still flourishes, of political appeals to separatism and parochialism, to the frequent neglect of the common aims and interests of all Americans. To a degree and in many ways that belie the cherished philosophy of the "melting pot," ethnic differences have survived and even intensified despite the radically altered conditions of life for the second and third generations of immigrants. The differences have survived in part—perhaps in large part—because politicians have encouraged them. The style, of course, has changed, as have the issues, since the days when the immigrant vote was solicited and sometimes paid for by big city bosses. The machines are mostly gone now and the ethnic groups have spread out and prospered, providing much of their political leadership. The basic appeal to ethnicity, however, has not changed, and the diversity that enriches our domestic life remains a recurrent cause of difficulties in our foreign relations.

There are two basic problems, the lesser being the imbalance between competing groups so that some exert disproportion-

ate influence at the expense of those who are weaker in numbers, unity and resources. The greater problem is the loss of cohesion in our foreign policy and the derogation from the national interest when, as Washington and Madison feared, factions among us lead the nation toward excessive foreign attachments or animosities. Even if the groups were balanced— if Turkish-Americans equaled Greek-Americans or Arab-Americans equaled Jewish-Americans—the result would not necessarily be a sound, cohesive foreign policy because the national interest is not simply the sum of our special interests and attachments. It is not, to be sure, wholly separate from these, nor can the national interest be antithetical to the strong preferences of large segments of the population, but the overall requirements of the United States—strategic, economic, political and moral—constitute a whole larger than the sum of its parts. Ethnic preferences figure in that whole but cannot be permitted to preempt it.

As long as the United States remained largely isolated from the conflicts of Europe, ethnic pressures had limited foreign policy impact. Even when Mayor "Big Bill" Thompson of Chicago, seeking Irish support, threatened in 1918 "to make the King of England keep his snoot out of America," the external consequences were minimal. After World War I, however, and to a far greater extent after World War II, when the United States acquired world responsibility, ethnic politics took on a new significance. It mattered little in world affairs, for example, when Senators heaped denunciation on the Tsar of Russia for his brutal suppression of the Hungarian revolution in 1849. It was a more consequential matter when Congress, under pressure from East European nationality groups, in July 1959 unanimously adopted a resolution calling on the President to proclaim an annual "Captive Nations Week." By that time ethnic foreign policy pressures had become, in Walter Lippmann's phrase, a "morbid experience."[9]

The oldest and most redoubtable of American ethnic interest groups are the Irish, who are credited with major historical exertions, and no little success prior to World War II, in setting the United States at odds with Great Britain. Irish-American as well as German-American opinion strongly resisted and probably delayed American intervention in both world wars.

Speaking of Britain's Irish policy, President Wilson told an adviser before World War I that, "there can never be a real comradeship between America and England until this issue is definitely settled and out of the way."[10] Pressed by Congress and by Irish-American groups to secure Irish home rule at the Paris Peace Conference, Wilson finally lost patience when an Irish-American delegation, for which he had secured permission to visit Ireland, traveled about making incendiary speeches and denouncing British "atrocities." "I don't know how long I shall be able to resist telling them what I think of their miserable mischiefmaking," Wilson complained. "They can see nothing except their own small interest."[11]

In 1940 President Roosevelt referred privately to "wild Irish" isolationist opposition to his policies.[12]

In more recent times the status of Northern Ireland has continued to stir ethnic repercussions in the United States, and although no royal "snoots" have been menaced, the issue still generates some tension between the transatlantic allies. Since British troops entered Northern Ireland in 1969 to suppress violence, recurrent incidents and the failure of the British to find a solution for the Protestant-Catholic conflict in Ulster have aroused the concern and indignation of Irish-Americans, including such highly placed Irish-Americans as the Speaker of the House of Representatives, the Governor of New York and the senior Senators from New York and Massachusetts.

Proposals by American officeholders to mediate the Ulster dispute, or to suspend arms sales to the police in Northern Ireland, along with warnings of an end to American patience, have been less than warmly received in London. The British were distinctly unenthusiastic about the joint appeal of the "Four Horsemen," Senators Kennedy and Moynihan, Speaker O'Neill and Governor Carey, in 1979 for a united Ireland, all the more as the appeal also charged the British government with "negligence" and "acquiescence" in the face of "gross violations of human rights." Noting that the four American leaders had repeatedly warned Irish-Americans against financing violence in Ulster by contributing to the illegal Provisional Irish Republican Army, *The Economist* of London declined to join in charges of meddling, observing that "the leaders have been consistently intelligent and cautious in their suggestions."[13]

Considerably less cautious have been the activities of a lobbying group known as the Irish National Caucus, which both the Irish and British governments have accused of aiding the Provisional IRA, and of the Ad Hoc Committee for Irish Affairs consisting, during the 96th Congress, of over 130 members of Congress. The Ad Hoc Committee has periodically pressed for congressional hearings on Northern Ireland and has also tried to play a peacemaking role, but in fact has had less impact than the size of its membership would suggest, partly because of lack of support from the "Four Horsemen," and also because of the opposition of the Irish government. Speaker O'Neill has steadfastly opposed congressional hearings lest they serve as a propaganda forum for the IRA. The then Irish Prime Minister, Jack Lynch, appealed to members of Congress not to join the Ad Hoc Committee and accused the Irish National Caucus of having been "closely associated with violence in Northern Ireland."

Among the American Irish, as among other ethnic groups, nationalism sometimes runs higher and stronger than in the home country. The Dublin government pursues a careful, conciliatory policy toward Northern Ireland and the British government, and deplores the violence of the Provisional IRA. When the Ancient Order of Hibernians, a major Irish-American organization, went to Ireland for its annual meeting in 1978, it was less than eagerly received by the Irish government and responded in kind. An unnamed Irish official said, "If they want to solve the Northern Ireland problem, let them come over here and let them live here."[14]

The moderation and statesmanship of the Irish government, strongly reinforced by leading Irish-American political leaders, have effectively curbed extremist impulses within some of the Irish-American organizations. Whatever international complications may have been generated by Irish-American political activities in the past, it cannot be said that the Irish lobby today represents a disruptive influence on American foreign policy or a threat to the national interest. Among other reasons for this salutary state of affairs, the restraint and responsibility of Irish-American political leaders, who could probably exploit the issue to their advantage if they chose, is critical, and also exemplary.

When Congress, on July 17, 1959, unanimously adopted the resolution calling for a "Captive Nations Week," it is doubtful that many members considered themselves to have made a major foreign policy enactment. The resolution was "churned out," according to a syndicated columnist of the day, "along with other casual holiday proclamations, such as National Hot Dog Month."[15] To members of Congress the resolution (which President Eisenhower promptly implemented) was a more or less routine response to the wishes of Americans whose countries of origin had fallen under Soviet domination. It had been strongly promoted by such groups as the Assembly of Captive European Nations, which had been formed in 1954 to work for the freedom and independence of the nations of Eastern and Central Europe, and was adopted by Congress verbatim from a draft submitted by Professor Lev Dobriansky of Georgetown University, a zealous advocate of East European causes who became well known in the corridors and committees of Congress. Thereafter, each year, Representatives and Senators have been reminded of the annual observance so they could place appropriate statements in the *Congressional Record.*

The Soviet government, noting that the "captive nations" listed in the 1959 resolution included not only the officially independent communist states of Eastern Europe but also integral units of the Soviet Union such as the Ukraine, Armenia, Georgia and Byelorussia, took the resolution somewhat more seriously, despite the milder tone of President Eisenhower's proclamation, his tactful exclusion of a list of "captives," and the omission of any promise to take action to secure their liberation. As it happened, during the first annual observance of Captive Nations Week in July 1959, then-Vice President Nixon was on a visit to the Soviet Union, and exchanges of visits between President Eisenhower and Premier Khrushchev were about to be announced. Premier—or at that time First Secretary—Khrushchev took the occasion to express strong displeasure with what he read as blatant interference in the internal affairs of the Soviet Union. Nixon felt obliged to explain and, in effect, apologize for Congress' actions, telling Khrushchev that "actions of this type cannot, as far as their timing is concerned, be controlled even by the President, because when Congress moves, that is its prerogative. Neither the President nor I would have deliberately chosen to have a resolution of this type passed just before we were to visit the U.S.S.R."[16]

Congress, of course, had not "moved" in the sense of having taken an autonomous policy initiative based on debate and deliberation. Congress had, in fact *been* moved by interest groups whose goal, although desirable, was practically unattainable. The Eisenhower Administration had already been compelled by practical circumstances to abandon early, facile statements about "liberating" Eastern Europe from Soviet domination. The inability of the West to challenge the Soviet Union on its borders without incurring unacceptable risks had been convincingly demonstrated by the events in Poland and especially Hungary in 1956. By implicitly threatening the Soviet Union with action that the Soviet leaders must have felt reasonably certain, though perhaps not absolutely certain, the United States would not take, Congress created an unnecessary element of tension with the other superpower, while at the same time casting doubt on its own right to be taken seriously in the foreign policy arena. By encouraging on the part of the suppressed populations of Poland, Hungary, Czechoslovakia and other East European countries hopes that almost certainly

could not be realized, Congress, for no better purpose than to appease an insistent domestic pressure group, acted in a capricious manner that could only lead to bitterness, if it did not actually incite the taking of dangerous risks, on the part of people who had looked to America with confidence and hope.

If achievement of stated goals is the measure of a lobby's success, the East European lobby must be accounted generally unsuccessful. The stated goal of such groups as the Assembly of Captive European Nations—freedom and full independence for the peoples of Eastern Europe—is no closer to attainment in 1981 than it was when ACEN was founded in 1954. The failure to achieve the ultimate objective does not, however, demonstrate either incompetence or ineffectiveness on the part of the East European ethnic lobby. Liberation has not been achieved for the simple, compelling reason that it cannot be achieved without incurring the risk of World War III. East European ethnic groups have been successful at times in achieving limited, discrete objectives, such as the delay in the early 1960s in extending most-favored-nation trade treatment to Yugoslavia, the organizing of import boycotts of East European products such as Polish hams, and cancellation of a sizable manufacturing contract in 1964 between the Firestone Rubber Company and the government of Romania. The three examples cited were not random in their effect; collectively, along with other lobbying initiatives, they effectively obstructed President Johnson's policy of "building bridges" to Eastern Europe.

Over the years, as one or another East European nation acquired a measure of autonomy from the Soviet Union, many Americans of ethnic descent from these countries have come to favor American trade, assistance and support for their countries of origin. Feelings of national affiliation came to outweigh dislike of the former homelands' communist governments as these governments acquired some freedom from Soviet control, and as it came to seem possible that the United States could bolster that freedom. There are no apparent pressures upon Congress now—none at least of which I am aware—to thwart possible American efforts to bolster the current Polish government as long as it is attempting to accommodate the Polish workers' demands for greater freedom without provoking Soviet intervention. In the 1950s and 1960s East European ethnic pressures effectively slowed, if they did not thwart, moves toward more normal relations with the countries of Eastern Europe and toward détente with the Soviet Union. As it has become obvious that the original objective of the "captive nations" movement—liberation from communist rule as well as Soviet domination—was unattainable, an accommodation to reality has been made.

Captive Nations Week is still proclaimed in the third week of July every year, and Senators and Representatives, with varying degrees of conviction, still make the required statements. The majority, however, and apparently too the majority of Americans of East European origin, have accepted what seem to be the logical conclusions drawn from accumulated experience: that the United States cannot now or at any time in the foreseeable future bring freedom and self-determination to Eastern Europe; that efforts to do so will jeopardize the chances of limited improvements being achieved while incurring the risk of dangerous confrontation between the superpowers; that the United States, through judicious political and economic initiatives, can strengthen and thus contribute to better-

ing the lives of their people; and that what can be done, although short of our preferences, is nevertheless well worth doing.

Since the enunciation of the Truman Doctrine on March 12, 1947, the United States has exercised the primary responsibility, previously held by Great Britain, for the strategic support of Greece and Turkey as barriers to the expansion of Soviet influence in the Mediterranean. Together, the two countries, both members of NATO, tie down perhaps 26 Warsaw Pact divisions, although their effectiveness in NATO has been chronically impaired by their quarrel over Cyprus. Turkey, in addition to maintaining an army of half a million, larger than that of any European member of NATO, has made available to the United States military installations from which critical intelligence is obtained regarding Soviet air and naval activities and missiles and weapons tests. By any tangible measure Turkey makes a substantial contribution to the Western alliance and to the national interest of the United States. When they are both active members of NATO, Greece and Turkey contribute substantially to each other's security because, as a Greek Defense Minister once told me, the value of Greece and Turkey acting together is much greater for the alliance than either or both acting separately. Accordingly, the signing in March 1980 of a five-year defense cooperation agreement between Turkey and the United States, after a period of sorely strained relations owing to the arms embargo imposed on Turkey by Congress following its military intervention in Cyprus in 1974, signaled a significant strategic gain for the Western alliance. The reintegration of Greece in October 1980 into the NATO command structure, from which Greece had withdrawn during the crisis of 1974, further strengthened NATO's southern flank, but it is by no means clear that the damage to relations between the United States and its two partners has been or will be completely repaired.

The historic conflict between Greece and Turkey, which erupted once again in 1974 with the Greek-engineered coup in Cyprus and the Turkish military intervention, quickly spilled over into the internal politics of the United States. Whereas the Turks heavily outweighed the Greeks in their own region, the Greeks, with a powerful ethnic lobby mobilized for their cause, held the upper hand in Washington. Armed with the fact that the Turks, in violation of the Foreign Military Sales Act, had used American arms in their invasion of Cyprus, the Greek-American organizations, spearheaded by the newly formed and largely foreign-supported American Hellenic Institute (AHI), worked assiduously and successfully to bring about the congressional vote for the arms embargo, which went into effect on February 5, 1975.

Greek-Americans were supported in their lobbying efforts by Americans of Armenian descent. The lobbying groups continued their campaign thereafter to prevent repeal of the embargo, bombarding Senators and Representatives with letters, telegrams, phone calls, personal visits, and even, in some cases, gifts of wine and cheese. A Senate vote in May 1975 to repeal the arms ban aroused the lobby to renewed efforts in the House of Representatives. In the week preceding the vote in the House, Greek-American rallies were held on the Capitol steps and Representatives were flooded with appeals and messages. On July 24, by a vote of 223 to 206, the House voted to uphold the embargo. One member of the House, on whom heavy constituent pressure had been applied, was quoted as saying, "Maybe I wouldn't have lost my seat over this, but who wants the hassle?"[17]

Failure to repeal the embargo prompted Turkey on the day following the House vote to close 26 U.S. bases and listening posts on its territory. In the domestic arena, however, 45,000 Americans of Turkish origin, most of them recent arrivals and not yet politically acculturated, were heavily outgunned by organizations claiming the support of three million Greek-Americans. The Turks had one domestic windfall: efforts by the Greek lobby to form, or at least create the appearance of, an alliance with the influential Israeli lobby failed. Israel, on the contrary, fearing the consequences to itself of the loss of U.S. listening posts in Turkey, which had proven valuable to Israel during the 1973 Arab-Israeli War, signaled its supporters to that effect, whereupon the leading Jewish organizations lent quiet but effective support to the Ford Administration's continuing efforts to secure repeal or modification of the embargo. Intensive efforts by President Ford and Secretary of State Kissinger culminated in congressional approval in October 1975 of a partial lifting of the arms embargo against Turkey.

Further relaxation of the embargo occurred over the next two years, but Congress did not finally repeal it until the summer of 1978. In the meantime relations between the United States and Turkey remained strained, and although the Turks gave no indication of wishing to withdraw from the Western alliance, they showed increasing interest in expanding their economic ties with the Soviet Union. Upon returning from Moscow in June 1978, Prime Minister Bulent Ecevit commented that "the embargo certainly affects our thinking in many ways and encourages us to be more imaginative regarding solutions to our economic problems and to our defense problems."[18]

The Senate and House debates of the

summer of 1978 were accompanied by intensive lobbying campaigns. President Carter in a news conference on June 14, 1978, said that lifting the embargo was "the most immediate and urgent foreign policy decision" before Congress. A leading supporter of repeal, Representative Paul Findley of Illinois, was quoted at the time as saying that the President was going to have to do a lot more than "make a few phone calls and have some Congressmen over to the White House for breakfast," because "the opposition is dedicated and strong, and it's been gearing up for this fight for a long time."

Opponents of repeal, including respected and influential leaders in both the Senate and the House, argued that they were prepared to have the embargo lifted as soon as Turkey began seriously negotiating a settlement on Cyprus. The Carter Administration and supporters of repeal in Congress pointed out that the embargo, after three and a half years, had failed to spur a large-scale withdrawal of Turkish forces from Cyprus or bring the Turks to the negotiating table, while having the undesired effects of alienating Turkey from the United States, impairing its armed forces, denying the United States intelligence on missile tests and troop movements in the Soviet Union, and thus seriously weakening the southeastern flank of NATO. In my own Senate speech in support of repeal I stressed that the action was needed to uphold NATO and was in no way anti-Greek; I cited the strategic arguments for repeal made by five former supreme allied commanders of NATO; I recommended that the Senate's decision "be based on a perception of American as well as of Greek or Turkish interests"; and I quoted Plato: "There can be no affinity nearer than our country."[19]

Although the Senate, overwhelmingly, and the House, by a narrow margin, voted to lift the embargo, the issue did not end in the summer of 1978. The following year, abetted by pro-Greek lobbyists, a protracted argument between the Senate and the House over a small item—whether $50 million in military assistance to Turkey was to be a grant or a loan—demonstrated to Turkey, in the words of a Library of Congress study, that "the arms embargo has not ended psychologically, even if it has legislatively."[20]

The ethnic Greek lobby, which demonstrated its considerable clout in helping bring about and then defending the Turkish arms embargo, has sometimes been compared with the potent Israeli lobby. There are only about three million Greek-Americans, compared to six million Jewish-Americans, but, like the Jews, the Greeks are concentrated in a relatively few urban states where they represent sizable and important voting blocs. In addition, like the American Jewish community, the Greek community in the United States is generally well organized, internally cohesive and motivated, well represented in business and the professions, and politically active in both political parties. The Greeks too, like the Jews, have had a real grievance: the Turks *did* violate the conditions of American military aid, and, in violation of both equity and international law, have maintained a tight military grip on nearly half of the island of Cyprus since 1974. The point should not be overlooked: for all the technique involved, and despite frequently exaggerated claims and arguments, neither Greek nor Jewish lobbies would command the support they do in Congress and with the American people if their case did not have substantial merit.

This, however, is about as far as the similarity between the two communities and their respective lobbies goes. By any objective measure of power and influence, the Greeks are "Number Two," and a fairly distant second at that.

"Fear undoubtedly is the greatest single factor accounting for Jews' high level of political activity," Steven D. Isaacs wrote in his book, *Jews and American Politics.*[21] The fear, Isaacs writes, antedates the Nazi Holocaust, going back to the Jew-baiting, discrimination and pogroms of Eastern Europe in the nineteenth and early twentieth centuries, from which over two million Jews, mostly penniless but with compelling motivation, sought and found refuge in America. Between 1880 and 1924 an estimated two and a half million Jews, representing one-third of East European Jewry, came to the United States, and like other East European immigrants, they came not as individuals but as a society, united in the experience of oppression, united and isolated too in confrontation with the gentler but still unfriendly gentile society surrounding them in the new land.

"The fear," writes Isaacs, "is pandemic among Jews and, whether that fear is at the surface of those Jews who involved themselves in politics, or buried deep within them, it *is* there and is the prevailing motive for a great part of their activity."[22] Carrying the analysis further to account for the extraordinary phenomenon of Jewish generosity in both charity and politics, Isaacs suggests that Jews are "paying to put in power the kind of men who will neither confiscate Jews' assets, wall them into ghettos, nor annihilate them." Or as New York's distinguished former Senator Jacob K. Javits summarized the Jewish ethic, "Give me a just society and I'll give you everything else."[23]

Jews have not always been active in American politics. Before World War II many American Jews hesitated to awaken the "sleeping giant" of anti-Semitism, but the growing acceptance and rising self-confidence of Jews during the Roosevelt era encouraged an increasingly active role. What galvanized Jewish political energies, however, were the Nazi Holocaust as its enormity became known, and above all, the birth and subsequent tribulations of an embattled, imperiled State of Israel. Determined that never again would the Jewish people be subjected to such unspeakable horrors as the genocide of World War II, the postwar generation of American Jews, by now familiar with the workings of the system, and with the sympathy and support of non-Jewish Americans, mobilized political, economic and intellectual resources to ensure the survival of the Jewish state.

President Truman, who is revered in Israel for his contributions to the creation of the Jewish state, was by no means committed to the Zionist cause when he became President in 1945. He was impressed by arguments made by the State and Defense Departments and by his military advisers that a pro-Zionist policy would militate against the national interest by alienating the Arabs in a period of mounting cold war with the Soviet Union. Dean Acheson, who served as Under Secretary and later as Secretary of State in the Truman Administration, opposed the creation of a Jewish state. Of those who had urged a pro-Zionist policy on the President, Acheson later wrote, "They had allowed, so I thought, their emotion to obscure the totality of American interests."[24] General Marshall, Secretary of State at the time of Israel's independence, urged that decisions on Palestine not be based on domestic politics.

Truman, however, came down repeatedly on the side of political advisers who warned of the risk of alienating Jewish voters. He first officially endorsed the creation of a Jewish state in Palestine on

October 4, 1946, the day of Yom Kippur, and one month before the congressional election. Over the next year and a half, pressures for further commitments mounted, to the President's considerable annoyance. "As the pressure mounted," Truman wrote in his memoirs, "I found it necessary to give instructions, that I did not want to be approached by any more spokesmen for the extreme Zionist cause."[25] For a time, in early 1948, Truman refused to receive Dr. Chaim Weizmann, who was to be Israel's first President, but he relented when his former business partner, Eddie Jacobson of Kansas City, at the request of American Jewish leaders, appealed to the President personally.[26] In the spring of 1948 Truman was warned repeatedly of the political risks of delay in recognizing the State of Israel. On May 12, 1948, for example, Jacob Arvey, the Democratic leader in Chicago, wrote Truman, "I fear very much that the Republicans are planning to exploit the present situation to their further advantage. This ought not to be permitted."[27] At a White House conference on Palestine on the same day Clark Clifford, then Special Counsel to the President, argued, against the State Department, the electoral advantages of prompt recognition. The State of Israel was proclaimed at 6 P.M., Washington time, on May 14, 1948. At 6:11 P.M. the White House announced the United States' recognition of the new state.

The decision-making as well as the decisions of the Truman Administration leading to the recognition of Israel stand as a paradigm of Middle East policymaking over the three decades following. With the exception of the Eisenhower Administration, which virtually compelled Israel's withdrawal from Sinai after the 1956 war, American Presidents, and to an even greater degree Senators and Representa-

tives, have been subjected to recurrent pressures from what has come to be known as the Israel lobby. For the most part they have been responsive, and for reasons not always related either to personal conviction or careful reflection on the national interest. When, for example, the American Israel Public Affairs Committee (AIPAC) mounted its 1975 campaign to negate the effect of a Ford-Kissinger "reassessment" of policy toward Israel, initiated following the breakdown of Sinai disengagement talks in March, it chose as its medium a letter from Senators strongly endorsing aid to Israel. Seventy-six of us promptly affixed our signatures although no hearings had been held, no debate conducted, nor had the Administration been invited to present its views. One Senator was reported to have candidly expressed a feeling that in fact was widespread: "The pressure was just too great. I caved." Another was reported to have commented, "It's easier to sign one letter than answer five thousand."[28]

The "letter of seventy-six" was perhaps the most spectacular, but not necessarily the most important of the operating successes of AIPAC, the group that works most directly for Israeli interests in Congress. More important, in the long run, had been the success of the Jewish organizations in maintaining solid congressional support for a high level of military and economic aid to Israel. This is not to suggest that Congress supports Israel for no better reason than fear of the Israel lobby; on the contrary, I know of few members of either house of Congress who do not believe deeply and strongly that support of Israel is both a moral duty and a national interest of the United States. It is rather to suggest that, as a result of the activities of the lobby, congressional conviction has been measurably reinforced by the knowledge that political sanctions will be applied to any who fail to deliver. When an issue of importance to Israel comes before Congress, AIPAC promptly and unfailingly provides all members with data and documentation, supplemented, as circumstances dictate, with telephone calls and personal visits. Beyond that, signs of hesitation or opposition on the part of a Senator or a Representative can usually be relied on to call forth large numbers of letters and telegrams, or visits and phone calls from influential constituents.

To a lesser degree lobbying has been generated as well in recent years from the relatively small Arab-American community. Before World War II only about a quarter of a million Arabs had come to the United States as immigrants, most of them Christians from Lebanon and Syria. A sizable number of Palestinian refugees and other Arabs—including professionals, technicians and students—found their way to the United States in the years after the 1948 war, and there are now two million Americans of Arab origin. Neither the old nor the new immigrants formed a cohesive ethnic political force until after the 1967 War, which awakened Arab-Americans to a sense of their origins and of their bonds with the Arab world. The National Association of Arab-Americans (NAAA) was founded in 1972 by prominent professional people of Arab descent "to protest and to register their disagreements with American policies of unquestioning support to Israel and total disregard for the security of Arab states in the Middle East."

Both lobbies, with heavy backing from their respective foreign counterparts, participated vigorously in the debate in the spring of 1978 over a Middle East arms sale package including the sale of 60 F-15 fighter planes to Saudi Arabia. While the Saudis relied primarily on professional lobbyists, including a public relations firm with whom they contracted for the express purpose of securing the F-15s, the Israelis relied on their own representatives and officials as well as on AIPAC and other American Jewish organizations to try to thwart the Saudi transaction. AIPAC, for example, in the candidly expressed hope of influencing votes on the arms sale, distributed to every member of Congress complimentary copies of the novel *Holocaust,* based on the widely viewed television series. On April 27, 1978, Israeli Foreign Minister Moshe Dayan met with members of the Senate Foreign Relations Committee at the Watergate Hotel to argue against the arms package. In hearings before the Senate Foreign Relations Committee, Morris J. Amitay of AIPAC warned of a "cycle of blackmail" if Saudi Arabia were permitted to buy warplanes as a "reward" for restraint on oil prices; John P. Richardson, speaking for NAAA, disavowed submission to oil or any other kind of blackmail but urged the Committee to "face up to the fact that interests included continuing access to the one community that makes this whole thing go."[29]

The Senate debate of May 15, 1978, on the Saudi arms sales was a fundamental one, ranging beyond military technicalities to embrace basic questions of the national interest and where it lay. In my own statement in support of the arms sale I noted that the planes had become symbols of the "American connection" on both sides, affirmed that the American commitment to Israel was "unique and unalterable," emphasized the importance of Middle East oil for ourselves and for our allies, and stated my belief that the range of American interests in the Middle East pointed to a relationship with Israel that was unique but not exclusive.[30]

I also made a point that seems even clearer today. I said:

The Soviet noose around the Middle East is tightening. This is no time for us to make mistakes. In this area the interests of Saudi Arabia and Israel coincide. Both are anti-Soviet. Both actively promote our interests, as well as their own by combating radicalism in the region. Both are good friends to the United States. And both need our support. [31]

The Senate approved the arms package by a vote of 54 to 44. Although it was interpreted at the time as a defeat for the Israel lobby, a more sober and objective interpretation is that the Senate withstood strong countervailing pressures to recognize the *variety* of American interests in the Middle East and the necessity of a policy aimed at *reconciling* these interests as distinguished from choosing one and sacrificing others. Something of the emotional, judgmental atmosphere surrounding the arms sale issue was evident in a letter to a Jewish newspaper in New York in which the writer, noting correctly that Senator Mathias had supported the arms package and cited oil as a necessary factor in the Senate's decision, commented: "Mr. Mathias values the importance of oil over the well-being of Jews and the State of Israel. The Jewish people cannot be fooled by such a person, no matter what he said because his act proved who he was."

One of the notable successes of lobbying by Jewish-Americans, the Jackson-Vanik Amendment of 1974, appears in retrospect to have been a Pyrrhic victory. A major effort by AIPAC, working in collaboration with Senate aides, had quickly secured over three-quarters of the Senate as sponsors of the amendment. The linkage of nondiscriminatory trade with freedom of emigration so angered the Soviets that, upon adoption of the trade act as amended, they canceled the 1972 Soviet-American trade agreement and stopped payment on World War II lend-lease debts. Jewish emigration, which had reached a peak of 35,000 in 1973, was reduced to 21,000 in 1974, the year Jackson-Vanik was adopted, 13,000 in 1975, 14,000 in 1976 and 17,000 in 1977. With a SALT II arms limitation agreement and expanded trade seemingly in prospect, Jewish emigration rose to 29,000 in 1978 and a record 51,000 in 1979, but then, with the December 1979 Soviet invasion of Afghanistan and the subsequent American grain embargo, fell to 21,000 in 1980.

The Jackson-Vanik Amendment not only failed of its own purpose but proved highly consequential as well for overall Soviet-American relations. The amendment put a lasting strain on the détente of the early 1970s, although it is unlikely that the congressional majorities who supported Jackson-Vanik had much thought for anything except an affirmation of the human rights of Russian Jews. The larger political consequence, whether in retrospect one welcomes or deplores it, was not intended at the time. In a meeting with Jewish leaders on June 15, 1975, Secretary of State Henry Kissinger said, "No country could allow its domestic regulations to be dictated as we were pushing the Soviets to do.... I think it was a serious mistake that the Jewish community got hung up on it."[32] Hyman Bookbinder, a respected and thoughtful leader of the American Jewish Committee, was quoted in 1975: "Logic told us we might lose the gamble, and it seems like we lost it. What we hoped we would get out of the Jackson Amendment did not come to pass."[33] A product of ethnic politics, the Jackson Amendment remains on the books, a failure on its own terms, an inadvertency in its larger consequences.

The "secret weapon" of ethnic interest groups is neither money nor technique, which are available to other interest groups as well, but the ability to galvanize for specific political objectives the strong emotional bonds of large numbers of Americans to their cultural or ancestral homes. As stated by a congressional aide with strong sympathies for Israel: "We don't do it for money the way some paid lobbyists do. We do it out of a very, very passionate commitment."[34]

The effects of these emotional bonds on American foreign policy are in some respects salutary. Ethnic groups awaken their fellow citizens to interests and injustices that might otherwise be overlooked or sacrificed to more tangible interests. But for the activities of Greek-Americans we might have overlooked, for larger strategic reasons, the injustices suffered by the Greek population of Cyprus. It is a plausible proposition too that, if it were not for the fact that over 20 million Americans are black, we would have been less active in efforts to secure racial justice in southern Africa. In the case of the Middle East there seems little doubt that, but for the efforts of American Jews, our military and economic aid to Israel would be less than it is, although I remain convinced that, even if there were no Israel lobby, the American people would remain solidly committed to Israel's survival.

Granting these benefits, ethnic politics, carried as they often have been to excess, have proven harmful to the national interest. Bearing out George Washington's warning, they have generated both unnecessary animosities and illusions of common interest where little or none exists. There are also baneful domestic effects: fueled as they are by passion and strong feelings about justice and rectitude, debates relating to the interplay of the national interest with the specific policies favored by organized ethnic groups generate fractious controversy and bitter recrimination. Public debate becomes charged with accusations of "betrayal" and "sellout," which is to say, of moral turpitude, when in truth the issues that divide us are, with few exceptions, questions of judgment and opinion about what is best for the nation. Ethnic advocacy represents neither a lack of patriotism nor a desire to place foreign interests ahead of American interests; more often it represents a sincere belief that the two coincide. Similarly, resistance to the pressures of a particular group in itself signals neither a sellout nor even a lack of sympathy with a foreign country or cause, but rather a sincere conviction about the national interest of the United States. There is a clear and pressing need for the reintroduction of civility into our public discussions of these matters.

Both the President and the Congress can help to reduce the fractiousness and strengthen our sense of common American purpose. The President, with his national constituency, is in a unique and powerful position not only to resist parochial pressures but to lead and educate the American people in matters of their common bonds and shared purposes. The Congress, although more vulnerable to group pressures, is not without resources to respond to them. Although Senators and Representatives do not usually have a national forum, they have ready access to their own constituents and there is nothing in the book of rules that prevents them from being leaders as well as followers of public opinion.

Sam Rayburn, longtime Speaker of the House, used to say that a legislator's first duty is to get reelected. It is a compelling but insufficient formula. An elected representative has other duties as well—to formulate and explain to the best of his or her ability the general interest, and to be prepared to accept the political consequences of having done so. In Edmund Burkes' famous formulation: "Your representative owes you, not his industry only but his judgment: and he betrays instead of serving you if he sacrifices it to your opinion."

As to the interest groups themselves, beyond the occasional tightening or reform of the lobbying and registration laws, it is difficult to conceive of any legally binding restraints upon them that would not be worse than their occasional excesses. As Madison noted, the only available methods for eliminating the "mischiefs of faction" are by destroying liberty, which is a cure far worse than the disease, or by giving everybody the same interests and opinions, which is altogether impracticable.[35] The desirable alternative is the encouragement on the part of ethnic groups of an entirely voluntary appreciation of what Irving Howe has called the "limits of ethnicity" and the "grandeur of the American idea." Ethnicity enriches our life and culture, and for that purpose should be valued and preserved; but the problems of the modern world and their solution have broken past the boundaries of ethnic group, race and nation. Howe summarizes: "The province, the ethnic nest, remains the point from which everything begins and without which, probably, it could not begin; but the province, the ethnic nest, is not enough, it must be transcended."[36]

NOTES

1. Michel-Guillaume-Jean de Crèvecoeur, "What Is an American?," Letter III of *Letters from an American Farmer* (1782).
2. Alexis de Tocqueville, *Democracy in America*, Vol. 1, Part II, Chapter 5.
3. *Public Papers of Woodrow Wilson, The New Democracy*, Vol. I (New York: Harper & Row, 1926), pp. 109-10.
4. National Television Address, January 14, 1981.
5. *Loc. cit.* footnote 3.
6. Nathan Glazer and Daniel P. Moynihan, *Ethnicity* (Cambridge, Mass.: Harvard University Press, 1975), pp. 23-24.
7. Meg Greenfield, *The Washington Post*, August 22, 1979.
8. See Louis L. Gerson, *The Hyphenate in Recent American Politics and Diplomacy* (Lawrence, Kan.: University of Kansas Press, 1964), especially pp. 3-10.
9. *Ibid.*, p. 19.
10. Joseph P. Tumulty, *Woodrow Wilson As I Know Him* (Garden City, N.Y.: Doubleday Publishing, 1921), pp. 394-95.
11. Seth Tillman, *Anglo-American Relations at the Paris Peace Conference of 1919* (Princeton, N.J.: Princeton University Press, 1961), p. 199.
12. Lawrence H. Fuchs, "Minority Groups and Foreign Policy," in *American Ethnic Politics* (New York: Harper Torchbooks, 1968), p. 149.
13. *The Economist*, March 24, 1979, p. 48.
14. *The New York Times*, July 6, 1978, p. A5.
15. Quoted by Gerson, *op. cit.* footnote 8, p. 27.
16. Quoted *ibid.*, p. 27.
17. See Russell Warren Howe and Sarah Hays Trott, *The Power Peddlers* (Garden City, N.Y.: Doubleday Publishing, 1977), p. 444.
18. Congressional Research Service, Issue Brief Number IB79089, *Turkey and U.S. Interests*, p. 13.
19. *Congressional Record—Senate*, July 25, 1978, p. S11707.
20. Congressional Research Service, *loc. cit.*, p. 12.
21. Steven D. Isaacs, *Jews and American Politics* (Garden City, N.Y.: Doubleday Publishing, 1974), p. 15.
22. *Ibid.*, p. 16.
23. *Ibid.*, pp. 19, 119, 129.
24. Dean Acheson, *Present at the Creation* (New York: W. W. Norton & Co., 1969), p. 169.

25. Harry S Truman, *Memoirs,* Vol. 2 (Garden City, N.Y.: Doubleday Publishing, 1956), p. 160.

26. John Snetsinger, *Truman, the Jewish Vote, and the Creation of Israel* (Stanford, Ca.: Hoover Institution Press, 1974), pp. 75-77.

27. *Ibid.,* pp. 105-09.

28. Howe and Trott, *op. cit.* footnote 17, pp. 272-73.

29. Middle East Arms Sales Proposals, *Hearings before the Senate Foreign Relations Committee,* 1978, pp. 166, 180.

30. *Congressional Record—Senate,* May 15, 1978, p. S7396.

31. *Ibid.*

32. Department of State Memorandum of Conversation.

33. Howe and Trott, *op. cit.* footnote 17, p. 318.

34. William J. Lanouette, "The Many Faces of the Jewish Lobby in America," *National Journal,* May 13, 1978, p. 755.

35. James Madison, *The Federalist,* Paper Number 10.

36. Irving Howe, "The Limits of Ethnicity, " *The New Republic,* June 25, 1977, pp. 17-19.

26. THE PETRODOLLAR CONNECTION

Steven Emerson

The best kept secret of the sale of AWACS reconnaissance planes to Saudi Arabia is that it was saved from defeat in the U.S. Senate by a massive and unprecedented corporate lobbying campaign. That lobbying campaign was carried out by American business from the top of the Fortune 500 to the ricegrowers in Arkansas, and largely orchestrated by Saudi Arabia and its American agents.

A three-month investigation has determined that the Saudi lobbying campaign resulted in one of the most successful manipulations of American business and American foreign policy ever attempted by a foreign power. Saudi Arabia demanded and received the aggressive support of the most powerful corporations in America. Scores of other business interests joined the campaign in order to protect existing petrodollar contracts or to obtain new ones. Still thousands of others were indirectly induced to join by pressure from their own domestic suppliers, purchasers, or business partners. And many others with no commercial stake in the sale, or even in Saudi Arabia, jumped into the lobbying fray because they were prevailed upon to believe that not upsetting the Saudis was vital to the U.S. economy. In the end, the effort to obtain Senate approval of the sale produced the most extensive involvement by the American business community in any major foreign policy decision since World War II. Not only energy and

munitions companies, but also farmers, toy manufacturers, airlines, trade associations, health care management firms, rice growers, banks, bus companies, construction firms, and other commercial interests from nearly every state pressed hard for the sale. In addition, evidence has been uncovered that points to possible widespread violations of the Foreign Agents Registration Act by major American corporations and their officers.

The AWACS strategy was devised in an elegant suite in Washington's Fairfax Hotel, where, beginning last September, a group of five men met every morning. The group consisted of three registered agents for Saudi Arabia—Frederick Dutton, Stephen N. Connor, and J. Crawford Cook—and two Saudis—Prince Bandar bin Sultan, son of the Saudi Defense Minister, and Abdullah Dabbagh, a former commercial attaché. A centerpiece of the campaign was to convince the American business community to lobby for the sale.

At the Fairfax meetings, Senators were targeted who were considered politically vulnerable and critical to the final vote. Corporations were broken down state by state and matched up with individual Senators. The White House and Senate Majority Leader Howard Baker provided the latest Senate head counts. Lists of American firms doing business in Saudi Arabia were collected, and political information on the progress of the lobbying efforts in Congress and in the business community was exchanged with other centers of corporate organizing: the Busi-

Source: *The New Republic*, 186 (February 17, 1982), pp. 18–25. Reprinted by permission of Steven Emerson.

ness Roundtable, United Technologies Corporation, and the Boeing Company.

The Saudis and their American agents tried to create an impression that Prince Bandar and other Saudi officials were unobtrusive presences, and were there only to answer questions if asked. *The Wall Street Journal* quoted Bandar as saying, "I am here for any Senator who wants to know our side of the story." In fact, Bandar played a much more active role. He took the initiative in making the rounds on Capitol Hill, setting up meetings, and arranging briefings with various Senators. He was even provided with an office off the Senate floor.

Crawford Cook and Stephen Connor, in the words of one informed source, "worked the hell out of the private sector. They were the hot and heavy guys." Hundreds of chief executive officers and corporate presidents and vice presidents were contacted and strongly urged to write or call their Senators. In the six weeks preceding the Senate vote, scores of Washington representatives of major American corporations were invited to attend "receptions" at the Saudi Embassy and other Saudi-designated locations, where the importance of the sale to Saudi Arabia was communicated. Prince Bandar and other Saudi officials made daily phone calls to chief executive officers, asking them to help by contacting Senators. Many American corporations were led to believe that much of American's trade with the Saudis—including their own—would disappear if the sale did not go through. Some were left with the unambiguous impression that their lobbying efforts would be monitored. And, in other cases, the promise of contracts was dangled in front of corporations, one corporate official said, "like raw meat before a hungry dog."

But by October the AWACS still seemed unlikely to pass in Congress, despite the intense lobbying by the Saudis and the Administration. So officials of Saudi Arabia made a formal decision to increase the pressure beyond the level of strong requests and implicit threats. Sources close to the Saudis have revealed that in an unprecedented move, Saudi Arabia held up final contract negotiations with American firms during the time when the sale was before Congress. Contracts awaiting final signatures were frozen and discussions on new contracts postponed. Several companies were warned if the sale did not go through, or if they did not lobby hard enough, renewals of their contracts would be in jeopardy. An examination of American, Middle Eastern, and Saudi trade publications which cover business developments in the region and monitor major contracts awarded by Saudi Arabia confirms that —with one exception—no American contracts in Saudi Arabia were awarded or renewed during the period from October 5 to October 28, 1981.

The exception was the Whittaker Corporation. Last August Whittaker's president, Joseph Alibrandi, published an article headlined "If I Were a Saudi Arabian" in *Newsweek's* "My Turn" column. Alibrandi extolled the altruistic and pro-Western policies of Saudi Arabia ("the primary peacemaker and defender of American interests in the Middle East") and attacked the West's ungrateful response. *Newsweek* identified Alibrandi as a "corporation president [who] has done business in Saudi Arabia for nearly twenty years." During half that time, Alibrandi was a Raytheon executive, and he had helped install ground-to-air Hawk missiles for the Saudis. When he took over at Whittaker in 1970, it was a diversified manufacturing company with no experience in hospital management. But Alibrandi's contacts in the Saudi Ministry of Defense and Aviation helped his new company to enter the health care field in a significant way. In 1974 the Whittaker Corporation was awarded a $100-million contract to manage and operate three Saudi hospitals, and the contract eventually grew to $500 million. After the *Newsweek* article appeared, Alibrandi mailed a copy to every member of the Senate. On October 26, 1981, two days before the scheduled vote on the AWACS sale, Whittaker announced that Saudi Arabia had awarded it a contract to expand the corporation's health care program to include five hospitals. The new fee was $834 million, a 67 percent increase and a sum equal to more than half the company's total revenue for 1981. (In late January, Whittaker announced a takeover attempt of the Brunswick Corporation. It offered $320 million in cash. Brunswick has resisted, charging that "Whittaker is subject to the influence of Saudi interests. Sheik al Fassi of Saudi Arabia has been quoted [in the *Washington Post*] as saying, 'This is one of the biggest companies in the world and I control it. Joe Alibrandi is my employee.' ")

Whittaker was not the only corporation to receive a lucrative contract after actively promoting the sale. In mid-October, the Greyhound Corporation, which is based in Arizona, contacted the state's two Senators to tell them that the company regarded the AWACS sale as important. Greyhound became involved, according to its vice president for public relations and advertising, Dorothy Lorant, because "the AWACS controversy had the potential to become disruptive for all, economically and politically." Lorant added that "it is not our style to knuckle under to any type of pressure," and that "it was a matter of conscience. The sale of AWACS would serve the coun-

try, the U.S. public, and this corporation as well." Eight days after the sale of AWACS was approved by the Senate, Greyhound Food Management, a wholly owned subsidiary of the Greyhound Corporation, was awarded a $90-million contract extension by the Saudi Ministry of Defense and Aviation. Before the Senate vote, Greyhound reportedly had to be reminded of its pending contract renewal.

On July 18, 1981, an official of National Medical Enterprises, a health care management corporation based in California, wrote to all members of the California delegation and to some other out-of-state members. The letters strongly supported the sale of AWACS and enhanced F-15 equipment to Saudi Arabia, and said, "My perception is that the sale is in the best interests of the United States." In September Saudi Arabia signed an original contract with National Medical Enterprises for the management of a hospital in Riyadh. The contract was worth $84 million.

As the lobbying effort gathered steam, there was greater coordination among the corporate participants. Representatives of forty companies, primarily in defense, aerospace, and petroleum-related areas, attended meetings held at the downtown Washington offices of the Business Roundtable, the country's most powerful business lobby. The meetings were organized by Richard M. Hunt, director of government relations for NL Industries, a manufacturer of petroleum equipment and supplies. Hunt denies that NL Industries was motivated by any economic gain, saying, "We appreciated the role Saudi Arabia played in maintaining moderate oil prices and also the need to maintain Middle East stability."

Hunt refuses to discuss details of the meetings, but according to one corporate representative, the sessions became intense and frank. The White House sent a staff person from its business liaison office, who, like the organizers of the meetings at the Fairfax Hotel, determined which Senators were considered vulnerable to political pressure. The question of which Senators were Jewish was discussed. And in one of the final sessions, a representative of a major corporation rose and told his Business Roundtable colleagues, "The children of Israel will stub their toes on this one." Hunt, however, denies that anti-Semitic comments were made. "There was not one comment made about Jews," he said. "I have a lot of respect for the little people."

Two corporate giants that became heavily involved in the lobbying campaign were Boeing, the main contractor for the AWACs planes, and United Technologies, which estimated that it had some $100 million at stake. According to their spokesmen, Boeing president E. H. Boullion and United Technologies president Harry Gray together sent out more than 6,500 telegrams to subsidiaries, vendors, subcontractors, suppliers, and distributors throughout the country. Boullion's telegram asserted that unless the deal went through, the "AWACS production line would be ended," a view not shared by officials of the Defense Department. Gray, in addition to mailing thousands of his own telegrams "requesting" support for the sale, pressured the chiefs of his subsidiaries (including Pratt & Whitney, Carrier Air Conditioning, Otis Elevator, and Ideal Electric) to send out the same telegram to hundreds of their vendors and distributors. The result was one of the most successful chain letter operations in history. One vendor said that the head of a United Technologies subsidiary told him confidentially that in the end over 10,000—and possibly as many as 20,000— telegrams were sent to businesses across the country. "Anybody who had ever done business with UT was asked to support the sale," he added. Ultimately letters filtered down to valve companies, small businesses with fewer than twenty employees, and even some mom-and-pop industrial distributor operations.

In his telegram, Gray couched his support for the AWACS in lofty foreign policy terms: "The Saudis are in the forefront of resistance to the spread of Soviet influence." But his vice president, Clark MacGregor (formerly chairman of Richard Nixon's reelection committee), appealed to partisan political sentiment. He sent out last minute warnings to the Republican leadership and Republican opponents of the AWACS sale that the Republicans would lose their majority in the Senate in the 1982 elections if the sale was defeated.

Gary's telegram ended on an ominous note: "Please wire your two U.S. Senators today asking them to sustain the President's position. Would you also send me a copy of your communication to the Senators?" Corporate officials, many dependent on United Technologies' goodwill, responded overwhelmingly. I reviewed more than 2,000 letters sent in by corporate supporters of the AWACS. More than 1,400 of these telegrams and letters paraphrased or quoted, in varying degrees, the points made by the United Technologies and Boeing telegrams. Some firms copied the telegrams verbatim; others tried to enhance their authenticity by claiming in an introductory paragraph that the impetus for writing came out of "internal discussions" with all the employees. One corporation had every one of its twenty officers send in the same telegrams. And other officials actually included at the bottom: "cc: Harry Gray, United Technologies Corporation." To many Senators, who receive weekly mail counts, the number of corporate supporters of the AWACS seemed impressive. But two companies, Boeing and United Technologies, may have been responsible for generating approximately 70 percent of the "grass roots" corporate mail.

The pressure exerted on the recipients of the United Technologies telegrams was extraordinary. One vendor with annual sales of under $15 million said that he was subjected to what he felt was "raw economic blackmail." He continued, "At our level, all small vendors are engaged in intense economic competition with each other. Very few have a big edge over the other in price—the final selection is sometimes arbitrary. So when Harry Gray asks vendors to lobby on AWACS, what choice do we have? How do we know that our refusal to support the AWACS won't be used against us later?"

The lobbying campaign also drew on the resources of construction companies with large Saudi interests. For example, two prominent firms in this area were Brown & Root, which provided pro-AWACS position papers to at least a dozen Sun Belt Senators, and Bechtel, Inc., whose actual and potential Saudi contracts are in the $40-billion range. (Secretary of Defense Caspar Weinberger, who was urging President Reagan to endorse the AWACS sale from the earliest weeks of the Administration, is a former vice president of Bechtel.) Like United Technologies, Bechtel has many subcontractors that are dependent on its business.

But even firms without substantial business interests in Saudi Arabia became active supporters of and lobbyists for the AWACS sale. The list of the many hundreds of companies that played a part in the campaign includes (to pick at random) the John Deere farm equipment manufacturing firm, Republic Steel, Alcoa (aluminum), Westvaco Corporation (a pulp and paper manufacturer), Barnes and Tucker (coal mining), Centex Corporation (a multi-industry holding company), PVI Industries, Inc. (a small business manufacturer of commercial water heaters), Fisher Price Toys Inc., Cubic Corporation (manufacturer of automatic fare card machines), SmithKline Corporation (drugs), and even some Pepsi-Cola bottling companies.

One of the oddest recruits to the AWACS cause was the Association of the Wall and Ceiling Industries-International, a nonprofit association representing American contractors from carpenters to plasterers. This group's interest in radar planes for Saudi Arabia would appear to be somewhat tangential. Nevertheless, its executive vice president, Joe Baker, attended meetings at the Business Roundtable to help organize the business community. Baker denies that he ever participated in these meetings, and said that he contacted only one Senator. Yet a White House staff member and another participant of the Business Roundtable each singled out Baker for his active support of the AWACS. President Reagan even wrote him a letter thanking him for his help. Baker also said that as far as he knew none of the contractors in his association had any Saudi Arabian connection. This may not be true much longer. A few weeks after the AWACS vote in the Senate, Baker was in the Middle East attempting to generate business for his members.

Nor was the petrodollar connection limited to oil, manufacturing, and construction industries. Agricultural groups—including the rice lobby and some farm co-ops—also became aggressive supporters of the AWACS sale. Riceland Foods, a major Arkansas rice producer and distributor, lobbied the Arkansas Congressional delegation. Officials of American Rice Inc. and other rice growers based in

Texas reportedly contacted members of the Texas delegation. The Rice Millers' Association, the rice industry's trade association, held a board of directors meeting on September 18, 1981, and voted to support the AWACS deal. It then contacted Senators from Florida, Mississippi, Missouri, Arkansas, Louisiana, and Texas. Why? A spokesman for Riceland Foods said it became involved because it was concerned with "foreign policy, Middle East peace, and trade." A spokesman for the Rice Miller's Association initially cited the need for "stability in the Middle East," but then added that sale of AWACS was "just a matter of economic sense." He said that American rice exports to Saudi Arabia from August 1980 to July 1981 totaled $150 million, and represented a 50 percent increase over the previous year. The sale of rice to Saudi Arabia was "strictly a cash market," and "the Saudis pay premium prices."

Cenex, a huge Minnesota-based farm cooperative, is part of a consortium with four oil refiners known as Interdependent Crude and Refining. Cenex lent support to a lobbying effort that included retaining a Washington law firm to promote the AWACS sale on Capitol Hill. And ICR delivered a slick brochure, prepared by its managing director, John Venners, to all Senators. According to the ICR brochure, the consortium was moved to act because

... the Saudis are asking for our help—a display of our faith and support, a renewal of trust, and a commitment to friendship. ... Even though we do not purchase oil from Saudi Arabia, we are concerned. We're concerned because we are well aware of the strategic importance of Saudi oil ... concerned because of the unsettled nature of the region and the threat to attack. ... We cannot afford to lose their [Saudi] friendship and continued cooperation.

There are other reasons, too. ICR was formed twenty-one months ago exclusively to obtain a direct crude oil supply contract with Saudi Arabia. But by September 1981, ICR had not met with any success. A source familiar with ICR said that the consortium decided to go all out for the AWACS because "it would provide a great entrée with the Saudis if they could prove they were in the forefront on the lobbying efforts. Up until then, ICR couldn't even get the Saudis to look at them [ICR]."

Cenex is a member of the National Farmers Union, a progressive general farm organization, many of whose board members were in fact opposed to the AWACS sale. But Cenex approved ICR's decision to lobby in support of the sale. According to the *Political Finance/Lobbying Reporter,* a spokesman for Cenex also said, "We're not opposed to the lobbying ... our members need the crude."

A high-ranking official of one of the major American farm organizations says, "all of the major farm co-ops were pressured" to lobby for the AWACS sale. Many have substantial investment in petroleum products, refineries, gasoline stations, and fertilizer production. But even farmer organizations became involved. The National Farmers Organization is a collective bargaining organization designed to secure the highest prices for farmers and producers. NFO's Washington director, Charles Fraser, sent out numerous letters on NFO stationery to Senators expressing support of the AWACS sale. Although the board of NFO never took a position, Fraser reportedly had been told to go ahead from key individuals in NFO.

Fraser was not the only one to move without the formal blessing of the organization for which he worked. Richard Lesher, president of the U.S. Chamber of Commerce, sent out letters to all Senators the day before the vote, in which he reported on his October trip to the Middle East. Lesher noted that the sale of AWACS was "not a one-nation, isolated issue." He wrote that "recommendations for approval" of the AWACS sale came from American businessmen and foreign officials in all the countries he visited. Though the U.S. Chamber never formally took a position, it did host a reception in October for the Saudi Minister of Commerce, Soliman Sulaim, where he asked business to support the AWACS sale. In addition, the Chamber included an article in its 860,000-circulation newsletter sent out in September that warned of the adverse consequences for all U.S. trade if the sale were to be defeated.

Even the Florist Insurance Companies sent letters in support of the AWACS sale to various Senators and Representatives. "The AWACS sales will provide a general spur to the economy and it will also put some more people to work in this country," a spokesman explained. "And the more people working in this country and the more they have in their pockets, the more they will spend on flowers." The spokesman said that letters of opinion are routinely sent out by the Florist Insurance Companies to Congressmen on various issues, but acknowledged that this was its first active venture in foreign policy.

In late October, with the Senate vote still hanging in the balance, a traveling contingent of the American corporate elite decided to provide an added push for the AWACS sale. A group of top corporate executives was touring Eastern Europe and the Persian Gulf on a "fact-finding mission" sponsored by Time Inc. On the morning of October 28—the day of the AWACS vote—a confidential telex was sent from Riyadh to a select group of wavering Senators. The telex, signed by 23 of the 24 visiting executives, pleaded for approval of the sale and claimed that

its defeat could "substantially impair U.S. ability to protect its legitimate interests in the Middle East." Many corporations whose officials signed the telex have done business in Saudi Arabia, some even have offices located there, and nearly all are looking to expand their markets in that country. When asked about the telex, one corporate spokesman suggested that it was Time Inc.'s idea. In fact, it has been learned that Theodore Brophy, chief executive officer of General Telephone and Electronics, came up with the idea on the night of October 27, and presented a draft of the telex to his colleagues the next morning. Significantly, until 1980 GTE was subjected to the Arab boycott. Some political observers believe that Brophy may have been trying to demonstrate to the Saudis the correctness of the Arab decision to drop GTE from the boycott list. One of the participants wondered about the possible embarrassment that could ensue if the telex was disclosed publicly, especially since it had emanated from Riyadh. But this objection was immediately dismissed, and, with the exception of one noncorporate leader—Vernon Jordan—the telex was signed by all the junketeers.

Though the signers wrote that their appeal was "personal," and that they were writing "individually," each of them (with the exception of Matina Horner, who signed the appeal but did not identify herself as president of Radcliffe College and a member of the board of Time Inc.) provided his title and the name of his corporation. (See below.)

The sale was approved by a 52-48 vote, although at least four other Senators had promised to vote for the sale if their votes were needed. The corporate lobby was decisive in achieving that margin, reversing the overwhelming opposition to the sale that had existed only a week before the vote.

Roger Jepsen, Republican of Iowa, had

been a leader in the anti-AWACS coalition, but he was turned around at the last moment with the help of farm manufacturing companies, farm co-ops, and defense contractors. David Boren, Democrat of Oklahoma, who had been leaning against the sale but voted for it in the end, was targeted by oil interests. Edward Zorinsky and James Exon, both Nebraska Democrats, were exposed to fierce pressure from major corporate interests in

---

THE RIYADH 23

The names and titles of corporate officials who signed the telex from Riyadh to Senators on the morning of the AWACS vote.

Robert Anderson
Chairman, Chief Executive Officer
Rockwell International Corporation

John R. Beckett
Chairman of the Board
Transamerica Corporation

Theodore F. Brophy
Chairman, Chief Executive Officer
General Telephone & Electronics
   Corporation

Philip Caldwell
Chairman, Chief Executive Officer
Ford Motor Company

Albert V. Casey
Chairman, Chief Executive Officer
American Airlines, Inc.

Richard P. Cooley
Chairman, Chief Executive Officer
Wells Fargo Bank, N.A.

Donald W. Davis
Chairman, Chief Executive Officer
The Stanley Works

Edwin D. Dodd
Chairman, Chief Executive Officer
Owens-Illinois, Inc.

Myron DuBain
Chairman, President, Chief
   Executive Officer
Fireman's Fund Insurance
   Companies

Henry J. Heinz II
Chairman of the Board
H. J. Heinz Company

Matina S. Horner

T. Lawrence Jones
President, Chief Executive Officer
American Insurance Association

Robert E. Kirby
Chairman, Chief Executive Officer
Westinghouse Electric Corporation

William E. LaMothe
Chairman, Chief Executive Officer
Kellogg Company

William S. Litwin
President
KeroSun, Inc.

Stewart G. Long
Vice President-Sales & Services
Trans World Airlines, Inc.

Henry Luce III
President
The Henry Luce Foundation, Inc.

Robert H. Malott
Chairman, Chief Executive Officer
FMC Corporation

John J. Nevin
Chairman, President, Chief
   Executive Officer
The Firestone Tire & Rubber
   Company

Paul C. Sheeline
Chairman, Chief Executive Officer
Intercontinental Hotels
   Corporation

John G. Smale
President, Chief Executive Officer
The Proctor & Gamble Company

Thomas J. Watson Jr.
Chairman Emeritus
International Business Machines
   Corporation

L. Stanton Williams
Chairman, Chief Executive Officer
PPG Industries, Inc.

their states. Both voted for the sale. In explaining what had influenced his vote, Zorinsky reportedly said he had discovered that the lamp posts of the city of Riyadh were made in Nebraska. According to the *Omaha World Herald,* a "top Saudi official" congratulated the head of Valmont Industries, which organized the Nebraska lobbying effort, over the telephone on the morning after the vote.

Howell Heflin, Democrat of Alabama, was confronted by a delegation of twenty-seven Alabama businessmen, some with contracts in Saudi Arabia. According to one source, the message was clear: "either you support the AWACS or you are our ex-Senator from Alabama." In the end, however, Heflin voted against the AWACS sale. Another Senator, a Midwesterner, said he was called by every chief executive officer in his state. And executives of FMC Corporation initiated appointments with various Senators and their staffs to lobby personally. At one meeting, said a Congressional source, the FMC representative emphatically told a Senator that FMC—a diversified heavy manufacturing and chemical comapny—considered the sale of AWACS to be its "number one foreign policy issue." The FMC representative warned the Senator, who remained opposed to the sale until the day of the vote, "We will remember this vote five years from now, when you are up for reelection."

According to government officials, the systematic political activity and lobbying in support of the AWACS sale strongly suggest that the Foreign Agents Registration Act has been violated. The act requires that a person register with the Department of Justice as a foreign agent if he acts at the request or under the direction or control of a foreign principal, or indirectly through an agent or a foreign principal, and does one of the following: (1) engages in political activities for, or in the interest of, a foreign principal; (2) acts as a public relations counsel, or publicity agent, or political consultant for a foreign principal; (3) engages in the transaction of money on behalf of a foreign principal; or (4) represents the interests of a foreign principal before any official of the U.S. government.

Violations of the foreign agents act may well have been committed by persons in the following four categories: (1) corporate officials who lobbied or contacted their Senators or Representatives at the request of Prince Bandar and other Saudi officials; (2) company officers who lobbied and contacted members of Congress under the threat or inducement, implicit or explicit, of losing or gaining Saudi contracts; (3) company officials who lobbied or contacted members of Congress at the request of Saudi registered agents; and (4) companies that passed along Saudi propaganda or surreptitiously promoted the interests of Saudi Arabia as their own before U.S. government officials.

It will be up to the Justice Department to determine whether corporate officals acted under the "direction or control" of the Saudis. And it would be misleading to suggest that all corporate lobbying originated from Saudi pressure. Some stemmed from economic self-interest abetted by Administration pressure and Republican loyalty. But much of the lobbying was engineered, directly and indirectly, by Saudi Arabia.

The Mobil Oil Corporation deserves special mention, for its role as a prime corporate propagandist for the Saudi cause. In addition, its activities may have constituted a violation of the Foreign Agents Registration Act. Beginning in October, Mobil spent more than half a million dollars on a media blitz with a series of full-page advertisements in at least twenty-six U.S. newspapers and magazines. There was no reference to AWACS or even to arms sales. Mobil focused exclusively on the "profound and rapidly growing economic partnership between the U.S. and Saudi Arabia." Mobil explained that Saudi business extends to forty-two states, that "hundreds of thousands" of jobs have been created by Saudi contracts, and that $35 billion will accrue to our balance of trade as a result of Saudi friendship. "Saudi Arabia is far more than oil—it means trade for America, jobs for Americans and strength for the dollar." In another full-page advertisement, under the headline "$35 Billion in Business for U.S. Firms," Mobil simply listed the names of two hundred U.S. corporations involved in Saudi Arabia.

In addition to avoiding any mention of the AWACS, the advertisements also represented a sharp departure from Mobil's previously published political "commentaries" on the Arab-Israeli conflict. As recently as last August, Mobil printed a column in its "Observer" style, praising selected statements by Yasser Arafat and heaping praise on the Saudis for their "peace plan." In the last line, Mobil called for "evenhanded treatment in the sale of military equipment to our friends in the Middle East, especially Saudi Arabia—the nation whose stability is so critical to the economic well-being of the free nations of the world."

The August 1981 advertisement was the third such commentary on the Middle East Mobil had published since June 1973, when it first began advertising in the *New York Times*. It was later discovered that Mobil's 1973 advertisement and numerous other oil company lobbying actions had been ordered by the Saudis. Documents subpoenaed from Aramco (the oil consortium consisting of Mobil, Exxon, Texaco, and Standard Oil of California) in 1974 and 1975 by the Senate Subcommittee on Multinationals, chaired by Frank Church, revealed that the Saudis had demanded and received the cooperation of the American oil companies in a surreptitious scheme to change American public opinion on the Arab-Israeli conflict. In one document dated May 1973, for example, King Faisal warned Aramco that it would lose its concession unless it informed both the U.S. public and government leaders of its "true interests in the area." Less than one month later, Mobil placed a pro-Saudi ad in the *New York Times* and then brought it to the attention of Saudi officials. Oil Minister Sheik Yamani commended Mobil, but remarked that this was "just a beginning" of what had to be done by the oil companies.

In shifting its advertising focus from an "analysis" of Middle East politics to the economic advantages of Saudi trade, Mobil hit upon a successful theme. But in light of the documentary evidence that previous Mobil activities were initiated at Saudi request, the most recent media campaign raises serious questions about whose interest Mobil was representing.

From this investigation, it becomes clear that most corporations that lobbied on the AWACS attempted to keep their involvement secret, except, of course, from the two groups of people that counted the most—members of Congress and the Saudis. One source close to the Saudis said that even if the sale had not gone through, the U.S. corporations could have gone back to the Saudis with evidence of their loyalty. He said, "It was a process of building up chits."

Many corporate officials denied taking any position on the sale, but when presented with hard evidence of their involvement, they tried to dismiss it as a spontaneous expression of civic responsibility. Upon further questioning, especially when asked if the Saudis communicated with them, they would drop the civics and maintain that their activities were spurred by economic self-interest. When asked whether the Saudis have pressed United Technologies into lobbying, a spokesman for the company said, "They [the Saudis] didn't have to. It was a matter of pure economic self-interest."

Most tellingly, it has been discovered that a handful of the major corporations agonized over the issue of lobbying for AWACS and finally decided not to do so. Some of them actually attended meetings of the Business Roundtable and receptions at the Saudi Embassy to give the impression that they backed the sale. Spokesmen for these firms have pleaded that they not be identified. One corporate official said, "If our absence on lobbying becomes conspicuous, there will be hell to pay."

From discussions with scores of corporate officials and spokesmen, it is also clear that most were unfamiliar with the substantive issues underlying the controversy behind the AWACS, nor did many of them care. But once these executives were made to feel that their contracts might be in jeopardy, or once they received a call from Prince Bandar, or a request from the registered agents, or the telegrams from Boeing and United Technologies, or the memo from the American Businessmen's Group of Riyadh (a business lobby based in Saudi Arabia), or the message from Mobil Oil's editorial ads—they quickly called Western Union and started sending out telegrams.

Beyond the specific case of a particular arms deal, the corporate lobbying effort for the AWACS sale raises the more general question of whether American corporations will not play a broader role in the formulation of American foreign policy, particularly in the Middle East. Are the Saudis now guaranteed an American lobby—perhaps the most powerful there is—on future issues? Will the Saudis and their American surrogates now press for their interests extending beyond arms sales? The push so far has been in lobbying. The next step will be pegging corporate campaign contributions to candidates with the right views not only on business concerns but also on the Arab-Israel issue. The National Association of Arab Americans has begun pressuring chief executive officers on this basis.

Some corporations have already begun to use financial pressure in a negative way. According to Congressional and Republican Party sources, several major corporations refused to attend two fundraisers held on behalf of two Senators last fall, and others withdrew from participation in the fundraisers out of anger against the Senators' opposition to the AWACS sale. Arab-backed corporate contributions will become increasingly important in future elections. Oil-related interests alone in the 1980 election campaign are conservatively estimated as having accounted for over $5 million in contributions, and, according to a CBS News report broadcast on October 19, "more than half a million dollars in contributions to Senate candidates last year [was] from companies within the American Businessmen's Group of Riyadh." Of the six largest recipients, all supported the sale.

In the end, the fierce corporate lobbying campaign on behalf of the AWACS deal—and the powerful alliance between American business and the House of Saud that appears to be aborning—has little to do with the U.S. national interest. The alignment with Saudi Arabia is the product of vested interests, not national interests, and the proliferation of those vested interests creates an illusory impression of spontaneous and broad American support for Saudi Arabia. Eight years after Saudi Arabia invoked its oil embargo with the goal of forcing a change in American Middle East policy, that goal now seems within its reach. But oil is no longer the weapon of choice. The Saudis are acutely aware of the military and political dangers of another embargo, and they also understand that such an embargo would be ineffective in a world of oil gluts. The oil weapon has been transformed into a money weapon—one that can be wielded even in the absence of a cartel. The Saudis have discovered that quintessential American vulnerability, the love of money, and the petrodollar connection has become diffused throughout American society.

27. AMERICAN OPINION: CONTINUITY, NOT REAGANISM

John E. Rielly

Two years after Ronald Reagan assumed the presidency, both the American people and the country's opinion leaders emphasize a desire for continuity in their foreign-policy priorities and oppose some of the major foreign-policy initiatives of the Reagan administration. Despite startling changes during the last few years—including the seizure of American hostages in Iran, the Soviet invasion of Afghanistan, the crushing of the now-banned independent trade union Solidarity in Poland, the U.S. failure to ratify the SALT II treaty, the war in the Falkland Islands, the severe global inflation followed by worldwide recession, and the dramatic foreign-policy changes proposed by Reagan two years ago—foreign-policy attitudes among the American public remain remarkably stable.

When both leaders and the public were asked to rank 13 foreign-policy goals in order of importance, the results on 11 out of 13 remained the same as four years ago. Concern with economic issues tops the list, with unemployment replacing inflation as the dominant issue. The gap between public and leadership attitudes and between the views of those two groups and the Reagan administration is great and growing on some major issues.

Both the public and U.S. leaders are less concerned about the military balance between the United States and the Soviet Union than four years ago. Support for

increased defense spending has dropped substantially. Peace and arms control issues have become higher priorities. Both the public and leaders are wary of direct intervention in Central America, yet they are more willing than before to commit American troops in crisis situations in priority areas such as Western Europe and Japan.

These are the principal findings of a new national survey of American public opinion on foreign-policy issues. In a time of deep recession, the U.S. preoccupation with domestic economic issues has reinforced the general concern with self-interest evident four years ago. The desire both to protect jobs and to insure access to energy supplies takes priority over more altruistic objectives such as promoting democracy abroad and upgrading the standard of living or promoting human rights in foreign countries. Americans continue to resist new commitments abroad but are more willing to honor some existing ones. The ideological fervor and determination to reverse certain long-time policies, so evident in Reagan's 1980 campaign for the presidency, evokes little support in popular or leadership opinion today.

The survey, sponsored by the Chicago Council on Foreign Relations (CCFR), was conducted by the Gallup Organization. Between October 29 and November 6, 1982, a systematic, stratified national sample of 1,547 American men and women was interviewed in person. In addition, between early November and mid-

Source: *Foreign Policy*, 50 (Spring, 1983), pp. 86–104.

December 1982, a leadership sample of 341 was interviewed by telephone or in person. Leaders were selected from the Reagan administration, Congress, international business, labor, the media, academia, religious institutions, foreign-policy organizations, and special interest groups.

This is the third CCFR study of the foreign policy attitudes of Americans. The first, conducted in November and December 1974, followed the resignation of President Richard Nixon. The second, conducted in November and December 1978, came two years into the presidency of Jimmy Carter and shortly before the fall of Shah Mohammad Reza Pahlavi of Iran. From 1940 until 1973, according to a series of Gallup Organization polls, the American public and its leaders nearly always assigned top priority to foreign-policy and security issues. In the past decade these priorities have been reversed. Americans are most concerned with domestic economic issues [see Table 27-1]: Sixty-four per cent of the public lists unemployment as the most important problem facing the country. Inflation follows with 35 per cent. Over one-half of the American leaders interviewed list the economy in general (54 per cent) and unemployment (53 per cent) as the top two priorities. Only 19 per cent list inflation, down from 85 per cent in 1978.

When asked which government programs should be expanded or cut back, a relatively high percentage of the public favored expansion of education (59 per cent), social security (49 per cent), and welfare and relief programs (27 per cent). Of three international programs listed, only one, defense spending (24 per cent), emerged as a leading priority for expansion, and it ranked lower than any of the domestic programs.

Most Americans view foreign policy as having a major impact on the U.S. economy (72 per cent), on gasoline prices (81 per cent), on the value of the dollar abroad (72 percent), and on unemployment at home (66 per cent). In selecting foreign-policy goals, protecting the jobs of American workers, raising the value of the dollar, and securing access to adequate supplies of energy are regarded as "very important" by more Americans than those citing arms control or containment of communism.

The 1982 results show a continuing erosion of the post-World War II public consensus that the national interest requires active participation by the United States in world affairs. Only a bare majority of the public now believes that such international activism best insures the future of the country, while over one-third now say the United States should stay out of world affairs. The country's leaders, however, remain virtually unanimous in their support of an active U.S. world role.

The perception that the United States plays a less important and less powerful role as a world leader today than in the past continues to grow about Americans and their leaders. Only a small minority of the public and very few leaders, however, would like to see the United States play a less important role as a world leader in the future. In an apparent contradiction, both groups generally believe the United States should play a more important role in the future.

Barely one-half of the public favors giving economic aid to other countries, and a majority opposes extending military aid or even selling military equipment. As in previous years, a majority of the public wants to cut back spending on both foreign economic and military aid.

Attitudes toward trade and commerce reveal a trend toward nationalism in the American public but not among leaders.

TABLE 27-1

Problems Facing the United States

"What do you feel are the two or three biggest problems facing the country today?"*

	Public			Leaders		
	1978	1982	Per Cent Change	1978	1982	Per Cent Change
Inflation	67%	35%	-32%	85%	19%	-66%
Unemployment	19	64	+45	25	53	+28
Taxes	18	6	-12	6	3	-3
Energy/energy crisis	11	3	-8	23	2	-21
Big government	6	2	-4	10	1	-9
Excessive government spending	9	5	-4	13	12	-1
Corruption	6	4	-2	2	2	0
World peace	3	6	+3	5	7	+2
Middle East	1	2	+1	4	2	-2
Foreign policy	3	6	+3	10	13	+3
Too much foreign aid	5	2	-3	0	1	+1
National defense	5	3	-2	21	9	-12
International economy	4	21	+17	10	60	+50

* The 1978 question was slightly different. It read the same as the current question and then included the phrase: " . . . that you would like to see the Federal Government do something about?"

TABLE 27-2

Foreign Policy Goals for the United States

	Public						Leaders					
	Very Important		Somewhat Important		Not Important		Very Important		Somewhat Important		Not Important	
	1978	1982	1978	1982	1978	1982	1978	1982	1978	1982	1978	1982
1. Protecting jobs of American workers	78%	77%	15%	17%	3%	3%	34%	43%	57%	46%	7%	10%
2. Keeping up the value of the dollar	86	71	8	22	2	2	73	38	25	50	2	10
3. Securing adequate supplies of energy	78	70	15	23	2	3	88	72	11	27	1	1
4. Worldwide arms control	64	64	23	25	5	6	81	86	16	12	3	2
5. Containing communism	60	59	24	27	10	8	45	44	47	46	7	8
6. Combating world hunger	59	58	31	33	5	5	67	64	31	35	2	1
7. Defending our allies' security	50	50	35	39	7	5	77	82	21	16	1	1
8. Matching Soviet military power	–	49	–	34	–	12	–	52	–	40	–	7
9. Strengthening the United Nations	47	48	32	32	13	13	26	25	49	47	25	28
10. Protecting interests of American business abroad	45	44	40	43	9	9	26	25	64	66	9	9
11. Promoting and defending human rights in other countries	39	43	40	42	14	9	35	41	56	54	8	5
12. Helping to improve the standard of living in less developed countries	35	35	47	50	12	11	64	55	33	44	3	1
13. Protecting weaker nations against foreign aggression	34	34	47	50	10	9	30	43	63	52	5	3
14. Helping to bring democratic forms of government to other nations	26	29	44	47	21	17	15	23	62	57	23	19

A comfortable majority (67 per cent) of U.S. leaders favors eliminating tariffs and other restrictions and only 28 per cent considers them necessary. The public supports tariffs, as 57 per cent considers them necessary and only 22 per cent wants to eliminate them. Both groups oppose restrictions on trade for political reasons. Only 15 percent of the public supports Reagan's sanctions against U.S. allies helping the USSR build a natural gas pipeline to Western Europe.

The American public considers four specific areas of the world vital to U.S. interests: Western Hemisphere countries, for reasons of geographic proximity; Western Europe where the United States has strong cultural and economic ties and where U.S. security interests in relation to the Soviet Union are clearest; Japan, America's principal trading partner, economic rival, and Asian security outpost; and the Middle East, including Israel, Egypt, and the oil-producing Arab countries. The leaders tend to have a broader view of American vital interests, although they rank various foreign countries in about the same order of importance.

Concern about energy supplies remains high, and the public views Saudi Arabia as one of the top five countries in which the United States has a vital interest (77 per cent). The public considers the prospect of communists seizing power in Saudi Arabia more of a threat to American interests than their taking power in France, Iran, El Salvador, or Taiwan. A substantial proportion of the public (39 per cent) would support U.S. military intervention if the Arabs cut off all oil shipments to the United States. One-quarter of the public and a majority of the leaders would back sending troops if Iran invaded Saudi Arabia.

American leaders consider relations with the USSR the main U.S. foreign policy problem (53 per cent). A smaller percentage of the public (15 per cent) lists U.S.-Soviet relations as the top problem. If this figure is combined, however, with the response concerning the nuclear arms race (13 per cent) and keeping peace (8 per cent), issues involving U.S.-Soviet relations have top priority for the American public.

When respondents were asked to express the intensity of their feelings toward 24 different countries, the Soviet Union elicited the coolest response. Willingness to send troops if the Soviet Union invaded Western Europe or Japan increased significantly among the public. Late Soviet President Leonid Brezhnev received very low ratings in relation to other world leaders, above only PLO leader Yasir Arafat and Iran's Ayatollah Ruhollah Khomeini. The American popular commitment to the North Atlantic Treaty Organization (NATO) remained steady. Public support for restricting U.S.-Soviet trade and cultural contacts has risen somewhat since 1978. Nevertheless, only 28 per cent of the public favors and 57 per cent opposes forbidding grain sales to the Soviet Union. Of the leaders, 81 per cent oppose the grain embargo and 69 percent oppose the restrictions on Soviet trade generally. Both the public (59 per cent) and the leaders (79 per cent) favor limiting the sale of advanced computers to the Soviet Union.

Significant change occurred among both the public and the leaders on the question of whether the Soviet Union is clearly stronger militarily than the United States. The proportion of the public that views the Soviets as having achieved equality increased from 26 per cent in 1978 to 42 per cent in 1982. Among leaders, 62 per cent agree the two superpowers possess roughly equal military power, 20 per cent

TABLE 27-3

U.S. Foreign Policy Problems

"What are the two or three biggest foreign policy problems facing the U.S. today?"

	Public		Leaders	
	1978	1982	1978	1982
Middle East	20%	19%	47%	39%
Reduce foreign aid	18	16	4	1
Relations with Soviet Union	13	15	46	53
Balance of trade	12	13	19	22
Arms race	7	13	16	14
War/nuclear war	—	11	—	13
Stronger foreign policy, loss of respect	—	10	2	18
Stay out of other countries' affairs	11	8	2	1
Keeping peace	9	8	13	17
Oil problem	9	5	7	2
Latin America	2	5	5	21
Third World	—	3	18	17
Stronger defense	3	2	7	7
Dealing with communism	2%	2%	6%	2%
World economy	2	2	7	11
Western Europe/Allies	1	2	6	14
Changing relations with African countries	4	1	18	2
Cuba	3	1	3	—
Relations with China	3	1	17	6
Iran crisis	1	1	8	1
Decline of the dollar	6	—	7	—
Human rights	1	—	7	2
Panama Canal	1	—	1	—
Taiwan	—	—	6	—
Vietnam	1	—	1	—

believe the United States is stronger, and 15 per cent think the Soviets are stronger. Diminished concern about the U.S.-Soviet military balance may reflect the greater confidence of the American people and leaders in U.S. military strength after two years of substantially increased defense budgets. Or it may indicate dwindling concern about the Soviet invasion of Afghanistan after three years or waning interest in Soviet pressure on Poland after two years.

Attitudes on defense spending have fluctuated over the past eight years. In 1974 a 3 to 1 majority favored cutting back defense spending. From 1974 to 1978 a 20 per cent shift in favor of increased spending for defense occurred. During the last four years, support for an expanded military budget has dropped by 10 per cent, reversing the trend of the previous four years. In the context of expanding or curtailing government programs, 24 percent of the public favors increasing defense spending and 34 percent favors cutting it back—an exact reversal of the percentages in 1978. The number that favors maintaining defense spending at the current level has remained about the same, and 34 per cent in 1978 and 36 percent in 1982. In the context of foreign-policy issues, with no domestic policy trade-offs, the results differ slightly, but the trend remains the same.

TABLE 27-4

The Military Balance

"At the present time, which nation do you feel is stronger in terms of military power, the United States or the Soviet Union—or do you think they are about equal militarily?"

	Public	Leaders
U.S. stronger	21%	20%
USSR stronger	29	15
About equal	42	62
Don't know	8	3

Twenty-four per cent of the public favors cutting back, 52 per cent wants to maintain the same level of spending, and 21 per cent favors expansion. The comparable figures for 1978 were 16 per cent, 45 per cent and 32 per cent.

The same trend is evident among the opinion leaders. In 1978, 31 per cent favored expanding the defense budget and 28 per cent wanted to cut back. By 1982 these figures changed to only 20 per cent in favor of expansion and 41 per cent supporting curtailment.

Independent surveys by the Gallup Organization, the National Opinion Research Center, and others taken in early 1981 indicate that popular support for increased defense spending reached its highest point in January 1981, when about two-thirds of the public favored an increase. It has diminished steadily since, and both the public and the leaders have a greater sense of military security. In addition to the sharp increase in the defense budget under Reagan, the sharp cuts in other government programs—including governmental welfare programs—have undoubtedly stiffened resistance to higher defense spending. It would appear the Reagan's administration's original priorities of sharply cutting back domestic spending and increasing military expenditures are the reverse of the public's current priorities.

Five years ago, a strong correlation existed between support for defense spending and concern that the military balance between the Soviet Union and the United States was tilting increasingly toward the Soviet advantage. This perception has become less significant in 1982. In 1978, 69 per cent of those supporting an expansion of defense expenditures also felt the United States was falling behind the Soviet Union in the military competition. In 1982, 55 per cent of those supporting a larger defense budget felt the Soviet Union possessed greater military strength. But of those who believe the Soviet Union has pulled ahead militarily, one half still want to keep the defense budget at the current level.

Growing support for arms control and increased concern about maintaining peace have accompanied the rapid military build-up of the first two years of the Reagan administration and the strong opposition to higher defense spending. Only one-third of the public opposes a nuclear arms freeze or endorses the Reagan position that a freeze should follow a further U.S. military build-up. A majority (58 per cent) favors an immediate mutual freeze.

The American public and leadership remain interested in cooperation with the USSR in non-military areas. Seventy-seven per cent of the public and 96 per cent of the leaders favor negotiating arms-control agreements; 64 per cent of the public and 78 per cent of the leaders support joint solutions to energy problems; and 57 per cent of the public and 81 per cent of the leaders oppose imposing a grain embargo on the Soviet Union. At the same time almost a majority of the public (47 per cent) and more than two-thirds (69 percent) of the leaders favor trade restrictions.

Although both the U.S. public and its leaders seem to accept Soviet military equality with a measure of equanimity, American support for NATO remains strong. In 1982, as in 1974 and 1978, the majority of the American public favored maintaining the U.S. commitment to NATO at its present level. Popular support for NATO increased slightly between 1974 and 1978 and has remained constant since then (58 per cent). Support for increasing the commitment (9 per cent) or decreasing it (11 percent) has also not changed in the past four years. Among opinion leaders a greater shift occurred: A smaller number favors an increase in the commitment, and over three-quarters (79 per cent) believe that the United States should maintain its commitment to NATO at the same level, an increase of 14 points since 1978.

Both the public and leadership show a marked unwillingness to become involved militarily in areas such as Central America or Taiwan but are more prepared to intervene in areas considered to be of vital interest—Western Europe, Japan, and to a lesser extent the Middle East. The willingness of the American public to support the use of American troops against a Soviet invasion of Western Europe increased between 1978 and 1982 from 54 per cent to 65 per cent. The opinion of American leaders remained constant at an overwhelming 92 per cent in favor of using U.S. troops in Europe. Similarly, support for military intervention in the case of Soviet invasion of Japan increased from 42 percent to 51 per cent among the public and stayed about the same among the leadership, roughly 78 per cent. An increased proportion of the public and the leadership would also send troops if the Arabs cut off oil shipments to the United States or if Arab forces invaded Israel. In contrast, only 20 per cent of the public and 10 per cent of the leaders would support the use of troops if leftist guerrillas appeared on the verge of victory in El Salvador. The public is substantially more inclined than the leaders to send troops if the Soviet Union invades Poland.

Most Americans continue to view their foreign policy with ambivalence. An overwhelming percentage of both public and leaders remain convinced that the United States has been a force for good in the world since 1945. At the same time,

TABLE 27-5

U.S.-Soviet Relations

"Relations between the Soviet Union and the United States have been the subject of disagreement for some time. Please tell me if you favor or oppose the following types of relationships with the Soviet Union."

| | Per Cent in Favor | | | |
| | Public | | Leaders | |
	1978	1982	1978	1982
Negotiating arms control agreements between the U.S. and the Soviet Union	–%	77%	–%	96%
Signing another arms agreement to limit some nuclear weapons on both sides	71	–	92	–
Signing an agreement to ban all nuclear weapons on both sides	62	–	61	–
Undertaking joint efforts with the Soviet Union to solve energy problems	68	64	90	78
Limiting the sale of advanced U.S. computers to the Soviet Union	51%	59%	59%	79%
Restricting U.S.-Soviet trade	39	47	17	28
Prohibiting the exchange of scientists between the U.S. and the Soviet Union	34	35	11	18
Resuming cultural and educational exchanges between the U.S. and the Soviets	–	70	–	94
Forbidding grain sales to the Soviet Union	–	28	–	16

TABLE 27-6

U.S. Response to Crisis Situations—1982

"There has been some discussion about the circumstances that might justify using U.S. troops in other parts of the world. I'd like to ask your opinion about several situations. Would you favor or oppose the use of U.S. troops if: . . . [if opposed, how far do you feel the U.S. should be willing to go?]"*

Situations:	Public							Leaders						
	Opposed to Sending Troops	Do Nothing	Try to Negotiate	Refuse to Trade	Send Military Supplies	Send Troops	Don't Know	Opposed to Sending Troops	Do Nothing	Try to Negotiate	Refuse to Trade	Send Military Supplies	Send Troops	Don't Know
1. Soviets invade Japan	49%	—%	—%	—%	—%	51%	—%	22%	—%	—%	—%	—%	78%	—%
2. Arabs cut off oil to U.S.	61	4	33	15	2	39	10	64	—	47	26	4	36	1
3. N. Korea invades S. Korea	78	—	—	—	—	22	—	50	—	—	—	—	50	—
4. Leftist guerrillas about to win in El Salvador	80	18	29	7	11	20	15	90	15	43	7	36	10	2
5. Iran invades Saudi Arabia	75	—	—	—	—	25	—	46	—	—	—	—	54	—
6. Arabs invade Israel	70	—	—	—	—	30	—	53	—	—	—	—	47	—
7. China invades Taiwan	82	—	—	—	—	18	—	85	—	—	—	—	15	—
8. Soviets invade Poland	69	10	27	13	9	31	13	94	10	40	49	11	6	3
9. Soviets invade W. Europe	35	5	14	4	4	65	9	8	—	5	2	4	92	1
10. Soviets invade China	79	—	—	—	—	21	—	94	—	—	—	—	6	—

* The portion of the question in brackets was asked only for situations 2, 4, 8, and 9.

TABLE 27-7

Role of Different Institutions in the Making of Foreign Policy

| | Per Cent "Very Important" | | | | Per Cent "More Important" | | | |
| | "How important a role do you think the following currently play in determining the foreign policy of the United States—a very important role, a somewhat important role or hardly an important role at all?" | | | | "Do you feel the role of the following should be more important than they are now, should be less important than they are now, or should be about as important as they are now?" | | | |
Institutions	Public 1974	Public 1978	Public 1982	Leaders 1982	Public 1974	Public 1978	Public 1982	Leaders 1982
President	49%	72%	70%	91%	45%	44%	39%	17%
Secretary of State	73	61	64	83	30	35	33	22
State Department	38	45	47	38	39	35	34	34
Congress	39	45	46	34	48	43	44	34
American business	41	41	35	22	21	27	23	22
Military	36	40	40	36	19	29	26	3
United Nations	28	31	29	2	41	39	37	33
CIA	28	29	28	20	15	18	16	9
Public opinion	19	26	23	15	59	62	54	36
Labor unions	24	25	17	3	17	17	17	14
Private foreign policy organizations	—	12	9	3	—	11	10	21
National Security Adviser	—	—	35	46	—	—	31	13

TABLE 27-8

Differences Between Foreign Policy Leaders and the Public—1982

	Public	Leaders	Gap (Leaders minus Public)
1. Best to take an active part in world affairs	54%	98%	+44%
2. Favor economic aid to other nations for economic development and technical assistance	50	94	+44
3. Favor economic aid to Central American nations	45	91	+46
4. Favor eliminating tariffs and restrictions	22	67	+45[a]
5. We should take a more active role in opposing apartheid in South Africa	45	79	+34
6. Favor giving military aid—arms and equipment—to other nations	28	59	+31
7. Favor selling military equipment to other nations	39	68	+29
8. Favor re-establishing relations with Cuba	48	81	+33
9. Goal of defending our allies' security is very important	50	82	+32
10. Agree Vietnam war fundamentally wrong and immoral	72	45	-27
11. Feel the CIA should not work secretly inside other countries to try to weaken or overthrow governments unfriendly to the U.S.	37	58	+21
12. Favor a mutual freeze on nuclear weapons right now, if the Soviets would agree	58	79	+21
13. Goal of protecting Americans' jobs very important	77	43	-34
14. Goal of keeping up the value of the dollar very important	71	38	-33

[a]Editor's Note: The entry was corrected from 47, based upon another reporting of these survey results in John E. Rielly, ed., *American Public Opinion and U.S. Foreign Policy 1983* (The Chicago Council on Foreign Relations, 1983), p. 37.]

Americans have not changed their opinion about the American involvement in Vietnam. In 1982 and in 1978 nearly three-quarters of the public (72 per cent) concurred in the statement "the Vietnam war was more than a mistake; it was fundamentally wrong and immoral." Opinion leaders, however, were less inclined to share this view (45 per cent). At the same time a larger number of both leaders and the public believe the United States is less respected in the world than a decade ago.

In evaluating the principal shapers of American foreign policy, both the public and leadership consider the president the dominant actor. Seventy per cent of the public and 91 per cent of the leaders believe that he plays a "very important role" in making foreign policy, a level unchanged from four years ago. The secretary of state's role is perceived to be slightly more important than four years ago by the public and substantially more significant by American leaders (63 and 83 percent, respectively), reflecting the dominant role played by both former Secretary Alexander Haig, Jr. and current Secretary of State George Shultz as compared with their predecessors in the Carter administration. Among the leaders, a sharp rise occurred in the number of those who considered the role of Congress as "very important" (45 per cent from 34 per cent).

When it came to indicating preferred roles for various actors in the foreign-policy process, the populist trend of the last decade continued. The proportion of Americans who consider the role of Congress too strong dropped slightly from 16 to 14 per cent, and the percentage that view the role of Congress as too weak increased significantly, if less dramatically, than in 1974 just after the Watergate crisis and the resignation of Nixon. American leaders also show increased support for a stronger congressional role, a view quite different from 1978 when both the public and leaders favored a diminished role for Congress.

Almost one-half (44 per cent) of the public believes that Congress should play a larger role in the foreign-policy process and over one-half (54 per cent) thinks that public opinion should as well, a conclusion consistent with the results of previous years. The Congress and public opinion received strongest support for an increased role, substantially more than the president, the secretary of state, or the State Department. In the current survey both the public and leaders favor a weaker role for the military in U.S. foreign policy.

The media were not listed among the alternative actors, but television remains by far the most reliable source of information on foreign policy in the eyes of Americans, more reliable than the presidency, the State Department, or foreign-policy leaders in Congress. Similarly, the public continues to rely on television as the principal source of information about foreign policy (75 per cent), newspapers second with 54 percent, radio third, and magazines fourth.

The gap between the preferences of leaders and public has not closed in the last four years, and the views of both conflict with the Reagan administration's in a number of areas. The leaders continue to favor a more active role for the United States in world affairs, are more interventionist, support free trade and oppose tariffs, and back economic and military aid.

Leaders are substantially (about 30 per cent) more likely to favor the use of troops in situations such as a Soviet invasion of Western Europe or Japan, invasion of Saudi Arabia by Iran, or invasion of South

Korea by North Korea. In low-priority areas, the leaders are less inclined to favor the use of troops, most notably in the case of the Soviet invasion of Poland and to a lesser extent in the case of a Soviet invasion of China or of imminent victory of the rebels in El Salvador.

At the same time leaders are more likely to see communism as a threat in areas of vital interest. Leaders are more inclined to favor cooperative relations with the Soviet Union in trade, grain sales, arms-control negotiations, as well as cultural, educational, and scientific exchanges. They also show a much greater inclination than the public to re-establish economic and political relations with Cuba. On military questions, they express slightly greater support than the public for cuts in the defense budget. Leaders favor arms control and endorse the mutual freeze on nuclear weapons right now in greater numbers. They are less supportive than the general public of domestic measures to protect the jobs of American workers or maintain the value of the American dollar.

In relation to the policies of the Reagan administration, the leaders tend to support the White House on trade as well as economic and military aid more than the public. On such issues as arms control, defense spending, intervention in El Salvador, and renewing ties with Cuba, they differ sharply with the administration. The public also differs substantially with the administration on foreign economic and military aid, defense spending, trade and tariff issues, the nuclear freeze, and sanctions against the West European allies over the Soviet natural gas pipeline. The public generally assigns higher priority to cooperation with the Soviet Union and is wary of the confrontational approach of the Reagan administration during its first two years in office. Finally, spending priorities continue to differ, with the public favoring increased domestic spending and the administration favoring the opposite.

In all three surveys one trend is evident: None of the last four administrations has been able to reverse the erosion of public support for a more active and powerful U.S. role in the world. The discouraging conclusion is partly offset by a substantial increase in the last two surveys—to a level of over 70 per cent in 1982—in the number of those who believe that the United States should play as important or a more important and powerful role as a world leader 10 years from now. Whether this second trend prevails will depend to a considerable extent on the success in shaping popular opinion by American leaders, who are unanimous in favoring an active U.S. world role.

SUGGESTED READINGS–PART II

Emerson, Steven. *The American House of Saud.* New York: Franklin Watts, 1985.

Franck, Thomas M., and Weisband, Edward. *Foreign Policy by Congress.* New York: Oxford University Press, 1979.

Hughes, Barry B. *The Domestic Context of American Foreign Policy.* San Francisco: W. H. Freeman, 1978.

Rielly, John E. *American Public Opinion and U.S. Foreign Policy 1983.* Chicago: Chicago Council on Foreign Relations, 1983.

Rubin, Barry. *Secrets of State: The State Department and the Struggle over U.S. Foreign Policy.* New York: Oxford University Press, 1985.

Schlesinger, Arthur M., Jr. *The Imperial Presidency.* Boston: Houghton Mifflin, 1973.

Spiegel, Steven L. *The Other Arab-Israeli Conflict: Making America's Middle East Policy, from Truman to Reagan.* Chicago: University of Chicago Press, 1985.

Stoessinger, John G. *Henry Kissinger: The Anguish of Power.* New York: W. W. Norton, 1976.

Talbott, Strobe, *Deadly Gambits,* New York: Alfred A. Knopf, 1984.

Turner, Stansfield. *Secrecy and Democracy: The CIA in Transition.* Boston: Houghton Mifflin, 1985.

Whalen, Charles W., Jr. *The House and Foreign Policy: The Irony of Congressional Reforms.* Chapel Hill: The University of North Carolina Press, 1982.

American Foreign Policy and the Future

With the breakdown in the postwar foreign policy consensus, and the failure of a new one to replace it, Part III offers three selections that focus on possible values and beliefs—or at least strategies—to shape policy in the future. The first reading suggests a return to democratic principles to guide American foreign policy, the second argues for the development of more ad hoc coalitions if a new consensus cannot be achieved, and the third outlines a strategy based largely upon current policy, albeit grounded in America's political traditions. While none of these may be wholly accepted or adequate, these three views should offer an important beginning point for discussing the values and beliefs that may guide future U.S. foreign policy.

The first selection, "Consensus Lost," by George Quester identifies the nature of the consensus that was destroyed by the Vietnam War, discusses the effect of that shattered consensus on how the United States now addresses international politics, and argues for the need to resurrect that earlier agreement on basic foreign policy beliefs. In essence, Quester argues, the Vietnam War undermined "the common agreement among Americans about what positive goals the United States could accomplish through its foreign policy." No longer were Americans assured about their previous efforts to bring democratic ideals to the rest of the world. Instead, Americans became divided among those who saw the United States as responsible for global problems, those who remained committed to political freedom as a primary foreign policy value, and those who were willing to compromise this commitment to political freedom for economic development—especially in assessing American relations with the Third World. The real consequence of these divisions has been the weakening of democratic values as the benchmark for shaping policy with other nations—at least until the human rights efforts of the Carter administration. Quester argues that this abandonment may well have been "premature and unjustified by events." His conclusion best summarizes his view on this lost consensus: "The Vietnamese drive for national unity may have convinced Americans that their values were no longer relevant to the future. Soviet human rights violations may persuade them that they are."

The second reading, "Prospects for Consensus in the 1980s," is taken from the final chapter of Ole R. Holsti and James N. Rosenau's excellent book entitled *American Leadership in World Affairs.* In that larger work, they illustrate that in the post-Vietnam period, American foreign policy leaders are divided into three major groups. The first group is the Cold War Internationalists, who basically still adhere to the beliefs of the cold war consensus and see all international politics as a struggle between East and West. For this group, the actions of the Soviet Union remain the pivotal point for understanding international affairs. The second group is the Post-Cold War Internationalists, who take a more differentiated view of international politics. They see international politics as shaped not only by East-West concerns but also North-South (i.e., rich-poor) issues. The third group is the Semi-Isolationists, who desire to reduce America's involvement in the world or at least to adopt a more self-interested strategy in dealing with other nations.

In light of these divisions, a consensual approach to foreign policy will be quite difficult in the near future, Holsti and Rosenau argue in the essay included here. Instead, they contend that "American administrations may be forced to rely upon shifting foreign policy coalitions, the composition of which will vary from issue to issue." Beyond that ad hoc strategy to developing foreign policy, Holsti and Rosenau also suggest some possible ways to build a new consensus, ranging from simple presidential directives to a full-blown domestic discussion of the ends and means of foreign policy. At this juncture, too, they provide an extensive series of crucial questions which should be included in any debate on a new foreign policy consensus. Despite this effort on their part, they remain skeptical whether any new consensus can be developed.

The final reading, "The Future of American Foreign Policy: New Realities and New Ways of Thinking," by Secretary of State George Shultz is taken from hearings before the Senate Foreign Relations Committee in early 1985. These hearings were initiated by the new chairman of that committee, Senator Richard Lugar of Indiana, as a means of reviewing past policy and devising a strategy for the future.

In his statement, Secretary Shultz argues that " . . . America's traditional goals and values have *not* changed. Our duty must be to help shape the evolving trends in accordance with our ideals and interests; to help build a new structure of international stability that will ensure peace, prosperity, and freedom for coming generations" (emphasis in original). He then proceeds to outline an approach focusing on a stable policy between the superpowers, the building of common goals and policies with allies and friends, and seeking change in areas such as southern Africa and the Middle East, consistent with our principles of justice and security. In addition, though, Secretary

Schultz argues that the United States must confront directly the new wave of terrorism with the help of other nations around the world.

What holds together these threads of policy, Shultz argues, are two important values and beliefs: *(a)* the essential unity of these policy goals among the American people—even to the point of a new consensus; and *(b)* the underlying commitment to democratic principles and political freedom. Unlike some in the past who have questioned the relevance of democratic ideals as the guide to policy, Secretary Shultz concludes that "these values are the source of our strength, economic as well as moral, and they turn out to be more central to the world's future than many may have realized."

28. CONSENSUS LOST

George Quester

Since the fall of Saigon, it has been commonplace to state that the United States has lost its postwar, anticommunist foreign policy consensus. Some attribute the U.S. reluctance to use force, unwillingness to provide aid, and refusal to support a strong intelligence community to this loss. By this view, the Soviet invasion of Afghanistan may even prove a cloud with a silver lining. Faced with the reality of Soviet military aggression, those concerned with foreign policy may decide that the postwar consensus based on anticommunism retains its validity. Coherence and a rise in American influence in the world could follow the reestablishment of this earlier opposition to communism as the basic goal of American foreign policy.

But there is another explanation of the decreased American foreign policy activism: What the United States lost in Vietnam was not so much the strong belief that communism was behind most of the world's problems and must be resisted, but something much more vital— the common agreement among Americans about what positive goals the United States could accomplish through its foreign policy. Lost in Vietnam, in other words, was agreement on what produces progress in the world. Regaining that consensus may be fundamental to a new balance in American diplomacy; and, in this regard, even conservative critics should hesitate before they so cavalierly disdain the Carter administration's concern for human rights.

Before the Vietnam war, most Americans accepted that U.S. political practice would, if adopted in any corner of the globe, increase the happiness of the people living there. In effect, the politics of Minnesota would also work in Burma or Kenya or Cuba or Algeria. For the first time in their history, Americans now doubt the moral desirability of implanting a duplicate of the American political system in foreign countries. They are turning isolationist not primarily in reaction to the costs of having influence abroad, but in response to doubts about the appropriateness of such influence.

Americans often tell themselves, rather lightheartedly, that the United States has been a revolutionary force in world events. The Voice of America constantly reminds Africans and Asians that the United States was the first new nation. Marxist critcs view this as hypocritical nonsense. Americans say the United States is a force for beneficial change; Marxists say the United States acts only to defend the economic status quo.

Yet for much of its history, the United States was an example of revolutionary change and, indeed, a supporter of such change. It served as an example of republican rule among nations governed by various forms of autocracy. The United States was openly supportive of the French Revolution after 1789 and was enthusiastic about the Latin American declarations of independence from Spain. The United States was pleased with the prospects of Greek independence from Turkey after 1831 and accorded diplomatic recogni-

Source: *Foreign Policy* 40 (Fall 1980), pp. 18–32.

tion to the Frankfurt Assembly in Germany during the revolutions of 1848.

When revolutionary leaders fled Germany or Hungary as the movements toward political democracy were suppressed, they came to the United States. America was the Algeria or Cuba of its time—an irritating safe haven for troublemakers; a vocal sounding board for grievances of the oppressed; a challenge, as Cuba has been, to the idea that the old way of doing things is the only way of doing things.

THE AMERICAN CENTURY

Why was the United States able to play this role? At the risk of oversimplification, the reason is that for the first century of American independence the outside world was governed by an ascriptive authority based neither on nationalism nor on liberalism. Hereditary authority continued to govern, irrespective of the languages people spoke or of any desire such people might have had to elect their own rulers. In the United States, the issue of ethnic nationalism played less of a role; the Atlantic crossing tended to standardize most Americans on the speaking of English. Meanwhile, the issue of republican government counted for a great deal.

The revolutions sweeping Europe in 1848 demanded both republican rule and ethnic self-determination. The subsequent accommodation made by Count Otto von Bismarck, Emperor Louis Napoleon, and others was to satisfy the demand for ethnic national identity without making the parallel concession of full political democracy. The masses of much of Europe were in effect bought off after 1848 with half the loaf of what they had been demanding, precisely the opposite half from what most Americans cared about.

Until 1918 for Europe and 1945 for Europe's overseas possessions, America remained a revolutionary society. Only since 1945, or since 1960, have both republican rule and ethnic self-determination been offered and rejected. Only in these years have Americans seen what they stood for rejected by forces of the future rather than by forces of the past. Today, many in the world would give priority not to political democracy but to social or economic democracy: the redistribution of material wealth from rich to poor. And that is the rub.

The economic part of the American system was not geared to any substantial equalization of results, but toward equal opportunity. The result has not been an unhappy one. Widespread inequality of economic returns has been balanced by substantial prosperity and overall economic success; the rich have become richer but the poor have not done so badly either, at least by the standards of the rest of the world. Thus, immigrants have seen America not only as a country of political freedom but also of economic liberation.

Revisionist interpretations of post-World War II American foreign policy tend to make a great deal of American commentators like Henry Luce, founder of Time, Inc., who spoke of the "American Century," which evokes earlier political and military hegemonies like *Pax Romana* or *Pax Britannica*. However, Luce was not seeking simple power in the sense of earlier hegemonies, with peace and the conduct of human affairs being dictated to the globe by the enforcement of naked military or economic power. Rather, he saw U.S. influence increasing through the magnetic power of the American example. This was indeed to be the American century in the sense that the world would make progress by voluntarily deciding to do things as Americans had done them.

Many observers have noted that axiomatic and unchallenged propositions in American life sometimes have the deepest hold precisely because they grip Americans subliminally. One of the best statements of this argument is in Louis Hartz's *The Liberal Tradition in America.* According to Hartz, American frontier society and physical remoteness from Europe produced a political culture of Lockean ideas, embedded so deep in the political subconscious that they never required explicit articulation. Not having to struggle aginst the remnants of aristocratic privilege, Americans in effect took for granted their own political system, with which they were largely satisfied.

The basic consensus in the United States was powerful precisely because no one ever thought that it needed to be articulated. Would Cuba or Burma or Bavaria be better off with contested elections? The American answer in 1885 or 1945 would have been automatic; but will it be so in 1985?

A DOUBLE STANDARD

What then has happened to the United States since World War II? Several broad generalizations can be offered. The outside world caught up with the United States in shaking off the aspects of traditional and ascriptive rule that have all along struck Americans as anachronistic. But most of the outside world was unable to achieve success on the economic side. This lower level of economic accomplishment generated a greater concern for economic equality or what some might style economic democracy.

Therefore, much of the outside world no longer saw the United States as a model for the future, but, rather, as a model of the past. Having been offered the essence of political democracy—freely contested elections with a free press—country after country around the world chose to give it up, often asserting that it was inconsistent with the achievement of economic equality and progress. Americans reacted to this development with frustration, confusion, and disappointment.

As a result, Americans divided into three groups. A few, of Marxist or other radical persuasion, claimed that the decision of much of the Third World to abandon democracy contained a lesson for America itself. They questioned whether the political processes of the United States are not overrated, given the economic inequalities and insufficiencies that also persist in America. If other countries can reduce poverty by curbing free elections and the free press, perhaps the United States should make the same choice.

A considerably larger number of Americans remained convinced that no degree of economic progress is worth abandonment of traditional political freedoms. They believed this to be true everywhere in the world. They regarded the termination of contested elections in Third World countries merely as the result of the insidious machinations of world communism or as misguided short cuts by the leaders of underdeveloped countries.

A third group of Americans has now appeared: those who accept a double standard, who would be resolute in defending political democracy for the United States, Canada, and most of Western Europe, but who would treat most of the economically underdeveloped and non-Europeanized portions of the world as governed by different priorities and standards, as being historically unprepared for free elections and too poor to have a free press.

The out-and-out Marxists were not, and are not, numerous enough to upset the American sense of consensus. The last point of view, however, has greater currency now across the political spectrum, and the consensus Americans knew is gone.

The exact boundaries of the "free-world capable" zone will sometimes be ambiguous. Japan is included. Spain and Portugal may find themselves included, depending on how deep democratic roots can set following decades of rule under Francisco Franco and Antonio Salazar.

Canada, Australia, and New Zealand are included without question, as are Scandinavia, the Low Countries, France, Germany, and Israel. India may objectively deserve to be included, given its renewed commitment to democratic elections. But in recent years many Americans have overlooked this massive exception to their pessimistic outlook, perhaps because they could no longer bring themselves to hope that any economically underdeveloped country would maintain such an attachment for long.

One reason for the especially strong American opposition to communism in Eastern Europe as opposed to Asia may be that the level of economic development in the former has not been low enough to justify any repression of political freedom. But the tendency for too many Americans may be to view much of Africa and Asia (and perhaps much of underdeveloped Latin America) as places where economic sharing may now have to take priority over political freedom. The geographical limitations Americans are placing on their concern for liberty abroad could provide the basis for a new isolationism that is very different from what they remember historically.

"OUR S. O. B."

Prior to World War II, the United States intervened in Asia and Latin America but it avoided intervention in Europe, not because it cared more about one area than the other, but because in simple power terms it had more of a chance to exert influence in Asia and Latin America. The balance of power in the nineteenth century might have kept European states from threatening the United States, but it also prevented the United States from intervening effectively in Europe. Just the opposite was true in Asia and Latin America.

The isolationism of the future promises to be the reverse geographically of the past. The United States would see its interests as located primarily in Europe, less so in Asia and Latin America. It is the reverse because the limit is now America's motives, not its capabilities.

Skeptics will voice dissent at this point. What about all the right-wing dictatorships with which the United States has enjoyed cordial relations? What about friendly U.S. relations with Soviet Premier Joseph Stalin during World War II or with Beijing today?

The answer involves a distinction between ends and means. The United States has as a nation been more prone than others to treat foreign people and countries as ends in themselves, rather than as means. Yet no nation can ever serve its optimal ends without giving some concern to power.

The difficulty with the analysis of real-politikers is that it suggests that power is the only concern, as if power were an end in itself. A naive idealist might, by contrast, be accused of never being concerned about power. American foreign policy has not been naively unaware of power, but it has been inclined to use power for what it believed, rightly or wrongly, would work in the end for the betterment of the people involved.

Franklin Delano Roosevelt's comment about Rafael Trujillo, a former dictator of the Domincan Republic, that "he may be an S. O. B., but he's our S. O. B.," does not suggest that the United States was pleased with the prospect of Trujillo in office for as long as he cared to hold it. The comment came at a time when Trujillo was ready to declare himself opposed to Nazi Germany, while the United States was fearful of Axis penetration of Latin America and the Caribbean. American support for Trujillo hardly demonstrates that the United States would not have preferred a democratic electoral system in the Dominican Republic, but rather that it needed him at the moment.

The U.S. rationalization has been that post-1945 relations with right-wing dictatorships have been alliances of convenience: The communist alternative seemed a more serious worldwide threat, as communist dictatorships appeared permanent while those of the army or of the right wing were not. Franco's death produced elections in Spain; Salazar's death resulted in a democratic Portugal. The colonels in Greece gave way to a democratic form of government. So did the Nigerian generals. Where has a communist dictatorship similarly evolved once it gained control of the ministry of the interior?

Everyone in the world who compromises ideals, even if rationally to serve ends, can be accused of hypocrisy and of having less-noble ends than professed. Hypocrisy is widespread in international affairs; nevertheless, even the most idealistic nation must make accommodation to the limits of its influence. In the end, the question is whether Americans, had they been able, would not have replaced Trujillo's system with the constitution of Minnesota. Until very recently, they most plausibly would have.

In a Machiavellian world, the United States has often been forced to employ less than perfect partners. Nevertheless, the United States can still make this claim: It has never had a political democracy as an enemy. So sweeping a claim would include Britain in 1776 and 1812 (close calls, perhaps), Spain in 1898, and Germany in 1914 (by today's standards, also not so far off the mark).

Mexican President Santa Ana may or may not have been a popular dictator, but he was definitely a dictator. U.S. conflicts with Mexico were not intended to win self-government for Mexicans: in a sense, however, they were intended to win self-government for the populations of Texas and California, which had changed character in the years after 1821. For World War II, the claim is salvaged only by U.S. failure to declare war on Finland, which as a democracy, and after Soviet invasion, became enrolled as an ally to Nazi Germany; the U.S. semi-alliance with Pakistan against India provides another close call. Yet the claim is still not really compromised.

Thus, if any country wishes to get along with the United States, let it merely, regardless of the economic system it pursues, make a complete and unconditioned commitment to free elections and the other attributes of democracy. This is what Cuban Premier Fidel Castro promised but failed to deliver. This was something Chilean President Salvador Allende Gossens could not bring himself to offer.

ARMY FATIGUES

But there is another challenge to the thesis. Has U.S. concern with free press and free elections simply not masked a desire to spread capitalism and win markets? Undeniably, free speech and free trades often go together. But the American need for markets in China or Latin America or Eastern Europe is often overstated in the radical analysis. Americans like steady customers abroad; who does not? Yet the urgency of this preference cannot explain the Spanish-American War, the American revulsion at the Japanese invasion of China, or the American reaction to the suppression of pluralism in Eastern Europe after World War II.

Americans felt concerned about the denial of multiparty elections in Eastern Europe after World War II because a new tyranny made the war against Nazi tyranny seem pointless. Compared to this deep popular feeling, the urgency of any need for markets (markets that are stressed by the radicals and revisionists but that had never amounted to much before 1939) in Poland, for example, becomes less striking.

A different approach would be to contrast societies that maintain their political democracy while going far toward the control of the economic sector with societies that follow the opposite course. Sweden would approximate the former, while Brazil a few years back looked much like the latter. U.S. relations with anticommunist Brazil continue to be troubled. Conversely, despite Sweden's imposition of backbreaking taxation and bureaucratic regulation of the private economic sector and its irritatingly independent positions on many international issues, American foreign policy toward Sweden has been basically friendly. In large part, this is because (as in the United States itself) there is no prospect of a compromise of its political democratic system.

What of U.S. opposition to Allende in Chile? Defenders of the Allende regime note that it was freely elected and that it made no real move to undo political democracy. No doubt, the special interests of American firms such as International Telephone and Telegraph Corp. and the devious proclivities of the Nixon admin-istration help explain the U.S. decision to destabilize the regime, which finally produced a military coup and the most blatant dictatorship in Chile's history.

Yet would the American people have tolerated the Nixon administration's hostile attitude toward the Allende regime if that government had made a genuine commitment to political freedom? History lacks the evidence for a fully convincing answer. However, would the regime not have drawn American tolerance rather than antagonism? Would Nixon not have found it more difficult to exert pressure against a government that promised to abide by the electoral process?

Allende's position, however, was that a recourse to political democracy would be attempted as long as it had the prospect of achieving economic democracy. The gist of this message was that he would not tamper with the liberal election process, as long as he could make progress toward socialism through it.

For this, Allende was attacked by Castro and others on the left, who argued that progress toward socialism, that is, toward economic democracy, could not be made within the framework of political democracy. But such a position was also bound to be objectionable from an American perspective. If a nation cannot achieve socialism in an atmosphere of free elections, most Americans feel that it is socialism that has to be dispensed with, not free elections.

It is seldom remembered that Castro's insurgency against the dictatorial regime of Fulgencio Batista at the end of the 1950s enjoyed widespread American popular support. Castro did not get his money or his arms from the Soviet Union, but from a more traditional exporter of revolution, the United States. Students today may not appreciate the piquant irony of Castro's constant wearing of the 1950s-style U.S. Army fatigues, instead of Soviet-style uniforms. Deliberately or otherwise, these uniforms of Castro's armed forces serve as a memorial to the original source of their support. Castro drew this support from individual American citizens, rather than the U.S. government, just as had the revolutionaries of the nineteenth century, drawing it on the promise of instituting free elections if he won. Without such support, it is plausible that he would not have succeeded.

Castro's ascent to power was followed by a repudiation of his commitment to free elections and the constitution Batista had suspended. Predictably, Castro's support in the United States disappeared with this change of commitment.

Such arguments may not satisfy the radical critic. Yet the revisionist who sees American foreign policy as the defense and projection of capitalism, rather than of political freedom, will have trouble accounting for the fact that Americans are now going through second thoughts about their espousal of political freedom for others. How can this be according to radical analysis? Have Americans become any less capitalistic, as they become more reluctant to project their power—whether military, economic, or political—into far corners of the world? Or is it instead that they have become less convinced that the United States has something to say to the outside world, something relevant to its political and economic future?

The revisionist or radical position has been mistaken in its explanations of past American foreign policy, even though this position is very much in step with changes of attitudes that have recently shaped policy. It was not economic greed or the defects of the capitalist system that made the United States send warships or dispense aid abroad. But Americans may now be deciding that the economic defects and inequities of the status quo abroad require that the United States cease to provide warships or to defend political democracy.

ABANDONING THE DEMOCRATIC IDEAL

The change is not in the U.S. domestic system or in its alleged needs, but in U.S. experience with the outside world. With regard to this world, Americans may be tired, but more important, they are confused.

Perhaps it takes political and economic success at home to breed generosity. For whatever reason, more than others the United States has generally cared about the fate of foreign people—from the starving Soviets saved by American food missions after World War I to the starving Khmer people saved by a U.N. program financed primarily by the United States. In the past, this concern was the result of consensus. Today this concern is weakening as the consensus is disappearing.

As Americans conclude that the developing world will not respect democratic values, they are losing the humanitarian impulse that traditionally distinguished them from others. Nor should this be unexpected. An elementary interpretation of human psychology suggests that altruism and sympathy are a function of how much people see other creatures as similar to themselves. Thus it is also no accident that American empathy with the outside world has declined as Americans have decided that, in terms of future political trends, most outsiders no longer resemble them.

The American belief in free elections is sometimes ridiculed as a Western cultural bias that has no relevance to China or Vietnam or Kenya or Bolivia. Such

charges of cultural parochialism reinforce the double standard, according to
which Africans and Asians are deemed
unfit for the freedoms accorded Scandi-
navians or Englishmen. What began as a
radical argument soon enough converges
with a form of racism: free elections and
free press are not appropriate for the less
developed countries (LDCs), and the
LDCs are not appropriate for free elections and free press. So why should the
United States lose any sleep over the formation of one more "peoples' democracy"?

How many Americans would regard
the U.S. endorsement of literacy for others as just another cultural parochialism,
a projection of American success to other
continents where it is not appropriate?
Would anyone argue that Americans favor
literacy for Africans, Asians, and Latin
Americans merely because, realpolitik
style, it increases U.S. power or because,
Marxist style, it will put underemployed
American publishing houses to work?
Most Americans still believe that anyone
on this earth will be happier for being
able to read. A few might conclude that
free elections are just as globally appropriate. The consensus the United States
lost may be a consensus it should have
fought to protect.

The shift in American foreign policy
since 1967 is, then, unique. Yet it may
well be that this U.S. abandonment of
the democratic ideal was premature and
unjustified by events. Thus, Americans
prematurely shrugged off the possibility
of a return to political freedom in India.
They ignored encouraging moves in that
direction in Nigeria, Brazil, and several
countries in Latin America. They also
failed to see the true impact of Carter's
human rights campaign.

Carter's statements criticizing political
repression in foreign countries became
one of the more distinctive aspects of his
foreign policy style. Among more experienced foreign policy practitioners, however, they were the object of great disgust.
Yet in some ways, his focus on human
rights was merely a return to the American stress on political democracy, for despite an effort to give equal priority to all
human rights, it was framed almost entirely in terms of civil and political liberties, rather than toward new economic
rights.

The cost of such a stress on human
rights seemed obvious. As additional em-
barrassments and discomforts were directed at the Soviet Union, it could cause
a more beleaguered politburo leadership
to feel less able and less willing to pursue
détente and international cooperation with
the United States. If prices as substantial
as these were to be paid, many asked what
the president of the United States thought
he was doing in so indelicately calling a
spade a spade. His predecessor has refused
to invite exiled Soviet dissident Alek-
sandr Solzhenitsyn to the White House
in order to avoid offending the Soviet
Union. Carter seemed eager to remind
the world of what was obvious: that the
USSR was a country that delivered little,
if anything at all, in the way of political
freedom.

Was this all inadvertent? Was it like so
much else in the Carter administration,
inconsistent and disorganized? Whatever the president's real motivations, historians may subsequently view the human
rights campaign of the Carter administration in a special light. The Vietnam
defeat had severely undercut American's
self-confidence in any of their altruistic
impulses, enough so to worry any American president. A country that had become so confused by right and wrong in
Vietnam might become inclined to confusion everywhere; but the confusions

might disappear—right and wrong might become identifiable again—if the focus were shifted to human rights and particularly to Soviet performance.

With China, the American man on the street might conclude that the Chinese do not have much freedom, but at least they are not starving anymore. By contrast, he might say with regard to the Soviet Union that the people have lost their freedom, but their economic gains do not make up for it. The trade-off that suggests that loss of political democracy can be justified by greater accomplishments in the areas of economic democracy is not relevant to the Soviet case. Some might be sympathetic to Marxist movements and Marxist solutions in Asia and Africa, but very few will want to think of themselves as apologists for President Leonid Brezhnev and the Soviet Union.

Carter's campaign against the Soviet Union could reduce Soviet interest in détente. It could also have the consequence of persuading the American people that at a certain point in a nation's development the American model again becomes a relevant standard by which the United States judges foreign behavior.

The Vietnamese drive for national unity may have convinced Americans that their values were no longer relevant to the future. Soviet human rights violations may persuade them that they are.

29. PROSPECTS FOR CONSENSUS IN THE 1980s

Ole R. Holsti and James N. Rosenau

American foreign policy is in disarray, and only the truest of true believers any longer believe that Reaganite nostalgia and nostrums will create order out of shambles. But the roots of disarray can be traced to the war in Vietnam, which long preceded Reagan's entry into the White House.

The Vietnam War abounds in ironies, not the least of which is that an American effort to prevent the unification by force of Vietnam ended in a unified Vietnam and in a disunited United States. It is too early for a final assessment of the war's full impact on the United States, its society and economy, but the profound and persisting impact of the Vietnam undertaking on the foreign policy beliefs of American leaders has emerged repeatedly from the evidence. The principal findings can be summarized briefly:

1. American leaders are strikingly divided on a broad range of foreign policy questions; there is good reason to believe that dissensus far exceeds that of the period between Pearl Harbor and the mid-1960s; and these divisions appear to have congealed into several rather distinct, almost mutually-exclusive belief systems. The domestic cleavages appear to be at least as strong as those that characterized the United States during the years preceding World War II.

2. The war in Vietnam represented a major landmark in American history, comparable to what students of domestic politics call "watershed elections," those that fundamentally alter voter alignments and loyalties. Among casualties of the longest war in American history are propositions that for two decades prior to Vietnam were regarded as virtually self-evident truths about international affairs. They are now among the most contentious points in discussions of American foreign policy.

3. The effects of the Vietnam War have persisted beyond the immediate period following military defeat of the Saigon regime in 1975. Both survey and anecdotal evidence indicates that neither efforts of the past several administrations to develop a foreign policy consensus nor dramatic events since the evacuation of the last Americans from Saigon have successfully bridged the cleavages arising from the war in Vietnam.

As long as this condition exists, American administrations may be forced to rely upon shifting foreign policy coalitions, the composition of which will vary from issue to issue. *Ad hoc* coalitions might take several forms.

Cold War Internationalists (the dominant perspective within the Reagan Administration) and Post-Cold War Internationalists believe in the practical and moral necessity of an active American foreign policy; in international re-

Source: *American Leadership in World Affairs* by Ole R. Holsti and James N. Rosenau, pp. 249–59. Reprinted by permission of the publishers, George Allen & Unwin Publishers, Ltd.

sponsibilities arising from power and wealth; and in the potentially disastrous consequences of abdication, leaving it to others, or to no one at all, to create and sustain a more effective international order. What kinds of American undertakings would draw sufficiently upon these shared values is rather hard to predict because it would require muting the far greater differences between the two groups. They agree that American security is inextricably linked to the international system, but they share little in either their diagnoses of those links or in their prescriptions on how to deal most effectively with them. . . .

Post-Cold War Internationalists and Semi-Isolationists generally agree more than they disagree in interpreting Soviet foreign policy actions and adducing their sources. They tend to describe the Soviet Union as a conservative nation beset with sufficient problems at home and abroad to render it at worst an uncooperative adversary, but one that is neither capable nor willing to pose a mortal threat to the United States or to the other industrial democracies. The Soviet Union, according to this perspective, is thus a typical great power with finite goals, rather than a revolutionary one with boundless global ambitions. Leaders in these two groups might thus join in supporting certain types of arms control agreements and other efforts at accommodation with the USSR but, of course, any prospects for such arrangements will also depend significantly on Soviet policies during the post-Brezhnev era. Such adventures as Afghanistan will virtually rule out any American consensus in favor of tension-reducing measures.

Finally, the Semi-Isolationists and Cold War Internationalists are united in a skeptical attitude about inflated definitions of economic interdependence; a denial of the thesis that Third World problems can be traced back to inequitable treatment at the hands of the Western industrial nations; and a rejection of the corollary that the United States has either special responsibilities or unique capabilities for assuring the material well-being of the less developed nations, especially of those that have demonstrated an unwillingness or inability to exercise the self-discipline for effective growth, or who remain wedded to values, ideologies and institutions that have demonstrably failed.[1] It is also not inconceivable that these two groups will also find a common cause in a significant redefinition of America's relationship to Western Europe and NATO, although probably for quite divergent reasons. Withdrawal of some or all American troops from Europe would be more consistent with the basic tenets of isolationism than with those of Cold War Internationalism. As indicated earlier, however, there are increasingly visible signs that some adhering to the latter viewpoint are more or less ready to write off Western Europe as hopelessly neutralist, if not defeatist, in its obsession for preserving détente, even in the face of Afghanistan, martial law in Poland, and other violations of the Helsinki accords. Some Cold War Internationalists who are troubled by the unprecedented magnitude of budget deficits also perceive that a reduction or total withdrawal of American forces for Europe offers the possibility of reducing the immense defense budgets proposed by the Reagan Administration.

Except in severe crises, persisting dissensus on foreign affairs would appear to rule out more enduring coalitions that might sustain long-term projects and ambitious American undertakings to cope with or to direct significant international changes. Bruising battles in the Congress—

comparable to those marking the Panama Canal Treaties, the SALT II Treaty (before it was withdrawn), the sale of AWACS aircraft to Saudi Arabia and the MX missile—seem likely to emerge in the wake of many major foreign policy initiatives. To gain a victory on one issue an administration might well deplete its political resources in the Congress, consequently reducing its leverage on others. The Panama Canal Treaties were sufficiently divisive for both parties that President Carter was forced to invest virtually all of his political capital to ensure their acceptance by the Senate. It was widely believed that several key Senators (for example, Republican leader Howard Baker) would be forced, by virtue of their votes supporting the Administration on the Panama Canal, to oppose the President on the SALT II Treaty. Moreover, the absence of general agreement on guiding principles of foreign policy may enhance the prospects for success of single-issue political factions, be they ethnic groups determined to redress perceived grievances abroad (for example, Greek-Americans, who have been notably successful in shaping and constraining American policy toward Turkey), or any of a score of industry-labor coalitions determined to protect such fledgling industries as automobiles, steel, textiles, machine tools, dairy products, shoes, sugar, consumer electronics, and others against the ravages of international competition.

The preceding discussion may appear to have taken an excessively static view, writing off prematurely the ability of an administration, especially one that gained a substantial victory, to forge a new foreign policy consensus. That Richard Nixon did not do so after his landslide victory in 1972 may perhaps be attributed to the Watergate scandal and its corrosive effects, as Nixon's energies and po-

litical resources were increasingly expended in a futile effort to stay in office. That Jimmy Carter failed to do so has been variously attributed to the narrowness of his electoral victory in 1976 and to a lack of political skill and acumen. Ronald Reagan suffers neither from the taint of major scandal nor from the ambiguities and constraints attending a close electoral victory. He has also demonstrated some political abilities in dealing with the public and the Congress that surpass those of his immediate predecessor. The 1981 tax bill is evidence of the latter point. However, as suggested [previously], his Administration has been less successful in gaining domestic support for his foreign and defense policies. What strategies might an administration then pursue for building a consensus? Several possibilities come to mind.

One approach to the problem is illustrated by a memorandum written by Secretary of State William Seward at a moment when the United States were becoming visibly disunited. To remedy what Seward perceived as the fact that "We are at the end of a month's administration, and yet without a policy, either domestic or foreign," he advised Abraham Lincoln:

I would demand explanation from Spain and France, categorically, at once.

I would seek explanations from Great Britain and Russia, and send agents to Canada, Mexico, and Central America to rouse a vigorous continental spirit of independence on this continent against European intervention.

And, if satisfactory explanations are not received from Spain and France,

Would convene Congress and declare war against them.[2]

Fortunately, Lincoln had the wisdom to reject Seward's mad suggestion—appropriately offered on April Fools Day, 1861—for dealing with domestic dissensus. War or external adventures may be perceived as tempting strategies for diverting attention away from seemingly intractable problems and domestic failures. Troubled dictatorships as varied as those in Argentina, Cuba, Libya, Iran, and Iraq have done so in recent years. It is, of course, a more dangerous strategy for major powers, but it may still be quite tempting to employ rhetorical fusillades against external adversaries as vehicles for creating national unity. At his confirmation hearing, Secretary of State Alexander Haig asserted that it is essential to "seek actively to shape events, and, in the process, attempt to force a consensus of likeminded people."[3] One cannot dismiss as totally implausible the hypothesis that repeated verbal clashes between Washington and Moscow during the initial months of the Reagan Administration were partly a consensus-building strategy.

Nor, of course, should one underestimate Moscow's ability to take precisely the actions that will sustain and add legitimacy to a hardline American policy toward the USSR. The Soviet invasion of Afghanistan may have been crucial to Reagan's nomination and election, both by offering vivid supporting evidence for his thesis of Soviet aggressiveness and by making the more optimistic Carter theory of Soviet behavior appear, in the eyes of many, to be naive and misguided. Soviet actions in and around Poland could have similar effects, although to date (1983) the situation in Poland appears to have had an impact very similar to that of events in Iran and Afghanistan: it has confirmed for many the validity of their prior foreign policy beliefs. Some examples will illustrate this point. Several Cold War Internationalists have asserted that neglect of American armed forces rendered the Administration impotent to deal

effectively with the issue. They failed to note, however, that the Eisenhower Administration, which possessed clear military superiority, responded similarly to the East German and Hungarian uprisings. Many Post-Cold War Internationalists found in Poland's tragedy evidence of Soviet restraint. They therefore supported resumption of aid to Poland and of arms control negotiations with the USSR, and opposed efforts to establish linkages between issues. Finally, a leading Semi-Isolationist suggested that Poland was too vital to Soviet security to warrant demands that Moscow keep its hands out of affairs in that country, and warned against driving the USSR "to desperation by pressing it mercilessly against a closed door."[4]

The imposition of martial law on Poland thus illustrates once again the durability of belief systems and their impact on the interpretation of events. However, an outright Soviet military invasion of that unfortunate country, especially if it leads to large-scale resistance and heavy casualties, could well prove to be the catalyst for creating a hard-line anti-Soviet consensus. Some of Reagan's critics have gone beyond attacking him for a "do nothing" policy on Poland, suggesting that the erosion during recent years of anti-communist zeal lies at the root of the problem because it has eliminated the moral foundations of American foreign policy. Evidence presented here, however, indicates no overwhelming enthusiasm for anti-communist crusades. Indeed, even many of the staunchest Cold War Internationalists favor entering into an alliance with China as a means of containing Soviet expansion.[5]

A second road to consensus brings to mind the somewhat wistful comments of a Carter Administration official when the SALT II Treaty was about to be presented to the Senate for ratification: "If Eisenhower was [sic] President, all he'd have to do is say: 'I've read the treaty, and I think it's good,' and he'd get a tremendous number of people to follow him."[6] More generally, an administration might invoke all of the symbols and practices of the early post-World War II decades in an effort to gain public and congressional support for the main outlines of its external policies. Appeals to "the national interest," "bipartisanship," "politics stops at the water's edge," "national security requirements," and the like might be called into service. By themselves, however, they are more likely to prove effective for the short run, especially in times of genuine and acute crisis, than for the longer-range goal of building domestic support for major international undertakings.

Moreover, structural and other changes in the Congress during the past two decades have rendered the task more difficult. The premise that "the Executive knows best" on matters of foreign policy has not fared well in recent years; as one Congressman recently put it, "For us, it is conventional wisdom that the President of the United States lies. That was unthinkable before the 1960s."[7] The same period has also witnessed a significant decentralization of power in the Congress. During the Eisenhower era, if the President could gain the support of House Speaker Sam Rayburn and Senate Majority Leader Lyndon Johnson, that was usually sufficient to ensure Congressional support, but the power of legislative leaders and committee chairmen has since declined. In any case, it seems unlikely that, either by virtue of widely-perceived expertise or of overwhelming public popularity, Reagan and his top foreign policy advisers can come close to matching the Congressional and public support almost

routinely accorded to Eisenhower.[8] Moreover, aside from anti-Soviet rhetoric, the Administration has been less than articulate in identifying the major conceptions that inform its foreign and defense policies, thus enhancing doubts about its competence to deal effectively with foreign affairs.

A third and far more modest approach is to follow the advice of the Semi-Isolationists, who propose that the United States should pursue external policies of retrenchment across a broad range of undertakings and commitments in part because such policies would not require a domestic consensus. That this approach would strike a responsive chord among a not insignificant minority of Americans seems clear from the evidence presented ... [previously]. This is not the place to debate the merits or demerits of the Semi-Isolationist prescription. Suffice it to say that, although the Reagan Administration may well adopt some isolationist measures (for example, despite rhetoric about the virtues of free trade, it has been somewhat protectionist in international trade), in most respects this approach to foreign policy appears to be too fundamentally at odds with the stated philosophies and goals of the President and his supporters to serve as the foundations of their foreign policies. However, future administrations might well find greater appeal in the isolationist approach.

There is at least one other approach to the task of consensus-building, but in many ways it is the most difficult of all to pursue effectively. Moreover, it offers no guarantee of success. It requires substantial political skills and perhaps more patience than one could reasonably expect, given the premium on short-run successes that arises from the frequency of elections and the ever-lengthening, virtually non-stop, electoral campaigns. This alternative requires a leadership capable of developing and articulating a vision of the world, of the American role within in, and of appropriate strategies and tactics that is persuasive in its diagnosis (what is the nature of the international system, what are the major trends, what are the primary threats and opportunities), its value component (what is desirable), and the assessment of the balance between available resources and existing constraints (what is feasible). It might stimulate an informed debate, not only to diagnose the threats from an international system that appears more firmly on the path to anarchy than to a "global village," but also to depict a vision of a preferred world order, of how the United States might best contribute toward its achievement, and of the means of doing so. According to this view, "The 'present danger' may be the failure to debate what it really is."[9] A short list of questions for discussion might include, but not necessarily be limited to, America's relations with each major sector of the international system.

What goals and strategies should govern American relations with the Soviet Union? Neither "détente" nor "human rights plus arms control," the dominant themes of the winning candidates in the 1972 and 1976 presidential elections proved especially effective, either for purposes of creating a post-Vietnam foreign policy consensus at home or for developing and sustaining more stable and cooperative relations with the USSR. It would be premature to pass final judgment on the Reagan approach to Soviet-American relations but, after two years, evidence of eroding domestic support for some of its key elements is not especially hard to find. Even some of Reagan's strongest supporters in 1980 have been

critical of what they judge to be weak responses to the imposition of martial law in Poland and the KAL 007 incident whereas others fear that worsening relations between Moscow and Washington will lead, at best, to a costly and futile race and, at worst, to armed conflict. Farmers, who have welcomed the cancellation of the Carter grain embargo, may be a notable exception to this observation.

Recent years have witnessed a combination of rapidly increasing Soviet military strength and brutal interventions in both contiguous and non-contiguous areas, on the one hand, and, on the other, a growing list of seemingly intractable domestic problems, including but not confined to agriculture, economic growth, corruption, infant mortality rates, and rampant alcoholism. Even the nuclear "balance of terror," which could have been described as reasonably stable during the 1960s and 1970s, is becoming unstable owing to emerging technologies (especially those that are increasing the accuracy of missile guidance systems), the Lilliputian successes of SALT and other arms control negotiations, nuclear proliferation, and the deployment of weapons with clear "first strike" capabilities. If the land-based version of the powerful and highly accurate MX missile and its Soviet counterpart (the SS-18) represent the wave of the future in strategic deterrence, then that future is likely to be unstable, expensive, and unburdened by serious progress in arms control. And if the debates on the MX and its basing mode are indicative, the future will also be bankrupt in any creative ideas, for example, about strategies for enhancing crisis stability. This volatile combination hardly augurs well for Soviet-American relations during the 1980s. Moreover, the costs of a policy toward the Soviet Union that is all sticks and no carrots may be quite high, both at home (for example, among disaffected farmers if grain sales are once again cut off, and among the growing upper-middle class anti-nuclear movement), and among those allies who, wisely or otherwise, tend to prefer détente to a Cold War.

What kinds of arrangements should be established with the other industrial democracies for dealing not only with defense issues (for example, strengthening NATO, or the perpetual issue of defining a proper division of contributions and responsibilities within the alliance), but also with such common problems as inflation, unemployment, energy and trade? During the period immediately following World War II, rapid and stable economic growth, fueled in part by cheap and ample oil, and supported by stable exchange rates and a strong American dollar, made possible a dramatic expansion of trade that was widely perceived as mutually beneficial. The "economic lessons of the 1930s" had seemingly been well learned. Today energy is scarce, expensive, and its availability is subject to political whim, in some cases of unstable and decidedly unattractive authoritarian regimes; high inflation and unemployment are the common lot of most industrial democracies; lack of confidence, not only in the dollar but also in other currencies, is reflected in the gyrating price of gold; and protectionist pressures have increased to the point that the danger of a trade war cannot be dismissed casually. Under these conditions, will the temptation to achieve a temporary advantage (that is, at least until the next election) by returning to the "beggar thy neighbor" economics of the 1930s prove too powerful? Or, can the industrial democracies establish new "regimes" for dealing creatively and cooperatively with these and other common problems? Can they establish the legitimacy of doing so among their respective domestic constituencies, or will they find that it is easier to mollify increasingly impatient electorates, first by placing the blame squarely on other nations, and then by taking actions that are consistent with such xenophobic diagnoses?

What relationships can be established with the less developed nations in order to cope with both the reality of a vast gap between the rich and poor nations, and the perception that the existing international order is structured so as to exacerbate rather than mitigate the problem? What kinds of risks should the United States be prepared to run for the luxury of being dependent for much of its oil on nations that have proven to be less than consistently sympathetic to American foreign policy, or with whom it has only a partial community of interest? What policies may be most effective in averting the economic collapse of one or more developing nations, or, should that occur, how can its results be contained so as to prevent a global economic collapse? How should the United States cope with what is certain to be a growing phenomenon: strident and reflexive anti-Americanism generated by leaders who, unable or unwilling to deal with their own domestic problems, require an external scapegoat? Although the Soviet Union has made it clear that it feels no responsibility for bettering the lot of the poor nations, asserting that the source of those problems is "capitalist exploitation," there is every reason to expect that Washington rather than Moscow will be the target of choice. Finally, what role, if any, might the United States play in local and regional disputes in the Third World? What are the costs and benefits of a persistent tendency to define these conflicts as facets of the Cold

War? Does the tendency to assert that disputes in the Middle East and elsewhere are linked to Soviet-American competition, without offering compelling evidence that this is so, risk offending all parties and so reducing American credibility as virtually to rule out any effective role in working out effective settlements? Conversely, what are the risks of a predisposition to "local-itis," the propensity to regard all turmoil as reflecting only unique local conditions, or of "Robin Hood-itis," the tendency to regard all revolutionaries as selfless democrats who seek power only to share it equitably?

Declining concern, if not disillusionment, with the less developed nations is fed and sustained by the growth there of authoritarian, sometimes totalitarian, rather than liberal institutions; by the murderous antics of the Khaddafis, Mengistus, Idi Amins, Castros, Bokassas, Khomeinis, Pinochets, Pol Pots, and Pham Van Dongs; by fears that some forms of assistance to the LDCs may be the first step into another Vietnam-like quagmire; and by the sentiment that, after all, charity begins at home. Plummeting public support for foreign aid may be found in poll after poll, but leadership views reveal a greater concern for the plight of poor nations, perhaps in recognition that benign neglect may be both a practically ineffective and morally inappropriate answer to the challenges posed abroad by responsible spokesmen for the "Group of 77" and in this country by former World Bank President Robert McNamara.[10]

A list of questions organized along geographical lines is bound to be a very incomplete one. Other issues that may merit serious discussion include these. *To what extent, and how, should the United States work cooperatively on problems that are international in both etiology and consequences: population control; population movements and refugees; pollution of the atmosphere, land, and oceans; proliferation of nuclear technologies and materials; periodic famines; protectionist pressures; and the like?*

It is naive to expect informed debate and clarification of such complex issues during election campaigns. The history of American elections does not offer a great deal of encouragement in this respect. In the best of times, they rarely provide a congenial setting for a "great debate" on monumental issues. Even less may be expected when there is a bull market in confusion, frustration, anger, and disillusionment about foreign affairs.[11] Recall the disgraceful tone of much campaigning during the 1950 and 1952 elections, when Americans were frustrated by the "loss" of China and the stalemated Korean War. Nor was the 1980 election especially illuminating.

A political campaign may preclude a high-quality discussion of foreign policy issues, but its end does not ensure that the discussion will take place in the less frenetic post-election atmosphere. The period since the 1980 election has certainly offered little to sustain the hopes of the optimists. Not only has the Reagan Administration failed almost completely to articulate a convincing set of fundamental principles that underlie its policies, but the Democratic opposition has not done much better. The content and tone of debates among spokesmen for various viewpoints does not augur well for informed discussion of these important issues. Perhaps some consolation may be found in the fact that most contestants have steered clear of the tactics espoused by Joseph McCarthy, Richard Nixon and other demagogues of an earlier generation.[12]

A century and a half ago, a sympathetic French observer of the American experiment wrote:

As for myself, I do not hesitate to say that it is especially in the conduct of their foreign affairs that democracies appear to be decidedly inferior to other governments ... [A] democracy can only with great difficulty regulate the details of an important undertaking, persevere in a fixed design, and work out its execution in spite of serious obstacles.[13]

In the face of the deep domestic cleavages described here, and an abundant agenda of critical international problems, the 1980s promise to provide an especially challenging decade for the United States to demonstrate that de Tocqueville's observation was fundamentally in error.

NOTES

1. See, for example, the similarities in diagnoses of Third World development in George F. Kennan, *The Cloud of Danger* (Boston: Little, Brown, 1977); and Michael Novak, *The Spirit of Democratic Development* (New York: Simon & Schuster, 1982).
2. J. G. Nicolay and John Hay, *Abraham Lincoln: A History,* Vol III (New York: The Century Co., 1890), p. 446.
3. Haig continued: "Such a consensus will enable us to deal with the more fundamental tasks I have outlined; the management of Soviet power, the reestablishment of an orderly international economic climate, and economic and political maturation of developing nations to the benefit of their peoples and the achievement of a reasonable standard of international civility." *New York Times,* January 10, 1981, p. 9.
4. See, for example, Seymour Weiss, "The Reagan Response on Poland," *The Wall Street Journal,* December 29, 1981, p. 20; ...; Anthony Lewis, "Who Lost Poland?," *New York Times,* January 7, 1982, p. A27; Flora Lewis, "The Gravest Loss," *New York Times,* December 21, 1981, p. A27; George F. Kennan, "Jaruzelski's Course," *New York Times,* January 5, 1982, p. A15; and Kennan, "As the Kremlin Sees It," *New York Times,* January 6, 1982.
5. See, for example, Irving Kristol, "Consensus and Dissent in U.S. Foreign Policy," in Anthony Lake (ed.), *The Vietnam Legacy* (New York: New York University Press, 1976); and Norman Podhoretz, "Neo-conservative Anguish over Reagan's Foreign Policy," *New York Times Magazine,* May 2, 1982, pp. 30-3ff. Evidence on the issue of an alliance with China is summarized in ... [previously].
6. Quoted in Steven V. Roberts, "Arms Pact Friends and Foes Rally for Senate Battle," *New York Times,* April 13, 1979, p. A2.
7. Representative Gerry E. Studds, quoted in Steven V. Roberts, "A Critical Coterie on Foreign Policy," *New York Times,* April 5, 1982, p. A20.
8. Aside from Secretaries of State Alexander Haig and George Shultz, the total international experience of top leaders in the Reagan administration (including the President, Secretary of State, Secretary of Defense, Director of the Central Intelligence Agency, and National Security Adviser) is very thin indeed. Caspar Weinberger had been a domestic official throughout his previous public career, and CIA Director William Casey had only limited service in the OSS. Richard V. Allen served briefly in a minor role in the Nixon Administration, and William Clark had no demonstrable experience or expertise in foreign affairs. The latter two appointments also drew some unfavorable reaction because both Allen and Clark failed to earn the degrees they sought in postgraduate schools (University of Munich and Loyola Law School). Clark failed even to earn a BA degree. Following his confirmation hearing for the position of Undersecretary of State, Republican Senator Charles Percy warned: "Never again can we accept a man who professes no

knowledge in the area for which he has been nominated." Clark later served until 1983 as National Security adviser, a position from which he apparently wielded very substantial power. *The Wall Street Journal,* February 4, 1981, p. 1.

9. James Reston, "The Present Danger," *New York Times,* November 17, 1978, p. A29.

10. For a comparison of public and leadership views on foreign aid, see the figures in the 1975, 1979, and 1982 Chicago Council on Foreign Relations surveys. John E. Rielly, *American Public Opinion and Foreign Policy,* 1975; Rielly, *American Public Opinion and Foreign Policy,* 1979, both published by the CCFR; and Rielly, "American Opinion: Continuity, not Reaganism," *Foreign Policy,* no. 50 (Spring 1983), pp. 86-104.

11. The data on performance ratings presented in Chapters 3 (Table 3.3) and 6 (Table 6.5) appear to justify this interpretation of leadership moods [not reprinted here].

12. There are, however, exceptions. See, for example, the vitriolic attacks in Noam Chomsky, *Toward a New Cold War* (New York: Pantheon Books, 1982); and Irving Kristol, "What Choice Is There in Salvador?," *The Wall Street Journal,* April 4, 1983, p. 16. The latter writes that, "the very idea of fair play, like the idea of gentlemanly conduct, is part of a conservative political tradition, not of a liberal—and definitely not of a left-liberal tradition."

13. Alexis de Tocqueville, *Democracy in America* (ed. Phillips Bradley), Vol. 1 (New York: Alfred A. Knopf, 1945), p. 235.

30. THE FUTURE OF AMERICAN FOREIGN POLICY: NEW REALITIES AND NEW WAYS OF THINKING

George Shultz

I am honored to lead off this important series of hearings on the future of American foreign policy. This is an auspicious moment: the beginning of a new presidential term, of a new Congress, and of the term of a distinguished new chairman [Senator Richard G. Lugar]. It is, for many reasons, a time of great promise and opportunity for the United States in world affairs.

Therefore, I commend the chairman for focusing the attention of the Congress and the American people on the fundamental issues we will face—not just the day-to-day issues that make the news but the underlying trends at work and the most important goals we pursue.

My presentation today is thus of a special kind. I would like to step back a bit and look at the present situation in perspective—the perspective of recent history, the perspective of the intellectual currents of our time, and the perspective of America's ideals and their relevance to the world's future.

THE CHANGING INTERNATIONAL SYSTEM

Soon after the dawn of the nuclear age, Albert Einstein observed that everything had changed except our ways of thinking. Even so dramatic a development as the nuclear revolution took a long time to be fully understood; how much longer has it

Source: Statement before the Senate Foreign Relations Committee, January 31, 1985.

usually taken to understand the implications of more subtle, intangible historical changes taking place around us.

Nineteen hundred and forty-five, everyone knows, marked a major turning point. An international system that had lasted for more than a century had broken down under the weight of two world wars and a great depression. An international order centered on Europe and dominated by Europe was replaced in the early postwar period by a new arrangement—a world dominated by two new superpowers, torn by ideological conflict, and overshadowed by nuclear weapons that made a new world war potentially suicidal. At the same time, an integrated international economic system established by America's initiative—based on the dollar and on a strong commitment to the freest possible flow of trade and investment—replaced the unbridled economic nationalism that had helped undermine international peace between the wars.

But history never stops. The postwar order, too, evolved and changed its shape. The breakup of colonial empires brought scores of new states onto the world stage. The so-called Third World became the scene of a growing number of local and regional conflicts. America, after Vietnam, retreated for a time from its active role of leadership. Europe, China, and Japan came into their own again as important economic and political actors; the energy crisis dramatized both the diffusion of economic power and the vulnerability of the postwar economic system. The

United States and the Soviet Union attempted a political dialogue to stabilize relations and control nuclear arms; then the dialogue broke down under the weight of the Soviet military buildup and geopolitical offensive.

Today, the cycle is turning again. Change is constant. America has recovered its strength and self-confidence. Power continues to be dispersed and the structure of political relations more complex, even as the interdependence of states increases. And as we head toward the 21st century, is a stable new pattern of international relations emerging? Einstein's observation takes on new relevance: our ways of thinking must adapt to new realities; we must grasp the new trends and understand their implications.

But we are not just observers; we are participants, and we are engaged. America is again in a position to have a major influence over the trend of events—and America's traditional goals and values have *not* changed. Our duty must be to help shape the evolving trends in accordance with our ideals and interests; to help build a new structure of international stability that will ensure peace, prosperity, and freedom for coming generations. This is the real challenge of our foreign policy over the coming years.

What are the forces of change? And what are the possible elements of a new and more secure international system?

RELATIONS BETWEEN THE SUPERPOWERS

Relations between the superpowers remain crucial, even though their political predominance is less than it was a few decades ago. Over 50 years' experience of U.S.-Soviet relations has given us by now a mature understanding of what is possible and what is not possible in this rela-

tionship. Yet conditions are evolving and the problem remains a conceptual challenge.

True friendship and cooperation will remain out of reach so long as the Soviet system is driven by ideology and national ambition to seek to aggrandize its power and undermine the interests of the democracies. We must resist this Soviet power drive vigorously if there is to be any hope for lasting stability. At the same time, in the thermonuclear age the common interest in survival gives both sides an incentive to moderate the rivalry and to seek, in particular, ways to control nuclear weapons and reduce the risks of war.[1] We cannot know whether such a steady Western policy will, over time, lead to a mellowing of the Soviet system; perhaps not. But the West has the same responsibility in either case: to resist Soviet encroachments firmly while holding the door open to more constructive possibilities.

After the failure of their political campaign to divide NATO, their propaganda to thwart deployment of intermediate-range nuclear missiles in Europe, and their boycott of talks, the Soviets have now returned to the arms control dialogue. We welcome this. My meeting in Geneva with Soviet Foreign Minister Gromyko was a constructive beginning of what the United States hopes will be a fruitful negotiation.

My able interlocutor, Andrei Gromyko, is, in a sense, the living embodiment of some of the Soviet Union's great advantages—continuity, patience, the ability to fashion a long-term strategy and stick to it. When the Soviets shift tactics, it is more often than not an adjustment to objective conditions without basic diversion from their long-term aims.

The democracies, in contrast, have long had difficulty maintaining the same consistency, coherence, discipline, and sense of strategy. Free societies are often impatient. Western attitudes have fluctuated between extremes of gloom and pessimism, on the one hand, and susceptibility to a Soviet smile on the other. Our ways of thinking have tended too often to focus either on increasing our strength or on pursuing negotiations; we have found it hard to do both simultaneously—which is clearly the most sensible course and probably the only way we can sustain either our defense programs or our ability to negotiate.

It is vital, for example, to carry through with the modernization of our strategic forces—in particular, the MX—to avoid undercutting our negotiators just as they begin the quest for real reductions in nuclear arms. The Soviets will have little incentive to negotiate seriously for reductions to lower, equal levels if we hand them on a silver platter their long-cherished goal of *unilateral* American reductions. Likewise, as we pursue such agreements, we are obliged to bear in mind the Soviets' record of violating previous accords and to insist on effective verification provisions in any new agreements.

In the last four years, the underlying conditions that affect U.S.-Soviet relations have changed dramatically. A decade or so ago, when the United States was beset by economic difficulties, neglecting its defenses, and hesitant about its role of leadership, the Soviets exploited these conditions. They continued their relentless military buildup; they and their clients moved more boldly in the geopolitical arena, intervening in such places as Angola, Cambodia, Ethiopia, and Afghanistan, believing that the West was incapable of resisting. They had reason for confidence that what they call the global "correlation of forces" was shifting in their favor.

Today, the West is more united than

ever before. The United States is restoring its military strength and economic vigor and has regained its self-assurance; we have a President with a fresh mandate from the people for an active role in leadership. The Soviets, in contrast, face profound structural economic difficulties, a continuing succession problem, and restless allies; its diplomacy and its clients are on the defensive in many parts of the world. We have reason to be confident that the "correlation of forces" is shifting back in *our* favor.

Nevertheless, history won't do our work for us. The Soviets can be counted upon periodically to do something, somewhere, that is abhorrent or inimical to our interests. The question is how the West can respond in a way that could help discipline Soviet international behavior but does not leave our own strategy vulnerable to periodic disruption by such external shocks. We must never let ourselves be so wedded to improving relations with the Soviets that we turn a blind eye to actions that undermine the very foundation of stable relations; symbolic responses to outrageous Soviet behavior have their place, and so do penalties and sanctions. At the same time, experience shows we cannot deter or undo Soviet geopolitical encroachments except by helping, in one way or another, those resisting directly on the ground. And many negotiations and endeavors we undertake with the Soviets serve mutual interests—indeed, they *all* should.

This leaves us with tough choices. Whether important negotiations ought to be interrupted after some Soviet outrage will always be a complex calculation. When the Soviets shot down the Korean Air Lines passenger plane in 1983, President Reagan made sure the world knew the full unvarnished truth about the atrocity; nevertheless, he also sent our arms control negotiators back to Geneva because he believed that a reduction in nuclear weapons was a critical priority.

In short, our "way of thinking" must seek sustainable strategy geared to American goals and interests, in the light of Soviet behavior but not just a reaction to it. Such a strategy requires a continuing willingness to solve problems through negotiation where this serves our interests (and presumably mutual interests). Our leverage will come from creating objective realities that will give the Soviets a growing stake in better relations with us across the board: by modernizing our defenses, assisting our friends, and confronting Soviet challenges. We must learn to pursue a strategy geared to long-term thinking and based on both negotiation and strength simultaneously, if we are to build a stable U.S.-Soviet relationship for the next century.[2]

The intellectual challenge of a new era faces us in a related dimension, namely *arms control*. The continuous revolution in technology means that the strategic balance—and the requirements of deterrence—are never static. Unfortunately, conventional ways of thinking about many of these questions continue to lag behind reality.

For decades, standard strategic doctrine in the West has ultimately relied on the balance of terror—the confrontation of offensive arsenals by which the two sides threaten each other with mass extermination. Certainly deterrence has worked under these conditions; nevertheless, for political, strategic, and even moral reasons, we should seek to do better than the proposition that our defense strategy *must* rely on offensive threats and *must* leave our people unprotected against attack. The Soviets, for their part, have *always* attached enormous importance to strategic defense, including not only air defense and civil defense but a deployed and modernized antiballistic missile system around Moscow—and intensive research into new defensive technologies.

The past of technological advance now opens possibilities for new ways of strategic thinking—never an easy process. The vehemence of some of the criticism of the President's Strategic Defense Initiative (SDI) seems to come less from the argument over technical feasibility—which future research will answer one way or another in an objective manner—than from the passionate defense of orthodox doctrine in the face of changing strategic realities. We are proceeding with SDI research because we see a positive and, indeed, revolutionary potential: defensive measures may become available that could render obsolete the threat of an offensive first strike. A new strategic equilibium based on defensive technologies and sharply reduced offensive deployments is likely to be the most stable and secure arrangement of all.

Our concept can be described as follows: during the next 10 years, the U.S. objective is a radical reduction in the power of existing and planned offensive nuclear arms, as well as the stabilization of the relationship between offensive and defensive nculear arms, whether on earth or in space. We are even now looking forward to a period of transition to a more stable world, with greatly reduced levels of nuclear arms and an enhanced ability to deter war based upon an increasing contribution of non-nuclear defenses against offensive nuclear arms. This period of transition could lead to the eventual elimination of all nuclear arms, both offensive and defensive. A world free of nuclear arms is an ultimate objective to which we, the Soviet Union, and all other nations can agree.

THE GROWING UNITY AND STRENGTH OF FRIENDS AND ALLIES

As the political dominance of the superpowers began to erode in the last few decades, some saw a five-power world emerging—with the United States, Soviet Union, Western Europe, China, and Japan as the major players. After the energy crisis of the early 1970s, others emphasized the increasing importance of the North-South relationship. The fact is, none of these concepts adequately describes the evolving pattern of world politics. In my view, the most striking trend is something else: the growing dynamism, cohesion, and cooperation of like-minded nations that share an important set of positive goals.

Equilibrium is not enough. American foreign policy is driven by positive goals—peace, democracy, liberty, and human rights; racial justice; economic and social progress; the strengthening of cooperation and the rule of the law. These are not Soviet goals. Yet they are at the core of any durable international system, because they are the goals that inspire peoples and nations around the world.[3]

The new spirit and unity of peoples that share these goals is a new trend we can see in many regions of the world and in many dimensions of foreign policy.

We see a new spirit of collaboration and friendship in our ties with our immediate neighbors, **Canada and Mexico** —ties whose importance is self-evident and which are a priority interest of the President.

In the **Atlantic community,** our time is marked by a new degree of political harmony and intimate collaboration among the Western allies. Just as striking, Japan, too, has emerged as a partner on key political and security issues. There is a new awareness, for example, of the importance of strengthening conventional defenses, as a way of bolstering Europe's security while reducing NATO's reliance on nuclear weapons. A strong Western deterrence posture is the most solid basis for engaging the East in constructive negotiations. Under Lord Carrington's wise leadership, NATO is taking steps for the short run to improve its readiness and infrastructure. For the longer run, the alliance is addressing other critical deficiencies, including the fundamental challenge of improving the efficiency of allied defense procurement.

Amid all the changes in the world, the security and well-being of Western Europe continue to be a vital interest of the United States. We have always supported West European unity, knowing that a strong Europe, while it would be a competitor in some ways, was in the overall interest of the free world. We wish the European Community well; we encourage our European friends to make further progress in developing a true European-wide market and in breaking down structural rigidities that impede both economic expansion and effective economic cooperation with us.

We see also, in Europe, new and creative thinking about the continuing pursuit of political unity and about strengthening West European cooperation in the defense field. We support both these goals. The West can only benefit from a major European role in world affairs. And the peoples of Western Europe should see defense as an endeavor they undertake for their own future, not as a favor to the United States. With statesmanship and a spirit of collaboration on both sides of the Atlantic, this evolution will strengthen the common defense and heighten the sense of common political purpose among the democracies.

As we think about Europe's evolution, we cannot forget **Eastern Europe.** Since the days of the Marshall Plan, when the West invited the East to join, we have always wanted the success of Western Europe to be a beacon to *all* of Europe. The present political division of the continent is wholly artificial; it exists only because it has been imposed by brute Soviet power; the United States has never recognized it as legitimate or permanent. Behind this cruel barrier lie political repression and economic stagnation. In certain countries, there are efforts at liberalization. But *all* the peoples of Eastern Europe are capable of something better, deserve something better, and yearn for something better. We have witnessed in recent years the powerful aspiration for free trade unions, for economic reform, for political and religious freedom, for true peace and security, for human rights as promised by the Helsinki accords.[4] We hope to see the day when the Soviet Union learns to think anew of its own security in terms compatible with the freedom, security, and independence of its neighbors.

In **East Asia and the Pacific,** another new reality is changing our thinking about the world. The economic dynamism of this region is taking on increasing importance, not only as a factor in America's foreign trade but as an economic model for the developing world and as a unique and attractive vision of the future. We see the countries of free Asia growing at 7% a year over the past decade; for the past five years, our trade with East Asia and the Pacific has been greater than our trade with any other region and is expanding at an accelerating rate. ASEAN [Association of South East Asian Nations] has become one of the world's most impressive examples of economic development and regional political co-operation. The Republic of Korea is a spectacular economic success story. Japan is playing a larger role—responsibly, positively, and cooperatively—commensurate with its growing strength. Experience is proving that economic openness is the formula for prosperity.

Pragmatism is now the watchword in the People's Republic of China, where the hopes for economic modernization have been invested—wisely—in a bold program of reform. China's long march to market is a truly historic event—a great nation throwing off outmoded economic doctrines and liberating the energies of a billion talented people. We wish China well in this exciting endeavor.

There are, of course, problems that post dangers to this bright economic future: the Soviet military buildup in the region; aggression by the Soviet Union and its clients in Afghanistan and Cambodia; unresolved tensions on the Korean Peninsula; internal problems in various countries. East Asia has a rich heritage of civilization—and also a turbulent history of bitter conflict. The tragedy that two of Asia's great ancient monuments—Angkor Wat and Borobudur—have suffered damage from modern violence is both a paradox and a warning.

The United States is conscious of its responsibility to contribute, in its way, to security and stability in East Asia and the Pacific. Our diplomacy seeks peaceful solutions to Asia's problems so that the fullest potential of its promise can be realized. We welcome, in particular, the role of ASEAN, including the front-line state of Thailand, which is working effectively to curb Vietnamese expansionism and aggression and to achieve a just settlement of the Cambodian conflict.

Overall, we are enormously encouraged by the new trend we see toward wider collaboration among many Asian nations with an extraordinary diversity of cultures, races, and political systems. A sense of Pacific community is emerging. There is an expanding practice of regional consultation and a developing sense of common interest in regional security. In this sense, a decade after Vietnam, the United States has more than restored its position in Asia. We can be proud of the vitality of our alliances, friendships, and productive ties in this promising region. If nations act with wisdom and statesmanship, we may well be at the threshold of a new era in international relations in the Pacific Basin.[5]

In **Latin America,** another kind of trend is apparent—the steady advance of democracy. Democracy is hardly a new idea, but this new development is revising some earlier assumptions in some quarters about the world's political future. A few years back, pessimists maintained that the industrial democracies were doomed to permanent minority status in the world community. Today, there is mounting evidence that the ideal of liberty is alive and well. In the Western Hemisphere, almost 95% of the population of Latin America and the Caribbean today live under governments that are either democratic or clearly on the road to democracy—in contrast to only one third in 1979. Over the last 5 years, popularly elected leaders have replaced military rulers or dictators in Argentina, Bolivia, Ecuador, El Salvador, Honduras, Panama, Peru, and Grenada. Brazil and Uruguay will inaugurate new civilian presidents in March. Guatemala is in transition to democracy. After a long twilight of dictatorship, the trend toward free elections and popular sovereignty in this hemisphere is something to cheer about. [6]

The United States has always been a champion of democracy. Democratic institutions are the best guarantor of human rights and also the best long-term guarantor of stability. The National Endowment for Democracy, with bipartisan support, is one reflection of this American commitment. On every continent, we see a trend toward democracy or else a yearning for democracy; both are vivid demonstrations that the idea of liberty is far from a culture-bound aspiration or monopoly of the industrialized West.

In fact, after years of guerrilla insurgencies led by communists against pro-Western governments, we now see dramatic and heartening examples of popular insurgencies *against* communist regimes. Today, in a variety of different circumstances—in Nicaragua, in Afghanistan, in Cambodia, in Ethiopia, and elsewhere in Africa—Marxist-Leninist rulers have found that the aspiration for representative government is not so easy to suppress. Americans have a long and honorable tradition of supporting the struggle of other peoples for freedom, democracy, independence, and liberation from tyranny. In the 19th century we supported Simon Bolivar, Polish patriots, and others seeking freedom—reciprocating, in a way, the aid given to us in our own revolution by other nations like France.

As the President put it a week ago: "[W]e, who are committed to free government and democratic institutions, must maintain a sense of fraternity between ourselves and other freedom-loving peoples." This is a proud heritage and a moral responsibility, and it poses some practical questions that we must face up to early in the 99th Congress.

The future of democracy is precisely what is at stake in **Central America.** U.S. policy is to promote democracy, reform, and human rights; to support economic development; to help provide a security shield against those who seek to spread tyranny by force; and to support dialogue and negotiation both within and among the countries of the region. Acting directly and through Cuba, the Soviet Union is abetting the establishment of a new communist dictatorship in Nicaragua.

We are backing democratic government and democratic political forces throughout Central America against extremists of both the left and the right. If we abandon those seeking democracy, the extremists will gain and the forces of moderation and decency will be the victims. This is why the Administration has worked so hard, and will continue to work hard, for effective negotiations, for economic and security assistance and for the bipartisan plan that emerged from the Kissinger commission [National Bipartisan Commission on Central America]. If the forces of dictatorship continue to feel free to aid and abet insurgencies in the name of "proletarian internationalism," it would be absurd if the democracies felt inhibited about promoting the cause of democracy, even by collective self-defense against such actions. Our nation's vital interests *and* moral responsibility require us to stand by our friends in their struggle for freedom.[7]

THE DYNAMIC OF CHANGE

The process of change is inexorable. In **southern Africa** we have a role to play in working for democratic change in South Africa. We are also key to efforts to help create a climate of regional security that will enable and encourage countries to get on with the priority of building decent and prosperous societies. In short, U.S. policy must pursue the dual objectives of racial justice and regional security. These two goals are not in conflict; they reinforce each other. But achieving them requires responsible, prudent, and dedicated diplomacy.

These twin challenges call for serious analysis and sober thinking, not emotional responses. We have already accomplished much, but our influence is not infinite. Today, there is less cross-border violence in southern Africa than at any time in more than a decade. Progress is being made toward a Namibia settlement. We have strengthened ties with Mozambique and other regional states. And South Africa itself has developed cooperative relations with many of its neighbors.

President Reagan has made clear that we regard South African apartheid as repugnant. He spoke loud and clear on December 10 when he said:

> We . . . call upon the Government of South Africa to reach out to its black majority by ending the forced removal of blacks from their communities and the detention, without trial, and lengthy imprisonment of black leaders. . . . [W]e ask that the constructive changes of recent years be broadened to address the aspirations of all South Africans. . . . We urge both the Government and the people of South Africa to move toward a more just society.

Within South Africa, a dynamic of change is already at work: more positive change is occurring now than in the 1970s or 1960s or 1950s. The positive influence of our relationship—our diplomacy, our companies, our assistance programs for black South Africans—is helping to build the basis for further change. Apartheid must go. But the only course consistent with American values is to engage ourselves as a force for constructive, peaceful change while there is still a chance. It cannot be our choice to cheer on, from the sidelines, the forces of polarization that could erupt in a race war; it is not our job to exacerbate hardship, which could lead to the same result.

Another region of change is the **Middle East.** Recent events have reminded us that the Arab-Israeli conflict is far from the only source of tension in that part of the world. There are other deep-seated national, ethnic, and religious conflicts like the Iran-Iraq war; there are diverse sources of radical extremism ranging from Marxist-Leninist ideology, to Islamic fundamentalism, to Qadhafi's bizarre personal brand of fanaticism; the Soviets seek to reinforce rejectionist elements and to exploit regional tensions for their own advantage.

The United States will continue its efforts to promote peaceful solutions in this vital area. This mediation is, of course, a traditional American role, but new conditions always call for new ways of thinking about how to pursue it. We are committed to the support of diplomatic efforts to end the conflicts in the gulf, in Lebanon, and in the Sahara. We are committed to the President's September 1 initiative as the most promising route to a solution of the Palestinian problem. We will be intensively engaged this year in consultations with our Arab and Israeli friends to explore opportunities for progress.[8]

In the **global economy,** an important shift of another kind is taking place—an intellectual shift, reflecting some lessons from experience. Lord Keynes's point about practical men being in thrall to some defunct economist may be less true now than in the past. Or perhaps the views first expressed by Adam Smith over two centuries ago on the creation of the "wealth of nations" are once again gaining practical prominence. At any rate, reality is intruding on some long-held notions about economic policy.

In both industrialized and developing countries, the economic difficulties of recent years are reminding us of some old truths about the real sources of economic progress. Some of us never forgot those truths. But recent experience has fueled a broad and long-overdue skepticism about statist solutions, central planning, and government direction.

This intellectual shift is partly the product of the extraordinary vigor of the American recovery. The United States has revised its tax system to provide real incentives to work, to save, to invest, to take risks, to be efficient. We have reduced government regulation, intervention, and control. We have opened opportunities for freer competition in transportation, finance, communication, manufacturing, and distribution. Last year's real growth in GNP [gross national product] was the sharpest increase since 1951; inflation was the lowest since 1967. The overall result has been the extraordinary creation of over 7 million new jobs in 2 years.

Success inspires emulation. Not only in East Asia, as I noted, but on every continent—Europe, Latin America, Africa, and elsewhere in Asia—we see movement to decentralize, to deregulate, to denationalize, to reduce rigidity, and to enlarge the scope for individual producers and consumers to cooperate freely through markets. In Africa, for example, if there is to be a long-term solution to the problem of hunger, it will have to come not just from relief efforts but from training, productive investment, and liberalizing reforms in agriculture; our aid policy is encouraging the efforts of African countries to move further in this direction.[9]

A worldwide revolution in economic thought and economic policy is underway. And it is coming just in time, because it coincides with yet another revolution—a revolution in the technological base of the global economy. This is what Walter Wriston has called "the onrushing age of information technology"—the combination of microchip computers, advanced telecommunications, and continuing innovation that is transforming almost every aspect of human endeavor.

The implications of this revolution are not only economic. First of all, the very existence of these technologies is yet another testimony to the crucial importance of entrepreneurship—and government policies that give free rein to entrepreneurship—as the wellspring of technological creativity and economic growth. The closed societies of the East are likely to fall far behind in these areas—and Western societies that maintain too many restrictions on economic activity run the same risk.

Second, any government that resorts to heavyhanded measures to control or regulate or tax the flow of electronic information will find itself stifling growth of the world economy as well as its own progress. This is one of the reasons why the United States is pressing for a new round of trade negotiations in these service fields of data processing and transfer of information.

Third, the advance of technology in this dimension is bound to challenge many cherished notions of sovereignty. But here, too, the West has the advantage, because the free flow of information is inherently compatible with our political system and values. The communist states, in contrast, fear this information revolution perhaps even more than they fear Western military strength. If knowledge is power, then the communications revolution threatens to undermine their most important monopoly—their effort to stifle their people's information, thought, and independence of judgment. We all remember the power of the Ayatollah's message disseminated on tape cassettes in Iran; what could have a more profound im-

pact in the Soviet bloc than similar cassettes, outside radio broadcasting, direct broadcast satellites, personal computers, or Xerox machines?

Totalitarian societies face a dilemma: either they try to stifle these technologies and thereby fall further behind in the new industrial revolution, or else they permit these technologies and see their totalitarian control inevitably eroded. In fact, they do not have a choice, because they will never be able entirely to block the tide of technological advance however hard they try.

The march of technology also compels us to continue our efforts to prevent the **spread of nuclear weapons.** The United States has long been the leader of an international effort to establish a regime of institutional arrangements, legal commitments, and technological safeguards to control the proliferation of nuclear weapons capabilities. This program has, in fact, had considerable success, in that the number of states that have acquired the means to produce nuclear explosives is far lower than doomsayers predicted 20 years ago. At the same time, the potential dangers of nuclear weapons proliferation remain as serious and menacing to international stability as has long been predicted.

The Reagan Administration will pursue this essential endeavor with a realistic appreciation of its complexities. Our thinking on this issue takes account of the growing international reliance on peaceful nuclear energy, the security concerns that give rise to the incentive to seek nuclear weapons, and the need for broad multilateral collaboration among nuclear suppliers if a nonproliferation regime is to be effective. We have made progress in restoring a relationship of confidence and a reputation for reliability with our nuclear trading partners. We have had fruitful talks with the Soviet

Union on this subject; we have worked to promote comprehensive safeguards and stricter export controls.[10]

NEW CHALLENGES TO OUR WAYS OF THINKING

These broad trends I have described are mostly positive trends, but not all. We see social dislocation arising from economic change; we see urban alienation, political turbulence, and the many potential sources and forms of disorder I have mentioned. The changes in the international system will follow the positive trends only if we—the United States and the free world—meet our responsibility to defend our interests and seek to shape events in accordance with our own ideals and goals.

In at least one respect, the modern world—with its spreading technology and prosperity and democratic aspirations—is ironically becoming also more and more vulnerable. I am thinking, of course, about **terrorism**. Even as the world becomes more secure from the danger of major war, paradoxically the democratic world now faces an increasing threat from this new form of warfare.

Terrorism these days is becoming less an isolated phenomenon of local fanatics and increasingly part of a new international strategy resorted to by the enemies of freedom. It is a vicious weapon used deliberately against democracies; against the interests, policies, and friends of the democracies; and against completely innocent people. There are disturbing links, as well, to international drug trafficking. Terrorism is a problem that, more than many others, is forcing us into new ways of thinking about how to safeguard our future. During the year ahead we must be prepared for serious terrorist threats in Western Europe, in the Middle East, and

in Latin America, much of it supported by or encouraged by a handful of ruthless governments.

As you know, I have been speaking out frequently on this subject, to stimulate public consideration and discussion of the complex issues involved.[11] A counter-strategy for combating terrorism, in my view, must encompass many things.

1. We and our allies must work still harder to improve security, share information, coordinate police efforts, and collaborate in other ways to defeat international terrorism. Much has been done in the past year, but much more remains to be done.
2. We in this country must think hard about the moral stakes involved. If we truly believe in our democratic values and our way of life, we must be willing to defend them. Passive measures are unlikely to suffice; means of more active defense and deterrence must be considered and given the necessary political support.
3. Finally, while working tirelessly to deny terrorists their opportunities and their means, we can—and must—be absolutely firm in denying them their goals. They seek to blackmail us into changing our foreign policies or to drive us out of countries and regions where we have important interests. This we *cannot* permit; we cannot yield position or abandon friends or responsibilities under this kind of pressure. If we allow terrorists even one such victory, we embolden them further; we demoralize all who rely on us, and we make the world an even more dangerous place.

There is, of course, a broader issue here, which I have also been discussing in several public statements. This is the basic question of the use of American power in the defense of our interests and the relevance of our power as the backstop to our diplomacy. It is reflected, for example, in what are often called "gray-area challenges"—namely, the kind of regional or local conflicts and crises that are likely to persist in a turbulent world, below the threshold of major war but nonetheless affecting important Western interests. Most of the major conflicts since 1945, indeed, have originated in such conflicts in the developing world. The end of the colonial order has not brought universal peace and justice; much of the developing world is torn by the continuing struggle between the forces of moderation and the forces of radicalism—a struggle actively exploited and exacerbated by the Soviet Union.

It is absurd to think that America can walk away from such challenges. This is a world of great potential instability and many potential dangers. We live, as is commonly said, on a shrinking planet and in a world of increasing interdependence. We have an important stake in the health of the world economy and in the overall conditions of global security; the freedom and safety of our fellow human beings will always impinge on our moral consciousness. Not all these challenges threaten vital interests, but at the same time an accumulation of successful challenges can add up to a major adverse change in the geopolitical balance.

We must be wise and prudent in deciding how and where to use our power. Economic and security assistance to allies and friends is clearly the preferred course—and is of crucial importance to our foreign policy; the direct American use of force must always be a last resort. The United States will always seek political solutions to problems, but such solutions will never succeed unless aggression

is resisted and diplomacy is backed by strength. We are reasonably well prepared to deter all-out Soviet nuclear aggression—provided we continue with our strategic modernization—but we must be sure we are as well prepared, physically and psychologically, for this intermediate range of challenges.[12]

PEACE, PROGRESS, AND FREEDOM

I have touched on a wide variety of topics, but two very important, and very basic, conclusions can be drawn from them.

First, the agenda for the immediate future seems to me to be an agenda on which the American people are essentially united. These are goals that are widely shared and tasks that are likely to reinforce another important trend: namely, the reemergence of a national consensus on the main elements of our foreign policy.[13] This, indeed, may be the most important positive trend of all, because so many of our difficulties in recent decades have been very much the product of our own domestic divisions. I hope that our two parties and our two branches of government will find ways to cooperate in this spirit, which would enormously strengthen our country in the face of the new opportunities and challenges I have described.

Second, all the diverse topics I have touched upon are, in the end, closely interrelated. President Reagan made this point in his speech to the United Nations last September.[14] The United States seeks peace and security; we seek economic progress; we seek to promote freedom, democracy, and human rights. The conventional way of thinking is to treat these as discrete categories of activity. In fact, as we have seen, it is now more and more widely recognized that there is a truly profound connection among them. And this has important implications for the future.

It is no accident, for example, that America's closest and most lasting international relationships are its alliances with its fellow democracies. These ties with the Atlantic community, Japan, and other democratic friends have an enduring quality precisely because they rest on a moral base, not only a base of strategic interest. When George Washington advised his countrymen to steer clear of permanent alliances, his attitude was colored by the fact that there were hardly any other fellow democracies in those days. We were among the first, and we had good reason to be wary of entanglements with countries that did not share our democratic principles. In any case, we now *define* our strategic interests in terms that embrace the safety and well-being of the democratic world.

Similarly, as I have already discussed, it is more and more understood that economic progress is related to a political environment of openness and freedom. It used to be thought in some quarters that socialism was the appropriate model for developing countries because central planning was better able to mobilize and allocate resources in conditions of scarcity. The historical experience of Western Europe and North America, which industrialized in an era of limited government, was not thought to be relevant.

Yet the more recent experience of the Third World shows that a dominant government role in developing economies has done more to stifle the natural forces of production and productivity and to distort the efficient allocation of resources. The real engine of growth, in developing as well as industrialized countries, turns out to be the natural dynamism of socie-

ties that minimize central planning, open themselves to trade with the world, and give free rein to the talents and efforts and risk-taking and investment decisions of individuals.

Finally, there is almost certainly also a relationship between economic progress, freedom, and world peace. Andrei Sakharov has written:

I am convinced that international trust, mutual understanding, disarmament, and international security are inconceivable without an open society with freedom of information, freedom of conscience, the right to publish, and the right to travel and choose the country in which one wishes to live. I am also convinced that freedom of conscience, together with other civic rights, provides both the basis for scientific progress and a guarantee against its misuse to harm mankind.

The implication of all this is profound: it is that the Western values of liberty and democracy—which some have been quick to write off as culture bound or irrelevant or passe—are not to be so easily dismissed. Their obituary is premature. These values are the source of our strength, economic as well as moral, and they turn out to be more central to the world's future than many may have realized.

After more than a century of fashionable Marxist mythology about economic determinism and the "crisis of capitalism," the key to human progress turns out to be those very Western concepts of political and economic freedom that Marxists claimed were obsolete. They were wrong. Today—the supreme irony—it is the communist system that looks bankrupt, morally as well as economically. The West is resilient and resurgent.

And so, in the end, the most important new way of thinking that is called for in this decade is our way of thinking about ourselves. Civilizations thrive when they believe in themselves; they decline when they lose this faith. All civilizations confront massive problems—but a society is more likely to master its challenges, rather than be overwhelmed by them, if it retains this bedrock self-confidence that its values are worth defending. This is the essence of the Reagan revolution and of the leadership the President has sought to provide in America.

The West has been through a difficult period in the last decade or more. But now we see a new turn. The next phase of the industrial revolution—like all previous phases—comes from the democratic world, where innovation and creativity are allowed to spring from the unfettered human spirit. By working together, we can spread the benefit of the technological revolution to all. And on every continent—from Nicaragua to Cambodia, from Poland to South Africa to Afghanistan—we see that the yearning for freedom is the most powerful political force all across the planet.

So, as we head toward the 21st century, it is time for the democracies to celebrate their system, their beliefs, and their success. We face challenges, but we are well poised to master them. Opinions are being revised about which system is the wave of the future. The free nations, if they maintain their unity and their faith in themselves, have the advantage—economically, technologically, morally.

History is on freedom's side.

NOTES

1. See Current Policy No. 577, "Realism and Responsibility: The U.S. Approach to Arms Control," Detroit, May 14, 1984.
2. See Current Policy No. 492, "U.S.-Soviet Relations in the Context of U.S. Foreign Policy." Testimony to the Senate Foreign Relations Committee, June 15, 1983; Current Policy No. 624, "Managing the U.S.-Soviet Relationship over the Long Term," Los Angeles, October 18, 1984.
3. See Current Policy No. 551, "Human Rights and the Moral Dimension of U.S. Foreign Policy," Peoria, February 22, 1984.
4. See Current Policy No. 508, "The Challenge of the Helsinki Process," Madrid, September 9, 1983.
5. See Current Policy No. 598, "Asia-Pacific and the Future," Honolulu, July 18, 1984.
6. See Current Policy No. 550, "Democratic Solidarity in the Americas," Bridgetown, Barbados, February 8, 1984.
7. See Current Policy No. 478, "Struggle for Democracy in Central America," Dallas, April 15, 1983.
8. See Current Policy No. 528, "Promoting Peace in the Middle East," Atlanta, November 19, 1983.
9. See Current Policy No. 487, "The U.S. and the Developing World: Our Joint Stake in the World Economy," New York, May 26, 1983.
10. See Current Policy No. 631, "Preventing the Proliferation of Nuclear Weapons," New York, November 1, 1984.
11. See Current Policy No. 589, "Terrorism: The Challenge to the Democracies," Washington, D.C., June 24, 1984; Current Policy No. 629, "Terrorism and the Modern World," New York, October 25, 1984; Current Policy No. 642, "The Ethics of Power," New York, December 9, 1984.
12. See Current Policy No. 561, "Power and Diplomacy in the 1980s," Washington, D.C., April 3, 1984.
13. See Current Policy No. 625, "A Forward Look at Foreign Policy," Los Angeles, October 19, 1984.
14. See Current Policy No. 615, "Reducing World Tensions," the President's address before the UN General Assembly, New York, September 24, 1984.

SUGGESTED READINGS–PART III

Bloomfield, Lincoln P. *In Search of American Foreign Policy.* New York: Oxford University Press, 1974.

Destler, I. M., Leslie H. Gelb, and Anthony Lake. *Our Own Worst Enemy: The Unmaking of American Foreign Policy.* New York: Simon & Schuster, 1984.

Hoffmann, Stanley. *Primacy or World Order.* New York: McGraw-Hill, 1978.

Holsti, Ole R., and James N. Rosenau. *American Leadership in World Affairs.* Boston: Allen & Unwin, 1984.

Hughes, Thomas L. "The Price of Collective Irresponsibility," *Foreign Policy* 40 (Fall 1980), pp. 33-60.

Quester, George. *American Foreign Policy: The Lost Consensus.* New York: Praeger Publishers, 1982.

Contributors

Jack N. Barkenbus is a political scientist at the Institute for Energy Analysis at the Oak Ridge Associated Universities.

Richard K. Betts is a Senior Fellow in foreign policy studies at The Brookings Institution in Washington, D.C.

Zbigniew Brzezinski was the Assistant to the President for National Security Affairs during the Carter administration. He is now Professor of Political Science at Columbia University.

Jimmy Carter was the 39th President of the United States.

Warren Christopher was Deputy Secretary of State from 1977 to 1981. He was particularly prominent in leading the negotiations to free the American hostages from Iran in 1979 to 1981.

Cecil V. Crabb, Jr., is Professor of Political Science at Louisiana State University at Baton Rouge. He has written several volumes on American foreign policy.

Arthur Cyr is the vice president and director of programming at the Council on Foreign Relations in Chicago.

I. M. Destler is a Senior Fellow at the Institute of International Economics in Washington, D.C.

Steven Emerson is a former staff member of the Senate Subcommittee on Foreign Economic Policy of the Senate Foreign Relations Committee and a former aide to the late Chairman of the Senate Foreign Relations Committee, Frank Church.

Richard A. Falk is Alfred G. Milbank Professor of International Law and Practice and Professor of Politics and International Affairs at Princeton University.

Alexander M. Haig, Jr. was Secretary of State from January 1981 to June 1982.

Stanley Hoffmann is Professor of Government at Harvard University and a member of Harvard's Center for International Affairs and Harvard's Center for European Studies.

Ole R. Holsti is the George V. Allen Professor of International Affairs at Duke University.

George Kennan has served as Ambassador to the Soviet Union and Yugoslavia and is presently Professor Emeritus from the Institute for Advanced Study at Princeton University.

Henry A. Kissinger was the Assistant for National Security Affairs to Presidents Nixon and Ford and served as Secretary of State from 1973 to 1976.

Walter LaFeber is the Marie Underhill Noll Professor of American History at Cornell University.

Charles McC. Mathias has been a U.S. Senator from the state of Maryland since 1969.

The late **Hans J. Morgenthau** was Albert A. Michelson Distinguished Service Professor of Political Science at The University of Chicago and Leonard Davis Distinguished Professor of Political Science at City College of the City University of New York, among other appointments. He was the principal proponent of the realist approach to the study of international politics through his seminal work, *Politics among Nations.*

Richard M. Nixon was the 37th President of the United States.

Dexter Perkins was University Professor Emeritus at Cornell University and Professor Emeritus at the University of Rochester.

George Quester is Professor of Government and Politics at the University of Maryland.

John E. Rielly is the president of the Chicago Council on Foreign Relations.

Ronald Reagan is the 40th President of the United States.

James N. Rosenau is Director of the Institute of Transnational Studies at the University of Southern California and Professor of Political Science and International Relations.

Marshall Shulman is Director of the W. Averell Harriman Institute for Advanced Study of the Soviet Union at Columbia University and Adlai E. Stevenson Professor of International Relations. He was an Ambassador and a Special Adviser to the Department of State during the Carter administration.

George Shultz has been Secretary of State since June 1982.

Strobe Talbott is diplomatic correspondent for *Time* magazine. He has written extensively about American foreign policy including *Endgame: The Inside Story of SALT II* and *The Russians and Reagan.*

George Thibault was special assistant to the Director of Central Intelligence during the Carter administration and currently serves as a teacher in the department of military strategy at the National War College.

John G. Tower was Senator from Texas from 1961 to 1984 where he chaired the Armed Services Committee. He is currently one of the American negotiators at the arms control talks in Geneva.

Harry S Truman was the 33rd President of the United States.

Stansfield Turner was Director of the Central Intelligence Agency during the Carter administration.

Cyrus Vance was Secretary of State from 1977 to 1980.

Alvin M. Weinberg is the Director of the Institute for Energy Analysis at the Oak Ridge Associated Universities.

Name Index

Subject Index

A Reader in American Foreign Policy was typeset at Compositors, Cedar Rapids, Iowa. Printing and binding was by Kingsport Press, Inc., Kingsport, Tennessee. Cover design was by John Goetz, Chicago, Illinois. Internal design was by F.E. Peacock Publishers' art department. The typeface is Times Roman.